The Globalization and Environment Reader

D1477074

The Globalization and Environment Reader

Edited by
Peter Newell and J. Timmons Roberts

WILEY Blackwell

Contents

Editors' Introduction: The Globalization and Environment Debate

J. Timmons Roberts and Peter Newell

Introduction

Just before the massive People's Climate March in 2014, author and activist Naomi Klein released a book which argued that we as a global society face a choice: either unregulated capitalism, or a livable Earth. The book, *This Changes Everything: Capitalism vs. the Climate* (Klein, 2014), cited climate scientists who believe we are on a collision course and so must drastically and immediately change the direction of our development path. Klein put it in stark terms: "What the climate needs to avoid collapse is a contraction in humanity's use of resources; what our economic model demands to avoid collapse is unfettered expansion. Only one of these sets of rules can be changed, and it's not the laws of nature" (21).

Klein argued that the time for half-measures is past, having been lost in the 1990s and 2000s when the process of globalization was deepening and intensifying. "Gentle tweaks to the status quo stopped being a climate option when we supersized the American Dream in the 1990s, and then proceeded to take it global" (22). She argued that the profound changes that need to be made could build a more sustainable and fairer society, such as "radically cutting our fossil fuel emissions and beginning the shift to zero-carbon sources of energy … with a full-blown transition underway within the decade" (18). But, she concluded, "we are not stopping the fire," because doing those things would "fundamentally conflict with deregulated capitalism … [and] are extremely threatening to an elite minority." She continued that it was "our great collective misfortune that the scientific community made its decisive diagnosis of the climate threat at the precise moment … that marked the dawning of what came to be called 'globalization.'"

Klein recounts the three policy pillars of the "market fundamentalism" of global-ization that "systematically sabotaged our collective response to climate change … privatization of the public sphere, deregulation of the corporate sector, and lower corporate taxation, paid for with cuts to public spending" (19). She describes how globalization made it impossible for the United Nations negotiations on climate to succeed, and quotes a Canadian college student who spoke at the 2011 United Nations climate talks in South Africa: "You have been negotiating all my life" (11). This was not an exaggeration: as we'll describe below, those talks began in the early 1990s in the build up to the 1992 UN Framework Convention on Climate Change. For Klein the overwhelming issue of climate change requires that we acknowledge its magnitude and horror, and think creatively about how we can reorganize society in a new and positive way. "Because of our lost decades, it is time to turn this around now. Is it possible? Absolutely. Is it possible without challenging the fundamental logic of deregulated capitalism? Not a chance."

The question of whether the globalization of the world's economy is compatible with the requirement for humans to live sustainably on planet Earth is one of the most pressing we face. Despite nearly a half-century of environmental diplomacy, institu-tion building and a bewildering array of environmental policy tools from regulation to environmental markets and voluntary measures, the health of the global environ-ment continues to deteriorate at an alarming rate (Newell, 2012). While some envi-ronmental problems are being more successfully dealt with, others continue to get worse, such as the total consumption of Earth's resources and soaring levels of gases in the atmosphere that are believed to be destabilizing the atmosphere in which our civilization developed and upon which it depends for our collective survival. While the global economy has increased in size by 22-fold since 1900, our use of construction minerals has increased 34-fold, ores 27-fold, and fossil fuels (coal, oil and gas) have seen a 12-fold increase (Krausmann et al., 2009). We use 3.6 times as much crops, residues, and wood as we did back then. Sadly, it is the same with the gases that are causing climate change (Boden et al., 2010). We are not bending the often exponential curves in these trends the way we need to. Radical change is needed.

Amid accumulating evidence that humanity has already passed and threatens to cross yet more planetary limits (Rockström et al., 2009), debate is intensifying about how to respond. For some the answer is to try to harness the vast and growing power of business, since their decisions have so much impact and they hold so much leverage in political circles. Articulating a claim often repeated in debates about globalization and the environment, Maurice Strong put it succinctly in 1992: "The environment is not going to be saved by environmentalists. Environmentalists do not hold the levers of economic power" (Bruno and Karliner, 2002: 22). Many people have faith in the ability of markets to solve society's problems to properly price nature. They believe that if the costs of environmental harm could be "inter-nalized" (or priced) into economic decision-making so that nature is valued in such a way that ecological limits become a feature of business-as-usual decision-making, then a sustainable economy would develop. Others believe that a global-izing capitalist world economy has been the driver and cause of the current predicament, and that the whole system needs to be reformed for environmental problems to be adequately addressed. Placing further power in the hands of market actors to "solve" the environmental crisis would be, as Nicolas Hildyard suggests in this volume, equivalent to putting the "foxes in charge of the chickens." For critics, therefore, we need to revisit our commitment to a globalizing, export-driven model of economic growth, not re-arrange the chairs on a sinking ship.

As we'll see throughout this volume, the debate about globalization and the environment is intimately connected to the debate about economic development's environmental impact. We need to understand the nature of development – how it takes place, who is influencing its direction, who benefits and who tends to be left behind. Over the past few decades, humanity has seen huge increases in economic development, bringing important overall improvements in indicators of health, education, and physical wellbeing (e.g. Norberg, 2007). The most recent phases of international development have also taken place while international trade has swung rapidly upward, part of what observers have called the unstoppable trend of "globalization" (e.g. Roberts, Hite, and Chorev, 2015). However, this pace of development and globalization has led to immense environmental degradation, and for over four decades many scientists have been arguing that the scale of the degradation threatens humanity. Yet most of the debate on development has for years ignored the environmental impacts that potentially undermine the entire model being held up as an ideal for poor nations to emulate: boundless economic growth and industrialization (Sutcliffe, 2000).

Along with economic globalization has come the globalization of environmental damage. The crux of the problem is that while economic development and globalization threaten the environment, many scholars and politicians argue that development is the key to achieving decent human wellbeing and in solving these same environmental problems (e.g. World Bank, 1992; Grossman and Kreuger, 1995; Selden and Song, 1995). As Mexican President Carlos Salinas was reported to have said on US television, Mexico needed first to pollute itself in order to meet its basic needs, and then environmental concerns could come later. The core issue is how to reconcile the two goals of economy and ecology. As we will see in this book, much research and policy is based on the premise that they can be brought together, but this might be wishful thinking.

To complicate things further, efforts to reconcile economy and ecology have taken place in a context of deepening and dramatic inequalities across the world and within countries. The third "leg" of the tripod of sustainability then is equity: how to harmonize development and environmental sustainability against a background of unequal development and international injustice. Forty years of negotiations, high-level reports, and "grand bargains" (which we review briefly below and which are discussed by a number of this volume's readings) leave us still grasping for solutions that will bring economy, ecology, and equity into alignment. This is not simply in any direction: economic growth in no way guarantees that equity and ecology will be addressed. Some types of environmental protection measures can create economic stagnation and even leave some parts of society behind. This has generated calls for a "just transition" to a green economy, for example, protecting vulnerable groups in the context of radical re-orderings of production and technology. This means ensuring that resource inequalities and workplace exploitation are not exacerbated by changing the technology but leaving poor working conditions in place and environmental injustices untouched. Examples include poorer immigrant women and child laborers assembling solar photovoltaic panels, or the dispossession of communities of their land to make way for wind farm projects (Swilling and Annecke, 2012; Newell and Mulvaney, 2013). Much previous work assumed that by dealing with equity and justice we would solve problems of environmental sustainability (Agyeman et al., 2003), but there is no reason to assume that democratic or just solutions alone will solve environmental crises. Indeed the urgency of the environmental crisis may sometimes be invoked as a rationale for the suspension of normal democratic procedures, however problematic that may be, in order to rush through the approval of "green" projects (Stirling, 2015).

In this brief introduction to the volume, we provide some background to the readings that follow by laying out some of the debate about environment and development, going back to the first United Nations Conference on the Human Environment, held in Stockholm, Sweden in 1972. We then spend some time discussing globalization and what it means, and exploring the complex relationship between globalization and the environment. We describe the difference between globalization and development, and where this leaves the politics of development today. The concluding two sections raise issues around the popular control of the social and environmental impacts of globalization. There are no easy solutions here – the tension between globalizing economic development and environmental protection is profound. It is, however, a tension we cannot fail to resolve. As Naomi Klein put it, "A whole lot of stuff we have been told is inevitable … simply cannot stand. And…a whole lot of stuff we have been told is impossible has to start happening right away" (2014: 28). Our hope is that this volume can inform better understanding of key actors, global forces of change, the barriers to improvement, and how they might be overcome, so that seemingly impossible "stuff" might start happening, right away.

Sustaining Development or "Sustainable Development"?

Though concern for protection of the environment has a much longer history, doomsday scenarios about a shrinking resource base, booming human populations, and spreading pollution intensified fears of ecological crises from the 1960s onwards (Carson, 1962; Meadows et al., 1972; Ehrlich, 1970). These fears in turn drove the rapid growth of a citizens' movement in the wealthier "Global North" countries of Japan, North America, and Europe. After the vast "Earth Day" protests drew 20 million people into the streets in the US on April 22, 1970 and a series of other protests, the Swedish government submitted a proposal to the UN declaring an "urgent need for intensified action at the national and international level, to limit and, where possible, to eliminate the impairment of the human environment." The UN Economic and Social Council (ECOSOC) approved the idea and sent it to the General Assembly, which endorsed it and convened "The UN Conference on the Human Environment." One hundred and thirteen nations met in Stockholm, Sweden in 1972, where conference Chair Maurice Strong told thousands of protesters outside the event that they were successfully pushing the nations of the world to address the environmental crisis.

The conference put the Global North on a head-on collision course with the priorities of nations in the "Global South," who saw poverty driving their own set of environmental problems: soil erosion, deforestation, desertification, and diminishing water resources. Developing country representatives argued that basic human needs must come before the work of environmental clean-up. Of great concern was that wealthy nations might use concepts of "our Spaceship Earth" and the "common heritage of mankind" embodied in international environmental treaties to limit their sovereign rights as nations to their own resources, which they argued were not global, but national, and which they held the right to exploit just as wealthier Northern countries had before them (and continue to do today). Southern nations argued that those in the North should stop claiming that all nations have a share of the Earth's resources which form a "common pool" or "World Trust." One Brazilian delegate argued that this "beautiful assumption" requires sharing also of economic and political power, industry, and financial control, which wealthy nations found quite unthinkable (Guimarães, 2000).

What emerged from the conference was a formal statement, the "Stockholm Declaration," which contained language for both those nations wanting an acknowledgment of the gravity of environmental issues and those wanting assurance that addressing the issue would not hamper their growth. The declaration included 26 principles on everything from environmental education and law to urbanization and population. Principle 1 began with "the fundamental right to freedom, equality and adequate conditions of life," a series of issues which imply economic development, but which have remained contentious up to the present. The "Action Plan for the Human Environment" agreed upon at Stockholm had 109 recommendations: for the scientific assessment of environmental problems, for ambitious institution-building for their management, and for a new United Nations Environment Programme (UNEP) to coordinate all UN actions on the environment. However the UNEP was based in Nairobi, Kenya, which for a series of reasons caused the agency to struggle to function as a coordinating agency (Reed, 1992; Ivanova, 2006). The principles were not the basis of international laws, and the 109 recommendations were largely overlooked. However Reed (1992) argues that Stockholm "successfully crystallizes the underlying issues" of global environmental politics, and forged a fragile compromise for future actions on the environment, such as a series of international treaties which were developed over the next decades.

The ten-year follow-up to Stockholm was the 1982 UN conference in Nairobi, which hardly anyone remembers anymore. It was described as "a complete disaster," as US President Ronald Reagan's delegate "succeeded in completely sabotaging the conference" (Vaillancourt, 2000). To pick up the pieces, in 1983, the UN General Assembly set up a World Commission on Environment and Development (WCED) which became known as the Brundtland Commission (under former Prime Minister Ms. Gro Harlem Brundtland of Norway). It included six representatives from wealthy industrialized countries, three East-Europeans, and 12 representatives of developing nations. In 1987, the commission issued the influential report *Our Common Future*, which popularized the term "sustainable development." It defined the term as "Development that meets the needs of the present without compromising the ability of future generations to meet their own needs" (1987: 43) (see this volume). The report's authors conceptualized sustainable development as having three dimensions: economic-developmental, environmental-ecological, and social-political (equity) (Vaillancourt, 2000).[1]

The concept of "sustainable development" gained immediate and wide acceptance, partly because it sounded positive but was so vague that everyone could sign up to it (Clapp and Dauvergne, 2004; Humphrey, Lewis, and Buttel, 2002). The Brundtland Report allowed all sides to embrace this concept of sustainable development, including the business community. "The chemical industry can help to make sustainable development a reality," claimed Dow Chemical's CEO Frank Popoff. The American Chemistry Council's Vice President Terry Yosie said that "Sustainable development is an appropriate framework for integrating the environmental, economic, and social issues that are facing industry and society…We endorse that framework" (Sissel, 2002).

However the concept of sustainable development was problematic from the start. It seemed to mean whatever people wanted it to mean: everyone had something different in mind when claiming it as their practice or visualizing the future with it as their goal. Whose idea of sustainable is to prevail? Whose and which development is to be sustained? People are still debating about what it means: David Pearce years ago collected 13 pages of definitions of sustainable development, all placing different emphasis upon the three elements of economic growth, environmental protection, and equity. Sociologists Craig Humphrey, Tammy Lewis, and Fred Buttel wrote that sustainable development, in the Brundtland Report and after, ignored any "limits to growth," assuming that environmental protection and economic growth were at least potentially entirely complementary. Instead, it obtained its rapid adoption and seeming instant consensus by "focusing on how sustainable development can be achieved" (Humphrey, Lewis, and Buttel 2002: 222). They concluded that the sustainable development approach is thus inherently "pro-technology, pro-growth, and compromise oriented" (Humphrey, Lewis, and Buttel 2002: 222). It fits well, they argued, with the technocratic approach to environmental crises, which holds that these crises can be resolved by scientific management (see Sachs, this volume). As Steven Bernstein has also shown, it sought to ensure that responses to environmental threats were compatible with a liberal (free market) economic order – what he calls "the compromise of liberal environmentalism" (Bernstein, 2001).

From Rio to Rio: The Rise of the Green Economy

After years of negotiating and four crucial preparatory conferences, the Rio Earth Summit (UN Conference on Environment and Development) in 1992 was a watershed event, with 168 countries represented, 117 heads of state, and a huge parallel

"People's Forum." The great numbers of Non-Governmental Organizations (NGOs) at the event took a two-pronged approach, working inside the convention hall as they could through their country delegations, and outside they built networks and collaborations with groups from around the world. In this way, the event effectively globalized the environmental movement in which new regions were represented and given voice in new and more global networks, even if national, regional, and international inequalities persisted.

Sensing key risks and the potential for widespread anti-industry attitude and a potential new wave of global regulations, international industry had a huge delegation at Rio in 1992 and at the next big summit in Johannesburg in 2002, and sought actively to redirect the debate. In fact, industry significantly funded the conferences, and was well placed in major discussions (Vaillancourt, 2000, Humphrey, Lewis, and Buttel, 2002, Bruno and Karliner, 2002; Chatterjee and Finger, 1994). This explains also the emergence of voluntary approaches to sustainable development – in which businesses and nations were allowed and encouraged to put forward their own pledges and approaches to solving environmental problems – and the presentation of the "business case" for sustainable development grounded in eco-efficiency (see Schmidheiny, this volume).

Coming out of Rio were several key treaties and documents, including the Convention on Biological Diversity, the Framework Convention on Climate Change, the Document on Forest Principles, and the Rio Declaration. A massive consensus document called *Agenda 21* attempted to lay out how to attain a strong economy and environmental protection for all people on Earth. An 800-page plan of action, with more than 100 recommendations, *Agenda 21* addressed environmental protection, socio-economic development, equity, justice and nearly everything else. Vaillancourt (2000) describes its "drab style," as it was written by many experts and technocrats from around the world, edited and re-edited, and condensed into summaries. These suggestions were not legally binding, and except for the "Local Agenda 21" approach for municipal planning, most have been ignored and forgotten.

A "Grand Bargain" at Rio emerged in which poor countries agreed to work on environmental protection if their growth was secured and if the costs of their cleaning up were borne by the wealthy nations. Promises of huge amounts of aid to address global environmental issues like ozone and climate change were made: the price tag placed on achieving sustainable development in the Third World was estimated at US$561.5 billion a year, with the Global North expected to bankroll US$141.9 billion in low or no-interest "concessional" assistance (or 20% of the total cost; Hicks et al., 2008). Developing countries were expected to foot the rest of the bill. Of the US$125 billion in concessional assistance, about US$15 billion a year was supposed to be devoted to global environmental issues, with the rest targeted at sustainable development programs in developing countries (Robinson, 1992).

Built into the treaties was a profound inequality in interests, in part because of the unequal representation of scientists and negotiators at Rio and the other Earth summits. At the sixth Conference of the Parties of the UNFCCC, for example, the US brought 99 formal delegates and the European Commission brought 76, while many small-island and African states were lucky if they could put together a one, two, or three person delegation. The problem is reflected as well in the number of authors drafting policy and key documents. In the 1995 Intergovernmental Panel on Climate Change Working Groups I, II, and III, out of 512 WGI authors, 212 were United States citizens and 61 were from the United Kingdom, while only 12 authors came from India and China combined. Working Groups II and III also showed very wide inequalities in representation (Kandlikar and Sagar, 1999). There is little question that these documents would look very different if written with equal representation from the Global South. One of the clearest differences would certainly be that the right to development would gain equal attention with environmental protection.

The struggle to reconcile economy, ecology, and equity through grand bargains and global summitry, new initiatives and discursive accommodations continues today. Twenty years after the original Rio summit many of the debates discussed above were replayed at the Rio+20 summit in 2012. Here however, sustainable development had given way to a focus on "green growth" and the development of Green Economies (Brand, 2012; Wanner, 2015). While interpretations and differences between the various organizations' use of the terms vary, the core meaning of green growth is simply stated: "It is economic growth (growth of gross domestic product or GDP) which also achieves significant environment protection" (Jacobs, 2012: 4). Strong emphasis is put on creating jobs and challenging investment through policy and market incentives into "green" and especially low carbon sectors of the economy. Since 2007 and the financial crisis and the ensuing great recession, the concepts of green growth and the green economy have come to occupy prominent positions in the policy discourse of international economic and development institutions (e.g. World Bank, 2012; UNEP, 2011). Alongside this, the creation of new institutions such as the Global Green Growth Institute in 2012 and explicit commitments to green growth as a policy objective at G20 summits are helping to ensure that green growth is firmly established, at least rhetorically, within the global economy.

Critical responses to green growth, as we'll see in the contribution from Barbara Unmüßig and colleagues in this volume include concerns about reproducing dominant paradigms about the nature of the crisis while neglecting some of the social aspects that were also at the heart of ideas about sustainable development in relation to equity and respect for people's rights to resources. They worry that the green economy debate could reproduce all the dynamics that caused concern at the time of the Rio summit: deference to elite expertise to define planetary boundaries within which we should live; and a privileging of technocratic responses that place great faith in technology and pricing ecosystem "services" as ways of managing the planet's resources (Scoones et al., 2015). The Rio+20 summit also generated heated debates about what forms of institutional and governance reform are required without regard to the systematic and structural drivers of environmental degradation and social exclusion which need to be addressed. This requires not just looking to more, different or better global institutions for the answers, but greater attention to the everyday production and distribution of environmental harm and social injustice within the global economy. Increasingly this occurs along and through complex supply chains which distribute costs, benefits, and value unevenly between social groups and ecosystems in different parts of the world, and over which states and international institutions have very little direct oversight. It is to these shifts in production and consumption in the global economy that have taken place alongside the global summitry discussed here that we now turn our attention.

Production, Labor, and the Environment

An iconic image of globalization is a massive container ship, bringing cheap toys, electronics, clothing and furniture halfway around the world. This choice of icons is well supported: about nine-tenths of world trade of goods is by ship, and most of the value is now carried in containers (People's Daily Online 2004). Staring at a shipload of containers is also like gazing at the Sphinx: its meaning is entirely obscured from our view. Hidden in each corrugated steel box are thousands of products produced around the world with "stuff" mined, farmed or pumped from far corners of the Earth. The wages, working conditions, and lives of workers whose labor is embodied in those products are organized differently in varied types of workplaces and communities, under the purview of either local, national, or international firms, under formal work rules and contracts, or in entirely informal arrangements, in small family-owned, publicly-held corporations, or state-owned enterprises. The same products could be produced under strict or extremely lax environmental and health conditions. Each firm may differ in its strategy of production, but facing global competition, we know they all share one criterion: they are required to keep production costs down.

Many environmentally or socially concerned consumers are asking retailers for labels on products documenting that they were produced in a "fair trade," "sweatshop free," "rainforest friendly," or even documenting its "ecological" or "carbon footprint" as part of "big-brand sustainability" (Dauvergne and Lister, 2013). However, the environmental implications of global production and global sourcing are massive, and extremely complex. To understand them, we need to understand the "commodity chain" running from the place where the raw material was extracted, to its transport, processing, marketing, consumption, and final disposal (Gereffi and Korzeniewitz, 1994). With cheaper transportation systems, the production, consumption and disposal of goods can be done in many locations and organized very differently. Even services have commodity chains and ecological footprints that often reach around the globe, as they rely on workers, equipment and energy produced in diverse locales, including processor chips and electricity to power massive computer "server farms." Environmental impacts and risks to workers and communities are great at certain nodes in this chain, and the social development benefits are often concentrated at very different nodes. This is often to the detriment of poorer countries, who have difficulty attracting industries doing the high-value stages of production (Selwyn, 2014).

Building on Dependency and World-Systems theories (which focused on *labor* as the basis of the value of products), Stephen Bunker advanced the idea that extraction of resources degrades both natural resources and the societies in those regions, while enriching the "core" and especially urban parts of the world economic system (Bunker, 1985; see also Galeano, 1971). This was an old but under-studied type of "unequal exchange" between the rich and poor regions of the world: each cycle of boom and bust from exporting raw materials makes the developing nations more desperate to extract greater volumes of whatever they can sell on global markets. The debt crisis of the 1980s, which faced many nations who borrowed heavily in the petrodollar boom days of the 1970s, is frequently considered a prime way that globalization has caused deeper environmental damage in the extractive regions of the world (e.g. Reed, 1992), part of broader resource flows from South to North (Khor, 1994). Joan Martínez-Alier and his colleagues advanced the idea of "environmentally unequal exchange" and an "ecological debt" which is owed by the North as a result of its unfairly profiting at the expense of the South (Martinez-Alier, 2003; Muradian et al., 2002). These ideas have finally begun to be quantitatively analyzed and confirmed by comparisons of impacts and benefits in different world regions (Giljum and Eisenmenger, 2004; Eisenmenger, Ramos-Martin, and Schandl, 2007; see also Steinberger et al. this volume).

The poorest nations of Africa and Latin America extract natural resources and "mine the soil" for greater export cash crop harvests. But the "New International Division of Labor" first described by Fröbel, Heinrichs, and Kreye in 1980 has now seen a nearly complete rearrangement of the factories to nations with lower labor costs. Manufacturers in countries like China and India are increasingly doing much more than that: they are assembling components or doing final assembly of manufactures which were until very recently done in the wealthy nations of the Global North. In turn, the changing geographies of production and consumption mirror closely the shifting profile and intensifying nature of pollution. The simultaneous de-industrialization of wealthier countries and industrialization of poorer ones, a strategy aimed at overcoming the power of unions to insist on higher wages and creating a new international division of labor, has meant that countries such as China, India, Brazil, and South Africa have seen their contributions to global problems such as climate change increase significantly. China's CO_2 emissions amounted to 407 million tonnes in 1980 to 1,665 million tonnes in 2006, while India's went from 95 million tonnes in 1980 to 411 million tonnes in the same period (Peet et al., 2011: 21). The final destination for many of the goods produced during this surge of industrialization remains the rich Global North. Forty per cent of China's product is exported, as is 20 per cent of India's (Peet et al., 2011: 22), raising the question of "embedded carbon" and who is responsible for the pollution embodied in the products that flow through the veins of the global economy.

The role of factors like weak environmental regulations and enforcement and cheap energy in driving the flight of industries to developing nations have been much debated. The main point here is that development efforts based on either an extractive or manufacturing model brings environmental damage, and often without securing much social improvement. That is, countries rushing to industrial models of national development risk gaining neither environmental protection nor positive social development. Both could potentially be done with reasonable protection of the human and natural environment, but combining them within a new model of "sustainable development" is not easy nor particularly likely in the current global economic climate.

Globalizing Consumption

The flip-side of production is of course consumption. And over-production, which can be endemic in the capitalist system, necessitates over-consumption. One of the most indelible features of the global capitalist economy over the last 70 years has been the exponential increase in mass consumption that has been achieved through advertising and marketing strategies, as well as the internationalization of production and transport networks, fueled by relatively cheap and abundant energy supplies. The importance of this aspect of the globalization of material desire through global advertising and media is reflected in the growth of activism aimed at questioning wasteful consumption, while raising awareness about the social and environmental costs of the ever increasing use of resources. The "shadows of consumption" that are left behind by the rising tide of mass consumption leave a trail of destruction in their wake. Ecological shadows, in this sense, refer to the global patterns of harm that result not just from the direct consequences of consuming, but also from the "environmental spill-overs from the corporate, trade, and financing chains that supply and replace consumer goods" (Dauvergne, 2008: xi).

The distribution of wealth and waste generated by this frenetic intensification of economic activity has been unevenly distributed, reflecting and exacerbating existing inequalities along the lines of class, race, and gender, as a vast literature on environmental justice has documented in detail (Pellow and Park, 2002; Newell, 2005). Whether it is toxic, plastic, or the sorts of e-waste (computers and the like) that end up on landfill sites in Ghana (Carmin and Agyeman, 2011), global accumulation strategies enabled by trade and investment agreements create greater distance between sites of production and sites of consumption and of disposal. But they also allow "spatial fixes" (Harvey, 1981) for the need to privatize gain and socialize risk and the externalities of production in sites, within and between societies, where opposition is weak and regulation either non-existent or weakly enforced.

Some of the greatest corporate icons of globalization and consumerism, whose ecological and social shadows stretch far and wide, are fast food giants. This is captured nicely in the phrase the "McDonaldization" of global society (Ritzer, 1993). Global brands like McDonalds or Kentucky Fried Chicken are building global franchises and displacing locally-produced and traded products every day. The main products these establishments are selling are six-fold: low price, consistency, the biological attraction of fat, sugar and salt, and the glamour of modernity. One company, Yum! Brands, Inc., based in Louisville, Kentucky, USA, "is the world's largest restaurant company in terms of system restaurants with over 34,000 restaurants in over 100 countries," in 2005 generating over US$9 billion in total revenue (Yum! 2007). In the third quarter of 2006, Yum! China Division alone had more than 2,400 system restaurants (Yum! 2007), and the firm was opening three restaurants a day around the world.

To open these restaurants, franchise owners and managers need to pay substantial monthly rent and fees to the corporation, and follow extremely detailed methods of management, production, sourcing, publicity, and almost everything else (Schlosser, 2001). The homogenization of textures and flavors of food requires that crops be uniform, and heavily processed in closely supervised factories. Fast food animals (like many others in "modern production") are often fattened on soybeans or other feed grains, which to meet demand are sometimes grown in areas previously covered in rainforests, savannah, or used to grow food for local human consumption. The social and environmental profile of agriculture is being transformed, as large-scale production of animals and crops is heavily favored in sourcing fast food chains over local family farming (e.g. Magdoff et al., 2000). High levels of chemical inputs are needed to maintain soil fertility, control pests, and to protect animal health. Large amounts of energy and inputs are needed for transport, processing, and packaging. Less discussed is the loss of local food systems, in which people have built their local cultural traditions around food production and consumption over centuries or millennia, and which tie people to their place and its protection. Finally, there is the obesity epidemic, which is spreading from the US along with these high-fat, high-sugar foods.

So from this one simple example one can see many elements of the arguments raised by activists and observers lumped into the "anti-globalization" camp. These are not all blamed on one brand or even solely on fast foods, but on the whole complex of changes in food and consumption systems going on in developing countries today. First, that globalization changes the way people make decisions, so it reorients local labor, land and other resources towards meeting the needs of the market, especially the global market, at the expense of local subsistence and improvement. Second, this loss of local markets for smallholder-grown products can drive migration from rural to urban residence, which creates another cascading set of social and environmental impacts in both sending and receiving locations. Third, global production and distribution means massive increases in the energy needed to transport products around, when compared to earlier systems of local provisioning. Fourth, globalization is increasing overall levels of consumption, which when combined with growing world populations, means increasing damage to ecosystems. Fifth, globalization increases risks by decreasing diversity in native food systems, with the adoption of homogenous hybrid and genetically-modified crops. Sixth, the current wave of globalization appears to be increasing inequality both within nations and between them, as local entrepreneurs or state politicians profit from working with transnational corporations or investors, while others gain only seasonal and menial work paying barely survival wages, and may lose other resources such as access to communal lands. And seventh, under pressure to increase their exports to gain hard currency to pay off international debts, developing nation governments look for resources to export, and often these have devastating impacts on rainforests and native peoples in these ecosystems.

While free market advocates rightly point out globalization's increasing global wealth overall, and the security of food supply that can come with trade and aid, these arguments animate a growing and sometimes converging movement of activists fighting for social justice, workers' rights, fair trade, and the environment that rally around "food justice" or food sovereignty, "climate justice" and energy sovereignty or for access to water or to defend the rights of forest dwellers and tribal groups. Numerous movements around the world are fighting to keep "the oil in the soil" and "the coal in the hole" for a variety of different motivations, from resource autonomy to health impacts and increasingly the fact that vast swathes of the world's fossil fuel resources will need to remain unburned if we are to keep climate change within tolerable limits. Environmentalists and labor unions have joined together occasionally to fight free trade treaties such as NAFTA (North American Free Trade Area), the Trans-Pacific Partnership, and trade bodies like the World Trade Organization (Newell, 2007). Indigenous people in Colombia, Ecuador, and Nigeria have fought big oil companies like Occidental Petroleum and Shell, attempting to force them to clean up environmental impacts on their local lands. People affected by dams are becoming more organized and linked internationally, and have fought for proper attention and the rethinking of some massive projects in key nations. The list is growing, and some authors argue that there are increasingly strong "transnational advocacy networks" which allow local peoples to more effectively fight national or international actors like corporations, governments, or international financial institutions like the IMF and the World Bank (e.g. Keck and Sikkink, 1997; Edwards and Gaventa, 2001).

One can find grounds in these trends for hope. Yet social-environmental NGOs are notoriously under resourced and ephemeral, growing rapidly and then dispersing, or being de-radicalized or co-opted by governments and corporations or professionalization of their leaders, what Dauvergne and LeBaron refer to as "the corporatization of activism" or just "Protest Inc" (2014). "Compassion fatigue" and the brutally short cycle of attention in the news media make it ever more difficult to mobilize protests in the wealthy nations, and even to secure long-term commitments to foreign assistance that might address environmental and social problems caused by development. The "Grand Bargain at Rio" is threatening to collapse. Global treaties to protect environmental-social systems (such as the Convention on Biological Diversity, the Kyoto Protocol and the Paris Agreement) were notoriously excruciating to negotiate through the international system, and almost entirely lack effective enforcement mechanisms. Meanwhile many corporate leaders that led the way in promoting corporate social responsibility have yet to seriously shift their investment portfolios out of forms of resource extraction that are pushing beyond planetary boundaries.

Many observers argue that stronger and more effective global institutions (like the UN agencies and treaties) are needed to push for a balancing of the need for economic development with the need for protecting the environment that sustains society, with some calling for a new World Environment Organization able to stand up to the institutions of global economic governance (Biermann, 2001, see this volume). For national politicians to support giving power over to such global institutions requires enduring pressure on them at the national and local levels. Local support in turn requires strong social movements, which in turn require an open, democratic political space in which to mobilize. The basic conditions for participatory democracy, in turn, are the rule of law (an independent and effective policy and court system), transparency in government, constitutional sharing of power, freedom of association, the press and expression, and so on. To achieve the *underlying conditions* for combining the three elements of sustainable development – economy, environment, and equity – requires revisiting the core issues of the bargain at Rio and before that, the core conflict at Stockholm. Development pathways, ecologically-unequal exchange, and the ecological debt need all to be addressed.

There is clearly not one route, roadmap, or blueprint for action. There is an array of state-led, citizen-led, market and technology-led pathways to sustainability (Scoones et al., 2015) that each imply a different model of globalization. As the contributors to this collection clearly show, there are also different theories of change at work: how much we can expect governments, corporations, citizens and international institutions to do, where power lies and whose ideas of change are best able to address social and environmental justice simultaneously. At this time in history all pathways to change need to be evaluated if there is to be any prospect of securing a global economy that is both just and sustainable.

Outline of the Book

We have included in this book summaries of each reading at the beginning of each section. Here, we describe the logic of the five sections of readings, while acknowledging that there is useful overlap in issues and approaches across the volume. We begin Part I, "Going Global," with some strong statements sounding the alarm on the devastating impacts of globalization on the ecosystems that sustain our species as we enter what some are calling the "Anthropocene," a new geological era in which human influence over the planet is overwhelming natural forces. It maps the terrain of the debate about globalization and the environment by providing some historical background on the institutions and actors that feature heavily in these discussions. It provides a critical look at discourses and framings: of globality, of who gets to define the terrain, of whose nature is subject to discussion and management, and on which globalizations are subject to debate and considered to be in need of control.

Part II, "The Nature of Globalization," addresses the debate about the fundamental cause and direction of globalization, and how that is affecting the natural environment. The readings identify the key dimensions of how nature is being marketed, valued, and brought within global systems of exchange. In particular, it highlights themes such as the privatization of sectors such as energy and water, the commodification and financialization of natural resources through trading and payments for ecosystem services, as well as the social and ecological consequences of marketization in its various forms for the realization of social and environmental justice. The section describes each trend with separate and overlapping readings, and locates them historically: are they really new phenomena, or are they part of evolving political and economic structures? What claims are made about their effectiveness and ability to use markets in the service of environmental protection and how credible are they? What are the strategies of different actors in creating or resisting these changes?

Part III, "Explaining the Relationship Between Globalization and the Environment," seeks to introduce readers to different ways of understanding how globalization and the environment are related. It offers a spectrum of views. On the one side are market liberal and institutionalist perspectives, which hold that markets (of a more or less regulated nature) provide the most efficient and effective vehicle for valuing and therefore protecting the environment. On the other are more critical views which suggest that either existing institutions, or more fundamentally, the economic system which they seek to defend and advance, lie at the root of the problem. A "social green" perspective argues that economic inequality drives the perpetuation and worsening of environmental problems. This enables readers to position their own thinking and the pieces in this volume in relation to these competing accounts of the relationship between globalization and the environment and the positive and negative aspects of globalization.

Part IV, "Governing Globalization and the Environment," introduces readers to debates about regulating and governing globalization. The core question is the extent to which regulation is possible, and the different forms it might take. We look both at debates about system-wide global governance (or what is increasingly being referred to as Earth Systems Governance), as well as the rise and proliferation of private regulation and "civil regulation," a term used to refer to civil-society-based attempts to construct forms of social control over the operations of business in a globalized economy. The section also touches upon the extent to which and the ways in which globalization might be having an impact upon existing governance arrangements and forms of environmental regulation. Here the readings touch on debates about whether in standards of environmental protection in a globalizing world there is evidence of a "race to the bottom," "a race to the top," or to somewhere in the middle.

Part V, "Can Globalization be Greened?" seeks to introduce readers to broader debates about whether and how globalization might be made compatible with protecting the global environment, from those that emphasize alternative measurements, goals, and institutional changes, to those that think a profound system change is necessary – that is, that capitalist globalization itself is inherently unsustainable as Naomi Klein suggests in the quotes that open this introduction. The section sets out to introduce readers to debates about the reformability of globalization, and whether its key institutions can be positively reshaped. And it provides an introduction to debates about insider or outsider strategies for achieving change.

What we hope the collection provides is a high quality "taster menu," rather than a comprehensive overview of the now vast literature on globalization and the environment. The greatest challenge for us was deciding what to include and what to leave aside, when there are so many different dimensions to this issue and such a wide range of viewpoints on the compatibility of globalization and sustainable development. While some readers will hone in on those sections that address aspects of the debate they are most interested in, others may read across the volume and thereby gain a clearer sense of the history and lineage of this debate and the variety of ways of engaging with it. However readers choose to use this volume, and which-ever way they seek to connect with its content, both parts which they disagree with and those which they might be sympathetic to, we hope that it inspires us all to reflect upon and engage in a process of change, even if we have very different the-ories and ideas about how change can be best be brought about. After all, the urgent necessity to address global environmental challenges and the goal of living more sustainability is rarely contested these days. But the debate rages about which glob-alizations are environmentally and socially compatible with which types of development, and ultimately what sort of world it is that we want to live in.

Note

1   Vaillancourt (2000) argues that the concept was not new. In 1976 an ecological manifesto by British Greens spoke at length about need to establish sustainable society; in 1973 and 1977 Ignacy Sacks from France promoted "ecodevelopment" in the Third World. His 1980 book on strategies of ecodevelopment described ways to "harmonize ecology and economics." The WWF, IUCN, UNESCO, and FAO in 1980 put out a report calling for long-term costs and benefits to be included in planning. In 1980 Lester Brown published *Building a Sustainable Society*, and there were many other roots of this idea (Vaillancourt 2000).

References

Agyeman, J., Bullard, R., and Evans, B. (eds) (2003) *Just Sustainabilities: Development in an Unequal World*, MIT Press, Cambridge, MA.

Bernstein, S. (2001) *The Compromise of Liberal Environmentalism*. New York: Columbia University Press.

Biermann, F. (2001) The emerging debate on the need for a World Environment Organization: a commentary. *Global Environmental Politics*, 1 (1), 45–56.

Boden, T.A., Marland, G., and Andres, R.J. (2010) *Global, regional, and national fossil-fuel CO_2 emissions,* Carbon Dioxide Information Analysis Center, Oak Ridge National Laboratory, U.S. Department of Energy, Oak Ridge, TN.

Boyd, E., Hultman, N.E., and Timmons Roberts, J., et al. (2007) The clean development mechanism: current status, perspectives and future policy. Environmental Change Institute/Tyndall Centre for Climate Research, Working Paper, June, 2007.

Brand, U. (2012) *Beautiful Green World: On the Myths of a Green Economy*, Rosa Luxemburg Foundation, Berlin.

Bruno, K. and Karliner, J. (2002) *Earthsummit.Biz: The Corporate Takeover of Sustainable Development*, Corpwatch and Food First Books, San Francisco and Oakland, CA.

Bunker, S. (1985) *Underdeveloping the Amazon: Extraction, Unequal Exchange and the Failure of the Modern State*, University of Illinois Press, Urbana, IL.

Carmin, J. and Agyeman, J. (eds) (2011) *Environmental Justice Beyond Borders: Local Perspectives on Global Inequities*, MIT Press, Cambridge, MA.

Carson, R. (1962) *Silent Spring*, Houghton-Mifflin, Boston, MA.

Chatterjee, P. and Finger, M. (1994) *The Earth Brokers: Power, Politics and World Development*, Routledge, London.

Clapp, J. and Dauvergne, P. (2004) *Paths to a Green World: The Political Economy of the Global Environment*, MIT Press, Cambridge, MA.

Dauvergne, P. (2008) *The Shadows of Consumption: Consequences for the Global Environment*, MIT Press, Cambridge, MA.

Dauvergne, P. and LeBaron, G. (2014) *Protest Inc: The Corporatization of Activism*, Polity Press, Cambridge.

Dauvergne, P. and Lister, J. (2013) *Eco-Business: A Big-Brand Takeover of Sustainability*, MIT Press, Cambridge, MA.

Dicken, P. (2007) *Global Shift: Mapping the Changing Contours of the World Economy*, 5th edn, Sage Publications, London and Guilford Press, New York.✓

Dobson, A. (2003) Social justice and environmental sustainability: ne'er the twain shall meet?, in *Just Sustainabilities: Development in an Unequal World* (eds, J. Agyeman, R. Bullard, and B. Evans), MIT Press, Cambridge, MA, pp. 83–98.

Edwards, M. and Gaventa, J. (eds) (2001) *Global Citizen Action*, Lynne Rienner, Boulder, CO.

Ehrlich, P. (1970) *The Population Bomb*, Ballantine Books, Boston, MA.

Eisenmenger, N., Ramos-Martin, J., and Schandl, H. (2007) Transition in a changed context: patterns of development in a globalizing world, *Socio-ecological Transitions and Global Change: Developments in Societal Metabolism and Land Use* (eds, M. Fischer-Kowalski and H. Haberl) Edward Elgar, Cheltenham, pp. 179–222.

Fischer-Kowalski, M. and Christof, A. (2001) Beyond IPAT and Kuznets Curves: globalization as a vital factor in analyzing the environmental impact of socio-economic metabolism. *Population and Environment*, 23, 7–47.

Fröbel, F., Heinrichs, J., and Kreye, O. (1980) *The New International Division of Labor*, Cambridge University Press, Cambridge, UK.

Galeano, E.H. (1971) (English 1973). *Open Veins of Latin America: Five Centuries of the Pillage of a Continent*, Monthly Review Press, New York.

Gereffi, G. and Korzeniewicz, M. (eds) (1994) *Commodity Chains and Global Capitalism*, Praeger, Westport, CT.

Giljum, S. and Eisenmenger, N. (2004) North-South trade and the distribution of environmental goods and burdens. A biophysical perspective. *Journal of Environment and Development*, 13 (1), 73–100.

Grossman, G.M. and Krueger, A.B. (1993) Environmental impacts of a North American free trade agreement, in *The U.S.-Mexico Free Trade Agreement* (ed. P. Garber), MIT Press, Cambridge, MA.

Guimarães, R. (2000) Brazil and global environmental politics: same wine in new bottles? In *Sustainability and Unsustainability on the Road from Rio* (eds, J. Timmons Roberts, E. Viola, F. Buttel, and A. Hite). Book manuscript in revision.

Harvey, D. (1981) The spatial fix: Hegel, von Thünen and Marx. *Antipode*, 13, 1–12.

Hicks, R.B., Parks, C., Timmons Roberts, J., and Tierney, M.J. (2008) *Greening Aid? Understanding Foreign Assistance for the Environment*, Oxford University Press, Oxford.

Humphrey, C., Lewis, T.L., and Buttel, F.H. (2002) *Environment, Energy, and Society: A New Synthesis*, Wadsworth, Boston.

Ivanova, M. (2006) Understanding UNEP: myths and realities in global environmental governance, Ph.D. Dissertation, Yale University.

Jacobs, M. (2012). Green growth. Centre for Climate Change Economics and Policy Working Paper No. 108, Grantham Research Institute on Climate Change and the Environment Working Paper No. 92.

Kandlikar, M. and Sagar, A. (1999) Climate change research and analysis in India: an integrated assessment of a south-north divide. *Global Environmental Change*, 9 (2), 119–138.

Keck, M.E. and Sikkink, K. (1997) *Activists Beyond Borders: Advocacy Networks in International Politics*, Cornell University Press, Ithaca, NY.

Khor, M. (1994) South-North resource flows and their implication for sustainable development. *Third World Resurgence*, 46, 4–25.

Klein, N. (2014) *This Changes Everything*, Allen Lane, London.

Krausmann, F. et al. (2009) Growth in global materials use, GDP and population during the 20th century. *Ecological Economics*, 68 (10), 2696–2705.

Magdoff, F., Bellamy Foster, J., and Buttel, F. (eds) (2000). *Hungry for Profit: The Agribusiness Threat to Farmers, Food, and the Environment*, Monthly Review Press, New York.

Meadows, D.H., Meadows, D., Randers, J., and Behrens III, W.W. (1972) *The Limits to Growth: A Report for the Club of Rome's Project on the Predicament of Mankind*, Universe Books, New York.

Muradian, R., O'Connor, M., and Martínez-Alier, J. (2002) Embodied pollution in trade: estimating the "environmental load displacement" of industrialised countries. *Ecological Economics*, 41 (1), 41–57.

Martínez-Alier, J. (2003) *The Environmentalism of the Poor: A Study of Ecological Conflicts and Valuation*, Edward Elgar, Cheltenham.

Newell, P. (2005) Race, class and the global politics of environmental inequality. *Global Environmental Politics*, 5 (3), 70–94.

Newell, P. (2007) Trade and environmental justice in Latin America. *New Political Economy*, 12 (2), 237–259.

Newell, P. (2012) *Globalization and the Environment: Capitalism, Ecology and Power*, Polity Press, Cambridge.

Newell, P. and Mulvaney, D. (2013) The political economy of the just transition, *The Geographical Journal*, 197 (2), 132–140.

Norberg, J. (2007) In defense of global capitalism, in *The Globalization and Development Reader* (eds, J. Timmons Roberts and A. Hite), Wiley-Blackwell, Oxford.

OECD (2011) *Towards Green Growth*, Organization for Economic Cooperation and Development, Paris.

Peet, R., Robbins, P., and Watts, M. (eds.) (2011) *Global Political Ecology*, Routledge, London.

Pellow, D. and Park, L.S-H. (2002) *The Silicon Valley of Dreams: Environmental Injustice, Immigrant Workers, and the High-Tech Global Economy*, New York University Press, New York.

People's Daily Online (2004) Huge room for China to develop containers, says shipping giant. Online at http://english.people.com.cn/200408/13/eng20040813_152880.html (accessed November 30, 2015).

Qi, Wu (2006) China's surging foreign trade: joy tempered with sorrow (29/09/2006). Web Features, Embassy of the People's Republic of China in the United Kingdom of Great Britain and Northern Ireland. Online at http://www.chinese-embassy.org.uk/eng/zt/Features/t274358.htm (accessed November 30, 2015).

Reed, D. (ed.) (1992) *Structural Adjustment and the Environment*, Westview Press, Boulder, CO.

Ritzer, G. (1993) *The McDonaldization of Society*, Pine Forge Press, Thousand Oaks, CA.

Robinson, N.A. (ed.) (1992) *Agenda 21 and UNCED Proceedings*, vols 1 and 2, Oceana Publications, New York.

Rockström, J., Steffen, W., and Noone, K. et al. (2009) A safe operating space for humanity. *Nature*, 461, 472–475.

Schlosser, E. (2001) *Fast Food Nation: The Dark Side of the All-American Meal*, Houghton Mifflin, Boston.

Schmidheiny, S. (1992) *Changing Course*, MIT Press, Cambridge, MA.

Scoones, I., Leach, M., and Newell, P. (eds) (2015) *The Politics of Green Transformations*, Routledge, London.

Selden, T.M. and Song, A. (1995) Neoclassical growth, the J curve for abatement and the inverted U curve for pollution, *Journal of Environmental Economics and Management*, 29, 167–168.

Selwyn, B. (2014) *The Global Development Crisis*, Polity, Cambridge.

Sissel, K. (2002) Brazil and Chile begin third-party verification. *Chemical Week*, July 3, (10), 63.

Stirling, A. (2015) Emancipating transformations: from controlling "the transition" to culturing plural radical progress, in *The Politics of Green Transformation* (eds, I. Scoones, M. Leach, and P. Newell), Abingdon: Routledge, pp. 54–68.

Sutcliffe, B. (2000) Development after ecology, in *From Modernization to Globalization: Perspectives on Development and Social Change* (eds, J. Timmons Roberts and A. Hite), Blackwell, Oxford, pp. 328–339.

Swilling, M. and Annecke, E. (2012) *Just Transitions: Explorations of Sustainability in an Unfair World*, UCT Press, South Africa

Timmons Roberts, J. and Thanos, N.D. (2003) *Trouble in Paradise: Globalization and Environmental Crises in Latin America*, Routledge, New York.

UNEP (2011) *Towards a Green Economy: Pathways to Sustainable Development and Poverty Eradication*, United Nations Environment Programme, Nairobi. Online at www.unep.org/greeneconomy (accessed July 12, 2014).

Vaillancourt, J.G. (2000) Sustainability and Agenda 21, in *Sustainability and Unsustainability on the Road from Rio* (eds, J. Timmons Roberts, E. Viola, F. Buttel and A. Hite). Book manuscript in revision.

Wanner, T. (2015) The new "passive revolution" of the green economy and growth discourse: maintaining the "sustainable development" of neoliberal capitalism. *New Political Economy*, 20 (1), 21–41.

World Bank (1992) *World Development Report 1992: Development and the Environment*, World Bank, Washington, DC.

World Bank (2012) *Inclusive Green Growth: The Pathway to Sustainable Development*, World Bank, Washington, DC.

Yum! Brands Co. (2007) "About Yum! Brands." Online at http://www.yum.com/about/default.asp

Part I
Going Global

Introduction

The debate about whether contemporary globalization is or can be made compatible with sustainable development takes us to the heart of one of the key controversies of our times. Does a globalizing economy provide new technologies, services, and sources of finance that are a pre-requisite for tackling problems of environment and development? Or is a globalizing economy the source of the problem, intensifying patterns of resource consumption and social inequalities and unable to respect finite natural limits because of its obsession with infinite growth?

The chapters in this section of the book reflect both these polarized views, from a faith in gradual ecological modernization of the global economy as institutions, norms, and behavior begin to address environmental challenges (see the contribution by Mol), to a more radical ecological perspective that questions the viability of growth and of an ever globalizing economy (as argued by Goldsmith). Between these polarities there are positions that occupy more of a middle ground, where the answer to the question "is globalization good or bad for the environment?" is more often than not: "It depends." It depends on the sector and region, how integrated they into the global economy and how vulnerable they are to price fluctuations and global environmental changes, for example, and it depends on how effective institutions are at reducing harm, regulating impacts, and maximizing the positive aspects of globalization. This is the position adopted by Najam et al. in this section.

The debate has a long and contested history which the chapters in this section speak to, providing an account of how our current predicament came to be in the context of debates about the "Anthropocene": a new geological era in which "human" forces and societies have become a global geophysical force (see Steffen et al.), and by charting some of the early attempts to articulate politically and institutionally what a more sustainable model of development might look like, most notably

The Globalization and Environment Reader, First Edition. Edited by Peter Newell and J. Timmons Roberts.
Editorial material and organization © 2017 John Wiley & Sons, Ltd. Published 2017 by John Wiley & Sons, Ltd.

through the work of the Brundtland Commission whose famous report *Our Common Future* we provide a summary of here.

Steffen and his colleagues in their now-famous contribution on the Anthropocene show that "human forces have become so pervasive and profound that they rival the great forces of nature and are pushing the Earth into 'terra incognita.'" The Anthropocene is often said in these accounts to have started in the late eighteenth century, when analyses of air trapped in polar ice showed the beginning of growing global concentrations of carbon dioxide (Crutzen, 2002: 23). The "major steps" in this shifting alignment of forces include the period from the end of the eighteenth century to 1950 and, "from the perspective of the functioning of the Earth System as a whole, the very significant acceleration since 1950" (Crutzen and Steffen, 2003: 253). This latter period, in particular, is marked out as "the one in which human activities rapidly changed from merely influencing the global environment in some ways to dominating it in many ways" (Crutzen and Steffen, 2003: 253). If we extend the analysis to the other planetary boundaries which have been "overshot" (Rockström et al., 2009) such as the nitrogen cycle and biodiversity and species loss, the evolving nature of the global political economy and the intensification of specific patterns of production, exploitation, and consumption associated with globalization, necessarily feature centrally in any explanation of causation.

If this provides the long historical background to the mounting sense of an environmental crisis, the 1987 Brundtland report *Our Common Future* constituted one of first attempts to articulate a global response to it, a section of which we reproduce. Indeed as the address by Gro Harlem Brundtland declares, the commission "grew out of an awareness that over the course of this century, the relationship between the human world and the planet that sustains it has undergone a profound change." The report first coined the term "sustainable development" which it defined as "development which meets the needs of current generations without compromising the ability of future generations to meet their own needs." In many ways it sought to reconcile differences of opinion about whether development or the environment should come first as well as respond to the critiques of mainstream development models that followed in the wake of the Club of Rome report *Limits to Growth* in 1972. This report painted an alarming picture of resource scarcity produced by a growing economy and a rapidly increasing population putting unsustainable pressure on a finite resource base. What followed was an attempt to show how the international community could protect the environment, address poverty, and do so as part of its quest for growth. This can be observed in the emphasis on changing "the quality of growth," integrating "environment and economics in decision-making" but unquestioningly as a project to "revive growth."

In the essay that follows by ecologist Nicolas Hildyard, what Brundtland (and the "Earth Summit" that followed five years later in Rio de Janiero) did was seek to obscure the role of development and economic growth in causing the environmental crisis and instead, through careful political maneuvering and diplomatic stage management, present it as the necessary solution to global environmental problems. He shows how big business, from being seen as culprits for environmental damage, were now being rehabilitated as the saviors of the planet with their capital, green technologies, and cleaner production processes, hence the title of his contribution "Foxes in Charge of the Chickens." Interestingly for Hildyard and others writing in this "political ecology" tradition, the key fault lines were not so much the global North and South, but rather between two other groups. On the one hand he saw global elites from states, corporations, the scientific community and conservative elements of the environmental movement, for whom "global management" of the environment offered the prospect of new roles, new funding, and new legitimacy. On the other hand Hidyard saw poorer communities and radical movements, for whom questions of sustainability and social justice are two sides of the same coin, excluded and marginalized by this growing "eco-cracy" of global managers that "threaten to unleash a new wave of colonialism in which the management of people, even whole societies, for the benefit of commercial interest is now justified in the name of environmental protection." For Hildyard the question is "whose common future are we fighting for?" (The Ecologist, 1993).

Following in a similar vein of a radical ecological position, though focused less on the global governance of the environment and more on the global economy itself, the piece by Edward Goldsmith holds that globalization is antithetical to any notion of sustainability. His starting point is that "By now, it should be clear that our environment is becoming ever less capable of sustaining the growing impact of our economic activities." What globalization does in this view is globalize and export an unsustainable model of development in the Global North to the Global South. This is achieved through investment flows and production overseen by Transnational Corporations and with the backing of powerful global institutions such as the World Trade Organization, the World Bank, and the International Monetary Fund. These huge organizations pressure countries to open up their natural resource sectors (such as forests and mineral reserves) to foreign exploitation. The effect is, as Goldsmith claims, "to generalize this destructive process, which means transforming the vast mass of still largely self-sufficient people living in the rural areas of the Third World into consumers of capital-intensive goods and services."

In the chapter that follows, Arthur Mol develops a very different position. He claims that the global economy, albeit unevenly, is actually undergoing a process of "greening." He calls this a process of "ecological modernization" whereby through shifts in business practices, institutional reforms at the regional and global level and an active global environmental movement, environmental values and perspectives are creeping into the everyday functioning of the global economy. This means that "economic processes of production and consumption are increasingly analyzed and judged, as well as designed and organized from both an economic *and* an ecological point of view" according to Mol. The effect of these "actors, institutions and mechanisms" that are in the making is to "tame the global treadmill of capitalism" as he puts it, by opening up opportunities for de-coupling and de-linking growth from increased pollution. This is similar in many ways to the stance taken in the essay that follows by Najam et al. who, while raising concern about the environmental consequences of the current trajectory of globalization, argue that "better governance is the key to both managing globalization and the global environment," and "More importantly, it is also the key to managing the relationship between the two." They lay out a series of propositions about globalization and the environment, which helpfully frame many of the essays that follow.

In terms of laying down the historical context of debates about the effect of a globalizing economy on the environment, of highlighting key milestones in global responses to environmental crisis, the Brundtland Commission and the Earth Summit, and articulating sharply contrasting views about both the adequacy and appropriateness of those responses and the overall compatibility of globalization and sustainability, this section sets up the rest of the collection.

References

Crutzen, P. (2002) "Geology of mankind." *Nature*, 415, 23.

Crutzen, P. and Steffen, W. (2003) "How long have we been in the anthropocene?" *Climatic Change*, 61: 251–257.

Ecologist, The (1993) *Whose Common Future? Reclaiming the Commons*, Earthscan, London.

Rockström, J., Steffen, W., and Noone, K. et al. (2009) "A safe operating space for humanity." *Nature*, 461, 472–475.

1

The Anthropocene: Are Humans Now Overwhelming the Great Forces of Nature? (2007)

Will Steffen, Paul J. Crutzen, and John R. McNeill

Introduction

Global warming and many other human-driven changes to the environment are raising concerns about the future of Earth's environment and its ability to provide the services required to maintain viable human civilizations. The consequences of this unintended experiment of humankind on its own life support system are hotly debated, but worst-case scenarios paint a gloomy picture for the future of contemporary societies.

Underlying global change (Box 1.1) are human-driven alterations of *i*) the biological fabric of the Earth; *ii*) the stocks and flows of major elements in the planetary machinery such as nitrogen, carbon, phosphorus, and silicon; and *iii*) the energy balance at the Earth's surface [2]. The term *Anthropocene* (Box 1.2) suggests that the Earth has now left its natural geological epoch, the present interglacial state called the Holocene. Human activities have become so pervasive and profound that they rival the great forces of Nature and are pushing the Earth into planetary *terra incognita*. The Earth is rapidly moving into a less biologically diverse, less forested, much warmer, and probably wetter and stormier state.

The phenomenon of global change represents a profound shift in the relationship between humans and the rest of nature. Interest in this fundamental issue has escalated rapidly in the international research community, leading to innovative new research projects like Integrated History and future of People on Earth (IHOPE) [8].

Will Steffen, Paul J. Crutzen, and John R. McNeill. 2007. "The Anthropocene: Are Humans Now Overwhelming the Great Forces of Nature?" In *Ambio*, 36: 8 (Dec., 2007), pp. 614–621. Reproduced with permission from The Royal Swedish Academy of Sciences.

The objective of this paper is to explore one aspect of the IHOPE research agenda – the evolution of humans and our societies from hunter-gatherers to a global geophysical force.

To address this objective, we examine the trajectory of the human enterprise through time, from the arrival of humans on Earth through the present and into the next centuries. Our analysis is based on a few critical questions:

- Is the imprint of human activity on the environment discernible at the global scale? How has this imprint evolved through time?
- How does the magnitude and rate of human impact compare with the natural variability of the Earth's environment? Are human effects similar to or greater than the great forces of nature in terms of their influence on Earth System functioning?
- What are the socioeconomic, cultural, political, and technological developments that change the relationship between human societies and the rest of nature and lead to accelerating impacts on the Earth System?

Pre-Anthropocene Events

Before the advent of agriculture about 10,000–12,000 years ago, humans lived in small groups as hunter-gatherers. In recent centuries, under the influence of noble savage myths, it was often thought that preagricultural humans lived in idyllic harmony with their environment. Recent research has painted a rather different picture, producing evidence of widespread human impact on the environment through predation and the modification of landscapes, often through use of fire [9]. However, as the examples below show, the human imprint on environment may have been discernible at local, regional, and even continental scales, but preindustrial humans did not have the technological or organizational capability to match or dominate the great forces of nature.

The mastery of fire by our ancestors provided humankind with a powerful monopolistic tool unavailable to other species, that put us firmly on the long path towards the Anthropocene. Remnants of charcoal from human hearths indicate that the first use of fire by our bipedal ancestors, belonging to the genus *Homo erectus,* occurred a couple of million years ago. Use of fire followed the earlier development of stone tool and weapon making, another major step in the trajectory of the human enterprise.

Early humans used the considerable power of fire to their advantage [9]. Fire kept dangerous animals at a respectful distance, especially during the night, and helped in hunting protein-rich, more easily digestible food. The diet of our ancestors changed from mainly vegetarian to omnivorous, a shift that led to enhanced physical and mental capabilities. Hominid brain size nearly tripled up to an average volume of about 1,300 cm^3, and gave humans the largest ratio between brain and body size of any species [10]. As a consequence, spoken and then, about 10,000 years ago, written language could begin to develop, promoting communication and transfer of knowledge within and between generations of humans, efficient accumulation of knowledge, and social learning over many thousands of years in an impressive catalytic process, involving many human brains and their discoveries and innovations. This power is minimal in other species.

Among the earliest impacts of humans on the Earth's biota are the late Pleistocene megafauna extinctions, a wave of extinctions during the last ice age extending from the woolly mammoth in northern Eurasia to giant wombats in Australia [11–13]. A similar wave of extinctions was observed later in the Americas. Although there has been vigorous debate about the relative roles of climate variability and human predation in driving these extinctions, there is little doubt that humans played a significant role, given the strong correlation between the extinction events and human migration patterns. A later but even more profound impact of humans on fauna was the domestication of animals, beginning with the dog up to 100,000 years ago [14] and continuing into the Holocene with horses, sheep, cattle, goats, and the other familiar farm animals. The concomitant domestication of plants during the early to mid-Holocene led to agriculture, which initially also developed through the use of fire for forest clearing and, somewhat later, irrigation [15].

Box 1.1   Global Change and the Earth System

The term *Earth System* refers to the suite of interacting physical, chemical and biological global-scale cycles and energy fluxes that provide the life-support system for life at the surface of the planet [1]. This definition of the Earth System goes well beyond the notion that the geophysical processes encompassing the Earth's two great fluids – the ocean and the atmosphere – generate the planetary life-support system on their own. In our definition biological/ecological processes are an integral part of the functioning of the Earth System and not merely the recipient of changes in the coupled ocean-atmosphere part of the system. A second critical feature is that forcings and feedbacks *within* the Earth System are as important as external drivers of change, such as the flux of energy from the sun. Finally, the Earth System includes humans, our societies, and our activities; thus, humans are not an outside force perturbing an otherwise natural system but rather an integral and interacting part of the Earth System itself.

We use the term *global change* to mean both the biophysical and the socio-economic changes that are altering the structure and the functioning of the Earth System. Global change includes alterations in a wide range of global-scale phenomena: land use and land cover, urbanisation, globalisation, coastal ecosystems, atmospheric composition, riverine flow, nitrogen cycle, carbon cycle, physical climate, marine food chains, biological diversity, population, economy, resource use, energy, transport, communication, and so on. Interactions and linkages between the various changes listed above are also part of global change and are just as important as the individual changes themselves. Many components of global change do not occur in linear fashion but rather show strong nonlinearities.

Box 1.2   The Anthropocene

Holocene ("Recent Whole") is the name given to the postglacial geological epoch of the past ten to twelve thousand years as agreed upon by the International Geological Congress in Bologna in 1885 [3]. During the Holocene, accelerating in the industrial period, humankind's activities became a growing geological and morphological force, as recognised early by a number of scientists. Thus, in 1864, Marsh published a book with the title "Man and Nature," more recently reprinted as "The Earth as Modified by Human Action" [4]. Stoppani in 1873 rated human activities as a "new telluric force which in power and universality may be compared to the greater forces of earth" (quoted from Clark [5]). Stoppani already spoke of the anthropozoic era. Humankind has now inhabited or visited all places on Earth; he has even set foot on the moon. The great Russian geologist and biologist Vernadsky [6] in 1926 recognized the increasing power of humankind in the environment with the following excerpt "... the direction in which the processes of evolution must proceed, namely towards increasing consciousness and thought, and forms having greater and greater influence on their surroundings." He, the French Jesuit priest P. Teilhard de Chardin and E. Le Roy in 1924 coined the term "noosphere," the world of thought, knowledge society, to mark the growing role played by humankind's brainpower and technological talents in shaping its own future and environment. A few years ago the term "Anthropocene" has been introduced by one of the authors (P.J.C.) [7] for the current geological epoch to emphasize the central role of humankind in geology and ecology. The impact of current human activities is projected to last over very long periods. For example, because of past and future anthropogenic emissions of CO_2, climate may depart significantly from natural behaviour over the next 50,000 years.

According to one hypothesis, early agricultural development, around the mid-Holocene, affected Earth System functioning so fundamentally that it prevented the onset of the next ice age [16]. The argument proposes that clearing of forests for agriculture about 8,000 years ago and irrigation of rice about 5,000 years ago led to increases in atmospheric carbon dioxide (CO_2) and methane (CH_4) concentrations, reversing trends of concentration decreases established in the early Holocene. These rates of forest clearing, however, were small compared with the massive amount of land transformation that has taken place in the last 300 years [17]. Nevertheless, deforestation and agricultural development in the 8,000 to 5,000 BP period may have led to small increases in CO_2 and CH_4 concentrations (maybe about 5–10 parts per million for CO_2) but increases that were perhaps large enough to stop the onset of glaciation in northeast Canada thousands of years ago. However, recent analyses of solar forcing in the late Quaternary [18] and of natural carbon cycle dynamics [19, 20] argue that natural processes can explain the observed pattern of atmospheric CO_2 variation through the Holocene. Thus, the hypothesis that the advent of agriculture thousands of years ago changed the course of glacial-interglacial dynamics remains an intriguing but unproven beginning of the Anthropocene.

The first significant use of fossil fuels in human history came in China during the Song Dynasty (960–1279) [21, 22]. Coal mines in the north, notably Shanxi province, provided abundant coal for use in China's growing iron industry. At its height, in the late 11th century, China's coal production reached levels equal to all of Europe (not including Russia) in 1700. But China suffered many setbacks, such as epidemics and invasions, and the coal industry apparently went into a long decline. Meanwhile in England coal mines provided fuel for home heating, notably in London, from at least the 13th century [23, 24]. The first commission charged to investigate the evils of coal smoke began work in 1285 [24]. But as a concentrated fuel, coal had its advantages, especially when wood and charcoal grew dear, so by the late 1600s London depended heavily upon it and burned some 360,000 tons annually. The iron forges of Song China and the furnaces of medieval London were regional exceptions, however; most of the world burned wood or charcoal rather than resorting to fuel subsidies from the Carboniferous.

Preindustrial human societies indeed influenced their environment in many ways, from local to continental scales. Most of the changes they wrought were based on knowledge, probably gained from observation and trial-and-error, of natural ecosystem dynamics and its modification to ease the tasks of hunting, gathering, and eventually of farming. Preindustrial societies could and did modify coastal and terrestrial ecosystems but they did not have the numbers, social and economic organisation, or technologies needed to equal or dominate the great forces of Nature in magnitude or rate. Their impacts remained largely local and transitory, well within the bounds of the natural variability of the environment.

...

The Industrial Era (ca. 1800–1945): Stage 1 of the Anthropocene

One of the three or four most decisive transitions in the history of humankind, potentially of similar importance in the history of the Earth itself, was the onset of industrialization. In the footsteps of the Enlightenment, the transition began in the 1700s in England and the Low Countries for reasons that remain in dispute among historians [25]. Some emphasize material factors such as wood shortages and abundant water power and coal in England, while others point to social and political structures that rewarded risk-taking and innovation, matters connected to legal regimes, a nascent banking system, and a market culture. Whatever its origins, the transition took off quickly and by 1850 had transformed England and was beginning to transform much of the rest of the world.

What made industrialization central for the Earth System was the enormous expansion in the use of fossil fuels, first coal and then oil and gas as well. Hitherto humankind had relied on energy captured from ongoing flows in the form of wind, water, plants, and animals, and from the 100- or 200-year stocks held in trees. Fossil fuel use offered access to carbon stored from millions of years of photosynthesis: a massive energy subsidy from the deep past to modern society, upon which a great deal of our modern wealth depends.

Industrial societies as a rule use four or five times as much energy as did agrarian ones, which in turn used three or four times as much as did hunting and gathering societies [26]. Without this transition to a high-energy society it is inconceivable that global population could have risen from a billion around 1820 to more than six billion today, or that perhaps one billion of the more fortunate among us could lead lives of comfort unknown to any but kings and courtiers in centuries past.

Prior to the widespread use of fossil fuels, the energy harvest available to humankind was tightly constrained. Water and wind power were available only in favoured locations, and only in societies where the relevant technologies of watermills, sailing ships, and windmills had been developed or imported. Muscular energy derived from animals, and through them from plants, was limited by the area of suitable land for crops and forage, in many places by shortages of water, and everywhere by inescapable biological inefficiencies: plants photosynthesize less than a percent of the solar energy that falls on the Earth, and animals eating those plants retain only a tenth of the chemical energy stored in plants. All this amounted to a bottleneck upon human numbers, the global economy, and the ability of humankind to shape the rest of the biosphere and to influence the functioning of the Earth System.

The invention (some would say refinement) of the steam engine by James Watt in the 1770s and 1780s and the turn to fossil fuels shattered this bottleneck, opening an era of far looser constraints upon energy supply, upon human numbers, and upon the global economy. Between 1800 and 2000 population grew more than six-fold, the global economy about 50-fold, and energy use about 40-fold [27]. It also opened an era of intensified and ever-mounting human influence upon the Earth System.

Fossil fuels and their associated technologies – steam engines, internal combustion engines – made many new activities possible and old ones more efficient. For example, with abundant energy it proved possible to synthesize ammonia from atmospheric nitrogen, in effect to make fertilizer out of air, a process pioneered by the German chemist Fritz Haber early in the 20th century. The Haber-Bosch synthesis, as it would become known (Carl Bosch was an industrialist) revolutionized agriculture and sharply increased crop yields all over the world, which, together with vastly improved medical provisions, made possible the surge in human population growth.

The imprint on the global environment of the industrial era was, in retrospect, clearly evident by the early to mid 20th century [28]. Deforestation and conversion to agriculture were extensive in the midlatitudes, particularly in the northern hemisphere. Only about 10% of the global terrestrial surface had been "domesticated" at the beginning of the industrial era around 1800, but this figure rose significantly to about 25–30% by 1950 [17]. Human transformation of the hydrological cycle was also evident in the accelerating number of large dams, particularly in Europe and North America [29]. The flux of nitrogen compounds through the coastal zone had increased over 10-fold since 1800 [30].

The global-scale transformation of the environment by industrialization was, however, nowhere more evident than in the atmosphere. The concentrations of CH_4 and nitrous oxide (N_2O) had risen by 1950 to about 1,250 and 288 ppbv, respectively, noticeably above their preindustrial values of about 850 and 272 ppbv [31, 32]. By 1950 the atmospheric CO_2 concentration had pushed above 300 ppmv, above its preindustrial value of 270–275 ppmv, and was beginning to accelerate sharply [33].

Quantification of the human imprint on the Earth System can be most directly related to the advent and spread of fossil fuel-based energy systems [...], the signature of which is the accumulation of CO_2 in the atmosphere roughly in proportion to the amount of fossil fuels that have been consumed. We propose that atmospheric CO_2 concentration can be used as a single, simple indicator to track the progression of the Anthropocene, to define its stages quantitatively, and to compare the human imprint on the Earth System with natural variability [...].

Around 1850, near the beginning of Anthropocene Stage 1, the atmospheric CO_2 concentration was 285 ppm, within the range of natural variability for interglacial periods during the late Quaternary period. During the course of Stage 1 from 1800/50 to 1945, the CO_2 concentration rose by about 25 ppm, enough to surpass the upper limit of natural variation through the Holocene and thus provide the first indisputable evidence that human activities were affecting the environment at the global scale. We therefore assign the beginning of Anthropocene to coincide with the beginning of the industrial era, in the 1800–1850 period. This first stage of the Anthropocene ended abruptly around 1945, when the most rapid and pervasive shift in the human-environment relationship began.

The Great Acceleration (1945–ca. 2015): Stage 2 of the Anthropocene

The human enterprise suddenly accelerated after the end of the Second World War [27] Population doubled in just 50 years, to over 6 billion by the end of the 20th century, but the global economy increased by more than 15-fold. Petroleum consumption has grown by a factor of 3.5 since 1960, and the number of motor vehicles increased dramatically from about 40 million at the end of the War to nearly 700 million by 1996. From 1950 to 2000 the percentage of the world's population living in urban areas grew from 30 to 50% and continues to grow strongly. The interconnectedness of cultures is increasing rapidly with the explosion in electronic communication, international travel and the globalization of economies.

The pressure on the global environment from this burgeoning human enterprise is intensifying sharply. Over the past 50 years, humans have changed the world's ecosystems more rapidly and extensively than in any other comparable period in human history [37]. The Earth is in its sixth great extinction event, with rates of species loss growing rapidly for both terrestrial and marine ecosystems [38]. The atmospheric concentrations of several important greenhouse gases have increased substantially, and the Earth is warming rapidly [39]. More nitrogen is now converted from the atmosphere into reactive forms by fertilizer production and fossil fuel combustion than by all of the natural processes in terrestrial ecosystems put together [...] [40].

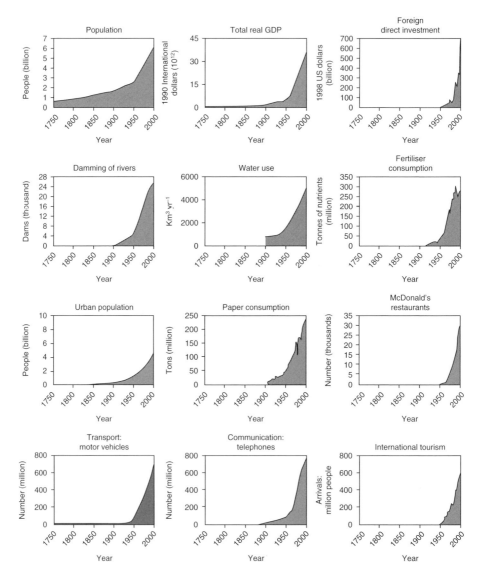

Figure 1.1   The change in the human enterprise from 1750 to 2000. [28]. The Great Acceleration is clearly shown in every component of the human enterprise included in the figure. Either the component was not present before 1950 (e.g., foreign direct investment) or its rate of change increased sharply after 1950 (e.g., population).

The remarkable explosion of the human enterprise from the mid-20th century, and the associated global-scale impacts on many aspects of Earth System functioning, mark the second stage of the Anthropocene – the Great Acceleration [41]. In many respects the stage had been set for the Great Acceleration by 1890 or 1910. Population growth was proceeding faster than at any previous time in human history, as well as economic growth. Industrialization had gathered irresistible momentum, and was spreading quickly in North America, Europe, Russia, and Japan. Automobiles and airplanes had appeared, and soon rapidly transformed mobility. The world economy was growing ever more tightly linked by mounting flows of migration, trade, and capital. The years 1870 to 1914 were, in fact, an age of globalization in the world economy. Mines and plantations in diverse lands such as Australia, South Africa, and Chile were opening or expanding in response to the emergence of growing markets for their products, especially in the cities of the industrialized world.

At the same time, cities burgeoned as public health efforts, such as checking waterborne disease through sanitation measures, for the first time in world history made it feasible for births consistently to outnumber deaths in urban environments. A major transition was underway in which the characteristic habitat of the human species, which for several millennia had been the village, now was becoming the city. (In 1890 perhaps 200 million people lived in cities worldwide, but by 2000 the figure had leapt to three billion, half of the human population). Cities had long been the seats of managerial and technological innovation and engines of economic growth, and in the Great Acceleration played that role with even greater effect.

However, the Great Acceleration truly began only after 1945. In the decades between 1914 and 1945 the Great Acceleration was stalled by changes in politics and the world economy. Three great wrenching events lay behind this: World War I, the Great Depression, and World War II. Taken together, they slowed population growth, checked – indeed temporarily reversed – the integration and growth of the world economy. They also briefly checked urbanization, as city populations led the way in reducing their birth rates. Some European cities in the 1930s in effect went on reproduction strikes, so that (had they maintained this reluctance) they would have disappeared within decades. Paradoxically, however, these events also helped to initiate the Great Acceleration.

The lessons absorbed about the disasters of world wars and depression inspired a new regime of international institutions after 1945 that helped create conditions for resumed economic growth. The United States in particular championed more open trade and capital flows, reintegrating much of the world economy and helping growth rates reach their highest ever levels in the period from 1950 to 1973. At the same time, the pace of technological change surged. Out of World War II came a number of new technologies—many of which represented new applications for fossil fuels – and a commitment to subsidized research and development, often in the form of alliances among government, industry, and universities. This proved enormously effective and, in a climate of renewed prosperity, ensured unprece-dented funding for science and technology, unprecedented recruitment into these fields, and unprecedented advances as well.

The Great Acceleration took place in an intellectual, cultural, political, and legal context in which the growing impacts upon the Earth System counted for very little in the calculations and decisions made in the world's ministries, boardrooms, laboratories, farmhouses, village huts, and, for that matter, bedrooms. This context was not new, but it too was a necessary condition for the Great Acceleration.

The exponential character of the Great Acceleration is obvious from our quantification of the human imprint on the Earth System, using atmospheric CO_2 concentration as the indicator [...]. Although by the Second World War the CO_2 concentration had clearly risen above the upper limit of the Holocene, its growth rate hit a take-off point around 1950. Nearly three-quarters of the anthropogenically driven rise in CO_2 concentration has occurred since 1950 (from about 310 to 380 ppm), and about half of the total rise (48 ppm) has occurred in just the last 30 years.

Stewards of the Earth System? (ca. 2015–?): Stage 3 of the Anthropocene

Humankind will remain a major geological force for many millennia, maybe millions of years, to come. To develop a universally accepted strategy to ensure the sustainability of Earth's life support system against human-induced stresses is one of the greatest research and policy challenges ever to confront humanity. Can humanity meet this challenge?

Signs abound to suggest that the intellectual, cultural, political and legal context that permitted the Great Acceleration after 1945 has shifted in ways that could curtail it [41]. Not surprisingly, some reflective people noted human impact upon the environment centuries and even millennia ago. However, as a major societal concern it dates from the 1960s with the rise of modern environmentalism. Observations showed incontrovertibly that the concentration of CO_2 in the atmosphere was rising markedly [42]. In the 1980s temperature measurements showed global warming was a reality, a fact that encountered political opposition because of its implications, but within 20 years was no longer in serious doubt [39]. Scientific observations showing the erosion of the earth's stratospheric ozone layer led to international agreements reducing the production and use of CFCs (chlorofluorocarbons) [43]. On numerous ecological issues local, national, and international environmental policies were devised, and the environment routinely became a consideration, although rarely a dominant one, in political and economic calculations.

This process represents the beginning of the third stage of the Anthropocene, in which the recognition that human activities are indeed affecting the structure and functioning of the Earth System as a whole (as opposed to local- and regional-scale environmental issues) is filtering through to decision-making at many levels. The growing awareness of human influence on the Earth System has been aided by *i*) rapid advances in research and understanding, the most innovative of which is interdisciplinary work on human-environment systems; *ii*) the enormous power of the internet as a global, self-organizing information system; *iii*) the spread of more free and open societies, supporting independent media; and *iv*) the growth of democratic political systems, narrowing the scope for the exercise of arbitrary state power and strengthening the role of civil society. Humanity is, in one way or another, becoming a self-conscious, active agent in the operation of its own life support system [44].

This process is still in train, and where it may lead remains quite uncertain. However, three broad philosophical approaches can be discerned in the growing debate about dealing with the changing global environment [28, 44].

Business-as-usual. In this conceptualisation of the next stage of the Anthropocene, the institutions and economic system that have driven the Great Acceleration continue to dominate human affairs. This approach is based on several assumptions. First, global change will not be severe or rapid enough to cause major disruptions to the global economic system or to other important aspects of societies, such as human health. Second, the existing market-oriented economic system can deal autonomously with any adaptations that are required. This assumption is based on the fact that as societies have become wealthier, they have dealt effectively with some local and regional pollution problems [45]. Examples include the clean-up of major European rivers and the amelioration of the acid rain problem in western Europe and eastern North America. Third, resources required to mitigate global change proactively would be better spent on more pressing human needs.

The business-as-usual approach appears, on the surface, to be a safe and conservative way forward. However, it entails considerable risks. As the Earth System changes in response to human activities, it operates at a time scale that is mismatched with human decision-making or with the workings of the economic system. The long-term momentum built into the Earth System means that by the time humans realize that a business-as-usual approach may not work, the world will be committed to further decades or even centuries of environmental change. Collapse of modern, globalized society under uncontrollable environmental change is one possible outcome.

[...]

Mitigation. An alternative pathway into the future is based on the recognition that the threat of further global change is serious enough that it must be dealt with proactively. The mitigation pathway attempts to take the human pressure off of the Earth System by vastly improved technology and management, wise use of Earth's resources, control of human and domestic animal population, and overall careful use and restoration of the natural environment. The ultimate goal is to reduce the human modification of the global environment to avoid dangerous or difficult-to-control levels and rates of change [47], and ultimately to allow the Earth System to function in a pre-Anthropocene way.

Technology must play a strong role in reducing the pressure on the Earth System [48]. Over the past several decades rapid advances in transport, energy, agriculture, and other sectors have led to a trend of dematerialization in several advanced economies. The amount and value of economic activity continue to grow but the amount of physical material flowing through the economy does not.

There are further technological opportunities. Worldwide energy use is equivalent to only 0.05% of the solar radiation reaching the continents. Only 0.4% of the incoming solar radiation, 1 W m^{-2}, is converted to chemical energy by photosynthesis on land. Human appropriation of net primary production is about 10%, including agriculture, fiber, and fisheries [49]. In addition to the many opportunities for energy conservation, numerous technologies – from solar thermal and photovoltaic through nuclear fission and fusion to wind power and biofuels from forests and crops – are available now or under development to replace fossil fuels.

Although improved technology is essential for mitigating global change, it may not be enough on its own. Changes in societal values and individual behaviour will likely be necessary [50]. Some signs of these changes are now evident, but the Great Acceleration has considerable momentum and appears to be intensifying [51]. The critical question is whether the trends of dematerialization and shifting societal values become strong enough to trigger a transition of our globalizing society towards a much more sustainable one.

Geo-engineering options. The severity of global change, particularly changes to the climate system, may force societies to consider more drastic options. For example, the anthropogenic emission of aerosol particles (e.g., smoke, sulphate, dust, etc.) into the atmosphere leads to a net cooling effect because these particles and their influence on cloud properties enhance backscattering of incoming solar radiation. Thus, aerosols act in opposition to the greenhouse effect, masking some of the warming we would otherwise see now [52]. Paradoxically, a clean-up of air pollution can thus increase greenhouse warming, perhaps leading to an additional 1°C of warming and bringing the Earth closer to "dangerous" levels of climate change. This and other amplifying effects, such as feedbacks from the carbon cycle as the Earth warms [53], could render mitigation efforts largely ineffectual. Just to stabilize the atmospheric concentration of CO_2, without taking into account these amplifying effects, requires a reduction in anthropogenic emissions by more than 60% – a herculean task considering that most people on Earth, in order to increase their standard of living, are in need of much additional energy. One engineering approach to reducing the amount of CO_2 in the atmosphere is its sequestration in underground reservoirs [54]. This "geo-sequestration" would not only alleviate the pressures on climate, but would also lessen the expected acidification of the ocean surface waters, which leads to dissolution of calcareous marine organisms [55].

In this situation some argue for geo-engineering solutions, a highly controversial topic. Geo-engineering involves purposeful manipulation by humans of global-scale Earth System processes with the intention of counteracting anthropogenically driven environmental change such as greenhouse warming [56]. One proposal is based on the cooling effect of aerosols noted in the previous paragraph [57]. The idea is to artificially enhance the Earth's albedo by releasing sunlight-reflective material, such as sulphate particles, in the stratosphere, where they remain for 1–2 years before settling in the troposphere. The sulphate particles would be produced by the oxidation of SO_2, just as happens during volcanic eruptions. In order to compensate for a doubling of CO_2, if this were to happen, the input of sulphur would have to be about 1–2 Tg S y^{-1} (compared to an input of about 10 Tg S by Mount Pinatubo in 1991). The sulphur injections would have to occur for as long as CO_2 levels remain high.

Looking more deeply into the evolution of the Anthropocene, future generations of *H. sapiens* will likely do all they can to prevent a new ice-age by adding powerful artificial greenhouse gases to the atmosphere. Similarly, any drop in CO_2 levels to low concentrations, causing strong reductions in photosynthesis and agricultural productivity, might be combated by artificial releases of CO_2, maybe from earlier CO_2 sequestration. And likewise, far into the future, *H. sapiens* will deflect meteorites and asteroids before they could hit the Earth.

For the present, however, just the suggestion of geo-engineering options can raise serious ethical questions and intense debate. In addition to fundamental ethical concerns, a critical issue is the possibility for unintended and unanticipated side effects that could have severe consequences. The cure could be worse than the disease. For the sulphate injection example described above, the residence time of the sulphate particles in the atmosphere is only a few years, so if serious side-effects occurred, the injections could be discontinued and the climate would relax to its former high CO_2 state within a decade.

The Great Acceleration is reaching criticality [...]. Enormous, immediate challenges confront humanity over the next few decades as it attempts to pass through a bottleneck of continued population growth, excessive resource use and environmental deterioration. In most parts of the world the demand for fossil fuels overwhelms the desire to significantly reduce greenhouse gas emissions. About 60% of ecosystem services are already degraded and will continue to degrade further unless significant societal changes in values and management occur [37]. There is also evidence for radically different directions built around innovative, knowledge-based solutions. Whatever unfolds, the next few decades will surely be a tipping point in the evolution of the Anthropocene.

References

1   Oldfield, F. and Steffen, W. 2004. The earth system. In: *Global Change and the Earth System: A Planet Under Pressure*. Steffen, W., Sanderson, A., Tyson, P., Jägeir J., Matson, P., Moore, B. Ill, Oldfield, F., Richardson, K., et al. (eds). The IGBP Global Change Series, Springer-Verlag, Berlin, Heidelburg, New York, p. 7.

2   Hansen, J., Nazarenko, L., Ruedy, R., Sato, M., Willis, J., Del Genio, A., Koch, D., Lacis, A., et al. 2005. Earth's energy imbalance: comfirmation and implications. *Science 308*, 1431–1435.

3   *Encyclopaedia Britannica*. 1976. Micropaedia, IX. London.

4   Marsh, G.P. 1965. *The Earth as Modified by Human Action*. Belknap Press, Harvard University Press, Cambridge, MA, 504 pp.

5   Clark, W.C. 1986. Chapter 1. In: *Sustainable Development of the Biosphere*. Clark, W.C. and Munn, R.E. (eds). Cambridge University Press, Cambridge, UK, 491 pp.

6   Vernadski, V.I. 1998. *The Biosphere (translated and annotated version from the original of 1926)*. Copernicus, Springer, New York, 192 pp.

7   Crutzen, P. J. 2002. Geology of mankind: the anthropocene. *Nature 415*, 23.

8   Costanza, R., Graumlich, L. and Steffen, W. (eds). 2006. *Integrated History and Future of People on Earth*. Dahlem Workshop Report 96, MIT Press, Cambridge, MA, 495 pp.

9   Pyne, S. 1997. *World Fire: The Culture of Fire on Earth*. University of Washington Press, Seattle, 379 pp.

10   Tobias, P.V. 1976. The brain in hominid evolution. In: *Encyclopaedia Britannica*, Macropaedia Volume 8. Encyclopedia Britannica, London, p. 1032.

11   Martin, P.S. and Klein, R.G. 1984. *Quaternary Extinctions: A Prehistoric Revolution*. University of Arizona Press, Tucson. 892 pp.

12   Alroy, J. 2001. A multispecies overkill simulation of the End-Pleistocene Megafaunal mass extinction. *Science 292*, 1893–1896.

13   Roberts, R.G., Flannery, T.F., Ayliffe, L.K., Yoshida, H., Olley, J.M., Prideaux, G.J., Laslett, G.M., Baynes, A., et al. 2001. New ages for the last Australian Megafauna: continent-wide extinction about 46,000 years ago. *Science 292*, 1888–1892.

14   Leach, H.M. 2003. Human domestication reconsidered. *Curr. Anthropol. 44*, 349–368.

15   Smith, B.D. 1995. *The Emergence of Agriculture*. Scientific American Library, New York, 231 pp.

16   Ruddiman, W.F. 2003. The anthropogenic greenhouse era began thousands of years ago. *Climat. Chang. 61*, 261–293.

17   Lambin, E.F. and Geist, H.J. (eds). 2006. *Land-Use and Land-Cover Change: Local Processes and Global Impacts*. The IGBP Global Change Series, Springer-Verlag, Berlin, Heidelberg, New York, 222 pp.

18   EPICA Community Members. 2004. Eight glacial cycles from an Antarctic ice core. *Nature 429*, 623–628.

19   Broecker, W.C. and Stocker, T.F. 2006. The Holocene CO_2 rise: anthropogenic or natural? *Eos 87*, (3), 27–29.

20   Joos, F., Gerber, S., Prentice, I.C., Otto-Bliesner, B.L. and Valdes, P.J. 2004. Transient simulations of Holocene atmospheric carbon dioxide and terrestrial carbon since the Last Glacial Maximum. *Glob.I Biogeochem*. Cycles 18, GB2002.

21   Hartwell, R. 1962. A revolution in the iron and coal industries during the Northern Sung. *J. Asian Stud. 21*, 153–162.

22   Hartwell, R. 1967. A cycle of economic change in Imperial China: coal and iron in northeast China, 750–1350. *J. Soc. and Econ. Hist. Orient 10*, 102–159.

23   TeBrake, W.H. 1975. Air pollution and fuel crisis in preindustrial London, 1250–1650. *Technol. Culture 16*, 337–359.

24   Brimblecombe, P. 1987. *The Big Smoke: A History of Air Pollution in London since Medieval Times*. Methuen, London, 185 pp.

25   Mokyr, J. (ed). 1999. *The British Industrial Revolution: An Economic Perspective*. Westview Press, Boulder, CO, 354 pp.

26   Sieferle, R.-P. 2001. *Der Europäische Sonderweg: Ursachen und Factoren*. Stuttgart, 53 pp. (In German).

27   McNeill, J.R. 2001. *Something New Under the Sun*. W.W. Norton, New York, London, 416 pp.

28   Steffen, W., Sanderson, A., Tyson, P.D., Jäger, J., Matson, P., Moore, B. III, Oldfield, F., Richardson, K., et al. 2004. *Global Change and the Earth System: A Planet Under Pressure*. The IGBP Global Change Series, Springer-Verlag, Berlin, Heidelberg, New York, 336 pp.

29   Vörösmarty, C.J., Sharma, K., Fekete, B., Copeland, A.H., Holden, J., Marble, J. and Lough, J.A. 1997. The storage and aging of continental runoff in large reservoir systems of the world. *Ambio 26*, 210–219.

30   Mackenzie, F.T., Ver, L.M. and Lerman, A. 2002. Century-scale nitrogen and phosphorus controls of the carbon cycle. *Chem. Geol. 190*, 13–32.

31   Blunier, T., Chappellaz, J., Schwander, J., Barnola, J.-M., Desperts, T., Stauffer, B. and Raynaud, D. 1993. Atmospheric methane record from a Greenland ice core over the last 1000 years. *J. Geophys. Res. 20*, 2219–2222.

32   Machida, T., Nakazawa, T., Fujii, Y., Aoki, S. and Watanabe, O. 1995. Increase in the atmospheric nitrous oxide concentration during the last 250 years. *Geophys. Res. Lett. 22*, 2921–2924.

33   Etheridge, D.M., Steele, L.P., Langenfelds, R.L., Francey, R.J., Barnola, J.-M. and Morgan, V.I. 1996. Natural and anthropogenic changes in atmospheric CO_2 over the last 1000 years from air in Antarctic ice and firn. *J. Geophys. Res. 101*, 4115–4128.

34   Barnola, J.-M., Raynaud, D., Lorius, C. and Barkov, N.I. 2003 Historical CO_2 record from the Vostok ice core. In: *Trends: A Compendium of Data on Global Change*. Carbon Dioxide Information Analysis Cener, Oak Ridge National Laboratory, U.S. Department of Energy, Oak Ridge, TN.

35   Etheridge, D.M., Steele, L.P., Langenfelds, R.L., Francey, R.J., Barnola, J.-M. and Morgan, V.I. 1998. Historical CO_2 records from the Law Dome DE08, DE08-2, and DSS ice cores. In: *Trends: A Compendium of Data on Global Change*. Carbon Dioxide Information Analysis Center, Oak Ridge National Laboratory, U.S. Department of Energy, Oak Ridge, TN.

36   Indermuhle, A., Stocker, T.F., Fischer, H., Smith, H.J., Joos, F., Wahlen, M., Deck, B., Mastroianni, D., et al. 1999. High-resolution Holocene CO_2-record from the Taylor Dame ice core (Antarctica). *Nature 398*, 121–126.

37   Millennium Ecosystem Assessment. 2005. *Ecosystems & Human Well-being: Synthesis*. Island Press, Washington.

38   Pimm, S.L., Russell, G.J., Gittleman, J.L. and Brooks, T.M. 1995. The future of biodiversity. *Science 269*, 347–350.

39   Intergovernmental Panel on Climate Change (IPCC). 2007. *Climate Change 2007: The Physical Science Basis. Summary for Policymakers*. IPCC Secretariat, World Meteorological Organization, Geneva, Switzerland, 18 pp.

40   Galloway, J.N. and Cowling, E.B. 2002. Reactive nitrogen and the world: two hundred years of change. *Ambio 31*, 64–71.

41   Hibbard, K.A., Crutzen, P.J., Lambin, E.F., Liverman, D., Mantua, N.J., McNeill, J.R., Messerli, B. and Steffen, W. 2006. Decadal interactions of humans and the environment. In: *Integrated History and Future of People on Earth*. Costanza, R., Graumlich, L. and Steffen, W. (eds). Dahlem Workshop Report 96. MIT Press, Cambridge, MA, pp 341–375.

42   Keeling, C.D. and Whorf, T.P. 2005. Atmospheric CO_2 records from sites in the SIO air sampling network. In: *Trends: A Compendium of Data on Global Change*. Carbon Dioxide Information Analysis Center, Oak Ridge National Laboratory, U.S. Department of Energy, Oak Ridge, TN.

43   Crutzen, P. 1995. My life with O_3, NO_x and other YZO_xs. In: *Les Prix Nobel (The Nobel Prizes) 1995*. Almqvist & Wiksell International, Stockholm, pp. 123–157.

44   Schellnhuber, H.-J. 1998. Discourse: Earth System analysis: the scope of the challenge. In: *Earth System Analysis*. Schellnhuber, H.-J. and Wetzel, V. (eds). Springer-Verlag, Berlin, Heidelberg, New York, pp. 3–195.

45   Lomborg, B. 2001. *The Skeptical Environmentalist: Measuring the Real State of the World*. Cambridge University Press, Cambridge, UK, 548 pp.

46   Rahmstorf, S. 2007. A semi-empirical approach to projecting future sea-level rise. *Science 315*, 368–370.

47   Schellnhuber, H.J., Cramer, W., Nakicenovic, N., Wigley, T. and Yohe, G. (eds). 2006. *Avoiding Dangerous Climate Change.* Cambridge University Press, Cambridge, UK, 406 pp.

48   Steffen, W. 2002. Will technology spare the planet? In: *Challenges of a Changing Earth: Proceedings of the Global Change Open Science Conference. Amsterdam, The Netherlands, 10–13 July 2001.* Steffen, W., Jäger, J., Carson, D. and Bradshaw, C. (eds). The IGBP Global Change Series, Springer-Verlag, Berlin, Heidelberg, New York, pp 189–191.

49   Haberl, H. 2006. The energetic metabolism of the European Union and the United States, decadal energy inputs with an emphasis on biomass. *J. Ind. Ecol. 10*, 151–171.

50   Fischer, J., Manning, A.D., Steffen, W., Rose, D.B., Danielle, K., Felton, A., Garnett, S., Gilna, B., et al. 2007. Mind the sustainability gap. *Trends Ecol.* Evol. in press.

51   Rahmstorf, S., Cazenave, A., Church, J.A., Hansen, J.E., Keeling, R.F., Parker, D.E., Somerville, R.C.J., et al. 2007. Recent climate observations compared to projections. *Science, 316,* 709.

52   Andreae, M.O., Jones, C.D. and Cox, P.M. 2005. Strong present day aerosol cooling implies a hot future. *Nature 435,* 1187–1190.

53   Friedlingstein, P., Cox, P., Betts, R., Bopp, L., von Bloh, W., Brovkin, V., Doney, V.S., Eby, M.I., et al. 2006. Climate-carbon cycle feedback analysis, results from the C^{4}MIP model intercomparison. *J. Clim. 19,* 3337–3353.

54   Intergovernmental Panel on Climate Change (IPCC). 2005. *Carbon Dioxide Capture and Storage. A Special Report of Working Group III.* Intergovernmental Panel on Climate Change, Geneva, Switzerland, 430 pp.

55   The Royal Society. 2005. *Ocean Acidification Due to Increasing Atmospheric Carbon Dioxide.* Policy document 12/05. The Royal Society, UK, 68 pp.

56   Schneider, S.H. 2001. Earth systems engineering and management. *Nature 409,* 417–421.

57   Crutzen, P. J. 2006. Albedo enhancement by stratospheric sulfur injections: A contribution to resolve a policy dilemma. *Clint. Chang. 77,* 211–220.

58   Raupach, M.R., Marland, G., Ciais, P., Le Quere, C., Canadell, J.G., Klepper, G. and Field, C.B. 2007. Global and regional drivers of accelerating CO_2 emissions. *Proc. Nat. Acad. Sei.* USA. in press.

59   This paper grew out of discussions at the 96th Dahlem Conference ("Integrated History and future of People on Earth [IHOPE]"), held in Berlin in June 2005. We are grateful to the many colleagues at the Conference who contributed to the stimulating discussions, and to Dr Julia Lupp, the Dahlem Conference organizer, for permission to base this paper on these discussions.

60   First submitted 31 May 2007. Accepted for publication October 2007.

2

Address at the Closing Ceremony of the Eighth and Final Meeting of the World Commission on Environment and Development and the Tokyo Declaration (1987)

Gro Harlem Brundtland

Address by
Mrs Gro Harlem Brundtland
Chairman
at the Closing Ceremony of the
Eighth and Final Meeting of the
World Commission on Environment and Development
27 February 1987
Tokyo, Japan

Ministers, Excellencies, Distinguished Guests

The World Commission on Environment and Development is honoured and pleased that you have joined us here today at the close of the Eighth and Final Meeting of the Commission.

We are most grateful to the Government of Japan for being our host at this important meeting. We believe it is appropriate that Tokyo be the venue of our final meeting. In holding our meeting here, we pay tribute to Japan for its steadfast support of our work. It was on the initiative of Japan in 1982 at the Special Session of UNEP's Governing Council that our independent Commission was called for by the General Assembly in the fall of 1983.

Since then, your country has not only given us very generous financial backing. It has also contributed greatly to our political and intellectual deliberations by

Address by Gro Harlem Brundtland, Chairman, at the Closing Ceremony of the Eighth and Final meeting of the World Commission on Environment and Development, 27 February 1987, Tokyo, Japan. Reproduced with permission from Prime Minister, Dr G. H. Brundtland.

providing us with such a distinguished member, the world renowned economist, statesman and devoted environmentalist, Dr. Saburo Okita.

It gives me the greatest pleasure also to be able to confirm that our meeting in Tokyo has been a success and that we have finalized our report which we shall shortly be presenting to the United Nations organs and issuing to the public in April. We have been able to agree because we were unanimous in our conviction that the prosperity and very survival of the planet depended on it.

Indeed, our Commission grew out of an awareness that over the course of this century, the relationship between the human world and the planet that sustains it has undergone a profound change.

When the century began, neither human numbers nor technology had the power radically to alter planetary systems. As the century closes, not only do vastly increased human numbers and their activities have that power, but major, unintended changes are occurring in the atmosphere, in soils, in waters, among plants and animals, and in the relationships among all of these. The rate of change is outstripping the ability of scientific disciplines to assess and advise. It is frustrating the attempts of political and economic institutions, which evolved in a different, more fragmented world, to adapt and cope. And it deeply worries many ordinary people who are seeking ways to place those concerns on political agendas.

Ladies and Gentlemen

The Commission first wants to make absolutely clear that we did not begin our task with the aim of adding our voices to those who predict a gloomy future. In fact, there are certain very positive trends which have appeared over the last decades: Infant mortality is falling, human life expectancy is increasing, the proportion of the world's adults who can read and write is climbing and the proportion of children starting school is rising. Globally, food production is increasing faster than the population is growing.

Even so, since the Commission began its work, some 850 days ago, concern, even fear, has been growing among people in all walks of life about the state of our world and the quality of life of millions who inhabit it, and there is an increasing awareness that we face great problems.

Let me remind you of a few of the most dramatic occurrences in this context since we began our work, occurrences which have contributed to this spreading sense of alarm:

- The crisis in Africa peaked putting 35 million people at risk, killing perhaps a million.
- An estimated 60 million of the World's people died of diarrhoeal diseases from contaminated drinking water and malnutrition; most of the victims were children.
- The Chernobyl nuclear reactor explosion sent nuclear fallout far across Europe, damaging food and water and increasing the threat of cancers in the future.
- A leak at the pesticide factory in Bhopal, India killed 2,000 people and blinded or injured 200,000 thousand more.
- Agricultural chemicals, solvents and mercury flowed into the River Rhine during a warehouse fire in Basle, Switzerland, resulting in large scale destruction of fish and the poisoning of drinking water in the Federal Republic of Germany and the Netherlands.

During our three years of deliberations, we have also witnessed a pervasive spread of poverty, especially in developing countries as well as the life-threatening challenges of desertification and deforestation confronting them. We have watched with alarm as countries in Africa and Latin America have been compelled to use earnings from resources to service their debt and thereby impair their continued development. And we have witnessed the enormous pressures imposed on many countries by rapid population growth.

Coupled with these developments, we have recognized an increasing number of threats to the planet itself: the depletion of the ozone layer, the accumulation of carbon dioxide in the atmosphere and its accompanying "greenhouse effects", the death of forest from acidification and the loss of tropical forest and the species and ecosystems they harbour.

And we have been constantly faced with the irreparable damage that could be caused by nuclear war.

Our Commission's mandate, rightly called for us to develop "concrete and real-istic" action proposals to deal with these alarming trends. We were asked to propose the changes needed. We were asked to see if the institutions we have created together were sufficient, and effective enough, to provide us with the tools that we need to manage the challenges imposed upon us by the pace and scale of these changes.

As a group, we have shared the conviction that it is possible to build a future that is more prosperous, more just and more secure for all. We share the conviction that it is possible to sustain and to expand the ecological basis for development. We have, from the outset, been acutely aware that we were not called upon to deal with the environment alone, but with development and the environment. The two are inti-mately interwoven in the real world.

This is true all over the world. "Development" can not be the narrow notion of "what poor nations should have so as to become richer". Just as the environment is where we all live, "development" is what we all do within that abode. Development takes place everywhere, in the Sahel, in the Arctic, in the industrial cities of the World, in the great farmlands, in the forests, wherever man is active.

And yet, the international mood surrounding our work has posed a dilemma. We obviously could not confine ourselves within the restraints of the political mood of the 1980s which is reflected in a retreat from multilateralism and international cooperation. That mood is not the answer to global issues. But what might seem difficult or even impossible today must be made possible for the future.

The Commission is convinced that the present disturbing trends and develop-ments cannot continue. We believe that humanity has reached a crossroads in its relationship with nature. We are also cognizant that the choices we make today will determine the future of our planet and the prosperity and well-being of the people who will inhabit it.

But we also recognize that we do not have all the answers, that the problems are too complex, that they are too inter-related and the required solutions to them too diverse to permit us to issue a detailed blueprint for action to deal with them. What is impor-tant is that the twenty two members of this Commission, people from different regions and of different beliefs and experiences, have engaged in a common evaluation and analysis of the problems. Our endeavour has resulted in a common under-standing of the alarming and unacceptable trends which face the globe and an urgent call for serious and drastic action to be taken.

But we are also convinced that our ability to deal with problems has never been greater. Advances in information systems, in health services, in forestry, in agriculture, in the efficient use of energy, and in monitoring global change provide us with reason to hope.

And we believe there are actions that can and must be taken now. That there are options for a sustainable future. These we will include in our report.

What we must do now is to direct our common endeavours towards our common future. We have witnessed, during our public hearings, that the will of the people to make the changes is there, in abundance. Now is the time for us to provide leadership.

We must learn not only to think, but to act upon, the knowledge that we are all responsible for this, our only earth. We can no more tolerate waste, misery and suffering on our shared globe than we can tolerate it in our own homes. We all have responsi-bility for one another, for our neighbours – that is what we are all – neighbours.

The concept of sustainable development is the overriding and global political concept that this commission will present and call for. What we have undertaken is to elaborate upon this concept, to analyse what it should mean and to draw conclu-sions as to how our behaviour must change so that development can be sustainable. The need for change is compelling. The will for change must be created.

Clearly the interventions needed to achieve sustainable development must be conceived and executed by processes that integrate environmental, social and economic considerations. The day when environmental management and economic development seemed to be in conflict has to be put far behind us.

The next few decades are crucial. The time has come to break away from the past. Attempts to maintain social and ecological stability through old approaches to development and environmental protection will increase instability. Security must be sought through change. The Commission has noted a number of actions that must be taken to reduce risks to survival and to put future development on paths that are sustainable. The Commission is aware that such a reorientation on a continuing basis is simply beyond the reach of present decision structures and institutional arrangements, both national and international.

Those structures must be remodelled so that development policies are policies for sustainable human progress far into the next century. Institutions whose policies and actions damage the resource base must be made responsible for that damage.

This Commission has been careful to base its recommendations on the realities of present institutions, on what can and must be accomplished today. We are not calling for action in the future by future generations. They will have their own tasks and needs, including perhaps the establishment of a world order whereby planetary con-siderations always take precedent over national considerations, and whereby an international, enforceable set of laws plays its part in creating a more equitable world. Those are among their options. But to keep options open for future genera-tions, present generations must begin now, and begin together, their efforts to achieve sustainable development.

Ladies and Gentlemen

Our report will not be a dismal prediction of ever increasing poverty, hunger and hardship. The concept of sustainable development implies human progress and improvement. Sustainable development is a goal not just for the developing nations, but for industrialized nations too. But the overriding priority should be given to the world's poor and to the needs of future generations.

Let me just touch upon a few of the problem areas we address in our report.

Human beings are a resource. But in many parts of the world population is growing at rates which cannot be sustained by available environmental resources, and therefore has to be addressed as an important part of broad social and economic policies. Access to education must be improved, in particular for girls, whose enrolment rates still lag behind those of boys. This gap must be closed as a matter of priority.

Agricultural policies in the developing nations tend to support export-oriented cash-crop farming and to neglect the small farmers – the food growers. Industrialized nations must alter present incentive systems to reduce surpluses and do away with unfair competition with nations which may have real comparative advantages. We should promote farming practices which make the best use of resources. To help in this, aid agencies should become ever more sensitive to agricultural needs in Third World countries.

Sustainable development recognizes that developing nations will require more, not less, total energy. Their industrialization and rapidly growing populations depend on this. But even the present global energy consumption creates serious environmental risks. Energy efficiency policies must therefore become the cutting edge of national energy strategies.

Energy efficiency is not the final solution, but will be an absolute must in the years to come, if the world is to develop a low energy future where renewable sources play a dominating role. This will require large scale research, and much strengthened international cooperation.

Sustainable development means nothing less than a new industrial era, where the energy and raw materials content of the end products must be way below present day levels. In the future, we expect that the best economists will also be the best ecologists. One measure of industrial development and competitiveness should be the level of waste output reduction. Toxic and poisonous products must receive the greatest attention. Under no circumstances should they be exported without the informed prior consent of the receiving countries. Our international institutions at present are clearly not sufficient to manage the international trade in dangerous substances.

Finally, ladies and gentlemen, let me say that to achieve sustainable development will require the involvement of people in decision making at all levels. Indeed, the Commission's work has been first and foremost concerned with people, of all countries and all walks of life, and it is to people that we shall now be addressing ourselves.

The radical change in human attitudes foreseen by acceptance of the concept of sustainable development depends upon a vast campaign of public education and re-education, a worldwide debate around these life-and-death issues. Changing the attitudes of people, everywhere is a fundamental prerequisite if the priorities of human society and therefore of human government are to be rewritten.

This campaign of public information is therefore viewed by the Commission as the next great priority. This campaign requires the collaboration and cooperation of the mass media, of parents and teachers and of all informed people.

We believe that the Report of the Commission will contribute to the generation of a global awareness of the urgency of the challenges which face us and a renewed commitment to action. As a first step towards this goal, the Commission this day submits to the peoples and governments of the world the following declaration to be known as the Tokyo Declaration.

World Commission on Environment and Development

Tokyo. Japan
27 February, 1987

Tokyo Declaration

The World Commission on Environment and Development was constituted in 1984 as an independent body by the United Nations General Assembly and set out to:

(a) re-examine the critical issues of environment and development, and formulate innovative, concrete, and realistic action proposals to deal with them;
(b) strengthen international cooperation on environment and development, and assess and propose new forms of cooperation that can break out of existing patterns and influence policies and events in the direction of needed change; and
(c) raise the level of understanding and commitment to action on the part of individuals, voluntary organizations, business, institutes and governments.

As we come in Tokyo to the end of our task, we remain convinced that it is possible to build a future that is prosperous, just and secure.

But realizing this possibility depends on all countries adopting the objective of sustainable development as the overriding goal and test of national policy and international cooperation. Such development can be defined simply as an approach to progress which meets the needs of the present without compromising the ability of future generations to meet their own needs. A successful transition to sustainable development through the year 2000 and beyond requires a massive shift in societal objectives. It also requires the concerted and vigorous pursuit of a number of strategic imperatives.

The World Commission on Environment and Development now calls upon all the nations of the World, both jointly and individually, to integrate sustainable development into their goals and to adopt the following principles to guide their policy actions.

1   *Revive Growth* Poverty is a major source of environmental degradation which not only affects a large number of people in developing countries but also undermines the sustainable development of the entire community of nations – both developing and industrialized. Economic growth must be stimulated, particularly in developing countries, while enhancing the environmental resource base. The industrialized countries can and must contribute to reviving world economic growth. There must be urgent international action to resolve the debt crisis; a substantial increase in the flows of development finance; and stabilization of the foreign exchange earnings of low-income commodity exporters.

2   *Change the Quality of Growth* Revived growth must be of a new kind in which sustainability, equity, social justice and security are firmly embedded as major social goals. A safe, environmentally sound energy pathway is an indispensable component of this. Education, communication, and international cooperation can all help to achieve those goals. Development planners should take account in their reckoning of national wealth not only of standard economic indicators, but also of the state of the stock of natural resources. Better income distribution, reduced vulnerability to natural disasters and technological risks, improved health, and preservation of cultural heritage – all contribute to raising the quality of that growth.

3   *Conserve and Enhance the Resource Base* Sustainability requires the conservation of environmental resources such as clean air, water, forests and soils; maintaining genetic diversity; and using energy, water and raw materials efficiently. Improvements in the efficiency of production must be accelerated to reduce per capita consumption of natural resources and encourage a shift to non-polluting products and technologies. All countries are called upon to prevent environmental pollution by rigorously enforcing environmental regulations, promoting low-waste technologies, and anticipating the impact of new products, technologies and wastes.

4   *Ensure a Sustainable Level of Population* Population policies should be formulated and integrated with other economic and social development programmes – education, health care, and the expansion of the livelihood base of the poor. Increased access to family planning services is itself a form of social development that allows couples, and women in particular, the right to self-determination.

5   *Reorient Technology and Manage Risks* Technology creates risks, but it offers the means to manage them. The capacity for technological innovation needs to be greatly enhanced in developing countries. The orientation of technology development in all countries must also be changed to pay greater regard to environmental factors. National and international institutional mechanisms are needed to assess potential impacts of new technologies before they are widely used. Similar arrangements are required for major interventions in natural systems, such as river diversion or forest clearance. Liability for damages from unintended consequences must be strengthened and enforced. Greater public participation and free access to relevant information should be promoted in decision-making processes touching on environment and development issues.

6   *Integrate Environment and Economics in Decision-Making* Environmental and economic goals can and must be made mutually reinforcing. Sustainability requires the enforcement of wider responsibilities for the impacts of policy decisions. Those making such policy decisions must be responsible for the impact of those decisions upon the environmental resource capital of their nations. They must focus on the sources of environmental damage rather than the symptoms. The ability to anticipate and prevent environmental damage will require that the ecological dimensions of policy be considered at the same time as the economic, trade, energy, agricultural and other dimensions. They must be considered on the same agendas and in the same national and international institutions.

7   *Reform International Economic Relations* Long term sustainable growth will require far-reaching changes to produce trade, capital, and technology flows that are more equitable and better synchronized to environmental imperatives. Fundamental improvements in market access, technology transfer, and international finance are necessary to help developing countries widen their opportunities by diversifying their economic and trade bases and building their self-reliance.

8   *Strengthen International Cooperation* The introduction of an environmental dimension injects an additional element of urgency and mutual self-interest, since a failure to address the interaction between resource degradation and rising poverty will spill over and become a global ecological problem. Higher priorities must be assigned to environmental monitoring, assessment, research and development, and resource management in all fields of international development. This requires a high level of commitment by all countries to the satisfactory working of multilateral institutions; to the making and observance of international rules in fields such as trade and investment; and to constructive dialogue on the many issues where national interests do not immediately coincide but require negotiation to be reconciled. It requires also a recognition of the essential importance of international peace and security. New dimensions of multilateralism are essential to sustainable human progress.

The Commission is convinced that if we can make solid progress towards meeting these principles in the balance of this century, the next century can offer a more secure, more prosperous, more equitable and more hopeful future for the whole human family.

3

Foxes in Charge of the Chickens (1993)

Nicholas Hildyard

The Earth Summit debacle

The United Nations Conference on Environment and Development, the self-styled Earth Summit, finished where it began. After ten days of press conferences, tree planting ceremonies and behind-the-scenes wheeling and dealing, the diplomats went home to their various other assignments and the politicians to their next round of international talks. Rio gave way to the Economic Summit at Munich and the more familiar territory of GATT, G-7 power politics and interest rates.

For the major players, the Earth Summit was a phenomenal success. The World Bank not only emerged with its development policies intact but with control of an expanded Global Environmental Facility (GEF), a prize that it had worked for two years to achieve. The US got the biodiversity convention it sought simply by not signing the convention on offer. The corporate sector, which throughout the UNCED process enjoyed special access to the Secretariat, also got what it wanted: the final documents not only treated TNCs with kid gloves but extolled them as key actors in the 'battle to save the planet'. Free-market environmentalism – the philosophy that TNCs brought to Rio through the Business Council on Sustainable Development – has become the order of the day, uniting Southern and Northern leaders alike. For many environmental groups, too, the Summit was a success: careers have been made, credibility achieved (some even having seats on government delegations) and their concerns are no longer marginalized. They are now recognized as major players themselves.

Nicholas Hildyard. 1993. "Foxes in charge of the chickens". In *Global Ecology: A New Arena of Political Conflict*, ed. W. Sachs. London: Zed Books. pp. 22–35. Reproduced with permission from Zed Books and N. Hildyard.

In brief, the Summit went according to plan. The net outcome was to minimize change to the status quo, an outcome that was inevitable from the outset of the UNCED process three years ago. Unwilling to question the desirability of economic growth, the market economy or the development process itself, UNCED never had a chance of addressing the real problems of 'environment and development'. Its Secretariat provided delegates with materials for a convention on biodiversity but not on free trade; on forests but not on agribusiness; on climate but not on auto-mobiles.[1] Agenda 21 – the Summit's 'action plan' – featured clauses on 'enabling the poor to achieve sustainable livelihoods' but none on enabling the rich to do so; a section on women but none on men. By such deliberate evasion of the central issues which economic expansion poses for human societies, UNCED condemned itself to irrelevance even before the first preparatory meeting got under way.

Conflicting Interests, Differing Perceptions

In that respect, the best that can be said for the Earth Summit is that it made visible the vested interests that stand in the way of the moral economies that local people are seeking to re-establish in the face of day to day degradation of their rivers, lakes, streams, fishing grounds, rangelands, forests and fields. For those who rely on the commons, such degradation means a loss of dignity and independence, security, livelihood and health. Defending the commons is thus often a matter of life and death. By contrast, figures in government, business and international organizations whose livelihoods do not depend directly on what is around them tend to view environmental degradation and the protests it provokes as threats to their political interest. For them the environment is not what is around their homes but what is around their economies. Northern leaders within UNCED, for example, were pre-occupied with how to keep a growing South from tapping resources and filling up waste sinks which the North has grown accustomed to using, while simultaneously maintaining the global capital flows which would help the global economy expand. Southern leaders, responding to prodding from Northern capital and hoping to benefit themselves as well, were equally preoccupied with extending the boundaries of their economies by bringing more land under the plough, logging more forests, diverting more water to industry and so on.

Not surprisingly, the three groups approach environmental degradation differently. For those who rely on the commons, the only response that makes sense is to concentrate on what has proved to be effective in the past, a response that entails maintaining or creating a space in which local commons regimes can root themselves. Such a strategy entails pushing for an erosion of the power of those who would undermine the commons, so that capital flows around the globe can be reduced, local control increased, consumption cut and markets limited. The demands of grassroots groups are thus not for more 'management' – a buzzword at Rio – but for agrarian reform, local control over local resources, the power to veto developments and a decisive say in all matters that affect their livelihoods. For them, the question is not *how* their environment should be managed – they have the experience of the past as their guide – but *who* will manage their environment and in *whose* interest. They reject UNCED's rhetoric of a world where all humanity is united by a common interest in survival, and instead they ask, 'Whose common future is to be sustained through the conventions and deals cut at UNCED?' Their struggle is not to win greater power for the market or the state, but to reinstate the community as the ultimate source of authority – in effect, to reclaim the commons.

By contrast, the preferred response of world leaders and mainstream environmentalists is to seek further enclosure of the commons by the market and the state, in the hope that whatever troublesome environmental damage has been caused by previous enclosure can be remedied by more far-reaching enclosure in the future. This approach seeks to preserve economic expansion through a programme of global management of both the environment and people. It has never been attempted before on the scale proposed. Previous less ambitious attempts, moreover, have not only failed to arrest environmental degradation, they have exacerbated it. Nonetheless, it is this path which has been chosen by the Secretariat and virtually all delegations at UNCED, as well as by the major multilateral development agencies and many scientific and conservation organizations.

The Threat of Environmentalism

The issues under discussion at UNCED were not new: on the contrary, from the smokestacks of Victorian Britain to the logged-out moonscapes of modern-day British Columbia or Sarawak, environmental degradation has gone hand-in-hand with economic expansion, as commercial interests have sacrificed local livelihoods and environments in order to obtain raw materials, transform them into commodities, market them and dispose of the wastes. Nor has the destruction gone unchallenged. In the South, local cultures have fought successive attempts – first by colonial regimes and then by their 'own' post-independence governments, acting in consort with commercial interests and international development agencies – to transform their homelands and themselves into 'resources' for the global economy. Timber operations have been sabotaged, logging roads blockaded, dams delayed, commercial plantations uprooted, factories and installations burned, mines closed down and rallies held in a constant effort to keep outside forces at bay.

Likewise in the North, the history of protest against the ravages of industrialism is a long one, coalescing initially around the machine-breaking and public health movements of the 19th century and emerging latterly in the many and diverse groupings now challenging environmental pollution, declining food quality, countryside destruction, health hazards in the home and workplace, and the erosion of community life. As in the South, such movements have expressed their concerns using whatever channels are available to them – from civil disobedience to legal challenges, boycotts and alliances with like-minded groups. Toxic waste dumps have been picketed, sites for nuclear power plants occupied, polluting pipelines capped, companies boycotted, whaling ships buzzed, and media campaigns mounted in an attempt both to combat environmental degradation and to put the environment on the political agenda.

Where environmental destruction was limited to the local level – a clear-cut forest here, a leaking toxic waste dump there, a polluted river here, a salinized tract of land there – and where protest was restricted to isolated movements, the threat that they posed to established patterns of power could be contained with relative ease. Commercial and industrial interests were able to follow a strategy of simply denying the problem or of justifying the destruction in the name of 'the greater good' or the 'national interest'. Opposition could be met by force or played down as 'uninformed', 'reactionary', 'luddite' or subversive. The reaction of the Velsicol Corporation to the publication in the early 1960s of Rachel Carson's *Silent Spring*, the book which in many respects launched the 'green' movement in the North, is illustrative. In a five-page letter to Carson's publishers, Velsicol accused her of being in league with 'sinister influences, whose attacks on the chemical industry have a dual purpose: (1) to create the false impression that all business is grasping and immoral, and (2) to reduce the use of agricultural chemicals in this country and in the countries of western Europe so that our supply of food will be reduced to east-curtain parity.'[2]

Crude as such attacks are, they still persist. Recently, Bill Holmes, a former member of the California State Board of Forestry, told the 1991 Redwood Region Logging Conference:

> In California we continue to plunge toward new ill-fated experiments in socialized timber management. The Hollywood crowd and other people in the US who hate America while worshipping Russia and its totalitarian system have jumped into bed with their environmental friends who welcomed them with open arms. They already had a great deal in common because, although not all left-wing radicals are environmentalists, certainly all environmentalists embrace some form of left-wing radical collectivism. As a result, the greatest threat to you, to me, to our communities, to our state and to our nation is no longer communism, it is not drugs, not AIDS, not crime, not poverty, not even liberal democrats, but radical environmentalism.[3]

Bill Holmes' vision of a communist conspiracy is clearly absurd, but he is right to be worried by the way in which alliances are being formed between formerly isolated, local or national citizens' groups, in order to resist the powerful interests that are threatening their commons. Indeed, it is arguably only as a result of such alliances that the previously marginalized discourse of environmentalism has been forced into the political mainstream, transforming ecological destruction from a 'side issue' that corporations and governments felt able to disregard, into lost markets and lost votes. If timber companies are now making noises about moving towards 'sustainable' logging practices, it is not because they have suddenly become aware of the damage they are causing to the environment (in many instances, they still deny the problem) but because timber boycotts and local protests have forced them to respond to growing public outrage over their activities. Likewise, if the landfilling of toxic wastes in the US is now being phased out, it is not because US companies themselves view landfill as an environmentally unacceptable means of waste disposal (US companies see no problems in landfilling their wastes in Britain or the Third World, for instance, where standards are lower) but rather because the spread of popular protest in the US had made it clear that 'not in my backyard' means 'not in anybody's backyard', leaving corporate executives with no option but to seek other waste disposal strategies. As Andrew Szasz notes:

> Community-based popular organization was the key factor. Indirectly, community protest pushed Washington to strengthen regulatory controls. Directly, local opposition … blocked the expansion of waste disposal and treatment capacity… Popular pressure worked on two levels: in Washington, mainstream environmental groups and members of Congress facing constituency pressure recognized how salient and volatile the issue was and supported stronger regulations. At the same time, local opposition to new facilities interacted with these stronger regulations to drive up disposal costs, and thus to raise economic pressures for waste reduction.[4]

The Threat of Economic Contraction

But the threat of environmentalism goes deeper than simply upsetting individual corporate apple carts. Tighter environmental standards – not to speak of environmental degradation itself – now threaten the *throughput* of resources in the global economy. As the Brundtland Commission, whose report *Our Common Future* initiated the UNCED process, puts it: 'We have in the past been concerned about the impacts of economic growth upon the environment. We are now forced to concern ourselves with the impacts of ecological stress … upon our economic prospects.'[5]

It is not clear whose 'economic prospects' Brundtland is referring to (at the local level, environmental degradation has been threatening local economic prospects for many decades): what is clear, however, is that environmental stress – and the pressure to ease it – is already denying *resources* to the global economy, whilst simultaneously depriving it of *sinks* into which the waste products of industrialism can readily (and cheaply) be disposed. As soils are eroded, so land is taken out of production; as the seas are overfished and rivers polluted, so fisheries crash; as forests are logged out or succumb to damage from air pollution, so timber supplies are threatened; and as the economic costs of mitigating damage rise, so capital is diverted away from productive growth. In the US alone, soil compaction – the direct result of modern mechanized agriculture – is estimated to have cost farmers some $3 billion in lost yields in 1980 alone. The damage already incurred through acid rain and pollution-related forest die-back in Europe and the US has been put at $30 billion, whilst the estimated cost of cleaning up the 2,000 worst polluting toxic waste dumps in the US has been put at $100 billion. No realistic figure can even be put on the social and economic disruption that will be incurred through global warming and ozone depletion. The likely loss of species alone makes the price tag incalculable.

Both Northern and Southern governments – voicing the concerns of industrial interests – argue that such costs could not be borne without sending the global economy into a tail-spin. For those whose livelihoods are being daily undermined by the growth economy, however, economic contraction is not the threat that the mainstream would have us believe: on the contrary, it brings the possibility of reclaiming the commons, of restoring what development has destroyed, and of living with dignity. As Gustavo Esteva, a social activist living in Mexico City, reports:

> With falling oil prices, mounting debts, and the conversion of Mexico into a free trade zone so that transnational capital can produce Volkswagen 'Beetles' in automated factories for export to Germany, the corruption of our politics and the degradation of Nature – always implicit in development – can finally be seen, touched and smelled by everyone. Now the poor of Mexico are responding by recreating their own moral economy. As Mexico's Rural Development Bank no longer has sufficient funds to force peasants to plant sorghum for animal feed, many have returned to the traditional inter-cropping of corn and beans, improving their diets, restoring some village solidarity and allowing available cash to reach further. In response to the decreasing purchasing power of the previously employed, thriving production co-operatives are springing up in the heart of Mexico City. Shops now exist in the slums that reconstruct electrical appliances; merchants prosper by imitating foreign trademarked goods and selling them as smuggled wares to tourists. Neighbourhoods have come back to life. Street stands and tiny markets have returned to corners from where they had disappeared long ago. Complex forms of non-formal organization have developed, through which the barrio (village) residents create protective barriers between themselves and intruding development bureaucracies, police and other officials; fight eviction and the confiscation of their assets; settle their own disputes and maintain public order.[6]

But whereas economic contraction provides a space in which the commons can regain some of its authority, it poses a direct threat to those whose power rests on the ability to sustain productive growth. The prospect of such contraction becoming a *permanent* feature of the economy as a result of environmental degradation and environmental protest has thus caused alarm bells to ring in corporate headquarters and other centres of power. Indeed, in a leaked memorandum, the US Environmental Protection Agency has described America's 'environmental justice movement', best known for its work in opposing toxic waste dumps, as the greatest threat to political stablity since the anti-war movement of the 1960s.

Containing Challenges

It is not the first time in history that movements for social change have threatened the power of established commercial and political élites. As in the past, the ability of those élites to survive with their power intact will ultimately depend on how far they are able to turn that challenge to their advantage. Now that it has become clear that environmentalism and environmental degradation can no longer be ignored, outright resistance to change is giving way to strategies for *managing* that change.

At one level, the emphasis has been on blocking those demands that cannot be contained without loss of power. Within UNCED, for example, elaborate mano-euvring enabled individual industries to head off measures that would impose too heavy a cost on their activities. Most notably, corporate interests effectively blocked discussion of the environmental impact of Transnational Corporations (TNCs): recommendations drawn up by the UN's own Centre for Transnational Corporations (UNCTC), which would have imposed tough global environmental standards on TNC activities, were shelved and instead a voluntary code of conduct, drawn up by the Business Council on Sustainable Development, a corporate lobbying group, was adopted as the Secretariat's input into UNCED's Agenda 21. The UNCTC's carefully crafted proposals were not even circulated to delegates. Meanwhile, a few months before the Rio Summit, the Centre itself was quietly closed down. Instead of being subject to a mandatory code of conduct, negotiated multilaterally, the TNCs emerged from UNCED without their role in causing environmental destruction even having been scrutinized in the official process, let alone curtailed.

On the contrary, governments, both North and South, have done everything in their power to protect the interests of their industrial and commercial lobbies. The US government's negotiating position, for example, has consistently reflected the close ties between the Bush administration and corporate interests: the guidelines issued to US delegates negotiating the Climate Convention faithfully reflected the position of the oil industry. Delegates were advised that it was not beneficial to discuss whether there is or is not warming, or how much or how little warming. In the eyes of the public, we will lose this debate. A better approach is to raise the many uncertainties that need to be understood on this issue.[7]

Instead, the negotiators were told to stress that 'the world community is making great strides towards understanding the science of global change, but many fundamental questions remain unanswered'; and that 'the economic impacts of potential global changes and possible responses are not well understood – more work is needed.'

A similar approach was adopted in the negotiations on biodiversity, the main priority of US negotiators being to block any measures that might harm the interests of biotechnology companies or undermine the patenting of 'intellectual property'. During the fourth Preparatory Meeting for UNCED, for example, the US delegation insisted that references in Agenda 21 to the hazards of biotechnology should be deleted, arguing that the risks have been exaggerated. In this, the position taken by the US delegation was identical to that of the Heritage Foundation, an influential US think-tank with close links to the US administration. The US also deleted major sections of the Agenda 21 text which would have imposed safeguards against 'the experimentation with unsafe fertility regulating drugs on women in developing countries'. A proposed ban on 'medical technologies in developing countries for purposes of experimentation in reproductive processes' was similarly deleted at the US' insistence.

Capturing the Debate

Beyond such wrecking tactics, however, UNCED saw a conscious attempt by corporate and other mainstream interests to 'capture' the debate on environment and development and to frame it in terms that suit their purposes. Here a number of strategies came into play:

First, there was a concerted effort on the part of government and industry to distance themselves from the destructiveness of 'past' policies. Constant references within the official documents to 'recent' satellite data, 'new' studies, 'latest statistics' and the like conveyed the impression that ecological degradation was a *recent* phenomenon – and one, moreover, that had primarily come to light through the diligence and foresight of *government* scientists, *international* institutions and *industrial* planners, thereby protecting the credibility and authority of those who bear prime responsibility for the activities that have created the current ecological crisis. The past disappeared from view, discreetly curtained off from scrutiny. Instead, the public was asked to look towards the future and with it, a new age of environmental awareness in which industry – now aware of the environment – had put its house in order to the satisfaction of earthworm and corporate executive alike. Industry's record was thus wiped clean: the fox could now be put in charge of the chickens.

Second, there was an attempt to deny the many conflicts of interests underlying the crisis. Neither the institutional framework of global society nor the material interests and values it reflects received serious scrutiny. Instead, the ills under discussion were cast as having somehow 'happened' by themselves. No one would appear to have promoted the destruction, except by way of lack of knowledge, foresight or alternatives. No one was gaining power or profit from current policies; no one stood in the way of solutions. Instead, UNCED promoted a rosy-tinted view of a world where all humanity is united by a common interest in survival, and in which conflicts of class, race, culture and gender are characterized as of secondary importance to humanity's supposedly common goals. Constant references to 'humanity's common resources', for example, neatly obscured the fact that the vast majority of people have no access to those resources, which they neither own nor control, and which are selfishly exploited for the narrow ends of a few. (In Brazil, for example, multinational companies own more land than all the peasants put together. In Britain, just nine per cent of the population owns 84 per cent of the land.) Likewise, the flows of resources from humanity's supposedly 'common resource base' are grossly unequal. In the last 50 years, the US has single-handedly consumed more fossil fuels and minerals than the rest of humanity has consumed in all recorded history. The US beef industry alone consumes as much food as the populations of India and China combined, an orgy of consumption that is possible only by starving other people.

Third, by removing environmental problems from their local setting and accentuating the global nature of the environmental crisis, UNCED gave currency to the view that *all* humans share a common responsibility for environmental destruction, either because of the demands they are currently placing on the environment or because of the demands they are expected to exert in the future. Thus, instead of ozone depletion being blamed – as it should be – on local corporate interests (Dupont, for example) using their global reach to globalize sales of CFCs and other ozone-depleting chemicals regardless of the known environmental impact, responsibility for the ozone hole was pinned on the future demand for fridges in the Third World.

Fourth, by portraying environmental degradation as a global problem requiring global solutions, UNCED gave added impetus to those multinational interests who would extend their global reach. By definition, only international institutions and national governments were up to the task in hand.

Fifth, and closely allied to the above, there was an attempt to frame environmental problems in terms of 'solutions' which only the North (and its allies in the South) can provide. Underpinning Agenda 21, for example, is the view that environmental and social problems are primarily the result of *insufficient capital* (solution: increase Northern investment in the South); *outdated technology* (solution: open up the South to Northern technologies); a *lack of expertise* (solution, bring in Northern-educated managers and experts); and *faltering economic growth* (solution: push for an economic recovery in the North). The prior questions of whether money can solve the environmental crisis, of who benefits from capital and technology transfers, and of *whose* environment is to be managed and on *whose* behalf, were simply sidelined. The development process itself went unchallenged and instead the environmental crisis was reduced to chequebook diplomacy: a big enough cheque and the Earth would be 'saved', too small a cheque and humanity would disappear down the tube. All of which was music to the ears of politicians, corporate executives, bankers and business interests in both North and South.

And *sixth*, UNCED attempted to inspire environmentalist and industrialist alike with a 'crisis management mentality', in which the need for action was deemed more important than settling differences on what action should be taken, by whom, on whose say-so and with whose interests paramount. Few environmentalists would argue that environmental degradation has reached critical proportions – destroying local livelihoods, condemning species to extinction, blighting landscapes, and (if climatic disruption occurs on the scale predicted by some climatologists) possibly threatening the very future survival of humans and other mammals. But within UNCED the critical nature of such threats was used to justify giving those currently in power still more authority; to legitimize programmes which would remove control still further from local people; and to sanction more management, more top-down development, more policing and still greater control of people. With 'crisis management' has come 'war-room environmentalism'. The environmental crisis, it has been argued by some commentators, should be treated as if it were 'a military threat to national security' requiring 'fast-acting intervention instruments, such as an international environmental police force which should intervene whenever and wherever ecological threats are posed in or by a given country for the international community of nations.'

UNCED's Prescriptions: Further Enclosure

That such thinking has gone unchallenged by mainstream environmental groups – indeed, in many instances, it is part of their rhetoric too – reflects the degree to which élites have been able to capture environmentalism and use it as a tool to increase their power. In that respect, now that UNCED is over, any hopes NGOs may have entertained about working on an equal footing with representatives of industrial interests have been delusions: they have constantly been outmanoeuvred. Worse still, the rhetoric they have embraced in the hope of nudging business and government in a more green direction is now being used to legitimize an agenda that, if unchallenged, threatens a new round of enclosure as devastating to the interests of ordinary people as anything that has gone before it. Consider the likely outcome of the new management regimes, capital flows and technology transfers that UNCED has set in motion.

Whilst local peoples have long managed their environments to sustain their livelihoods and cultures, the new environmental managers behind Agenda 21 have very different priorities. What is to be 'managed' are those aspects of the environment that have value to the global economy – from germplasm for biotechnology to pollution sinks and other commodities that can be traded. Increasingly, environmental managers assume the right to 'protect' the environment from demands that conflict with the 'needs' of commercial interests – a formula that labels local people, the main 'competitors' for 'resources', as the prime agents of environmental destruction. Once that premise is accepted, it is easy to demean the ways local people traditionally care for their environment. The way is thus opened for new institutions, administered for the needs of trade and commerce, to assume environmental management at all levels.

Within agriculture, for example, the policies promoted by the UN Food and Agriculture Organization at UNCED forsee the best land in Third World countries being zoned for cash crops. Only in those areas where 'natural resource limitations' or 'environmental or socioeconomic constraints' preclude intensification would farmers be allowed to grow their own food for their own use. Coupled to this zoning policy is the recommendation that governments should 'evaluate the carrying and population supporting capacity of major agricultural areas', and, where such areas are deemed to be 'overpopulated', take steps to change the 'man/land ratio' (their terminology) by 'facilitating the accommodation of migrating populations into better endowed areas'.[8] Transmigration programmes are explicitly recommended as a possible way forward.

Peasants who have been forced onto marginal lands as a result of 'high potential areas' being taken over for intensive export-oriented agriculture will thus be liable to resettlement at the whim of any government that deems them a threat to the environment. Since it is admitted that there are few 'better endowed areas' that can be opened for agriculture, the majority of the new transmigrants will have no option but to move to the slums of large cities or to clear land in forests. Many of the displaced are likely to wind up as labourers or 'tied producers' growing cash crops under contract to large corporations. Predictably, perhaps, the proponents of such 'sustainable agriculture' policies do not consider the possibility that ecological stress in marginal areas would be better relieved by reclaiming 'high potential areas' for peasant agriculture.

The global managers thus threaten to unleash a new wave of colonialism, in which the management of people – even whole societies – for the benefit of commercial interests is now justified in the name of environmental protection. Whereas in the past 'crown sovereignty' and 'poverty alleviation' were used to legitimize the appropriation of local resources and the dismantling of local institutions for the national good, under the new regime, integral local practices are to be broken down yet further in the service of systemic goals. This time these goals are not simply to provide raw materials, cheap labour, and markets to an international economic system, but also to supply environmental repair or caretaker services to mitigate the problems that system itself has created. Carbon-dioxide-absorbing tree farms will supplant peasants' fields and fallows, tropical forests will be taken away from their inhabitants to provide services to Northern industry, researchers and tourists, and population control efforts will be redoubled as a way of taking pressure off Northern-controlled resources.

The new and additional financial resources agreed at Rio are likely further to reinforce that management strategy. The loans agreed during the pilot phase of the Global Environment Facility (GEF), which aims to 'help' developing countries to 'contribute towards solving global environmental problems', give an indication of how green funds will be used to further élite interests. At the time, GEF's terms of reference restricted it to funding environmental projects which are of 'global' – rather than local – significance and which would therefore be 'of benefit to the world at large', its four priorities being the 'protection of biodiversity', the mitigation of global warming, the control of pollution in international waters, and the management of stratospheric ozone depletion. Few would deny that these are all areas of major concern: it is also incontestable that the chief perpetrators of the destruction in all four areas are Northern interests, acting in conjunction with southern élites. But GEF has not singled out these areas in order to take on the world's dominant élites: rather it is concerned with securing control of those aspects of the environment – the atmosphère, the seas and biodiversity – that are necessary to the continued throughput of resources in the global economy. Thus, by designating the atmosphere and biodiversity as 'global commons', the GEF was able to override the local claims of those who rely on local commons and effectively assert that everyone has a right of access to them, that local people have no more claim to them than a corporation based on the other side of the globe. Pressing problems with a direct impact on local peoples – desertification, toxic waste pollution, landlessness, pesticide pollution and the like, all of which could be judged as being of 'global concern' – are thus pushed to one side while the local environment is sized up for its potential benefit to the North and its allies in the South. It is surely no coincidence, for example, that 59 per cent of projects approved under the first tranche of the GEF should have been for 'biodiversity protection'. Nor is it surprising that the chair of the GEF, Mohamed El-Ashry, singled out areas which 'include important gene pools or encompass economically significant species' as the priority for funding. Biodiversity protection is thus translated into protecting biodiversity not for its own sake but for the global economy.

Likewise, the GEF uses the notion of 'internalizing' ecological costs as a formula not for preventing inherently destructive projects but for providing additional resources to them in the guise of green funding. Thus, El-Ashry told *World Bank News:* 'We now know that the environmental costs of building dams can be considerable. The belief in the past was that environmental considerations were additional costs that could be postponed until a country became fully developed. But we've learned that these costs should be considered investments. Postponing these investments can only result in higher costs later on.'[9] The message to dam builders was clear: not only does the GEF believe it possible to mitigate the damage done by dams, but it is willing to pay for such mitigatory measures. Such cynicism in the face of the overwhelming evidence of the destructiveness of large dams is unforgivable. For, in reality, no amount of animal rescue schemes, education programmes, biosphere reserves or direct monetary compensation can undo the ecological damage done by dams, or make good the psychological and social rape inflicted by such projects on local people. Internalizing these externalities by reducing them to figures on a balance sheet that can then be magicked away by setting them against supposed benefits may be politically expedient but it does not make the projects any more defensible morally, ecologically or socially. For what the GEF refers to as 'externalities' are flesh and blood: they are real people, real animals. They are not simply 'germplasm' or 'biodiversity'. They bleed when bulldozers crush them. They cry when they are uprooted from their homes. They are 'externalities' only in the sense that they are 'external' to the interests of those who determine the GEF's priorities. They are in the way.

Nothing could be more revealing of the agenda that UNCED set itself to promote.

Notes

1   W. Sachs (1992) 'Theatre on the Titanic', *Guardian,* 29 May.
2   F. Graham (1980) 'The Witch-hunt of Rachel Carson', *Ecologist*, Vol. 10, No. 3, March.
3   Quoted in *Earth Island Journal,* Summer 1991, p. 48.
4   A. Szasz (1991), 'In Praise of Policy Luddism: strategic lessons from the hazardous waste wars', *Capitalism, Nature, Socialism*, Vol. 2, No. 1, Issue 6, pp.17–43.
5   World Commission on Environment and Development (1987) *Our Common Future,* Oxford University Press, Oxford, p. 5.
6   G. Esteva (1991) 'Development: the modernization of poverty', *Panoscope,* November, p. 28.
7   World Commission on Environment and Development, op. cit.
8   UN Food and Agriculture Organization (1991) *SARD Draft Proposals,* 's-Hertogenbosch, The Netherlands, April, pp. 12 and 16; and FAO (1991) *The Den Bosch Declaration and Agenda for Action on Sustainable Agriculture and Rural Development,* 's-Hertogenbosch, The Netherlands, April, p. 9.
9   Mohamed El-Ashry (1991) 'Sustainable Development Requires Environmental Protection', *World Bank News,* 22 August.

4

Can the Environment Survive the Global Economy? (1997)

Edward Goldsmith

By now, it should be clear that our environment is becoming ever less capable of sustaining the growing impact of our economic activities. Everywhere our forests are overlogged, our agricultural lands overcropped, our grasslands overgrazed, our wetlands overdrained, our groundwaters overtapped, our seas overfished, and just about the whole terrestrial and marine environment overpolluted with chemical and radioactive poisons. Worse still, if that is possible, our atmospheric environment is becoming ever less capable of absorbing either the ozone-depleting gases or the greenhouse gases generated by our economic activities without creating new climatic conditions to which we cannot indefinitely adapt.

In such conditions, there can be only one way of maintaining the habitability of our planet and that is by setting out methodically to reduce this impact. Unfortunately, it is the overriding goal of just about every government in the world to maximize world trade and create a **global economy** – which has now been institutionalized with the signing of the GATT Uruguay Round Agreement. To increase trade is justified because it is seen to be the most effective way of increasing economic development, which we equate with progress, and which in terms of the world-view of modernism, is made out to provide a means of creating a material and technological paradise on Earth, from which all the problems that have confronted us since the beginning of our tenancy of this planet will have been methodically eliminated.

Unfortunately, economic development, by its very nature, must necessarily further increase the impact of our economic activities on the environment. This could not be better illustrated than by the terrible environmental destruction that has occurred

Edward Goldsmith. 1997. "Can the Environment Survive the Global Economy?" In *The Ecologist*, 27(6).

in Taiwan and South Korea, the two principal newly industrial countries (NICS) that in the last decades have achieved the most stunning rates of economic growth, and that are currently held up as models for all Third World countries to emulate.

In the case of Taiwan, as Walden Bello and Stephanie Rosenfeld have carefully documented in their book *Dragons in Distress* [1], forests have been cleared to accommodate industrial and residential developments and plantations of fast-growing conifers. The virgin broadleaf forests that once covered the entire eastern coast have now been almost completely destroyed. The vast network of roads built to open up the forests to logging, agriculture and development, has caused serious soil erosion, especially in the mountain areas where whole slopes of bare soil have slid away.

Efforts to maximize agriculture production in export oriented plantations have led to the tripling of fertilizer use between 1952 and 1980, which has led to soil acidification, zinc losses and decline in soil fertility, with water pollution and fertilizer run-off contaminating ground water – the main source of drinking water for many Taiwanese.

The use of pesticides has increased massively, and it is a major source of contamination of Taiwan's surface waters and ground waters; and their sale is subject to no effective government controls. The food produced is so contaminated with pesticides that, according to the sociologist Michael Hsias, "Many farmers don't eat what they sell on the market. Instead, they grow an organic crop, and that is what they consume [2]."

A substantial number of Taiwan's 90,000 factories have been located in the countryside, on rice fields along waterways and near private residences. In order to maximize competitiveness, their owners have disregarded what waste-disposal regulations there are and much of the waste is simply dumped into the nearest waterway. Not surprisingly, 20 per cent of farmland, according to the government itself, is now polluted by industrial waste water. Nor is it surprising that 30 per cent of the rice grown in Taiwan is contaminated with heavy metals, including mercury, arsenic and cadmium. Human waste, of which only about 1 per cent receives even primary treatment, is flushed into rivers, providing nutrients for the unchecked growth of weeds which use up the available oxygen, killing off the fish life. This largely explains why Taiwan now has the world's highest incidence of hepatitis. Agricultural and industrial poisons and human waste have now severely polluted the lower reaches of just about every one of Taiwan's major rivers – many of which "are little more than flowing cesspools, devoid of fish, almost completely dead". In Hou Jin, a small town near the city of Kaohsiung, forty years of pollution by the Taiwan Petroleum Company has made the water not only unfit to drink but actually combustible.

The prawn-farming industry has achieved a fantastic growth-rate – with prawn production increasing 45 times in just ten years. Prawn-farmers, however, have themselves become deprived of the fresh clean water that they need because of the build-up of toxic chemical wastes from upstream industries in rivers and wells. As a result the mass deaths of prawn and fish have become a regular occurrence.

Air pollution has also increased massively. Sulphur dioxide and nitrous oxide pollution in Taiwan are now intolerable, regularly reaching levels that are double those judged harmful in the USA. Not surprisingly, the incidence of asthma among children in Taiwan has quadrupled in the last ten years. Not surprisingly too, cancer has now become the leading cause of death, its incidence having doubled over the last 30 years.

Even if the annual rate of economic growth in Taiwan were cut to 6.5 per cent, stresses on Taiwan's already degraded environment would double by the year 2000. Even if this were vaguely feasible, can one really believe that it could be allowed to double again, and yet again, without rendering the island almost totally unfit for human habitation? Already, many people are abandoning Taiwan and buying houses in such places as Australia and New Zealand, partly at least to escape the Taiwan environmental nightmare.

It could be argued of course that once Taiwan has achieved a certain level of GNP, it will be able to afford to install the technological equipment required for mitigating the destructiveness of the development process. This argument was credible until recently. However, with the development of the **global economy**, competitiveness has become the order of the day. This has meant deregulation – that is, the abandonment of regulations, including environmental regulations, that increase costs to industry. This implies, in effect, that much of the legislation that has been forced on recalcitrant governments by environmental groups in the rich industrial countries is being systematically repealed. Not even the rich countries, in fact, can now "afford" environmental controls.

Creating Consumers

Creating a **global economy** means seeking to generalize this destructive process, which means transforming the vast mass of still largely self-sufficient people living in the rural areas of the Third World into consumers of capital-intensive goods and services, mainly those provided by the transnational corporations (TNCs). For this to be possible, the cultural patterns with which most Third World people, at least in rural areas, are still imbued and that commit them to their largely self-sufficient life styles must of course be ruthlessly destroyed by American television and Western advertising companies and supplanted by the culture and values of Western mass-consumer society. Of course, it is mainly the appetite for this lifestyle that can be exported – the lifestyle itself, only an insignificant minority will ever enjoy, and even then for but a brief period of time, for the whole enterprise is completely impossible, the biosphere being incapable of sustaining the impact on it of the increased economic activities required.

Thus it has been calculated that to bring all Third World countries to the consumption level of the USA by the year 2060 would require 4 per cent economic growth a year. This, of course, would have to be properly distributed, which in itself would not be easy. The annual world output, however, and, in effect, the annual impact of our economic activities on the environment, would be 16 times what it is today – which is of course not even remotely conceivable. However, this consideration could not be further from the minds of those who are promoting the **global economy**. Thus America's Big Three automakers soon hope to finalize deals in China, whose object is to bring automobiles to each person who now rides a bicycle or simply walks. Merely the extra carbon-dioxide emissions from several hundred million more automobiles would make nonsense of the UN's Intergovernmental Panel on Climate Change's tentative prognostics by leading to a massive escalation in the rate of global warming with all its concomitant horrors. If every Chinese were also to have a refrigerator, as the Chinese government proudly promises, emissions of CFCs and HCFCs would escalate to the point of making nonsense of any agreements reached on the basis of the Montreal protocol to cut down on emissions of ozone depleting substances in order to save what remains of the ozone layer.

Production for Export

One of the principles of economic globalization and "free trade" is that countries should specialize in producing and exporting a few commodities that they produce particularly well and import almost everything else from other countries. This means that such production is not limited by local demand but only by world demand, hence a massive increase in production for export. It is worth considering what an enormous proportion of the world's production of the most basic commodities is already produced for export – 33 per cent in the case of plywood, 84 per cent in the case of coffee, 38 per cent in the case of fish, 47 per cent in the case of bauxite and alumina, 40 per cent in the case of iron ore, 46 per cent in the case of crude oil [3].

Timber is also above all an export crop. In Malaysia, more than half the trees that are felled for timber are exported. This brings in $1 1/2 billion a year in foreign exchange, but at a terrible environmental cost. Peninsular Malaysia was 70 per cent to 80 per cent forested 50 years ago. Today, mainly because of the export trade, it has been largely deforested. The result has been escalating soil erosion, the fall of the water-table in many areas, and a general increase in droughts and floods. The Malaysian States of Sarawak and Sabah are being stripped so rapidly that it is but a matter of a few years before all but the most inaccessible forests will have been destroyed, annihilating, at the same time, the culture and lifestyle of the local tribal people.

As country after country is logged out, the loggers simply move elsewhere. In South-East Asia it is to New Guinea, Laos, Myanmar and Cambodia, the last countries that remain still largely forested – significantly the only ones too that have remained, up till now, outside the orbit of the world trading system. At the current rate of forest destruction, these countries will have been largely deforested within the next decade.

It is probable that so long as a market can be found for the timber, forests will continue to be logged. Effective measures to control logging are unlikely, since in most countries in South-East Asia it is the politicians and their families who own the concessions, and the logging companies with whom they deal are in any case too powerful and too corrupt to control [4]. It is probable that only a collapse of the world economy could save the remaining loggable forests.

Plantation crops mass-produced for export tend also to cause terrible environmental destruction. This is clear in the US Mid-West, where the intensive cultivation of maize and soya beans, largely for export, is leading to such serious soil-erosion that what was once the most fertile agricultural area in the world will, on current trends, be almost entirely deprived of its topsoil within the next 50 years [5].

Tobacco is another crop that is largely grown for export worldwide. In the case of Malawi it represents 55 per cent of that country's foreign exchange earnings. Robert Goodland notes that "tobacco depletes soil nutrients at a much higher rate than most other crops, thus rapidly decreasing the life of the soil [6]." But the heaviest environmental cost of tobacco production lies in the sheer volume of wood needed to fuel tobacco-curing barns. Every year the trees from an estimated 12,000 square kilometres are cut down, with 55 cubic metres of cut wood being burnt for every tonne of tobacco cured. Some experts put the figure even higher – at 50,000 square kilometres [7].

Coffee is largely an export crop, and its production also causes the most serious environmental degradation. Georg Borgstrom notes how the coffee planters have destroyed the soils of Brazil. "The almost predatory exploitations by the coffee planters", he writes, "have ruined a considerable proportion of Brazil's soils. In many areas, these abandoned coffee lands are so mined that they can hardly ever be restored to crop production. In others, a varying portion of the topsoil has been removed, or the humus content of the soil has been seriously reduced. In most regions, a mere one-tenth now remains of the amount of humus present when coffee cultivation was started. Therefore the coffee plantations have always been on the march, grabbing new lands and leaving behind eroded or impoverished soils [8]."

The same can be said of groundnut plantations in French West Africa. Indeed it has been estimated, Franke and Chasin write, that "after only two successive years of peanut growing, there is a loss of thirty per cent of the soil's organic matter and sixty per cent of the colloidal humus. In two successive years of peanut planting, the second year's yield will be from twenty to forty per cent lower than the first [9]."

What the export-oriented logging industry is doing to our forests and the export-oriented livestock rearing schemes and intensive plantations are doing to our land, the high-tech fishing industry, itself dependent on exports – with 38 per cent of fish caught worldwide exported – is doing to the seas. Today, nine of the world's seventeen major fishing grounds are in decline and four are already "fished out" commercially. Total catches in the Northwest Atlantic have fallen by almost a third during the last 20 years. In 1992, the great cod fisheries of the Grand Banks off Newfoundland in Canada were closed indefinitely, and in Europe mackerel stocks in the North Sea have decreased by 50 times since the 1960s [10].

As fish stocks are depleted in the North, it is in the South that the fleets are now congregating, but the volume of fish exported from developing nations has already increased by nearly four times in the last 20 years, and Southern fisheries are already under stress [11].

The predictable result is the depletion of Third World fisheries too, with the most drastic consequences for local fishing communities.

The expansion of many export-oriented industries gives rise to a whole range of adverse environmental consequences affecting most aspects of people's lives. An obvious case in point is the intensive prawn-farming industry that has been expanding rapidly throughout Asia and some parts of the Americas and Africa. Its export market for intensively farmed prawns is now worth 6.6 billion dollars.

Already about half of the world's mangrove forests have been cut down, many of them in order to accommodate prawn farms. In Ecuador for instance, in 1987 120,000 hectares of mangroves have been destroyed for this purpose. In Thailand the figure is 100,000 hectares. The consequences of mangrove destruction are catastrophic for local fishing communities, as many fish species necessarily spend part of their life cycle in mangrove forests. If they are destroyed, fishing catches tend to fall dramatically.

Another environmental consequence of prawn farms is a reduction in the availability of fresh water for irrigation in nearby rice paddies, the reason being that prawn farms require large amounts of fresh water to mix with sea water in order to produce the brackish water that the prawns like living in. In the Philippines the overextraction of ground water for prawn farms in Negros Occidental "has caused shallow wells, orchards and ricelands to dry up, land to subside and salt water to intrude from the sea [12]."

Chemical pollution is another problem, as some intensive prawn farms can use up to 35 chemicals and biological products as disinfectants, soil and water conditioners, pesticides, fertilizers and feed-additives. In South Thailand's "rice bowl" between the provinces of Nakhon Si Thammarat and Songkhla, yields have crashed as chemical runoff from 15,000 acres of prawn farms have polluted irrigation canals [13].

As more and more land is required for the cultivation of export crops, the food needs of rural people must be met by production from an ever-shrinking land-base. Worse, it is always the good land that is devoted to export crops – land that lends itself to intensive, large-scale mass-production. Production for export always has priority since it offers what governments are keenest to obtain: foreign exchange. The rural population is thus increasingly confined to rocky and infertile lands, or steep slopes that are very vulnerable to erosion and totally unsuited to agriculture. These areas are rapidly stripped of their forest-cover, ploughed up and degraded. This has occurred, and continues to occur, just about everywhere in the Third World with the growth of the export trade to the world economy.

An example is provided by the rapid growth of soya bean cultivation in Brazil, which is now the second largest soya bean exporter after the United States. One of the results of such growth has been the forced migration of vast numbers of peasants from their lands in the southern state of Rio Grande do Sul and into Amazonia, in particular to the states of Rondonia and Para, where they have cleared vast areas of forest to provide the land from which they must now derive their sustenance. This land, which is largely lateritic, is totally unsuitable to agriculture and after a few years becomes so degraded that it is no longer of any use. This forces the peasants to clear more forest, which provides them with land for another few years – a process that could theoretically continue until all available forest has been destroyed.

Increased Transport

So far we have only considered some of the local effects of extractive export industries, such as logging, ranching, fishing and in particular intensive prawn-farming. But the produce of such industries, as well as minerals such as oil, coal, natural gas, and mass-produced manufactured goods, must be transported to the countries that import them. With the development of the **global economy** the volume of such produce and the distances over which it must be transported can only increase very significantly.

Already in 1991, 4 billion tonnes of freight were exported by ship worldwide, and this required 8.1 exajoules of energy, which is as much as was used by the entire economies of Brazil and Turkey combined. 70 million tonnes of freight that year were sent by plane, and this used 0.6 exajoules, which is equal to a total annual energy use of the Philippines [14].

A European Union task force has calculated that the creation of the single market in Europe in 1993 would increase cross-border traffic with the consequent increase in air pollution and noise by 30 per cent to 50 per cent. With the increase in trade between North America and Mexico, cross-border trucking has doubled in the last five years and this was even before trade barriers were reduced between the two countries. The US government predicted that after the signature of the North American Free Trade Agreement (NAFTA) cross-border trucking would increase by nearly seven times. The ratification of the GATT Uruguay Round Agreement can only further increase the worldwide transport of goods even more dramatically – and to accommodate it a vast number of new highways, airports, harbours, warehouses, etc., must be built, which in itself can only cause serious environmental destruction.

The trans-Amazonian highway for instance, which is designed to supply Asian markets with more timber and minerals, will rip through one of the biologically-rich forested areas of the tropics. Like previous World Bank funded highways carved through primary forests, it will fragment habitat and open up previously inaccessible lands to loggers, miners, ranchers and settlers, just as occurred in the case of the World Bank's notorious Polonoereste project, which triggered off the deforestation of the State of Rondonia and the annihilation of most of its tribal groups.

In its aim to expand and accelerate the transport of goods along the Rio de la Plata, the Hidrovia project of the Mercosur countries will dry out Brazil's Pantanal (the world's largest wetland which contains the highest diversity of mammals) while worsening flooding downstream. The building of more ports, essential for exporting and importing goods, destroys coastal habitats by demolishing wetlands and mangrove forests, increasing chemical spillage, and dredging the bottoms of bays and lagoons. The increased transport itself, will of course give rise to even more environmental devastation, if one takes into account the pollution caused by the extra combustion of fossil fuels – and in particular the effect of increased carbon-dioxide emissions on global warming, not to mention the accidents during transport, leading to oil spills and spills of dangerous chemicals etc. Indeed, it is likely that if merely the environmental costs of increased transport were really taken into account – that is, if they Were "internalized" – then much of world trade would be totally uneconomic and we would return to a very much more localized and less environmentally destructive trading system [15].

The Environmental Effects of Increased Competition

A recent EC report has seriously questioned the effectiveness of current environmental regulations in protecting our environment as the impact on it continues to grow.

It points out there has already been a 13 per cent increase in the generation of municipal wastes between 1986–1991, a 35 per cent increase in the EC's water withdrawal rate between 1970–1985, and a 63 per cent increase in fertilizer use between 1986 and 1991. It predicts that if current growth rates continue, carbon-dioxide emissions must increase by 20 per cent by the year 2010, making nonsense of the EU countries' commitment to stabilize them by the year 2000.

Clearly then these regulations must be seriously strengthened. However, in the free-for-all of the **global economy** no country can strengthen environmental regulations that increase corporate costs without putting itself at a "comparative disadvantage" vis-a-vis its competitors.

The push for a global carbon tax illustrates this problem. The European Union and Japan both proposed adopting an international tax on fossil fuels as a first step in a campaign to reduce carbon-dioxide emissions. The United States refused, saying that imposing such a tax on Americans would be "electorally impossible". Not wanting to impose costs on themselves alone, the EU and Japan dropped the idea. Fossil-fuel use and carbon-dioxide emissions thereby remain almost entirely out of control [16].

In other words, responsible producers who seek to minimize environmental costs must compete against those who do not, and are thereby more competitive. This, among other things, endangers, indeed condemns, the world's remaining ecologically sustainable economic activities.

An example is Amazonia's rubber tappers, who extract latex from the rubber trees scattered throughout much of the Amazonian forests, in a perfectly sustainable manner. They will encounter increasing difficulty in competing with rubber grown on plantations in Asia that have been obtained by clearing tropical forests, especially as under pressure from transnational tyre companies with plants in Brazil, such as Pirelli, Michelin and Goodyear, tariffs on natural rubber imports are due to be eliminated in the next decade [17].

Competition and Environmental Disaster

In order to increase competitivity, corporations are increasingly undertaking cost-cutting measures which generally involve cutting down, often drastically, on the number of employees. This can seriously increase the incidence of environmental accidents. A case in point is the Exxon Valdez disaster, which would probably not have occurred if Exxon had not eliminated 80,000 jobs, among other things reducing the crews of its supertankers by a third [18]. In addition the supertanker would normally have navigated in a safe but slow shipping lane. Instead, also in order to cut costs, it was moved to a much faster shipping lane, but one which was incomparably more dangerous, since it meant having to navigate through ice floes from the Columbia glacier. David Dembo considers that the Bhopal environmental disaster would probably not have occurred if Union Carbide had not indulged in all sorts of cost-cutting measures [19].

Deregulation

Until recently corporations have been limited in their efforts to cut costs by a host of regulations that have been passed, mainly in the last decades, in order to protect the interests of labour, the unemployed, the poor, the old and the sick, local community, local economics, and of course the environment. To the hard-nosed businessman these regulations are so much bureaucratic red tape and serve above all to increase costs and reduce competitivity. As a result pressure has mounted everywhere to get rid of these regulations as quickly as possible. The term used for achieving this cynical and incredibly shortsighted goal is deregulation, and not surprisingly it has been the order of the day for fifteen years or more, in both the US and the UK. Thus when George Bush was Vice-President, he headed the Reagan administration's "Task Force on Regulatory Relief" which, according to the World Public Citizens Congress Watch, was involved in thwarting workers' safety regulations; obstructing consumer products' safety controls; rolling back highway safety initiatives and weakening environmental protection. In 1989, during the Bush administration, this work was taken over by Vice-President Quayle with his "Council on Competitiveness" which did much the same thing. Among other things it was active in opening up the commercial exploitation of possibly as much as half the United States' protected wetlands and tabled more than 100 amendments to the EPA's implementation proposals for the 1990 Clear Air Act.

Free-Trade Zones

What are likely to be the effects of deregulation at a world level can be gauged from the experience with "free-trade zones" or "export-processing zones", of which there are now some 200 in the Third World – usually situated near key communication centres. Foreign industries are enticed to establish themselves in these zones by the simple expedient of eliminating any effective regulations to protect the interests of labour or the environment.

Needless to say, wherever free-trade zones have been established, there has been environmental devastation on a literally horrific scale. Alexander Goldsmith argues that with the ratification of the GATT Treaty we are transforming the world into what is in effect little more than one vast "free-trade zone" – a truly horrifying thought [20].

The Environmental Effects of Structural Adjustment Programmes (SAPs)

What provides another eloquent illustration of the environmental consequences of increased competitiveness and deregulation among export-oriented industries is the experience of those Third World countries that in the last ten years have been subject to IMF and World Bank Structural Adjustment Programmes.

For instance, Costa Rica was subjected to no fewer than nine IMF and World Bank structural adjustment programmes between 1980 and 1989. Greatly increased exports were made possible by the massive expansion of the banana industry and of cattle-ranching. The latter was heavily subsidized (a form of government intervention that free-traders do not seem to disapprove of), a third of state agricultural credit going to the cattle ranchers. Expansion took place at the cost of the country's forest cover which dropped from 50 per cent in 1970 to 37 per cent in 1987 and has dropped still further since. Increasing banana production has also been very destructive to the environment. Huge amounts of chemical fertilizers and pesticides have been used, which are washed into the rivers and end up in the sea – leading among other things to the destruction of coral reefs – 90 per cent of these having been annihilated in some areas [21].

Walden Bello shows that structural adjustment programmes have led to the same sort of environmental destruction in Chile, Ghana and in the Philippines – one of the most structurally adjusted countries in the world. Among other things, the forests, soils and coral reefs of that country have suffered terribly in the last 20 years, as have its mangroves, which have been systematically converted into prawn farms geared to the export trade, their extent having been reduced from the original 500,000 hectares to a mere 30,000 [22].

The relevance of the experience of countries subject to SAPs is clear if we consider that by signing the GATT Uruguay Round Agreement we have in effect subjected the entire world to one vast structural adjustment programme.

Cross-Deregulation

More effective than deregulation carried out by national governments within their own country is that which is conveniently imposed on them by their trading partners under the GATT Uruguay Round Agreement. In the EU's April 1994 Report on US Barriers to Trade and Investment, it is suggested that the commissioners should seek to overturn a large number of Californian and US Federal environmental laws which it is felt can successfully be classified as GATT-illegal trade barriers. These include, in the first category, California's Safe Drinking Water and Toxic Enforcement Act (proposition 65) which requires sticking warning labels on products containing known carcinogenic substances.

Among the Federal laws targeted are the "Gas Guzzler" and other taxes which aim at encouraging the production of small, more cost-fuel efficient cars, which is of course essential if we are to reduce pollution levels in cities and more important still if we are to cut down on greenhouse-gas emissions.

Other Federal laws which the European Union hopes to overturn are the Nuclear Non-Proliferation Act and a number of laws designed to protect fish stocks by limiting the use of large-scale drift nets and other devices that lead to the over-exploitation of fish stocks.

A US Federal environmental law that the World Trade Organization (WTO) has already declared GATT-illegal is the Marine Mammal Protection Act (MMPA) which limits the number of dolphins that can be killed when fishing for tuna in a country that exports tuna to the US. Mexico successfully challenged this act before a GATT panel in 1991, though the panel decision was blocked on technical grounds. Since then the World Trade Organization set up by the GATT has declared the act GATT-illegal, hence repealing this important environmental legislation.

It has been estimated by the US chief negotiator at one of the UNCED prepcoms that 80 per cent of America's environmental legislation could be challenged in this way and most of it declared illegal before WTO panels [23].

At the same time, the US and other countries can conveniently challenge European Union environmental laws in the same way, as indeed they are doing. Already the US has successfully challenged the legality of the European Union's decision to ban the import of beef from America that contains growth hormone residues. A WTO secret panel has thus ruled to repeal yet another important piece of environmental legislation, and this is only the beginning [24].

Harmonizing Standards

Free trade has been institutionalized by a series of free-trade agreements, such as the FTA between the US and Canada, NAFTA and GATT. It is important to realize that these free-trade agreements were designed and promoted by associations of business people, for whom environmental regulations are no more than costs that must be reduced to the minimum.

Not surprisingly, from the very start of the different negotiations that led to the signing of these treaties, the environmental issue has, when possible, been avoided altogether. The Canadian government sought to justify this in the case of the FTA by insisting at the time that "it is a commercial accord between the world's two largest trading partners. It is not an environmental agreement," and "the environment is not therefore a subject for negotiation; nor are environmental matters included in the text of the agreement." As Steven Shrybman comments: "This is an astonishing statement, in view of the fact that the agreement explicitly deals with such issues as energy, agriculture, forest management, food safety and pesticide regulations, matters that could not bear more directly on the environment [25]."

Nor is it surprising that the very word "environment" appears nowhere in the mandate of the GATT, nor is it mentioned in the constitution of the WTO save in a very cursory manner in the preamble.

Public pressure has, of course, forced the bureaucrats to take some notice of environmental issues, and there is even talk of "greening the GATT". But, whatever the rhetoric, when it comes to adopting environmental standards that will increase costs to industry, they are invariably rejected. Thus in 1971 the GATT secretariat stated that it was inadmissible to raise tariffs so as to take into account pollution abatement costs. In 1972 it refused to accept "the polluter pays principle", even though it had been adopted by the OECD Council that same year. Shrybman summed up the situation at the time in the following words: "GATT is being renegotiated with virtually no consideration of its environmental implications. The governmental institutions that have responsibility for trade negotiations have no mandate to address environmental issues, nor the expertise to do so. Environmental organizations are neither being consulted nor being given an opportunity to comment on the various proposals that are being advanced by their respective governments. Instead, participation is restricted to large corporations and trade associations which pursue an agenda of economic growth, profit maximization and deregulation. The shroud of secrecy which surrounds trade negotiations allows these objectives to be advanced in private and without regard to their environmental consequences [26]."

It is thereby not surprising that the international standards for food safety set by the Codex Alimentarius [a little known UN Agency that now fixes international food safety standards in accordance with the principles established by the Agreement on the Application of Sanitary and Phytosanitary Measures (SPM) and the Agreement on Technical Barriers to Trade (TBT)] are not designed to influence countries to raise their still pitifully lax environmental standards, but on the contrary, to lower them still further so as to reduce costs to industry. Thus 42 per cent of the Codex standards for pesticides are lower than EPA and FDA standards. Fifty times more DDT, for instance, may be used on peaches and bananas, and 33 times more DDT may be applied on broccoli [27].

Such EPA and FDA standards are thereby considered too strict, and can be challenged, as almost certainly they will, in the interests of the international harmonization of standards. On the other hand, standards cannot be challenged on the grounds that they are too low and they do not reflect the true environmental costs of destructive corporate activities.

As Ralph Nader puts it: "The international standards provide a ceiling but not a floor for environmental and health protection [28]."

It may be argued that governments can theoretically set standards that are higher than the WTO standards – but only if they satisfy a number of conditions that are so designed as to make it virtually impossible to avoid their being classified as non-tariff barriers to trade, and hence as GATT-illegal. Moreover, the conditions are vague, and thus subject to all sorts of interpretations, and since the WTO Dispute

Resolution Panel is largely made up of corporate representatives who meet, what is more, in total secret, it's unlikely to come to a decision that will lead to an increase in corporate costs [29].

Under such conditions, it must be clear that there is no way of protecting our environment within the context of a global "free-trade" economy, committed to continued economic growth, and hence to increasing the impact of our economic activities on an environment incapable of sustaining even the present impact without undergoing increasingly serious and ever less tolerable degradation.

Of course, measures could be taken to ban or at least limit activities that are particularly destructive – and channel economic development into those areas that are less so. But with the development of the **global economy**, even this is no longer possible – for by its very nature it must be controlled by increasingly stateless, unaccountable and ungovernable transnational corporations, that have set up, via the World Trade Organization, a new international legal system that is designed to make it virtually impossible to adopt environmental controls that could increase their costs and thereby reduce their competitiveness.

There is no evidence that trade or economic development are of any great value to humanity. World trade has increased by eleven times since 1950 and economic growth by five times, yet during this same period there has been an unprecedented increase in poverty, unemployment, social disintegration and environmental destruction. The environment on the other hand is our greatest wealth. To kill it, as the TNCs are methodically doing, is an act of unparalleled criminality. Nor can it be in anything but their very short-term interests to do so, for, as it might be worth pointing out to their leaders, there can be no international trade, no economic development and indeed no TNCs on a dead planet.

This article is an edited and extended version of Chapter 7 "Global Trade and the Environment" that appeared in *The Case Against the Global Economy*, by Jerry Mander and Edward Goldsmith, published by Sierra Club Books, San Francisco, available in the UK from Random House, London.

References

1   Walden Bello & Stephanie Rosenfeld, *Dragons in Distress*.
2   Michael Hsias, quoted by Walden Bello, ibid.
3   Hilary French, *Costly Tradeoffs. Reconciling Trade and the Environment*, Worldwatch Institute, Washington DC, 1993.
4   George Marshall, The Bennett Report, *The Ecologist* vol. 20, no.5, October 1990.
5   J. Krohe, "Illinois – The US Breadbasket. Where has all the soil gone?" *The Ecologist* vol. 14, no. 5/6, 1984.
6   Robert Goodland, *Environmental Management in Tropical Agriculture*, Westview Press, Colorado, 1984.
7   Edward Goldsmith & Nicholas Hildyard, *The Earth Report* no. 2, Mitchell Beazley, London, 1990.

8   Georg Borgstrom, *The Hungry Planet*, Collier Books, New York, 1967.

9   R. Franke & B. Chasin "Peasants, Peanuts, Profits and Pastoralists". *The Ecologist*, vol. 11, no. 4, 1981

10   The editors of *The Ecologist*, vol. 25, nos. 2–3, 1995.

11   Hilary French, op. cit.

12   Alex Wilks "Prawns, Profits and Protein: Aquaculture and Food Production" *The Ecologist*, vol. 25, no. 2–3, 1995.

13   Alex Wilks, op. cit.

14   Hilary French, op. cit.

15   Victor Menotti, unpublished paper.

16   Victor Menotti, ibid.

17   Victor Menotti, ibid.

18   Hawken, *The Ecology of Commerce*, San Francisco, 1993.

19   David Dembo et alia, *The Abuse of Power: Social Performance of Multinational Corporations. The Case of Union Carbide*, New York, NY, New Horizons Press, 1990.

20   Alexander Goldsmith "Free Trade Zones" in Mander & Goldsmith, *The Case Against the Global Economy and for a Turn Towards the Local.*

21   Walden Bello, *Dark Victory*.

22   Walden Bello, ibid.

23   Nicholas Hildyard, personal communication.

24   Simon Retallack, "The WTO's Record So Far", *The Ecologist*, vol. 27, no. 4, 1997.

25   Steven Shrybman, *The Ecologist*, vol. 20. no. 1, Jan/Feb 1990.

26   Steven Shrybman, ibid.

27   John Hulgren, *Final Paper*, International Honors Programme, Boston, 1992.

28   Testimony before the House Small Business Committee on The Uruguay Round Agreement on the General Agreement on Tariffs and Trade, April 26 1994.

29   Ralph Nader & Lori Wallach, "GATT, NAFTA & The Subversion of the Democratic Process" in Mander & Goldsmith, op. cit.

5

Ecological Modernization and the Global Economy (2002)

Arthur P. J. Mol

1. Introduction

Arguably ecological modernization ideas – and to some extent ecological modernization practices – have gained solid ground in at least the West European nation-states.
It is not only the increasing amount of literature that points in that direction, but even
more the fact that the fundamental debates around ecological modernization ideas seem
to have disappeared in Europe. While the ecological modernization perspective met
severe criticism and skepticism in the 1980s and early 1990s, during the second half of
the 1990s this debate faded away. Some of the causes are to be found in the maturation
of ecological modernization ideas. But the changing nature of the environmental
discourse, and the changes in the social practices and institutional developments
related to environmental deterioration and reform have also contributed to this.

But that does not mean that ecological modernization is no longer subject to
doubts, controversies and debates. It only indicates that these controversies and
debates transcend the level of the European nation-state. Today, discussions on the
adequacy of ecological modernization – both as interpretation scheme and as
normative trajectory for environmental reform – are to be found outside Europe, for
example, with regard to the US and the newly industrializing countries and with
respect to the global economy. In this paper, I want to focus on the latter challenge.
What is the relevance of ecological modernization ideas with respect to understanding global environmental reforms? Can we already identify ecological
modernization mechanisms and dynamics that direct a still dominant market driven
global capitalism into more sustainable directions? What trajectories can we envisage

Arthur P. J. Mol. 2002. "Ecological Modernisation and the Global Economy". In *Global Environmental
Politics*, 2(2): 92–109, 112. Reproduced with permission from MIT Press Journals.

for a more comprehensive system of global environmental governance? What does this mean for the agenda of ecological modernization studies?

In dealing with these questions I will shortly summarize the ecological modernization ideas (section 2). I will then elaborate upon the discussions and ambivalences of globalization processes in relation to environmental decay and reform, especially entering into a discussion with neo-Marxists (sections 3 and 4). Subsequently, I will analyze from an ecological modernization perspective what actors, institutions and mechanisms are presently in the making to tame the global treadmill of capitalism (sections 5 to 7). Finally, I return to ecological modernization theory by outlining the consequences globalization should have for ecological modernization studies.

2. Ecological Modernization Theory

Several empirical studies identify from the mid-1980s onward a rupture in the long established trend of parallel economic growth and increasing ecological disruption in most of the ecologically advanced nations, such as Germany, Japan, the Netherlands, the US, Sweden and Denmark. This slowdown is often referred to as the decoupling or delinking of material flows from economic flows. In a number of cases (regarding countries and/or specific industrial sectors and/or specific environmental issues) environmental reform can even result in an absolute decline in the use of natural resources and discharge of emissions, regardless of economic growth in financial or material terms (product output). The social dynamics behind these changes, that is the emergence of actual environment-induced transformations of institutions and social practices in industrialized societies, are encapsulated in the ecological modernization theory. This theory tries to understand, interpret and conceptualize the nature, extent and dynamics of this transformation process.

The basic premise of ecological modernization theory is the centripetal movement of ecological interests, ideas and considerations in social practices and institutional developments. This results in ecology-inspired and environment-induced processes of transformation and reform going on in the core practices and central institutions of modern society. Within ecological modernization theory these processes have been conceptualized at an analytical level as the growing autonomy or independence of an ecological perspective and ecological rationality vis-à-vis other perspectives and rationalities. In the domain of policies, politics and ideologies, the growing independence of an ecological perspective took place in the seventies and early eighties. The construction of governmental organizations and departments dealing with environmental issues dates from that era, followed later by the emergence of green parties in the political system of many countries of the Organization for Economic Cooperation and Development (OECD). In the ideological domain a distinct green ideology – as manifested by, for instance, environmental NGOs and environmental periodicals – started to emerge in the 1970s. Especially in the 1980s, this ideology assumed an independent status and could no longer be interpreted in terms of the old political ideologies of socialism, liberalism and conservatism. But the crucial transformation, which makes the notion of the growing autonomy of an ecological perspective and rationality especially relevant, is of more recent origin. In the economic domain, ecological rationality has started to challenge the dominant economic rationality. And since, according to most scholars, the growing independence of an ecological rationality and perspective from their economic counterparts in the domain of production and consumption is crucial to "the ecological question," this last step is the decisive one. It means that economic processes of production and consumption are increasingly analyzed and judged, as well as designed and organized from both an economic *and* an ecological point of view. Some profound institutional changes in the economic domain of production and consumption have been discernible from the late 1980s onward. Among these changes were the widespread emergence of environmental management systems, the introduction of an economic valuation of environmental goods via the introduction of eco-taxes, the emergence of environment-inspired liability and insurance arrangements, the increasing importance attached to environmental goals such as natural resource saving and recycling among public and private utility enterprises, and the articulation of environmental considerations in economic supply and demand. The fact that we analyze these transformations as *institutional* changes indicates their semi-permanent character. Although the process of ecology-induced transformation should not be interpreted as linear and irreversible, as was common in the modernization theories in the 1950s and 1960s, these changes have some permanency and would be difficult to reverse.

Various ecological modernization scholars have elaborated on the social mechanisms, dynamics and processes through which social practices and institutional developments at the national level take up environmental interests and considerations. Most attention has been paid to technological change, market dynamic and economic actors, political modernization and new forms of governance, and the strategies and ideologies of social movements.

3. Challenging Ecological Modernization: Globalization and AntiGlobalization

This ecological modernization perspective of ongoing institutional transformations triggered by relatively independent environmental ideas and interests has been challenged since the late 1990s by economic globalization. Perceptions on economic globalization, as I will argue below, have brought neo-Marxist perspectives on the treadmill-of-production and on the second contradiction of capital strongly back into the environmental debate.

Globalization reflects a kind of common sense view of the global transformations and interdependencies that most people claim – or are told – to witness. The idea of the nation-state as the rule, the organizing principle and unit, and everything outside it as the exception that proves and fortifies this "rule," has been discarded by an increasing number of people. Global networks and flows, rather than countries, are the "true architectures of the new global economy." This is particularly important for environmentalists and environmental reforms in OECD countries, where the combating of environmental problems has relied firmly for at least the last quarter of the twentieth century on strong nationstates, albeit in vain. Consequently, environmentalists have always been hostile to infringements on the nation-state, whether they be the result of privatization, deregulation or, now, globalization. For instance, the anti-globalization movement that became well known after its protests at the 1999 World Trade Organization (WTO) summit in Seattle, has a strong environmental signature.

In most studies globalization is often closely associated with, if not limited to, the dynamics of global capitalism. The internal dynamics of the capitalist mode of production explains to a large extent the emergence, shape and dynamics of what is called "globalization." Consequently, globalization may lead to the same kind of social disasters that befell capitalism. While arguably on a national scale most industrialized societies have to a greater or lesser extent managed to reduce and neutralize the most severe consequences of the "free" capitalist market, we are now witnessing the return of these very same problems, especially on a global scale and within developing societies. It is globalization – or, more precisely, global capitalism – that is the root cause of this new round of social and environmental destruction.

Some scholars conclude that globalization might lead to the end of the global capitalist economic order, because it jeopardizes the sustenance base of production and consumption. This line of thinking was implicit in the ideas of some protesters at Seattle in 1999 and is articulated explicitly by a number of neo-Marxist environmental sociologists such as Ted Benton, Peter Dickens, Allan Schnaiberg and his colleagues, and James O'Connor. They have combined the idea of an aggressive global expansion of the capitalist economy with the ongoing and intensifying (global) environmental crisis to formulate the "second contradiction of capitalism" argument. According to them, the economic growth and expansion that are inherent within the global capitalist economy will run up against environmental boundaries that will, in the end, turn the tide of the global capitalist economic order and change it beyond recognition. "A systematic answer to the question, 'Is an ecologically sustainable capitalism possible?' is, 'Not unless and until capital changes its face in ways that would make it unrecognizable to bankers, money managers, venture capitalists, and CEOs looking at themselves in the mirror today.'" One of the great historians of our time, Eric Hobsbawm, reaches a similar conclusion on the environmental crisis in the last chapter of his study on the *Age of Extremes*.

Should we thus conclude that an ecological modernization perspective has nothing to offer when we move from the level of the national state to the level of the global economy? I do not think so. Before focusing our attention on the contribution of an ecological modernization perspective to the understanding of the relationship between globalization and the environment, I want to clarify the distinctions between ecological modernization scholars, on the one hand, and neo-Marxists, on the other.

4. Ecological Modernization and Neo-Marxism

Neo-Marxist inspired scholars focus on the continuity of capitalist exploitation of nature, trivialize any environmental improvement and blame the ecological modernization perspective for their failure to get at the "roots of the environmental crisis." More systematically, five major points can be raised to clarify the differences between the two schools of thought (see Table 5.1).

First, ecological modernization studies concentrate on "environmental radicalism" rather than on "social radicalism." That is, in their assessments of existing patterns of change-in-the-making ecological modernization perspectives tend to focus on the contributions to environmental reform, and not primarily on the effects of these changes in terms of various other criteria. "Small" deviations from existing institutions and practices *can* produce substantial environmental improvements, just as "big" changes in terms of a radical or fundamental reorganization of the economic relations of production *can* have limited environmental benefits (as we know from former communist Eastern Europe). Ecological modernization is first and foremost an *environmental* social theory, analyzing the environmental origins and environmental consequences of social change. Neo-Marxist scholars seem to be primarily interested in changes that involve a transformation of the capitalist or treadmill character of production and consumption. The hypothesized one-to-one relationship between the "relations of production" and environmental disruption causes them to count changes as significant only if they undermine the treadmill.

Furthermore, the analysis of change in the two perspectives differs in terms of what might be called "absolute" (neo-Marxist) versus "relative" (ecological modernization). Criticizing ecological modernization theory for its rather naive ideas on environmental improvements, neo-Marxist scholars claim that all – or the overwhelming majority – of production and consumption practices are still governed by treadmill logics, and that ecological, environmental or sustainability criteria will seldom, if ever, become dominant in the organization and design of production and

Table 5.1   Comparing Contrasting Perspectives on Environmental Reform

	Treadmill-of-Production	Ecological Modernization
Main emphasis	Institutional continuity	Institutional transformations
Kind of radicalism	Economic radicalism	Environmental radicalism
Environmental improvements	Absolute sustainability	Relative improvements
Assessment of environmental change	Window dressing	Real changes
Relation between changes analyzed and changes proposed	Weak relation	Strong relation
Object of evaluation	High consequence risks	"Conventional" environmental problems

consumption. In my view, however, this is not so much what contemporary ecological modernization theorists will or should deny. I would agree that treadmill (or economic) criteria and interests play a crucial and dominant role in organizing and designing global production and consumption, and that they will probably always remain at least as important as ecological or other criteria. But the innovation is that ecological interests and criteria are slowly but steadily catching up with economic criteria. Compared to some decades ago, environmental interests can no longer be ignored and increasingly make a difference in organizing and designing production and consumption. In that sense, ecological modernization theory looks at relative (but significant) changes into more environmentally sound directions, in contrast to the "absolute" sustainability sought by neo-Marxist scholars.

Thirdly, there is a major difference between the two perspectives in their assessments of the environmental changes that have been set into motion from the late 1980s onwards: window-dressing (neo-Marxists) versus structural changes in institutions and social practices (ecological modernization). It goes without saying that empirical evidence to underpin either of the two can easily be found and constructed. After all, the large variety in data sets, criteria, variables, time intervals and the like rule out the possibility of any "objective" final answer or conclusion. Neo-Marxist scholars insist that they see no real, lasting environmental improvements and therefore define all environmental initiatives and institutional changes as window dressing. Ecological modernizationists claim that an assessment of environmental transformations in terms of window-dressing seems to bypass the differences that exist between the current period of institutionalization of the environment – regardless of all the shortcomings and limited successes – and that of the 1970s.

Fourthly, a distinction should be made between the nature of the changes advocated by the two frameworks. Both neo-Marxist and ecological modernization perspectives contain analytical as well as normative, and even prescriptive, dimensions. This means that they both analyze contemporary processes of social continuity and change, but also seek to contribute to the development of normative, political trajectories of transformation that ought to take place in order to turn the tide of environmental destruction. Most neo-Marxist studies display a major gap between the quite advanced and detailed theoretical analyses of the immanently destructive character of the treadmill of (global) capitalist production, on the one hand, and the suggestions made for concrete trajectories towards social change, on the other. David Pepper, James O'Connor and Goldfrank's world-system theory volume put forward detailed and refined neo-Marxist analyses of the destructive pattern of the capitalist world economy, but rather "meager" and utopian countervailing strategies for environmental reform. It seems to me that the strategies for change developed within neo-Marxist inspired perspectives have not been improved and refined in step with their analyses of environmental disruption. They are founded only marginally on existing patterns of social transformation and thus have a highly "utopian" character. In contrast, within ecological modernization theory there is a closer link between the analyses of existing changes-in-the-making in the main institutions and social practices, and the design of "realist-utopian" trajectories for environmental reform for the near future.

Finally, a distinction can sometimes be found in the kind of environmental problems that form the object of evaluation. We have already touched upon this in an earlier stage in noticing that the "apocalyptic horizon of environmental reform," usually more dominant in neo-Marxist inspired studies, is often only related to the so-called "high-consequence risks" of climate change, biodiversity, ozone layer depletion and the like. At the same time, "conventional" environmental problems such as surface water pollution, solid waste, local and regional air pollution, and noise are, or at least have been until the mid 1990s, the more typical objects of ecological modernization studies. This difference in object sometimes contributes to differences in evaluations. One of the clearest examples of this contrast is the debate around the presentations of the Environmental Sustainability Index at the World Economic Forum in 2001.[1] The Environmental Sustainability Index (ESI) is a measure of overall progress towards environmental sustainability, developed for 122 countries. The ESI scores are based upon a set of 22 core "indicators," each of which combines two to six variables for a total of 67 underlying variables. It is used to rank countries from most environmentally sustainable (Finland, Norway and Canada being the top three) to least environmentally sustainable (Haiti, preceded by Saudi-Arabia and Burundi). The New Economics Foundation (NEF), among others, attacked the report and calculations as "global misleadership." It was especially critical of the fact that the US was listed 11th on the index, when its ecological footprint placed it 129th out of 151 countries, and carbon dioxide/climate change indicators placed it 149th. While these latter indicators – and the NEF – take a global perspective, the Environmental Sustainability Index is preoccupied with local and national successes in combating environmental pollution, incorporating global issues such as climate change as just one out of the 67 variables that make up the ESI.

In the remaining part of this paper I illustrate that an ecological modernization perspective can balance the idea of an all-determining global capitalism that only results in further environmental decay. Also, at a global level, we can identify the emergence of actors, institutions and mechanisms that tame the treadmill of global capitalism, although these reflexive dynamics differ from their national equivalents (that emerged some twenty years earlier in the most developed countries).

5. Taming the Treadmill of Global Capitalism: Political Modernization

Political scientists and international relations theorists, in particular, have concentrated on the construction of global, multilateral or supra-national environmental organizations, institutions and regimes as instruments to contribute to environmental reform of a globalizing world order. Especially since the early 1990s, international relations scholars have identified environmental issues as a new and interesting issue for multilateral actions, institutions and regimes. They have devoted a great deal of attention to the numerous multilateral environmental agreements (MEAs), most of which focus on one or a limited number of environmental issues (such as the protection of the ozone layer, the export of waste, transboundary air pollution, the protection of the oceans, or the Framework Convention on Climate Change). Although they remain a set of "piecemeal or issue-specific arrangements," the expanding number of multilateral environmental agreements are increasingly moving towards common denominators in terms of legal and policy principles (via spill-over and other mechanisms), and thus becoming more relevant as building blocks for universal international environmental law and policy. In that sense, they jointly contribute to the emergence of a relatively independent environmental realm in national and global politics.

Nevertheless, I would argue that, in the end, the regional, originally economic, institutions such as the European Union (EU) and to a lesser extent the North American Free Trade Agreement (NAFTA) are probably of greater relevance for the future taming of transnational capitalism. The "institutionalization of the environment" in these regions has proceeded beyond a level of piecemeal or issue-specific environmental arrangements. The design of overarching political institutions and arrangements, originally intended to further economic integration, increasingly includes environmental protection. The same is true for the economic arrangements, albeit to a lesser extent. In most of the other regions – including the upcoming economic region centered around Japan – organizations and institutions such as Asia-Pacific Economic Cooperation (APEC), the Association of Southeast Asian Nations (ASEAN), ASEAN Free Trade Area (AFTA) and Mercosur have until now remained dedicated to trade liberalization and economic integration. And although this environmental inclusion in the EU and NAFTA is far from ideal from an environmental interest perspective, most scholars looking for promising developments and prospects in the taming of transnational capitalism are turning their attention to the European Union and to a lesser extent the NAFTA. The preference for the European Union above NAFTA as a model for future global governance is due to its relatively strong supra-national institutions (such as the Commission, the European Parliament and the European Court of Justice), which are to a major extent lacking in MEAs, as well as in NAFTA, the greenest trade agreement to date. This makes the EU unique, not only because it has the supra-national power to counteract the environmental side-effects of global capitalism, caused or facilitated by member states and transnational corporations (TNCs) linked to these states, but because it is the first experiment in supra-national democratic governance, as advocated so strongly by David Held and his colleagues.

Beyond the Up-Scaling of National Environmental Arrangements

From an environmental reform perspective, most of the new and primarily political supranational entities are to some extent the equivalent of the national political arrangements that inspire them. The industrialized nation-states have produced national political arrangements from the 1970s onward, which have had some success in turning structural ecological deterioration into environmental improvements. The basic idea now seems to be that since environmental problems have moved to supra- and transnational levels, in terms of both causes and manifestations, the political institutions and arrangements to deal with them must also be "upgraded" to those levels in order to remain effective: "es handelt sich letzten Endes um die Strategie eines 'Weiter-so' auf gehobenem Niveau."[2]

But there are some serious shortcomings in this rather simple idea of up-scaling. First, in the age of globalization, environmental deterioration has taken on an entirely different aspect as compared to the situation in the 1970s and 1980s. This change goes much further than a change in scale, and therefore merely up-scaling the nation-state institutions and political arrangements for environmental reform to the global level will not do. The dynamics of environmental deterioration and effective reform in an era of globalization are not so much related to geographical scale but to the specific characteristics of the globalization processes. The actors involved in triggering political innovations, the legal status, the absence of a sovereign entity and the "democratic" limitations of alternatives for such a sovereign entity, the changing character of capitalism itself, and the disenchantment of science are but a few of the factors that cause supra-national or global political institutions to deviate fundamentally rather than marginally from their national counterparts.

A second and partly related reason is that supra-national, transnational or global political institutions do not have a similar relevance for all countries. There are profound differences between countries in terms of economic development, political and economic integration in the global system, national political institutions and "environmental reform capacity." Moreover, with respect to environmental decision-making and implementation, the global political system still depends to a large extent on nation-states. As a result of all these factors, countries will be involved unequally in and react differently to "upscaling" in different parts of the planet. Developing countries in sub-Saharan Africa are hardly involved in and barely "touched" by the emerging global political institutions and agreements aiming at environmental reform, so they have little to gain from them in terms of alleviating their environmental problems and crises. Other industrializing economies, such as those in Southeast and East Asia, directly or indirectly, for political or economic reasons, show more interest in taking up "universal" or global environmental norms and standards. The situation in the most developed parts of the economy appears even more promising, as global environmental harmonization seems more and more the objective of these countries.

Third, under conditions of globalization, political arrangements and institutions dealing with environmental reform are no longer restricted to the nation-state system. Decentralized forms of government (such as municipalities or regions) are also appearing on the global stage of environmental politics. Furthermore, global environmental politics, regardless of the level, now also involves actors other than the traditional political agents and institutions. Subpolitical developments – environmental politics involving actors and mechanisms outside the traditional political domains "occupied" by (the system of) nation-states, parliaments and political parties – are interpreted by some as a new answer to environmental deterioration, following some of the typical features of globalization. Nongovernmental environmental organizations have always been at the forefront of environmental reform in the OECD countries, but until recently their role in environmental politics was basically restricted to pressing the traditional political agents – national environmental authorities – to act. Conversely, the role of transnational enterprises has traditionally been one of either simply causing environmental deterioration or (hesitantly, reactively or even symbolically) complying with reform measures in response to pressures from, primarily, national governments. These traditional patterns seem to be changing: both the agents of "civil society" and the agents of economic interests are beginning to become active and powerful in environmental politics at the national, the sub- and the supra-national levels.[3] Such innovations along the lines of ecological modernization can only be understood against the background of a weakening system of sovereign states, the limited achievements of these nation-states, emerging globalization processes and the institutionalization of the environment in political and economic domains. The following two sections focus on these sub-political innovations, and their role in taming the global treadmill.

6. Taming the Treadmill of Global Capitalism: Economic Dynamics

One major – and disputed – innovation of the ecological modernization theory and related interpretation frameworks has been the notion that market dynamics and economic actors have a distinct role to play on the stage of environmental reform, and are already doing so in the most developed nations. What is referred to here is not the isolated "free" markets, the ideal-typical capitalist settings or the short-term profit-maximizing companies that have no regard for continuity. Environmental reform is coming about in the interplay between economic markets and actors on the one hand, and (organized) citizen-consumers and political institutions seeking to condition them on the other. Such interplay allows environmental considerations, requirements and interests to slowly but increasingly become institutionalized in the economic domain. If such market/economy-induced environmental reforms have come about in national settings in the OECD countries, will they also hold in an era marked by globalization, and what would be the difference?

Market-Induced Environmental Reforms

Numerous scholars, including those writing in an ecological modernization tradition, have identified several "economic" mechanisms and dynamics which redirect global capitalist developments and trigger or mediate environmental innovations and reform. As a rule, such economic mechanisms and dynamics do not originate in the economic domain itself. In that sense "market failure" in the provision of common or collective goods, such as the environment, is also – or even more – evident on a global scale. In this sense, also, credit is due to the neo-Marxist scholars warning us not to be over-optimistic about the environmental motives and contributions of economic actors and dynamics per se.

As a rule, the self-regulating economic actors have to be put under "pressure" first before they contribute to environmental improvements (leaving the few "win-win" situations aside). Political decisions, civil pressure, and citizen-consumer demand are decisive. But while they may arise in one corner of the globe at a certain point in time, the economic "domain" has a strong role to play in articulating, communicating, strengthening, institutionalizing and extending (in time and place) these environmental reforms across the globe by means of its own (market and monetary) "language," logic and rationality and its own "force." Transnational industrial companies, global markets and trade, global information and communi-cation networks and companies, and global economic institutions (such as the European Union, multilateral trade treaties such as NAFTA, investment banks like the World Bank, the Asian Development Bank (ADB) and the European Bank for Reconstruction and Development (EBRD), and international financial institutions) play – or, rather, are beginning to play – a vital role in this dynamism. Moreover, developing regions are generally more deeply affected by the global markets and economic actors than by supranational political institutions, although this varies according to each country's degree of integration in the global economy. The envi-ronment becomes to some extent institutionalized in the economic domain. And thus (global) economic institutions, rules and actors operate less and less according to economic principles alone and they can no longer be understood in mere economic logics and terms.

However, we cannot be clear enough about two points. First, these economic dynamics behind environmental reform cannot be understood as established "fact" in all countries, or the majority of foreign investments or trade, nor as an evolutionary development that will "automatically" unfold. These dynamics can only be interpreted as developments taking place, a transformation in-the-making in the global economy that can be identified and which might very well develop on an increasing scale in the decades to come. But, at the moment, it is still a process in *status nascendi,* accompanied by power struggles, standstills and even regression. While various developments point towards an institutionalizing of the environ-ment in the economic domain, there is no fundamental reason or principle pre-venting the stagnation or reversal of this process of ongoing institutionalization. Second, the economy-mediated environmental innovations and transformations as they are developing now are significant and a major first step, but they are far from sufficient. Economic mechanisms, institutions and dynamics will always first follow economic logics and rationalities, which implies they will always fall short in fully articulating environmental interests and pushing environmental reforms, if they are not constantly paralleled and propelled by environmental institutions and envi-ronmental movements. Neo-liberals who would have us believe that we can leave the environment to the economic institutions and actors are wrong. Besides, since economic interests are distributed unequally, any environmental reform brought about by economic players will display similar inequalities, making the results sometimes ambivalent.

The role of global economic dynamics in environmental reform, as well as the ambivalences involved, can be illustrated by the adoption of the ISO 14000 standards. The increasing need to have ISO 14000 standards in order to get access to certain international markets has triggered a drive for environmental harmonization. However, in their analysis of the global introduction of the ISO 14001 standard for environmental management systems, Krut and Gleckman show that this economic push for environmentally harmonized reform can also have its drawbacks. For one thing, a major part of the developing nations were excluded from the design process of the standard. Another drawback is that the existence of the standard disables countries from moving beyond compliance towards more stringent environmental goals. Both the reluctance of global firms to work towards such new environmental "standards" as well as the limits imposed on the possibilities of governments to move beyond the WTO regulations that sanction these ISO standards can hamper progressive environmental developments. In a similar way, the global regime of foreign direct investments has led to a "stuck in the mud" situation, as it fails to provide the incentives for nation-states to engage in a "race to the top" of the environmental standards.[4]

Thus, in conclusion, environmental reforms induced and articulated by economic dynamics, institutions and actors do take place, and we may expect them to become increasingly important. In ecological modernization terminology, the environment is slowly becoming institutionalized in the economic domain. But this process will continue to be challenged and criticized for some time, with the traditional economic interests on the one side, and those who belittle the environmental gains and emphasize the related and unequally distributed social drawbacks, on the other.

Dialectics of Markets and Politics

In analyzing the role global economic actors and mechanisms can and to some extent already do play in environmental reform, it should be stressed that these economic actors and mechanisms are not footloose, neither in the political sense nor in the geographical sense. Firstly, markets and economic actors have always been and will remain phenomena that in the end are politically sanctioned. It is not only that contemporary markets are organized and regulated by political systems and that they could not function as absolutely *free* markets these days. It is also that global companies and global markets depend in the end on a political legitimation of their products and production processes, and increasingly environmental controversies are part and parcel of this legitimacy question. This was so when they operated primarily on a national level and this is not fundamentally different at the global level, however flexible all forms of capital have become in moving around the globe. Environmental groups and their (global) networks, international media, global political actors and institutions, and states intervene in markets and condition the actions of global producers. Secondly, markets and global firms have to settle in geographical locations. This is evident when it comes to material operations in terms of production, distribution and consumption of capital and consumer goods, but it is no less true for the operations of monetary capital. Although geographical flexibility has vastly increased, "even in a globalizing world, all economic activities are geographically localized." And in these localities, the economic interactions are organized, designed and shaped by extra-economic logics such as the local social, cultural, political and physical conditions, even if they engage with actors on the other side of the globe. So if, from an ecological modernization perspective, we emphasize the growing importance of market dynamics in global environmental reform, we have to be aware that "das Projekt der Marktwirtschaft war immer auch ein politisches Projekt – eng verbunden mit der Demokratie."[5] The global market economy and its representatives are under constant scrutiny for the legitimacy of their performance regarding the environment, exactly because they are not footloose.

Political backing (in the broadest sense) is always needed to get markets and economic actors moving in a desirable direction, before market and economic actors can "take over" by articulating and institutionalizing the environment in their domain. It remains a fact that the political drive to activate global markets and economic relations for environmental reform still comes mainly from the most developed countries. This is something that is rooted in history, since these countries were the first to experience very severe environmental problems, as well as protests, and are currently less occupied with the basic economic needs or scarcity. For this reason, and due to unequal power distributions, the environmental priorities and definitions of the developed countries are dominant in global economic institutions (and often also in multilateral environmental agreements), while developing countries often see their environmental priorities neglected. From that perspective one could also have sympathy with the Environmental Sustainability Indicator ESI of the World Economic Forum (see above). Furthermore, developing countries are at a disadvantage in initiatives to redesign economic institutions to incorporate environmental priorities (for example, the WTO), or initiatives to conclude multilateral environmental agreements (for example, the developments in the Framework Convention on Climate Change). The re-negotiations on the Multilateral Agreement on Investment MAI (either in the framework of the OECD or, more likely, in that of the WTO) as well as the greening of the WTO (such as eco-labels, precautionary principle, article XX revisions) will be future cases where these environmental disparities between developed and developing countries will re-emerge. Only strong political backing from beyond the economic and political elites of the most developed countries can ensure that these global economic institutions contribute to future environmental reform in a mode that is less "biased" towards the northern hemisphere.

7. Taming the Treadmill of Global Capitalism: Global Civil Society

It often seems that those who are furthest removed from the actual practice of what has become known as the global civil society, are the first to emphasize and acknowledge the growing countervailing powers of the global environmental movement and the universality of environmental norms and principles. Among them are not only the captains of transnational industries such as Shell and General Electrics, leaders of economic institutions such as the OECD, or neo-liberal economic scholars such as Kenichi Ohmae and World Bank president James Wolfensohn, but also (former) political world leaders such as the German President Roman Herzog and the US Vice-President Al Gore. All of them have stressed the major role of a globalizing civil society, tightly connected to the communication and information revolution, in achieving environmental reforms by taming global capitalism. Meanwhile, environmentalists, and the social scientists and political commentators closely linked to environmental movements, are much more cautious, ambivalent or even pessimistic as to the achievements of a global civil society. In most of their messages they continue to underline the dominant pattern of global capitalist developments, almost as if it had not been touched by the relentless efforts and pressures coming from environmental movements, "green" politicians, relatively marginal global environmental organizations such as UNEP and a diffuse and intangible global environmental consciousness. How can such contrasting evaluations be explained?

In fact, there are several explanations. One of them is the political "game," in which the environmental movement creates for itself an underdog position in order to be able to "beg" for the massive support it needs to beat the Goliath of global capitalism. By the same token, representatives of global capital overstate the strength of this movement, in order to suggest that sufficient countervailing power exists to balance global capital or even stress the dangers of these powerful groups and ideas and legitimize a "green backlash." To some extent it will also be caused by the view that the neighbor's grass is always greener, while the moss and ill weeds are most easily spotted in one's own backyard. From the perspective of transnational companies, Greenpeace must look like a powerful, well-organized and influential organization that manages to articulate environmental anxieties and consciousness into well-coordinated campaigns that attract widespread media attention and increasingly force global economic players into retreat (and reform). The Brent Spar campaign is an illustration. From the inside, the perception is much more that of the difficulties of co-ordination between and within national groups, the failures in campaigns, the limited environmental results and the ambivalent relations with the media, or the tensions between the professional NGO offices and the large population of supporters and grassroots environmentalists.

Finally, it makes a difference whether one takes as one's point of reference the OECD members, the newly industrializing economies, or the developing countries of, for instance, sub-Saharan Africa. The newly industrializing countries in particular have witnessed a major fortification of the environmental movement and environmental consciousness under the recent conditions of globalization. The Latin American environmental movement, for example, has become much stronger during the last decade of the second millennium, and so have those in a number of newly industrializing economies in Asia (e.g. Thailand, Taiwan and the Philippines). Most African states and countries like Vietnam and China, however, have not spawned more than a rather scattered environmental movement, strong in some localities on specific issues, but rather powerless on a national level and poorly integrated into global networks. Nevertheless, even if civil society initiatives are still weak in African countries, the changing global power relations on environmental issues can have profound repercussions on transnational companies investing in the continent, as Shell has experienced in Nigeria and a consortium of oil multinationals and the World Bank are experiencing in planning – and from October 2000 onward implementing – a major oil pipeline through Chad and Cameroon.

Global Environmentalism

The global civil society is not global in the sense that it has a global network of environmental NGOs covering every locality of the world. Nor does it have a common frame of reference similarly articulated in every corner of our planet. That will take some time to be accomplished. One obstacle is that any "shared" environmental frame of reference falls apart in different parts of the world. People's environmental priorities are different in different parts of the world (climate change versus clean water; nature conservation versus the "brown agenda"), and definitions of environmental problems diversify as they are mediated by local backgrounds, history, and traditions. Environmental universalism is prevented by local factors articulating in heterogeneous cultural frameworks, as is widely acknowledged. But the most important reason for the absence of a global frame of reference is the fact that the capacities and resources to articulate an environmental discourse in civil society are unequally distributed, especially – but not only – along the economic divides.

The main reasons why we can still speak of global environmentalism are the following: (i) the ethics and principles of environmental behavior as regards the investments, production and trade of transnational companies and investment banks are increasingly applied in a similar way to practices anywhere around the globe; (ii) the potential to monitor environmental (mis)behavior of transnational corporations and institutions has moved far beyond the major centers of the global environmental movement in the developed world; (iii) environmental misbehavior and information are communicated around the globe; and (iv) sanctions can transcend the boundaries of one state and are no longer limited to the localities of misbehavior. However, even though environmentalism has become global, transnational investors that are not strongly connected to the most developed countries have less to "fear" from a global civil society. In Vietnam, for instance, American multinationals such as Nike are more vulnerable to environmental protests from global civil society than are regional investors from South Korea, Taiwan or Indonesia.

The emergence of a global civil society and its growing power to challenge the environmental destructiveness of global capitalism has made some of the major global economic players more aware of the need to move beyond mere compliance with formal political requirements laid down in laws and agreements. We can witness new forms of global environmental (sub)politics, arising especially in situations where (i) nation-states are losing control of national and global developments, (ii) scientific "proof" is no longer taken for granted, but increasingly seen as both an instrument of social interests and an object of social conflict, and (iii) information and communication systems heighten the transparency of the world-wide actions of global economic actors. The controversies surrounding genetically modified organisms are of course a typical example where formal political requirements are overtaken by civil society politics. The representatives of global capitalism are finding it increasingly difficult to ignore civil society environmental protests and sensibilities, while formal environmental policies (both nationally and internationally) are "lagging behind." TNCs are experiencing that they can less and less afford to restrict their environmental performance to compliance with formal political requirements. We can identify an increasing need, particularly for the visible multinationals from the OECD countries, to justify their actions not only towards the states, MEAs and conventional political actors, but also towards representatives of civil society, resulting in new forms of (global) environmental politics. Major European food companies are developing various strategies to get into contact with (organized) consumers and concerned citizens, in order to become aware of their ideas and "sensibilities" at an early stage of product development. This does not result automatically in major environmental improvements, as many concerned citizens experience today, but it does give us a first glance of the potential stepping stones along the way towards future global environmental governance.

8. Conclusions: Ecological Modernization Perspectives in an Era of Globalization

For a relatively long time, ecological modernization theory focused both theoretically and empirically on the environmental reforms taking place in a number of industrialized, Western countries, even though the importance of supranational and global dynamics for these new patterns of (national) environmental reform had been recognized […].

We should remain suspicious of ideas that claim that environmental reform processes show universal forms, dynamics and characteristics, in view of the fact that nations and regions differ and that environmental reform mechanisms vary accordingly, no matter how strongly such environmental reforms are triggered and influenced by global processes. Local refinements and contextualization of the ecological modernization theoretical framework, which until recently could rightfully be criticized for being too monolithic and too Eurocentric, is essential […].

Notes

1 This study was done by the Columbia University Center for International Earth Science Information network (CIESIN), the Yale Center of Environmental Law and Policy, Yale University, and the World Economic Forum's Global Leaders for Tomorrow Environment Task Force. See http://www.ciesin.columbia.edu/indicators/ESI.

2 "In the end, it is a strategy of 'more of the same thing" on an elevated level." Beck, Ulrich. 1997. *Was ist Globalisierung? Irrtümer des Globalismus—Antworten auf Globalisierung.* Frankfurt am Main: Suhrkamp, 221.

3 An illustrative example might be the breakdown of the Global Climate Coalition, a group of large energy-intensive multinationals that claim that there is insufficient scientific evidence on climate change to justify political measures such as those negotiated in Kyoto. After BP, Shell and Dow Chemicals, Ford Motors also left the coalition in December 1999, emphasizing the need for pro-active measures and R&D.

4 The idea of a 'race to the bottom' of national environmental regimes following competition for foreign direct investment is not supported by empirical studies carried out on this issue (see, among others, the studies of the World Bank, the OECD, and political scientists such as Leonard and Janicke).

5 "The project of the market economy has always been a political project as well – closely connected to democracy." Beck 1997, 232–233.

6

Environment and Globalization: Five Propositions (2010)

Adil Najam, David Runnalls, and Mark Halle

The processes that we now think of as "globalization" were central to the environmental cause well before the term "globalization" came into its current usage. Global environmental concerns were born out of the recognition that ecological processes do not always respect national boundaries and that environmental problems often have impacts beyond borders; sometimes globally. Connected to this was the notion that the ability of humans to act and think at a global scale also brings with it a new dimension of global responsibility – not only to planetary resources but also to planetary fairness. These ideas were central to the defining discourse of contemporary environmentalism in the 1960s and 1970s and to the concept of sustainable development that took root in the 1980s and 1990s.

The current debate on globalization has become de-linked from its environmental roots and contexts. These links between environment and globalization need to be re-examined and recognized. To ignore these links is to misunderstand the full extent and nature of globalization and to miss out on critical opportunities to address some of the most pressing environmental challenges faced by humanity.

[…]

Although the contemporary debate on globalization has been contentious, it has not always been useful. No one doubts that some very significant global processes – economic, social, cultural, political and environmental – are underway and that they affect (nearly) everyone and (nearly) everything. Yet, there is no agreement on exactly how to define this thing we call "globalization," nor on exactly which parts of it are good or bad, and for whom. For the most part, a polarized view of globalization, its potential and its pitfalls has taken hold of the public imagination. It has often

Adil Najam, David Runnalls, and Mark Halle. 2010. *Environment and Globalization: Five Propositions.* Winnipeg: International Institute for Sustainable Development. pp. 1, 4–35.

been projected either as a panacea for all the ills of the world or as their primary cause. The discussion on the links between environment and globalization has been similarly stuck in a quagmire of many unjustified expectations and fears about the connections between these two domains.

Although the debates on the definition and importance of globalization have been vigorous over time, we believe that the truly relevant policy questions today are about who benefits and who does not; how the benefits and the costs of these processes can be shared fairly; how the opportunities can be maximized by all; and how the risks can be minimized.

[…]

1   Globalization of the economy. [...]
2   Globalization of knowledge. [...]
3   Globalization of governance. [...]

While the importance of the relationship between globalization and the environment is obvious, our understanding of how these twin dynamics interact remains weak. Much of the literature on globalization and the environment is vague (discussing generalities); myopic (focused disproportionately only on trade-related connections); and/or partial (highlighting the impacts of globalization on the environment, but not the other way around).

Box 6.1   Defining Globalization

What is Globalization?
There are nearly as many definitions of globalization as authors who write on the subject. One review, by Scholte, provides a classification of at least five broad sets of definitions:

Globalization as internationalization. The "global" in globalization is viewed "as simply another adjective to describe cross-border relations between countries." It describes the growth in international exchange and interdependence.

Globalization as liberalization. Removing government-imposed restrictions on movements between countries.

Globalization as universalization. Process of spreading ideas and experiences to people at all corners of the earth so that aspirations and experiences around the world become harmonized.

Globalization as westernization or modernization. The social structures of modernity (capitalism, industrialism, etc.) are spread the world over, destroying cultures and local self-determination in the process.

Globalization as deterritorialization. Process of the "reconfiguration of geography, so that social space is no longer wholly mapped in terms of territorial places, territorial distances and territorial borders."

It is important to highlight that not only does globalization impact the environment, but the environment impacts the pace, direction and quality of globalization. At the very least, this happens because environmental resources provide the fuel for economic globalization, but also because our social and policy responses to global environmental challenges constrain and influence the context in which globalization happens. This happens, for example, through the governance structures we establish and through the constellation of stakeholders and stakeholder interests that construct key policy debates. It also happens through the transfer of social norms, aspirations and ideas that criss-cross the globe to formulate extant and emergent social movements, including global environmentalism.

In short, not only are the environment and globalization intrinsically linked, they are so deeply welded together that we simply cannot address the global environmental challenges facing us unless we are able to understand and harness the dynamics of globalization that influence them. By the same token, those who wish to capitalize on the potential of globalization will not be able to do so unless they are able to understand and address the great environmental challenges of our time, which are part of the context within which globalization takes place.

The dominant discourse on globalization has tended to highlight the promise of economic opportunity. On the other hand, there is a parallel global discourse on environmental responsibility. A more nuanced understanding needs to be developed – one that seeks to actualize the global opportunities offered by globalization while fulfilling global ecological responsibilities and advancing equity. Such an understanding would, in fact, make sustainable development a goal of globalization, rather than a victim. As a contribution towards this more nuanced understanding of these two dynamics, we will now outline five propositions related to how environment and globalization are linked and how they are likely to interact.

The Five Propositions

By way of exploring the linkages between environment and globalization, let us posit five key propositions on how these two areas are linked, with a special focus on those linkages that are particularly pertinent for policy-making and policy-makers. The purpose of these propositions is to highlight the possible implications of the dominant trends. This is neither an exhaustive list nor a set of predictions. It is rather an identification of the five important trajectories which are of particular importance to policy-makers because (a) these are areas that have a direct bearing on national and international policy and, (b) importantly, they *can* be influenced by national and international policy.

Proposition #1:

The rapid acceleration in global economic activity and our dramatically increased demands for critical, finite natural resources undermine our pursuit of continued economic prosperity.

Table 6.1 Environment and Globalization: Some Examples of Interaction

How does globalization affect the environment?	Means of influence	How does environment affect globalization?
- *Scale* and composition of economic activity changes, and consumption increases, allowing for more widely dispersed externalities. - *Income* increases, creating more *resources* for environmental protection. - *Techniques* change as technologies are able to extract more from nature but can also become *cleaner*.	Economy	- Natural *resource scarcity or/and abundance* are *drivers of globalization*, as they incite supply and demand *forces* in global markets. - The need for *environmental amelioration* can extract costs from economy and siphon resources away from development goals
- Global interactions *facilitate exchange of environmental knowledge and best practices.* - *Environmental consciousness* increases with emergence of global environmental networks and civil society movements. - Globalization facilitates the spread of existing *technologies* and the emergence of new technologies, often replacing existing technologies with more extractive alternatives; greener technologies may also be spurred. - Globalization helps spread a homogenization of *consumption-driven aspirations.*	Knowledge	- Signals of environmental stress travel fast in a compressed world, *environmentally degraded and unsustainable locations* become marginalized from trade, investment, etc. - Sensibilities born out of environmental stress can push towards *localization* and *non-consumptive development* in retaliation to the thrust of globalization. - Environmental stress can trigger alternative technological paths, e.g., dematerialization, alternative energy, etc., which may not have otherwise emerged.
- Globalization makes it increasingly difficult for states to rely only on *national regulation* to ensure the well-being of their citizens and their environment. - There is a *growing demand and need for global regulation,* especially for the means to enforce existing agreements and build upon their synergies to improve environmental performance. - Globalization facilitates the involvement of a growing *diversity of participants and their coalitions* in addressing environmental threats, including market and civil society actors.	Governance	- Environmentalism becomes a global *norm.* - Environmental standards *influence patterns of trade and investment* nationally and internationally. - The nature of environmental challenges requires the incorporation of environmental governance into other areas (e.g., trade, investment, health, labour, etc.). - Stakeholder participation in *global environmental governance* – especially the participation of NGOs and civil society – has become a model for other areas of global governance.

The premise of this proposition is that a sound environment is essential to realizing the full potential of globalization. Conversely, the absence of a sound environment can significantly undermine the promise of economic prosperity through globalization.

The notion that rising pressures on, and dwindling stocks of, critical natural resources can dramatically restrain the motors of economic growth is not new. What *is* new, however, is the realization that the spectacular economic expansion we have been seeing has made the resource crunch a pressing reality that could easily become the single biggest challenge to continued economic prosperity.

The premise of the proposition is fairly simple. First, natural resources – oil, timber, metals, etc. – are the raw materials behind much of global economic growth. Second, there is ultimately a finite amount of these resources available for human use. Third, and importantly, the quantum of resources being used has grown exponentially in recent years, especially with the spectacular economic expansion of large developing economies – such as India and China – and increasing global prosperity. Fourth, we are already witnessing increasing global competition for such resources; and not just market, but geopolitical forces are being mobilized to ensure continued supplies and controls over critical resources.

[...] degradation of ecological processes – especially fragile ecological systems that are central to the preservation of our essential life systems – could cause a major hiccup in continued global economic growth, and possibly become the single most important threat to the continuation of current globalization trajectories. [...]

Although scares about "limits to growth" have proved less than credible in the past, simple economic logic (and available trends) argues that, as competition for scarce natural resources increases, prices will be driven up – and sooner than we might have assumed. In the past, technology has – and in the future, it certainly could – help to alleviate some of these pressures by developing new solutions and by more widely deploying existing technological solutions. However, the prospects of higher demand, growing prices and dwindling stocks are already propelling new races for control over key resources. The race is now on not just for oil, but for metals, minerals, timber and even for recyclable waste. For many developing countries endowed with critical resources in high demand, this provides an opportunity to harness the power of globalization and pull themselves out of poverty. Past experience suggests that national and global economies have not been particularly good at allowing for the benefits of resources to flow down to the poor; the challenge today is to find the ways and means to do exactly that.

A parallel challenge is to decrease the adverse effects of resource competition on the poor. [...]

Environmental degradation could also impact productivity through damages to health. For example, international agencies found that 2.5 million people in the Asia-Pacific region die every year due to environmental problems including air pollution, unsafe water and poor sanitation. Ignoring environmental costs destroys value. The "natural capital" of ecosystem services (such as watersheds, which provide clean water) is drawn down, creating a need to pay for services (like water filtration plants) that could have been provided for free, in perpetuity, if sustainably managed.

Similarly, environmental degradation, global and local, will affect the agricultural sector, on which the majority of the world's poor depend directly for their survival. For example, recent data suggest that global climate change could reduce South Asia's wheat area by half. While gains in productivity in temperate areas could partially offset the difference, whether poorer tropical countries could afford to buy food from richer regions of the world is uncertain. To avoid famine, the Consultative Group on International Agricultural Research has already called for accelerated efforts to develop drought-, heat- and flood-resistant strains of staple crops. The Worldwatch Institute estimates that 17 per cent of cropland in China, and a staggering 28 per cent in India, is seriously degraded by erosion, water-logging, desertification and other forms of degradation.

It is most likely, therefore, that decreased environmental stability will create more hostile conditions for economic growth and also place new pressures on international cooperation. Two recent reports have documented and drawn global attention to this discussed "possibility," which has started to become a reality. On one hand, the *Millennium Ecosystem Assessment* has meticulously documented the slide in the environmental health of the planet and how we are pushing the limits of many critical resources. The recent rise in oil prices has had the effect of making this connection tangible and recognizable even to ordinary citizens. On the other hand, the recently released *Stern Review* has bluntly suggested that these environmental pressures have now begun impacting global economic processes and that impacts of climate change could create losses of 5–10 per cent of global GDP, and decrease welfare by up to 20 per cent if damages include non-market impacts and are weighted for ethical/distribution effects. This calculation includes estimations of damages caused by flooding, lower crop yields, extreme weather-related damages, and other direct impacts on the environment and human health.

[...]

Proposition #2:

The linked processes of globalization and environmental degradation pose new security threats to an already insecure world. They impact the vulnerability of ecosystems and societies, and the least resilient ecosystems. The livelihoods of the poorest communities are most at risk.

With globalization, when insecurity increases and violence erupts, the ramifications become global in reach. The forces of globalization, when coupled with those of environmental degradation, expand concepts of threat and security, both individually and through their connections. We have already begun recognizing new global threats from non-state groups and individuals, and security is now being defined more broadly to include, among others, wars between and within states; transnational organized crime; internal displacements and migration; nuclear and other weapons; poverty; infectious disease; and environmental degradation.

To take one pressing example, the World Resources Institute (WRI) reports that:

Water scarcity is already a major problem for the world's poor, and changes in rainfall and temperature associated with climate change will likely make this worse. Even without climate change, the number of people affected by water scarcity is projected to increase from 1.7 billion today to 5 billion by 2025. In addition, crop yields are expected to decline in most tropical and sub-tropical regions as rainfall and temperature patterns change with a changing climate. A recent report by the Food and Agriculture Organization estimates that developing nations may experience an 11 per cent decrease in lands suitable for rain-fed agriculture by 2080 due to climate change. There is also some evidence that disease vectors such as malaria-bearing mosquitoes will spread more widely. At the same time, global warming may bring an increase in severe weather events like cyclones and torrential rains.

All of this imperils human security, which in turn drives societal insecurity and, in many cases, violence. Placed in the context of globalization, violence and insecurity can spill out since now they can travel further, just as people, goods and services can.

Security is about protecting people from critical and pervasive threats. This ranges from the security of nations to that of individuals and of societies. Human security is about creating systems that give individuals and communities the building blocks to live with dignity. Livelihoods are, therefore, an essential element of human security. Acting together, globalization and environmental stress may directly threaten the livelihoods of the poor, i.e., the capabilities, material and social assets and activities required for a means of living, and decrease their ability to cope with, and recover from, environmental stresses and shocks.

For "winners" of the process, globalization becomes an integrating phenomenon – one that brings together markets, ideas, individuals, goods, services and communications. For the "losers" in the process, however, it can be a marginalizing phenomenon. Just as the winners come closer to each other they become more "distant" from the losers. The dependence within society on each other becomes diminished as transboundary dependence increases. To use a basic example, as West African consumers develop a liking for imported rice, their "links" to farmers on other continents who export rice to them increase even as their "links" to farmers in their own country growing cassava decrease. Environmental stress can have a similarly marginalizing impact on the vulnerable and the weak. It is quite clear from the evidence now that even though climate change will eventually impact everyone, it will impact the poorest communities first and hardest. In the case of desertification, we already see the poorest and most vulnerable communities being displaced the most. In essence, the already insecure and vulnerable are pushed to greater depths of insecurity and vulnerability.

The combined effects of globalization-related marginalization and environment-related marginalization can wreak havoc on whatever resilience poor communities might otherwise have possessed. An illustrative example is the case of small fishers in the Caribbean. On one hand, globalization forces of advanced extraction technologies, reduced transportation costs, increased ability to keep fish-stock fresh over long distances and increasing global demands from far-away markets combine to drive the small fisher out of the market. On the other, the very same forces dramatically decrease the amount of fish in the ocean, thereby further reducing the resilience of the small fisher. As globalization changes the patterns of environmental dependence, it may marginalize parts of Caribbean society and disintegrate local security networks.

In many ways, climate change is the ultimate threat to global security because it can existentially threaten security at every level from the individual to the planetary. [...]

International experience with the linkage between natural resources and conflict calls for resolute action as natural resources can fuel and motivate violent conflict (e.g., conflict diamonds funding rebel groups in Angola and Sierra Leone; conflicts over distribution of resource profits from timber and natural gas in Indonesia; oil as key factor in Iraqi invasion of Kuwait). Environmental stress unleashed by potential climate change could trigger international migration and, possibly, civil wars. In fragile circumstances, environmental stress could act as an additional destabilizing factor exacerbating conflict as it combines with other political and social factors. [...]

Conflict sets back the prospects for sustainable development, often by decades, by setting in motion a negative spiral – environmental degradation leads to more competition for scarce resources, leading the powerful to secure the resources for their use, leading to conflict, which leads to worsened social relations, smash-and-grab resource use, greater resentment, etc. Security – from national to human – is, therefore, a prerequisite for realizing the benefits of sustainable development as well as those of globalization.

PROPOSITION #3:

The newly prosperous and the established wealthy will have to come to terms with the limitations of the ecological space in which both must operate, and also with the needs and rights of those who have not been as lucky.

[...]

- "By one calculation, there are now more than 1.7 billion members of 'the consumer class' – nearly half of them in the developing world. A lifestyle and culture that became common in Europe, North America, Japan and a few other pockets of the world in the twentieth century is going global in the twenty-first." [...]

The rapid rise of this set of erstwhile developing countries should also trigger reflection within established industrialized economies on the questions of growth and consumption. It is not viable – nor was it ever – to urge consumption restraint on the newly prosperous while continuing on paths of high consumption oneself. [...] the newly prosperous as well as those who have been affluent for much longer will now have to come to terms with the limitations of the ecological space in which both must operate and also with the needs and rights of those who have not been as lucky.

The interaction of globalization and environment are writ large in the new realities unleashed by the focus of global possibilities in terms of both processes moving southwards. For example, it is popular to say that "China is the workshop to the world"; but it is also worth asking "who is the customer of this workshop's products?" and "who are the suppliers to the workshop?" [...] To consider the "workshop" metaphor seriously requires placing the "workshop" within a supply chain that is (a) truly global in nature, and (b) not just an economic supply chain, but an environmental one.

[...]

The question is whether these emerging economies of the South will have the foresight to embrace the opportunity and to chart a development path that is different from that which had been followed by those who came before them, and whether the "old" affluent economies of the North will demonstrate a shared commitment to assist the developing world in charting such a path and by demonstrably taking the lead in curtailing their own unsustainable patterns.

PROPOSITION #4:

Consumption – in both North and South – will define the future of globalization as well as the global environment.

To put this proposition most bluntly, the central challenge to the future of environment and globalization is consumption, not growth. Fueled by the aspirational "norms" of consumption that also become globalized through, in part, the global media and advertising, consumption changes magnify the footprints of growth. For example, while global population doubled between 1950 and 2004, global wood use more than doubled, global water use roughly tripled, and consumption of coal, oil, and natural gas increased nearly five times.

A focus on consumption immediately draws our attention to the challenge of inequity. That challenge cannot be brushed aside. A simple but powerful illustration suggests that on average, in 2000, one American consumed as much energy as 2.1 Germans, 12.1 Colombians, 28.9 Indians, 127 Haitians or 395 Ethiopians. [...] national averages hide massive consumption inequity within nearly all societies. The very affluent within developing countries over-consume just as the poor within affluent countries under-consume.

[...] Humanity's ecological footprint – the demand people place upon the natural world – has increased to the point where the Earth is unable to keep up in the struggle to regenerate. The key to resolving this challenge is to de-link consumption from growth, and growth from development: to provide the poor with the opportunity to increase their use of resources even as the affluent reduce their share so that a sustainable level and global equity can be achieved.

Technology is one key element in meeting this challenge. The policy decisions we now take that will influence future trajectories of technology development and deployment – and of consumption choices – will shape the interaction between globalization and the global environment. The good news is that these trajectories *can* be shaped by policy. Technology has been one of the great drivers of modern globalization. It has also become one of the principal drivers of environmental processes. Transport technologies, for example, have not only made the world a smaller and more "global" planet, they have also resulted in new environmental stress, especially through increased atmospheric carbon concentrations. Technology has sped up prosperity for many, but it has also allowed extraction of resources – fish, timber, metals, minerals, etc. – at unprecedented rates, thereby placing new and massive pressures on stocks.

At the same time, technological advances have allowed, in some areas, reduced environmental stress. Evidence suggests, for example, that China's economic growth has come with a relatively lesser increase in emissions than what had happened earlier in Europe and North America because China has been able to "leapfrog" to technologies that are much cleaner than Europe and North America were using at similar stages in their development. Although its emission rates per GDP are still high, they are decreasing and have been halved in the last decade. For example, their fuel economy standards are higher than those of the United States.

Technological solutions will inevitably determine the future of globalization as well as the global environment. But they will do so within the context of global consumption demands. Technology cannot change the demands or help us satisfy all of them but it can, through globalization, help meet these demands in a more planet-friendly way.

[...]

Ultimately, the trajectories of the future – as well as the technologies available – will be shaped by our aspirations of what a "good life" really is. The moral and spiritual dimension of planetary aspirations may not seem like an appropriate subject for policy discussions, but it lies at the very heart of the type of global society that we want to live in and the type of global society that we are constructing. Not only are policy discussions impacted by aspirational decisions of society, they can in fact shape these aspirations. The Brundtland Report released 20 years ago was very much an attempt to shape global aspirations on environment as well as what we now call globalization. Agenda 21, which emerged from the Rio Earth Summit 15 years ago, was another such attempt. Since then, an array of other influential ideas have come from governments, civil society and business. For example, concepts of "natural capitalism," industrial ecology, eco-efficiency, "Factor Ten" efficiency improvements, and "Global Transitions" have been proposed and some have gained currency in civic discourse, business strategy and government policy.

[...]

The purpose of this proposition, therefore, is not simply to say that consumption is the key to understanding globalization and the environment. It is to propose that de-linking consumption from growth, and growth from development is possible. That the promise of sustainable development is – or can be – an honest promise; honestly kept. It is also to suggest that policy interventions are necessary to make this transition and to offer the hope that slowly – albeit too slowly – this realization is coming to be accepted by decision-makers. The challenge, of course, is whether this slow realization will be able to trigger the much larger change in global consumption trajectories before it is too late.

PROPOSITION #5:

Concerns about the global market and global environment will become even more intertwined and each will become increasingly dependent on the other.

Although still unrecognized by many, it is nonetheless a fact that a large proportion of existing global environmental policy is, in fact, based on creating, regulating and managing markets. The most obvious examples are direct trade-related instruments like the Convention on International Trade in Endangered Species of wild fauna and flora (CITES) or the Basel Convention on Trade in Hazardous Waste. But even less obvious instruments such as the Climate Convention (especially through its emission trading provisions) or the Biodiversity Convention (through, for example, the Cartagena Protocol on living modified organisms) operate within created or existing marketplaces and markets are a central element of their design and implementation.

For their part, the managers of market interactions – most prominently in the area of international trade, but also in investment, subsidies, etc. – have also belatedly come to the conclusion that they cannot divorce market policies from environmental policy for long. To take international trade as an example, we see that a significant part of international trade is in environment-related goods – ranging from trade in resources such as timber or fish to flowers and species, and much more. Moreover, trade in just about all goods has environmental relevance in the manufacture, transport, disposal and use of those goods. The Preamble to the Marrakech Agreements establishing the World Trade Organization (WTO) recognizes this clearly. And following its lead, the Doha Round of WTO negotiations has also acknowledged this intrinsic connection by placing environment squarely on the trade negotiation agenda. Although those negotiations are currently stalled, the principle of the inclusion of environmental concerns on the trade agenda is no longer in question and is not in doubt.

Importantly, there is a synergy in the stated goals of the trade and the environment system. Both claim to work in the context of, and for the attainment of, sustainable development. Given that international trade is a principal motor of globalization, one can argue that sustainable development should be considered an ultimate goal of globalization, just as it is the stated end-goal of the international trading system.

[...]

Looking at the larger picture, one does begin to see the emerging recognition of the need for better integration among the key players. On the trade side, for example, the Doha Declaration and its reaffirmation of sustainable development as the meta-goal of global trade policy was a manifestation of this recognition. Soon afterwards, the World Summit on Sustainable Development (WSSD) of 2002 also reaffirmed the centrality of the trade and environment connections in its Declaration and all its deliberations. However, the move from the declaratory to the regulatory remains mired in institutional challenges since our systems of global governance have been designed to keep the two issues apart rather than to inspire collaboration for the achievement of common goals.

The central point of this proposition, then, is that even though the reality of the global marketplace and the global environment are intrinsically intertwined and becoming ever more so – through the mechanisms of international trade; manifestations of environmental stress; the changes in peoples' livelihoods; and the actions of business and civil society – the processes of decision-making in these two areas are still far apart and only occasionally interact. The good news is that recent developments have nudged policy-makers in the two areas to talk to each other just a little bit more. To be meaningful, however, this nudge must soon convert into a real push and the stated common goal of sustainable development should become a central driver of coordinated policies.

Avenues for Action: What Can We Do?

Better global governance is the key to managing both globalization and the global environment. More importantly, it is also the key to managing the relationship between the two. The processes of environment and globalization are sweepingly broad, sometimes overwhelming, but they are not immune to policy influence. Indeed, the processes as we know them have been shaped by the policies that we have – or have not – put in place in the past. Equally, the direction that globalization, the global environment and the interaction of the two will take in the years to come will be shaped by the policy decisions of the future. Governance, therefore, is the key avenue for action by decision-makers today.

However, it is also quite clear that both globalization and environment challenge the current architecture of the international system as it now exists. Both dynamics limit a state's ability to decide on and control key issues affecting it. Globalization does it largely by design as states commit to liberalize trade and embrace new technologies. The environment challenges the system by default as ecosystem boundaries rarely overlap with national boundaries and ecological systems are nearly always supra-state. The role of the state in the management of the international system has to evolve to respond to the evolution of the challenges facing it.

This evolution is already happening, but often in painful, even contorted, ways. Having outgrown its old structure, the international system is designing a new, more inclusive one. Many problems have been identified in the current system of global governance: it is too large; it is chronically short of money and yet also wasteful of the resources it has; it has expanded in an ad hoc fashion; it lacks coordination and a sense of direction; it is often duplicative and sometimes different organizations within the system work at crosspurposes to each other, etc. In terms of environment and globalization, we see three important goals for the global governance system as it exists today.

Managing institutional fragmentation: Although there already exist organs within the system to address most problems thrown up by environment and globalization, the efforts of these institutions are fragmented and lack coordination or coherence. The efforts and the instruments for making the "system" work as a whole either do not exist or are under-utilized. [...] There is a pressing need, therefore, for meaningful global governance reform that creates viable and workable mechanisms for making existing institutions work together more efficiently and effectively than they have so far.

Broadening the base of our state-centric system: Despite some headway over the last two decades, the essential architecture of the international governance system remains state-centric, even though neither the problems nor the solutions are any longer so. [...] Whether it is companies creating new global norms and standards through their procurement and supply chains, or NGOs establishing voluntary standards in areas such as forestry or organic products, we see that policy in practice is no longer the sole domain of the inter-state system. It should be acknowledged that both civil society and business are beginning to be integrated into global governance mechanisms – for example, through their presence and participation in global negotiations and summits and through closer interactions with environmentally progressive businesses. This process needs to be deepened and accelerated, and meaningful ways need to be found to incorporate them as real partners in the global governance enterprise.

Establishing sustainable development as a common goal: The post-World War II international organizational architecture was originally designed to avoid another Great War. In terms of what the system does and in terms of the types of goals that it has set for itself (e.g., the Millennium Development Goals; stabilization of atmospheric concentrations of CO_2; eradication of diseases such as Malaria; control of HIV/AIDS; etc.), the system has evolved to a broader understanding of what we mean by "security" as well as of what its own role is. Yet, it is not always clear that the entire system of global governance is moving towards a common goal. This creates undue friction between the organizations that make up the system and results in disjointed policies. [...]

- The last few years have seen a number of different initiatives on *international institutional reform,* and the next few will invariably see more. Many of these have been focused on organizational reform relating to management, operations, financing, etc. Some have been focused more precisely on strengthening key institutions in specific issue areas (e.g., UNEP for global environmental governance). The success of such initiatives is important in making the system efficient and these processes should be supported and strengthened. [...]
- The challenge, however, is larger than efficiency alone. It is also about making the various components of the system work together and towards a shared vision. As an initial step, one could envisage choosing just one area with which to begin and establishing modalities for *deep and permanent links between institutions that are dealing with clearly related issues.* [...]
- Effectively responding to the challenges of environment and globalization requires a concerted effort to find *new and meaningful ways to engage non-state actors from business and civil society.* [...]
- The existing instruments that do relate to environment and globalization tend to come either from the direction of environmental policy (e.g., the climate convention) or from the direction of economic policy (e.g., WTO rules). [...] However, we will soon also need to start *creating new instruments that emerge not*

from one of the two dynamics – environment or globalization – but from the inter-action of the two. [...] One option might be to promote systems of payment for ecological services (domestically, internationally and possibly globally). Or, at a minimum, to account for the value of such services in national accounts so that more reasoned and reasonable decision-analysis can be done for and by policy-makers. Another option, at a more extreme end of the spectrum of possibilities, may be to consider new legal instruments: a possible "Global Compact on Poverty Reduction" or a "Global Treaty on Consumption." [...]

- Another area of global governance that needs attention in terms of environment and globalization is that of *security – and insecurity.* [...] There is a need to even more explicitly broaden the mandate of global security organizations to include non-traditional security mandates, including those related to environmental security.

- Although discussions of environment and globalization may take place at the global level, the implications of these dynamics are invariably national and local. It is evident that the ability to manage these processes, to benefit from the poten-tial of globalization and to minimize the threats of environmental degradation are all functions of *preparedness, information and capacity.* Investments in these areas – and particularly in developing countries – can have immediate as well as long-term benefits vis-à-vis sustainable development. As has been suggested, globalization has great potential to bring economic prosperity to the poor. But this potential cannot be realized without the capacity to do so and a readiness within those communities and societies to actualize these benefits. The role of international assistance in creating such readiness and enhancing such capacities is critical. Addressing domestic capacity constraints – including, for example, in early warning; technology choice and innovation; decision analysis; long-term investment analysis; etc. – should, therefore, be a key area of international cooperation.

- Finally, we do need *better assessments* of the full potential as well as the full costs of environment and globalization interactions. [...] What are the economic costs of various environmental stresses? What are the long-term impacts of alternative technology decisions? What is the potential for de-materialization and de-linking growth from consumption? A first step, therefore, would be to conduct a large-scale global assessment of the state of knowledge on environment and globalization. [...]

Part II

The Nature of Globalization – Cases and Trends in Globalization

Introduction

Should governments be strongly involved in managing key resources, instituting strict regulations on pollution, and heavily shaping the space in which firms operate? Or should they rather just set the context with prices on environmental goods and allow firms to find the cheapest ways to meet targets for pollution by trading permits for example? If the pieces in the previous section were contentious, this section sees equally opposed visions of the great value or the great peril of adopting a neoliberal economic model to resolve critical environmental problems. Can we get beyond this polarized debate and find a world where cooperation between environmentalists and businesses "replaces confrontation," as one author envisions? Is this an all-or-nothing issue, or are they many flavors, degrees, and elements of "the neoliberal turn" in managing environmental problems?

We begin with the remarkable result of a one-week intensive workshop in 1996 at the National Center for Ecological Analysis and Synthesis (NCEAS) in the United States. There, environmental economist Robert Constanza and his 12 co-authors took on the audacious task of estimating the monetary value of all ecosystems on Earth. Their controversial 1997 article appeared in one of the world's top scientific journals, *Nature*, and it launched a whole movement among economists and conservation biologists. Its influence has steadily grown over time, and now the piece has been cited over 12,000 times, including by major global assessments, biodiversity prioritization efforts, and scenario-building efforts. Despite this, an influential 2009 piece described an "increasing consensus about the importance of incorporating these 'ecosystem services' into resource management decisions," but acknowledged that "quantifying the levels and values of these services has proven difficult" (Nelson et al., 2009).

The Globalization and Environment Reader, First Edition. Edited by Peter Newell and J. Timmons Roberts.
Editorial material and organization © 2017 John Wiley & Sons, Ltd. Published 2017 by John Wiley & Sons, Ltd.

In their piece, Constanza and his co-authors argue that there is a need to put a price on all the benefits that nature provides: clean water, breathable air, flood protection, pollination for food crops, and so on. Though they acknowledge the difficulties and uncertainty of doing so and anticipate the future work that will be needed to hone the numbers, the authors estimated that ecosystems provide about US$33 trillion of services each year. About half of those benefits are from the recycling of nutrients, and nearly two-thirds of all the benefits come from marine systems, followed by forests and wetlands. To give an idea of the scale of these services' value, the total was about twice the total global GNP at the time. Their point is that without such valuation, these services will continue to be neglected. They also make the point that the global price system would be very different if ecosystem services were actually paid for, and they call for national accounting (in indicators like the GNP) to better reflect them.

Michael Jacobs adopts a more critical approach to the role of economics in safeguarding the environment. He argues that "markets have become a central organizing principle of environmental policy," at the expense of an understanding of the role of the state. He argues that sustainability has characteristics that simply make it impossible to reduce to economic logic, and that by trying to fit this square peg (of sustainability) into the round hole (of economics) we are bound to fail in achieving a sustainable society. Like many others, he describes environmental problems as having limits that humans could overstep. But crucially, he describes how natural goods like clean air and water are "collective": we all survive together by protecting the climate, for example, or none of us does. Nicely, Jacobs states then that "individuals cannot be 'sustainable.' Sustainability is either something which the whole of a society achieves, or it does not happen at all." And while we can never know the changes required to get to sustainability, the certain thing is that they "will be large." Vast might be a better word, as Jacobs envisions profound transformations of how we live and work to get us to a truly sustainable state.

Jacobs describes neoclassical economics' approach of turning environmental goods into commodities, such as by putting a price on carbon in the atmosphere or by calculating and "internalizing" the costs and benefits of protecting species and rainforests as Costanza's group proposed. He concludes that the massive task of changing society so that it becomes sustainable – for example by getting people out of their cars and use public transport, "will need to be promoted through regulatory, tax and other measures which will affect the prices of goods and services in the market." His critique is damning, arguing that neoclassical economics sheds "almost no light" on the deep "structural" changes that society needs. Instead he points to the "French regulation theory" pioneered by Michel Aglietta and Alain Lipietz as a broader perspective on how society is organized and the complex deal that is struck in each period of history on how people should live, and on how governments should function. Car use and food habits are "locked in" by years of investments and cultural habits, which constrain decisions. This is not to say that change is impossible, but Jacobs argues that a better understanding of society is needed to design pathways to a sustainable future. And after arguing for the leading role that states must take in the ecological restructuring of society, Jacobs ends with a question that goes to the heart of many debates on globalization: "In a globalized economy, are national states powerful enough, or are supranational states, or state structures, required?"

In direct opposition to Jacob's argument is the next piece by two analysts at the massive McKinsey management consulting firm (Jeremy Hockenstein and Bradley Whitehead) and a Harvard University government school professor (Robert Stavins). They begin their 1997 piece claiming that market-based environmental tools that were barely used at that time should be receive much greater attention. This statement is fairly shocking to hear today, since market mechanisms lie at the core of many major environmental policy areas such as fisheries and forests management and include pollution trading in sulfur dioxide and carbon markets that lay at the core of the Kyoto Protocol, drafted later that same year and much discussed in other pieces in this section and volume.

Hockenstein, Stavins, and Whitehead argued that in spite of some disappointing results with market-based management of the environment, it was not time to turn back to "command-and-control" (state led) regulatory approaches. Rather, they argued that new and improved market tools were needed. They described the inflexibility and cost of "command-and-control regulations …[which] force all firms to shoulder identical shares of the mitigation burden, regardless of the relative cost of the burden to them." They review five categories of market-based instruments of environmental policy; the two most commonly discussed are taxes and fees on pollution, which push firms to clean up, and the creation of permits to pollute, which can then be traded to reduce costs. Hockenstein et al. argue that both create incentives for the firms to green in the cheapest way possible. They also discuss "bottle bill" type deposit and refund systems and cutting subsidies for resource extraction, such as for fossil fuel extraction and use. These subsidies are increasingly criticized across the spectrum of opinion for creating massive waste by keeping prices too low. In this article, which appeared in the widely read magazine *Environment*, Hockenstein and his co-authors directly criticize the magazine's main readers, accounting for the slow uptake of market mechanisms to fear among environmentalists, environmental experts and government bureaucrats about their own skills becoming obsolete in a new world. But they also describe hesitation and resistance among the business community, who still consider them regulatory and risky. In sum, these are unashamedly pro-market authors arguing that we need to "double down" on neoliberal approaches to solving the environmental crisis.

A more different approach could barely be found than the contribution from Heidi Bachram. She takes a deeply critical look at market environmentalist mechanisms, focusing on the system set up by the Kyoto Protocol to allow the trade in permits to release greenhouse gases such as carbon dioxide and methane. Central to her study is the Clean Development Mechanism (CDM), which allows wealthy countries to buy permits from emissions reductions generated from projects set up in developing countries which they then claim against their own reduction targets. As Bachram puts it: "The amount of credits earned by each project is calculated as the difference between the level of emissions with the project and the level of emissions that would occur in an imagined alternative future without the project." For example, credits are issued for the difference in emissions between using solar panels paid for through the CDM instead of constructing a planned coal-fired power plant. The basic idea was that wealthy countries would increase the level of ambition of their actions to tackle climate change if they could pay for emissions to be reduced in parts of the world where it is cheaper to do so and, at the same time, incentivize emissions reductions in developing countries that might also capture associated "sustainable development" benefits from hosting projects, such as jobs, clean technology, or health benefits.

This system, Bachram argues, however, is a recipe for fraud. Some of the same companies that act as consultants developing the projects also monitor and verify the volume of permits generated by a project. The collusion between corporations and the auditors they pay to produce the reports of emissions reductions from these projects presents ample opportunities for exaggeration and papering over uncertainty. In a second line of critique Bachram also describes the risk of "carbon colonialism" in this system, as companies in the Global North seek to "go carbon neutral" by buying up land to store carbon in tree plantations, on land that would be used for local food production and livelihoods as well as cases of poorer groups being dispossessed of their land to make way for offset projects. Bachram describes the "arm-twisting" of rich countries to push this approach and the "moral cover" these schemes provide to consumers of fossil fuels, leaving the system intact and unreformed.

Bachram describes the way the carbon trading system made its way into UN climate treaties through the early and profound influence of corporations in the negotiation process and the "hypnotizing," and co-opting of environmental groups. The complex language and process in the UN for addressing climate change has led to a non-democratic situation where a few technocratic "climate experts" have to translate what is going on for NGOs and the public. Inevitably, they do not emphasize the justice and community-based concerns of the mechanisms they are helping to create. Bachram ends by calling for a sharp turn back to government regulation as a solution: "taxation, penalties for polluting, and imposed technological 'fixes,' such as scrubbers and filters on smokestacks." Instead of corporate-led approaches to renewable energy, Bachram calls for community-based solutions that empower and educate, even as they develop renewable energy options to address climate change.

Stephen Schmidheiny, a man from one of most important industrial dynasties in Switzerland, whose asbestos business he assumed control of, was asked by Maurice Strong to lead the business involvement in the 1992 UNCED process. He led the creation of the World Business Council on Sustainable Development (WBCSD), bringing in 50 top corporate leaders from around the world. We here reprint "The Business of Sustainable Development," the Introduction to Schmidheiny's book *Changing Course*, which lays out the case for business action. He reviews positive and negative trends in population, environment, and development, and describes the value of seeing these environmental threats "from a business perspective, [since it can] help guide both governments and companies towards plausible policies that offer protection from disaster while making the best of the challenges." Uncertainty needn't lead to inaction, he argues: businesses deal with this stuff all the time. Schmidheiny uses insurance as an example of how businesses should think about the future. Buying insurance has costs, but "these are costs the rational are willing to bear and costs the responsible do not regret."

Schmidheiny describes "the precautionary principle", the approach that one acts to prevent harm even in the absence of full scientific certainty about risks in cases, "remains the best practice in business as well as in other aspects of life." He concludes that "There are many opportunities for business," and regulations often lead to great competitiveness – for example Japan, Germany, and the United States all have highly regulated sectors like the chemical industry. He reviews the impact of the report *Our Common Future*, which was adopted by the UN General Assembly and the Group of Seven major economies, and by businesses. He acknowledges the controversy over the need for rapid growth in developing countries and the core problem of asking politicians and business people to act with future generations in mind, when they don't vote or buy stuff. But we need "a new vision," and Schmidheiny has mustered a *Who's Who* of major corporate leaders to sign *The Declaration of the Business Council for Sustainable Development*. It calls for companies to look at and address the impacts of their products over their full life cycle, at the eco-efficiency of their operations, and to take actions sooner rather than later. Their declaration calls for free market approaches by governments and "more streamlined regulatory systems," whereby "inertia is overcome and cooperation replaces confrontation."

Water has been one of the key battlegrounds in debates about the appropriate role of the state, market, and communities in protecting, pricing and providing access to key resources. Amid claims about the "right to water" and civil unrest and social conflict in response to water privatizations in countries such as Argentina, Bolivia, South Africa, and Uruguay, the contribution from Karen Bakker takes stock of the debate and the effectiveness of "anti-privatization" and "alter-globalization" movements engaged in efforts to construct alternative community economies and cultures of water, centered on concepts such as the commons and "water democracies." In particular she alerts to the danger of seeing "rights" as an all-encompassing antidote to the drive to privatize resources and access to them. Human rights discourse has even been adopted by private companies themselves and human rights are often individualistic, anthropocentric, state-centric, and compatible with private sector provision of water supply; and as such, a limited strategy for those seeking to refute water privatization. "Rights talk" runs the risk of reinforcing the public/private binary upon which this confrontation is based and therefore diminishing possibilities for collective action beyond corporatist models of service provision. In contrast, she suggests, the "alter-globalization" debate opened up by disrupting the public/private binary has created space for the construction of alternative community economies of water.

Importantly and usefully she takes a critical look at activist campaigning and academic scholarship on market environmentalism which in her view needs to collapse very different types of policies and reforms into an over-simplified and monolithic category of "neoliberalism." She joins Noel Castree (2003) in criticizing those who would lump and conflate privatization, commercialization, and commodification. Reforms can be undertaken in distinct categories, and are not necessarily concomitant; one may privatize without deregulating, deregulate without marketizing, and commercialize without privatizing. Commercialization, she points out, involves focusing the whole system on the top goals of efficiency, cost-benefit analysis, and profit maximization. Her big point is that one can have any combination of these three neoliberal elements, and different combinations of these exist in diverse settings. She describes how different "cultures of water use" exist everywhere, and that local people fight against the globalization of preferred ways of managing water, making its commodification contested, partial, and transient. Her piece therefore is a useful counterpoint to scholarly and activist literatures that make neoliberal globalization seem like a uni-linear, homogenizing and all-encompassing force that has similar effects and cannot be reversed. Some social-natural systems simply "fail to cooperate with the market" and there is significant scope for diverse strategies of resistance to contest and then re-shape the governance of water for the common good.

So we end this section with a far more complex picture of what is happening in the world as capitalist production and market systems are spreading across the globe. Valuing nature as proposed by Costanza and colleagues, and the utilization of a series of market instruments to manage environmental problems as proposed by Hockenstein et al., are advancing and deepening the logics and practices of neoliberalism. The large number of corporate co-signers of the piece by Schmidheiny and the World Business Council for Sustainable Development calling for eco-efficiency and market-based environmentalism shows the popularity of these ideas, as they became nearly universal in the 1990s and 2000s. But it is not a one-way street. Critiques by Bachram and Jacobs, and the piece by Karen Bakker show the complexity of neoliberalization and that it is not a uniform process that unfolds in predictable ways, nor is it inevitable. Different deals, negotiations, and compromises have been struck everywhere, even if a major shift has occurred in the terrain upon which this happens.

References

Castree, N. (2003) "Commodifying what nature?" *Progress in Human Geography*, 27 (3), 273–297.

Nelson, E., Mendoza, G., and Regetz, J. (2009) "Modeling multiple ecosystem services, biodiversity conservation, commodity production, and tradeoffs at landscape scales". *Frontiers in Ecology and the Environment*, 7 (1), 4–11.

7

The Value of the World's Ecosystem Services and Natural Capital (1997)

Robert Costanza, Ralph d'Arge, Rudolf de Groot, Stephen Farber, Monica Grasso, Bruce Hannon, Karin Limburg, Shahid Naeem, Robert V. O'Neill, Jose Paruelo, Robert G. Raskin, Marjan Van den Belt, and Paul Sutton

Because ecosystem services are not fully 'captured' in commercial markets or adequately quantified in terms comparable with economic services and manufactured capital, they are often given too little weight in policy decisions. This neglect may ultimately compromise the sustainability of humans in the biosphere. The economies of the Earth would grind to a halt without the services of ecological life-support systems, so in one sense their total value to the economy is infinite. However, it can be instructive to estimate the 'incremental' or 'marginal' value of ecosystem services (the estimated rate of change of value compared with changes in ecosystem services from their current levels). There have been many studies in the past few decades aimed at estimating the value of a wide variety of ecosystem services. We have gathered together this large (but scattered) amount of information and present it here in a form useful for ecologists, economists, policy makers and the general public. From this synthesis, we have estimated values for ecosystem services per unit area by biome, and then multiplied by the total area of each biome and summed over all services and biomes.

Although we acknowledge that there are many conceptual and empirical problems inherent in producing such an estimate, we think this exercise is essential in order to: (1) make the range of potential values of the services of ecosystems more apparent; (2) establish at least a first approximation of the relative magnitude of

Robert Costanza, Ralph d'Arge, Rudolf de Groot, Stephen Farber, Monica Grasso, Bruce Hannon, Karin Limburg, Shahid Naeem, Robert V. O'Neill, Jose Paruelo, Robert G. Raskin, Marjan van den Belt, and Paul Sutton. 1997. "The value of the world's ecosystem services and natural capital." In *Nature*, 387: 253–260. Reproduced with permission from Macmillan.

global ecosystem services; (3) set up a framework for their further analysis; (4) point out those areas most in need of additional research; and (5) stimulate additional research and debate. Most of the problems and uncertainties we encountered indicate that out estimate represents a minimum value, which would probably increase: (1) with additional effort in studying and valuing a broader range of ecosystem services; (2) with the incorporation of more realistic representations of ecosystem dynamics and interdependence; and (3) as ecosystem services become more stressed and 'scarce' in the future.

Ecosystem Function and Ecosystem Services

Ecosystem functions refer variously to the habitat, biological or system properties or processes of ecosystems. Ecosystem goods (such as food) and services (such as waste assimilation) represent the benefits human populations derive, directly or indirectly, from ecosystem functions. For simplicity, we will refer to ecosystem goods and services together as ecosystem services. A large number of functions and services can be identified [1–4]. Reference [5] provides a recent, detailed compendium on describing, measuring and valuing ecosystem services. For the purposes of this analysis we grouped ecosystem services into 17 major categories. These groups are listed in Table 7.1. We included only renewable ecosystem services, excluding non-renewable fuels and minerals and the atmosphere. Note that ecosystem services and functions do not necessarily show a one-to-one correspondence. In some cases a single ecosystem service is the product of two or more ecosystem functions whereas in other cases a single ecosystem function contributes to two or more ecosystem services. It is also important to emphasize the interdependent nature of many ecosystem functions. For example, some of the net primary production in an ecosystem ends up as food, the consumption of which generates respiratory products necessary for primary production. Even though these functions and services are interdependent, in many cases they can be added because they represent 'joint products' of the ecosystem, which support human welfare. To the extent possible, we have attempted to distinguish joint and 'addable' products from products that would represent 'double counting' (because they represent different aspects of the same service) if they were added. It is also important to recognize that a minimum level of ecosystem 'infrastructure' is necessary in order to allow production of the range of services show in Table 7.1. Several authors have stressed the importance of this 'infrastructure' of the ecosystem itself as a contributor to its total value[6,7]. This component of the value is not included in the current analysis.

Natural Capital and Ecosystem Services

In general, capital is considered to be a stock of materials or information that exists at a point in time. Each form of capital stock generates, either autonomously or in conjunction with services from other capital stocks, a flow of services that may be

Table 7.1   Ecosystem services and functions used in this study

Number	Ecosystem service[*]	Ecosystem functions	Examples
1	Gas regulation	Regulation of atmospheric chemical composition.	CO_2/CO_2 balance, O_3 for UVB protection, and SO_x levels.
2	Climate regulation	Regulation of global temperature, precipitation, and other biologically mediated climatic processes at global or local levels.	Greenhouse gas regulation, DMS production affecting cloud formation.
3	Disturbance regulation	Capacitance, damping and integrity of ecosystem response to environmental fluctuations.	Storm protection, flood control, drought recovery and other aspects of habitat response to environmental variability mainly controlled by vegetation structure.
4	Water regulation	Regulation of hydrological flows.	Provisioning of water for agricultural (such irrigation) or industrial (such as milling) processes or transportation.
5	Water supply	Storage and retention of water.	Provisioning of water by watersheds, reservoirs and aquifers.
6	Erosion control and sediment retention	Retention of soil within an ecosystem.	Prevention of loss of soil by wind, runoff, or other removal processes, storage of stilt in lakes and wetlands.
7	Soil formation	Soil formation processes.	Weathering of rock and the accumulation of organic material.
8	Nutrient cycling	Storage, internal cycling, processing and acquisition of nutrients.	Nitrogen fixation, N, P and other elemental or nutrient cycles.
9	Waste treatment	Recovery of mobile nutrients and removal or breakdown of excess or xenic nutrients and compounds.	Waste treatment, pollution control, detoxification.
10	Pollination	Movement of floral gametes.	Provisioning of pollinators for the reproduction of plant populations.
11	Biological control	Trophic-dynamic regulations of populations.	Keystone predator control of prey species, reduction of herbivory by the predators.
12	Refugia	Habitat for resident and transient populations.	Nurseries, habitat for migratory species, regional habitats for locally harvested species, or overwintering grounds.

(Continued)

Table 7.1   (*Continued*)

Number	Ecosystem service*	Ecosystem functions	Examples
13	Food production	That portion of gross primary production extractable as food.	Production of fish, game, crops, nuts, fruits by hunting, gathering, subsistence farming or fishing.
14	Raw materials	That portion of gross primary production extractable as raw materials.	The production of lumber, fuel or fodder.
15	Genetic resources	Sources of unique biological materials and products.	Medicine, products for materials science, genes for resistance to plant pathogens and crop pests, ornamental species (pets and horticultural varieties of plants).
16	Recreation	Providing opportunities for recreational activities.	Eco-tourism, sport fishing, and other outdoor recreational activities.
17	Cultural	Providing opportunities for non-commercial uses.	Aesthetic, artistic, educational, spiritual, and /or scientific values of ecosystems.

* We include ecosystem 'goods' along with ecosystem services.

used to transform materials, or the spatial configuration of materials, to enhance the welfare of humans. The human use of this flow of services may or may not leave the original capital stock intact. Capital stock takes different identifiable forms, most notably in physical forms including natural capital, such as trees, minerals, ecosystems, the atmosphere and so on; manufactured capitals, such as machines and buildings; and the human capital of physical bodies. In addition, capital stocks can take intangible forms, especially as information such as that stored in computers and in individual human brains, as well as that stored in species and ecosystems.

Ecosystem services consist of flows of materials, energy, and information from natural capital stocks which combine with manufactured and human capital services to produce human welfare. Although it is possible to imagine generating human welfare without natural capital and ecosystem services in artificial 'space colonies', this possibility is too remote and unlikely to be of much current interest. In fact, one additional way to think about the value of ecosystem services is to determine what it would cost to replicate them in a technologically produced, artificial biosphere. Experience with manned space missions and with Biosphere II in Arizona indicates that this is an exceedingly complex and expensive proposition. Biosphere I (the Earth) is a very efficient, least-cost provider of human life-support services.

Thus we can consider the general class of natural capital as essential to human welfare. Zero natural capital implies zero human welfare because it is not feasible to substitute, in total, purely 'non-natural' capital for natural capital. Manufactured and human capital require natural capital for their construction [7]. Therefore, it is not very meaningful to ask the total value of natural capital to human welfare, nor to ask the value of massive, particular forms of natural capital. It is trivial to ask what is the value of the atmosphere to humankind, or what is the value of rocks and soil infrastructure as support systems. There value is infinite in total.

However, it is meaningful to ask how changes in the quantity or quality of various types of natural capital and ecosystem services may have an impact on human welfare. Such changes include both small changes at large scales and large changes at small scales. For example, changing the gaseous composition of the global atmosphere by a small amount may have large-scale climate change effects that will affect the viability and welfare of global human populations. Large changes at small scales include, for example, dramatically changing local forest composition. These changes may dramatically alter terrestrial and aquatic ecosystems, having an impact on the benefits and costs of local human activities. In general, changes in particular forms of natural capital and ecosystem services will alter the costs or benefits of maintain human welfare.

Valuation of Ecosystem Services

The issue of valuation is inseparable from the choices and decisions we have to make about ecological systems [6, 8]. Some argue that valuation of ecosystems is either impossible or unwise, that we cannot place a value on such 'intangibles' as human life, environmental aesthetics, or long-term ecological benefits. But, in fact, we do so every day. When we set construction standards for highways, bridges and the like, we value human life (acknowledged or not) because spending more money on construction would save lives. Another frequent argument is that we should protect ecosystems for purely moral or aesthetic reasons, and we do not need valuations of ecosystems for this purpose. But there are equally compelling moral arguments that may be in direct conflict with the moral argument to protect ecosystems; for example, the moral argument that no one should go hungry. Moral arguments translate the valuation and decision problem into a different set of dimensions and a different language of discourse [6]; one that, in our view, makes the problem of valuation and choice more difficult and less explicit. But moral and economic arguments are certainly not mutually exclusive. Both discussions can and should go on in parallel.

So, although ecosystem valuation is certainly difficult and fraught with uncertainties, one choice we do not have is whether or not to do it. Rather, the decisions we make as a society about ecosystems imply valuations (although not necessarily expressed in monetary terms). We can choose to make these valuations explicit or not; we can do them with an explicit acknowledgement of the huge uncertainties involved or not; but as we are forced to make choices, we are going through the process of valuation.

The exercise of valuing the services of natural capital 'at the margin' consists of determining the differences that relatively small changes in these services make to human welfare. Changes in quality or quantity of ecosystem services have value insofar as they either change the benefits associated with human activities or change the costs of those activities. These changes in benefits and costs either have an impact on human welfare thorough established markets or through non-market activities. For example, coral reefs provide habitats for fish. One aspect of their value is to increase and concentrate fish stocks. One effect of changes in coral reef quality or quantity would be discernible in commercial fisheries markets, or in recreational fisheries. But other aspects of the value of coral reefs, such as recreational diving and biodiversity conservation, do not show up completely in markets. Forests provide timber materials through well established markets, but the associated habitat values of forests are also felt through unmarketed recreational activities. The chains of effects from ecosystem services to human welfare can range from extremely simple to exceedingly complex. Forests provide timber, but also hold soils and moisture, and create microclimates, all of which contribute to human welfare in complex, and generally non-marketed ways.

Valuation Methods

Various methods have been used to estimate both the market and non-market components of the value of ecosystem services [9–16]. In this analysis, we synthesized previous studies based on a wide variety of methods, noting the limitations and assumptions underlying each.

Many of the valuation techniques used in the studies covered in our synthesis are based, either directly or indirectly, on attempts to estimate the 'willingness-to-pay' of individuals for ecosystem services. For example, if ecological services provided $50 increment to the timber productivity of a forest, then the beneficiaries of this service should be willing to pay up to $50 for it. In addition to timber production, if the forest offered non-marketed, aesthetic, existence, and conservation values of $70, those receiving this non-market benefit should be willing to pay up to $70 for it. The total value of ecological services would be $120, but the contribution to the money economy of ecological services would $50, the amount that actually passes through markets. In this study we have tried to estimate the total value of ecological services, regardless of whether they are currently marketed.

Figure 7.1 shows some of these concepts diagrammatically. Figure 7.1a shows conventional supply (marginal cost) and demand (marginal benefit) curves for a typical marketed good or service. The value that would show up in gross national product (GNP) is the market price p times the quantity q, or the *pbqc*. There are three other relevant areas represented on the diagram, however. The cost of production is the area under the supply curve, *cbq*. The 'producer surplus' or 'net rent' for a resource is the area between the market price and the supply curve, *pbc*. The 'consumer surplus' or the amount of welfare the consumer receives over and above the price paid in the market is the area between the demand curve and the market price, *abp*. The total economic value of the resource is the sum of the producer and consumer surplus (excluding the cost of production), or the area *abc* on the diagram. Note that total economic value can be greater or less than the price times quantity estimates used in GNP.

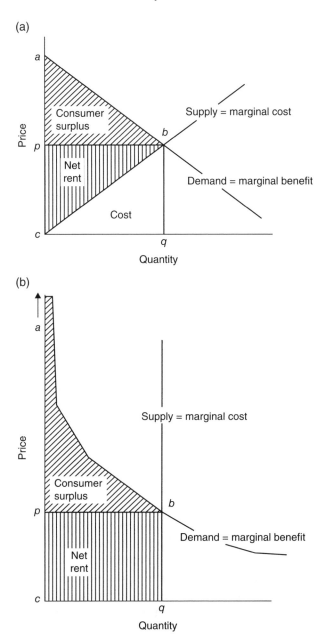

Figure 7.1 Supply and demand curves, showing the definitions of cost, net rent and consumer surplus for normal goods (a) and some essential ecosystem services (b). See text for further explanation.

Figure 7.1a refers to a human-made, substitutable good. Many ecosystem services are only substitutable up to a point, and their demand curves probably look more like Fig. 7.1b. Here the demand approaches infinity as the quantity available approaches zero (or some minimum necessary level of services,) and the consumer surplus (as well as the total economic value) approaches infinity. Demand curves for ecosystem services are very difficult, if not impossible, to estimate in practice. In addition, to the extent that ecosystem services cannot be increased or decreased by actions of the economic system, their supply curves are more nearly vertical, as shown in Fig. 7.1b.

In this study we estimated the value per unit area of each ecosystem service for each ecosystem type. To estimate this 'unit value' we used (in order of preference) either: (1) the sum of consumer and producer surplus; or (2) the net rent (or producer surplus); or (3) price times quantity as a proxy for the economic value of the service, assuming that the demand curve for ecosystem services looks more like Fig. 7.1b than Fig. 7.1a, and that therefore the area *pbqc* is a conservative underestimate of the area *abc*. We then multiplied the unit values times the surface area of each ecosystem to arrive at global totals.

Ecoystem Values, Markets and GNP

As we have noted, the value of many types of natural capital and ecosystem services may not be easily traceable through well functioning markets, or may not show up in markets at all. For example, the aesthetic enhancement of a forest may alter recreational expenditures at that site, but this change in expenditure bears no necessary relation to the value of the enhancement. Recreationists may value the improvement at $100, but transfer only $20 in spending from other recreational areas to the improved site. Enhanced wetlands quality may improve waste treatment, saving on potential treatment costs. For example, tertiary treatment by wetlands may save $100 in alternative treatment. Existing treatment may cost only $30. The treatment cost savings does not show up in any market. There is very little relation between the value of services and observable current spending behavior in many cases.

There is also no necessary relationship between the valuation of natural capital service flows, even on the margin, and aggregate spending, or GNP, in the economy. This is true even if all capital service flows had an impact on well functioning markets. A large part of the contributions to human welfare by ecosystem services are of a purely public goods nature. They accrue directly to humans without passing through the money economy at all. In many cases people are not even aware of them. Examples include clean air and water, soil formation, climate regulation, waste treatment, aesthetic values and good health, as mentioned above.

Global Land Use and Land Cover

In order to estimate the total value of ecosystem services, we needed estimates of the total global extent of the ecosystems themselves. We devised an aggregated classification scheme with 16 primary categories as shown in Table 7.2 to represent current global land use. The major division is between marine and terrestrial systems. Marine was further subdivided into open ocean and coastal, which itself includes estuaries, seagrass/algae beds, coral reefs, and shelf systems. Terrestrial systems were broken down into two types of forest (tropical and temperate/boreal), grasslands/rangelands, wetlands, lakes/rivers, desert, tundra, ice/rock, cropland, and urban. Primary data were from ref. [17] as summarized in ref. [4] with additional information from a number of sources [18–22]. We also used data from ref. [23], as a cross-check on the terrestrial estimates and refs [24] and [25] as a check on the marine estimates. The 32 landcover types of ref. [17] were recategorized for Table 7.2 [...]. The major assumptions were: (1) chaparral and steppe were considered rangeland and combined with grasslands: and (2) a variety of tropical forest and woodland types were combined into 'tropical forests'.

Synthesis

We conducted a thorough literature review and synthesized the information, along with a few original calculations, during a one-week intensive workshop at the new National Center for Ecological Analysis and Synthesis (NCEAS) at the University of California at Santa Barbara. Supplementary Information lists the primary results for each ecosystem service and biome. Supplementary Information includes all the estimates we could identify from the literature (from over 100 studies), their valuation methods, location and stated value. We converted each estimate into 1994 US$ ha^{-1} yr^{-1} using the USA consumer price index and other conversion factors as needed. These are listed in the notes to the Supplementary Information. For some estimates we also converted the service estimate into US$ equivalents using the ration of purchasing power GNP per capita for the country of origin to that of the USA. This was intended to adjust for income effects. Where possible the estimates are stated as a range, based on the high and low values found in the literature, and an average value, with annotated comments as to methods and assumptions. We also included in the Supplementary Information some estimates from the literature on 'total ecosystem value', mainly using energy analysis techniques [10]. We did not include these estimates in any of the totals or averages given below, but only for comparison with the totals from the other techniques. Interestingly, these different methods showed fairly close agreement in the final results.

Each biome and each ecosystem service had its special considerations. Detailed notes explaining each biome and each entry in Supplementary Information are given in notes following the table. More detailed descriptions of some of the ecosystems, their services, and general valuation issues can be found in ref. [5]. Below we briefly discuss some general considerations that apply across the board.

Source of Error, Limitations and Caveats

Our attempt to estimate the total current economic value of ecosystem services is limited for a number of reasons, including:

1   Although we have attempted to include as much as possible, our estimate leaves out many categories of services, which have not yet been adequately studied for

Table 7.2 Summary of average global value of annual ecosystem services

Biome	Area (ha × 10⁶)	1 Gas regulation	2 Climate regulation	3 Disturbance regulation	4 Water regulation	5 Water supply	6 Erosion control	7 Soil formation	8 Nutrient cycling
Marine	36,302								
Open ocean	33,200	38							118
Coastal	3,102			88					3,677
Estuaries	180			567					21,100
Seagrass/ algae beds	200								19,002
Coral reets	62			2,750					
Shelf	2,660								1,431
Terrestrial	15,323								
Forest	4,855		141	2	2	3	96	10	361
Tropical	1,900		223	5	6	8	245	10	922
Temperate/ boreal	2,955		88		0			10	
Grass/ rangelands	3,898	7	0		3		29	1	
Wetlands	330	133		4,539	15	3,800			
Tidal marsh/ Mangroves	165			1,839					
Swamps/ floodplains	165	265		7,240	30	7,600			
Lakes/rivers	200				5,445	2,117			
Desert	1,925								
Tundra	743								
Ice/rock	1,640								
Cropland	1,400								
Urban	332								
Total	51,625	1,341	684	1,779	1,115	1,692	576	53	17,075

Numbers in the body of the table in \$ ha⁻¹ yr⁻¹. Row and column totals are in \$ yr⁻¹ × 10⁹, column totals are the sum of the products of the per ha services in the table and the area of each biome, not the sum of the per ha services themselves. Shaded cells indicate services that do not occur or are known to be negligible. Open cells indicate lack of available information.

many ecosystems. In addition, we could identify no valuation studies for some major biomes (desert, tundra, ice/rock, and cropland). As more and better information becomes available we expect the total estimated value to increase.

2 Current prices, which form the basis (either directly or indirectly) of many of the valuation estimates, are distorted for a number of reasons, including the fact that they exclude the value of ecosystem services, household labour and the informal economy. In addition to this, there are differences between total value, consumer

9 Waste treatment	10 Pollination	11 Biological control	12 Habitat/refugia	13 Food production	14 Raw materials	15 Genetic resources	16 Recreation	17 Cultural	Total valute per ha ($ha^{-1}yr^{-1})	Total global flow value ($yr^{-1}) × 10^9
									577	20,949
		5		15	0			76	252	8,381
		38	8	93	4		82	62	4,052	12,568
		78	131	521	25		381	29	22,832	4,110
					2				19,004	3,801
58		5	7	220	27		3,008	1	6,075	375
		39		68	2			70	1,610	4,283
									804	12,319
87		2		43	138	16	66	2	969	4,706
87				32	315	41	112	2	2,007	3,813
87		4		50	25		36	2	302	894
87	25	23		67		0	2		232	906
4,177			304	256	106		574	881	14,785	4,879
6,696			169	466	162		658		9,990	1,648
1,659			439	47	49		491	1,761	19,580	3,231
665				41			230		8,498	1,700
	14	24		54					92	128
2,277	117	417	124	1,386	721	79	815	3,015		33,268

surplus, net rent (or producer surplus) and $p \times q$, all of which are used to estimate unit values (see Fig. 7.1).

3   In many cases the values are based on the current willingness-to-pay of individuals for ecosystem services, even though these individuals may be ill-informed and their preferences may not adequately incorporate social fairness, ecological sustainability and other important goals [16]. In other words, if we actually lived in a world that was ecologically sustainable, socially fair and where everyone had perfect knowledge of their connection to ecosystem services,

both market prices and surveys of willingness-to-pay would yield very different results than they currently do, and the value of ecosystem services would probably increase.

4   In calculating the current value, we generally assumed that the demand and supply curves look something like Fig. 7.1a. In reality, supply curves for many ecosystem services are more nearly inelastic vertical lines, and the demand curves probably look more like Fig. 7.1b, approaching infinity as quantity goes to zero. Thus the consumer and producer surplus and thereby the total value of ecosystem services would also approach infinity.

5   The valuation approach taken here assumes that there are no sharp thresholds, discontinuities or irreversibilities in the ecosystem response functions. This is almost certainly not the case. Therefore this valuation yields an underestimate of the total value.

6   Extrapolation from point estimates to global totals introduces error. In general, we estimated unit area values for the ecosystem services (in $ha^{-1} yr^{-1}) and then multiplied by the total area of each biome. This can only be considered a crude first approximation and can introduce errors depending on the type of ecosystem service and its spatial heterogeneity.

7   To avoid double counting, a general equilibrium framework that could directly incorporate the interdependence between ecosystem functions and services would be preferred to the partial equilibrium framework used in this study (see below).

8   Values for individual ecosystem functions should be based on sustainable use levels, taking account of both the carrying capacity for individual functions (such as food-production or waste recycling) and the combined effect of simultaneous use of more functions. Ecosystems should be able to provide all the functions listed in Table 7.1 simultaneously and indefinitely. This is certainly not the case for some current ecosystem services because of overuse at existing prices.

9   We have not incorporated the 'infrastructure' value of ecosystems, as noted above, leading to an underestimation of the total value.

10 Inter-country comparisons of valuation are affected by income differences. We attempted to address this in some cases using the relative purchasing power GNP per capita of the country relative to the USA, but this is a very crude way to make the correction.

11 In general, we have used annual flow values and have avoided many of the difficult issues involved with discounting future flow values to arrive at a net present value of the capital stock. But a few estimates in the literature were stated as stock values, and it was necessary to assume a discount rate (we used 5%) in order to convert them into annual flows.

12 Our estimate is based on a static 'snapshot' of what is, in fact, a complex, dynamic system. We have assumed a static and 'partial equilibrium' model in the sense that the value of each service is derived independently and added. This ignores the complex interdependencies between the services. The estimated could also

change drastically as the system moved through critical non-linearities or thresholds. Although it is possible to build 'general equilibrium' models in which the value of all ecosystem services are derived simultaneously with all other values, and to build dynamic models that can incorporate non-linearities and thresholds, these models have rarely been attempted at the scale we are discussing. They represent the next logical step in deriving better estimates of the value of ecosystem services.

We have tried to expose these various sources of uncertainty wherever possible in Supplementary Information and its supporting notes, and state the range of relevant values. In spite of the limitations noted above, we believe it is very useful to synthesize existing valuation estimates, if only to determine a crude, initial magnitude. In general, because of the nature of the limitations noted, we expect our current estimate to represent a minimum value of ecosystem services.

Total Global Value of Ecosystem Services

Table 7.2 is a summary of the results of our synthesis. It lists each of the major biomes along with their current estimated global surface area, the average (on a per hectare basis) of the estimated values of the 17 ecosystem services we have identified from Supplementary Information, and the total value of ecosystem services by biome, by service type and for entire biosphere.

We estimated that at the current margin, ecosystems provide at least US$33 trillion dollars worth of services annually. The majority of the value of services we could identify is currently outside the market system, in services such as gas regulation (US$1.3 trillion yr^{-1}), disturbance regulation (US$1.8 trillion yr^{-1}), waste treatment (US$2.3 trillion yr^{-1}) and nutrient cycling (US$17 trillion yr^{-1}). About 63% of the estimated value is contributed by marine systems (US$20.9 trillion yr^{-1}). Most of this comes from coastal systems (US$10.6 trillion yr^{-1}). About 38% of the estimated value comes from terrestrial systems, mainly from forests (US$4.7 trillion yr^{-1}) and wetlands (US$4.9 trillion yr^{-1}).

We estimated a range of values whenever possible for each entry in Supplementary Information. Table 7.2 reports only the average values. Had we used the low end of the range in Supplementary Information, the global total would have been around US$19 trillion. If we eliminated nutrient cycling, which is the largest single service, estimated at US$17 trillion, the total annual value would be around US$16 trillion. Had we used the high end for all estimates, along with estimating the value of desert, tundra and ice/rock as the average value of rangelands, the estimate would be around US$54 trillion. So the total range of annual values we estimated were from US$16–$54 trillion. This is not a huge range, but other sources of uncertainty listed above are much more critical. It is important to emphasize, however, that despite the many uncertainties included in this estimate, it is almost certainly an underestimate for several reasons, as listed above.

There have been very few previous attempts to estimate the total global value of ecosystem services with which to compare these results. We indentified two, based on completely different methods and assumptions, both from each other and from the methods used in this study. They thus provide an interesting check.

One was an early attempt at a static general equilibrium input–output model of the globe, including both ecological and economic processes and commodities [26, 27]. This model divided the globe in to 9 commodities or product groups and 9 processes, two of which were 'economic' (urban and agriculture) and 7 of which were 'ecological', including both terrestrial and marine systems. Data were from about 1970. Although this was a very aggregated breakdown and the data was of only moderate quality, the model produced a set of 'shadow prices' and 'shadow values' for all the flows between processes, as well as the net outputs from the system, which could be used to derive an estimate of the total value of ecosystem services. The input–output format is far superior to the partial equilibrium format we used in this study for differentiating gross from net flows and avoiding double counting. The results yielded a total value of the net output of the 7 global ecosystem processes equal to the equivalent of US$9.4 trillion in 1972. Converted to 1994 US$ this is about $34 trillion, surprisingly close to our current average estimate. This estimate broke down into US$11.9 trillion (or 35%) from terrestrial ecosystem processes and US$22.1 trillion (or 65%) from marine processes, also very close to our current estimated. World GNP in 1970 was about $14.3 trillion (in 1994 US$), indicating a ratio of total ecosystem services to GNP of about 2.4 to 1. The current estimate has a corresponding ration of 1.8 to 1.

A more recent study [28] estimated a 'maximum sustainable surplus' value of ecosystem services by considering ecosystem services as one input to an aggregate global production function along with labour and manufactured capital. Their estimates ranged from US$3.4 to US$17.6 trillion yr^{-1}, depending on various assumptions. This approach assumed that the total value of ecosystem services is limited to that which has an impact on marketed value, either directly or indirectly, and thus cannot exceed the total world GNP of about US$18 trillion. But, as we have pointed out, only a fraction of ecosystem services affects goods traded in existing markets, which would be included in measures such as GNP. This is a subset of the services we estimated, so we expect this estimate to undervalue total ecosystem services.

The results of both of these studies indicate, however, that our current estimate is at least in approximately the same range. As we have noted, there are many limitations to both the current and these two previous studies. They are all only static snapshots of a biosphere that is a complex, dynamic system. The obvious next steps include building regional and global models of the linked ecological economic system aimed at a better understanding of both the complex dynamics of physical/biological processes and the value of these processes to human well-being [29, 30]. But we do not have to wait for the results of these models to draw the following conclusions.

Discussion

What this study makes abundantly clear is that ecosystem services provide an important portion of the total contribution to human welfare on this planet. We must begin to give the natural capital stock that produces these services adequate weight in the decision-making process, otherwise current and continued future human welfare may drastically suffer. We estimate in this study that the annual value of these services is US$16–54 trillion, with an estimated average of US$33 trillion. The real value is almost certainly much larger, even at the current margin. US$33 trillion is 1.8 times the current global GNP. One way to look at this comparison is that if one were to try to replace the services of ecosystems at the current margin, one would need to increase global GNP by at least US$33 trillion, partly to cover services already captured in existing GNP and partly to cover services that are not currently captured in GNP. This impossible task would lead to no increase in welfare because we would only be replacing existing services, and it ignores the fact that many ecosystem services are literally irreplaceable.

If ecosystem services were actually paid for, in terms of their value contribution to the global economy, the global price system would be very different from what it is today. The price of commodities using ecosystem services directly or indirectly would be much greater. The structure of factor payments, including wages, interest rates and profits would change dramatically. World GNP would be very different in both magnitude and composition if it adequately incorporated the value of ecosystem services. One practical use of the estimates we have developed is to help modify systems of national accounting to better reflect the value of ecosystem services and natural capital. Initial attempts to do this paint a very different picture of our current level of economic welfare than conventional GNP, some indicating a levelling of welfare since about 1970 while GNP has continued to increase [31–33]. A second important use of these estimates is for project appraisal, where ecosystem services lost must be weighed against the benefits of a specific project [8]. Because ecosystem services are largely outside the market and uncertain, they are too often ignored or undervalued, leading to the error of constructing project whose social costs far outweight their benefits.

As natural capital and ecosystem services become more stressed and more 'scarce' in the future, we can only expect their value to increase. If significant, irreversible thresholds are passed for irreplaceable ecosystem services, their value may quickly jump to infinity. Given the huge uncertainties involved, we may never have a very precise estimate of the value of ecosystem services. Nevertheless, even the crude initial estimated we have been able to assemble is a useful starting point (we stress again that it only a starting point). It demonstrates the need for much additional research and it also indicates the specific areas that are most in need of additional study. It also highlights the relative importance of ecosystem services and the potential impact on our welfare of continuing to squander them.

Notes

1   de Groot, R. S. Environmental functions as a unifying concept for ecology and economics. *Environmentalist* 7, 105–109 (1987).
2   Turner, R. K. *Economics, Growth and Sustainable Environments* (eds Collard, D. *et al.*) (Macmillan, London, 1988).
3   Turner, R. K. Economics of wetland management, *Ambio* 20, 59–63 (1991).
4   de Groot, R. S. *Functions of Nature: Evaluation of Nature in Environmental Planning, Management, and Decision Making* (Wolters-Noordhoff, Groningen, 1992).
5   Daily, G. (ed.) *Nature's Services: Societal Dependence on Natural Ecosystems* (Island, Washington DC, 1997).
6   Turner, R. K. & Pearce, D. in *Economics and Ecology: New Frontiers and Sustainable Development* (ed. Barbier, E. D.) 177–194 (Chapman and Hall, London, 1993).
7   Costanza, R. & Daly, H. E. Natural capital and sustainable development. *Conserv. Biol.* 6, 37–46 (1992).
8   Bingham, G. *et al.* Issues in ecosystem valuation: improving information for decision making, *Ecol. Econ.* 14, 73–90 (1995).
9   Mitchell, R. C. & Carson, R. T. *Using Surveys to Value Public Goods: the Contigent Valuation Method* (Resources for the Future, Washington DC, 1989).
10 Costanza, R., Farber, S. C. & Maxwell, J. Valuation and management of wetlands ecosystems. *Ecol. Econ* 1, 335–361 (1989).
11 Dixon, J. A. & Sherman, P. B. *Economics of Protected Areas* (Island, Washington DC, 1990).
12 Barde, J. -P. & Barbier, E. B. Valuing environmental functions in developing countries, *Biodiv. Cons.* 1, 34 (1992).
13 Aylward, B. A. & Barbier, E. B. Valuing environmental functions in developing countries. *Biodiv. Cons.* 1, 34 (1992).
14 Pearce, D. *Economic Values and the Natural World* (Earthscan, London, 1993).
15 Goulder, L. H. & Kennedy, D. in *Nature's Services: Societal Dependence on Natural Ecosystems* (ed. Daily, G.) 23–48 (Island, Washington DC, 1997).
16 Costanza, R. & Folke, C. in *Nature's Services: Societal Dependence on Natural Ecosystems* (ed. Daily, G.) 49–70 (Island, Washington DC, 1997).
17 Matthews, E. Global vegetation and land-use: new high-resolution data bases for climate studies. *J. Clim. Appl. Meteorol.* 22, 474–487 (1983).
18 Deevey, E. S. Mineral cycles. *Sci. Am.* 223, 148–158 (1970).
19 Ehrlich, R., Ehrlich, A. H. & Holdren, J. P. *Ecoscience: Population, Resources, Environment* (W. H. Freeman, San Francisco, 1997).
20 Ryther, J. H. Photosynthesis and fish production in the sea. *Science* 166, 72–76 (1969).
21 United Nations Environmental Programme *First Assessment Report, Intergovernmental Panel on Climate Change* (United Nations, New York, 1990).
22 Whittaker, R. H. & Likens, G. E. in *Primary Production of the Biosphere* (eds Leith, H. & Whittaker, R. H,) 305–328 (Springer, New York, 1975).
23 Bailey, R. G. *Ecosystem Geography* (Springer, New York, 1996).
24 Houde, E. D. & Rutherford, E. S. Recent trends in estuarine fisheries: predictions of fish production and yield. *Estuaries* 16, 161–176 (1993).
25 Pauly, D. & Christensen, V. Primary production required to sustain global fisheries. *Nature* 374, 255–257 (1995).

26   Costanza, R. & Neil, C. in *Energy and Ecological Modeling* (eds Mitsch, W. J., Bosserman, R. W. & Klopatek, J. M.) 745–755 (Elsevier, New York, 1981).

27   Costanza, R. & Hannon, B. M. in *Network Analysis of Marine Ecosystems: Methods and Applications* (eds Wulff, F., Field, J. G. & Mann, K. H.) 90–115 (Springer, Heidelberg, 1989).

28   Alexander, A., List, J., Margolis, M. & d' Arge, R. Alternative methods of valuing global ecosystem services. *Ecol. Econ.* (submitted).

29   Costanza, R., Wainger, L., Folke, C. & Mäler, K.-G. Modeling complex ecological economic systems: toward an evolutionary, dynamic understanding of people and nature *BioScience* 43, 545–555 (1993).

30   Bockstael, N. *et al.* Ecological economic modeling and valuation of ecosystems. *Ecol. Econ.* 14, 143–159 (1995).

31   Daly, H. E. & Cobb, J. *For the Common Good: Redirecting the Economy Towards Community, the Environment, and a Sustainable Future* (Beacon, Boston, 1989).

32   Cobb, C. & Cobb, J. *The Green National Product: a Proposed Index of Sustainable Economic Welfare* (Univ. Press of America, New York, 1994).

33   Max-Neef, M. Economic growth and quality of life: a threshold hypothesis. *Ecol. Econ.* 15, 115–118 (1995).

8

Sustainability and Markets: On the Neoclassical Model of Environmental Economics (1997)

Michael Jacobs

The purpose of this article is to discuss the role of markets in the concept and the practical achievement of environmental sustainability. As in other spheres of political and economic life, markets have become a central organising principle of environmental policy, at least in theory and conceptual framework. The vehicle for this has been the development of neoclassical environmental economics, which has gradually assumed a significant influence in the way environmental policy is perceived. In this article I argue that the prominent role given to the market in environmental-economic policy debate is misplaced. The neglected issue in environmental policy is the nature of the state: how (and how far) states can influence market behaviour towards environmental ends in a global capitalist economy.

The article falls into two halves. In the first half three crucial features of sustainability as an environmental-economic objective are set out: its biophysical basis, its collective character and the scale of the socioeconomic changes it requires. The approach to environmental policy taken by neoclassical environmental economics is then explained, including the central role given in this to markets. In the second half I attempt to show how these features of the sustainability objective make the neoclassical 'market model' inadequate. The model cannot describe the concept of sustainability; it fails to illuminate its structural character; and its discussion of different policy instruments is too limited. A brief concluding section suggests some key features required by any coherent theory of the 'sustainability state'.

For the purposes of this article I define environmental sustainability as a path of economic and social development whose impacts on the natural environment are constrained within ecological limits. These limits are defined, in general terms, as

Michael Jacobs. 1997. "Sustainability and markets: On the neoclassical model of environmental economics". In *New Political Economy*, 2(3): 365–385. Reproduced with permission from Taylor & Francis.

those which maintain over time the health or integrity of ecosystems and the capacity of the biosphere to provide essential 'environmental services', such as clean air and water, climate regulation, the maintenance of genetic diversity, nutrient recycling and so on.

This concept of sustainability [...], is founded on the notion of biophysical limits to economic activity. That is, it starts from the premise that certain conditions of the natural environment which may be caused by human activity would be intolerable, either because they would involve major ecological disruption or degradation or because of their effects on human health and quality of life. The idea of 'intolerability' makes sustainability a fundamentally social notion: human societies must choose what they regard as (in)tolerable. But sustainability is not *simply* social: it does not permit societies to choose just any condition of the environment and describe that as 'sustainable'. For the term to be meaningful, the argument over what is tolerable must be couched in terms of environmental health and integrity and the capacity of the biosphere to maintain the provision of environmental services over time. There will always be room for argument, as discussed above, as to what precisely constitutes these concepts; but they cannot simply be ignored if the term 'sustainability' is to be used. In this sense, sustainability is inescapably biophysical in origin. It is the condition of the natural environment, ultimately, which determines whether or not a society can be described as sustainable and to which the social argument must refer.

It is important to note exactly what this biophysical emphasis does and does not imply, since the notion of 'environmental limits' has been the subject of much misunderstanding. It *does* imply that there are limits to particular uses of environmental stocks and flows of material and energy through the economy. But there is almost no-one who disagrees with this: who thinks (for example) that we can go on adding mercury to rivers or lead to air forever, or that we can concrete over the entire world's agricultural land. These flows and stocks, like others, are subject to limits of tolerability. But this does *not* imply that therefore there are (imminent) limits to *all* material and energy throughputs: one material can substitute for another, and some new materials (and some sources of energy) might become available in such huge supply, with minimal waste disposal effects, that their physical limits are not relevant. These are ultimately empirical-cum-speculative questions (on which there is much dispute). Certainly, sustainability as a concept does not imply that *economic growth* must be subject to limits: this depends on whether efficiency of resource use can be raised sufficiently (and sufficiently cheaply), which is also an empirical question.

Only the first limit, to particular material and energy flows and stocks, is definitely implied by the concept of sustainability. But this is enough, for the scientific evidence appears to show that many of these limits are being, or have already been, reached. Of course, this is where the social construction of sustainability becomes crucial, for (as well as scientific uncertainty) there is by no means universal agreement on where many of the most important limits lie. Disputes arise about the possibility of substitutions and efficiency improvements in relation to future scarcities, about the nature of ecosystem health and human quality of life and about the intrinsic value of the natural world. But so long as these arguments are conducted in terms of the health and integrity of ecosystems and the capacity of the biosphere to provide environmental services, they are about sustainability, not a denial of it.

Sustainability and Collectivity

The second feature of sustainability which bears on the arguments of this article is its inescapably collective character. Nearly all environmental goods are public goods. That is, they are in general 'indivisible' between individuals benefiting from them (the air you breathe is the same air I breathe) and it is difficult to restrict access only to people willing to pay. The public good character of most environmental goods means that they must be collectively provided (individual purchase is always liable to free riding), generally by regulation or taxation. In turn, this means that decisions about how much of the environment should be protected, or to what level, must be made collectively and politically by the community or society as a whole; in practice, by the state.

This much is commonplace. But there is a stronger sense in which sustainability is collective in character. Some environmental goods, such as clean air or beautiful landscapes, can plausibly be represented as contributing to individual welfare or well-being, and therefore as objects of individual 'consumption'. Although they must generally be collectively provided, their benefits can meaningfully be described as accruing to individuals. But this cannot be said of many of the goods (and bads) with which sustainability is concerned. Some, perhaps, fall into an intermediate category of 'social risks'. Toxic waste, for example, is clearly a contributor to individual 'diswelfare' when and if it causes health problems to people living near disposal sites. But it is not clear that it is an individual or private concern for people not living in these areas. Such people do generally have concerns about such waste (as opinion surveys show), but the problem is surely better described as belonging to the society in which individuals live than directly to the individuals themselves. It is at best an indirect risk.

For most of the major issues with which sustainability is concerned, even a limited ascription of private benefit or disbenefit to individuals appears inappropriate. It makes little sense to speak of an individual 'consuming' the control of climate change, the prevention of desertification or the maintenance of species; to see these goods as making an identifiable contribution to *individual* well-being. Rather, they seem to provide the essential life-support framework *within which* individuals can achieve well-being. It is of course possible to trace the effects of impairment of such 'environmental services' to the lives of individuals [...]. But there is something odd about individualising these issues in this way: quintessentially, if climate change or species loss occurs, it occurs to society as a whole. This is not to downgrade the importance of differential distributions of environmental goods and bads: some groups of people will suffer far worse effects than others. But it is to assert the inescapably *collective* nature of global environmental problems. The language of the popular sustainability discourse gives a clue to this: overwhelmingly couched in terms of the problems faced by 'the world' and 'our children', caused by 'society', it urges actions which 'we' must take in response. To put it another way, individuals cannot be 'sustainable'. Sustainability is either something which the whole of a society achieves, or it does not happen at all.

The Scale of the Sustainability Objective

The third important feature of sustainability is the scale of the changes required to achieve it. Acknowledgement of this is often lacking in discussion of environmental policy. [...]

What scale of reductions in impact are required for sustainability, and in which aspects of the environment? [...] 'environmental space'. Estimates are made, from scientific evidence and judgement, of total global environmental capacities: that is, those levels of air and water quality, land use, materials consumption and energy consumption, etc., which can sustain ecosystem and human health over time. These global totals are then divided by the figure for current global population to produce global per capita 'allowances' on the equality principle. [...]

[...]

[...] But they suggest the sort of scale of the changes in current patterns of environmental consumption required by the sustainability objective.

Economic growth has a second important effect. With respect to raw materials and waste discharges, environmental policy is generally able only to address the rate of environmental consumption *per unit of output*. That is, for example, a new technology can be prescribed which cuts polluting emissions from a manufacturing process by half. But the half relates only to emissions from a constant volume of output. If output doubles, the actual (absolute) emissions remain constant. We have so far expressed sustainability targets in absolute terms. But for the purposes of policy it will often be necessary to express them as improvements to the 'environmental efficiency of production': that is, to the rate of resource use and waste production per unit of output. [...]

[...]

None of these possible elements of sustainable production and consumption patterns can be projected with certainty. In particular, whether or not sustainability is compatible with continued economic growth, and/or whether overall consumption or 'standard of living' will have to decline in value terms remains open. It will depend partly on the extent of efficiency improvements and material substitutions in the provision of existing goods and services, and partly on the extent to which new, less-material goods and services (e.g. education and health care) arise in response to higher material prices [...]. What can be stated, though, with reasonable certainty, given the scale of the reductions in material throughput required, is that sustainability is a tough objective for industrial societies to meet. The changes required will be large.

Neoclassical Environmental Economics

Over the last few years, at the same time as the concept of sustainability has become more prominent in environmental policy debate, the discourse of neoclassical environmental economics has also come to play an increasingly dominant role. Broadly speaking, the neoclassical approach can be characterised as an attempt to render environmental issues amenable to conventional microeconomic analysis, by turning discrete environmental goods (clean air, species preservation, acceptable climate change and so on) into priced commodities. This takes place through two 'stages' of policy making.

The first stage specifies the *objective* of policy, answering the question: 'How much environment should be protected?' Drawing on its marginalist traditions, the neoclassical answer to this question is that the environment should be protected up to the point at which the costs of protecting it outweigh the benefits from so doing. This involves a cost-benefit calculus, in which the 'benefits of the environment' must be calculated in monetary terms and then compared over time with the monetary costs of protection. The second stage is then concerned with the *instruments* of policy, answering the question: 'How can the objectives best be achieved?' The neoclassical answer focuses in general on the criterion of efficiency: the 'best' achievement of the objective is the one which incurs the least total cost to society. Efficiency is secured, it is generally argued, through the use of 'market-based instruments' such as taxes, charges and tradable pollution permits, which give producers and consumers financial incentives to reduce environmentally damaging behaviour.

At the heart of the neoclassical approach is a model of the market. Environmental problems are seen as examples of 'market failure': cases where markets fail to achieve their otherwise socially optimal result. This failure arises because environmental goods are (in general) not priced. This results in 'external' or 'social' costs (environmental damage) being imposed on third parties. The first stage of policy making seeks to discover the magnitude of these costs. It does this by discovering the 'market value' or 'shadow price' of different kinds of environmental costs and benefits. The market value is defined as consumers' average willingness to pay for benefits or avoid costs. This can be discovered either by examining market values for goods associated with the environment (such as travel to the countryside, or houses with pleasant views) or by asking the public their willingness to pay directly in 'contingent valuation' surveys. In either case, the value of the environment is given by consumer behaviour in markets, rather than being imposed by government bureaucracies.

Once the values of the external costs have been discovered, the aim of the second stage is then to 'internalise' them: that is, to bring them back within the market by raising the prices of damaging activities via taxes, charges, tradable permits and so on. This forces those responsible for causing the costs to face them directly. Having to pay higher prices or taxes will change their market behaviour: they will reduce the environmental damage they cause. If the costs have been calculated correctly, and the taxes or other market instruments are effective, the total amount of environmental damage will be reduced to just that point at which its marginal costs equal its marginal benefits. Moreover, this will have been achieved at the lowest possible cost to society – in contrast to the use of 'non-market', regulatory ('command and control') instruments, whose inflexibility makes for much higher costs. The market failure will have been eliminated: the market will once again generate the socially optimal result.

This 'market model' of environmental damage and policy response has been intellectually highly influential. Even though, for a number of reasons, it has proved difficult to implement precisely in practice, the conceptual framework it provides increasingly underpins official environmental policy thinking in the UK, the USA and other industrialised countries. [...] Indeed, it is arguably *because* of this emphasis on the market that the neoclassical discourse has become so dominant. This emphasis appears to make orthodox environmental economics concordant both with mainstream economic rationality and with neoliberal ideology. It therefore appeals to those (such as the former British government) with commitments to these two streams of thought. Neoclassical economics appears to offer a 'market-based' alternative to the traditional approach to environmental policy, which is perceived as dealing with environmental problems through government planning and regulation. Indeed, the approach it recommends is often described as enabling policy to 'use market forces' to achieve environmental objectives.

Markets and the Concept of Sustainability

The neoclassical model is a powerful intellectual tool which has contributed a great deal to the economic analysis of environmental problems. Because it has risen to prominence at the same time as the concept of sustainability it is not unnaturally assumed (and by the advocates of the neoclassical school commonly asserted) that the two are connected: that neoclassical economics can contribute to the understanding and achievement of sustainability. But it is this claim that I wish to deny. I want to show that the central role given to markets in the neoclassical model is deeply unhelpful in understanding either the concept of sustainability itself or its policy implementation. This unhelpfulness arises from the three characteristics of sustainability we have discussed: its biophysical basis, its collective nature and the scale of the changes it requires.

The biophysical basis of sustainability represents a fundamental difference between it and the market model of environmental economics. The latter is essentially a branch of welfare economics, concerned with maximising well-being in society. The innovation it introduces is the inclusion of unpriced environmental benefits within the measurement of well-being; but its goal – the socially optimal result of equilibrating markets in which all external costs have been internalised – is explicitly concerned with the satisfaction of human preferences. Sustainability, by contrast, is ultimately concerned with the maintenance over time of biophysical stocks and flows and their environmental effects. There is no necessary connection between these and human preferences. Sustainability may or may not maximise the satisfaction of human preferences, now or in the future: this is not how it is defined. The neoclassical answer, of course, is that even on a biophysical definition sustainability must involve human judgement of 'tolerability', and this is where the market model enters. It is in the hypothetical markets of the first stage of neoclassical policy making that such judgements are made. In markets for environmental goods people express their views on what is tolerable.

But this approach cannot bridge the gap. In markets, people do not 'express their views'; they express their private willingness to pay for environmental benefits. There is no *necessary* reason to suppose that the social optimum in environmental markets (where marginal aggregate willingness to pay just equals the marginal cost of environmental protection) will fall within the biophysical limits of ecosystem health and maintenance of environmental capacities. It may do; it may not, particularly where incomes are low and the (opportunity) cost of environmental protection is high. If it does not, the neoclassical model cannot redefine sustainability out of its biophysical basis, saying that whatever the market chooses just *is* 'sustainable'. Of course, it may be argued that if markets generate this result this is the path society should choose: satisfying market preferences is a more important goal than sustainability. This is perfectly coherent. But it does not mean that the concept of sustainability can be defined or understood through the operation of markets. The biophysical basis of sustainability marks its logical separation from the neoclassical model.

In fact, this argument can go further. In proposing that markets are an appropriate institution through which society can make judgements about the tolerability of environmental change, the neoclassical school misunderstands the nature of such judgements. Here it is the collective character of sustainability which raises the problem. We saw above that most of the environmental problems with which sustainability is concerned are not experienced individually and do not directly contribute to individual well-being. They provide, rather, the general conditions of life-support and social stability within which individual well-being is meaningful. But then the use of markets to decide their fate – leaving it to the private willingness to pay of individuals – seems inappropriate. We might (perhaps) expect people to pay individually for clean air or a beautiful landscape, since these goods provide individual benefit. But there is something profoundly odd about the idea of privately 'purchasing' the control of climate change, prevention of desertification or maintenance of species (or even the elimination of toxic waste). These are, as we have said, quintessentially collective decisions, affecting everyone.

[...] If sustainability is a collective outcome affecting society as a whole, decisions about it should be made socially or collectively. Markets, including hypothetical markets, are essentially individualistic institutions, in which individuals make private choices in relation to their own self-interest, and these are aggregated to generate a social preference. But social choices, of which sustainability is one, must be public in character, involving debate and argument about the common good of society as a whole rather than simply the good of individuals. They require the deliberative institution of the 'forum' rather than the aggregative institution of the market.

There is a specific dimension to this which is of particular importance. Sustainability is a distributive aim. The goal of maintaining environmental capacities over time is often represented and justified as a fair distribution of resources between generations. As we have seen, it must also involve some principle of equity between different countries and regions within the present generation. But fair distribution can only be a political choice, not a market one.

In the first place, the market model is concerned with the allocation of resources, not their distribution. As standard welfare economics acknowledges, the socially optimal result (even adjusted for external costs) is efficient; it need not be equitable. The neoclassical school gets round this difficulty by introducing equity into the model as a consumer preference: people normally value their children's well-being, and if they are altruistic they may value other people's too. But this move simply fails to understand what equity or fairness is. It does not rely on private concern for other people's welfare, let alone willingness to pay for it. It is a moral outcome in its own right: it stands logically separate from any actual procedures generating particular outcomes. As such, it must be the subject of moral and political deliberation about social choices; it cannot simply flow from the aggregation of private preferences. In markets, not only is there no such deliberation, but the aggregated preferences are almost guaranteed not to achieve equity, since any individual's concern for the well-being of future and distant people will almost certainly be 'discounted' [...].

[...]

Markets and Structural Change

There is a more profound, if subtler, way in which the market model fails to illuminate the concept of sustainability. The concept of market equilibrium depends upon the assumption that demands and preferences (tastes) at given prices do not change. This assumption makes it possible to compare two alternative policy options – for example, one with environmental protection measures, one without – and judge which one is preferable. Only if tastes do not change will the idea of something being 'preferable' have the same meaning in both options. This assumption is at work, notably, in cost-benefit analysis, which the neoclassical school uses to evaluate the effects of policy proposals. It enables economists to say, for example, whether society would be better off if public funds were to be spent on public transport in order to reduce air pollution; or whether global warming is worth it, given the costs of its prevention.

But this is not as straightforward as it seems at first sight – or as it is taken to be in the neoclassical model. For the assumption of constant preferences only works in relation to small changes in market conditions over relatively short timescales. Small changes are required because such changes can safely be assumed not to change the prices of other goods and services in society. If other prices do change, then so will demands and preferences, since these are governed not just by the objective character of different products but by their prices *relative* to one another. If many of these prices are altered, because the policy option involves major changes in market conditions, the assumption falls. Whether or not this happens, the assumption becomes increasingly unstable the longer the timescale over which change is measured. It is hardly realistic to expect demands for goods and services to remain constant over a period of, say, 30 years.

The problem here, it should be clear, is the scale of the changes required by sustainability. It will be recalled that, on plausible calculations of environmental effects and economic growth, these changes are likely to be very large. New industrial technologies and processes will have to be developed, new products will need to be introduced, new kinds of infrastructure put in place. Some important aspects of lifestyles, such as transport demands, are almost certainly going to have to change. These changes will need to be promoted through regulatory, tax and other measures which will affect the prices of goods and services in the market. [...]

Sustainability will therefore involve major adjustments in relative prices. These adjustments will mean that demands and preferences themselves change. But, in turn, this will mean that the changes cannot simply be judged from the perspective of the present, when current demands and preferences apply. To put it another way: if sustainability is 'achieved' in, say, 30 years, the people living then will not judge their well-being in the same way as people would now. The very fact that substantial changes will have occurred will mean they have different tastes.

There are thus two perspectives from which sustainability can be judged. There is the *ex ante* one, in which demands and preferences are assumed unchanged. And there is the *ex post* one, in which demands and preferences have changed – in ways we cannot predict. The market model of cost-benefit analysis in relation to sustainability therefore does not tell the full story. By concentrating exclusively on the *ex ante* analysis, it fails to capture the sense in which the choice of sustainability is a choice to live in a different kind of society, one in which we (or our descendants) will have different kinds of demands and preferences: perhaps in which we will be different kinds of people altogether.

The inadequacy of the market model here runs deep. Sustainability, it is clear, requires long-term *structural change* in economy and society: changes not just in the demands for a wide variety of goods and services, but in technologies, infrastructures, lifestyles. But it is precisely these kind of shifts on which the model throws almost no light. It is well suited to understanding small, incremental changes in particular markets, where all else can be assumed constant: prices, tastes, basic technologies. But these conditions are precisely those which do not hold for the kind of shifts required by sustainability. Here we wish to know how to change these things, or what happens when they change. Our analysis must focus on the dynamic process by which one type or structure of market changes into another, not (or only secondarily) on what happens inside a particular market. The crucial missing element in the market model is *time*. The idea of the equilibrating market is essentially static, when what is needed is an understanding of the dynamics of the economy: of its historical, non-reversible adjustment and development.

Understanding sustainability, therefore, almost certainly requires the use of evolutionary and institutional approaches to economics. These approaches offer at least four important insights unavailable from the neoclassical market model. First, evolutionary theory offers a conceptual framework for understanding how market systems change over time. Though some economists have used an evolutionary approach to explain how imperfect markets generate optimal equilibria ('natural selection' rewards profit maximising behaviour), the crucial insight here is the role played by 'adaptive learning' among individual firms as they react to past experience. Achieving sustainability is likely to require particular attention to the processes of institutional learning – among consumers and public bodies as well as among firms.

This will require, second, an understanding of the conditions under which such adaptation occurs. Here institutional studies of technological innovation have shown the crucial role played by different organisational forms and cultures within firms, and by the financial and public policy environments in which they operate. The price mechanism, key variable in the market model, is shown to be of rather less importance. This finding has major implications for the kinds of policy instrument necessary to achieve sustainability: it suggests that price incentives such as taxes will need to be supplemented by policies aimed at firm culture and context. [...] The understanding of 'regulatory regimes' provided by French regulation theory – embracing firm organisation, consumption patterns and public policy – may be of particular help here, showing how different features of industrial and social organisation are interrelated.

This in turn leads to a third important insight of evolutionary-institutional models. This is the 'embeddedness', or condition of being 'locked-in', of particular products and forms of production in wider technological and institutional infrastructures. [...] The demand for cars, for example, is closely tied to the infrastructure of roads and public transport and the patterns of land-use planning which have grown up in the past 40 years – which themselves have been influenced by the demand for cars. [...] One of the hardest tasks in achieving sustainability will be to transform deeply embedded or 'locked-in' products and production processes of these kinds: again, there are obvious implications for the choice of appropriate policy instruments. These will have to address the wider institutional and technological contexts as well as the products or processes themselves.

[...] The fourth insight offered by evolutionary-institutional economics is that technical change is limited. Outside specific and rare periods where the whole 'techno-economic paradigm' shifts, technical change occurs along 'technological trajectories'. [...] Such change is 'path dependent': choices are constrained by decisions made in the past, and the circumstances that have arisen from them. Recognising these limitations of technical change is a crucial element in understanding sustainability. There are considerable technological opportunities for improving resource efficiency, but these must occur only within existing trajectories and will be constrained by the patterns of development which the past has bequeathed us. [...]

An evolutionary and institutional approach to economic analysis will not provide simple explanations and prescriptions: the complexity of socioeconomic conditions and the uncertainty inherent in innovatory change make this impossible. But they will surely prove more useful than the simplicities of the market model. The concept of 'market failure' exemplifies the inadequacy of the neoclassical approach. The idea that the current state of unsustainability is a 'failure' of the market system suggests that we should have expected it to be sustainable; it has gone wrong somewhere. But this model offers no help in understanding what has actually happened. Unsustainability is not a failure, since the present system of markets was never intended to be sustainable. Its historical trajectory has been given by other goals and interests. If society now wishes to change that trajectory, it should not see this as a process of 'correcting' markets, but as choosing a different future development path. In this sense sustainability can be described as a choice of 'ecological restructuring': of deliberate changes in the structure of economic activity (and therefore of wider social systems) so as to bring environmental impacts within the boundary of ecosystem health and environmental capacity maintenance.

Markets and Instruments

If the neoclassical market model throws little light on the objective of sustainability, it is hardly any clearer in relation to the instruments required to achieve the objective. The dominant distinction made in the second stage of neoclassical policy making is between market-based and regulatory instruments. The former are sometimes presented as a policy mechanism in tune with 'free markets', while the latter – slyly given the pejorative label 'command and control' by neoclassical economists – are draconian and bureaucratic. But of course this is nonsense. Both kinds of instrument are forms of government intervention in markets. Regulations affect market behaviour just as taxes, charges and tradable permits do. Both change the conditions under which market actors operate.

The force of the neoclassical distinction derives from the overriding criterion of efficiency given by the neoclassical definition of optimality. Regulatory mechanisms (such as technological standards, legal prohibitions) are said to achieve given objectives at greater total costs than financial incentives such as taxes and charges. But the scale of the changes required by sustainability makes the criterion of efficiency rather less important than that of *effectiveness:* actually achieving the objective in the first place. [...]

The fact that major price rises in basic commodities such as energy and water can have extremely regressive distributional effects provides another reason why price incentives alone are not sufficient to achieve sustainability. Such effects will have to be mitigated through other kinds of policy, particularly public investment in and subsidy for domestic energy efficiency, but also possibly through the welfare benefit system. Where environmental policy stimulates differential regional employment effects, these too will need to be mitigated.

The point of these arguments is not to deny the importance of market-based instruments in policies for sustainability. They will be essential. It is to expose the seriously misleading character of the market model of intervention. The model suggests that there are just two stages of environmental policy making: setting objectives, and then adjusting prices to achieve these objectives. Policy implementation in this model is seen as an essentially hands-off process: using taxes and charges to change market prices allows firms and households to make their own decisions about how to respond with the maximum amount of flexibility and market liberty. The detailed intervention in specific production and consumption decisions required by regulatory methods (setting product standards for example) is no longer necessary: government can simply pull the appropriate price strings from afar.

This model of the policy process is, however, a fiction. There are in fact three stages: in between setting objectives and determining instruments there is the choice of 'techniques'; that is, of the technical and social methods by which the objectives will be achieved. [...]

The market model's emphasis on incentive instruments assumes that governments do not have to be interested in techniques: the market can be left to sort these out on its own. But the importance of basic technologies and infrastructures in achieving sustainable reductions in environmental impact means that in many fields governments will have to get involved in choices of techniques. Much of the infrastructure will have to be publicly provided or regulated – transport, land-use planning, energy supply, water supply, telecommunications networks, waste disposal. Research and development in new basic technologies will almost certainly not be forthcoming from private industry alone. If public support is required, detailed involvement in the choice and assessment of technologies is inevitable. Investment in such technologies will also require detailed partnerships with the private sector, which will not be willing to undertake such investment unless it can be certain that it will be supported by appropriate infrastructure, financial and tax conditions (including quite possibly financial support) and regulatory regimes. Where major structural change is involved, governments cannot avoid hands-on involvement in choices over the form it takes.

Markets, Planning and the State

Understood as a process of ecological restructuring, therefore, sustainability will require detailed government involvement: in setting environmental-economic objectives, in choosing techniques, and in the use of instruments. This must be described as a form of planning. But it is not planning in opposition to markets. Here again traditional dichotomies merely obscure the argument, in two different ways. On the one hand, 'planning for sustainability' will not get rid of markets. What sustainability requires are changes in the conditions in which markets currently operate: the prices given to them by tax regimes (and by the structure of other markets), the infrastructure in which they are embedded, their legal framework, even their social (cultural and moral) context. This is not a question of *adding* such conditions: markets are already bounded and structured in these ways, both by cultural-historic legacy and deliberate policy. In this sense current environmental outcomes are already 'determined', if only by omission. Altering the outcomes by changing these conditions will redefine many markets, reducing the scale of some, enlarging others; new markets will be created. But though the scale of purposeful intervention will be higher than currently, this will still be a market economy.

[...]

But this immediately raises the question of the nature of the state which is expected to perform such a steering function. What kind of state would it be? After all, there is no more *logical* connection between sustainability and the state – no *a priori* reason for the state even to pursue the goal – than between sustainability and the market. This is an absolutely central question for sustainability, but the dominance of the neoclassical theory means that it has barely been addressed in the environmental literature. The deficiency of the market model here is one of omission. The flip-side of the emphasis on markets in environmental debate is the lack of consideration given to the state.

In neoclassical theory the state is a cipher: it is assumed simply to adopt in benign and disinterested fashion the socially optimum objective and to adjust taxes and charges until the optimum is achieved. But of course states are not like this: as the Austrian/public choice schools have pointed out, they engender their own bureaucratic self-interest, they are open to regulatory capture and they are subject to at least as much 'failure' as markets, if not more. [...] Markets cannot guarantee, and are in practice almost certainly unable to achieve, major reductions in environmental impact. Since the most important environmental goods are inescapably public and collective in character, only states can regulate their condition: only states have the coercive power which can overcome the free-riding problems of individual choice. For this reason sustainability needs a rather more substantive theory of the state in relation to late modern capitalism. Is the process of 'steering ecological restructuring' feasible? Under what conditions might states engage in such a process? A substantive theory of the 'sustainability state' must be the subject of another article. But some of the questions it would have to answer can be suggested.

First, such a theory would have to explain the relationship between the state and the processes of capital accumulation under the sustainability objective. Is the process of 'steering ecological restructuring' *economically and technologically feasible?* In capitalist societies it is reasonable to assume that even active states can only pursue economic directions which allow capital accumulation to continue: the collapse of accumulation would undermine the state. But this raises a serious issue for environmental sustainability. Sustainability requires economic activity to remain within biophysical limits. Is this compatible with long-run capital accumulation? If it is, evolutionary change led by the state may be theoretically feasible; if not, the role and nature of the state are not clear at all.

Second, a theory of the 'sustainability state' would need to explain the *political conditions* under which a state would wish to engage in the ecological restructuring project. Even if continuing accumulation is possible, its probable slower pace under the sustainability goal and the changed distributions it would enforce between industries and firms are likely to encounter resistance on the part of capital. In these circumstances, what balance of forces on and within the state, from which interests in society, might be strong enough to push it towards adopting the sustainability objective? Could a sustainability state win the *public legitimacy* to engage in the necessary steering activity?

Third, even if sustainability is economically feasible and has sufficient political motivation, do states have the *power* to direct or influence capital sufficiently to enable it to be pursued? This question requires particular consideration to be given both to the *scale* of the state and to its *form*. In a globalised economy, are national states powerful enough, or are supranational states, or state structures, required? We have argued that sustainability requires considerable government intervention. What kind of state apparatus is required to engage in such levels of intervention?

[...]

The way markets are understood and the emphasis they are given in dominant debates in environmental policy has been misplaced. This is not to say that markets are unimportant. Examined as empirical structures – different in every sector, socially embedded, constrained by external conditions and forces (both deliberately imposed and not) – the study of markets is crucial to sustainability policy. However, as a foundational conceptual construct – from which political objectives can be derived, the process of environmental change understood and the means of policy implementation designed – markets offer very little help. [...]

9

Crafting the Next Generation of Market-Based Environmental Tools (1997)

Jeremy B. Hockenstein, Robert N. Stavins, and Bradley W. Whitehead

The next generation of environmental policy will require innovative tools and strategies to meet both present and future challenges. Market-based instruments are one such tool. These instruments are by no means new. They have been part of the environmental policy landscape (though with varying degrees of prominence) for the past two decades because they are attractive in both theory and practice. But market-based instruments have generally failed to meet the great expectations that we have had for them. As a result, they now lie only on the periphery of environmental policy. Does this represent yet another breakdown between theory and practice? Was the effort to transform environmental regulations with these tools nothing more than tilting at windmills, and is it time to return to more established – if expensive – policy mechanisms?

A close analysis suggests that the answer is no. Market-based instruments have in fact produced attractive results and promise additional benefits. To date, their effectiveness has been undermined by some unrealistic expectations, lack of political will, design flaws, and limitations in the ability of private companies to respond to them. These flaws are all remediable, however, and we may now be at a point where we can profit from past experience.

Rather than abandoning the use of market-based instruments, policymakers on all levels should direct their efforts to making the next generation of these instruments work better than the last one. By examining the use of market-based instruments and highlighting some of their flaws to date, this article will

Jeremy B. Hockenstein, Robert N. Stavins, and Bradley W. Whitehead. 1997. "Crafting the Next Generation of Market-Based Environmental Tools". In *Environment*, 39(4): pp. 12–20, 30–33. Reproduced with permission from Taylor & Francis and R. N. Stavins.

attempt to identify some of the ingredients required for these instruments to become a fundamental and effective part of the next generation of environmental policy.

Market-Based Policy Instruments

There are two steps in the formulation of an environmental policy: the choice of an overall goal and the selection of a means to achieve that goal. In practice, these two steps are often linked within the political process because both the choice of a goal and the selection of a mechanism for achieving it have important political ramifications. This article, however, will focus exclusively on the second step, assessing the use of market-based instruments to achieve given environmental goals.

Market-based instruments are regulatory devices that shape behavior through price signals rather than explicit instructions on pollution control levels or methods. These instruments, which include such measures as tradable permits or pollution charges, are often described as "harnessing market forces" because, when properly implemented, they encourage firms and individuals to undertake actions that serve both their own financial interest and public policy goals. (For additional information on the nature and scope of these instruments, see Box 9.1)

The conventional approach to regulating environmental quality is referred to as the "command-and-control" approach because it allows relatively little flexibility as to the means of achieving goals. Early environmental policy, embodied in such laws as the Clean Air Act of 1970 and the Clean Water Act of 1972, relied almost exclusively on this approach.

In general, command-and-control regulations set uniform standards for firms, usually in the form of technology or performance standards. As a result, such regulations force all firms to shoulder identical shares of the mitigation burden, regardless of the relative costs of this burden to them. This is a significant drawback because experience has shown that some firms can lower pollution at much less cost than others. Thus, while the command-and-control approach can effectively limit emissions of pollutants, it typically exacts unduly high societal costs in the process. Furthermore, command-and-control regulations tend to freeze the development of technologies that might otherwise result in greater levels of control. They offer little or no financial incentive for businesses to exceed their control targets, and both technology-based and performance-based standards have the effect of discouraging experimentation with new technologies.

Market-based instruments have captured the attention of environmental policymakers because of their potential advantages over the traditional command-and-control approach. The two most notable advantages are cost effectiveness and dynamic incentives for technology innovation and diffusion. In theory, properly designed market-based instruments allow society to achieve any desired level of pollution reduction at the lowest possible cost. (Alternatively, they offer more reduction for the same commitment of resources.) They accomplish this by allowing

Box 9.1   Types of Market-based Instruments

Market-based instruments fall into five general categories, depending on whether they impose pollution charges, create tradable permit or deposit refund systems, or reduce market barriers or government subsidies.

Pollution charges consist of fees or taxes on the amount of pollution that a company produces, such as the amount of sulfur dioxide an electric utility emits in the process of generating electricity. By internalizing pollution costs, such charges encourage a company to reduce its pollution to the point where its marginal cost of mitigation equals the tax rate. Because the marginal cost of mitigation differs from firm to firm, however, not all firms will cut their pollution to the same degree. In general, those with lower costs will achieve greater reductions than those with higher costs, a result that will minimize the overall (societal) cost of mitigation.

The potential savings from such an approach to regulation are not just theoretical. Research indicates that control costs vary enormously as a result of differences in firms' physical configuration, age of assets, and so forth. By encouraging those firms with the lowest costs to bear the brunt of the mitigation burden – as distinct from requiring all firms to reduce pollution by the same amount – society can realize substantial savings. The challenge with pollution charges is figuring out how high to set them. Ideally, the amount of the tax should equal the benefits from the cleanup. However, it is often difficult to know beforehand how firms will respond to a given level of charges – and thus what level of cleanup will result from a particular charge.

Tradable permits can achieve the same cost-minimizing allocation of the pollution control burden as charges while avoiding the problem of uncertain responses by firms. Under a tradable permit system, the government establishes an allowable (overall) level of pollution and then allots it among the various firms by issuing them permits. Firms that keep their emissions below the allotted level may sell or lease the unused portion of their permit to other firms or use it to offset excess emissions in other parts of their operations.

Under a *deposit refund system*, consumers pay a surcharge when purchasing a potentially polluting product.

When they later return the product to an approved center for recycling or proper disposal, their deposit is refunded. A number of states have successfully implemented this system through "bottle bills" to control litter from beverage containers and reduce the flow of solid waste to landfills.

Reducing market barriers imposed by government can also help to promote optimal resource use. For example, measures that facilitate the voluntary exchange of water rights promote more efficient allocation and use of scarce water supplies.

Elimination of government subsidies can also create a powerful economic incentive for environmental protection. Subsidies are the mirror image of taxes and, at least in theory, they could provide important economic incentives to address environmental problems. In practice, however, many subsidies promote inefficient and environmentally unsound economic development. A prime example is the below-cost sale of timber by the U.S. Forest Service to private companies, where the prices charged do not even cover the cost of preparing the timber for harvest.

firms to share the burden of pollution control more efficiently – through encouraging those firms that can achieve reductions in pollution most cheaply to achieve the greatest reductions. In addition to this cost advantage, market-based instruments can provide stronger incentives for companies to adopt cheaper and better pollution-control technologies.

Limited Experience

Market-based instruments have had some notable applications in the United States, Europe, and the rest of the world during the last two decades. [...] Nonetheless, these instruments are still at the fringes of environmental policy and have generally not performed as well as predicted. Most importantly, they have not become a central component of private firms' environmental decisionmaking.

Market-based instruments represent only a small share of new regulations in the United States (and a trivial portion of existing ones). At the most basic level, there are two principal reasons for this. First, most of the major environmental legislation was enacted before such instruments became so prominent (since 1990, the Clean Air Act and the Safe Drinking Water Act are the only major environmental laws to be reauthorized). Second, Congress has generally lacked the political will to revise laws when not strictly necessary. Given that Title 40 of the *Code of Federal Regulations* (entitled "Protection of the Environment") contains more than 14,310 pages of environmental regulations, it could take a very long time for market-based instruments to become the core of environmental policy if Congress is not willing to use them for "old" problems as well as new ones.

Compounding the problem, however, is the fact that many of those with a stake in regulatory outcomes have not embraced market-based instruments wholeheartedly. Although the federal government's environmental bureaucracy clearly desires effective environmental regulation, most Environmental Protection Agency (EPA) employees were hired to oversee traditional command-and-control programs requiring technical and legal skills. Because market-based regulation would require people with a different set of skills (notably economists and MBAs), current employees are naturally worried about becoming obsolete. For this reason, one would not expect them to focus on promoting market-based instruments to achieve environmental goals.

Efforts to increase the use of market-based instruments are sometimes hampered by environmental organizations as well. Although some environmental groups have welcomed the selective use of such instruments, others are concerned that increased flexibility in environmental regulation will lead to less protection overall. Furthermore, some in the environmental community still see environmental quality as an inalienable right that market-based programs curtail by condoning the "right to pollute." Lastly, some environmental professionals, like their government counterparts, may be resisting the depreciation of their skills.

The ambivalence of the regulated community itself has also undermined the use and effectiveness of market-based instruments. Many industries and companies have applauded market-based instruments in the abstract because of their flexibility and cost effectiveness. For instance, in its landmark work *Changing Course*, the Business Council for Sustainable Development described how economic instruments could be used to meet environmental objectives at reduced costs. As a practical matter, however, the vast majority of these businesses have not responded enthusiastically to these market-based instruments.

Much of the hesitation stems from a reluctance to promote any regulation, no matter how flexible or cost effective. Businesses are cautious or even fearful of the regulatory process. On the basis of past experience, they tend to believe that political forces beyond their control might unfavorably distort the design and implementation of market-based instruments. Their first concern is that any cost savings will be taken away from them and simply used to increase the overall level of environmental cleanup. As one business representative noted, "These instruments are often seen as a way to up the ante." Second, businesses fear that the actual design of these instruments will lessen their flexibility and penalize companies. For instance, in implementing regulations to reduce sulfur dioxide emissions, several states that produce high-sulfur coal attempted to force companies to install expensive scrubbers instead of shifting to more economical low-sulfur coal.

A third factor dampening businesses' enthusiasm for market-based instruments is the fear that the rules will change over time. Environmental investments can be very costly, running into tens of millions of dollars. For businesses to get optimal return from these investments, environmental regulations have to be not only flexible but predictable over time. Many business leaders are skeptical that any presidential administration can "deliver the government" in the necessary way. Acid rain furnishes a good example: In that case, EPA proposed changes to the permit bidding process after it was underway. Furthermore, the American Lung Association has sued EPA in an attempt to force the agency to tighten standards for sulfur dioxide emissions. Whether or not such measures are desirable for environmental reasons, they represent a potentially significant change in the rules of the game for companies who invested under different assumptions.

Given the antiregulation climate pervading Washington, firms have been successful in arguing against *any* regulation rather than for *better* regulation. To the extent that environmentally sensitive industries have felt compelled to act, they have preferred voluntary to compulsory approaches. The chemical industry, for example, has developed its Responsible Care codes and argues that this obviates the need for intensive regulation. The petroleum and paper industries have established similar initiatives. The success of these programs – or at least the energy being directed toward them – may have diverted some attention away from market-based approaches, however.

Finally, firms are concerned that "buying the right to pollute" under emissions trading programs could lead to negative publicity. Even though purchasing emissions permits is completely legal and helps to improve the environment at a lower overall cost to society, uninformed citizens may perceive such behavior as unethical.

Lack of public understanding is another reason for the slow penetration of market-based instruments into environmental policies. Unfortunately, the benefits of such instruments are typically not visible while the perceived negatives are. Under traditional command-and-control policies, the costs of compliance are usually buried within a firm's capital and cost structure. While consumers may see prices go up, they tend not to associate this with environmental regulations. By the same token, they do not experience firsthand the cost effectiveness of market-based instruments: It is simply not readily apparent to consumers that gasoline or electricity prices are lower than they otherwise would have been because of the implementation of market-based programs to phase out lead or reduce sulfur dioxide emissions.

Moreover, market-based instruments (especially charges) may suffer from making environmental costs more transparent. While it may be valuable to encourage individuals to consciously link environmental costs and benefits, it can also dampen the enthusiasm with which they embrace market-based instruments. Finally, these instruments are an easy target for opponents because they conjure up images of companies simply paying for the right to pollute. While the fallacy of this view is unquestionable (after all, command-and-control instruments just *give away* the right to pollute), the public relations imagery surrounding it has been compelling.

Mixed Performance

As noted previously, market-based instruments have tended not to perform as well as predicted. One of the reasons for this is that the predictions themselves have often been unrealistic. They have generally been based on performance under ideal conditions, implicitly assuming that the cost-minimizing allocation of the pollution-control burden would result and that marginal abatement costs would be perfectly equated across all sources. This has tended to distort comparisons between market-based and other approaches. In a frequently cited table, for instance, one analyst compared the cost of an actual command-and-control program to that of a least-cost market-based program. Others have mistakenly used this comparison as an indicator of the potential gains from specific market-based instruments. (The appropriate comparison would be between actual command-and-control programs and either actual or reasonably constrained theoretical market-based programs.)

In addition, predictions made during policy debates have typically ignored a number of factors that can adversely affect performance, such as the transaction costs involved in implementing market-based programs; uncertainty as to the property rights bestowed under these programs; competitive market conditions; an existing regulatory environment that does not give firms appropriate incentives to participate; and the inability of firms to fully take advantage of program opportunities because of flaws in their internal decisionmaking processes.

The sulfur dioxide allowance trading program is a high-profile example of a case where overly optimistic predictions were made. Analysts originally predicted that the program would cut the cost of achieving emissions reductions by up to $3 billion annually. Now, however, the program is expected to result in savings of only about $1 billion annually. Furthermore, the volume of permit trading and the prices paid for permits have been lower than originally predicted. In a correctly functioning market, one would expect the price of a permit to equal the marginal cost of lowering emissions. One reason for the lower than expected permit prices is simply that marginal abatement costs have declined due to a fall in the price of low-sulfur coal and innovations in fuel blending that have enabled more switching to that type of coal. Permit prices may actually be lower than marginal abatement costs, however, owing to utilities' reluctance to consider new options; constraints imposed on them by existing contracts; the existing regulatory environment, including locally binding environmental and rate-of-return regulations; regulatory uncertainty; property rights questions; and transaction costs.

Flaws in the design of market-based instruments have also contributed to their failure to perform at full potential. While some of these flaws were simply due to ignorance as to how markets would react, others were known to be problematic from the start but nevertheless included to make the programs politically palatable. One striking example is the "20 percent rule" under EPA's Emission Trading Program. This rule, which was adopted at the insistence of the environmental community, stipulated that each time a permit was traded the amount of pollution it authorized was to be reduced 20 percent. Because traded permits became progressively less valuable under this rule, it discouraged trading and thereby increased regulatory costs.

A third explanation for the mixed performance of market-based instruments lies in the limitations imposed by firms' internal structures and the expertise of their management. Market-based instruments entail very different kinds of decisions than do more traditional regulatory approaches, and most firms are simply not equipped to make them. Because market-based instruments have not been widely used and business is uncertain as to how great a role they will play in the future, most companies have not reorganized their environmental, health, and safety (EH&S) departments to fully exploit these instruments. To the contrary, most firms continue to focus on minimizing the cost of complying with traditional regulations rather than making the strategic decisions required by market-based instruments.

There are exceptions, of course. Enron Corporation, a multinational energy company based in Texas, has attempted to use market-based instruments to its strategic benefit by creating new markets for acid rain permits. Other firms have appointed EH&S leaders who are familiar with a wide range of policy instruments and who bring a strategic focus to their pollution-control efforts. Generally, however, as lawyers and engineers rather than MBAs, EH&S personnel are more experienced in interpreting detailed regulations and designing technological solutions to comply with them than they are in exploiting the competitive advantages that market-based instruments allow.

EH&S departments are further impaired because their functions are not well integrated with those of the business units. Close links between the two functions are rare and, in many cases, environmental costs are not fully measured or attributed to the business units from which they derive. This has limited companies' ability to make the few strategic decisions required under command-and-control regulation (such as allocating production among different plants to minimize the costs of compliance). When companies face the much broader set of strategic questions raised by market-based instruments, the lack of integration of EH&S units with business units becomes a more pressing problem.

Futhermore, EH&S managers have traditionally been responsible mainly for risk management and problem avoidance. Seldom have they had real incentives to improve the bottom line. While business managers may try to push for more cost-effective environmental solutions, they often lack the knowledge (and confidence) to take on the technical experts. The firms that have been most effective in addressing these issues have moved their general managers through the EH&S department as part of their development and more closely integrated environmental issues into their capital and business planning processes. Absent this shift in mindset, the full potential of market-based instruments will not be realized.

The Next Generation

Given the relatively poor performance of market-based instruments so far, one might argue that they should be dropped from the regulatory toolkit. On the contrary, both the success with these instruments and the lessons learned from their failures suggest that we use them even more in the future.

At the beginning of the 1990s, EPA estimated that the United States was spending more than $100 billion annually to comply with some federal environmental laws and regulations – an amount that is likely to rise over time. As a result, environmental policymakers need to seek more cost-effective tools for maintaining and improving environmental quality. This means that market-based instruments, with their potential for reducing costs and providing incentives for new technology, are more important than ever. When used with other policy options, these instruments can play an exceptionally valuable role in helping society meet its overall environmental goals with minimum economic sacrifice. Making the best use of resources is especially important because we have other pressing social problems to address, including poverty, education, and violent crime.

Based on our experience with the current generation of market-based instruments, there appear to be four steps we could take to ensure that more such instruments are adopted and to realize greater benefits from them: improving their design; using them more at the state and local level; implementing a deposit refund system for hazardous wastes and a revenue-neutral carbon tax at the federal level; and changing the current regulatory structure to make greater use of market-based instruments.

Design Improvements

Improving the design of market-based instruments should help overcome the resistance that firms and environmental groups have shown toward them as well as ensure that more of their potential benefits are actually realized.

As noted previously, firms and environmental groups are both concerned about the lack of predictability associated with most market-based instruments – firms fearing that the rules of the game will be changed in midstream and environmental groups that flexible instruments will lead to less pollution control. The first step toward addressing such concerns should be to clarify precisely when market-based instruments are appropriate. Such instruments are not a panacea for all environmental problems but only one element of what should be a portfolio of policy instruments. In some cases, market forces alone may be sufficient to address an environmental problem (such as when consumers change their purchasing behavior after learning about its adverse environmental impacts). This, of course, is attractive because it avoids cumbersome rulemaking and monitoring. On the other hand, it may require the government to make sure that the public has the information it needs to make well-informed decisions (as it has done with the Toxics Release Inventory and various labeling laws). In other cases, the government may be able to negotiate an agreement with companies or industry groups to avoid direct regulation. When regulation is called for, however, market-based instruments should be the first option considered – even though many environmental problems will continue to require a traditional command-and-control solution.

When implementing market-based instruments, an overarching goal should be to make them more predictable in terms of being permanent, having set rules, and ensuring that pollution control targets are met. In addition, market-based instruments should be designed to deliver optimum benefits through reducing transaction costs; clarifying the rights bestowed on participants; ensuring competitive market conditions; offering incentives to participate; and providing sufficient information to program participants. When political pressures necessitate changes in a proposed program, they should be made so as not to detract from the program's efficiency. For example, the environmental community's goal of increasing the amount of pollution control achieved by EPA's emissions trading program could have been met more effectively if the 20 percent rule had been modified. Rather than reducing the quantity-value of traded permits only, the program might have been designed to reduce the quantity-value of all permits (by some amount less than 20 percent) over a designated period of time. This would not have diminished the program's antipollution impact, but by avoiding a disincentive to permit trading, it would have lowered the overall costs of regulatory compliance.

State and Local Efforts

In the current political climate, where power continues to be transferred from the federal government to the states, it is essential that state and local governments give greater emphasis to market-based instruments. Although federal spending for environmental control continues to outpace state spending ($18.2 billion in 1991, compared with $9.6 billion), state spending has been increasing while federal spending has been decreasing. As a result, the discussion regarding market-based instruments has begun to shift from federal initiatives to those at lower levels. One of the most exciting uses of market-based instruments at the state and local level has been in an area not generally regarded as environmental: the permitting process. The time required to issue permits pertaining to such matters as zoning, construction, and pollution discharge has been a great challenge for state and local governments – and a source of frustration for new and growing companies. Some states offer specific incentives (usually in the form of shorter delays) for firms to participate in new pollution prevention programs. While not market-based instruments in the strict sense, initiatives of this sort do embody the spirit of what is called for in the next generation of environmental policy. That is, they offer a relatively simple way to meet environmental goals without intricate legislation. There is also ample opportunity for state and local governments to use market-based instruments to address environmental issues in areas such as waste management, land use, and air quality.

Waste management. At the core of most municipal solid waste problems are flawed price signals that fail to convey to consumers and producers the true costs of the wastes they generate. In most communities, the costs of waste collection and disposal are not generally known because they are embedded in property or other taxes.

Market-based instruments can be used to ensure that waste creation and disposal decisions are more closely linked to the actual costs.

Some municipalities have highlighted the costs of waste disposal by including a separate charge for waste collection in their property tax assessments. However, because such charges are usually flat fees that do not vary with the quantity of waste, they provide no incentive for households, firms, and other organizations to modify their product purchasing and disposal decisions.

Fundamental to an effective waste management strategy is getting the prices right. Unit pricing is an attractive way to address this problem. By charging households for waste collection services in proportion to the actual amount of refuse that they leave at the curbside, unit pricing can link household charges to the real costs of collection and disposal. This method creates a strong incentive for households to reduce the quantity of waste they generate, whether through changes in their purchasing patterns, reuse of products and containers, or composting of yard wastes. Furthermore, by charging higher rates for unseparated refuse than for certain separated recyclables, local governments can create incentives for households to recycle parts of their trash. In addition to encouraging reductions in the solid waste flow, unit pricing provides flexibility to consumers and producers.

Municipalities that use unit pricing for collection and disposal services need to consider several important design and implementation issues. For instance, in some of the initial forays into unit pricing, several communities (including Seattle) billed households for the number and size of trash receptacles they left at the curbside. Although this led to a substantial reduction in the flow of solid waste into landfills, it also raised fairness concerns because low-income households were paying a higher percentage of their incomes for trash pickup than high-income households. Seattle addressed this issue much as electric utilities do – with low "life-line rates" for initial blocks of usage.

Clearly, unit charges are not a panacea for solid waste management problems, but by providing a high degree of choice to consumers and firms, this approach combines cost effectiveness with minimum inconvenience to them.

Land use. Increasingly, acrimonious public debates about economic growth versus environmental protection are centered on land-use decisions. And as economic and population growth continue, a larger share of environmental problems will entail tensions over the ways in which land is used. Market-based instruments have been employed to a limited extent in this area, and the opportunity may exist to widen their application.

Land trading systems, which are a type of tradable permit program, have been adopted in several states, including New Jersey, Florida, and California. Florida's wetlands mitigation banking program was established in 1993. It allows the state and five local water management districts to license wetlands owners who preserve (or improve) their property as "mitigation bankers" entitled to sell "credits" to developers. The amount of mitigation credits required to offset a development is based on the type of land that is to be developed. Even before the program was formally established, a group of entrepreneurs created a company called Florida Wetlandsbank, which now sells mitigation credits for $45,000 per acre and uses a portion of the proceeds to improve degraded wetlands.

Programs of this sort clearly come with complex implementation issues to be resolved. Devising methods to compare different types of land along such dimensions as their level of biodiversity, for instance, is a significant challenge. Nonetheless, market-based solutions have the potential to reduce the degree of conflict usually associated with such development decisions.

Air quality. Building on the much discussed RECLAIM trading program that the city of Los Angeles implemented in 1994, several states have launched (or are in the process of launching) their own air emissions trading programs. To be successful, these programs must incorporate the policy lessons we have learned from previous experiences with market-based instruments. Several are already in danger. One of these is Michigan's emissions trading program, which allows companies that exceed current regulatory requirements for volatile organic compounds (VOCs) and all other localized air pollutants except ozone to sell emissions credits to other companies. Although the program took effect in March 1996, it has yet to be approved by EPA due to administrative delays and concerns over the program's ability to meet regulatory control standards. Uncertainty as to whether the current rules will be the final ones is likely to dampen firms' enthusiasm for the program. As other emissions trading programs are instituted, such as New Jersey's program for nitrogen oxides and VOCs and Connecticut's program to authorize trading of New Jersey's emissions credits, officials must ensure that they are designed to encourage maximum participation.

Federal Efforts

While working to further the use of market-based instruments at the state and local level, policymakers should also push for new incentive programs at the federal level, particularly a deposit refund system for hazardous wastes and a revenue-neutral carbon tax (to reduce carbon emissions when and if the United States decides to participate in a binding world agreement).

Hazardous wastes. While unit pricing for municipal waste is useful in reducing the amount of waste created, it does not provide incentives for changing disposal methods, a problem that is particularly important in the case of hazardous wastes. Deposit refund systems can create these incentives. These systems combine a special front-end charge (the deposit) with a refund payable when the substance in question is turned in for recycling or proper disposal. (This, of course, is the concept behind the "bottle bills" that many states have adopted.) Although deposit refund systems have been used primarily at the state level, federal programs would be preferable in certain cases, such as when firms sell easily transportable products throughout the country and when the consequences of improper disposal do not vary significantly from one location to another. Geographic homogeneity of charges also reduces the cost and complexity of control, both to firms and to administering agencies.

Deposit refund systems are most appropriate for products for which the costs of improper disposal are high; in such cases, the benefits from proper disposal usually outweigh the costs of separation and redemption. One product for which a federal deposit refund system should be considered is lead-acid batteries. The amount of lead going into landfills and incinerators is a major hazard, particularly in view of the well-documented linkage between lead exposure and childhood learning disabilities. Most of the new lead entering the environment each year is from the improper disposal of batteries. Although a substantial amount of lead from motor vehicle batteries is recycled each year, the proportion of batteries recycled has been decreasing during the last 30 years. At present, more than 20 million unrecycled batteries enter the waste stream annually and this number may increase by more than 30 percent by the year 2000.

In addition to the lead-acid battery deposit program, the federal government should consider creating a deposit refund system for certain "containerizable" hazardous chemicals (largely liquid chemicals stored in metal drums). About 30 percent of industrial wastes are generated in small enough quantities to be containerized. One important category of such chemicals is chlorinated solvents.

While most chlorinated solvents are recycled to some degree by the thousands of firms using them, substantial amounts still reach the environment. Especially serious are the highly contaminated spent solvents that are uneconomical to recycle and that are often illegally dumped to avoid disposal costs.

Another potential application of the deposit refund approach is to used lubricating oil. The improper disposal of such oil, which current federal regulations do not address, is both a health and an ecological hazard. When used oil is dumped into storm sewers or placed in unsecured landfills, it can contaminate groundwater and surface water supplies; when it is burned as fuel it produces air pollution. Enforcing proper disposal of lubricating oil through conventional regulations would be exceedingly costly because hundreds of thousands of firms and millions of consumers would have to be monitored. A deposit refund system would be far more cost effective.

Carbon emissions. If the United States does decide to participate in a binding international agreement to reduce carbon emissions, policymakers will then have to devise a mechanism to meet this country's pollution reduction commitment. This would be easiest to accomplish by means of a revenue-neutral carbon tax (or other market-based instrument) rather than through the traditional command-and-control regulation.

A properly designed carbon tax regime would both increase the cost of carbon emissions (by imposing a tax, say, on the carbon content of fuels) and decrease the cost of creating or preserving carbon sinks (by allowing a tax credit for such activities). By altering the relevant price signals, such a regime would internalize the costs of climate change for both firms and individuals. Higher relative prices for fossil fuels would have the effect of both reducing carbon emissions and stimulating the development of new technologies that are less carbon intensive. This would enable the United States to achieve its emissions reductions goals at the lowest overall cost.

A properly designed carbon tax regime would also be revenue neutral, that is, it would combine the introduction of carbon charges with the reduction or elimination of other taxes, thus helping to reduce the distortions associated with those taxes. Designing an acceptable mechanism to achieve revenue neutrality is extremely complex, however.

Tradable permits are another market-based approach to reducing carbon emissions that is more cost effective than a traditional command-and-control approach. There are, however, important substantive differences between permit and tax programs that policymakers would need to consider prior to developing a permit-trading program.

Regulatory Structure

To date, market-based instruments have been adopted only in conjunction with new or reauthorized regulations. Because only a small percentage of the existing body of regulations comes up for renewal at any given time, the overall use of market-based instruments has been fairly small. If cost-effective regulation is a serious priority for environmental policymakers, the application of market-based instruments to existing regulations will have to be aggressively pursued. While reexamining existing regulations will be difficult in the current political climate, the growing support for reducing regulatory costs may make this avenue more viable. Only in this way will market-based instruments become an important part of future environmental policy.

The rewards for tackling the regulatory beast appear to be substantial. For example, an experiment conducted by Amoco Oil Company and EPA at Amoco's Yorktown, Virginia, refinery showed that more flexible approaches could yield a savings of 75 percent ($40 million) over existing regulations. Unfortunately, these savings will not be realized because the old regulations remain on the books. EPA has also been experimenting with Project XL, which seeks to work with industry groups across media (air, water, and land) to revitalize environmental policy. Eight pilot programs have recently been launched and preliminary results are encouraging. Most observers are skeptical that such cooperative programs will achieve meaningful results, but if they do they could well be the hallmark of the next generation of environmental policy.

Final Thoughts

In spite of a history of false starts and unmet expectations, market-based instruments remain an attractive tool for tackling environmental problems. Given the potential cost savings and positive societal impacts that such instruments offer, they should clearly be an integral part of the environmental policy landscape in the future. For this reason, policymakers and legislators need to work together to develop effective applications for them.

The roadmap laid out in this article – improving program design, applying market-based instruments at the state and local level, implementing new federal programs, and changing the basic approach to regulation – will help the environmental community develop and implement successful market-based regulation. By shifting organizational mindsets, developing new and needed skills, and overcoming the resistance of sometimes competing interest groups, we can make market-based instruments work for our collective benefit and bring environmental policy into the 21st century.

10

Climate Fraud and Carbon Colonialism: The New Trade in Greenhouse Gases (2004)

Heidi Bachram

The rush to make profits out of carbon-fixing engenders another kind of colonialism.

—Centre for Science and the Environment, India

Introduction

To understand the impact of "pollution permits" and "emissions trading"[1] on the ecological crisis, the findings of the international scientific community must be noted. The Intergovernmental Panel on Climate Change (IPCC), a UN advisory body numbering 3,000 scientists, concluded in 2001 that "the present CO_2 concentration has not been exceeded during the past 420,000 years and likely not during the past 20 million years." The clear and alarming consensus in the scientific community is that humankind is wreaking havoc on the atmosphere. Across the world 80 million people are at severe risk of their homes and livelihoods being destroyed by flash flooding as sea levels rise, fed by melting icecaps, and extreme weather events become more frequent. Although these weather changes will occur everywhere, poorer countries will have less ability to adapt. Meanwhile the emissions of greenhouse gases, that are creating the problems, come overwhelmingly from the richer industrialized countries that do have the resources to adapt. For example the US and the EU, with only 10 percent of the world's population, are responsible for producing 45 percent of all emissions of carbon dioxide (CO_2), the principal greenhouse gas.

Heidi Bachram. 2004. "Climate fraud and carbon colonialism: the new trade in greenhouse gases". In *Capitalism Nature Socialism*, 15(4): 1–16. Reproduced with permission from Taylor & Francis.

Three-quarters of all the CO_2 emitted by human activities is from burning fossil fuels. The rest mostly comes from deforestation. The IPCC concludes that an immediate reduction of 50–70 percent of carbon dioxide emissions is necessary to stabilize the concentrations in the atmosphere. In their most recent report, they state that "eventually CO_2 emissions would need to decline to a very small fraction of current emissions." Faced with this looming climate crisis, the global community of states response has been passage of the Kyoto Protocol in 1997, slowly ratified by 156 countries, and infamously rejected by the world's biggest polluter – the US. At the core of the Protocol is an agreement to reduce emissions by an average of 5.2 percent below 1990 levels of greenhouse gases by the year 2012.[2] Larry Lohmann vividly sums up the inadequacy:

> Shortly after the treaty was initialed in 1997, a scientific journal pointed out that 30 Kyotos would be needed just to stabilize atmospheric concentrations at twice the level they stood at, at the time of the Industrial Revolution. At this rate, 300 years of negotiations would be required just to secure the commitments necessary by the end of this decade.[3]

Also agreed upon in 1997 was the main mechanism for achieving this target, tabled by the US in response to heavy corporate lobbying: emissions trading. This market driven mechanism subjects the planet's atmosphere to the *legal* emission of greenhouse gases. The arrangement parcels up the atmosphere and establishes the routinized buying and selling of "permits to pollute" as though they were like any other international commodity. The Dutch institute RIVM estimate that with emissions trading the actual reductions achieved under Kyoto will only be 0.1 percent far below the already inadequate 5.2 percent reduction from 1990 levels.[4]

In addition, as we shall show, emissions trading is rife with controversy and the potential for exacerbating environmental and social injustice. The changes necessary to avert climate catastrophe are simple enough, namely, a switch away from fossil fuels and to renewable energy like solar and wind, along with a reduction in energy use generally. Instead, world leaders have taken ten years to agree to inadequate targets and the deeply flawed mechanism of emissions trading. Although emissions trading is represented as part of the solution, it is actually a part of the problem itself. Despite the scope and gravity of the dangers posed by greenhouse gases, and the major role of emissions trading in compounding them, this arrangement has not been seriously challenged in any international forum. The continuing acquiescence toward emissions trading is not an accident or bureaucratic oversight. The smooth sailing of this arrangement is attributable to the arm-twisting tactics of the richer nations and their constituencies of corporate polluters whenever global treaties are hammered out. The failure of the Kyoto Protocol to deal adequately and effectively with climate change is also representative of wider issues of democratic decisionmaking and symptomatic of the injustices that permeate international relationships between peoples.

What is Emissions Trading?

Under the Kyoto Protocol the "polluters" are countries that have agreed to targets for reducing their emissions of gases in a pre-defined time period. The polluters are then given a number of "emissions credits" equivalent to their 1990 levels of emissions minus their reduction commitment. These credits are measured in units of greenhouse gases, so one ton of CO_2 would equal one credit. The credits are licenses to pollute up to the limits set by the commitment to achieve the average reduction of 5.2 percent agreed in Kyoto. The countries then allocate their quota of credits on a nation-wide basis, most commonly by "grandfathering," so that the most polluting industries will receive the biggest allocation of credits. In this system it pays to pollute.

Several possibilities then exist:

1   The polluter does not use its whole allowance and can either save the remaining credits for the next time period (bank them), or sell the credits to another polluter on the open market.
2   The polluter uses up its whole allowance in the allotted time period, but still pollutes more. In order to remain in compliance, spare credits must be bought from another polluter that has not used up its full allowance.
3   The polluter can invest in pollution reduction schemes in other countries or regions and in this way "earn" credits that can then be sold, or banked, or used to make up shortfalls in its original allowance.

Credit-earning projects that take place in a country with no reduction target (mostly in the "developing" world) come under the contentious rubric of the "Clean Development Mechanism" (CDM). There have already been signs that traditional Overseas Development Aid (ODA) given by developed countries will be used to fund CDM projects. Instead of building wells, rich countries can now plant trees to "offset" their own pollution. Projects which take place in countries with reduction targets come under Joint Implementation (JI). For example, an energy efficiency program in Poland funded by a UK company could qualify.

It appears that JI projects will mainly take place in Eastern Europe and Russia, where equivalent reductions can be made more cheaply as costs and regulatory standards are lower.

Both CDM and JI projects can be of different kinds: monoculture tree plantations, which theoretically absorb carbon from the atmosphere (carbon sinks); renewable energy projects such as solar or wind projects; improvements to existing energy generation; and so on. The amount of credits earned by each project is calculated as the difference between the level of emissions with the project and the level of emissions that would occur in an imagined alternative future without the project. With such an imagined alternative future in mind, a corporate polluter can conjure up huge estimates of the emissions that would be supposedly produced without the company's

CDM or JI project. This stratagem allows for a high (almost limitless) number of pollution credits that can be earned for each project. It allows the company to pollute more at other sites, to sell its credits to other polluters, or to engage in a combination of these lucrative tactics. Its long-term consequences are (1) increased greenhouse gas emissions and (2) increased corporate profit obtained from their production.

There is yet another provision in emissions trading that introduces increasing levels of complexity and confusion: the pollutants are interchangeable. In effect, a reduction in the emission of one greenhouse gas (e.g., carbon dioxide) enables a polluter to claim reductions in another gas (e.g., methane). Thus, progress in "cleaning up" the atmosphere might appear to be going forward, while closer scrutiny reveals that no actual improvement is taking place.

Climate Fraud

While many hundreds of millions of dollars are being invested in setting up emissions trading schemes all over the world (the UK government alone has spent UK £215 million on its trial trading scheme), virtually no resources are being channeled into their regulation. This imbalance can only lead to an emissions market dangerously reliant upon the integrity of corporations to file accurate reports of emissions levels, and reductions. In practice, corporations such as PricewaterhouseCoopers are acting as both accountants for and consultants to polluting firms, and as verifiers of emission reduction projects. Some entrepreneurial firms such as CH2M Hill and ICF Consulting are also offering consultancy and brokerage as well as verification services. These potential conflicts of interest were at the heart of scandals relating to Enron and Arthur Andersen, who were both pioneers in emissions trading.

Opportunities for fraud abound as the poorly regulated emissions markets develop. This is inevitable in the *laissez-faire* environment in which emissions trading is conducted. In the first year of the UK's trial emissions trading scheme in 2002, Environmental Data Services (ENDS) exposed the main corporations involved in the scheme as having defrauded the system. They found that three chemical corporations had been given over £93 million in "incentives" by the UK government for their combined commitments to reduce pollution by participating in the voluntary trading scheme. However, the corporations had already achieved their promised reductions under separate compulsory EU-wide regulations. ENDS estimated that one corporation, DuPont, could make a further £7 million from the market value of the "carbon" credits generated. Therefore the corporations had received millions of UK taxpayers' money for doing nothing. This was only highlighted by the independent work of the ENDS service inasmuch as no government monitoring of the scheme revealed these instances of fraud. No subsequent action was taken by the government to respond to these revelations.

Monitoring the Monitors

At present, there is no consensus on the international monitoring of emissions trading or the means to verify claimed reductions in greenhouse gas emissions. The prospects for such monitoring and verification are still under discussion in the official negotiations. Nevertheless, hundreds of credit-generating projects are going ahead and at least three EU countries (Denmark, the Netherlands and the UK) have begun their own internal greenhouse gas trading schemes, with an EU-wide market set to begin in 2005. What has been emerging in place of UN or government-led guidance are initiatives taken by Non-Governmental Organizations (NGOs); corporate-led self-monitoring; and entrepreneurial verification schemes by consulting firms.

Environmental NGOs such as the World Wide Fund for Nature (WWF) are developing labeling standards for CDM projects, similar to other controversial labeling schemes such as the Forest Stewardship Council accreditation. Alongside this, more critical NGOs such as SinksWatch, World Rainforest Movement and the CDMWatch attempt to monitor trades and support communities affected by projects by providing them with crucial research and campaigning tools. However, these latter groups are often poorly funded and under-resourced, and it is impossible for NGOs to systematically monitor the thousands of transactions that are expected to take place globally once the greenhouse gas markets come into being.

Meanwhile, oil giants BP and Shell have been experimenting with internal trading schemes and have employed self-monitoring to report trades and verify reductions. There are obvious conflicts of interest affecting the reliability of data produced in this way. For example, BP state that their internal trading scheme achieved 5 percent reduction in CO_2 emissions, half of their voluntary commitment of 10 percent reductions below 1990 levels. The scheme also earned them US $650 million in extra profits as most reductions were achieved through energy efficiency and reducing gas flaring. They admitted that measuring reported emissions is "never 100 percent accurate." However, there is no independent corroboration for these figures as the data was monitored internally by BP itself.

Lastly, consulting firms such as Det Norske Veritas (DNV) have taken up the verification of emissions reductions. In 2002, for instance, DNV validated a eucalyptus plantation, a project funded by the World Bank's new Prototype Carbon Fund. The plantation is the target of local and international campaigns as monoculture eucalyptus causes severe problems for local peoples and the environment. While admitting in their report that they could not guarantee that the carbon would be permanently stored in the plantation, DNV nonetheless recommended the project to the Clean Development Mechanism Board.

There are serious concerns about the effectiveness and wisdom of relying upon any of these monitoring and verification practices, yet a reliable surveillance system is essential to prevent the Kyoto targets from being undermined by fraudulent and destructive projects. However, it is difficult to imagine how any organization, UN-sanctioned or otherwise, could cope with the vast amount of trade that will take place globally.

Carbon Colonialism

The Centre for Science and the Environment India observes that so-called carbon-fixing projects are in reality opening the door to a new form of colonialism, which utilizes climate policies to bring about a variation on the traditional means by which the global South is dominated. In particular this trend is seen in the use of monoculture plantations which allegedly "sequester" or remove CO_2 from the atmosphere. Scientific understanding of the complex interactions between the biosphere (trees, oceans, and so on) and the troposphere (the lowermost part of the atmosphere) is limited. Further, there is scientific consensus that the carbon stored above-ground (i.e. in trees) is not equivalent to the carbon stored below-ground (i.e. in fossil fuels). Therefore there is no scientific credibility for the practice of soaking-up pollution using tree plantations. Yet entrepreneurial companies such as FACE International are charging ahead with plantations while propagating the idea that consumers need not change their lifestyles. This new logic dictates that all that need be done is to become "carbon neutral" by planting trees. The majority of these projects are being imposed upon the South.

The key questions revolve around whether the concept of "carbon offsetting" is either tenable or desirable. The various schemes of Clean Development Mechanisms (CDM) and Joint Implementation Mechanisms of the Kyoto Protocol rely on the notion that emissions from a polluting source can be "nullified" through investments in renewables or "carbon sinks." These compensation mechanisms vary in complexity and design, but all are enthusiastically promoted by the emerging offset industry which is being developed to service the new markets. As a result, clients wishing to go "carbon neutral" are bombarded with a plethora of new, untested, and poorly thought-through offset products and services.

Companies such as Future Forests sell branded carbon offset products to promote so-called CarbonNeutral™ living. They offer a consumer the possibility to take CarbonNeutral™ flights, go CarbonNeutral™ driving, live in CarbonNeutral™ homes, and be a CarbonNeutral™ citizen, by planting trees which theoretically absorb carbon from the atmosphere. The gathering of global business elites, the World Economic Forum, promotes their events as CarbonNeutral™ with the aid of these self-styled "offset" businesses. The allure of offset culture is understandable. Corporations, ever conscious of cost and image, seek quick-fix solutions that do not require radical changes to fundamental business practice.

However, there are many problems with this approach. Offset schemes typically do not challenge the destructive consumption ethic, which literally drives the fossil fuel economy. These initiatives provide "moral cover" for consumers of fossil fuels. The fundamental changes that are urgently necessary, if we are to achieve a more sustainable future, can then be ideologically redefined or dismissed altogether as pipe dreams. Furthermore, land is commandeered in the South for large-scale monoculture plantations which act as an occupying force in impoverished rural communities dependent on these lands for survival. The Kyoto Protocol allows industrialized countries access to a parcel of land roughly the size of one small

Southern nation – or upwards of 10 million hectares – every year for the generation of CDM carbon sink credits.[5] Responsibility for over-consumptive lifestyles of those in richer nations is pushed onto the poor, as the South becomes a carbon dump for the industrialized world.

On a local level, long-standing exploitative relationships and processes are being reinvigorated by emissions trading. Indigenous communities, fisher folk, and other marginalized rural Brazilian peoples were systematically removed from land during the colonial obsession with plantations. Now the World Bank is funding a euca-lyptus plantation in Brazil run by an existing plantation company called Plantar, with the intention that it be approved as a CDM project. While plantations have their own ecologically destructive qualities such as biodiversity loss, water table dis-ruption and pollution from herbicides and pesticides, their social impact is equally devastating to a local community. Lands previously used by local peoples are enclosed and in some cases they have been forcibly evicted. This was the case in Uganda when a Norwegian company leased lands for a carbon sink project which resulted in the eviction of 8,000 people in 13 villages.

The workers on such plantations have little or no health and safety protection and are exposed to hazardous chemicals and dust particles. Plantar is a company with an especially sordid history. In March, 2002, the Regional Labour Office (DRT), prose-cuted 50 companies, among them Plantar, for the illegal outsourcing of labor, a pro-cess synonymous with extreme degrees of exploitation. Indeed, in the 1990s, the Montes Claros (MG) Pastoral Land Commission (CPT), an organization originating in the Catholic Church and well-respected in the region, verified that slave labor was used on the company's property.

Similar disregard exists for the natural environment. Thus local fisher folk in the regions around the plantations in Brazil are poverty-stricken and devastated due to the pollution caused by the over-use of pesticides and herbicides, which contami-nates rivers and water sources and kills fish. In some cases, the water in streams and rivers has entirely dried up because the non-indigenous eucalyptus is a thirsty tree. With the World Bank's assistance, this plantation will now expand by 23,400 hect-ares. This is a disaster for local agriculture and people dependent on water sources for subsistence. The ruination caused by the trafficking in pollution credits serves only to place the cloak of ecological respectability over local and global unequal power relations.

Might Makes Right

One of the more tragic ironies of the Kyoto Protocol is that "carbon sinks" (forests, oceans, etc.) can only qualify for emission credits if they are managed by those with official status. This means that an old-growth rainforest inhabited for thousands of years by indigenous peoples does not qualify under Kyoto rules as "managed," and cannot get credits. However, a monoculture plantation run by the state or a registered private company does qualify. This exposes the vested interests which are served by emissions trading, as ordinary people are not recognized by the official process. Neither does Kyoto offer protection for forests. Instead emissions trading provides an opportunity for extended encroachment on the lives of indigenous peoples by government and corporations, expanding the potential for neo-colonial land-grabbing. Further, other ecosystems such as grasslands are not protected under Kyoto, therefore a monoculture plantation could supplant them. Under the guise of creating solutions for one environmental problem, climate change, further destruction of diverse ecosystems has been legitimized.

Emissions trading represents the latest strategy in an ongoing process that stems from 16th century European land enclosures to the recent World Trade Organization (WTO) negotiations on public health and education, to privatize and liberalize the global commons and resources. By its very nature, an emissions credit entitles its owner to dump a certain amount of greenhouse gases into the atmosphere. Control of such credits effectively leads to control of how the atmosphere, perhaps the last global commons, is used. The Kyoto Protocol negotiations has not only created a property rights regime for the atmosphere. It has also awarded a controlling stake to the world's worst polluters, such as the European Union, by allocating credits based on historical emissions. A similar relationship applies to the process leading to the agreement of Kyoto.

The 1992 Rio Earth Summit and Climate Change

From the beginning of international discussions about climate change Northern governments and corporate polluters have been opposed to the structural changes needed to truly combat the problem. Before the Earth Summit, an International Negotiating Committee (INC) was set up to formulate a draft text. Within the INC, both the US and the EU argued against binding reductions in greenhouse gas emissions. The Earth Summit did however produce the United Nations Framework Convention on Climate Change (UNFCCC). Despite some obvious merits such as a recognition that climate change was an urgent issue for the first time in an international agreement, the UNFCCC did not include any commitment to legally binding emission reductions. Nor did it recognize the role of industry, over-consumption and free trade policies in exacerbating climate change.

Meanwhile in 1991, the UN Conference on Trade and Development (UNCTAD) had set up a department on the trade in greenhouse gases. Emissions trading then found its way onto the INC's agenda at its third session held in Nairobi in September, 1991. UNCTAD also setup the International Emissions Trading Association (IETA), a corporate lobby group dedicated to promoting emissions trading. These activities led to a May, 1992, report entitled "Combating Global Warming: Study on a global system of tradable carbon emission entitlements," produced with financial support from the governments of the Netherlands and Norway. The intimate connections between business and the UN is further evidenced in that the former head of UNCTAD's emissions trading division, Frank Joshua, is now the Global Director for greenhouse gas emissions trading at Arthur Andersen.

Formal proposals for trading emissions, however, were not made until the mid-1990s. By then UNCTAD's research on greenhouse gas trading was well advanced; it never pursued research on other alternatives, or even on other market-based instruments such as pollution taxes. The neo-liberal bias of the UN in this instance seems less a question of succumbing to corporate pressure than of an organizational culture oriented towards corporate-friendly solutions as a matter of course.

The Role of Corporations

Corporate lobby activity before the Earth Summit remains to be researched, but it is telling that most of industry's goals for the Earth Summit (i.e. promoting "cost-effective policies" and "self-regulation") were achieved. Considering the corporate connections to government delegations, it is unsurprising that they were so successful. For example, the chair of the Working Party on Sustainable Development in one of the most powerful corporate lobby groups in the world, the International Chamber of Commerce, was also a member of the UK official delegation in Rio. The ICC continues to have privileged access to policymakers and regularly makes statements to the International Negotiating Committee (INC) on climate change, representing the "voice of business." The voices of neo-liberal ideology seem consistently to be heard "loud and clear" in all international forums on climate change.

Corporations also promote business-friendly solutions through "partnerships" with NGOs, governments and the UN. This tactic is new, and exposes some dissension within corporate ranks. Enron, for example, saw that Kyoto "would do more to promote Enron's business than will almost any other regulatory initiative," and was one of the main proponents of emissions trading. Along with expensive PR campaigns such as British Petroleum's environmental "Beyond Petroleum" make-over, so-called progressive corporations have successfully advanced the concept of Public-Private-Partnerships (PPPs), wooing NGOs and public opinion with slick public relations campaigns and advertising. This approach was epitomized by what happened at the World Summit on Sustainable Development in Johannesburg in 2002. No legally binding agreements were reached at this second Earth Summit. Instead, over 280 PPPs were showcased, highlighting the lack of political will on the part of governments, and the extravagant enthusiasm of corporations for taking control of the issue.

Co-opting NGOs

Environmental NGOs have also been hypnotized by corporate "multistakeholder" dialogues. Part of the formula for developing an image of the "good corporate citizen" is to enlist the help of friendly NGOs in controversial activities, effectively outsourcing legitimacy. Environmental NGOs can therefore provide a moral stamp of approval for corporations involved in emissions trading. The conflict of interest involved in verifying the emissions of companies who are paying you to do so while also providing general funding for your organization, is obvious. "Working with business is as important to us as munching bamboo is for a panda," according to a World Wide Fund for Nature (WWF) representative. Unsurprisingly, since WWF receives approximately £1 million a year from corporations in the UK alone and has an operational budget larger than the World Trade Organization. Recently WWF stated that emissions trading in the European Union could be an "important element" in climate policy and help to "prevent dangerous climate change… as cost-effectively as possible."

However, it is not just conservative environmental NGOs that have been neutral-ized by strategies of corporate polluters. At the original Earth Summit in Rio the NGO Global Forum produced an alternative treaty, designed to influence the offi-cial Rio Declarations. In this visionary document, the NGOs declared that the cli-mate negotiators should "avoid any emission trading schemes which only superficially address climate change problems, perpetuate or worsen inequities hidden behind the problem, or have a negative ecological impact." After Kyoto, how-ever, the large NGOs that had helped produce the alternative treaty in Rio began to abandon their stand against emissions trading. By November, 2000, at the sixth meeting (COP6) of the signatories to the UN Framework Convention on Climate Change, even some of the more radical NGOs like Friends of the Earth had changed their position on emissions trading. At COP6 they moderated their demands to calling for a 20 percent limit on the use of emissions trading. Eight months later, after agreement was reached on key controversial issues in the Kyoto Protocol at COP6.2 in Bonn in July, 2001, press statements from Friends of the Earth International heralded the agreement as a "new hope for the future" – even though it placed no specific limits on the use of emissions trading, and was actually weaker than the deal they had described as "junk" in COP6.

In Johannesburg at the 2002 World Summit on Sustainable Development, Greenpeace and the World Business Council for Sustainable Development (WBCSD), which includes corporations such as Dow Chemical and General Motors, made a joint declaration on climate change, urging governments to move forward. This happened despite the fact that the WBCSD still does not necessarily endorse implementation of the 1997 Kyoto Protocol, in sharp contrast to the stated aims of Greenpeace. At the Earth Summit in 1992, Greenpeace and the WBSCD had been "fighting like cats and dogs." Ten years later they stood on the same platform, but without a substantial common vision of how governments should move forward.

A number of mainstream NGOs that have long campaigned for an international agreement on climate change are now persuaded that business support is crucial. Part of the reason is technocratic. In the lengthy negotiation process, the talks tend to become extremely technical and the language impenetrable to the point that most people participating do not understand fully the implications of the compromises made. In effect, environmental policy decisions are often left in the hands of "climate experts" in organizations with the knock-on effect that democracy and understanding within NGOs suffers and public statements are reduced to simplified slogans.

At times, even well-intentioned activists in NGOs are persuaded by the win-win scenario rhetoric that accompanies emissions trading. Talk of "technology transfer" and "leapfrogging industrialization" is seductive. Yet at the heart of this corporate paternalism lies the stone-cold logic of the free market. This has created a situation where the NGO world has been thrown into confusion and discord. While mostly Northern mainstream NGOs support, or do not resist, emissions trading, many social movements and smaller NGOs are vehemently opposed to it. Now that NGOs have been effectively diverted, corporate interests have been placed at the heart of political negotiations and industry has been defined as a legitimate stakeholder.

The Impact of the World Trade Organization on Emissions Trading

Proponents of emissions trading argue that as schemes are implemented the rules governing them can be tightened and improved, and fraud avoided. This view is at best naïve and at worst, dishonest. As emissions trading emerges as the principal component of government climate change policy, the rules for its use will have to conform to the general rules governing trade. Any efforts to improve the rules of emissions trading, or to curb its use, will be subject to the general forces of liberalization. Industry lobby groups and neo-liberal think-tanks want World Trade Organization (WTO) compliance across the board, with no exceptions made for other purposes or values. Many corporate lobby groups, in particular, want unrestricted free trade in greenhouse gas credits rather than government regulation and taxation to achieve emissions reductions. Since the rules for the Kyoto mechanisms are still being developed, and the WTO's Committee on Trade and Environment (the principal committee responsible for evaluating the relationship between Multilateral Environmental Agreements such as the Kyoto Protocol, and the WTO) is still deliberating, much remains speculative. However, there are already many areas of likely conflict. The net effect may be to water down regulation of emissions trading in order to avoid trade conflicts.

Environmental Justice

A further fundamental problem of emissions trading is its tendency to perpetuate and aggravate environmental injustice. The six greenhouse gases due to be traded all have toxic co-pollutant side effects.[6] This aggravates other dimensions of social injustice inasmuch as polluting industries are disproportionately located in low-income areas and communities of color. In the case of a sulphur dioxide trading scheme in Los Angeles, RECLAIM, where localized pollution of the local Latino communities around factories involved in the scheme continued unabated. It is likely that this phenomenon will be widely replicated with global greenhouse gas trading. Reductions will not need to take place at their source, allowing factories to continue polluting locally. And the communities affected are those with the least power to resist; "pollution ghettoes" are thereby created, bringing the seemingly abstract nature of the market into deadly focus.

The introduction of emissions trading means that precious time and resources are being channeled away from the solutions that could successfully resolve climate change in a just way. It took ten years to put the RECLAIM program into place in Los Angeles, and the Kyoto market will not officially begin trading until 2008. By then national governments will have spent millions setting up their internal schemes in preparation for the international market. Brokers, consultants, NGOs, corporations, PR firms, speculators, as well as opportunistic experts and consulting firms that offer "science for sale" will be created in anticipation of the new carbon economy. All this energy, investment and time could be put into more positive and effective strategies to resolve climate change, and at the same time, to combat environmental injustice. Besides central government measures, from taxation and subsidies to laws, grassroots initiatives of all kinds could provide answers at low cost while also successfully tackling issues of environmental injustice and carbon colonialism.

The Alternative

One alternative to corporate-led schemes such as emissions trading is government regulation. This can include taxation, penalties for polluting, and imposed technological "fixes," such as scrubbers and filters on smokestacks. Such an approach has been successfully adopted in Iceland (where 99 percent of electricity comes from geothermal sources) and Costa Rica (where 92 percent of energy comes from renewables). Additionally, government fossil fuel subsidies and tax breaks could be withdrawn and subsidies for small-scale renewables increased instead. However, there are problems with this approach as well. In Iceland, one of the main producers and distributors of renewable energy is the oil giant Shell. Although the product has changed from fossil fuels to renewables, the corporation is still the same. The power dynamic remains; often the renewable investments of large fossil fuel corporations are another tactic in a cleverly planned "greenwash" campaign to improve their public image. Additionally the failure to challenge corporate monopolies in the renewable energy sector could stifle diversity and innovation as was shown when comparing developments in the Netherlands and Germany. In the Netherlands, subsidies for the solar industry in the 1990s were concentrated on Shell and eco-consultants Ecofys. This limited the number of solar panel firms to just a few main players and Shell gained a virtual monopoly in solar panel installation. In contrast, German subsidies were distributed more fairly across different sized firms. By 2002 there were over 300 companies involved in supplying solar panels. Even a future where wind and solar are the main source of energy still fails to challenge underlying patterns of consumption and does not guarantee that transnational corporations will suddenly behave in an environmentally or socially just way.

Many grassroots initiatives have nevertheless arisen to tackle these problems and it is here that we can see the outlines of an holistic approach to the problem posed by climate change. Thousands of small-scale projects successfully balancing social and economic injustice with environmental sustainability have already sprung up around the world. The Centre for Alternative Technology in Wales, for example, is in the process of building a wind turbine, a project that was initiated and is managed by the local community. The energy will be used locally, and any surplus sold and the dividends are to be shared among the community group. Another initiative is in the process of being launched in Northern Spain by a project called ESCANDA who are engaged in planning and forming a renewable energy co-operative to invest, build and maintain wind and solar energy. This challenges corporate control of energy production and distribution, promoting empowerment and democracy as decision-making is held by the people producing and using the electricity generated. It is hoped that the project can provide a model for other communities in Spain and perhaps be applied Europe-wide.

Another method is employed by Khanya College in Johannesburg where a community education program to tackle issues of climate change from an environmental justice perspective is being planned. Community educators and activists will conduct workshops to both inform and train township residents in the province on the impacts and effects of climate change upon their lives. The workshops open up a safe political space where the community can explore the issues and create their own solutions. This unique synthesis of education and empowerment is absent from the official process, and diametrically opposed to the top-down solutions offered by proponents of emissions trading schemes. What all these community-based projects have in common is an innovative, yet practical, combination of economics, ecology, democracy and participation.

Conclusions

In the best case scenario that emissions trading is strictly regulated, it is still unlikely to achieve even the woefully inadequate reductions in greenhouse gas emissions enshrined in the Kyoto Protocol. This would be true even if the US joined the rest of the major polluting countries in ratifying the Protocol. Yet should a foolproof monitoring system be put in place, the whole system would lose its appeal of being cheap and unchallenging for corporations, and so any attempt to introduce such methods will be strongly opposed. Furthermore, the neo-liberal trends in international trade make it unlikely that emissions markets will ever be tightly regulated. The strategy and tactics of emissions trading have been adorned with the rationale of neo-liberal ideology; they have become so institutionalized in international forums that regulatory initiatives are unlikely to be proposed from within their circles.

Yet even if emissions trading were adequately regulated, the reality is that the trading in pollution best serves the needs of those with the most to lose from resolving the climate crisis. As climate change exposes fundamental flaws in the current world order, only the most challenging responses will have any prospect of success. Transnational fossil fuel corporations and the governments of industrialized countries will not concede power willingly. That is why emissions trading is being used to distract attention away from the changes that are urgently needed. In this way corporations and government are able to build the illusion of taking action on climate change while reinforcing current unequal power structures. Emissions trading therefore becomes an instrument by means of which the current world order, built and founded on a history of colonialism, wields a new kind of "carbon colonialism."

As with the colonialism of old, this new colonizing force justifies its interference through moral rhetoric. As the colonizers seek to resolve climate change, they conveniently "forget" the true source of the problem. With the looming climate crisis and the desperate need for action, the resulting course recommended by corporations and government is not analyzed critically. The debate is transformed, shifting the blame onto the poor masses of the global South. Lost in this discourse is the reality that the world's richest minorities are the culprits who have over-consumed the planet to the brink of ecological disaster. Instead of reducing in the rich countries, a carbon dump is created in the poor countries. Thus rich countries can continue in their unequal over-consumption of the world's resources.

> The poor countries are so poor that they will accept crumbs. They know that and they are taking advantage of it.
>
> –Sajida Khan, community organizer campaigning
> against an emissions trading project in Durban, South Africa.

On almost every level of emissions trading, colonial and imperialistic dimensions exist. There may be new labels for these phenomena, such as environmental injustice, but the fundamental issues are the same. The dynamics of emissions trading, whereby powerful actors benefit at the expense of disempowered communities in both North and South, is a modern incarnation of a dark colonial past. European colonialism extracted natural resources as well as people from the colonized world. In the 20th century, international financial institutions took on the role of economic colonizer in the form of Structural Adjustment Policies (SAPs) for the "Third World." Now an ecological crisis created by the old colonizers is being reinvented as another market opportunity. This new market brings with it all the built-in inequities that other commodity markets thrive upon. From the pumping of pollution into communities of color in Los Angeles to the land grabbing for carbon "sinks" in South America, emissions trading continues this age-old colonial tradition.

Notes

1   For the purposes of this paper, the term "emissions trading" refers to credit-and-trade (Clean Development Mechanism and Joint Implementation) as well as cap-and-trade systems in the Kyoto Protocol.

2   Kyoto Protocol, UNFCCC website:http://unfccc.int/resource/docs/convkp/kpeng.html

3   "The Kyoto Protocol: Neocolonialism and Fraud." Talk given at "Resistance is Fertile" gathering, The Hague. Larry Lohmann, April, 2002.

4   "Evaluating the Bonn Agreement and some Key Issues," The National Institute of Public Health and the Environment (RIVM) p. 22. The Netherlands, 2001.

5   "Sinks in the CDM are limited to 1 percent of Annex I countries annual emissions. Based on the average rate of growth of plantation trees this brings this figure. See the SinksWatch website for more information on sinks and Kyoto: http://www.sinkswatch.org

6   The six greenhouse gases focused upon in the international negotiations are: carbon dioxide (CO_2), methane (CH_4), nitrous oxide (N_2O), hydrofluorocarbons (HFCs), perfluorocarbons (PFCs), and sulphur hexafluoride (SF_6).

11

The Business of Sustainable Development (1992)

Stephen Schmidheney

"With greater freedom for the market comes greater responsibility."

Gro Harlem Brundtland Prime Minister, Norway

Running a company requires daily assessments of opportunities, risks, and trends. Corporate leaders who ignore economic, political, or social changes will lead their companies toward failure. So too will those who overreact to change and perceived risk.

Many global trends offer hope. Life expectancy, health care, and education have all improved dramatically in the second half of this century. World food production has stayed well ahead of population growth. Average per capita incomes have increased by the highest sustained rates ever. No shortage of raw materials looms in the foreseeable future. Given the right technology, the planet's soils can supply more than the basic food needs of much larger populations.

But neither business nor any other leaders can afford to see only the positive, especially when these optimistic signs are based on averages that mask alarming departures from the norm. Several other linked global trends demand any thinking person's attention. Each is replete with scientific uncertainty. To overreact to any of these would be dangerous, but to ignore any of them would be irresponsible.

First, the human population is growing extremely rapidly; according to the most optimistic estimates, an already crowded planet is likely to have to support twice as many people next century. Environmental ills have varying causes, but all are made worse by the pressure of human numbers.

Stephen Schmidheney. 1992. *Changing Course: A Global Business Perspective on Development and the Environment.* Cambridge: Massachusetts Institute of Technology Press. pp. 1–13. Reproduced with permission from MIT Press.

The Globalization and Environment Reader, First Edition. Edited by Peter Newell and J. Timmons Roberts.

Second, the last few decades have witnessed an accelerating consumption of natural resources – consumption that is often inefficient and ill planned. Resources that biologists call renewable are not being given time to renew. The bottom line is that the human species is living more off the planet's capital and less off its interest. This is bad business.

Third, both population growth and the wasteful consumption of resources play a role in the accelerating degradation of many parts of the environment. Productive areas are hardest hit. Agriculturally fruitful drylands are turning into desert; forests into poor pastures; freshwater wetlands into salty, dead soils; rich coral reefs into lifeless stretches of ocean.

Fourth, as ecosystems are degraded, the biological diversity and genetic resources they contain are lost. Many environmental trends are reversible; this loss is permanent.

Fifth, this overuse and misuse of resources is accompanied by the pollution of atmosphere, water, and soil – often with substances that persist for long periods. With a growing number of sources and forms of pollution, this process also appears to be accelerating. The most complex and potentially serious of these threats is a change in climate and in the stability of air circulation systems.

There are also alarming trends apparent in patterns of "development"; these, too, begin with population projections. More than 90 percent of population growth takes place in the developing world – that is, in poorer countries. This means that when the present world population of more than 5 billion doubles next century, there will be an extra 4.5 billion people in nations where today it is hardest to secure jobs, food, safe homes, education, and health care.

Already, population growth means that the number of people who belong to the underclass – those unable to secure such basics of life as adequate food, shelter, clothing, health care, and education – is rising yearly in much of the developing world. In the mid-1980s more than a billion people on the planet, almost a third of the population of the developing world, were trying to survive on an income equivalent to about $1 per day.

Poverty, rapid population growth, and the deterioration of natural resources often occur in the same regions, creating a huge imbalance between the quarter of the planet living in rich, industrial nations and the three quarters residing in developing nations. The national income of Japan's 120 million people is about to overtake the combined incomes of the 3.8 billion people in the developing world. The industrial nations have generally cut their aid to the developing world. And because of debt servicing and repayment and reduced foreign investment, total capital flows were reversed in the second half of the 1980s, with money flowing from poor to rich.

These two sets of alarming trends – environment and development – cannot be separated. Economic growth in most of the developing world will depend for some time on agricultural production, so a reduction in the productivity in ecosystems tends to mean declining farm production and loss of revenue. But increasing populations in stagnant economies mean that more people are directly relying on the environmental resource base for a living. Environmental and economic decline are in many areas an inseparable part of the same downward spiral.

The resulting global structural challenge was concisely summed up by Maurice Strong, Secretary General of the UN Conference on Environment and Development in Brazil in June 1992: "The gross imbalances that have been created by concentration of economic growth in the industrial countries and population growth in developing countries is at the centre of the current dilemma. Redressing these imbalances will be the key to the future security of our planet – in environmental and economic as well as traditional security terms. This will require fundamental changes both in our economic behavior and our international relations."

Clearly action is required. But which actions, and when, given the huge uncertainties involved? This is the sort of issue that business copes with daily. Corporate leaders are used to examining uncertain, negative trends, making decisions, and then taking action, adjusting, and incuring costs to prevent damage. Insurance is just one example. There are costs involved, but these are costs the rational are willing to bear and costs the responsible do not regret, even if things turn out not to have been as bad as they once seemed. We can hope for the best, but the"precautionary principle" remains the best practice in business as well as in other aspects of life.

This principle was agreed to at the World Industry Conference on Environmental Management in 1984 and at the 1989 Paris summit of the leaders of the seven richest industrial nations (the G7). It was strengthened in the Ministerial Declaration of the 1990 UN Economic Commission for Europe meeting in Bergen: "In order to achieve sustainable development, policies must be based on the precautionary principle. Environmental measures must anticipate, prevent and attack the causes of environmental degradation. Where there are threats of serious or irreversible damage, lack of full scientific certainty should not be used as a reason for postponing measures to prevent environmental degradation."

Yet risk and uncertainty are usually accompanied by new opportunities, and business has long been adept at seizing such chances. For example, using energy more efficiently, and thus reducing global and local pollution, decreases costs and increases competitiveness. Many of what politicians and economists call "no regrets policies" – actions that make sense no matter what the real threat of global warming – are from a business point of view opportunities and good investments; examples include improving energy efficiency and developing new energy sources, new drought-resistant crops, and new resource management techniques.

There will be many opportunities for business. Having researched various aspects of competitive advantage among nations, Harvard Business School Professor Michael Porter reported: "I found that the nations with the most rigorous [environmental standards] requirements often lead in exports of affected products....The strongest proof that environmental protection does not hamper competitiveness is the economic performance of nations with the strictest laws." He mentions the successes of Japan and Germany, as well as that of the United States in sectors actually subject to the greatest environmental costs: chemicals, plastics, and paints.

Viewing environmental threats from a business perspective can help guide both governments and companies toward plausible policies that offer protection from disaster while making the best of the challenges.

[...]

Sustainable Development

During the first great wave of environmental concern in the late 1960s and early 1970s, most of the problems seemed local: the products of individual pipes and smokestacks. The answers appeared to lie in regulating these pollution sources.

When the environment reemerged on the political agenda in the 1980s, the main concerns had become international: acid rain, depletion of the ozone layer, and global warming. Analysts sought causes not in pipes [...] and stacks but in the nature of human activities. One report after another concluded that much of what we do, many of our attempts to make "progress," are simply unsustainable. We cannot continue in our present methods of using energy, managing forests, farming, protecting plant and animal species, managing urban growth, and producing industrial goods. We certainly cannot continue to reproduce our own species at the present rate.

Energy provides a striking example of present unsustainability. Most energy today is produced from fossil fuels: coal, oil, and gas. In the mid-1980s, the world was burning the equivalent of 10 billion metric tons of coal per year, with people in industrial nations using much more than those of the developing world. At these rates, by 2025 the expected global population of more than 8 billion would be using the equivalent of 14 billion metric tons of coal. But if all the world used energy at industrial-country levels, by 2025 the equivalent of 55 billion metric tons would be burned. Present levels of fossil fuel use may be warming the globe; a more than five-fold increase is unthinkable. Fossil fuels must be used more efficiently while alternatives are being developed if economic development is to be achieved without radically changing the global climate.

Given such widespread evidence of unsustainability, it is not surprising that the concept of "sustainable development" has come to dominate the environment/development debate. In 1987, the World Commission on Environment and Development, appointed three years earlier by the UN General Assembly and headed by Norwegian Prime Minister Gro Harlem Brundtland, made sustainable development the theme of its entire report, *Our Common Future*. It defined the concept simply as a form of development or progress that "meets the needs of the present without compromising the ability of future generations to meet their own needs."

The phrase itself can be misleading, as the word development might suggest that it is a chore for "developing" nations only. But development is more than growth, or quantitative change. It is primarily a change in quality. More than a decade ago, the influential World Conservation Strategy, compiled by the United Nations and organizations representing governments and private bodies, defined development as "the modification of the biosphere and the application of human, financial, living and non-living resources to satisfy human needs and improve the quality of human life."

Thus all nations are, or would wish to be, developing. And sustainable development will require the greatest changes in the wealthiest nations, which consume the most resources, release the most pollution, and have the greatest capacity to make the necessary changes. These nations must also respond to the criticism from many leaders in the poor parts of the world that industrial countries risk reversing the relationship between production and the satisfaction of needs. They charge that increased production in wealthy nations no longer serves primarily to satisfy needs; rather, the creation of needs serves to increase production.

The idea that much of what humanity does in the name of progress is unsustainable and must be changed has gained rapid acceptance. In 1987, the UN General Assembly passed a resolution adopting the World Commission's report as a guide for future UN operations, and commending it to governments. Since then, many governments have tried to bend their policies to its recommendations. The July 1989 G7 summit called for "the early adoption, worldwide, of policies based on sustainable development."

Business has also taken up the challenge, at the international, national, and sectoral levels. The International Chamber of Commerce drafted a "Business Charter for Sustainable Development," which was launched in April 1991 at the Second World Industry Conference on Environmental Management. The Charter, endorsed by 600 firms worldwide by early 1992, encourages companies to "commit themselves to improving their environmental performance in accordance with these [the Charter's] 16 Principles, to having in place management practices to effect such improvement, to measuring their progress, and to reporting this progress as appropriate internally and externally."

The senior business group in Japan, the Keidanren, adopted an Environmental Charter in 1991 that sets out codes of behavior toward the environment. Malaysia has established a corporate environmental policy that calls on companies "to give benefit to society; this entails…that any adverse effects on the environment are reduced to a practicable minimum." The Confederation of Indian Industry has also urged an "Environment Code for Industry" upon its members.

Chemical industry associations in several countries have agreed to a Responsible Care program to promote continuous improvement in environmental health and safety. Begun in Canada and taken up in the United States, Australia, and many European countries, the scheme encourages associations to draft codes of conduct in many areas of operations, and it recommends that large companies help smaller ones with environmental and safety improvements.

Sustainable development will obviously require more than pollution prevention and tinkering with environmental regulations. Given that ordinary people – consumers, business people, farmers – are the real day-to-day environmental decision makers, it requires political and economic systems based on the effective participation of all members of society in decision making. It requires that environmental considerations become a part of the decision-making processes of all government agencies, all business enterprises, and in fact all people. It requires levels of international cooperation never before achieved, not least in agreeing to and enforcing treaties to manage global commons such as the atmosphere and oceans. It requires, beyond immediate environmental concerns, an end to the "arms culture" as a method of achieving security, and new definitions of security that include environmental threats.

Recently the nations of the world seem to have begun to move, albeit slowly, in these directions. Environmental concern has gradually begun to infuse all areas of decision making. Democracy has become a more prevalent form of government throughout the developing world, Eastern Europe, and the former Soviet Union. The Montreal protocol on the ozone layer […] suggests that nations may be able to cooperate along the harder paths toward a cleaner global environment. Definitions of security are changing, and the end of the cold war may free resources for work on environmental security.

Will these changes last, and are they happening fast enough?

The Growth Controversy

Perhaps the most controversial conclusion of the World Commission was that sustainable development requires rapid economic growth. This assumption is based on the reality that growing populations and poor populations require goods and services to meet essential needs and that "meeting essential needs depends in part on achieving full growth potential, and sustainable development clearly requires economic growth in places where such needs are not being met. Elsewhere, it can be consistent with economic growth, provided the content of growth reflects the broad principles of sustainability and non-exploitation of others."

There are critics who argue that the limits to economic growth have already been reached and there must be "zero growth" from now on. Some of them do not explain how zero growth will meet the needs of a planet with more than 10 billion people. But others who feel that the environmental limits to growth have been reached, such as Robert Goodland and Herman Daly of the World Bank's Environment Department, argue that "development by the rich must be used to free resources… for growth and development so urgently needed by the poor. Large-scale transfers to the poorer countries also will be required."

The World Commission itself noted that growth alone is not enough, as high levels of productivity and widespread poverty can coexist and can endanger the environment. So sustainable development requires societies to meet human needs both by increasing environmentally sustainable production and "by ensuring equitable opportunities for all."

The Commissioners argued that growth was limited at present by both the nature of technologies and the nature of social organization. For example, humanity will eventually be using much more energy than today, but an increasing part will have to come from sources other than fossil fuels. And if societies remain organized so that many people remain impoverished despite sustained economic growth, then this poverty will both degrade environmental resources and eventually act as a brake on growth.

The Business Challenge

The requirement for clean, equitable economic growth remains the biggest single difficulty within the larger challenge of sustainable development.

Proving that such growth is possible is certainly the greatest test for business and industry, which must devise strategies to maximize added value while minimizing resource and energy use. Given the large technological and productive capacity of business, any progress toward sustainable development requires its active leadership.

Open, prospering markets are a powerful force for creating equity of opportunity among nations and people. Yet for there to be equal opportunity, there must first be opportunity itself. Open, competitive markets create the most opportunities for the most people. It is often the nations where markets most closely approach the ideal of "free," open, and competitive that have the least poverty and the greatest opportunity to escape from that poverty.

The World Commission listed as the first prerequisite for sustainable development a political system in which people can effectively participate in decision making. But freedom to participate in political decisions and freedom to participate in markets are inseparable over the long run. The citizens of Central Europe, having achieved political freedom, are now building market freedom. The Asian nations that achieved thriving market economies under authoritarian regimes are now moving toward more democratic governments.

Yet no market can be called "free" in which the decisions of a few can cause misuse of resources and pollution that threaten the present and future of the many. Today, for instance, the earth's atmosphere is providing the valuable service of acting as a dump for pollutants; those enjoying this service rarely pay a reasonable price for it.

"Eco-efficiency"

The present limits to growth are not so much those imposed by resources, such as oil and other minerals, as was argued by the 1972 Club of Rome report *The Limits to Growth*. In many cases they arise more from a scarcity of "sinks," or systems that can safely absorb wastes. The atmosphere, many bodies of water, and large areas of soil are reaching their own absorptive limits as regards wastes of all kinds.

"We believe a business cannot continue to exist without the trust and respect of society for its environmental performance."

ShinrokuMorohashi
President
Mitsubishi Corporation

Business has begun to respond to this truth. It is moving from a position of limiting pollution and cleaning up waste to comply with government regulations toward one of avoiding pollution and waste both in the interests of corporate citizenship and of being more efficient and competitive. The economies of the industrial countries have grown while the resources and energy needed to produce each unit of growth have declined. Chemical companies in industrial nations have doubled output since 1970 while more than halving energy consumption per unit of production.

Industry is moving toward "demanufacturing" and "remanufacturing" – that is, recycling the materials in their products and thus limiting the use of raw materials and of energy to convert those raw materials. That this is technically feasible is encouraging; that it can be done profitably is more encouraging. It is the more competitive and successful companies that are at the forefront of what we call "eco-efficiency."

But eco-efficiency is not achieved by technological change alone. It is achieved only by profound changes in the goals and assumptions that drive corporate activities, and change in the daily practices and tools used to reach them. This means a break with business-as-usual mentalities and conventional wisdom that sidelines environmental and human concerns.

A growing number of leading companies are adopting and publicly committing themselves to sustainable development strategies. They are expanding their concepts of who has a stake in their operations beyond employees and stockholders to include neighbors, public interest groups (including environmental organizations), customers, suppliers, governments, and the general public. They are communicating more openly with these new stakeholders. They are coming to realize that "the degree to which a company is viewed as being a positive or negative participant in solving sustainability issues will determine, to a very great degree, their long-term business viability," in the words of Ben Woodhouse, director of Global Environmental Issues at Dow Chemical.

The Challenge of Time

As the World Commission noted, sustainable development requires forms of progress that meet the needs of the present without compromising the ability of future generations to meet their own needs. In the late twentieth century, we are failing in the first clause of that definition by not meeting the basic needs of more than 1 billion people. We have not even begun to come to grips with the second clause: the needs of future generations. Some argue that we have no responsibility for the future, as we cannot know its needs. This is partly true. But it takes no great leap of reason to assume that our offspring will require breathable air, drinkable water, productive soils and oceans, a predictable climate, and abundant plant and animal species on the planet they will share.

Yet it is a hard thing to demand of political leaders, especially those who rely on the votes of the living to achieve and remain in high office, that they ask those alive today to bear costs for the sake of those not yet born, and not yet voting. It is equally hard to ask anyone in business, providing goods and services to the living, to change their ways for the sake of those not yet born, and not yet acting in the marketplace. The painful truth is that the present is a relatively comfortable place for those who have reached positions of mainstream political or business leadership.

This is the crux of the problem of sustainable development, and perhaps the main reason why there has been great acceptance of it in principle, but less concrete actions to put it into practice: many of those with the power to effect the necessary changes have the least motivation to alter the status quo that gave them that power.

When politicians, industrialists, and environmentalists run out of practical advice, they often take refuge in appeals for a new vision, new values, a new commitment, and a new ethic. Such calls often ring hollow and rhetorical. But given that sustainable development requires a practical concern for the needs of people in the future, then it does ultimately require a new shared vision and a collective ethic based on equality of opportunity not only among people and nations, but also between this generation and those to come. Sustainability will require new technology, new approaches to trade to spread the technology and the goods necessary for survival, and new ways of meeting needs through markets. Business leadership will be required, and expected, in all these areas.

However, sustainable development will ultimately be achieved only through cooperation among people and all their various organizations, including businesses and governments. And leaders elected to decision-making and executive offices retain a fundamental obligation to inform and educate their constituencies about the urgent necessity and the reasons for changing course.

We believe that the best aspects of the human propensity to buy, sell, and produce can be an engine of change. Business has helped to create much of what is valuable in the world today. It will play its part in ensuring the planet's future.

Shaping the Future

The inevitable process of change toward sustainable forms of development will determine the future course of human civilization and shape our life-styles and thereby the way we do business. Yet many business leaders have so far been relatively passive in dealing with these issues.

Perhaps this ultimately has to do with the way we each react to the dimension of time. Those who have little interest in the future of nature and humanity will have little regard for the sustainability of their actions and will not be concerned to grapple with and understand the challenges facing us all. Those who do care about society and its progress have learned to understand that business never operates in a vacuum. It interacts at many levels with society, and society is now entering a period of rapid and fundamental changes.

Business has developed remarkable skills in market intelligence to spot and to a certain extent predict changing demand patterns. It must also construct a system of "social intelligence" to spot, understand, and interpret signals of change in development patterns. Those who are quickest to receive and act on such signals will have a great advantage over competitors who react only when changes in society become apparent in the form of changed consumer habits.

The environmental challenge has grown from local pollution to global threats and choices. The business challenge has likewise grown – from relatively simple technical fixes and additional costs to a corporate wide collection of threats, choices, and opportunities that are of central importance in separating tomorrow's winners from tomorrow's losers. Corporate leaders must take this into account when designing strategic plans of business and deciding the priorities of their own work.

Sustainable development is also about redefining the rules of the economic game in order to move from a situation of wasteful consumption and pollution to one of conservation, and from one of privilege and protectionism to one of fair and equitable chances open to all. Business leaders will want to participate in devising the rules of the new game, striving to make them simple, practical, and efficient.

No one can reasonably doubt that fundamental change is needed. This fact offers us two basic options: we can resist as long as possible, or we can join those shaping the future. *Changing Course* is an invitation and a challenge to business leaders to choose the more promising and more rewarding option of participation.

12

The "Commons" versus the "Commodity": Alter-globalization, Anti-privatization and the Human Right to Water in the Global South (2007)

Karen Bakker

Prologue

On a rainy Friday in 2003, the world's Water and Environment Ministers met in Kyoto to discuss the global water crisis. While Ministers met behind closed doors, participants at the parallel public World Water Forum were presented with alarming statistics: water scarcity had been growing in many regions; and over 20% the world's population was without access to sufficient supplies of potable water necessary for basic daily needs. In response, conference organizers had drafted an Inter-Ministerial declaration, based upon the view that the best response to increasing scarcity was the commercialization of water. International support for the commercialization of water supply had been growing since the controversial Dublin Statement on Water and Sustainable Development in 1992.[1] In light of endemic "state failure" by governments supposedly too poor, corrupt, or inept to manage water supply systems, increased involvement of the private sector in water supply management was openly advocated by many conference participants.

Reflecting this shift in international water policy, private water companies had been invited to meet with government delegations, international financial institutions, and bilateral aid agencies to develop solutions to the world's water problems. Yet many of the governments represented at the conference had themselves been accused of irresponsible water management by their citizens. The government of South Africa, for example, had continued to support the Lesotho Highlands Water Project (the largest in Africa), despite the participation of its then-Minister for Water

Affairs in the high-profile World Commission on Dams which comprehensively reviewed – and condemned – the social, environmental, and economic record of large dams around the world (Bond 2002). The private water companies in attendance at Kyoto were similarly targeted by activists, with corporations such as Enron under attack by an international alliance of anti-dam activists, environmentalists, public sector unions, international "bank-watcher" and "anti-globalization" think tanks, indigenous peoples, and civil society groups. These self-named "water warriors" protested both inside and outside the Forum, critiquing the Forum co-organizers (the Global Water Partnership and the World Water Council) for their close ties to private water companies and international financial institutions, and for an unrepresentative, opaque, and illegitimate process (ironically, similar critiques were directed by the Forum organizers at activists).

Activists' protests culminated with the disruption of a planned highlight of the Forum – a plenary session chaired by Michel Camdessus (former head of the IMF) promoting active government support for increased private sector involvement in the water sector in the South (Winpenny 2003). Chanting "water is life", activists stormed the stage and demanded the withdrawal of the private sector, a return to local "water democracy", a rejection of large dams as socio-economically and environmentally unsound, and a recognition of water as a human right. Yet activists' calls fell largely on deaf ears. Southern and northern ministerial delegates reached consensus; including, controversially, support for private sector financing, new mechanisms for private sector involvement in water supply management, and a conspicuous failure to refer to water as a human right.

Introduction: The Triumph of Market Environmentalism?

The Kyoto Declaration embodies an increasingly dominant philosophy of development, variously termed "liberal environmentalism" (Bernstein 2001), "green neoliberalism" (Goldman 2005), or market environmentalism (Bakker 2004): a mode of resource regulation which aims to deploy markets as the solution to environmental problems (Anderson and Leal 2001). Market environmentalism offers hope of a virtuous fusion of economic growth, efficiency, and environmental conservation: through establishing private property rights, employing markets as allocation mechanisms, and incorporating environmental externalities through pricing, proponents of market environmentalism assert that environmental goods will be more efficiently allocated if treated as economic goods – thereby simultaneously addressing concerns over environmental degradation and inefficient use of resources.

Critical research on market environmentalism frames this paradigm as the "neoliberalization of nature" (Bridge 2004; Mansfield 2004a; McAfee 2003; McCarthy 2004; McCarthy and Prudham 2004; Perrault 2006; Prudham 2004). The majority of this research focuses on the negative impacts of neoliberal reforms, including both environmental impacts and the distributional implications of the various forms of "accumulation by dispossession" enacted by neoliberalization (Glassman 2006), although some research also suggests that states can rationally administer environmental degradation and resource appropriation from local communities (Scott 1998), or that environmental improvements can occur in the context of state re-regulation which accompanies privatization (Angel 2000; Bakker 2005).

This debate is particularly acute in the water sector. The increasing involvement of private, for-profit multinational water corporations in running networked water supply systems around the world has inspired fierce debate internationally (see, for example, Finger and Allouche 2002; Johnstone and Wood 2003; Laurie and Marvin 1999; Swyngedouw 2005).[2] Proponents of market environmentalism in the water sector argue that water is an increasingly scarce resource, which must be priced at full economic and environmental cost if it is to be allocated to its highest-value uses, and managed profitably by private companies whose accountability to customers and shareholders is more direct and effective than attenuated political accountability exercised by citizens via political representatives (Rogers et al 2003; Winpenny 1994). Opponents of market environmentalism argue that water is a non-substitutable resource essential for life, and call for water supply to be recognized as a human right, which (they argue) both places an onus upon states to provide water to all, and precludes private sector involvement (see, for example, Bond 2002; Goldman 2005; Johnston, Gismondi and Goodman 2006; Laxer and Soron 2006; Morgan 2004b).

Several conceptual questions underlie this debate. Is water a human right? If so, is private sector provision incompatible with the human right to water? What is the relationship between property rights regimes and privatization? And how can we best conceptualize and mobilize alternatives to neoliberalization? This paper explores these questions, documenting the different constructions of property rights adopted by pro- and anti-privatization advocates, questioning the utility of the language of "human rights", and interrogating the accuracy of the (often unquestioned) binaries – rights/commodities, public/private, citizen/customer – deployed by both sides of the debate. In doing so, the paper undertakes two tasks: the development of a conceptual framework of market environmentalist reforms; and the application of this framework to the case of water supply.

The first part of the paper develops a typology of market environmentalist reforms in resource management, arguing that conceptual confusion frequently arises due to a lack of analytical precision about the wide range of ongoing reforms that are often over-simplified into a monolithic (and inaccurately labelled) "neoliberalism". The second section examines one example of these conceptual confusions: the positioning of "human rights" as an antonym to "commodities" by anti-privatization campaigners. After documenting the tactical failures of such an approach, the paper contrasts "anti-privatization" campaigns with "alter-globalization" movements engaged in the construction of alternative community economies and culture of water, centred on concepts such as the commons and "water democracies". In this third section of the paper, an attempt is made to complicate the public/private, commodity/rights, citizen/customer binaries underpinning much of the debate, through exploring the different socio-economic identities of citizens, and different property rights, invoked under different water management models around the world. In the concluding section, the conceptual and political implications of this analysis are teased out, focusing on the implications of this analysis for our understandings of "neoliberal natures".

Neoliberal Reforms and Resource Management: Clarifying the Debate

Much of the literature on "neoliberalizing nature" is concerned with the creation of private property rights for resources previously governed as common pool resources.[3] Of particular interest have been the impacts of "neoliberalism" on specific resources (Bakker 2000, 2001; Bradshaw 2004; Bridge 2004; Bridge and Jonas 2002; Bridge, McManus and Marsden 2003; Gibbs and Jonas 2000; Johnston 2003; Maddock 2004; Mansfield 2004a, 2004b; McAfee 2003; Robertson 2004; Smith 2004; Walker et al 2000). As Noel Castree notes in his review of this literature (Castree 2005), much of this work has emphasized case-specific analyses of very different types of processes broadly grouped under the rather nebulous banner of neoliberalization: privatization, marketization, deregulation, reregulation, commercialization, and corporatization, to name just a few.

Although Castree acknowledges the utility of this work in illustrating that "neoliberalism" is actually constituted of a range of diverse, locally rooted practices of neoliberalization, he identifies two analytical traps: failure to identify criteria by which different cases of neoliberalizing nature can be deemed sufficiently similar in order to conduct comparisons; and the occlusion of distinct types of neoliberal practices when subsumed under the broad (and overly general) label of neoliberalism. This paper responds to Castree's call for analytical frameworks with which to clarify these issues. As Sparke notes in a recent review (2006), this task is both analytically and politically crucial, insofar as the ideal types to which some of this work falls prey risk reinforcing or even reproducing the idealism of neoliberalism itself.

In developing such an analytical framework, an iterative approach is required which articulates (and revises) conceptual frameworks of neoliberalization (as a higher-order abstraction) and empirical analysis of the contingent mediation of neoliberal agendas by historically and geographically specific material conditions and power relations. In undertaking this analysis, it is important to distinguish between three categories of resource management upon which neoliberal reforms can be undertaken. Resource management *institutions* are the laws, policies, rules, norms and customs by which resources are governed. Resource management *organizations* are the collective social entities that govern resource use. And resource management *governance* is the process by which organizations enact management institutions; the practices by which, in other words, we construct and administer the exploitation of resources (Table 12.1).

As illustrated in Table 12.1, reforms can be undertaken in distinct categories, and are not necessarily concomitant; one may privatize without deregulating; deregulate without marketizing; and commercialize without privatizing, etc (Bakker 2004). To give a simple example: privatization of the water supply industry in England and Wales in 1989 did not entail marketization; that is, it did not entail the introduction of markets in water abstraction licenses. This example illustrates one of the main confusions which arises in the literature: reforms to institutions, organizations, and governance are all subsumed under the general term "neoliberalization", despite the fact that they often involve very different types of reforms, applied to different aspects of resource management. Another source of confusion arises when different types of reforms are assumed to be interchangeable, and when distinct terms (marketization, privatization) are assumed to be synonymous, when they are not.

How is such a typological exercise helpful in either analysis or activism? First, the failure to distinguish between categories of resource management, and between targets and types of reforms, obscures the specificity of the reform processes which are the object of analysis, and limits our ability to compare cases, as Castree has noted. For example, comparing the introduction of water rights for "raw" water (water in nature) (Haddad 2000) in California to private sector participation in water supply management in New York (Gandy 2002) is of limited interest,

Table 12.1   Resource management reforms: examples from the water sector

Category	Target of reform	Type of reform	Example drawn from the water sector
Resource management institutions	Property rights	Privatization (enclosure of the commons or asset sale)	Introduction of riparian rights (England; Hassan 1998); or sale of water supply infrastructure to private sector (England and Wales; Bakker 2004)
	Regulatory frameworks	De-regulation	Cessation of direct state oversight of water quality mechanisms (Ontario, Canada; Prudham 2004)
Resource management organizations	Asset management	Private sector 'partnerships' (outsourcing contracts)	French municipal outsourcing of water supply system management to private companies (Lorrain 1997)
	Organizational structure	Corporatization	Conversion of business model for municipal water supply: from local government department to a publicly owned corporation (Amsterdam, The Netherlands; Blokland, Braadbaart and Schwartz 2001)
Resource governance	Resource allocation	Marketization	Introduction of a water market (Chile; Bauer 1998)
	Performance incentives/ sanctions	Commercialization	Introduction of commercial principles (eg full cost recovery) in water management (South Africa; McDonald and Ruiters 2005)
	User participation	Devolution or decentralization	Devolving water quality monitoring to lower orders of government or individual water users (Babon River, Indonesia; Susilowati and Budiati 2003)

because two distinct processes are at work (marketization versus private sector participation). In contrast, comparing the introduction of water markets in Chile (Bauer 1998) and California (Haddad 2000) is worthwhile, because in both cases private property rights for water supply have been introduced via a process of marketization of water resource allocation. In short, the typology presented in Table 12.1 is analytically useful because it enables us to correctly compare different types of market environmentalist reforms, and to more accurately characterize their goals and evaluate their outcomes.

This typology is also useful in addressing the widespread failure to adequately distinguish between different elements of neoliberal reform processes, an analytical sloppiness that diminishes our ability to correctly characterize the aims and trajectories of neoliberal projects of resource management reform (Bakker 2005). Commercialization, for example, often precedes privatization in the water supply sector, which is sometimes followed by attempts to commodify water. The biophysical properties of resources, together with local governance frameworks, strongly influence the types of neoliberal reforms which are likely to be introduced: common-pool, mobile resources such as fisheries are more amenable to marketization, whereas natural monopolies such as water supply networks are more amenable to privatization (Bakker 2004). In other words, in failing to exercise sufficient analytical precision in analyzing processes of "neoliberalizing nature", we are likely to misinterpret the reasons for, and incorrectly characterize the pathway of specific neoliberal reforms.

As explored in subsequent sections of the paper, this typology may also be useful in clarifying activist strategies, and in structuring our analyses of activism and advocacy. For example, in much of the literature on "neoliberal nature" (and in many NGO and activist campaigning documents), water as a "commodity" is contrasted to water as a "human right". Careful conceptualization of the neoliberalization of water demonstrates that this is misleading, insofar as the term "commodity" refers to a property rights regime applicable to resources, and human rights to alegal category applicable to individuals. The more appropriate, but less widely used, antonym of water as a "commodity" would more properly be a water "commons". As explored in the following sections, this distinction has had significant implications for the success of "anti-privatization" and "alter-globalization" struggles around the world.

Debating Neoliberalization: Anti-privatization Campaigns and the "Human Right to Water"

The international campaign for a human right to water has grown enormously over the past decade. This campaign has its roots in the arguments of anti-privatization campaigners, who have fought numerous campaigns to resist, and then overturn water privatization projects around the world. Advocates of private sector involvement in water supply – private companies, bilateral aid agencies, and many governments – argue that it will increase efficiency, and deliver water to those who currently lack access. They point to the failure of governments and aid agencies to achieve the goal of universal water supply during the International Water and Sanitation Decade (1981–1990), and to the low efficiency and low levels of cost recovery of public utilities. Through efficiency gains and better management, private companies will be able to lower prices, improve performance, and increase cost recovery, enabling systems to be upgraded and expanded, critical in a world in which one billion people lack access to safe, sufficient water supplies. Privatization (the transfer of ownership of water supply systems to private companies) and private sector "partnerships" (the construction, operation and management of publicly owned water supply systems by private companies) have, it is argued, worked well in other utility sectors (see, for example, DFID 1998; Dinar 2000; Rogers et al 2002; Shirley 2002; Winpenny 2004).

This view has been strongly critiqued by those who argue that neoliberalization entails an act of dispossession with negative distributive consequences that is emblematic of "globalization from above" (Assies 2003; Barlow and Clarke 2003; Bond 2004a; Hukka and Katko 2003; McDonald and Ruiters 2005; Petrella 2001; Shiva 2002). According to its opponents, the involvement of private companies invariably introduces a pernicious logic of the market into water management, which is incompatible with guaranteeing citizen's basic right to water. Private companies – answerable to shareholders and with the over-riding goal of profit – will manage water supply less sustainably than public sector counterparts. Opponents of privatization point to successful examples of public water systems, and on research that private sector alternatives are not necessarily more efficient, and often much more expensive for users, than well-managed public sector systems (see, for example, Estache and Rossi 2002). They assert the effectiveness of democratic accountability to citizens when compared with corporate accountability to shareholders; an argument less easy to refute following the collapse of Enron, which by the late 1990s had become one of the largest water multinationals through its subsidiary Azurix.

Opponents of water supply privatization frequently invoke a human right to water to support their claims (Gleick 1998; Hukka and Katko 2003; Morgan 2004b, 2005; Trawick 2003). The argument for creating a human right to water generally rests on two justifications: the non-substitutability of drinking water ("essential for life"), and the fact that many other human rights which are explicitly recognized in the UN Conventions are predicated upon an (assumed) availability of water (eg the right to food).

The claim to a human right to water rests on shaky legal ground: no explicit right to water is expressed in the most relevant international treaty,[4] although the UN Committee on Economic, Social and Cultural Rights[5] issued a comment in 2002, asserting that every person has a right to "sufficient, safe, acceptable, physically accessible, and affordable water" (ECOSOC 2002; Hammer 2004). Accordingly, a significant element of anti-privatization campaigning of NGOs in both the North and South has been a set of intertwined campaigns for the human right to water, beginning with a set of declarations by activists in both the North and the South,[6] and growing to include well-resourced campaigns hosted by high-profile NGOs such as Amnesty International, the World Development Movement, the Council of Canadians, the Sierra Club, Jubilee South, Mikhail Gorbachev's Green Cross and Ralph Nader's Public Citizen.[7] Activists have also focused on country-specific campaigns for constitutional and legal amendments, notably Uruguay's 2004 successful referendum resulting in a constitutional amendment creating a human right to water in 2004.

As the anti-water privatization campaign has transformed into a campaign for the human right to water, activists have gained support from mainstream international development agencies including the World Health Organization and the United Nations Development Programme (ECOSOC 2002; UNDP 2006; UN Economic and Social Council 2003; WHO 2003). These agencies articulate several arguments in favour of the human right to water: higher political priority given to water issues; new legal avenues for citizens to compel states to supply basic water needs; and the fact that the right to water is implicit in other rights (such as the rights to food, life, health, and dignity) which have already been recognized in international law, and which are implicitly recognized through legal precedents when courts support right of non-payment for water services on grounds of lack of affordability (UNWWAP 2006).

Opponents have pointed out the difficulty of implementing a "right to water": lack of clear responsibility and capacity for implementation; the possibility of causing conflict over transboundary waters; and potential abuse of the concept as governments could over-allocate water to privileged groups, at the expense of both people and the environment. Others argue that a right to water will effect little practical change: the right to water enshrined in South Africa's post-apartheid constitution,[8] for example, has not prevented large-scale disconnections and persistent inequities in water distribution (Bond 2002; McDonald and Ruiters 2005). Another critique pertains to the anthropocentrism of human rights, which fail to recognize rights of non-humans (or ecological rights); providing a human right to water may, ironically, imply the further degradation of hydrological systems upon which we depend.

Another, more fundamental criticism is the argument that a human right to water does not foreclose private sector management of water supply systems. Critics of human rights doctrines argue that "rights talk" stems from an individualistic, libertarian philosophy that is "Eurocentric" (see, for example, Ignatieff 2003; Kymlicka 1995; Mutua 2002; Rorty 1993); as such, human rights are compatible with capitalist political economic systems. In other words, private sector provision is compatible with human rights in most countries around the world. A human right to water does not imply that water should be accessed free (although it might imply an affordable basic "lifeline" supply) (UNWWAP 2006), although this is at odds with cultural and religious views on water access in many parts of the world.[9] Indeed, the UN's Committee on Economic, Social and Cultural Rights recognized the ambivalent status which a human right conveys upon a resource when it defined water as a social, economic, and cultural good as well as a commodity (ECOSOC 2003).

Many citizens of capitalist democracies accept that commodities are not inconsistent with human rights (such as food, shelter), but that some sort of public, collective "safety net" must exist if these rights are to be met for *all* citizens. This is true for housing and food (as inadequate as these measures may be in practice). The situation with drinking water is more complicated, because drinking water is a non-substitutable resource essential for life, and because networked water supply is a natural monopoly subject to significant environmental externalities. In this case, strong market failures provide an overwhelming justification for public regulation and, in many cases, ownership of assets. Full privatization is thus inconsistent with a human right to water unless it is coupled (as it is in England) with a universality requirement (laws prohibiting disconnections of residential consumers), and with strong regulatory framework for price controls and quality standards.[10] Private sector participation in water supply, on the other hand, certainly fits within these constraints. In short, rooted in a liberal tradition that prioritizes private ownership and individual rights, the current international human rights regime is flexible enough to be fully compatible with private property rights, whether for water or other basic needs.

In summary, pursuing a "human right to water" as an anti-privatization campaign makes three strategic errors: conflating human rights and property rights; failing to distinguish between different types of property rights and service delivery models; and thereby failing to foreclose the possibility of increasing private sector involvement in water supply. Indeed, the shortcomings of "human right to water" anti-privatization campaigns became apparent following the Kyoto World Water Forum, as proponents of private sector water supply management began speaking out in favour of water as a human right. Senior water industry representatives identified water as a human right on company websites, in the media[11] and at high-profile events such as the Davos World Economic Forum.[12] Right-wing think tanks such as the Cato Institute backed up these statements with reports arguing that "water socialism" had failed the poor, and that market forces, properly regulated, were the best means of fulfilling the human right to water (Bailey 2005; Segerfeldt 2005). Non-governmental organizations such as the World Water Council, regarded by anti-privatization campaigners as being allied with private companies also developed arguments in favour of water as a human right (Dubreuil 2005,2006). Shortly after the Kyoto meeting, the World Bank released a publication acknowledging the human right to water (Salman and McInerney-Lankford 2004).

Two years later, at the Fourth World Water Forum in Mexico City in 2006, representatives of private water companies issued a statement recognizing the right to water, and recalling that the private sector had officially endorsed the right to water in 2005 at the 13th session of the UN's Commission on Sustainable Development (Aquafed 2006). At the Mexico City Forum, a somewhat contrived consensus across civil society, the private sector, and governments on the "right to water" emerged (Smets 2006). Despite dissenting views of Third World governments such as Bolivia, a "diluted" interpretation of the human right to water prevailed in the Ministerial Declaration of the Fourth World Water Forum, in regards to which private companies had an officially sanctioned role.

Ironically, this has occurred at the same time as private companies have been acknowledging the significant barriers to market expansion in the water supply sector in the South. Analysis of the discourse of the public statements of senior executives of water supply services firms reveals a retreat from earlier commitments to pursuing PSPs globally, with senior figures publicly acknowledging high risks and low profitability in supplying the poor (Robbins 2003). Some international financial institutions have begun officially acknowledging the limitations of the private sector (ADB 2003; UNDP 2003). High-profile cancellations of water supply concession contracts – including Atlanta, Buenos Aires, Jakarta, La Paz, and Manila – seem to bear out the hypothesis that water presents difficult, and perhaps intractable problems for private sector management. The private sector has indeed retreated from supplying water to communities in the South, but this has been largely due to the failure to achieve acceptable return on investment and control risk, not to anti-privatization, pro-human rights campaigns. Companies continue to insist that water is a human right, which they are both competent and willing to supply, if risk-return ratios are acceptable, but this is not a condition which cannot be met by most communities.

Alter-globalization and the Commons

In reflecting on the failure of the "human right to water" campaigns to foreclose the involvement of the private sector in water supply management, we broach a question often raised by "alter-globalization" activists: how can we negotiate resistance to neoliberalization? In raising this question, alter-globalization (as distinct from anti-privatization) activists are often dismissive of human rights, arguing that "rights talk" resuscitates a public/private binary that recognizes only two unequally satisfactory options – state or market control: twinned corporatist models from which communities are equally excluded (see, for example, Olivera and Lewis 2004; Roy 1999; Shiva 2002). Instead, activists have turned to alternative concepts of property rights, most frequently some form of the "commons", to motivate their claims, juxtaposing this view to that of water as a commodity (Table 12.2).

At the risk of over-simplification, the commodity view asserts that private ownership and management of water supply systems (in distinction from water itself) is possible and indeed preferable. From this perspective, water is no different than other essential goods and utility services. Private companies, who will be responsive both to customers and to shareholders, can efficiently run and profitably manage

Table 12.2   The commons versus commodity debate

	Commons	*Commodity*
Definition	Public good	Economic good
Pricing	Free or "lifeline"	Full-cost pricing
Regulation	Command and control	Market based
Goals	Social equity and livelihoods	Efficiency and water security
Manager	Community	Market

water supply systems. Commercialization rescripts water as an economic good rather than a public good, and redefines users as individual customers rather than a collective of citizens. Water conservation can thus be incentivized through pricing – users will cease wasteful behaviour as water prices rise with increasing scarcity. Proponents of the "commodity" view assert that water must be treated as an economic good, as specified in the Dublin Principles and in the Hague Declaration,[13] similar to any other economic good – such as food – essential for life.

In contrast, the commons view of water asserts its unique qualities: water is a flow resource essential for life and ecosystem health; non-substitutable and tightly bound to communities and ecosystems through the hydrological cycle (Shiva 2002; TNI 2005). From this perspective, collective management by communities is not only preferable but also necessary, for three reasons. First, water supply is subject to multiple market *and* state failures; without community involvement, we will not manage water wisely. Second, water has important cultural and spiritual dimensions that are closely articulated with place-based practices; as such, its provision cannot be left up to private companies or the state. Third, water is a local flow resource whose use and health are most deeply impacted at a community level; protection of ecological and public health will only occur if communities are mobilized and enabled to govern their own resources. In particular, those who advance the "commons" view assert that conservation is more effectively incentivized through an environmental, collectivist ethic of solidarity, which will encourage users to refrain from wasteful behaviour. The real "water crisis" arises from socially produced scarcity, in which a short-term logic of economic growth, twinned with the rise of corporate power (and in particular water multi-nationals) has "converted abundance into scarcity" (Shiva 2002). As a response to the Dublin Principles, for example, the P7 Declaration (2000) outlined principles of "water democracy", of decentralized, community-based, democratic water management in which water conservation is politically, socio-economically and culturally inspired rather than economically motivated.

Despite their divergent political commitments, opponents and proponents of neoliberalization of water supply share some common conceptual commitments, including an understanding (lacking in many "neoliberalizing nature" analyses) that commodification is fraught with difficulty.[14] In the language of regulatory economists and political scientists, water is conventionally considered to be an imperfect public good (nonexcludable but rival in consumption) which is highly localized in nature, and which is often managed as a common-pool resource, for which relatively robust community-controlled cooperation and management mechanisms exist in many parts of the world (Berkes 1989; Mehta 2003; Ostrom 1990). It is the combination of public good characteristics, market failures and common property rights which makes water such an "uncooperative" commodity, and so resistant to neoliberal reforms, as neoclassical economists recognize when referring to the multiple "market failures" that characterize resources such as water supply[15] (Bakker 2004). To rephrase this analysis in political ecological terms: water is a flow resource over which it is difficult to establish private property rights; is characterized by a high degree of public health and environmental externalities – the costs of which are difficult to calculate and reflect in water prices; and is a partially non-substitutable resource essential for life with important aesthetic, symbolic, spiritual, and ecological functions which render some form of collective, public oversight inevitable. Private property rights can be established for water resources or water supply infrastructure, but full commodification does not necessarily, and in fact rarely follows.

A high degree of state involvement, therefore, is usually found even in countries that have experimented heavily with neoliberal forms to water management. Here lies the second point of convergence between "commodity" and "commons" proponents: both neoliberal reformers and defenders of the "commons" invoke dissatisfaction with centralized, bureaucratic state provision (cf Scott 1998). Whereas over much of the 20th century, "public good" would have been opposed to "economic good" in defense of the state against private interests by antiprivatization activists, alter-globalization movements – such as ATTAC and the Transnational Institute – explicitly reject state-led water governance models (Shiva 2002; TNI 2005). In doing so, as explored below, they reinvigorate a tripartite categorization of service delivery which undermines the "public/private" binary implicitly underlying much of the debate on neoliberalism more generally (Table 12.3).

As indicated in Table 12.3, significant differences exist between the public utility, commercial, and community governance models, despite the fact that these models overlap to some degree in practice. One important distinction is the role of the consumer: a citizen, a customer, or a community member. Each role implies different rights, responsibilities, and accountability mechanisms. Yet this tri-partite categorization tends to compartmentalize water supply into ideal types. In fact, many governments have chosen to create hybrid management models. Some have chosen, for example, to retain ownership while corporatizing water services, as in the Netherlands. In France, private-sector management of municipally owned water supply infrastructure via long-term management contracts is widespread. Other countries such as Denmark, with a long tradition of cooperative management of the local economy, prefer the coop model – provision by a non-profit users "association in which local accountability is a key incentive". Moreover, this tripartite classification is clearly inadequate when applied to the global South, where "public" water supply systems often supply only wealthier neighbourhoods in urban areas, leaving poor and rural areas to self-organize through community cooperatives or informal, private, for-profit provision by water vendors, often at volumetric rates much higher than those available through the public water supply system. Indeed, most residents use multiple sources of water in the home, and rely on a mix of networked and artisanal water supply sources, through both state and private sector delivery systems, using a combination of household piped network water connections, shallow and deep wells, public hydrants, and water vendors for their water supply needs (see, for example, Swyngedouw 2004). A public/private binary, even where it admits to the possibility of a third "cooperative" alternative, is clearly insufficient for capturing the complexity of water provision in cities in the South (Swyngedouw 2004). Alternative community economies of water do, in fact, already exist in many cities in the South (Table 12.4), and represent "actually existing alternatives" to neoliberalism which

Table 12.3 Water supply delivery models: the cooperative, the state, and the private corporation

		State	Market	Community
Resource management institutions	Primary goals	Guardian of public interest Conformity with legislation/policy	Maximization of profit Efficient performance	Serve community interest Effective performance
	Regulatory framework	Command and control	Market mechanisms	Community-defined goals (not necessarily consensus based)
	Property rights	Public (state) or private property	Private property	Public (commons) or private property
Resource management organizations	Primary decision-makers	Administrators, experts, public officials	Individual households, experts, companies	Leaders and members of community organizations
	Organizational structure	Municipal department, civil service	Private company, corporation	Cooperative, association/network
	Business models	Municipally owned utility	Private corporate utility	Community cooperative
Resource governance	Accountability mechanism	Hierarchy	Contract	Community norms
	Key incentives	Voter/ratepayer opinion	Price signals (share movements or bond ratings), customer opinion	Community opinion
	Key sanctions	Political process via elections, litigation	Financial loss, takeover, litigation	Livelihood needs, social pressure, litigation (in some cases)
	Consumer role	User and citizen	User and customer	User and community member
	Participation of consumers	Collective, top-down	Individualistic	Collective, bottom-up

activists have sought to interrogate, protect, and replicate through networks such as the "Blue Planet Project", "Octubre Azul", World Social Fora (Ponniah 2004; Ponniah and Fisher 2003) and alternative "world water fora".[16]

In opening up space for the conceptual acknowledgement of alternative community economies (cf Gibson-Graham 2006), this tactic is to be welcomed. Yet caution is also merited, insofar as appeals to the commons run the risk of romanticizing

Table 12.4   Neoliberal reforms and alter-globalization alternatives

Category	Target of reform	Type of reform	Alter-globalization alternative
Resource management institutions	Property rights	Privatization	• Mutualization (re-collectivization) of asset ownership (Wales; Bakker 2004) • Communal water rights in village "commons" in India (Narain 2006)
	Regulatory frameworks	De-regulation	• Re-regulation by consumer-controlled NGOs such as "Customer Councils" in England (Franceys forthcoming; Page and Bakker 2005)
Resource management organizations	Asset management	Private sector "partnerships"	• Public-public partnerships (eg between Stockholm's water company (Stockholm Vatten) and water utilities in Latvia and Lithuania) (PSIRU 2006) • Water cooperatives in Finland (Katko 2000)
	Organizational structure	Corporatization	• Low-cost, community-owned infrastructure (eg Orangi Pilot Project, Pakistan; Zaidi 2001)
Resource governance	Resource allocation	Marketization	• Sharing of irrigation water based on customary law ("usos y costumbres") in Bolivia (Trawick 2003)
	Performance incentives/ sanctions	Commercialization	• Customer corporation (with incentives structured towards maximization of customer satisfaction rather than profit or share price maximization; Kay 1996)
	User participation	Devolution or decentralization	• Community watershed boards (Canada; Alberta Environment 2003) • Participatory budgeting (Porto Alegre, Brazil; TNI 2005)

community control. Much activism in favour of collective, community-based forms of water supply management tends to romanticize communities as coherent, relatively equitable social structures, despite the fact that inequitable power relations and resource allocation exist within communities (McCarthy 2005; Mehta 2001; Mehta, Leach and Scoones 2001). Although research has demonstrated how cooperative management institutions for water common pool resources can function effectively to avoid depletion (Ostrom 1990; Ostrom and Keohane 1995), other research points to the limitations of some of these collective action approaches in water (Cleaver 2000; Mehta 2001; Mosse 1997; Potanski and Adams 1998; St Martin 2005). Commons, in other words, can be exclusive and regressive, as well as inclusive and progressive (McCarthy 2005). Indeed, the role of the state in encouraging redistributive models of resource management, progressive social relations and redistribution is more ambivalent than those making calls for a "return to the commons" would perhaps admit.

Thus, the most progressive strategies are those that adopt a twofold tactic: reforming rather than abolishing state governance, while fostering and sharing alternative local models of resource management. In some instances, these alternative strategies tackle the anthropocentrism of neoliberalization (and "human right to water" campaigns) directly, recognizing ecological as well as human needs, the latter being constrained through a variety of norms, whether scientifically determined "limits", eco-spiritual reverence, or eco-puritan ecological governance. In other cases, they may make strange bedfellows with some aspects of neoliberal agendas, such as decentralization, through which greater community control can be enacted (Table 12.4).

These models are necessarily varied; no one model of water governance can be anticipated or imposed (cf Gibson-Graham 2006). Rather, they build on local resource management and community norms, whether rural water users' customary water rights ("usos y costumbres") in the Andes (Trawick 2003); revived conceptions of Roman "res publica" and "res commmuna" in Europe (Squatriti 1998); or community norms of collective provision of irrigation in Indian "village republics" (Shiva 2002; Wade 1988). In each instance, a place-specific model of what Indian activist Vandana Shiva terms "water democracy" emerges, offering a range of responses to the neoliberalization agendas identified earlier in the paper. In other words, these "really existing" alter-globalization initiatives are a form of what Gibson-Graham terms "weak theory": deliberately organic, tentative, local, place-based, and (at least at the outset) modest.

"Weak", does not, however, imply "insignificant". These reforms are, of course, necessarily local – because water is usually consumed, managed, and disposed of at a local scale. But they are nonetheless replicable, and thus represent potentially powerful "actually existing alternatives" to neoliberalization. One example is the recent proliferation of "public public partnerships", in which public water supply utilities with expertise and resources (typically in large cities in the North) are partnered with those in the South, or with smaller urban centres in the North (PSIRU 2005, 2006; Public Citizen 2002; TNI 2005). Activists have actively promoted these strategies as a tactic of resistance to water supply privatization initiatives, while acknowledging the political pitfalls of promoting public-public partnerships in the wake of failed private sector contracts, particularly the potential for such partnerships to be promoted as a strategy for less profitable communities, allowing more limited private sector contracts to "cherry pick" profitable communities. Institutional support from multilateral agencies may soon be forthcoming, as the newly commissioned UN Secretary General's

Advisory Board and Water and Sanitation has requested the UN to support the creation of an international association of public water operators.[17] Encouraged by the UN Commission on Sustainable Development's official acknowledgment of the importance of promoting public-public partnerships (TNI 2006; UNCSD 2005), and by specific campaigns by public water supply utilities – notably Porto Alegre – governments in Argentina, Bolivia, Brazil, Indonesia, Holland, Honduras, France, South Africa, and Sweden have initiated public-public partnerships, at times also entailing a radical restructuring of management-worker relationships within water supply utilities (TNI 2006).

Conclusions

As explored in this paper, the adoption of human rights discourse by private companies indicates its limitations as an anti-privatization strategy. Human rights are individualistic, anthropocentric, state-centric, and compatible with private sector provision of water supply; and as such, a limited strategy for those seeking to refute water privatization. Moreover, "rights talk" offers us an unimaginative language for thinking about new community economies, not least because pursuit of a campaign to establish water as a human right risks reinforcing the public/private binary upon which this confrontation is predicated, occluding possibilities for collective action beyond corporatist models of service provision. In contrast, the "alter-globalization" debate opened up by disrupting the public/private binary has created space for the construction of alternative community economies of water. These "alter-globalization" proposals counterpose various forms of the commons to commodity-based property and social relations. Greater progressive possibilities would appear to be inherent in the call of alter-globalization activists for radical strategies of ecological democracy predicated upon calls to decommodify public services and enact "commons" models of resource management (see, for example, Bond 2004a, 2004b; TNI 2005).

How does a more refined understanding of neoliberalization, as outlined in the typology introduced at the outset of this paper, assist in this task? First, it enables activism to be more precise in its characterization of "actually existing" neoliberalisms, and thus to develop alternatives which have more political traction. For example, the "commons" is an effective strategy for combating privatization because it correctly opposes a collective property right to private property rights. Second, in locating the application of neoliberalization in specific historically and geographically contingent contexts, it emphasizes what Sparke terms the "*dis*locatable" idealism of neoliberalism (Sparke 2006), both through generating alternatives and through demonstrating how ostensibly neoliberal reforms may be congruent with other political agendas. In so doing, it enables us to see that neoliberalism is not monolithic – and that it creates political opportunities that may be progressive. For example, some neoliberal reforms may be congruent with the goals of alter-globalization activists – such as decentralization leading to greater community control of water resources. Third, it reminds us to pay attention to the multiplicity of reforms that typically occur when "neoliberalizing nature", not all of which focus on property rights. Specifically, the typology presented in Table 12.1 allows us to refine our academic analyses and activist responses to different types of neoliberalization, which vary significantly, opening up the creation of a range of alternative community water economies (Table 12.4).

Many of these alternatives, it should be noted, are not produced in reaction to neoliberalization, but rather resuscitate or develop new approaches to governing the relationship between the hydrological cycle, and socio-natural economies and polities. Some aspects of these reforms are congruent with a neoliberal agenda, but the work of alter-globalization activists reminds us that they need not be subsumed by neoliberalization. Rather, these reforms open up new political ecological and socio-natural relationships through which an ethic of care – for non-humans as well as humans – can be developed. As this paper has argued, this "alter-globalization" agenda necessitates a refinement of our conceptual frameworks of neoliberalization, accounting for multiple modes of property rights and service provision. This conceptual reframing allows us both to accurately analyze neoliberalization in situ and also to generate politically progressive strategies with which to enact more equitable political ecologies – particularly if our definitions of prospective "commoners" are porous enough to include non-humans.

Notes

1   The 1992 International Conference on Water and the Environment set out what became known as the "Dublin Principles": including the principle that "water has an economic value in all its competing uses and should be recognized as an economic good". The Dublin Principles have been adopted by numerous international, multilateral and bilateral agencies. For assessments and critiques of commercialization in the water sector, see Bakker (2004), Finger and Allouche (2002), Huffaker and Whittlesey (2003), Johnstone and Wood (2001), Kaika (2003), Kijne (2001), Kloezen (1998), Kumar and Singh (2001), Landry (1998), McDonald and Ruiters (2005), Shirley (2002), Takahashi (2001), and Ward and Michelsen (2002).

2   For an NGO perspective critical of water privatization, see the Council of Canadians Blue Planet Project (http://www.canadians.org/blueplanet/index2.html). For academic studies critical of the privatization process, with a focus on developing countries, see the Municipal Services Project website (http://qsilver.queensu.ca/~mspadmin). The US-based Public Citizen runs a campaign on water supply (http://www. citizen.org/cmep/Water/). The Global Water Partnership is an influential network of companies, governments, and lending agencies committed to the Rio-Dublin principles (http://www. gwpforum.org/). For an international public sector union perspective, see the PSIRU website (http://www.psiru.org).

3   See, for example, articles in the recent special issue of *CNS* 16(1) (2005), or in the special issue of *Geoforum* on neoliberal nature (2004: 35(3)) edited by James McCarthy and Scott Prudham.

4   The International Covenant on Economic, Social and Cultural Rights, one of the keystones of international human rights law. None of the United Nations conventions on human rights (except article 24 of the Convention on the Rights of the Child) explicitly recognizes the right to water (Morgan 2004).

5   The Committee on Economic, Social and Cultural Rights (CESCR) is the body of independent experts that monitors implementation of the International Covenant on Economic, Social and Cultural Rights by its State parties.

6   These declarations include the Cochabamba Declaration, the Group of Lisbon's Water Manifesto (Petrella 2001), and the Declaration of the P8 (the world's poorest eight countries, organized as a counterpart to the G8) at their fourth summit in 2000.

7   Campaigns include the UK-based "Right to Water" (http://www.righttowater.org.uk) and "Blue October" campaigns, the Canada-based "Friends of the Right to Water Campaign", and the US-based "Water for All" campaign and "Green Cross" campaign for an international convention on the right to water (http://www.watertreaty.org).

8   The Constitution of the Republic of South Africa guarantees the right of citizens access to sufficient water (Act 108 of 1996, section 7(2)).

9   For example, water is defined as collective property ("waqf"), with water available free to the public, under Islam (Faruqui, Biswas and Bino 2003).

10 As recognized by the UN Committee in its comment on the human right to water, which stated that, in permitting third parties (such as the private sector) in addition to state actors to supply water, an additional burden is placed upon regulatory frameworks, including "independent monitoring, genuine public participation, and imposition of penalties for non-compliance" (ECOSOC 2002, article 24).

11 See Frérot (2006). Antoine Frérot was, at the time, the Director General of Veolia (one of the two largest private water companies in the world).

12 Veolia's French language website states, for example, that "L'eau est considérée a la fois comme un bien economique, social, ecologique et comme un droit humain" ["Water is considered an economic, social and ecological good as well as a human right"], http://www.veoliaeau.com/gestion-durable/gestion-durable/eau-pour-tous/bien-commun. See also the Open Forum on "Water: Property or Human Right?" at the 2004 Davos Forum, http://gaia.unit.net/wef/worldeconomicforum_annualmeeting2006/default.aspx?sn=15810

13 The Ministerial Declaration of the Hague on Water Security in the twenty-first century followed the inter-ministerial meeting known as the "2nd World Water Forum" in 2000. See http://www.worldwaterforum.net.

14 Commodification entails the creation of an economic good through the application of mechanisms to appropriate and standardize a class of goods or services, enabling them to be sold at a price determined through market exchange.

15 The classic definition of a market failure is a case in which a market fails to efficiently allocate goods and services, due to the "failure" to meet assumptions of standard neoclassical economic models. For example, market failures occur when property rights are not clearly defined or are unenforceable, when goods are non-excludable and non-rivalrous ("public goods"), when prices do not incorporate full costs or benefits ("externalities"), when information is incomplete, or in a situation of monopoly.

16 See, for example, the on-line chatroom at http://www.waterjustice.org; the website of the second alternative world water forum (http://www.fame2005.org).

17 See archived meeting session history on the Advisory Board website: http://www.unsgab.org.

References

ADB (2003) *Beyond Boundaries: Extending Services to the Urban Poor.* Manila: Asian Development Bank.

Alberta Environment (2003) *Water for Life: Alberta's Strategy for Sustainability.* Edmonton: Alberta Environment.

Anderson T and Leal D (2001) *Free Market Environmentalism.* New York: Palgrave.

Angel D (2000) The environmental regulation of privatized industry in Poland. *Environment and Planning C: Government and Policy* 18(5):575–92.

Aquafed (2006) Statement on the right to water and role of local governments by Gérard Payen, during the opening session of the World Water Forum. http://www.aquafed.org/pdf/WWF4-opening_GP_RTW-LocGov_Pc_2006-03-16.pdf.

Assies W (2003) David versus Goliath in Cochabamba: Water rights, neoliberalism, and the revival of social protest in Bolivia. *Latin-American-Perspectives* 30(3):14–36.

Bailey R (2005) Water is a human right: How privatization gets water to the poor. *Reason Magazine* 17 August. http://www.reason.com/news/show/34992.html.

Bakker K (2000) Privatizing water, producing scarcity: The Yorkshire drought of 1995. *Economic Geography* 96(1):4–27.

Bakker K (2001) Paying for water: Water pricing and equity in England and Wales. *Transactions of the Institute of British Geographers* 26(2):143–64.

Bakker K (2004) *An Uncooperative Commodity: Privatizing Water in England and Wales.* Oxford: Oxford University Press.

Bakker K (2005) Neoliberalizing nature? Market environmentalism in water supply in England and Wales. *Annals of the Association of American Geographers* 95(3):542–65.

Barlow M and Clarke T (2003) *Blue Gold: The Fight to Stop the Corporate Theft of the World's Water.* New York: Stoddart.

Bauer C (1998) Slippery property rights: Multiple water uses and the neoliberal model in Chile, 1981–1995. *Natural Resources Journal* 38:109–54.

Berkes F (1989) *Common Property Resources: Ecology and Community-based Sustainable Development.* London: Belhaven Press.

Bernstein S (2001) *The Compromise of Liberal Environmentalism.* New York: Columbia University Press.

Blokland M, Braadbaart O and Schwartz K (2001) *Private Business, Public Owners.* The Hague and Geneva: Ministry of Housing, Spatial Planning, and Development and the Water Supply and Sanitation Collaborative Council.

Bond P (2002) *Unsustainable South Africa: Environment, Development, and Social Protest.* London: Merlin Press.

Bond P (2004a) Water commodification and decommodification narratives: Pricing and policy debates from Johannesburg to Kyoto to Cancun and back. *Capitalism Nature Socialism* 15(1):7–25.

Bond P (2004b) Decommodification and deglobalisation: Strategic challenges for African social movements. *Afriche e Oriente* 7(4).

Bradshaw M (2004) The market, Marx and sustainability in a fishery. *Antipode* 36(1):66–85.

Bridge G (2004) Mapping the bonanza: Geographics of mining investment in an era of neoliberal reform. *The Professional Geographer* 56(3):406–21.

Bridge G and Jonas A (2002) Governing nature: The re-regulation of resource access, production, and consumption. *Environment and Planning A (guest editorial)* 34:759–66.

Bridge G, McManus P and Marsden T (2003) The next new thing? Biotechnology and its discontents. *Geoforum* 34(2):165–74.

Castree N (2005) The epistemology of particulars: Human Geography, case studies, and "context". *Geoforum* 36(5):541–666.

Cleaver F (2000) Moral ecological rationality, institutions, and the management of common property resources. *Development and Change* 31(2):361–83.

DFID (1998) *Better Water Services in Developing Countries: Public-Private Partnership – The Way Ahead.* London: Department for International Development.

Dinar A (2000) *The Political Economy of Water Pricing Reforms.* Washington: World Bank.

Dubreuil C (2005) *The Right to Water: From Concept to Implementation.* World Water Council.

Dubreuil C (2006) *Synthesis on the Right to Water at the 4th World Water Forum, Mexico.* World Water Council.

ECOSOC (2002) General comment 15. Geneva: United Nations Committee on Economic, Social and Cultural Rights.

Estache A and Rossi C (2002) How different is the efficiency of public and private water companies in Asia? *World Bank Economic Review* 16(1):139–48.

Faruqui N, Biswas A and Bino M (2003) *La gestion de l'eau selon l'Islam.* CRDI/Editions: Karthala.

Finger M and Allouche J (2002) *Water Privatisation: Transnational Corporations and the Re-regulation of the Water Industry.* London: Spon Press.

Franceys R (forthcoming) Customer committees, economic regulation and the Water Framework Directive. *Journal of Water Supply: Research and Technology–Aqua.*

Frérot A (2006) Parce que ce droit est fondamental, il doit devenir effectif. *Le Monde* 17 March.

Gandy M (2004) Rethinking urban metabolism: Water, space and the modern city. *City* 8(3):363–79.

Gibbs D and Jonas A (2000) Governance and regulation in local environmental policy: The utility of a regime approach. *Geoforum* 34(3):299–313.

Gibson-Graham J K (2006) *A Postcapitalist Politics.* Minneapolis: University of Minnesota Press.

Glassman J (2006) Primitive accumulation, accumulation by dispossession, accumulation by "extra-economic" means. *Progress in Human Geography* 30(5):608–25.

Gleick P (1998) The human right to water. *Water Policy* 1:487–503.

Goldman M (2005) *Imperial Nature: The World Bank and the Making of Green Neoliberalism.* New Haven, CT: Yale University Press.

Haddad B (2000) *Rivers of Gold: Designing Markets to Allocate Water in California.* Washington: Island Press.

Hammer L (2004) Indigenous peoples as a catalyst for applying the human right to water. *International Journal on Minority and Group Rights* 10:131–61.

Harvey D (2005) *A Short History of Neoliberalism.* Oxford: Oxford University Press.

Hassan J (1998) *A History of Water in Modern England and Wales.* Manchester: Manchester University Press.

Huffaker R and Whittlesey N (2003) A theoretical analysis of economic incentive policies encouraging agricultural water conservation. *International Journal of Water Resources Development* 19(1):3753.

Hukka J J and Katko T S (2003) Refuting the paradigm of water services privatization. *Natural Resources Forum* 27(2):142–55.

Ignatieff M (2003) *Human Rights as Politics and Idolatry.* Princeton: Princeton University Press.

Johnston B R (2003) The political ecology of water: An introduction. *Capitalism Nature Socialism* 14(3):73–90.

Johnston J, Gismondi M and Goodman J (2006) *Nature's Revenge: Reclaiming Sustainability in an Age of Corporate Globalization*. Toronto: Broadview Press.

Johnstone N and Wood L (2001) *Private Firms and Public Water. Realising Social and Environmental Objectives in Developing Countries*. London: International Institute for Environment and Development.

Kaika M (2003) The Water Framework Directive: a new directive for a changing social, political and economic European framework. *European Planning Studies* 11(3):299–316.

Katko T (2000) *Water! Evolution of Water Supply and Sanitation in Finland from the mid-1800s to 2000*. Tampere: Finnish Water and Waste Water Works Association.

Kay J (1996) Regulating private utilities: The customer corporation. *Journal of Cooperative Studies* 29(2):28–46.

Kijne J W (2001) Lessons learned from the change from supply to demand water management in irrigated agriculture: A case study from Pakistan. *Water Policy* 3(2):109–23.

Kloezen W H (1998) Water markets between Mexican water user associations. *Water Policy* 1:437–55.

Kumar M D and Singh O P (2001) Market instruments for demand management in the face of scarcity and overuse of water in Gujarat, Western India. *Water Policy* 3(5):387–403.

Kymlicka W (1995) *Multicultural Citizenship: A Liberal Theory of Minority Rights*. Oxford: Oxford University Press.

Landry C (1998) Market transfers of water for environmental protection in the Western United States. *Water Policy* 1:457–469.

Laurie N and Marvin S (1999) Globalisation, neo-liberalism and negotiated development in the Andes: Bolivian water and the Misicuni dream. *Environment and Planning A* 31:1401–15.

Laxer G and Soron D (2006) *Not for Sale: Decommodifying Public Life*. Toronto: Broadview Press.

Lorrain D (1997) Introduction – the socio-economics of water services: The invisible factors. In Lorrain D (ed) *Urban Water Management – French Experience Around the World* (pp 1–30). Levallois Perret: Hydrocom.

Maddock T (2004) Fragmenting regimes: How water quality regulation is changing political-economic landscapes. *Geoforum* 35(2):217–30.

Mansfield B (2004a) Neoliberalism in the oceans: "Rationalization", property rights, and the commons question. *Geoforum* 35(3):313–26.

Mansfield B (2004b) Rules of privatization: Contradictions in neoliberal regulation of North Pacific fisheries. *Annals of the Association of American Geographers* 94(3):565–84.

McAfee K (2003) Neoliberalism on the molecular scale. Economic and genetic reductionism in biotechnology battles. *Geoforum* 34(2):203–19.

McCarthy J (2004) Privatizing conditions of production: trade agreements as neoliberal environmental governance. *Geoforum* 35(3):327–41.

McCarthy J (2005) Commons as counter-hegemonic projects. *Capitalism Nature Socialism* 16(1):9–24.

McCarthy J and Prudham S (2004) Neoliberal nature and the nature of neoliberalism. *Geoforum* 35(3):275–283.

McDonald D and Ruiters G (2005) *The Age of Commodity: Water Privatization in Southern Africa*. London: Earthscan.

Mehta L (2001) Water, difference, and power: Unpacking notions of water "users" in Kutch, India. *International Journal of Water* 1(3–4).

Mehta L (2003) Problems of publicness and access rights: Perspectives from the water domain. In Kaul I, Conceicao P, Le Goulven K and Mendoza R (eds) *Providing Global Public Goods: Managing Globalization* (pp 556–75). New York: Oxford University Press and United Nations Development Program.

Mehta L, Leach M and Scoones I (2001) Editorial: Environmental governance in an uncertain world. *IDS Bulletin* 32(4).

Morgan B (2004a) The regulatory face of the human right to water. *Journal of Water Law* 15(5):179–86.

Morgan B (2004b) Water: frontier markets and cosmopolitan activism. *Soundings: a Journal of Politics and Culture* Issue on "The Frontier State" (27):10–24.

Morgan B (2005) Social protest against privatization of water: Forging cosmopolitan citizenship? In Cordonier Seggier M C and Weeramantry J (eds) *Sustainable Justice: Reconciling International Economic, Environmental and Social Law*. The Hague: Martinus Nijhoff.

Mosse D (1997) The symbolic making of a common property resource: History, ecology and locality in a tank-irrigated landscape in South India. *Development and Change* 28(3):467–504.

Mutua M (2002) *Human Rights: A Political and Cultural Critique*. Philadelphia: University of Pennsylvania Press.

Narain S (2006) Community-led alternatives to water management: India case study. Background paper: Human Development Report 2006. New York: United Nations Development Programme.

Olivera O and Lewis T (2004) *Cochabamba! Water War in Bolivia*. Boston: South End Press.

Ostrom E (1990) *Governing the Commons: The Evolution of Institutions for Collective Action*. New York: Cambridge University Press.

Ostrom E and Keohane R (eds) (1995) *Local Commons and Global Interdependence: Heterogeneity and Cooperation in Two Domains*. Cambridge, MA: Harvard University, Centre for International Affairs.

Page B and Bakker K (2005) Water governance and water users in a privatized water industry: Participation in policy-making and in water services provision – a case study of England and Wales. *International Journal of Water* 3(1):38–60.

Perrault T (2006) From the Guerra del Agua to the Guerra del Gas: Resource governance, popular protest and social justice in Bolivia. *Antipode* 38(1):150–72.

Petrella R (2001) *The Water Manifesto: Arguments for a World Water Contract*. London and New York: Zed Books.

Ponniah T (2004) Democracy vs empire: Alternatives to globalization presented at the World Social Forum. *Antipode* 36(1):130–33.

Ponniah T and Fisher W F (eds) (2003) *Another World is Possible: Popular Alternatives to Globalization at the World Social Forum*. New York: Zed Press.

Potanski T and Adams W (1998) Water scarcity, property regimes, and irrigation management in Sonjo, Tanzania. *Journal of Development Studies* 34(4):86–16.

Prudham W S (2004) Poisoning the well: Neoliberalism and the contamination of municipal water in Walkerton, Ontario. *Geoforum* 35(3):343–59.

PSIRU (2005) *Public Public Partnerships in Health and Essential Services*. University of Greenwich, Public Services International Research Unit.

PSIRU (2006) *Public-Public Partnerships as a Catalyst for Capacity Building and Institutional Development: Lessons from Stockholm Vatten's Experience in the Baltic Region*. University of Greenwich, Public Services International Research Unit.

Public Citizen (2002) *Public–Public Partnerships: A Backgrounder on Successful Water/Wastewater Reengineering Programs*. Washington: Public Citizen and Food and Water Watch.

Robbins P (2003) Transnational corporations and the discourse of water privatization. *Journal of International Development* 15:1073–1082.

Robertson M (2004) The neoliberalization of ecosystem services: Wetland mitigation banking and problems in environmental governance. *Geoforum* 35(3):361–73.

Rogers P, de Silva R, et al (2002) Water is an economic good: How to use prices to promote equity, efficiency, and sustainability. *Water Policy* 4(1):1–17.

Rorty R (1993) Human rights, rationality, and sentimentality. In S Shute and S Hurley (eds) *On Human Rights: The Oxford Amnesty Lectures*. New York: Basic Books.

Roy A (1999) *The Cost of Living*. London: Modern Library.

Salman S and McInerney-Lankford S (2004) *The Human Right to Water: Legal and Policy Dimensions*. Washington DC: World Bank.

Scott J (1998) *Seeing Like a State: How Certain Schemes to Improve the Human Condition have Failed*. New Haven: Yale University Press.

Segerfeldt F (2005) *Water For Sale: How Business and the Market Can Resolve the World's Water Crisis*. London: Cato Institute.

Shirley M (2002) *Thirsting for Efficiency*. London: Elsevier.

Shiva V (2002) *Water Wars: Privatization, Pollution and Profit*. London: Pluto Press.

Smets H (2006) Diluted view of water as a right: 4th World Water Forum. *Environmental Policy and Law* 36(2):88–93.

Smith L (2004) The murky waters of the second wave of neoliberalism: Corporatization as a service delivery model in Cape Town. *Geoforum* 35(3):375–93.

Sparke M (2006) Political geography: Political geographies of globalization (2) – governance. *Progress in Human Geography* 30(3):357–72.

Squatriti P (1998) *Water and Society in Early Medieval Italy, A.D. 400–1000*. Cambridge: Cambridge University Press.

St Martin K (2005) Disrupting enclosure in the New England fisheries. *Capitalism Nature Socialism* 16(1):63–80.

Susilowati I and Budiata L (2003) An introduction of co-management approach into Babon River management in Semarang, Central Java, Indonesia. *Water Science & Technology* 48(7):173–80.

Swyngedouw E (2004) *Social Power and the Urbanization of Water*. Oxford: Oxford University Press.

Swyngedouw E (2005) Dispossessing H_2O: The contested terrain of water privatization. *Capitalism Nature Socialism* 16(1):81–98.

Takahashi K (2001) Globalization and management of water resources: Development opportunities and constraints of diversified developing countries. *International Journal of Water Resources Development* 17(4):481–88.

TNI (2005) *Reclaiming Public Water: Achievements, Struggles and Visions from Around the World*. Amsterdam: Transnational Institute.

TNI (2006) *Public Water for All: The Role of Public-Public Partnerships*. Amsterdam: Transnational Institute and Corporate Europe Observatory.

Trawick P (2003) Against the privatization of water: An indigenous model for improving existing laws and successfully governing the commons. *World Development* 31(6):977–96.

UNCSD (2005) *Report on the Thirteenth Session*. New York: UN Commission on Sustainable Development. E/CN.17/2005/12.

UNDP (2003) *Millenium Development Goals: A Compact for Nations to End Human Poverty.* New York: United Nations Development Program.

UNDP (2006) *Beyond Scarcity: Power, Poverty, and the Global Water Crisis: UN Human Development Report 2006.* New York: United Nations Development Programme, Human Development Report Office.

UN Economic and Social Council (2003) *Economic, Social and Cultural Rights.* Report submitted to the 59th session of the Commission on Human Rights, by the Special Rapporteur on the Right to Food. E/CN.4/2003/54.

UNWWAP (2006) *Water: A Shared Responsibility.* New York: United Nations World Water Assessment Program.

Wade R (1998) *Village Republics: Economic Conditions for Collective Action in South India.* Cambridge: Cambridge University Press.

Ward F A and Michelson A (2002) The economic value of water in agriculture: concepts and policy applications. *Water Policy* 4(5):423–46.

Walker D L (1983) The effect of European Community directives on water authorities in England and Wales. *Aqua* 4:145–47.

WHO (2003) *The Right to Water.* Geneva: World Health Organisation.

Winpenny J (1994) *Managing Water as an Economic Resource.* London: Routledge.

Winpenny J (2003) *Financing Water for All: Report of the World Panel on Financing Water Infrastructure.* Geneva: World Water Council/Global Water Partnership/Third World Water Forum.

Zaidi A (2001) *From Lane to City: The Impact of the Orangi Pilot Project's Low Cost Sanitation Model.* London: WaterAid.

Part III

Explaining the Relationship between Globalization and the Environment

Introduction

This section brings together four pieces that set out to explain how globalization is affecting the environment. The first by Clapp and Dauvergne lays out a framework of four ways of looking at environmental problems, and the following pieces are examples of those approaches. The World Bank chapter exhibits a market environmentalist position on how to solve the problem. The Newell piece includes political economy and political ecology in what can be seen as a "social green" approach to globalization and the environment. Finally the Levy, Haas, and Keohane piece provides a classic "institutionalist" approach to solving global environmental issues. The issues covered in the pieces are diverse, and reveal quite different proposals of ways forward.

In their widely used teaching book on global environmental politics *Paths to a Green World*, Jennifer Clapp and Peter Dauvergne outline a series of different approaches or worldviews regarding the relationship between globalization and the environment. The framework places scholars, policy-makers, bureaucrats, business people and activists who consider themselves environmentalists into four categories. Their categorization is based on each group's beliefs about the roots of environmental problems, on their sense of whether the Earth is fragile or resilient, and whether they think governments, firms, or individuals are the most likely to contribute to solving the problems. Market liberal environmentalists – who we heard from in the last section – acknowledge failures of the economic system to include ecological impacts, and believe that pricing pollution or establishing trading systems provide the best ways of managing them. By 'internalizing' environmental costs, their true value gets factored into decisions about production and investment. Coming from a scientific background, bioenvironmentalists see problems inevitably coming from human societies that ignore ecological rules, damage habitats, and

The Globalization and Environment Reader, First Edition. Edited by Peter Newell and J. Timmons Roberts.
Editorial material and organization © 2017 John Wiley & Sons, Ltd. Published 2017 by John Wiley & Sons, Ltd.

contaminate global systems. As well as tighter controls on population growth and consumption, they are also comfortable with a more coercive role for global institutions in scientifically managing the global ecosystem. Institutionalists see environmental problems as worsening but manageable, and propose better design of government institutions and United Nations or other intergovernmental agencies as the way to manage them. Finally social greens see the roots of environmental damage in the unequal power within economic systems, and a globalizing capitalist economy in particular, and focus on addressing inequality and injustice as critical to addressing environmental problems.

What we find most useful about this categorization is that it acknowledges the roots and validity of a wide range of approaches to understanding globalization and its impacts on the environment, and clarifies why different groups propose such different paths to addressing environmental problems. In some ways, these four categories could describe the scholars we work with in environmental studies programs in universities, the individuals of all four sorts we interact with at UN climate change negotiations, and the balance of readings in this volume. They also consider what each of these four groups believes are the impacts of globalization on the environment – potentially positive (market liberals and institutionalists) or almost always destructive (bioenvironmentalists, social greens). Their framework is a gross simplification, of course: Clapp and Dauvergne anticipate a potential critique of their piece – that there are many other categories of worldviews, that single individuals might hold several of these views, and that people might shift depending on the issue of concern.

In their flagship annual *World Development Report*, the World Bank's research department seeks to show its leadership on emerging issues and suggest market-friendly pathways forward. As market liberals (following Clapp and Dauvergne's typology), they tend to focus on market failures such as when prices don't include key issues like environmental damage, and damaging government policies, like fossil fuel subsidies that inflate demand. Solutions in World Bank reports almost inevitably involve eliminating barriers to economic growth, decreasing subsidies, and increasing market-based incentives.

The bank's 2003 volume was a follow-on to a major report published in 1992, in which the bank pioneered and pushed forward economic approaches to major environmental problems. In both cases, they were timed to support, inform, and direct thinking at the major UN environmental summits discussed in the Editors' Introduction and many pieces in this volume. The 2003 report stated plainly upfront that economic growth itself, and basic development, required attention to protecting the environment and "transforming" society. To push thinking in that direction, they attempted to persuade economists and planners to think further into the future: 20 to 50 years.

Remarkably, they acknowledge that despite their own best efforts, that global poverty persists, inequality is widening, conflicts are widespread, air, water, soil, forests and biodiversity are threatened and worsening. They hope to foster the shaping of a "poverty-eliminating growth path that integrates social and environmental concerns in pursuit of the goal of sustained improvements in well-being". They acknowledge globalization's negative effects "if institutions … do not evolve fast enough to deal with the adverse spillovers." But characteristically they point to the opportunities that will come with proper management of the global commons, ones that will come as the global population growth slows and more people move to cities, for example. Related to this, the report seeks to bring a spatial perspective to improve understanding of problems of integrating economic, social, and environmental problems. They conclude by acknowledging that institutions to manage economic globalization are far ahead of those set up to address environmental and social change. In reading these sometimes progressive ideas it is important to remember when reading World Bank reports that they are written by the "research unit" of the bank, which is quite separate from its policy and lending arms.

Peter Newell, in a chapter from a larger book on "The Political Ecology of Globalization," takes us on a whirlwind tour of the landscape from a "political ecology" perspective. That term has been used in many ways, and he acknowledges it is a very eclectic field, taking on "questions of access to material and natural resources, and issues of resistance, equity, and justice in the negotiation and distribution of social and environmental benefits at multiple scales." This makes it a "social green" approach, in Clapp and Dauvergne's framework. Political ecology's contribution often is to show the local impacts of global capitalist production, extraction of resources, and exchange, in the far corners of the world. But Newell describes how the "dynamic also runs the other way," as local resistance against mining or logging or protests against particular sites of production force changes in national and global markets and systems of regulation. Newell describes the value of combing a political ecology with a political economy approach, focusing on how the vast changes occurring as the world's economy strengthen the hand of transnational companies that can threat to take "flight" to lower-regulation or lower-priced locations of production. He sees this threat as critical in driving the market-based environmental approaches described in the last section, as local and national governments themselves fear "pricing out" the firms they need to stay in their towns or countries to pay taxes and create jobs. Newell describes how environmental crises are often just displaced from one place to another: as companies and governments become aware of environmental crises such as climate change, they often take steps that create new environmental problems for other people because they are not tackling the causes of them. This is the case with the United States creating standards for how much biofuels must be used in gasoline, which in turn has driven land grabs to build plantations in Africa and disastrous rises in corn price across the world.

Newell raises a core question of this book and what we consider the trillion-dollar question of our day: can capitalism reinvent itself to function without fossil fuels? He answers that capitalism is constantly reinventing itself, based on different technologies and organizations of production and consumption. He then turns to look for positive signs of a low-carbon economy emerging, and finds several. Some insurance companies are leading the way in preparing for climate risks, and active movements to divest from fossil fuels are making headway. But fossil fuel companies still enjoy vast privileges in our economic system. The globalizing economy has empowered a new capitalist class, he argues, which has itself driven the neoliberal turn described in the last section, with free-trade treaties and new flexible styles of regulation. But following Antonio Gramsci's insights, Newell points out that the powerful never entirely get their way, and are forced to accommodate critics "and make concessions in the name of preserving the power of an historic bloc" that holds power. In short, Newell argues that the fields of political ecology, international political economy, and global environmental politics can all provide "analytical tools and resources that allow us to make sense of what is going on, on whose behalf and with what consequences." Everything is at stake, and nothing is certain, or simple.

A classic example of an "institutionalist" approach to global environmental issues, we here excerpt "Institutions for the Earth," a summary of an influential MIT Press book of the same name by political scientists Marc Levy, Peter Haas, and Robert Keohane. It was published just after the huge United Nations Conference on Environment and Development, better known as the Rio Earth Summit, or UNCED. They directly confront those who would say that international bodies cannot address big problems like the environmental crisis, pointing to cholera, the slave trade, and nuclear weapons testing as issues "successfully managed against great odds with the help of international institutions." They report on the outcomes of international efforts on seven issue areas: leaking oil tanker ships, acid rain, ozone, pollution of the North and Baltic Seas, overfishing, overpopulation, and pesticide abuse, and use those lessons to draw larger conclusions.

Levy et al. make three very clear points about why institutions might matter for saving the Earth. First, international institutions can help shape a positive agenda on environmental problems, bringing together scientific information and amplifying the political consensus and sometimes promoting greater concern among "laggard" governments. Second, they can help build treaties and policies which are agreed internationally, raising the profile of the issue. And third, they can boost better national policies to get the sources of pollution under control, and help those governments build their capacity to do the work of controlling issues like pollution or overfishing. This is especially important for the poorest states, where a big impact can come from aid and assistance that is directly transferred to create environmental agencies. They also suggest how a big impact can be generated from creating networks between organizations, like NGOs and those agencies, within those countries and across regions and the globe. They observe that "institutions can serve as magnifiers of public pressure when they foster competition among governments to be more pro-environmental." Unusually, they finish with direct advice to the then new Secretary General of the UN with regard to the UNCED process and in particular in relation to the climate change negotiations. Their greatest advice was to build pro-environmental coalitions. "Create and manipulate dynamic processes by which governments change conceptions of their interests and mobilize and coordinate complex policy networks involving governments, NGOs, subunits of governments, and industrial groups, as well as a variety of international organizations that have different priorities and political styles." They call for nonpartisan and untainted scientific information creation, and in the case of climate change, for public education and some "shaming" of laggard countries.

This piece and the World Bank's on the value of market-based solutions both offer widely held positions, and followers of these approaches will find useful material in each. It is also critical for all to understand well the positions of those with differing positions, in their own words. The missing fourth worldview, as it is outlined by Clapp and Dauvergne, is bioenvironmentalism. Different strands of this thinking can be found by readers in the work of Paul and Anne Ehrlich, William Ophuls, or Herman Daly, for example. Our estimation is that these four perspectives will continue to co-exist uneasily in the world of environmental politics (and environmental studies programs in universities). All may contain elements of an effective approach to addressing global environmental issues. But though they may be equally valid, some are more equal than others, in terms of the power they wield over key decision-makers charged with managing the relationship between globalization and the environment.

13

Peril or Prosperity? Mapping Worldviews of Global Environmental Change (2011)

Jennifer Clapp and Peter Dauvergne

The sun could well engulf the earth in about 7 or 8 billion years. "So what," you might shrug. "The extinction of earth, beyond the horizon of human time, ridiculous, not worth imagining." Yet some environmentalists believe that waves of smaller disasters – like global warming, deforestation, and biodiversity loss – are already destroying the planet. Without doubt, too, many of the world's poorest people have already collided with their sun, dying from disease, starvation, war, and abuse. The beginning of the end, these environmentalists lament, is already upon us. We, as a species, are now beyond the earth's carrying capacity, a trend accelerating in the era of globalization. Unless we act immediately with resolve and sacrifice, in a mere hundred years or so, humanity itself will engulf the earth. The future is one of peril.

Many environmentalists rebel against such catastrophic visions. Yes, there are undeniable ecological problems – like the depletion of the ozone layer, the pollution of rivers and lakes, and the collapse of some fish stocks – but some ecological disturbance is inevitable, and much is correctable through goodwill and cooperation. There is no crisis or looming crisis: to think so is to misread the history of human progress. This history shows the value of positive thinking, of relying on human ingenuity to overcome obstacles and create ever-greater freedom and wealth with which we can ensure a better natural environment. Globalization is merely the latest, though perhaps the most potent, engine of human progress. The future is one of prosperity.

Who is correct? Do the pessimists need Prozac? Do the optimists need a stroll through a toxic waste dump in the developing world? Less flippantly, what is the middle ground between these two extremes? What are the causes and consequences

Jennifer Clapp and Peter Dauvergne. 2011. *Paths to a Green World: The Political Economy of the Global Environment*. Cambridge: Massachusetts Institute of Technology Press. pp. 1–17. Reproduced with permission from MIT Press.

of global environmental change? Are ecological problems really as severe as some claim? Does the cumulative impact of these problems constitute a crisis? How is the global community handling them? Why are the efforts to resolve some problems more successful than others? Why are environmental problems worse in some parts of the world? And what is the relationship to global political and economic activity? These are tough questions, and we do not pretend to know the answers with absolute certainty. A quick survey of the typical answers to these questions reveals an almost endless stream of contradictory explanations and evidence. Each answer can seem remarkably logical and persuasive. The result for the thoughtful and "objective" observer is often dismay or confusion.

Given this, how does one even begin to understand global environmental change? It helps, we believe, to begin with the big picture, rather than delving immediately into in-depth studies of particular environmental issues. Understanding this big picture is, in our view, necessary *before* we can fully understand the various interpretations of the *specific* causes and consequences of environmental problems. In the quest for knowledge and a role in a world overloaded with information and experts, far too often this larger picture is ignored – or at least poorly understood. For problems as intricate as global environmental ones, this can lead to muddled analysis and poorly formulated recommendations. Without this broad perspective, for example, "solving" one problem can ignore other related problems, or create even greater problems elsewhere.

How polities and societies allocate financial, human, and natural resources directly influences how we manage local, national, and ultimately global environments. The issues that shape the relationship between the global political economy and the environment are, of course, often technical and scientific. But they are frequently also socioeconomic and political. Our hope is that by sketching the arguments and assumptions about socioeconomic and political causes with the broadest possible strokes, we will assist readers in a lifelong journey of understanding the causes and consequences of global environmental change, as well as the controversies that surround it. This is a small yet essential step to eventually solving, or at least slowing, some of these problems. To introduce these topics, we map out a new typology of worldviews on the political economy of global environmental change.

Four Environmental Worldviews

We present four main worldviews on global environmental change and its relationship to the global political economy: those of *market liberals, institutionalists, bioenvironmentalists,* and *social greens.* These labels are intentionally transdisciplinary. Many books on the global environment confine the analysis to one disciplinary box – by limiting it, say, to political science theories or to economic models. This leaves far too many questions badly answered and far too many questions unasked. But we have had to make some choices. It is, of course, impossible to cover all disciplinary perspectives in one book. In our case we have chosen to rely mostly on the tools of political science, economics, development studies, environmental studies, political geography, and sociology. This focus, we believe, is narrow enough to do justice to the literature in these disciplines while still broad enough to provide new insights into the sources of environmental change and the possible options – both theoretical and practical – for managing it.

These are "ideal" categories, exaggerated to help differentiate between them. They are designed as tools to help simplify a seemingly unmanageable avalanche of conflicting information and analysis. Within each category, we have tried to clump thinkers – not just academics, but equally policymakers and activists – with broadly common assumptions and conclusions. This we hope provides a sense of the debates in the "real" world – that is, within bureaucracies, cabinet meetings, international negotiations, and corporate boardrooms, as well as in classrooms. Our approach, in a sense, tries to capture the societal debates about environment and political economy rather than just the academic debates over the theories of the political economy of the environment.

Naturally, given the breadth of our labels, many disagreements exist among those in each category. We have tried to show the range of views subsumed under each of the four major worldviews, although at the end of this book you may still find that your own beliefs and arguments do not fit neatly into any of these categories. Or you may feel that you hold a mix of views – even ones that at first seem at opposite poles, such as market liberal and social green. This does not mean that our categories are erroneous. Or that you are inconsistent or hypocritical. Or that you should force your views into one category. Instead, it just shows the complexity and diversity of individual views on the issues.

Our typology, moreover, does not cover all possible views, although, while conscious to avoid creating dozens of labels, we do try to give a reasonable range. We only include thinkers who are *environmentalists* – that is, those who write and speak and work to maintain or improve the environment around us. This includes those highly critical of so-called environmental activists or radical greens. An economist at the World Bank is, in our view, just as much an environmentalist as a volunteer at Greenpeace, as long as the economist believes she or he is working for a better environment (however that is defined). Also, we focus principally on economic and political arguments, and tend to give less attention to philosophical and moral ones. Within the political and economic literature, we stress arguments and theories that try to *explain* global environmental change – that is, the literature that looks at an environmental problem and asks: Why is that happening? What is causing it? And what can be done?

With those introductory remarks, we now turn to our typology.

Market Liberals

The analysis of market liberals is grounded in neoclassical economics and scientific research. Market liberals believe that economic growth and high per capita incomes are essential for human welfare and the maintenance of sustainable development. Sustainable development is generally defined by these thinkers along the lines of the

1987 World Commission on Environment and Development (WCED): "development that meets the needs of the present without compromising the ability of future generations to meet their own needs." In terms of improving global environmental conditions, market liberals argue that economic growth (production and consumption) creates higher incomes, which in turn generates the funds and political will to improve environmental conditions. Rapid growth may exacerbate inequalities, as some of the rich become super rich, but in the long run all will be better off. In other words, all boats will rise. Market-liberal analysis along these lines is commonly found, for example, in publications of the World Bank, the World Trade Organization (WTO), and the World Business Council for Sustainable Development (WBCSD), as well as in the media in publications such as *The Economist*.

Market liberals see globalization as a positive force, because it promotes economic growth as well as global integration. They concede that as states pursue economic growth, environmental conditions – such as air and water quality – may deteriorate as governments and citizens give firms more scope to pursue short-term profits, thus stimulating further economic growth. But once a society becomes wealthy, citizens (and in turn governments and business) will raise environmental standards and expectations. *The Economist* magazine explains the global pattern: "Where most of the economic growth has occurred – the rich countries – the environment has become cleaner and healthier. It is in the poor countries, where growth has been generally meagre, that air and water pollution is an increasing hazard to health." The key, market liberals argue, is good policy to ensure that economic growth improves the environment in all countries.

The main drivers of environmental degradation, according to market liberals, are a lack of economic growth, poverty, distortions and failures of the market, and bad policies. The poor are not viewed as unconcerned or ignorant. Rather, to survive – to eat, to build homes, to earn a living – they must exploit the natural resources around them. They are, according to the World Bank, both "victims and agents of environmental damage." It is unrealistic, perhaps even unjust, to ask the poor to consider the implications of their survival for future generations. The only way out of this vicious cycle is to alleviate poverty, for which growth is essential. Restrictive trade and investment policies and a lack of secure property rights all hamper the ability of the market to foster growth and reduce poverty. Market failures – instances where the free market results in an environmentally suboptimal outcome – are viewed as possible causes of some environmental problems, although these are seen as relatively rare in practice. More often, market liberals argue, poor government policies – especially those that distort the market, such as subsidies – are the problem.

Market liberals frequently draw on more moderate estimates of environmental damage and more optimistic scenarios for the future. A few have become famous for declaring that the global environment is nowhere near a state of crisis – such as economist Julian Simon, popular columnist Gregg Easterbrook, and political scientist Bjørn Lomborg. But most recognize that many environmental problems are indeed serious, although all reject the image of the world spinning toward a catastrophic ecological crash. Instead market liberals tend to stress our scientific achievements, our progress, and our ability to reverse and repair environmental problems with ingenuity, technology, cooperation, and adaptation. For these thinkers, population growth and resource scarcity are not major concerns when it comes to environmental quality. A glance at the historical trend of better environmental conditions for all confirms this (especially statistics from the developed world). So do the global data on human well-being, such as medical advances, longer life expectancy, and greater food production. Furthermore, most environmental problems, if not currently responding to efforts to manage them more effectively, at least have the potential to improve in the longer term.

Thinkers from the market-liberal tradition place great faith in the ability of modern science and technology to help societies slip out of any environmental binds that may occur (if, for example, there are unavoidable market failures). Human ingenuity is seen to have no limits. If resources become scarce, or if pollution becomes a problem, humans will discover substitutes and develop new, more environmentally friendly technologies. Market liberals see advances in agricultural biotechnology, for example, as a key answer to providing more food for a growing world population. Their belief in science leaves most market liberals wary of precautionary policies that restrict the use of new technology, unless there is clear scientific evidence to demonstrate it is harmful.

Market liberals believe open and globally integrated markets promote growth, which in turn helps societies find ways to improve or repair environmental conditions. To achieve these goals market liberals call for policy reforms to liberalize trade and investment, foster specialization, and reduce government subsidies that distort markets and waste resources. Governments, too, need to strengthen some institutions, such as institutions to secure property rights or institutions to educate and train the poor to protect the environment. Governments are encouraged to use market-based tools – for example, environmental taxes or tradable pollution permits – to correct situations of genuine market failure. Innovative environmental markets – like a global scheme to trade carbon emissions or niche markets for environmental products such as timber from sustainable sources – and voluntary corporate measures to promote environmental stewardship are also reasonable ways to improve environmental management. But in most cases it is best to let the market allocate resources efficiently. Market liberals, such as the economist Jagdish Bhagwati and the business executive Stephan Schmidheiny, strongly argue that it makes economic sense for firms to improve their environmental performance, and for this reason it makes sense to let the market guide them.

Institutionalists

The ideas of institutionalists are grounded in the fields of political science and international relations. They share many of the broad assumptions and arguments of market liberals – especially the belief in the value of economic growth, globalization, trade, foreign investment, technology, and the notion of sustainable development.

Indeed, moderate institutionalists sit close to moderate market liberals. It is a matter of emphasis. Market liberals stress more the benefits and dynamic: solutions of free markets and technology; institutionalists emphasize the need for stronger global institutions and norms as well as sufficient state and local capacity to constrain and direct the global political economy. Institutions provide a crucial route to transfer technology and funds to the poorest parts of the planet. Institutionalists also worry far more than market liberals about environmental scarcity, population growth, and the growing inequalities between and within states. But they do not see these problems as beyond hope. To address them, they stress the need for strong institutions and norms to protect the common good. Institutionalist analysis is found in publications by organizations such as the United Nations Environment Programme (UNEP) and by many academics who focus their analysis on "regimes" (international environmental agreements and norms) in the fields of political science and law.

Institutionalists see a lack of global cooperation as a key source of environmental degradation. Ineffective cooperation partly arises because of the nature of the sovereign state system, which gives a state supreme authority within its boundaries. In such a system states tend to act in their own interest, generally leaving aside the interest of the global commons. Yet like market liberals, institutionalists *do not* reject the way we have organized political and economic life on the planet. Instead they believe we can overcome the problem of sovereignty as the organizing principle of the international system by building and strengthening global and local institutions that promote state adherence to collective goals and norms. This can be most effectively carried out through global-level environmental agreements and organizations.

The process of globalization makes global cooperation increasingly essential (and increasingly inevitable). But institutionalists stress that unfettered globalization can add to the pressures on the global environment. The task for those worried about the state of the global environment, then, is to guide and channel globalization, so it enhances environmental cooperation and better environmental management. This point has been stressed most forcefully by key policy figures such as former Norwegian Prime Minister Gro Harlem Brundtland in her role in the 1980s as head of the World Commission on Environment and Development and Canadian diplomat Maurice Strong as organizer of global environmental conferences. The aim of this approach is to ensure that global economic policies work to both improve the environment and raise living standards. Controls at all levels of governance, from the local to the national to the global, can help to direct globalization, enhancing the benefits and limiting the drawbacks.

For the global environment, institutionalists believe that institutions need to internalize the principles of sustainable development, including the decision-making processes of state bureaucracies, corporations, and international organizations. Only then will we be able to manage economies and environments effectively – especially for common resources. For many institutionalist academics, like political scientist Oran Young, the most effective and practical means is to negotiate and strengthen international environmental regimes. Many within the policy world, such as in the United Nations Environment Programme, add the need to enhance state and local capacity in developing countries. Thus, many institutionalists call for "environmental aid" for the developing world. It should be stressed, however, that institutionalists do not necessarily support all institutions uncritically. Some point to badly constructed institutions as a source of problems. Many point, too, to the difficulty of trying to measure the implementation and effectiveness of an international agreement or institution. But a defining characteristic of institutionalists is the assumption that institutions matter – that they are valuable – and that what we need to do is reform, not overthrow, them.

Institutionalists also argue that strong global institutions and cooperative norms can help enhance the capacity of *all* states to manage environmental resources. What is needed, from this perspective, is to effectively embed environmental norms in international cooperative agreements and organizations as well as state policies. Along these lines, many institutionalists support the precautionary approach, where states agree to collective action in the face of some scientific uncertainty. Institutionalists also advocate the transfer of knowledge, finances, and technology to developing countries. Organizations like the World Bank, the United Nations Environment Programme, and the Global Environment Facility (GEF) already play a role here. And many institutionalists point to the creation of, and changes within, these organizations as evidence of progress.

Bioenvironmentalists

Inspired by the laws of physical science, bioenvironmentalists stress the biological limits of the earth to support life. The planet is fragile, an ecosystem like any other. Some even see the earth as behaving like a living being, a self-regulating, complex, and holistic superorganism – the so-called Gaia hypothesis, as articulated by environmental scientist James Lovelock. The earth can support life, but only to a certain limit, often referred to as the earth's "carrying capacity." Many bioenvironmentalists see humans as anthropocentric and selfish (or at least self-interested) animals. Some, like the academic William Rees, even see humans as having "a genetic predisposition for unsustainability." All bioenvironmentalists agree that humans as a species now consume far too much of the earth's resources, such that we are near, or indeed have already overstepped, the earth's carrying capacity. Such behavior, without drastic changes, will push the planet toward a fate not much different from the ecological calamity of Easter Island of 300 years ago – where a once-thriving people became over a few centuries "about 2000 wretched individuals … eking out a sparse existence from a denuded landscape and cannibalistic raids on each other's camps." These scholars stress the environmental disasters around us, often citing shocking figures on such problems as overfishing, deforestation, species loss, and unstable weather patterns. Publications of the Worldwatch Institute and the WWF are illustrative of this perspective.

For most bioenvironmentalists population growth is a key source of stress on the earth's limits. The ideas of Thomas Malthus (1766–1834), who in "An Essay on the

Principle of Population" predicted that the human population would soon outstrip food supply, were revived in the late 1960s by writers such as biologist Paul Ehrlich. Sometimes known as neo-Malthusians, these writers argue that global environmental problems ultimately stem from too many people on a planet with finite resources. The principle of sovereignty, which divides the world into artificial territories, aggravates the effects of too many humans, because it violates the principles of ecology and creates what academic Garrett Hardin famously called a "tragedy of the commons." For him, too many people without overarching rules on how to use the commons creates a situation where individuals, rationally seeking to maximize their own gain at the expense of others, overuse and ultimately destroy the commons. This point, stressed by many bioenvironmentalists, is also made by many institutionalists, as discussed earlier.

Many bioenvironmentalists stress, too, that the neoclassical economic assumption of infinite economic growth is a key source of today's global environmental crisis. For these thinkers, a relentless drive to produce ever more in the name of economic growth is exhausting our resources and polluting the planet. Many argue that the drive to pursue ever more economic growth is what has taken the earth beyond its carrying capacity. For bioenvironmentalists, human consumption patterns are as great a problem as population growth, and the two are seen as inextricably linked. They argue that together rising populations and consumption are drawing down the earth's limited resources, and that we must respect the biophysical limits to growth: both for people and economies.

Not all bioenvironmentalists engage directly in discussions on economic globalization, but those that do tend to see globalization as a negative force for the environment. They agree with market liberals that globalization enhances economic growth. But instead of seeing this as positive for the environment, they see it as contributing to further environmental degradation, For them, more growth only means more consumption of natural resources and more stress on waste sinks. Globalization is blamed, too, for spreading Western patterns of consumption into the developing world. With much larger populations and often more fragile ecosystems (especially in the tropics), this spread of consumerism is accelerating the collapse of the global ecosystem. Globalization is also seen to encourage environmentally harmful production processes in poor countries that have lower environmental standards. For these reasons, these bioenvironmentalists argue that we must curtail economic globalization to save the planet.

Solutions proposed by bioenvironmentalists flow logically from their analysis of the causes of environmental damage: we need to curb economic and population growth. Those who focus on the limits to economic growth have been a core group in the field of ecological economics, pioneered by thinkers such as the economist Herman Daly and published in journals such as *Ecological Economics*. This group combines ideas from the physical sciences and economics to develop proposals to revamp economic models to include the notion of physical limits, which involves changing our measures of "progress" and the methods we use to promote it. Only then, these thinkers argue, can we reduce the impact of humans on the planet and prod the world toward a more sustainable global economy. Those bioenvironmentalists who focus more on overpopulation call for measures to lower population growth, like expanding family planning programs in the Third World, and for curbs on immigration to rich countries where consumption problems are the worst. At the more extreme end, some see a world government with coercive powers as the best way to control the human lust to fill all ecological space, destroying it, often inadvertently, in the process.

Social Greens

Social greens, drawing primarily on radical social and economic theories, see social and environmental problems as inseparable. Inequality and domination, exacerbated by economic globalization, are seen as leading to unequal access to resources as well as unequal exposure to environmental harms. While these views have long been important in debates over environment and development, and are themselves a mix of a variety of radical views, scholars in international political economy have only recently recognized them as a distinct perspective.

Many social greens from a more activist stance focus on the destructive effects of the global spread of large-scale industrial life. Accelerated by the process of globalization, large-scale industrialism is seen to encourage inequality characterized by overconsumption by the wealthy while at the same time contributing to poverty and environmental degradation. While agreeing broadly with this analysis, other, more academic-social greens draw on Marxist thought, pointing specifically to capitalism as a primary driver of social and environmental injustice in a globalized world. They argue that capitalism, and its global spread via neocolonial relations between rich and poor countries, not only leads to an unequal distribution of global income, power, and environmental problems, but is a threat to human survival. Also inspired by Marxist thought, some social greens take a neo-Gramscian, or historical materialist perspective, focusing on the way those in power frame and influence ecological problems, primarily hegemonic blocs consisting of large corporations and industrial country governments. Other social greens like Vandana Shiva draw heavily from feminist theory to argue that patriarchal relationships in the global economy are intricately tied to ecological destruction. The key concern of all of these strands of social green thought, then, is inequality and the environmental consequences related to it. Social green analysis can be found in magazines such as *The Ecologist* and in reports of groups such as the International Forum on Globalization (IFG) and the Third World Network (TWN).

Social greens sympathize with bioenvironmentalist arguments that physical limits to economic growth exist. Overconsumption, particularly in rich industrialized countries, is seen by social greens to put a great strain on the global environment. Many, perhaps most prominently Wolfgang Sachs and Edward Goldsmith, see this problem as accelerating in an era of economic globalization. The arguments of social greens on growth and consumption, and on the role of the global economy in accelerating both, are close to bioenvironmentalist arguments. But few social greens accept bioenvironmcntalisi arguments regarding population growth, instead maintaining that overconsumption, particularly among the rich in the First World, is a far greater problem. Unlike bioenvironmentalists, most social greens see population-control policies as a threat to the self-determination of women and the poor.

Whether it is viewed as spreading industrialism or capitalism (or both), social greens uniformly oppose economic globalization, arguing that it is a key factor behind much of what is wrong with the global system. In addition to feeding environmentally destructive growth and consumption, globalization is seen to breed injustice in a number of ways. It exacerbates the inequality within and between countries. It reinforces the domination of the global rich and the marginalization of women, indigenous peoples, and the poor. It assists corporate exploitation of the developing world (especially labor and natural resources). It weakens local community autonomy and imposes new forms of domination that are Western and patriarchal (local customs, norms, and knowledge are lost, replaced by new forms unsuited to these new locations). Globalization is also seen to destroy local livelihoods, leaving large numbers of people disconnected from the environment in both rich and poor countries. This globalization is viewed by many social greens as a continuation of earlier waves of domination and control. In the words of the prominent antiglobalization activist Vandana Shiva, "The 'global' of today reflects a modern version of the global reach of the handful of British merchant adventurers who, as the East India Company, later, the British Empire raided and looted large areas of the world."

From this analysis, it is not surprising that social greens reject the current global economy. Reactive crisis management in a globalized world, social greens believe, will not suffice to save the planet: tinkering will just momentarily stall the crash. In many instances the environmental solutions of market liberals and institutionalists, because they assume globalization brings environmental benefits, are part of the problem. For social greens major reforms are necessary, well beyond, for example, just strengthening institutions or internalizing environmental and social costs into the price of traded goods. Thus social greens, as the work of the International Forum on Globalization exemplifies, call for a dismantling of current global economic structures and institutions. To replace this, many social greens advocate a return to local community autonomy to rejuvenate social relations and restore the natural environment. Localization activist Colin Hines has mapped out a model for how this could occur. It entails a retreat from the large-scale industrial and capitalist life and a move toward local, self-reliant, small-scale economics. These thinkers stress the need to, in the words of some, "think globally, act locally." In other words, understand the global context, while at the same time acting in ways suitable to the local context. These thinkers advocate bioregional and small-scale community development – because they firmly believe that a stronger sense of community will fulfill basic needs and enhance people's quality of life. Such development would help to reduce inequities and levels of consumption that are out of balance with the world's natural limits.

As part of their strategy for promoting community autonomy and localization, social greens also stress the need to empower those voices that the process of economic globalization is marginalizing. They embrace indigenous knowledge systems, for example, arguing these are equally if not more valid than the Western scientific method. The process of economic "development," these critics argue, foists the latter onto the developing world, thus threatening ecologically sound local systems. Many social greens regard local cultural diversity as essential for the maintenance of biological diversity. The erosion of one is seen to lead to the erosion of the other. In advocating local and indigenous empowerment and input, social greens emphasize that effective solutions to environmental problems will continue to remain elusive unless the voices of women, indigenous peoples, and the poor are integrated into the global dialogue on environment and development, as well as into locally specific contexts.

Conclusion

Table 13.1 summarizes the main assumptions and arguments of market liberals, institutionalists, bioenvironmentalists, and social greens. We have tried hard to present these views fairly and accurately. Yet we also stress again that these are "ideal" categories, and within each there are a range of views and more subtle debates. Some authors you will read will fit neatly into one of these categories, while others are more difficult to classify. This just demonstrates the range of possible views. Moreover, there are alliances between various views on different issues, which makes the terrain difficult to map at times. For example, market liberals and institutionalists agree with one another that economic growth and globalization have positive implications for the environment, while social greens and bioenvironmentalists hold the opposite view. And institutionalists and bioenvironmentalists agree that population growth poses a problem for the world's resources, while market liberals and social greens put far less emphasis on this factor.

We stress that we do not want to leave the impression that any one of these is the "correct" view. Each, we believe, contains insights into the sources of today's environmental problems, as well as into potential solutions. Each view has its own logic, which fits with its assumptions. Understanding these views help to explain, too, the often markedly different interpretations of the condition of the global environment. One article, for example, may well declare global warming the most serious threat confronting today's governments. The next article may declare it a hoax, a ploy to raise funds or perhaps to scare world leaders into action. This, we believe, does not mean that there are no facts – or causality – or analysis – or statistics. It also does not mean that some authors lie and deceive. Rather it merely shows how different interpretations and different values – that is, different worldviews – can shape which information an analyst chooses to *emphasize*.

As you proceed through the rest of this book, we urge you to keep an open mind regarding the debates and evidence about the consequences of the global political

Table 13.1 Environmental perspectives

Focus	Market liberals Economies	Institutionalists Institutions	Bioenvironmentalists Ecosystems	Social greens Justice
A global environmental crisis?	No. Some inevitable problems, but overall modern science, technology, ingenuity, and money are improving the global environment.	Not yet. Potential for crisis unless we act now to enhance state capacity and improve the effectiveness of regimes and global institutions.	Yes. Near or beyond earth's carrying capacity. Ecological crisis threatens human survival.	Yes. Social injustice at both local and global levels feeds environmental crisis.
Causes of problems	Poverty and weak economic growth. Market failures and poor government policy (i.e., market distortions such as subsidies as well as unclear property rights) are also partly to blame.	Weak institutions and inadequate global cooperation to correct environmental failures, underdevelopment, and perverse effects of state sovereignty.	Human instinct to overfill ecological space, as seen by overpopulation, excessive economic growth, and overconsumption.	Large-scale industrial life (some say global capitalism), which feeds exploitation (of labor, women, indigenous peoples, the poor, and the environment), and grossly unequal patterns of consumption.
Impact of globalization	Fostering economic growth, a source of progress that will improve the environment in the long run.	Enhancing opportunities for cooperation. Guided globalization enhances human welfare.	Driving unsustainable growth, trade, investment, and debt. Accelerating depletion of natural resources and filling of waste sinks.	Accelerating exploitation, inequalities, and ecological injustice while concurrently eroding local-community autonomy.

The way forward	Promote growth, alleviate poverty, and enhance efficiency, best pursued with globalization. Correct market and policy failures, and use market-based incentives to encourage clean technologies. Promote voluntary corporate greening.	Harness globalization and promote strong global institutions, norms, and regimes that manage the global environment and distribute technology and funds more effectively to developing countries. Build state capacity. Employ precautionary principle.	Create a new global economy within limits to growth. Limit population growth and reduce consumption. Internalize the value of nonhuman life into institutions and policies. Agree to collective coercion (e.g., some advocate world government) to control greed, exploitation, and reproduction.	Reject industrialism (and/or capitalism) and reverse economic globalization. Restore local community autonomy and empower those whose voices have been marginalized. Promote ecological justice and local and indigenous knowledge systems.

economy for global environmental change. This is certainly not easy. These are emotional issues. And the evidence and arguments are often contradictory, almost as if analysts live in different worlds. Our hope [...] is not to confuse you, but to leave you with a better understanding of your own assumptions and arguments. Moreover, if you then decide to reject the arguments of others, you will do so with a genuine understanding of the complexity and historical sources of those views. Only then can the debates truly move forward.

14

Introduction to *World Development Report, 2003: Sustainable Development in a Dynamic Global Economy* (2003)

World Bank

Achievements and Challenges

World Development Report 2003 is about sustainable development. It is about people and how we deal with each other. It is about our home planet and its fabric of life. And it is about our aspirations for prosperity and posterity.

Any serious attempt at reducing poverty requires sustained economic growth in order to increase productivity and income in developing countries. But there is more to development than just economic growth – much more. This Report argues that ensuring sustainable development requires attention not just to economic growth but also to environmental and social issues. Unless the transformation of society and the management of the environment are addressed integrally along with economic growth, growth itself will be jeopardized over the longer term.

Environment and social issues, when not addressed, accumulate over time and have consequences that do not show up in the shorter time horizons typical of economic policymaking. That is why this Report adopts a longer time horizon of 20 to 50 years. Within this time frame it is possible to identify environmental and social problems – local, national, and global – that can have very costly or even irreversible consequences if not addressed immediately. For other problems, where the consequences are not irreversible, the longer time horizon provides the lead time to start changing attitudes and institutions and so make it possible to respond before the problems become crises.

In short, this Report takes a comprehensive, longer term, and dynamic view of sustainability, with a clear focus on poverty reduction.

World Bank. 2003. *World Development Report 2003: Sustainable Development in a Dynamic World – Transforming Institutions, Growth, and Quality of Life.* https://openknowledge.worldbank.org/handle/10986/5985. Licensed under the Creative Commons CC-BY 3.0 Generic license.

The Globalization and Environment Reader, First Edition. Edited by Peter Newell and J. Timmons Roberts.
Editorial material and organization © 2017 John Wiley & Sons, Ltd. Published 2017 by John Wiley & Sons, Ltd.

The Core Development Challenge

Most current estimates suggest that 2 billion people will be added to the world's population over the next 30 years and another billion in the following 20 years. Virtually all of this increase will be in developing countries, the bulk of it in urban areas. In these same countries, 2.5 billion to 3 billion people now live on less than $2 a day. The core challenge for development is to ensure productive work and a better quality of life for all these people. This will require substantial growth in productivity and incomes in developing countries.

The challenge may seem daunting – and it is. But over the past 30 years world population also rose by 2 billion. And this growth was accompanied by considerable progress in improving human wellbeing, as measured by human development indicators. Average income per capita (population-weighted in 1995 dollars) in developing countries grew from $989 in 1980 to $1,354 in 2000. Infant mortality was cut in half, from 107 per 1,000 live births to 58, as was adult illiteracy, from 47 to 25 percent.

Looking back to the 1950s and 1960s, it was feared at the time that the developing countries – particularly China, India, and Indonesia – would not be able to feed their rapidly growing populations. Thanks to the green revolution in agriculture, the doomsday scenarios of famine and starvation did not materialize in these, the most populous, developing countries. In the 1960s and 1970s the Club of Rome and many other groups forecast that the Earth would rapidly run out of key natural resources. So far, this has not happened, again because changes in technology and in preferences have allowed the substitution of new resources for existing ones – for example, fiber optics in place of copper. Global action has also led to major strides in eliminating disease scourges (smallpox and river blindness), and in addressing new problems (ozone depletion).

But accompanying these achievements were some negative social and environmental patterns that must not be repeated in the next 50 years if development is to be sustained.

- *Poverty: declining, but still a challenge.* There has been a significant drop in the percentage of people living in extreme poverty (that is, living on less than $1 per day). Even the absolute number of very poor people declined between 1980 and 1998 by at least 200 million, to almost 1.2 billion in 1998.[1] The decrease was primarily due to the decline in the number of very poor people in China as a result of its strong growth from 1980 onward.[2] Since 1993, there have also been encouraging signs of renewed poverty reduction in India. Sub-Saharan Africa, by contrast, has seen its number of very poor people increase steadily. Yet in 1998, despite the decline in Asia and the increase in Sub-Saharan Africa, East Asia and South Asia still accounted for two-thirds of the world's very poor people, and Sub-Saharan Africa for one-quarter. Development strategies will need to do better in eliminating abject poverty. The estimated 1 billion very poor people is of the same order of magnitude as the independently generated figures on the number of people who are undernourished and underweight.

- *Inequality: widening.* The average income in the richest 20 countries is now 37 times that in the poorest 20. This ratio has doubled in the past 40 years, mainly because of lack of growth in the poorest countries. Similar increases in inequality are found within many (but not all) countries.
- *Conflict: devastating.* In the 1990s, 46 countries were involved in conflict, primarily civil. This included more than half of the poorest countries (17 out of 33). These conflicts have very high costs, destroying past development gains and leaving a legacy of damaged assets and mistrust that impedes future gains.

The increased scale and reach of human activity have also put great pressure on local and global common property resources (water, soil, and fisheries), as well as on local and global sinks (the ability of the biosphere to absorb waste and regulate climate).

- *Air: polluted.* At the local level, hundreds of developing-country cities have unhealthy levels of air pollution. At the global level, the biosphere's capacity to absorb carbon dioxide without altering temperatures has been compromised because of heavy reliance on fossil fuels for energy. Global energy use traditionally has grown at the same rate as gross domestic product (GDP). Greenhouse gas (GHG) emissions will continue to grow unless a concerted effort is made to increase energy efficiency and move away from today's heavy reliance on fossil fuels. In the past 50 years excess nitrogen – mainly from fertilizers, human sewage, and combustion of fossil fuels – has begun to overwhelm the global nitrogen cycle, giving rise to a variety of ill effects ranging from reduced soil fertility to excess nutrients in lakes, rivers, and coastal waters. On current trends, the amount of biologically available nitrogen will double in 25 years.
- *Fresh water: increasingly scarce.* Fresh water consumption is rising quickly, and the availability of water in some regions is likely to become one of the most pressing issues of the 21st century. One-third of the world's people live in countries that are already experiencing moderate to high water shortages. That proportion could (at current population forecasts) rise to half or more in the next 30 years unless institutions change to ensure better conservation and allocation of water. More than a billion people in low-and middle-income countries – and 50 million people in high-income countries – lacked access to safe water for drinking, personal hygiene, and domestic use in 1995.
- *Soil: being degraded.* Nearly 2 million hectares of land worldwide (23 percent of all cropland, pasture, forest, and woodland) have been degraded since the 1950s. About 39 percent of these lands are lightly degraded, 46 percent moderately degraded, and 16 percent so severely degraded that the change is too costly to reverse. Some areas face sharp losses in productivity. Grasslands do not fare much better: close to 54 percent show degradation, with 5 percent being strongly degraded.
- *Forests: being destroyed.* Deforestation is proceeding at a significant rate. One-fifth of all tropical forests have been cleared since 1960. According to the Food and Agriculture Organization of the United Nations (FAO), deforestation has been concentrated in the developing world, which lost nearly 200 million hectares

between 1980 and 1995. In the Brazilian Amazon annual deforestation rates varied between 11,000 and 29,000 square kilometers a year in the 1990s. Deforestation in developing countries has several causes, including the conversion of forests to large-scale ranching and plantations and the expansion of subsistence farming. At the same time, forest cover in industrial countries is stable or even increasing slightly, although the forest ecosystem has been somewhat altered. According to a 1997 World Resources Institute (WRI) assessment, just one-fifth of the Earth's original forest remains in large, relatively natural ecosystems.

- *Biodiversity: disappearing.* Through a series of local extinctions, the ranges of many plants and animals have been reduced from those at the beginning of the century. In addition, many plants and animals are unique to certain areas. One-third of terrestrial biodiversity, accounting for 1.4 percent of the Earth's surface, is in vulnerable "hot spots" and is threatened with complete loss in the event of natural disasters or further human encroachment. Some statistics suggest that 20 percent of all endangered species are threatened by species, introduced by human activity, alien to the locality.
- *Fisheries: declining.* The aquatic environment and its productivity are on the decline. About 58 percent of the world's coral reefs and 34 percent of all fish species are at risk from human activities. Seventy percent of the world's commercial fisheries are fully exploited or overexploited and experiencing declining yields.

None of these social and environmental patterns is consistent with sustained growth in an interdependent world over the long term. Given the social and environmental stresses caused by past development strategies, the goal of raising human well-being worldwide must be pursued through a development process that "does better" – a poverty-eliminating growth path that integrates social and environmental concerns in pursuit of the goal of sustained improvements in well-being.

Windows of opportunity The development process is about change and transformation. Economies evolve. Societies and cultures evolve. Nature evolves. But they evolve at different speeds, creating stresses that need to be addressed and managed.[3] Moreover, in an era of globalization, the growing scale and speed of change in human activity are in some cases outpacing the rate at which natural processes and life-support systems can adapt. Globalization and faster technological change are also altering the nature of social interaction and affecting the efficacy of existing institutions. Although globalization and technological change offer many benefits, they can have deleterious side effects if institutions at local, national, and international levels do not evolve fast enough to deal with the adverse spillovers. The consequences of previous patterns of development are also beginning to bind, restricting certain growth paths or making them more costly.[4]

But these processes, if managed well, can create new opportunities. Of the many interrelated drivers of change and transformation, four stand out: scientific and technological innovation, income growth, population growth, and urbanization. The first two are likely to continue changing preferences and providing new opportunities to satisfy these preferences. The demographic and urban transitions, by contrast, are one-time changes, and the opportunities they offer are perhaps less well recognized. These are discussed in the next section.

- *Scientific and technological innovation.* The flow of information and ideas, boosted greatly by the Internet, can enable developing countries to learn more rapidly from each other and from industrial countries. It can also facilitate the emergence of networks to monitor a wider array of development impacts. Other technological changes can enable developing countries to leapfrog stages in the development process that rely on inefficient uses of natural resources. Science and technology can help address major socioeconomic problems. As noted, the green revolution was critical in enabling many developing countries to avoid widespread starvation. To benefit from these opportunities, institutions are needed that can stimulate and diffuse technological innovations and avoid or mitigate any deleterious consequences.
- *Income growth.* A projected growth in global income of 3 percent a year over the next 50 years implies a fourfold increase in global GDP. Increasing income growth may place a strain on the environmental and social fabric if there is too little attention to shifting consumption and production patterns. But this future economic growth will also require major investments in new human-made capital to expand capacity and to replace existing capacity as it ages. Making these investments (many of which are long lived) more environmentally and socially responsible through appropriate investment criteria will go a long way toward putting development on a more sustainable path – an opportunity not to be missed.

Opportunities in the demographic transition   When today's industrial countries were themselves developing, their population densities and growth rates were much lower than those of developing countries today, and the pressure on their resources was consequently lower. They also had a more evenly distributed age structure and lower dependency rates, allowing social institutions to adapt gradually to the requirements of a changing population.

Populations in industrial countries as a group were fairly stable for most of the second half of the 20th century. As a result, the growth in world population in this period has been driven primarily by population growth in developing countries. The stresses and spillovers from this population growth are generally observed not, as was originally expected, at the aggregate level (for example, in large-scale famines and food shortages) but, rather, in more insidious ways – in many smaller interactions between population, poverty, and resources. The outcomes are felt in greater pressures on fragile lands, in lower wages, and in persistent unemployment.

It is now clear that a global demographic transition is well underway, even if it is not yet complete. This is a major historic opportunity. World population is expected to stabilize by the end of this century at 9 billion to 10 billion people, 20 to 30 percent lower than forecast in the 1960s and 1970s. Many factors have contributed to this slowdown:

- More educated, employed women and smaller families
- Greater off-farm opportunities, creating a need for more education for children
- Widespread dissemination of modern contraceptive technology, making it easier for people to plan childbearing.

Of the expected population increase, 85 percent (3 billion) will be born in the next 50 years (Figure 14.1). But the speed of the transition, and the resulting population size and structure, will vary by region and by country. If fertility rates do not fall as rapidly as now projected, aggregate populations will be larger, putting greater pressures on natural resources and the social fabric. If they drop faster, many countries will have to deal sooner than expected with another problem – an aging population. This can have major consequences, especially for rural populations, for whom formal social safety nets are either nonexistent or not well developed. For example, one consequence of China's one-child policy – which dramatically and successfully lowered aggregate population – may be that by 2030 as much as one-third of the population will be over age 65.

   Influencing the demographic processes in many countries is the growing incidence of HIV/AIDS, malaria, and tuberculosis. For example, current estimates and projections in Sub-Saharan Africa indicate increasingly large losses of working-age people to the AIDS epidemic. The economic impact of such high mortality is especially serious because enormous private and public investments have already been made in members of this age group. The loss of their productive lives leaves large and unpredictable gaps

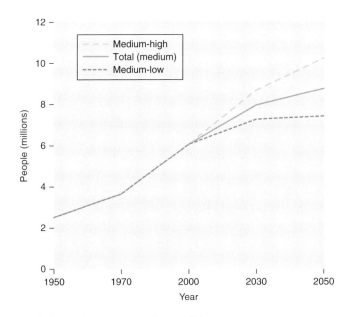

Figure 14.1   Global population approaching stability
Note: Medium-high and medium-low variants based on U.N. projections of medium-high and medium-low scenarios scaled to World Bank aggregates.
Source: World Bank estimates.

in the labor force. Malaria causes high levels of adult sickness rather than deaths, but this too inflicts heavy losses on labor productivity. Changes in the incidence of disease will have profound effects on health expenditures in these African countries.

With declining fertility, the age structure of the population changes, opening a window of opportunity in developing countries for a few decades – a window they can use for catching up and raising welfare for all. The proportion of the working-age population rises in relation to the proportions of children (those under 15) and the elderly (over 65), enabling societies to spend less on school construction and on old-age medical expenses and to invest the savings in generating economic growth. But such benefits will materialize only if the members of the working-age population are gainfully employed and have opportunities to expand their asset base. Eventually, dependency ratios rise again as these workers age, and the window of opportunity starts to close, as it will soon begin doing in East Asia and Eastern Europe.

Some regions, notably East Asia, have benefited substantially from the drop in the ratio of dependants to workers. Investment in forming a skilled, healthy labor force, combined with policy and institutional settings conducive to using this labor force effectively, helped generate strong economic growth. Two keys to success were maintenance of an open economy and investment in sectors with high growth potential. Since most developing regions will continue to experience relatively low dependency ratios for some decades, careful preparation now can help make the most of their windows of opportunity.

Until now, populations have been growing too rapidly for fiscally constrained governments to expand the provision of jobs, infrastructure, and public services enough to keep pace with people's needs. This task will become easier now that the global population is approaching stability. Governments in both urban and rural areas can move from catching up with the quantitative need for services, to upgrading their quality. Much of the social tension and frustration arising from unemployment and poor public services can then be attenuated.

Lower rates of population growth will reduce pressure on natural resources, but this will be offset by the increase in per capita consumption. The latter trend makes it essential to adopt the technologies and growth paths for production and consumption that will ensure the sustainable use of natural resources. To benefit from the opportunities a stabilizing population provides, it is critical to anticipate problems and identify development strategies for getting through the transition period (the next 20 to 50 years) without creating conditions that generate further conflict or resource degradation.

Opportunities in the urban transition   As countries move from poverty to affluence, the required growth in productivity involves a shift from heavy dependence on agriculture as a primary source of employment and income to nonagricultural activities that do not make intensive use of land. This is generally accompanied by a major shift in population from rural to urban areas. Indeed, the most important socioeconomic and cultural transformation over the past 150 years has been the transformation of relatively closed, exclusive, custom-based rural societies into relatively open, inclusive, innovation-oriented urban societies.[5]

Rural communities, especially in less accessible areas, have long adapted to their circumstances, developing vibrant, self-sufficient communities. As long as risks could be absorbed locally, these communities continued to learn and adapt. Dependence on local ecosystems, however, imposed limits on risk taking and innovation. This autonomous development path changes as rural areas become drawn into larger markets and strengthen their links with urban areas, making trade networks and distance from market centers more critical features of development opportunities and local resource pressures.

Increasing densities in towns and cities, and the greater connectivity between cities, as well as between urban and rural areas, increases the catchment area of markets and the returns to economic endeavor. If managed well, this transformation enables the emergence of new activities and productive job opportunities. Towns, as market centers for a rural hinterland, start the process of creating economies of scale for nonagricultural activities. Urban society also permits the spreading of risks over larger numbers of people and activities. Knowledge flows more readily, through increased opportunities for face-to-face contacts among various actors. And the need to accommodate diverse views and meet rapidly changing challenges stimulates innovation and new applications of technology. As a result, larger cities become incubators of new values – among them, risk taking and innovation.

Creativity, knowledge flow, the increasing scale of activities, and larger catchment areas are central to specialization and productivity growth. This is true not just for the production of goods but also for the provision of services. A village or neighborhood can support a primary school or basic clinic, and the local teacher or doctor can be a generalist. But providing higher, more sophisticated, and more differentiated education and health care requires more specialized skills. Because of the fixed costs of supporting these specialized skills, a larger catchment area (a town or a subsection of a city) is required. The higher population densities, lower transport costs, and lower communications costs in towns and cities make the more specialized operations possible. In moving further up the hierarchy of required specialization, the required catchment area also increases. So, the transition from villages to towns, and from cities to metropolitan areas, corresponds to the different functional capabilities of larger, higher-density conurbations. The potential benefits of higher densities and greater connectivity can be more easily realized if the investment climate is improved through better enabling rules and frameworks and better physical infrastructure. Stimulating and attracting investments – in particular, by the small and medium-size enterprises that provide most of the jobs for growing urban populations – is the key to accommodating the expected growth in urban populations and ensuring their ability to pay for needed urban services and amenities.

Seeing the socioeconomic transformations in spatial terms   Economists and engineers focus on the sectoral changes that accompany economic growth and technological innovations. This is understandable when focusing on GDP and the emergence or obsolescence of industries, but it is not very helpful for understanding the impact of these changes on society and nature. The most fundamental social and economic transformation – from traditional rural to modern urban – is manifested spatially. Except in the most populous countries, such as China and India, rural societies are relatively low in density and heavily dependent on agriculture as the primary source of employment and output. Modern urban societies are generally higher in density and dependent on activities that benefit from proximity and do not require a great deal of land, such as manufacturing and services. These activities and land use patterns generate different types of sociocultural and environmental problems.

Most ecosystems, too, are defined spatially. Much flora and fauna is locally unique and adapts gradually to changes in local circumstances. Local problems and stresses appear earliest, whether in the form of local extinctions, the reduction of the ranges of many plants and animals, or soil, air, and water pollution. These changes, the result of local development pressures, do not show up at national and global levels until they accumulate, but they provide early warning of problematic consequences of current development patterns.

The jurisdictions of many institutions that make or implement rules and laws (legislatures, constitutions, and government agencies) are also defined spatially. Often, the spatial jurisdiction of institutions does not match the spatial nature of the social and environmental problems generated by economic activity – one reason for the persistence of these problems.

Given our interest in people, where they live, and how they interact with each other and with nature, it is important to look at where people are now and where they are likely to be in the future. The world's population increased by more than 3.5 billion people in the past 50 years, and 85 percent of these added people were in developing and transition countries. The number of people living in fragile rural areas in developing countries doubled, in stark contrast to the declining numbers in this category in high-income countries. The number of cities with a population of more than 10 million people went from 0 to 15 in developing countries but only from 1 to 4 in high-income countries.

In the next 30 to 50 years the 2 billion to 3 billion increase in the world's population will be almost exclusively (97 percent) in developing and transition countries, and virtually all of it will be in urban areas. The growth of the urban population is driven by natural increase, rural-to-urban migration, and the incorporation of high-density rural areas on the urban fringe. The number of megacities in developing countries is likely to increase to 54, while it will stabilize at 5 in high-income countries. It is not yet clear whether the number of people living in fragile areas will continue to increase, but it probably will unless migration opportunities change. As many as 2 billion people will live in two areas that are difficult to manage: fragile rural areas and megacities. Dealing with these people's needs will be a major challenge, since there is not much experience in industrial countries that can be adapted to their needs.

The following are some of the key questions with local and global implications that will face the world's population over the next two to five decades:

- Will rural populations – especially those on fragile lands, in more commercially active areas, and on agricultural frontiers – be able to overcome poverty, improve their livelihoods, and adapt to new opportunities, including opportunities in towns and cities?

- Will the rapidly growing cities of the developing world live up to their potential as dynamic engines of growth and social modernization, or will they get mired in poverty, pollution, congestion, and crime?
- Will renewable resources – particularly forests, soil, water, biodiversity, and fisheries – be depleted, or will they be managed as indefinitely sustained sources of livelihood and well-being?
- Will societies be sufficiently creative, resilient, and forward-looking as they undergo sweeping transformations in patterns of growth and migration? Will they be able to promote more equitable development and cope with unexpected shocks?
- Will poor countries be able to accelerate their growth without destabilizing social and environmental stresses? Will the prospective $140 trillion world GDP at mid-century generate fewer environmental and social stresses than the much smaller global economy today?

These are difficult but important questions, which this Report cannot answer definitely. However, it identifies an approach and process that should generate more dialogue and creativity in finding answers.

The interactions among society, economy, and nature vary in the different spatial arenas, although problems across locations are linked. Productivity increases in agriculture help feed the cities. Innovation and productivity increases in the cities help raise productivity and the quality of life in rural areas. Geography matters because of the characteristics of local ecosystems, such as the cost of overcoming local diseases. Geography also matters because of geometry in the form of connectivity and distance to central nodes and markets; the cost of transport is more important here than that of communication. Indeed, the strong association between rural poverty in remote and fragile ecosystems becomes more apparent when the problem is viewed through a spatial lens.

For this reason, the Report is organized by spatial areas that have different characteristics and require correspondingly different approaches to their development.

Fragile lands. The estimated 1.3 billion people living on fragile lands have modest assets that can help bring them out of extreme poverty, but these assets are seldom nurtured by local or national institutions. The people have land that is subject to many constraints, making it vulnerable to degradation, erosion, floods, and landslides. They possess human capital, which is handicapped by restrictive traditions, limited mobility, lack of voice, and poor access to services. This is even more true for women, who are thus the most marginal group. The mainly poor people on fragile lands also face circumstances vastly different from their counterparts on Europe's rural periphery 50 to 100 years ago. Today, international migration is highly restricted, and while rural-to-urban migration is important for them, there are limited numbers of jobs at above-subsistence wages for unskilled workers, especially in the low-growth economies. As a result, as noted above, instead of declining sharply, the number of people living on fragile lands is estimated to have doubled in the past 50 years – despite some outmigration.

Rural areas with potential for commercial crops. The problem of feeding a growing and more urban population calls for better management of the interaction with nature, particularly with respect to land and water (extensification versus intensification of agriculture). Whether or not rural families have land, water, and education is critical to their current livelihood, as well as to their ability to move to cities in the future. More egalitarian access to these assets is also crucial for determining the quality of society's institutions. A successful rural-urban transition requires the elimination of poverty for those who stay in the countryside and better preparation of those who move to the cities. It also demands protection of remaining natural ecosystems and habitats, given their central role in maintaining life-support systems and biodiversity. This latter requirement is one reason to intensify agricultural production in areas already under commercial crops and pasture. Intensification in such areas not only minimizes pressure on biodiversity and on marginal agricultural areas but also increases the food available to cities and leads to dynamic rural-urban linkages. Higher population density in these rural areas would also make investments in health and education more cost-effective and would increase the potential for off-farm employment and help farmers accept risk and innovate.

Urban areas. Cities of the developing world face a formidable undertaking, given the expected rapid rate of growth and sheer numbers of urban residents to be employed, housed, and serviced. The characteristics of periurban settlements, towns, cities, and megacities – higher density, large scale of settlement, and greater social diversity – facilitate the creation of productive employment opportunities, efficient provision of services, and access to ideas and learning. But having many people at close quarters also creates the potential for social problems – crime and social dislocation – and for environmental spillovers that pose health and safety hazards, especially for those living in neighborhoods without sanitation or drainage and in potential disaster zones. The long life of urban physical capital stock can lock in certain development paths, making changes costly. If managed well, urban areas can be the future engines of growth. If not, their environmental and social problems will be concentrated and difficult to fix.

The discussion of problems affecting fragile lands, rural commercial areas, and urban settings, and of possible solutions, is important because many public goods and externalities are local in nature and are, in principle, amenable to action at the local level. An enabling framework for local action and the principie of subsidiarity require that public goods and externalities that affect wider catchments be addressed, at higher levels – national and global.

At the national level. The political, legal, and market domain for coordinating many activities is frequently the nation. Many externalities spill over beyond local communities and municipalities, and even across regional boundaries. The nation is thus often the level at which interests can be balanced, either directly or by facilitating negotiation among localities. National actors may be better placed to organize the provision of public goods and to take advantage of scale economies when the beneficiaries extend beyond subnational regions. Generating a strong investment climate, including sound macroeconomic fundamentals, good governance, and basic infrastructure, requires a framework that is typically national in scope. Dismantling perverse subsidies, husbanding forests and fisheries, and curbing water and air pollution in river basins and airsheds are major national challenges.

Managing foreign aid and avoiding civil conflict are other key national concerns that determine whether development is sustainable.

At the global level. Many economic, environmental, and social processes – knowledge, conflict, disease, pollution, migration, and finance – spill over national boundaries. A few of these processes generate problems that are purely global: depletion of the stratospheric ozone layer is an example. But most global problems and opportunities are experienced at the local level as well. Automobiles that pollute local airsheds also generate greenhouse gases; wetland destruction that disrupts local water resources also undermines biodiversity of global significance; new ideas that are generated in one place can benefit people in other places, near and far. The public goods nature of many of these issues and the need to address the negative externalities requires coordination across boundaries. The distinctive challenge for global issues is to balance interests and commit to solutions in the absence of a global authority.

Act Now – For Long-term Problems

Before proceeding to a discussion of local, national, and global issues, this Report sets forth a framework which argues that social and environmental outcomes have a bearing on human well-being both directly and through their effect on growth. When social and environmental issues are systematically neglected for long periods, economic growth will be affected. That is why improving the quality of life for those living in poverty today – and for the 2 billion to 3 billion people who will be added to the world's population over the next 50 years – will require a growth path that integrates environmental and social concerns more explicitly.

Some problems of sustainability are already urgent and require immediate action; examples are local ecosystems where population is pressing on deeply degraded soils, and forests and water stocks that have been nearly depleted. In such cases productivity is already on the decline and opportunities for correction or mitigation may even have been lost; abandonment of existing practices and outmigration may be necessary. The urgency of some of these problems has been overlooked because the people most affected are physically remote from centers of power, or because their voices are not heard, or both.

Some issues call for immediate action because there are good prospects for reversing the damage to the environment at relatively low cost, as in taking measures against air and water pollution. Even then, undoing some of the damage to the affected population (such as the respiratory damage caused by breathing air laden with particulates) may not be fully possible. But knowing the health impacts does create a moral imperative to protect those affected from further exposure, to compensate them to the extent possible, and to prevent others from becoming victims.

Another category of issues unfolds over a longer time horizon. The problems may not yet be urgent, but the direction of change is unmistakable. For these, it is essential to get ahead of the curve and prevent a worsening crisis before it is too costly. Biodiversity loss and climate change are in this category: there is already a need to adapt to the consequences of past and current behavior, but there is also still scope for mitigation, though not for complacency. Similarly, the need to anticipate urban growth by facilitating low-income settlements in safe areas and by setting aside major rights-of-way and spaces for public amenities makes it necessary to act now to avoid greater costs and regrets later.

What is clear is that almost all of the challenges of sustainable development require that action be initiated in the near term, whether to confront immediate crises, such as the health risks to children from unsanitary living conditions in existing slums, or to stem the tide of crises where concerted action in the near term could avert much greater costs and disruption to human development in the longer term.

In looking back over past successes and failures in solving development problems, it is clear that there have been more successes where markets function well (for example, in providing food to people with effective demand), even where the problems that markets have to solve (such as transport and communications) are relatively complex. The major problems that remain (inclusion, poverty reduction, deforestation, biodiversity, and global warming) are, however, generally not amenable to standard market solutions, although markets can help solve subsets of these problems.

One difficulty is that environmental and social assets suffer from underinvestment and overuse because they have the characteristics of public goods:

- Sometimes, ignorance of the consequences of action leads to overuse or underprovision. The ignorance is in part due to underinvestment in knowledge and understanding – itself a public good.
- In other cases there are no mechanisms for facilitating cooperation among individuals, communities, or countries even when it is clear to those involved that the returns to cooperation (especially in the long run), exceed the returns to unilateral action (especially in the short run).
- In still other cases the gains from acting in the broader interests of society fail to be realized because correcting a spillover has distributional consequences and the potential losers resist change.
- Sometimes underprovision is a response to perceived tradeoffs between growth and the costs of correcting externalities. These tradeoffs may be the unfortunate outcome of having been boxed into a corner through a past failure of foresight. Or there may be genuinely difficult choices in balancing legitimate interests and assessing the value of nonmarket benefits and risk reduction, especially if those who would benefit are dispersed over current and future generations.

Environmental and social stresses reflect the failure of institutions to manage and provide public goods, to correct spillovers, and to broker differing interests. Because the spatial extent of spillovers varies by problem, appropriate institutions are needed at different levels, from local through national to global.

Getting to socially preferred outcomes requires institutions that can identify who bears the burden of social and environmental neglect and who benefits – and who can balance these diverse interests within society. This perspective helps in understanding why technically sound policy advice (for instance, "eliminate perverse incentives" or "impose charges on environmental damages") is so seldom taken up.

The emphasis of this Report is not on identifying a specific set of policies or outcomes considered advantageous but on the processes by which such policies and outcomes are selected. Outcomes emerging from strong processes are more robust. In many cases, and increasingly, institutions respond too late or too poorly – or without the capacity to commit to a course of action. In today's world the lag between the emergence of a problem and the emergence of institutions that can respond to it is too long. We need to see farther down the road. Why? Because institutions that facilitate and manage national economic growth, and even globalization, are still inadequate, yet where such institutions are in fact emerging, they are developing faster than complementary institutions that might be able to avoid or cope with the deleterious environmental and social consequences of economic change.

Notes

1   The quality and coverage of the household survey data used to measure poverty have improved dramatically in the past 10 to 15 years, and the World Bank has played an important role in facilitating this improvement. Since 1990, the Bank's $1 per day poverty estimates have drawn fully on these new data. However, the paucity of adequate survey data for the past naturally makes estimation over longer periods more hazardous. In *Globalization, Growth and Poverty* (World Bank 2002), it was estimated that the number of people living below $1 per day had fallen by 200 million between 1980 and 1998. As noted in the Report, that estimate had to draw on two different sources that used different methods. Further checks using more consistent methods corroborate the earlier estimate. These estimates also suggest that if China were excluded, there would have been little or no net decline in the total number of poor people.

2   In 1978 China abandoned its reliance on collective agriculture, sharply increased the prices paid for agricultural goods, and dramatically increased the role of market signals and foreign investment.

3   Social change and cultural evolution have also been speeding up, but not uniformly within or across societies. Some cultures are less able to adapt to speed of change even if they wanted to, while others may not even want to.

4   Until recently, the carbon emissions generated by energy-intensive activities (that rely on fossil fuels, such as coal) did not affect global temperatures because they had not exceeded the biosphere's absorptive capacity. Now more expensive alternatives are needed to avoid further damage.

5   Much like the dynamics by which teams become more creative, populations moving to cities go through stages of forming, storming, norming, and performing. Forming occurs when individuals with different backgrounds come together; storming, when their different perspectives clash; norming, when more inclusive norms evolve; and performing, when constructive behavior replaces destructive behavior. The result is that cities, in the best cases, become centers where different cultural values come together and jointly develop more inclusive values to accommodate different perspectives and provide space for different subgroups to specialize and innovate.

15

The Political Ecology of Globalization (2012)

Peter Newell

This chapter seeks to contribute to debates about globalization and the environment by showing how the social forces that are central to contemporary capitalist globalization are also decisive shapers of environmental outcomes. The primacy of intensifying accumulation on a global scale creates critical ecological and political challenges, notably whether viable accumulation strategies can be identified that are less resource intensive or may even profit from reduced resource use, or whether environmental problems such as climate change create a crisis of capitalism because of its inability to respect ecological limits to growth.[1] This context is critical for understanding the "nature" and conduct of global environmental politics and the effectiveness of existing structures of global environmental governance. More specifically, it affects our understanding of whether such structures are capable of reshaping the global economy and steering it onto a more sustainable footing, or whether their role is more likely to advance and deepen capitalist globalization.

In such a rendition, global environmental governance, understood conventionally as what international environmental regimes do, is dislodged from a position of primacy in the analysis in favor of an account that attempts to "read" ecologically and socially the organization of the global political economy: the relations of power that create and sustain it and the ecological and social consequences of this way of ordering things. While such an account has implications for the orthodox study of global environmental governance since it problematizes liberal understandings of the state and the role of (international) law, its main focus is the relationship between capitalism and ecology:

Peter Newell. 2012. "The Political Ecology of Globalization". In *Handbook of Global Environmental Politics*, ed. P. Dauvergne. Cheltenham: Edward Elgar. pp. 263–274. Reproduced with permission from Edward Elgar Publishing.

a relationship that international institutions and powerful states within them mediate in important ways, but which requires an analytical focus that goes beyond that.[2]

This chapter argues first that since many aspects of (global) environmental change are produced by economic and social forces associated with contemporary capitalism, we need to develop an understanding of global environmental politics in which attempts to construct forms of global environmental governance are placed within the historical context in which they develop and the social and economic forces which shape (and are shaped by) the context within which cooperation and change is (or is not) possible, are taken seriously.[3] This is crucial to understanding the sources of environmental change and the possibilities of containing or reversing it given the prevailing organization of power and distribution of resources in the global system.

Second, the claim is made that such an understanding can be enriched and enhanced by combining insights from critical (international) political economy with an extensive body of work on "political ecology." This work explicitly seeks to explain environmental politics, often understood as struggles over access to (natural) resources, as a function of the social relations that structure issues of access, property, entitlement, and justice. The political ecology tradition is hugely eclectic, including feminist political ecology, cultural political ecology and poststructuralist accounts alongside work within a political economy tradition.[4] While traditionally focused on particular sites of struggle, a (return to) global political ecology is increasingly apparent which enables the sorts of cross-scalar, multi-site analysis that are critical to understanding the drivers and impacts of global environmental change and the drivers and impacts of attempts to manage that change through institutions of global environmental governance.[5] Here is it argued that historical materialist lines of enquiry are particularly well placed to connect a macro understanding of social forces in global politics with micro and site-specific manifestations of this organization of power which political ecologists document with such rigor.[6] The fusion of insights from these distinct, but related, theoretical traditions offers the possibility of reading contemporary capitalism (globalization) ecologically: capturing the nature of its material flows and their social and environmental consequences, and so gives as a more wide-ranging, multidimensional and multiscalar account of the everyday conduct of global environmental politics than global attempts to construct law around specific transborder effects of production (rather than regulate the sources of them).

Which Globalization?

The historical context which this chapter describes is the current neoliberal order that has emerged from the late 1970s onwards, but whose project of monetary discipline and global integration has deepened and intensified during the 1980s and 1990s.[7] It refers, for example, to attempts to rescale accumulation opportunities through bilateral, regional and global trade and investment agreements, state restructuring, privatization, and the use of monetary policy and enhanced capital mobility. Within this there are specific features of the organization of the existing global political economy that are of particular significance for understandings of the potential and limits of global environmental governance. These include the power and mobility of finance capital which has enabled the financialization of environmental services,[8] the critical though schizophrenic attitude toward the role of the state and regulation, particularly on the part of states in the "Lockean heartland"[9] which has left us with the plural but uneven ensemble of public and private institutions and initiatives that we have aimed at de-regulating public, and re-regulating through private means, different sectors of the economy, and the creation of new sites of accumulation to overcome the limits to capital: crises of overproduction and underconsumption.[10]

This context has shaped the willingness and, to some extent, ability of states to create forms of environmental regulation threatening to powerful fractions of capital amid fears of pollution flight and carbon leakage. Whether a race to the bottom, top, or to the middle is the appropriate term, or whether regulatory chill is a more accurate term,[11] depends very much on the country and sector in question and the degree of autonomy or "developmental space" they have to assert conditions on powerful investors.[12] The threat of capital flight, nonetheless, is a powerful weapon in the armoury of corporations wishing to check more stringent environmental regulations, and one many governments take extremely seriously and invoke themselves as a rationale for not imposing costs on their businesses which surpass those required of their competitors. It features prominently, for example, in efforts to check initiatives by activists to see new rules and regulations to govern the social and environmental behavior of transnational corporations operating overseas.[13] Instead, we have seen a growth of self and private regulation which confers on leading business actors, principally transnational companies, the power (and authority) to establish their own rules of conduct and restraint in a more open (for some) global economy.[14] Much of the proliferation of voluntary regulation through the negotiation of codes of conduct and certification schemes can be understood as an attempt to respond to popular anxieties about the ability of corporations to exploit lower social and environmental standards in a more open global economy and offers a concrete and visible way of taking action while not accommodating more critical demands for tougher forms of social and environmental regulation.

Beyond the question of governing globalization, what is interesting in environmental terms is the coincidence of early twenty-first-century capitalism with a growing realization that the energy base upon which modern capitalism has been built is unsustainable, whether because of scarcity induced by peak oil, concerns about climate change or a questioning of the social costs of imperial ventures to provide energy security. In this context a set of economic strategies predicated on the movement of goods and services over ever longer distances starts to look vulnerable. Pressures to account for carbon footprints and reduce "food miles" express anxiety about the environmental consequences of more globalized circuits of production and consumption. Indeed, half of all emissions of carbon released into the atmosphere from the burning of fossil fuels and cement production have occurred since the mid-1970s.[15] Then there are the unforeseen boomerang effects that reverberate around the global economy when the needs of food, energy, and water compete and conspire to produce tension and crisis. The drive in the US for biofuels as a solution to an energy crisis which pushes up the price of corn resulting in "tortilla riots" in Mexico; the drives toward land-grabs in countries such as Ethiopia and Sudan to secure future supplies of water and food for rapidly expanding economies, anticipating the exhaustion of their own resource bases, create new vulnerabilities at the very moment that they appear to provide a measure of resource security. As Harvey and many others have pointed out, capitalism does not resolve its crises, it merely moves them around.[16]

These issues raise the question of capitalism's relationship to fossil fuels. Clearly much of the history of the expansion of capitalism can be told through war, conquest, colonialism, and accumulation through dispossession. The pursuit of oil and coal in particular[17] has been decisive in the making of British and American power[18] and in fueling the industrial revolution. The need to secure reliable and affordable supplies of energy continues to be a significant shaper of foreign policy as any number of imperial ventures in the Middle East and elsewhere testify.[19] The question is whether in an age of "peak oil" and climate change, a different type of capitalism can emerge to drive large-scale investments in "clean" energy and related energy services[20] or whether climate change reflects a "crisis of the capitalist mode of production" as writers such as Brunnengräber claim[21] or, as Huber suggests, that "fossil fuels represent an historically specific and internally necessary aspect of the capitalist mode of production."[22] In other words can there be capitalism that is not "fossil capitalism"[23] and can we imagine a world beyond "hydro-carbon civilization"?[24]

Capitalism is nothing if not resilient and adaptable, revolutionizing forms of production in restless waves of innovation. As Marx and Engels famously stated, the bourgeoisie "cannot exist without constantly revolutionizing the means of production."[25] While certain "base technologies"[26] may characterize eras of capitalism, as Buck notes, it is important not to "confuse particular manifestations of capitalism – that is, particular historical social formations – with capitalism itself, thus underestimating the flexibility of the beast."[27] Even a post-oil economy, he argues, would be a capitalist one as long as there is an industrial reserve army without ownership or control of the means of production and as long as the production of commodities by commodities prevails. Hence, even peak oil can be reworked as an opportunity for growth where fossil fuels can be replaced by a "solar revolution."[28] Technological dynamism is at the heart of capitalism, and as a consequence, its technological trajectories are not necessarily set in stone. "Capital, as value in motion, does not care about what it makes, the machinery used or the motive source. It cares only about its own self-expansion and valorization," he claims.[29] These are the incessant waves of creative destruction that some argue might yet be harnessed toward the goal of a low carbon economy.[30]

One area where from whence this momentum may derive is finance capital's sensitivity to risk. Environmental activists have long targeted investment banks and insurance companies as powerful actors that wield significant influence over governments as well as the businesses that rely on them for capital. Greenpeace sought to work with the insurance and re-insurance industry exposed to large pay-outs as a result of "natural" disasters to encourage them to disinvest from fossil-fuel investments,[31] while other activists have pressured leading investment banks to screen their portfolios for large fossil-fuel projects which run the risk of attracting negative publicity and diminishing shareholder value.[32] While such strategies have, on occasion, enjoyed a limited degree of success, the question remains whether finance capital can afford to be indifferent to the fate of fossil-fuel industries and their dependants. It is important not to exaggerate the autonomy of financial from productive capital. After all banks and insurance companies have to have something to invest in. It is also the case that many CEOs and shareholders are rewarded with stock options tying their fate to the fortunes of the financial markets as increasing the price of stock itself becomes an objective of the corporation.[33] With the structures of regulation, tax, and subsidies that we currently have, fossil fuels, despite clear evidence of the environmental problems they generate, continue to be systematically privileged by state managers and therefore continue to offer highly profitable returns. This explains why, despite efforts of oil companies to rebrand themselves as "Beyond Petroleum" in the case of British Petroleum, or to dissociate themselves from business organizations that are openly hostile about the case for action on climate change, they continue to invest in highly destructive but highly lucrative investments such as the oil tar sands in Alberta Canada.

Overproduction of course necessitates overconsumption. One of the most indelible features of the global capitalist economy over the last 40 years has been the exponential increase in mass consumption that has been achieved through advertising and marketing strategies and the internationalization of production and transport networks, fueled until now by cheap and abundant energy supplies. The "shadows of consumption" that are left behind leave a trail of destruction, however.[34] The changing geographies of production and consumption mirror closely the shifting profile and intensifying nature of pollution. The simultaneous deindustrialization of wealthier countries and industrialization of poorer ones, a strategy aimed at overcoming the power of unions to insist on higher wages and creating a new international division of labor, has meant that countries such as China, India, Brazil, and South Africa have seen their contributions to global problems such as climate change increase significantly. China's CO_2 emissions amounted to 407 million tonnes in 1980 and 1,665 million tonnes in 2006, while India's went from 95 million tonnes in 1980 to 411 million tonnes in the same period.[35] The final destination for many of the goods produced during this surge of industrialization remains the rich West. Forty percent of China's product is exported as is 20 percent of India's,[36] raising the question of "embedded carbon" and who is responsible for the pollution embodied in the products that flow through the veins of the global economy.

The distribution of wealth and waste generated by this frenetic intensification of economic activity has been unevenly distributed, reflecting and exacerbating existing inequalities along the lines of class, race and gender as a vast literature on environmental justice has documented in detail.[37] Whether it is toxic, plastic or the sorts of e-waste (computers and the like) that ends up on landfill sites in Ghana,[38] global accumulation strategies enabled by trade and investment agreements create greater distance between sites of production and sites of consumption but also allow for "spatial fixes"[39] for the need to privatize gain and socialize risk and the externalities of production in sites, within and between societies, where opposition is weak and regulation either non-existent or weakly enforced. This dynamic is visible not just in relation to waste, but also through the commodification of carbon in offset markets that provide a spatial fix (and a temporal one by discounting the future) by displacing carbon reduction efforts to areas of the world where it can be done more cost-effectively.[40] It is a function, in many ways, of the triumph of efficiency over equity as the primary organizing principle in neoliberal environmental governance.

These then are just some of the ways in which capitalism's relationship to nature has evolved in the context of globalization. They suggest shifting alignments of power in the relationship between state and capital, though notably not a "hollowing-out" or "retreat" of the state in most areas of the world, or in areas of policy of most significance to environment as has been claimed for other areas of policy.[41] They point rather to a reconstitution of power whereby some parts of the state have internationalized, becoming embedded within, and responding to, the preferences of a transnational capitalist class, such as ministries of trade and finance, while others have diminished in importance such as ministries of labor grounded in social forces that have lost power and that exercise less structural influence in conditions of globalization.[42] They suggest a delegation of regulatory power to market actors to establish appropriate forms of labeling and certification and a strong preference for regulation *for* business than *of* business, one that can be traced through the history of failed and half-hearted attempts at business regulation and the simultaneous rise of trade and investment agreements that grant new powers to transnational corporations over states,[43] a manifestation of what Gill refers to as the "new constitutionalism."[44] The forms of globalization described here reflect the preferences and political project of a capitalist class which includes "globalising state bureaucrats"[45] and the business interests that they represent and seek to serve based in the epicenters of the world economy.

The landscape described here also reveals the ways in which strategies for responding to environmental crises have been aligned with the imperatives of capital accumulation. Whether it be the marketization of environmental governance and the preference for market-based over so-called "command and control" solutions, the rise of payments for ecosystem services approaches to conservation or the commodification of water, forests and carbon as responses to environmental problems, dominant responses serve to entrench capitalism rather than respond to the need for structural reform in advanced capitalist economies demanded by environmental crises. Problems generated by overconsumption of resources, such as fossil fuels, become an investment opportunity to buy and sell "offsets" which allow companies and individuals to purchase emissions reduction opportunities in the developing world and claim them as part of their own emissions reductions efforts, all the while keeping existing structures of production and consumption intact. Water scarcity is regarded as a problem produced by inefficient state institutions and a failure to incentivize conservation by allocating property rights. Privatization becomes the obvious solution. The 2003 World Bank World Development Report on "Sustainable Development in a Dynamic Economy" advances the idea that the spectacular failure to tackle poverty and environmental degradation over the last decade is due to a failure of governance, "poor implementation and not poor vision." The report notes, "Those [poverty and environmental problems] that can be coordinated through markets have typically done well; those that have not fared well include many for which the market could be made to work as a coordinator." The challenge for governments is therefore to be more welcoming of private actors through, among other things, "a smooth evolution of property rights from communal to private."[46]

So far the story of globalization and its relationship to environmental governance could be told through critical international political economy (IPE) accounts drawing on historical materialist analysis of (global) environmental politics[47] and broader bodies of critical scholarship on globalization and capitalism which usefully draw attention to the social forces underpinning the project of globalization, understood as the deepening, intensification and re-scaling of capitalism.[48] What is missing from such an account, however, is evidence of the social and environmental consequences of a global economy organized in this way and premised upon these relations of power. This is where I argue that work on political ecology can make a useful contribution, balancing the macro focus of critical IPE and grounding our analysis of the "socio-natures"[49] that produce and are produced by globalization.

Which Political Ecology?

What is political ecology and why does it help us to understand the relationship between globalization and the environment? At its broadest, political ecology seeks to provide a framework for understanding human-society or "socio-natural" relations.[50] More specifically, it examines the interrelations of politics and power, structures, and discourses with the environment. Here I highlight those elements which offer a bridge to IPE and critical traditions within global environmental politics (GEP):[51] materialist political ecologies that posit linkages between ecologies and the economies of which they are a part. For example, the global political ecology that Peet et al. engage in "emphasises global political economy as a main causal theme."[52] For them

> Political ecology is predicated on an ecologically conceptualised view of politics: it is attentive to the hard edges of capitalist accumulation and global flows of labour, capital and information, but also attuned to the complex operations of power-knowledge... all within a system prone to political-economic crisis.[53]

It is a research agenda that coalesces around the impact of capitalist development on the environment, the social and political implications of environmental protection and management, and the political economy of the way "new natures" are produced. Such lines of enquiry have been pursued through work on the practices of commodification of "neoliberal natures,"[54] as well as "classic" political ecology concerns around questions of access to material and natural resources, and issues of resistance, equity and justice in the negotiation and distribution of social and environmental benefits at multiple scales.[55]

One strand of political ecology that developed in the wake of, and by way of response to, the Rio Earth summit in 1992 was that associated with the work of Wolfgang Sachs, Nicolas Hildyard, Vandana Shiva and others, which perhaps resonates most directly with the traditional preoccupations of international relations scholars.[56] Critical of the contents of the Rio agenda, particularly what went "unsaid at UNCED" in terms of the role of militarism, debt and consumption in driving environmental degradation, and the actors that had secured for themselves a place at the negotiating table in deciding appropriate forms of global managerial action while deflecting attention away from their own implication in accelerating ecological crisis,[57] this work provided a powerful and timely antidote to the optimism and faith placed in the institutions of global governance to deliver effective environmental and development outcomes. It was critical of "the aspirations of a rising ecocracy to manage nature and regulate people worldwide," "largely devoid of any consideration of power relations, cultural authenticity and moral choice."[58]

But there is actually a much longer lineage of work on political ecology, which is "global," less in the *spatial* sense of privileging global institutions as the site of enquiry and the location of politics and more in a *causal* sense by exploring the ways in which particular ecologies and the social relations in which they are embedded are a product of broader social relations, particularly class relations. Piers Blaikie's work was particularly pioneering in this sense combining "the concerns of ecology and a broadly defined political economy":[59] studying, for example, how the nature of social erosion in Nepal could be usefully understood in relation to the global capitalist political economy.[60] Other work on metabolism, metabolic rifts[61] and entropy,[62] drawing on Marx, on ecology and on ecological economics is also useful here for its attention to ecological and energy flows in a way which is not bound by ontologies which privilege the state or international institutions as "units" of analysis. Instead the focus is on mapping and accounting for "ecologically unequal exchange,"[63] the social roots of global environmental change[64] or the points of tension between how ecological systems operate and how capitalism functions. Such work provides us with an invaluable account of the (economic) *causes* of global environmental change.

But it also affords insights into how the expansion of capitalist logics under globalization and their extension to the environmental realm has intensified conflicts over natural resources and how they are valued.[65] Studies on resistance to extraction, commodification, and privatization of resources[66] on the part of marginalized groups reveal the specific social and site specific ecological consequences of attempts to open up mining, forestry, and water to private investors.[67] Increasingly, attention is also being paid to the "local" social and environmental consequences of market-based initiatives deriving from global environmental institutions, whether it is the Clean Development Mechanism (CDM), REDD (Reduced Emissions from

Deforestation and Forest Degradation), or conservation efforts centered around payments for ecosystem services.[68] This complements work on the activities of key neoliberal economic institutions such as the World Bank as well as on environmental bodies such as the Global Environment Facility.[69] Because issues of access, property rights and livelihoods are affected by and enrolled in global circuits of capital, political ecology provides useful ways of identifying and tracing the social and environmental consequences of neoliberal forms of environmental governance. This contributes to lines of enquiry aimed at understanding who wins and who loses from particular (global) environmental governance arrangements.[70]

Given that site- and resource-specific conflicts increasingly result from and are embedded with "global" configurations of politics and social forces, strands of critical IPE usefully connect with "local" political ecologies, to show how broader structures of power are reproduced and present in struggles around natural resources which often embody inequalities based on class, race, or gender.[71] The globalizing reach of international regimes and their role in creating markets in, and determining access to, resources as crucial as water, energy, and seeds means that critical accounts of global environmental governance have to widen their analysis beyond the "international" level and beyond conventional theoretical foci to comprehend how the structures of power which shape and circumscribe "global" environmental governance may also configure "local" sites of resource governance. The dynamic also runs the other way. These sites, in turn, impact upon global regimes through the value they create or fail to produce as commodities to be exchanged on global markets (in the form of certified emissions reductions, for example) or the symbolic value rested in them as examples of successful projects (that bring "co-benefits" to communities beyond their value as a commodity), or because of the controversy generated through acts of resistance by affected communities and social movements.

Political ecology's focus on material, institutional, and discursive practices of power complements in many ways neo-Gramscian framings of power in GEP which illustrate how governance arrangements often serve to globalize particular sets of material and political interests.[72] As with all hegemonic projects, however, for the sorts of solutions to problems of global environmental change promoted by global institutions to maintain their "common-sense" status, strategies of accommodation are required to bring on board critics and make concessions in the name of preserving the power of a historic bloc. Hegemony is never complete and acts of resistance serve to remake them, producing legitimacy crises that their advocates then have to address. We see this clearly in both the governance reforms taking place within the CDM and the standards created in voluntary carbon markets aimed at tackling instances of climate fraud and double-counting of carbon credits exposed by activists, so as to contain threats to the credibility of the market as a whole.[73] Studies within political ecology also draw attention to the ways in which globalizing projects are resisted and rejected, or "reworked" into more positive local impacts. For example, how people create opportunities within the global carbon economy by "manoeuvring through and finding spaces at the interstices of the same political economy that in other ways simultaneously constrains and structures their agency."[74]

Conclusions

Contrary to much conventional analysis, it is suggested here that globalization is most usefully understood as a political and economic project, often incoherent and unevenly clearly applied, but one which seeks to overcome limits to capital accumulation by opening up markets through new suites of trade and investment agreements, securing property rights for investors and constructing institutions able to lock in an integrated global economy on terms set by its most powerful actors. This produces a range of environmental as well as social challenges that require theorists and practitioners to find analytical tools and resources that allow us to make sense of what is going on, on whose behalf and with what consequences. It has been suggested here that attempting to read globalization "ecologically" through the use of a diverse and eclectic set of work that falls under the umbrella of political ecology provides a useful starting point in this endeavor that complements insights gleaned from critical IPE and GEP. This is so because of political ecology's explicit attempt to link ecological concerns with political economy, because of its attention to the way in which social relations produce and reflect different "socionatures" and because of its lack of respect for analytical categories and distinctions that prevent us from capturing trans-scalar political, economic, and ecological dynamics that help to explain both the causes of global environmental change as well as the context in which they are being addressed by states, international institutions and a multitude of other actors trying to steer globalization in a more ecologically stable and socially responsible direction.

Notes

1   Kovel 2007; Magdoff and Bellamy Foster 2010; and Newell and Paterson 2010.
2   Newell 2011.
3   Newell 2008.
4   Blaikie 1985; Rocheleau et al. 1996; Stott and Sullivan 2000; and Forsyth 2003.
5   Carmin and Agyeman 2011; and Peet et al. 2011.
6   Mann 2009.
7   Harvey 2005.
8   Newell and Paterson 2010.
9   Van der Pijl 1998.
10   Harvey 2010.
11   Vogel 1997; and Neumayer 2001.
12   Gallagher 2005.
13   Newell 2001.
14   Lipschutz with Rowe 2005.
15   Peet et al. 2011, 22.
16   Harvey 2010.
17   Freese 2003; and Kaldor et al. 2007.
18   Rupert 1995.

19   Rees 2001.
20   Newell and Paterson 2010.
21   Brunnengräber 2006, 219.
22   Huber 2008.
23   Altvater 2006.
24   Peet et al. 2011, 10.
25   Marx and Engels 1998, 38.
26   Storper and Walker 1989.
27   Buck 2006, 60.
28   Altvater 2006, 53.
29   Buck 2006, 63.
30   Derber 2010.
31   Paterson 2001a.
32   Newell 2008.
33   Peet et al. 2011, 21.
34   Dauvergne 2008.
35   Peet et al. 2011, 21.
36   Peet et al. 2011, 22.
37   Pellow and Park 2002; and Newell 2005, 2006.
38   Carmin and Agyeman 2011.
39   Harvey 1981.
40   Bumpus and Liverman 2008.
41   Strange 1996.
42   Sklair 2002.
43   Muchlinski 1999; and Newell 2001.
44   Gill 2002, 47.
45   Breslin 2003.
46   World Bank 2003, 3.22.
47   Gale and M'Gonigle 2000; and Levy and Newell 2005.
48   Gill 2002; Sklair 2002; and Robinson 2004.
49   Castree and Braun 2001.
50   Robbins 2004.
51   Saurin 2001; Paterson 2001b; and Newell 2008.
52   Peet et al. 2011, 23.
53   Peet et al. 2011, 23.
54   Castree 2003, 2008; Budds 2004; Mansfield 2004, 2007; and Bakker 2005.
55   Peluso 1992; Bryant and Bailey 1997; Paulson et al. 2003; and Zimmerer and Bassett 2003.
56   Sachs 1993.
57   Chatterjee and Finger 1994; and thomas 1996.
58   Sachs 1993, xv.
59   Blaikie and Brookfield 1987, 17.
60   Blaikie 1985.
61   Clarke and York 2005; and Burkett and Bellamy Foster 2006.
62   Altvater 2006.
63   Martinez-Alier 2007.
64   Roberts et al. 2003.
65   Martinez-Alier 2002.

66   Goldman 1998.
67   Newell 2007.
68   Bachram 2004; Brockington and Igoe 2006; Lohmann 2006; and Adams and Hutton 2007.
69   Young 2002; and Goldman 2005.
70   Newell 2008.
71   Blaikie 1985; Blaikie and Brookfield 1987; and Peet and Watts 2004.
72   Levy and Newell 2002; and Mann 2009.
73   Newell and Paterson 2010.
74   Bebbington 2003, 300.

References

Adams, William and J. Hutton. 2007. People, Parks and Poverty: Political Ecology and Biodiversity Conservation. *Conservation and Society* 5: 147–83.

Altvater, Elmar. 2006. The Social and Natural Environment of Fossil Capitalism. In *Coming to Terms with Nature*, edited by Leo Panitch and Colin Leys, 37–60. London: Merlin Press.

Bachram, Heidi. 2004. Climate Fraud and Carbon Colonialism: The New Trade in Greenhouse Gases. *Capitalism, Nature, Socialism* 15 (4): 1–16.

Bakker, Karen. 2005. Neoliberalizing Nature? Market Environmentalism in Water Supply in England and Wales. *Annals of the Association of American Geographers* 95 (3): 542–65.

Bebbington, Anthony. 2003. Global Networks and Local Developments: Agendas for Development Geography. *Tijdschrift Voor Economische En Sociale Geografie* 94 (3): 297–309.

Blaikie, Piers. 1985. *The Political Economy of Soil Erosion in Developing Countries*. London: Longman.

Blaikie, Piers and Harold Brookfield. 1987. *Land Degradation and Society*. London: Methuen.

Breslin, Shaun. 2003. Reforming China's Embedded Socialist Compromise: China and the WTO. *Global Change, Peace and Security* 15 (3): 213–29.

Brockington, D. and J. Igoe. 2006. Eviction for Conservation: A Global Overview. *Conservation and Society* 4: 424–70.

Brunnengräber, Achim. 2006. The Political Economy of the Kyoto Protocol. In *Coming to Terms with Nature*, edited by Leo Panitch and Colin Leys. Socialist Register 2007, 213–31. London: Merlin Press.

Bryant, Raymond and Sinéad Bailey. 1997. *Third World Political Ecology*. London: Routledge.

Buck, Daniel. 2006. The Ecological Question: Can Capitalism Prevail? In *Coming to Terms with Nature*, edited by Leo Panitch and Colin Leys. Socialist Register 2007, 60–72. London: Merlin Press.

Budds, Jessica. 2004. Power, Nature and Neoliberalism: The Political Ecology of Water in Chile. *Singapore Journal of Tropical Geography* 25 (3): 322–42.

Bumpus, Adam and Diana Liverman. 2008. Accumulation by De-carbonization and the Governance of Carbon Offsets. *Economic Geography* 84 (2): 127–55.

Burkett, Paul and John Bellamy Foster. 2006. Metabolism, Energy and Entropy in Marx's Critique of Political Economy: Beyond the Podolinsky Myth. *Theory and Society* 35: 109–56.

Carmin JoAnn and Julian Agyeman, eds. 2011. *Environmental Justice beyond Borders: Local Perspectives on Global Inequities*. Cambridge MA: MIT Press.

Castree, Noel. 2003. Commodifying What Nature? *Progress in Human Geography* 27 (3): 273–97.

Castree, Noel. 2008. Neoliberalising Nature: The Logics of Deregulation and Reregulation. *Environment and Planning A* 40 (1): 131–52.

Castree, Noel and Bruce Braun. 2001. *Social Nature: Theory Practice and Politics*. Oxford and New York: Blackwell.

Chatterjee, Pratap and Matthias Finger. 1994. *The Earth Brokers: Power, Politics and World Development*. London: Routledge.

Clarke, Brett and Richard York. 2005. Carbon Metabolism: Global Capitalism, Climate Change and the Biospheric Rift. *Theory and Society* 34: 391–428.

Dauvergne, Peter. 2008. *The Shadows of Consumption: Consequences for the Global Environment*. Cambridge MA: MIT Press.

Derber, Charles. 2010. *Greed to Green: Solving Climate Change and Re-Making the Economy*. London: Paradigm.

Forsyth, Tim. 2003. *Critical Political Ecology: The Politics of Environmental Science*. London: Routledge.

Freese, Barbara. 2003. *Coal: A Human History*. London: Basic Books.

Gale, Fred and Michael M'Gonigle, eds. 2000. *Nature, Production Power: Towards an Ecological Political Economy*. Cheltenham, UK and Northampton, MA, USA: Edward Elgar.

Gallagher, Kevin, ed. 2005. *Putting Development First*. London: Zed Books.

Gill, Stephen. 2002. Constitutionalizing Inequality and the Clash of Globalizations. *International Studies Review* 4 (2): 47–65.

Goldman, Michael, ed. 1998. *Privatising Nature: Political Struggles for the Global Commons*. London: Pluto Press.

Goldman, Michael. 2005. *Imperial Nature: The World Bank and Struggles for Social Justice in an Age of Globalization*. New Haven, CT: Yale University Press.

Harvey, David. 1981. The Spatial Fix: Hegel, von Thünen and Marx. *Antipode* 13 (3): 1–12.

Harvey, David. 2005. *A Brief History of Neoliberalism*. Oxford: Oxford University Press.

Harvey, David. 2010. *Enigma of Capital: And the Crisis of Capitalism*. London: Profile Books.

Huber, Matthew. 2008. Energizing Historical Materialism: Fossil Fuels, Space and the Capitalist Mode of Production. *Geoforum* 40: 105–15.

Kaldor, Mary, Terry Lynn Karl and Yahia Said, eds. 2007. *Oil Wars*. London: Pluto Press.

Kovel, Joel. 2007. *The Enemy of Nature: The End of Capitalism or the End of the World*. London: Zed Books.

Levy, David and Peter Newell. 2002. Business Strategy and International Environmental Governance: toward a Neo-Gramscian Synthesis. *Global Environmental Politics* 3 (4): 84–101.

Levy, David and Peter Newell, eds. 2005. *The Business of Global Environmental Governance*. Cambridge, MA: MIT Press.

Lipschutz, Ronnie with James Rowe. 2005. *Globalization, Governmentality and Global Politics: Regulation for the Rest of Us?* New York: Routledge.

Lohmann, Larry. 2006. *Carbon Trading: A Critical Conversation on Climate Change, Privatisation and Power*. Sturminster Newton, UK: The Corner House.

Magdoff, Fred and John Bellamy Foster. 2010. What Every Environmentalist Needs to Know About Capitalism. *Monthly Review* (March): 1–30.

Mann, Geoff. 2009. Should Political Ecology be Marxist? A Case for Gramsci's Historical Materialism. *Geoforum* 40: 335–44.

Mansfield, Becky. 2004. Neoliberalism in the Oceans: "Rationalization," Property Rights, and the Commons Question. *Geoforum* 35 (3): 313–26.

Mansfield, Becky. 2007. Articulation between Neoliberal and State-Oriented Environmental Regulation: Fisheries Privatization and Endangered Species Protection. *Environment and Planning A* 39 (8): 1926–42.

Martinez-Alier, Joan. 2002. *The Environmentalism of the Poor: A Study of Ecological Conflicts and Valuation.* Cheltenham, UK and Northampton, MA, USA: Edward Elgar.

Martinez-Alier, Joan. 2007. Marxism, Social Metabolism and International trade. In *Rethinking Environmental History: World Systems History and Global Environmental Change,* edited by Alf Hornborg, John Robert McNeill and Joan Martinez-Alier, 221–39. Lanham, MD: Altamira.

Marx, Karl and Frederick Engels. 1998. *The Communist Manifesto.* London: Verso.

Muchlinski, Peter. 1999. A Brief History of Business Regulation. In *Regulating International Business: Beyond Liberalization,* edited by Sol Picciotto and Ruth Mayne, 47–60. Basingstoke: Macmillan.

Neumayer, Eric. 2001. Do Countries Fail to Raise Environmental Standards? An Evaluation of Policy Options Addressing "Regulatory Chill." *International Journal of Sustainable Development* 4 (3): 231–44.

Newell, Peter. 2001. Managing Multinationals: The Governance of Investment for the Environment. *Journal of International Development* 13: 907–19.

Newell, Peter. 2005. Race, Class and the Global Politics of Environmental Inequality. *Global Environmental Politics* 5(3): 70–93.

Newell, Peter. 2006. Environmental Justice Movements: Taking Stock, Moving Forward. *Environmental Politics* 15 (4): 656–60.

Newell, Peter. 2007. Trade and Environmental Justice in Latin America. *New Political Economy* 12 (2): 237–59.

Newell, Peter. 2008. The Political Economy of Global Environmental Governance. *Review of International Studies* 34: 507–29.

Newell, Peter. 2011. The Elephant in the Room: Capitalism and Global Environmental Change. *Global Environmental Change* 21 (1): 4–6.

Newell, Peter and Matthew Paterson. 2010. *Climate Capitalism: Global Warming and the Transformation of the Global Economy.* Cambridge: Cambridge University Press.

Paterson, Matthew. 2001a. Risky Business: Insurance Companies in Global Warming Politics. *Global Environmental Politics* 1 (3): 18–42.

Paterson, Matthew. 2001b. *Understanding Global Environmental Politics: Domination, Accumulation, Resistance.* Basingstoke: Palgrave.

Paulson, Susan, Lisa Gezon and Michael Watts. 2003. Locating the Political in Political Ecology: An Introduction. *Human Organisation* 62 (3): 205–17.

Peet, Richard, Paul Robbins and Michael Watts, eds. 2011. *Global Political Ecology.* London: Routledge.

Peet, Richard and Michael Watts, eds. 2004. *Liberation Ecologies: Environment, Development, Social Movements.* London: Routledge.

Pellow, David and Lisa Sun-Hee Park. 2002. *The Silicon Valley of Dreams: Environmental Injustice, Immigrant Workers, and the High-Tech Global Economy.* New York: New York University Press.

Peluso, Nancy. 1992. The Political Ecology of Extraction and Extractive Reserves in East Kalimantan, Indonesia. *Development and Change* 23 (4): 49–74.

Rees, John. 2001. Imperialism: Globalization, the State and War. *International Socialism 93*. Exeter: BPC Wheatons.

Robbins, Paul. 2004. *Political Ecology: A Critical Introduction*. Oxford: Blackwell.

Roberts, J. Timmons, Peter Grimes and Jodie Manale. 2003. Social Roots of Global Environmental Change: A World-Systems Analysis of Carbon Dioxide Emissions. *Journal of World-Systems Research* 9 (2): 277–315.

Robinson, William. 2004. *A Theory of Global Capitalism: Production, Class and State in a Transnational World*. Baltimore, MD: Johns Hopkins University Press.

Rocheleau, Diana, Barbara Thomas-Slayter and Esther Wangari. 1996. *Feminist Political Ecology: Global Issues and Local Experiences*. London: Routledge.

Rupert, Mark. 1995. *Producing Hegemony: The Politics of Mass Production and American Global Power*. Cambridge: Cambridge University Press.

Sachs, Wolfgang, ed. 1993. *Global Ecology: A New Arena of Political Conflict*. London: Zed Books.

Saurin, Julian. 2001. Global Environmental Crisis as "Disaster Triumphant:" The Private Capture of Public Goods. *Environmental Politics* 10 (4): 63–84.

Sklair, Leslie. 2002. *Globalization: Capitalism and Its Alternatives*. Oxford: Oxford University Press.

Storper, Michael and Richard Walker. 1989. *The Capitalist Imperative: Territory, Technology and Industrial Growth*. Cambridge: Blackwell.

Stott, Philip and Sian Sullivan. 2000. *Political Ecology: Science, Myth and Power*. Oxford: Oxford University Press.

Strange, Susan. 1996. *The Retreat of the State*. Cambridge: Cambridge University Press.

Thomas, Caroline. 1996. Unsustainable Development? *New Political Economy* 1 (3): 404–7.

Van der Pijl, Kees. 1998. *Transnational Classes and International Relations*. London: Routledge.

Vogel, David. 1997. *Trading Up: Consumer and Environmental Regulation in the Global Economy*. Cambridge, MA: Harvard University Press.

World Bank. 2003. *World Development Report: Dynamic Development in a Sustainable World Transformation in the Quality of Life, Growth, and Institutions*. New York: Oxford University Press.

Young, Zoe. 2002. *A New Green Order? The World Bank and the Politics of the Global Environment Facility*. London: Pluto Press.

Zimmerer, Karl and Thomas Bassett. 2003. *Political Ecology: An Integrative Approach to Geography and Environment–Development Studies*. New York: Guilford Press.

16

Institutions for the Earth: Promoting International Environmental Protection (1992)

Marc A. Levy, Peter M. Haas, and Robert O. Keohane

The United Nations Conference on Environment and Development (UNCED), held in Rio de Janeiro in June 1992 was the world's most comprehensive organized response to international environmental degradation. UNCED delegates sought to adopt conventions on greenhouse gases and biodiversity; to enunciate in an "Earth Charter" the principles by which humans should conduct themselves in relation to the environment; to adopt a program of action, called Agenda 21, to implement the Earth Charter; and to develop a set of institutional and financial arrangements to support such measures.

However, many critics are skeptical of the ability of national governments to solve the problems on UNCED's agenda. Because governments are ultimately concerned with protecting national security and maintaining economic growth, they may be incapable of adequately addressing the fundamental problems that have given rise to the environmental agenda. Thus, these critics argue, as long as governments protect national interests and refuse to grant significant powers to supranational authorities, the survival of the planet is in jeopardy.[1]

The skeptics are right to warn that the planet's ecosystem is in danger and that its protection will require modifications in traditional interpretations of state sovereignty. But development of a world government is not around the corner. Organized international responses to shared environmental problems will occur only through cooperation among states, not through the imposition of a supranational authority over them. Intergovernmental cooperation has achieved a number of major successes over problems that earlier seemed as daunting as does UNCED's present agenda. Such problems as the spread of cholera, the slave trade, and atmospheric

Marc A. Levy, Peter M. Haas, and Robert O. Keohane. 1992. "Institutions for the Earth: Promoting International Environmental Protection". In *Environment: Science and Policy for Sustainable Development*, 34(4): 12–36. Reproduced with permission from Taylor & Francis testing of nuclear weapons were all successfully managed against great odds with the help of international institutions. Here, institutions will be defined as persistent and connected sets of rules and practices that prescribe behavioral roles, constrain activity, and shape expectations. The focus here is on institutions that consist of organizations and constellations of organizations. Activities for which the rates of anthropogenic releases of pollutants to the environment have decelerated since 1955 – for example, sulfur, lead, and carbon tetrachloride emissions – are also areas for which international environmental institutions were developed and applied.[2]

The international community's ability to preserve the quality of the planet for future generations depends upon international cooperation. Successful cooperation, in turn, requires effective international institutions to guide international behavior toward sustainable development.

But how can international institutions, which necessarily follow the principle of state sovereignty, contribute to the solution of difficult global problems? What are the sources of effectiveness for institutions that lack enforcement power? A recently completed research project at Harvard University attempted to answer these questions by analyzing the factors influencing organized responses to seven international environmental problems: oil pollution from tankers, acid rain, stratospheric ozone depletion, pollution of the North and Baltic seas, mismanagement of fisheries, overpopulation, and misuse of agricultural chemicals.[3] In an analysis largely based on concepts and methods drawn from political science, the Harvard investigators identified the roles played by international environmental institutions in attempting to solve these problems. The researchers focused on institutional effectiveness, specifically whether the international institutions had a positive contribution to the treatment of the shared problems.

The establishment of truly effective international environmental institutions would improve the quality of the global environment. However, much of this activity is relatively new, and none of the studies on the seven issues has produced good direct data about changes in environmental quality as a result of international institutional action. Therefore, the researchers focused on the observable political effects of institutions, in addition to their direct environmental impacts.[4] This is not just a case of looking where the light is brighter. For international institutions to make a difference in the environment, they must spawn political change, and it is therefore appropriate to judge them according to how well they do so.

Effective institutions can influence the political process at three key points in the environmental policy-making and policy implementation process: by contributing to more appropriate agendas and reflecting the convergence of political and technical consensus about the nature of environmental threats; by contributing to more comprehensive and specific international policies agreed upon through a political process whose core is intergovernmental bargaining; and by contributing to national policy responses that directly control sources of environmental degradation. Although effectiveness in setting agendas and in international policy formulation is a facilitating condition, effectiveness in national policymaking is a necessary condition for improvement of environmental quality through the actions of international institutions.

The studies at Harvard reveal four types of national policy responses. Some countries simply avoid international obligations by failing to sign treaty commitments. Others accept commitments but fail to live up to them. A third group accepts commitments and achieves compliance. Finally, a fourth group surpasses the explicitly required obligations. Effective institutions nudge countries further along this continuum of commitment and compliance.

Countries that fall into the first two categories may be called laggards because they typically possess much weaker environmental measures than do others. The economic costs of strengthening these measures may be high, and noncompliant laggards may have agreed to regulation only reluctantly. Laggard countries may support collective policies even though they do not have the scientific, technical, or administrative capacity to implement the rules and may hope that "joining the club" would entitle them to receive assistance.

Countries in the latter two categories, or "leaders," willingly sign and comply with treaty commitments and often exceed these commitments. Leaders commonly possess more advanced domestic environmental policies and also are often subject to more intense domestic political pressures than are laggards. This was the case with U.S. leadership in the ozone and population case studies. Leaders are often motivated simply by being the first to suffer environmental damage, though being first frequently means being the most severely affected, as was the case for acid rain in Sweden and Norway and marine oil pollution off the coast of Britain. Domestic pressure, advanced policies, and disproportionate damage all give leaders higher levels of motivation and political capacity to effect change than others have. In the seven case studies, these differences prompted leaders to promote institutional solutions to environmental problems.[5]

Based on an examination of the political consequences of international environmental institutions, the Harvard research team formulated tentative general propositions and specific lessons for leaders and designers of international institutions who wish to use international organizations and regulations to improve the quality of the natural and human environment. The case studies reveal three distinctive functions of international environmental institutions: to promote concern among governments; to enhance the contractual environment by providing negotiating forums and creating ways to disseminate information; and to build national political and administrative capacity. These three functions dominate the attention of effective institutions. On the other hand, there is little evidence that international organizations enforce rules. Indeed, in the case studies, monitoring environmental quality and national policy measures was a far more influential institutional activity than was direct enforcement, and promoting re-evaluation of state interests was more effective than was forcing behavior against a state's interest.[6]

International Environmental Institutions

International environmental institutions can be considered to be responses to problems caused by inadequate responses by governments, acting without institutional support, to environmental threats. The inadequacy of governmental responses derives principally from three major factors: low levels of concern about the environmental threat, lack of capacity to manage it, and the inability to overcome problems of collective action. Institutions that help improve the quality of efforts to protect the environment – in other words, effective institutions – help to overcome each of these factors.

Increasing Governmental Concern

For each of the case studies, there were periods when some governments were motivated to solve an environmental problem but were unable to overcome the central bottleneck created by the fact that their concern was not shared by other governments. In such cases, it is unrealistic to expect institutions to promulgate effective regulatory rules; the laggard states will either block rules or insist on weak rules.

Institutions are not powerless in such settings, however, and several ways exist by which they can boost concern within laggard states. In cases where a laggard state's lack of concern was due to a misunderstanding of its own interests, normative pronouncements (to reduce transborder air pollution or to stop destroying the ozone layer) accompanied by collaborative scientific reviews sometimes contributed to a shift from low to high concern. The collaborative reviews of scientific evidence under the Vienna convention and Montreal protocol on protecting the ozone layer clearly played a major role in the increased concern of several governments for the problem of stratospheric ozone depletion.

Institutions can also serve as magnifiers of public pressure when they foster competition among governments to be more pro-environmental, as was seen in the Baltic Sea and North Sea Ministerial Conferences, in further ozone negotiations, and in acid rain "tote-board diplomacy". Under these circumstances, international institutions were important sounding-boards for politicians in a competitive game to impress the public. Although intergovernmental organizations are almost always extremely reticent to criticize governments, nongovernmental organizations (NGOs) do not face such constraints. NGOs typically play an active role, using information from formal international meetings and public statements made by governmental officials to embarrass and criticize a country's national policy. Under these conditions, each international institution is part of a complex network of governments, international institutions, nonprofit NGOs, mass media, and industry groups, in which public pressure may overwhelm industries' and governments' resistance.

International institutions can focus normative pressure on states, as well. When international principles and norms have been agreed upon, they may acquire legitimacy as intrinsically valuable premises rather than as contestable reflections of interest-based compromises. Just as the United Nations Educational, Scientific and Cultural Organization in the 1970s offered many resolutions under the theme "the collective legitimation of the world's doers of good or the delegitimation of its doers of evil," international environmental institutions can legitimize or delegitimize state practices.[7]

Institutions can also have an impact on how nations express their concern at the international level. International institutions that have open procedures for setting agendas may enable weak states or groups of states to put issues on the international agenda in ways that cannot be ignored by others. Furthermore, by providing established leadership roles, international organizational arrangements may allow proponents of action to have greater influence than they would have in a disordered international system. Thus, domestic concern about environment issues may be magnified at the international level, and it may be more feasible to mobilize coalitions for policy change because of the institution. The Convention on Long Range Transboundary Air Pollution is a good example.

Institutions can also increase concern by facilitating the linking of issues. A laggard state may have little concern for an environmental problem, but if an institution helps the environmental problem to other issues that are of concern, then the laggard may lose its reluctance. Such a link is direct in the case of material incentives, such as financial aid, the transfer of technology to developing countries and those in Eastern Europe, or the trade sanctions in the Montreal protocol. The link can also be less direct, as when governments exert diplomatic pressure within the context of an environmental institution, raising the prospect that life may be made difficult for the laggard in other areas if the country does not comply. Institutions help increase such diplomatic pressure, both by publicizing a laggard's opposition and by creating the opportunity to form international coalitions explicitly designed to put pressure on laggards. In the cases of stratospheric ozone and acid rain, pro-environmentalist "clubs" explicitly formed to exert pressure on opponents of emerging institutional rules. Other times, less formal international coalitions emerged, as in the cases of the pesticide trade and pollution in the North and Baltic seas.

Enhancing the Contractual Environment

The degree of concern that a government expresses about an international environmental problem reflects not only its view on the issues but also its calculations of both the feasibility of such action and the action's costs and benefits. Thus, concern is partly a function of the other two crucial factors: the nature of the contractual environment and a state's capacity. If levels of effective communication among states and their ability to make credible commitments to each other are low, it may seem futile to raise new issues for the international agenda. Environmental institutions, however, can enhance the quality of the contractual environment and thus facilitate the creation and maintenance of international agreements. Institutions create bargaining forums in which information is shared and thus reduce the transaction costs of negotiating agreements. Institutions that create ongoing negotiating processes help make commitments more credible by ensuring regular interaction among participants on the same set of issues.

Another way institutions can facilitate agreements is to provide monitoring and verification services. Frequently, uncertainty regarding the future actions of other countries can restrain otherwise willing countries from accepting mutual constraints. Monitoring by an institution can help overcome this obstacle in three ways: by measuring aspects of environmental quality; by observing potential sources of pollution, such as oil tankers; and by monitoring national policy. Institutions can also serve as a scapegoat, enabling governments to transfer blame for costly adjustment measures and, thus, lessen the domestic political cost of carrying out actions that are unpopular though beneficial.

Every institution that was studied monitored aspects of environmental quality, either directly or in conjunction with independent scientific laboratories. Although many of the institutions also gathered data on the activities of potential sources of pollution, only the acid rain monitoring program was able to validate national reports more or less independently; every other such program relied solely on national reports of behavior. In spite of countries' ability to falsify their own national reports (secretariats never challenge the reports), governments value them. In situations where public interest is high, NGOs and domestic bureaucracies that want more effective action can use the information in the reports to apply public or intragovernmental pressure on the government in question to make it live up to its promises. In terms of national policies, international institutions are also dependent on national reporting. However, in this area, even though states could misrepresent their policies in national reports, governments seem to value the exchange of information for its role in reducing uncertainty and in promoting public scrutiny.

For issues about which concern is very high, a nation's ability to monitor violations may not be essential for cooperation. Nations around the North and Baltic seas undertook significant new policy measures despite the lack of well-funded and integrated monitoring systems for either compliance or environmental quality. Monitoring arrangements for compliance with the Montreal protocol still have loopholes, are based on awkward economic proxies for actual environmental emissions, and do not generate prompt identification of violations. For example, the major industrialized countries appear to have incentives to reduce production of ozone-depleting chemicals that are so strong that they are satisfied with weak verification measures, and their concern about noncompliance is low.

Sometimes, however, monitoring is essential. Because systematic monitoring of oil tankers at sea is impractical, controls on vessel-source pollution only became effective when equipment regulations – which could easily be monitored – replaced discharge rules as the principal means of regulation. Prior to the adoption of exclusive economic zones in the late 1970s, the ability of fishing fleets to escape detection created a climate of distrust that contributed to the failure of collective efforts to manage fish stocks.

Enhancing the contractual environment is most relevant for international commons problems, where regulatory rules specifying mutual restraints are the dominant focus of bargaining. But, surprisingly, actions that are meant to improve the contractual environment are also relevant for national environmental problems, where mutual restraints are not an issue. The prior informed consent rules associated with pesticide trade, for example, are not intended to solve a commons problem but to assist national responses to the problem in developing countries. The rules provide points of accountability within national governments that may enable concerned groups within society and within governments of pesticide-importing countries to make exact commitments, to pressure for more effective controls on pesticide availability and use, to monitor compliance, and to apply strategies of reciprocity. In general, institutional activities that enhance the contractual environment can facilitate the negotiation of norms and principles governing national problems, as well as those operating at an international level for commons problems.

Regulations do more than regulate – they help generate political concern, they set normative standards, they communicate intensity of preferences, and they legitimize financial transfers that might otherwise be termed bribes or even blackmail. This dual role of regulatory rules explains why so many international institutional responses to environmental problems have been regulatory in nature. With the exception of population, regulatory standards were set (though not always formally enshrined in international law) in each of the case studies investigated by the researchers, even when it was clearly impossible or unrealistic for many states to apply them.[8]

Increasing National Capacity

For collective principles, norms, and rules to be promulgated and implemented, it is not sufficient for governments to be concerned only about environmental problems and for the contractual environment to be reasonably benign. Governments must also have the technical capacity to negotiate meaningful regulations that take into account both environmental realities and the political and economic incentives facing governments, firms, and other organizations that affect environmental quality. After such regulations have been specified and agreed on, the burden of action shifts to national responses, which are often inhibited by low political, legal, and administrative capacity. Leaders of weakly institutionalized states who want to conform to international norms and principles and to comply with regime rules may lack the political legitimacy or the loyalty of competent and honest bureaucracies necessary to develop and implement domestic initiatives. International regulations create an external demand for effective domestic action, and international coalitions, including NGOs, may prompt increasing internal demand as well. However, severe constraints may exist on the ability of the state to supply effective policy. When this problem becomes serious, international institutions can play an important role in helping to increase domestic capacity, sometimes by transferring resources to weak governments in the form of technical assistance or outright aid and, in other instances, by creating interorganizational networks that serve as catalysts and facilitators. Capacity building is particularly important for developing countries and the new Eastern European democracies, whose administrative and political abilities are generally limited by a lack of resources.

Technical assistance from international institutions is common. Many institutions offer training programs, policy-relevant information, and research grants to help weak governments create stronger policy programs. Typically, such programs are operated under the auspices of an international institution. In many of the cases studied, such programs helped weaker states improve their ability to develop and implement effective measures to protect the environment. For instance, the ozone fund enables less developed countries to find alternatives to chlorofluorocarbons (CFCs); family-planning experts help mothers in developing countries control population growth; technical assistance from the UN Food and Agriculture Organization helps national pesticide registrars and promotes integrated pest management; and fishery commissions train national fisheries managers. Institutions contributed to building private-sector capacity, as well. Fisheries commissions trained private fishermen as well as state managers. The International Maritime Organization's training seminars help educate ship captains in applying international and national environmental measures to their routine operations.

In addition to such familiar aid roles, international environmental institutions have developed networks with other agencies with related operational programs, such as the World Bank, various regional development banks, and the UN Development Programme. It is revealing that, in the case of marine oil pollution, where coalitions with operational organizations are absent, virtually no increase occurred in relevant developing countries' capacity to enforce or comply with treaties.

Therefore, effective international institutions tailor their activities according to the specific political obstacles they face. [...] Of course, increasing governmental concern, enhancing the contractual environment, and building state capacity are not strictly sequential activities, but they interact with one another synergistically. In other words, reinforcing one is likely to strengthen others, though weakness in one activity may drain another. Effective institutions will address these interactions with sophisticated strategies operating at multiple levels. The weak technical capacity of participating states, for example, may inhibit expressions of concern because governments that are technically ignorant are likely to take abstract, principled stands and may be reluctant to discuss specific costs and benefits for fear of being unable to evaluate others' arguments. And when a government prepares a national policy response, problems of low concern may re-merge. It may turn out that some regime members had enough concern to accept mutual commitments but had insufficient concern to make the necessary domestic adjustments. Or domestic political opponents who had been uninvolved during the negotiation of international rules may become more formidable obstacles once domestic adjustment measures are deliberated. If problems of low concern emerge during this phase, the networks formed by international environmental institutions can increase the influence of their domestic allies by providing them with information or by mobilizing transnational coalitions to influence their governments.

There are additional complex links that the research team did not explore systematically, such as the availability of technological options, which also enhanced institutional effectiveness. More aggressive international actions for protecting the ozone layer, for controlling acid rain, for protecting regional seas, and for controlling oil pollution from tanker operations were all facilitated by the availability of technological options that made such objectives appear feasible. However, technological change is partly a function of institutional influences and partly autonomous. Technology has been both a contributing cause and a consequence of institutional effectiveness. Corporate decisions to invest in new technologies are driven in part by signals from institutions regarding future market opportunities. For instance, although progress in the ozone case after the Montreal protocol was made easier by the creation of possible CFC substitutes, the availability of such commercial substitutes was itself the consequence of prior research and development decisions by the major producers, who had accurately perceived in the early 1980s that such products might become marketable if CFCs turned out to have negative environmental effects.

   In the course of carrying out this study, the researchers have become increasingly aware of the effects that international negotiations and the evolution of international institutions can have on the availability of new technologies relevant to environmental problems. Technology arises in response to anticipated economic demands and is conditional on the state of scientific knowledge and its underlying technical capabilities. Anticipated economic demand, as in the case of CFCs, is, to a considerable extent, the result of anticipated environmental regulation. An important issue in considering international environmental regulation is the degree of elasticity of the underlying technology. If increased demand, fostered by regulation, is likely to bring a valuable new technology into being, the case for regulation is strengthened. Conversely, if no such technology seems feasible, the costs of regulation may be very high.

Advice to the New Secretary General

What are the implications of these findings for those who wish to build effective international environmental institutions? Because only a small number of cases (which were not scientifically chosen) have been studied, definitive judgments cannot be offered on the entire range of practical questions being debated in the UNCED process. Nonetheless, certain conclusions emerge quite strongly.

Build Environment-centered Coalitions

The most general lesson that can be drawn from the case studies is that the most significant roles of international institutions – such as magnifying concern, facilitating agreement, and building capacity – do not require large administrative bureaucracies. Indeed, running such a bureaucracy may divert leaders of international organizations from their most important tasks, which are quintessentially political: to create and manipulate dynamic processes by which governments change conceptions of their interests and to mobilize and coordinate complex policy networks involving governments, NGOs, subunits of governments, and industrial groups, as well as a variety of international organizations that have different priorities and political styles.

In so far as capacity needs to be built, international environmental organizations should first seek to make operational arrangements with other international organizations, thus building mutually reinforcing networks and coalitions rather than establishing competing bureaucracies. Indeed, keeping the size of secretariats small forces them to build bridges to other groups and develop networks rather than hierarchies. A reputation for competent professionalism may induce others to cooperate as well.

The case studies reveal that a variety of environment-centered coalitions can be effective. Institutions can help create and nurture coalitions among like-minded governments, among action-oriented groups within other institutions and organizations, among supportive NGOs, and among environmental protection ministries. Institutions commonly perform better when environmental ministries serve as lead agencies in their deliberations. Although some responses are beyond an institution's control, institutional architects may have some influence over the shape of supporting coalitions.[9]

Foster Open-ended Knowledge Creation

Environmental institutions are typically constructed to deal with problems that are not well understood. The only reliable knowledge, when institutions are created, is that current understanding of the problem will be obsolete in 10 or 20 years. Hence, the rules and organizations that comprise institutions should not codify existing knowledge in rules that are difficult to change, but should, on the contrary, foster an open-ended process of knowledge creation.

Such a process would require routine scientific monitoring of the environment, and universal circulation of information should be encouraged. Monitoring should be nonpartisan and untainted by national concerns, to offset suspicions that such activities are politically controlled or are a disingenuous way to promote an economic advantage. Monitoring should be conducted through direct contracts with international organizations to guarantee insulation from national policy agendas but should be performed by national scientists because governments typically pay closer attention to the findings of their own scientists. The provision of information should be indirect rather than formal and institutionalized to eliminate distributional bargaining, government censorship and control, and myopia in reporting.[10] Also, information should be made available frequently and promptly. The United Nations Environment Programme (UNEP) could serve as a clearinghouse for such information. A particularly timely and effective means of information diffusion is the UNEP executive director's annual state of the environment report.

Institutions should also monitor and publicize state environmental policies. Secretariats should be authorized to gather information regarding their governments' actual environmental protection measures and to report this information to NGOs and other domestic groups. In this way, UNEP could provide information for less developed countries and governments that are not able to emulate this role themselves. Furthermore, this function, combined with its environmental monitoring role, would be useful for UNEP in the post UNCED order. The Organization for Economic Cooperation and Development (OECD) is already playing this policy review role among advanced industrial countries and is seeking to extend it to the new regimes of Eastern Europe.

In addition to monitoring governments, institutions can help promote the widespread development of scientific knowledge concerning the various causes of environmental damage and the various consequences of suspected pollutants. Without institutional intervention, knowledge that is relevant to policymaking is limited to those nations that are active in scientific research. Institutions can help speed up the diffusion process by establishing multinational assessment panels, working groups, and collaborative research programs. Such international, knowledge-based groups can often make effective use of innovative transnational experts, such as those at the International Institute for Applied Systems Analysis, the International Council of Scientific Unions, and the International Union for Conservation of Nature and Natural Resources, in ways that national efforts cannot.

National political agendas should focus on environmental harm rather than on particular pollutants. For instance, the fact that the Vienna convention did not mention CFCs by name was considered a failure by some activists; in fact, the opposite is true. Agendas that focus on harm rather than on pollutants encourage increasing knowledge, rather than limiting it, and make possible a broadening regulatory scope, which, as the case of the diminishing ozone layer indicates, can be a matter of human survival. Although the acid rain regime was prompted by concern over acidified lakes and damaged forests, it followed an agenda that encouraged consideration of any environmental harm from a pollutant that crossed national borders. The furor over acid rain has fostered considerable knowledge about a variety of pollutants, some of which have no role in acidification of lakes and forests. By contrast, the International Convention on the Prevention of Pollution from Ships (MARPOL) set very limited agendas, and most progress in building knowledge about marine pollution has occurred in spite of, rather than because of, the institution.

Move from Principles to Rules

None of the institutions in the study was successful from the outset, though some eventually became so. In fact, most international environmental institutions were first considered to be disappointing by their creators. But there is cause for optimism even for inauspicious beginnings, and effective institutions must seize the opportunities for expanding the consequences of their activity.

Effective institutions begin with commitments "merely" to norms and principles and either lack regulatory rules or possess only very weak ones. This is exactly as it should be. If states waited to form institutions until there was enough concern and scientific understand to adopt strong rules, they would wait much too long. Institutions are needed early on to help create the conditions that make strong rules possible.[11]

To switch from principles to rules, institutions must create a dynamic process of negotiation in which interests are discussed, possibilities for joint regulations are explored, and reasons for concern are investigated. Such a process serves as a focal point for action and permits the various coalition-building processes already discussed to develop at their own rates. Such a process also puts the elements of an effective institutional response into place piece by piece.

Many of the mechanisms that facilitate adoption of effective rules and national implementation of joint rules are time consuming to create. A major advantage of an ongoing negotiation process that strives to move from principles to rules is that it helps lay the groundwork for effective rulemaking. When major crises occur, an institution that has laid the groundwork with facilitating mechanisms will be much better positioned to seize the opportunity to lock in strong rules than is an institution that is waiting to put together a comprehensive package. The discovery of the ozone hole in 1987, for example, would not have galvanized a rapid response if it were not for the procedural mechanisms established by the Vienna convention and Montreal protocol.

An evaluation of policy measures must be sensitive to the political process of moving from principles to rules, as well as to issues of economic efficiency and ethics. For example, it is easy to be critical of across-the-board percentage reductions, which are commonly employed at an early stage in international environmental regulation. Such cuts are unlikely to be economically efficient because they do not target the worst polluters, who could attain the greatest improvements at the lowest cost. Also, because such cuts discriminate against governments that have already taken environmentally sound measures, they are not fair. And expectations of similar across-the-board cuts in the future could lead governments to refrain from taking early unilateral action to reduce environmental damage. Yet the political virtue of such across-the-board cuts is that the severity of required reductions is likely to correlate with the intensity of domestic support for environmental actions. In other words, the political support for pollution control is greatest in those countries that have reduced emissions most. Thus, for all their drawbacks, across-the-board cuts may facilitate building initial coalitions that support policy regulation, which more efficient or fair rules could foreclose.

Build National Capacity

Finally, it is necessary to appreciate the importance of building political and administrative capacity within both the state and civil society. When they are effective, international environmental institutions are not merely rule-making bodies.

They are also vehicles for transferring skills and expertise and for empowering domestic actors to solve domestic problems of international importance.

Institutions should foster capacity building by providing policy-relevant information that can be used by government allies to develop better programs and to justify their actions to domestic opponents. The information also can be used by private organizations, such as NGOs, to pressure governments to adopt improved regulatory practices. That capacity building is often a necessary condition for effectiveness is another reason for environmental institutions to begin by establishing norms and principles and move toward establishing rules. Often the initial norms and principles, even though they fail to alter state behavior directly through binding rules, set in motion a process that builds domestic capacity in member governments. When conditions become right for binding rules, the capacity is in place to implement them effectively. In the acid rain regime, the governments of Eastern Europe emerged from the Cold War with more sophisticated air pollution policy infrastructures than they would have had if they had not participated in international environmental institutions. This is a striking effect, given the antipathy of the communist regimes to environmental protection.

Contemporary Greenhouse-gas Negotiations

Some of the research team's findings are relevant to the current international negotiations on greenhouse gases. These negotiations can be traced back to the concern over greenhouse-gas emissions and global climate change first expressed at the 1979 World Climate Conference. In an October 1985 meeting in Villach, Austria, scientists from UNEP, the World Meteorological Organization (WMO), and the International Council of Scientific Unions concluded that the threat of a greenhouse warming was real and called for cuts in carbon dioxide emissions. The conferees established the Advisory Group on Greenhouse Gases composed of two representatives from each of the three organizations. The advisory group organized two scientific and expert workshops in 1987 that drafted reports on the extent of the problem of global warming and called for an "intergovernmental mechanism" in response. Three working groups submitted reports to the 1988 Toronto conference on the changing atmosphere and the implications for global security, which called for 20-percent reductions in overall carbon dioxide emissions by the year 2000.

The Intergovernmental Panel on Climate Change (IPCC) was created in November 1988 in response to the lessons learned from the ozone talks, where independent scientists had strongly shaped the agenda. The governments kept negotiations about greenhouse gases out of the hands of scientists, who had already caused a lot of political consternation at Villach and Toronto. Although IPCC was administered by UNEP and WMO, the panel's scientists were chosen and briefed by government officials, and the final reports of three IPCC working groups, released in August 1990, were closely edited to ensure that the scientists did not pursue agendas that are potentially threatening to broader national interests. In December 1990, the United Nations General Assembly moved the focus of authority from the IPCC to a newly created Intergovernmental Negotiating Committee (INC) with its own secretariat. Many delegates were tired of being browbeaten by UNEP's executive director Mostafa Tolba at UNEP-sponsored meetings, and they designed the greenhouse-gases institutions to avoid a repetition of that process.

To date, INC has met four times, but talks have been disappointing because countries are deadlocked. At the September 1991 meeting in Nairobi, for example, it was proposed that the meeting follow a procedure known as "pledge and review," in which delegates would present and discuss their national measures, but this format was discarded after a week. The United States continues to argue that science does not yet support the need for rapid responses and still opposes any emission controls. All other OECD countries have announced a willingness to restrict emissions, and many European governments have already announced unilateral plans to stabilize or reduce their national carbon dioxide emissions. Many developing countries seek a concessionary transfer of technology to enable them to reduce their greenhouse-gas emissions cost effectively. The difficulty of reaching an internationally coordinated political solution to global warming is exacerbated by the unprecedented high costs of adjustment. These costs exacerbate concerns about countries benefiting and not cooperating and make governments highly sensitive to imposing new adjustment costs on the politically powerful transportation, manufacturing, and energy sectors of their economies, particularly during a period of recession. The scientific understanding of the problem remains fragmentary and incomplete, and public awareness, particularly in the United States, remains weak and poorly informed.

Such conditions pose a daunting challenge to those concerned with applying institutional lessons to this particular commons problem. Specifically, the strategy of taking problems one at a time, within separate issue areas, does not seem appropriate. Greenhouse-gas emissions are caused by a wide array of human activities that cannot be treated in isolation. Consequently, harder political and economic choices must be made, and much broader and more intense opposition can be expected because virtually all groups in the world will be asked to make sacrifices. Thus, no rapid action to reduce greenhouse-gas emissions is likely.

Some suggestions, based on the team's findings, may nevertheless be offered. Publicity and public education could increase domestic concern, prompting greater demand for international action, particularly in such laggards as the United States. Autonomous, nonpartisan scientific advice from a group such as a reconstituted Advisory Group on Greenhouse Gases could help provide information that is not politically suspect and thus provide the scientific basis for convergence of views and for eventual monitoring of any agreements that might emerge. Because many Western European governments have already adopted brave targets for carbon dioxide reductions, a well-publicized "pledge-and-review" process could shame others into making pledges and initiating policy processes at home. Capacity-building techniques are unlikely to have a significant impact on industrialized countries, such as the

United States, but could help rapidly industrializing countries and the countries in transition in Eastern Europe to reduce greenhouse-gas emissions.

Sovereignty

Sovereignty remains the legal cornerstone of the environmental order.[12] States are, if anything, reinforced in their legal authority to make decisions for the environment. All significant actions analyzed in this study have stressed national regulatory action on behalf of the environment. The skeptic might ask, "Is it possible to mitigate environmental problems without changing the underlying political economic factors responsible for environmental degradation?"

Rather surprisingly, the answer seems to be "yes." Discrete, reformist, institutionalist measures have been effective at improving environmental quality in several of the cases studied. Although international institutions have not been integrated in a systematic way, their efforts have complemented each other better than one might have expected. For instance, although the International Maritime Organization deliberately focused entirely on oil pollution from tankers, other institutions were designed to deal with additional sources of marine pollution. Land-based sources of pollution and nonvessel sources of coastal pollution were treated by UNEP and by the Baltic Sea and North Sea institutions. UNEP and the Food and Agriculture Organization have worked together remarkably well on issues of chemical pesticides.

The achievements of international environmental institutions do not stem from large bureaucratic operations or the use of effective enforcement powers. On the contrary, such international institutions are extremely weak, in terms of budgets and authority. Their impact comes from performing three catalytic functions: increasing governmental concern, enhancing the contractual environment, and increasing national political and administrative capacity. International institutions, led by savvy executives who tailor their actions to overcome political obstacles, can design arrangements that increase the probability of achieving effective results in accord with the "art of the possible."

Although the nation-state remains the sole legitimate source of public policy, the range of legitimate policy options has shifted. People in advanced countries have demanded that their governments accept the responsibility for a clean environment, in addition to the responsibility of keeping prices stable and insuring economic growth and full employment. States with environmentally mobilized publics were the most fervent supporters of emission reductions in the Baltic Sea and North Sea cases. It is still too soon to appreciate or examine the extent of such a change in national motivations, but the people and governments of such states surely will continue to press for such arrangements on a widening set of environmental issues. International institutions must be designed and applied to allow motivated actors to heighten environmental concern, to solve problems of collective action, and to build and spread national capacity. These political changes are necessary to protect the natural environment upon which humans depend.

[...]

Notes

1 See, for example, J. T. Mathews, "Redefining Security," *Foreign Affairs* 68, no. 2 (Spring 1989):174; and L. K. Caldwell, International Environmental Policy: Emergence and Dimensions, 2nd revised edition Durham, N.C.: Duke University Press, 1990). See also C. Black and R. Falk, "Introduction: The Structure of the International Environment," The Future of The International Legal Order, vol. 4 (Princeton, N.J.: Princeton University Press, 1972), ix; D. Newsom, "The New Diplomatic Agenda: Are Governments Ready?" *International Affairs* 65, no. 1 (Winter 1988/1989); and Financial Times, 13 March 1989.

2 R. W. Kates, B. L. Turner II, and W. C. Clark, "The Great Transformation," The Earth As Transformed by Human Action (Cambridge, England: Cambridge University Press, 1990), 8. See also J. G. Speth, "Environmental Pollution," in Earth '88: Changing Geographic Perspectives (Washington, D.C.: National Geographic Society, 1988).

3 P. M. Haas, R. O. Keohane, and M. A. Levy, eds., Institutions for The Earth: Sources of Effective International Environmental Protection (Cambridge, Mass.: MIT Press, forthcoming).

4 This operationalization is meant to be compatible with that of M. A. Levy, G. Osherenko, and O. R. Young, "The Effectiveness of International Regimes: A Design for Large-Scale Collaborative Research" (Discussion paper, Institute for Arctic Studies, Dartmouth College, Hanover, N.H., 4 December 1991).

5 For a more general discussion of leadership, see O. R. Young, "Political Leadership and Regime Formation: On the Development of Institutions in International Society," *International Organization*, 45, no. 3 (Summer 1991):281–308.

6 See A. Chayes and A. Handler Chayes, "Compliance Without Enforcement: State Behavior Under Regulatory Treaties," *Negotiation Journal* 7 (July 1991):311–30.

7 J. P. Sewell, "UNESCO: Pluralism Rampant," in R. W Cox and H. K. Jacobson, eds., The Anatomy of Influence: Decision Making in International Organization (New Haven, Conn.: Yale University Press, 1973), 149. The concept of collective legitimation was first developed by I. L. Claude, The Changing United Nations (New York: Random House, 1967).

8 Whether reliance on command-and-control regulations, rather than on market-based incentives, is somehow necessitated by the nature of international politics or, instead, represents a failure of policy imagination is an issue that the authors did not explore.

9 For a useful discussion, see J. K. Sebenius, "Negotiating a Regime to Control Global Warming," in R. E. Benedick et al., Greenhouse Warming: Negotiating a Global Regime (Washington, D.C.: World Resources Institute, 1991), 69–98.

10 M. K. Tolba, "Building an Environmental Institutional Framework for the Future," Environmental Conservation 17, no. 2 (Summer 1990); E. L. Miles, "Science, Politics and International Ocean Management," *Policy Papers in International Affairs*, no. 33 (Berkeley, Calif.: Institute of International Studies, 1987).

11 A similar point is made by A. Chayes in "Managing the Transition to a Global Warming Regime or What to Do 'til the Treaty Comes," in R. E. Benedick et al., 61–68, note 9 above.

12 See R. O. Keohane, "Sovereignty, Interdependence and International Institutions," working paper no. 1 (Cambridge, Mass.: Center for International Affairs, Harvard University, February 1991). See also P. M. Haas, Saving the Mediterranean: The Politics of International Environmental Cooperation (New York: Columbia University Press, 1990); and P. M. Haas and T. Sungen, "The Evolution of International Environmental Law," in N. Choucri, ed., Global Environmental Accords (Cambridge, Mass.: MIT Press, forthcoming).

Part IV

Governing Globalization and the Environment

Introduction

One of the critical discussions in debates about globalization and the environment is how the impact of an increasingly globalized economy on the natural environment can be better governed, managed, or regulated. Put differently, what mechanisms, institutions, and policy processes might be required to harness the positive elements of globalization while avoiding its negative ones? Positive elements might include the diffusion of environmental norms (Mol, 2003) and the spread of "green" technology and business and policy best practice. On the negative side, there is the harmful outsourcing of pollution to poorer communities, the exploitation of weaker environmental laws and enforcement by multinational corporations when they operate in poorer nations, and the externalization of environmental harm by conducting the most damaging stages of production there.

This debate builds in turn on earlier concerns about whether states and international institutions any longer have the capacity to regulate businesses, even if they wanted to. Some have argued that corporations "rule the world" (Korten, 1995) and that the state has "retreated" (Strange 1996). Others call the idea that the state is powerless a "myth" (Weiss, 1998), and a third group have sought to nuance more general narratives about what forms of governance are desirable and possible in a context of globalization. This third group includes many of the contributors to this section.

In direct conflict with one another, and going to the heart of debates about the scope for "trading up" environmental standards or "racing to the bottom" by undermining environmental governance, are two classic contributions from David Vogel and Ken Conca. Vogel argues that far from leading to a competitive race whereby countries lower their environmental standards to attract increasingly mobile investors, globalization and greater market openness means that most firms

The Globalization and Environment Reader, First Edition. Edited by Peter Newell and J. Timmons Roberts.
Editorial material and organization © 2017 John Wiley & Sons, Ltd. Published 2017 by John Wiley & Sons, Ltd.

are forced to raise their standards of production and environmental performance in order to enter the richest markets in the world in Europe, North America, and Japan, where environmental standards, public and private, tend to be higher. In this sense he argues that current regional and international governance mechanisms are adequate to enable nations which have the resources and the commitment to improve environmental quality to do so, either on their own or in cooperation with other nations with similar values and resources. Indeed, he claims there is substantial evidence of nations increasingly adopting the standards of their richer, greener trading partners, and that trade agreements have played a critical role in strengthening many national environmental practices.

For Conca on the other hand, the effect of the World Trade Organization, as the main global governance institution charged with promoting trade liberalization, has been to jeopardize and undermine effective environmental governance. He argues that it does so by generating a chilling effect on national level regulation – governments fear tightening their rules because companies might flee to other places. Cases before the World Trade Organization's dispute settlement mechanism – and this was particularly the case at the time he was writing in the late 1990s – have tended to uphold exporting country claims that their products have been discriminated against by unfair environmental laws in importing countries. Hence his claim that "The WTO has proven to be profoundly anti-environmental both procedurally and substantively, handing down environmentally damaging decisions whenever it has had the chance to do so." From Conca's more critical environmental perspective "the hyperliberalization of trade is inimical to the quest for global ecological sustainability." He argues this is not just because of decisions handed down by the dispute settlement mechanism, but because of "the destabilization of several important international environmental regimes, and the commodification of critical global cycles and ecosystem services." His is a prescient anticipation of the current financialization and commodification of nature under the guise of "payments for ecosystem services," argued for in the Costanza et al. chapter in Part II.

Alongside these conflicts and tensions over the scope and effect of public regulation, we have also observed a huge increase in so-called private governance in the last decade. These are voluntary forms of governance set up by and for private actors, even if emulating some of the characteristics of public governance. From standards set by and for business in international organizations such as the ISO (International Organization of Standardization) to systems of certification, and the development of codes of conduct and partnerships, there has been a proliferation and thickening of private standard-setting (Pattberg, 2007; Gulbrandsen, 2010). What Robert Falkner brings to this debate is a useful reminder and account of the ongoing importance of public governance and state power for providing the frameworks within which this private governance is possible, and for providing the necessary enforcement and sanctions which private actors often lack. Much governance labelled private is often hybrid at best, involving strong elements of public and state authority. Falkner's argument is the transformative nature of private governance is greatly exaggerated, either as indicative of realignments of power associated with globalization and the demise of the state system in particular, or as a reflection of the consolidation of global control by transnational capital.

Peter Newell's contribution brings in a different dimension to the debate about governing globalization and the environment by exploring the question of the governance of investment for the environment. How, given the enormous increase in power and wealth produced and accumulated by global corporations, can states, civil society and international institutions ever hope to hold them to account for their social and environmental responsibilities when they span the globe and move between jurisdictions? This relates to a common concern about the mismatch between the global reach of many multinational companies and the limited reach of national governments. Newell explores a range of ways in which it might be possible to control corporations, from civil regulation and civil redress to international law, to novel attempts to use the law to hold corporations liable in their "home" countries for their social and environmental performance abroad through transnational litigation.

Civil regulation refers to a range of strategies of liberal and critical engagement, adopted by civil society organizations working with and against business to develop a normative framework for the social and environmental responsibilities of business in society. In other words, if governments and international institutions are either unwilling or unable to regulate globalizing businesses then civil society actors and social movements will. They do this through negotiating codes of conduct, setting up certification schemes, and many of the tools which Falkner labels as forms of private governance. Civil regulation also includes, however, more confrontational forms of activism such as consumer boycotts and shareholder activism, thereby challenging as well as working with business. The contribution raises important questions about who sets the appropriate standards for the conduct and on whose behalf. While increasingly businesses engage in what they call "corporate social and environmental *responsibility*" (Zadek, 2001), here the emphasis is on strengthening mechanisms of answerability and enforceability that underpin effective corporate accountability on terms not set by corporations themselves. He considers the pros and cons of different public and private strategies for promoting corporate responsibility and accountability both in terms of their environmental effectiveness and their ability to protect the needs of the poorest communities that are often in the front line of conflicts over access to and the extraction of natural resources.

For Frank Biermann, the challenge is a larger meta-scale one of reform of the global governance architecture and in particular the need for a UN Environment Organization (UNEO) or World Environment Organization (WEO). This is to counter the power of global economic institutions and ensure environmental issues are given adequate and proper weight in the global system. He outlines a series of ideal types around which a new global body could be modelled. The most far-reaching of these is a hierarchical intergovernmental organization on environmental issues that would be equipped with majority decision-making as well as enforcement powers vis-à-vis states that fail to comply with international agreements on the protection of global commons, a sort of world Environment Protection Council.

Biermann is hopeful that the establishment of a UN specialized agency on environmental issues could strengthen global norm-building and institutionalization. Such a body could also be enabled to approve by qualified majority vote certain regulations, which are then binding on all members. These would improve the overall implementation of earth system governance, for example, by a common comprehensive reporting system on the state of the environment and on the state of implementation in different countries. A UNEO would also importantly seek to enhance the participation of poorer countries in global environmental decision-making, those that are often on the front line of environmental degradation, despite playing an historically insignificant role in causing it. While critics have highlighted concerns about whether a new institution is politically viable and would be able to bypass the obstacles to previous reform proposals (Newell, 2001), Biermann argues that such a reform is desirable and urgently required. Indeed around the time of the Rio+20 conference in 2012 a number of countries again joined the call for a World Environment Organization to establish some of the failings in the current architecture of global environmental governance. Its time might yet come.

References

Gulbrandsen, L.H. (2010) *Transnational Environmental Governance: The Emergence and Effects of the Certification of Forests and Fisheries*, Edward Elgar, Cheltenham.

Korten, D. (1995) *When Corporations Rule the World*, Kumarian Press, West Hartford, CT.

Mol, A. (2003) *Globalization and Environmental Reform: The Ecological Modernization of the Global Economy*, MIT Press, Cambridge, MA.

Newell, P. (2001) New environmental architectures and the search for effectiveness. *Global Environmental Politics*, 1 (1), 35–45.

Pattberg, P. (2007) *Private Institutions and Global Governance: The New Politics of Environmental Sustainability*, Edward Elgar, Cheltenham.

Strange, S. (1996) *The Retreat of the State*, Cambridge University Press, Cambridge.

Weiss, L. (1998) *The Myth of the Powerless State*, Polity Press, Cambridge.

Zadek, S. (2001) *The Civil Corporation: The New Economy of Corporate Citizenship*, Earthscan, London.

17

Trading Up and Governing Across: Transnational Governance and Environmental Protection (1997)

David Vogel

The Impact of Economic Interdependence

Contrary to the fears of many environmentalists, the increase in economic interdependence has not led to a weakening of national environmental standards. International trade as a proportion of GNP has significantly increased in every industrial nation since the late 1960s. Yet during this same period, environmental regulations have become progressively stricter in all industrial nations and a number of industrializing ones as well. Virtually all nations now devote substantially more resources both in absolute and relative terms to environmental protection than they did in 1970.

Since the early 1970s few major economies have experienced a greater increase in their exposure to the global economy than the United States: between 1970 and 1980 both its imports and exports as a share of GNP more than doubled. At the same time, American regulatory standards have become substantially stronger during the last quarter century. The proportion of America's GNP devoted to pollution control stood at 1.5 percent in 1972; it has been higher every year since, averaging more than 1.7 percent between 1980 and 1986 and increasing to 2.2 percent in 1992. Annual expenditures on compliance with federal environmental regulations totaled $90 billion in 1990 and increased by approximately $30 billion following passage of the 1990 Clean Air Act Amendments.

In Europe, the goal of creating a single market was in large measure motivated by the interests of business managers and political leaders in making European industry more competitive in the global economy. Yet the Single European Act also

David Vogel. 1997. "Trading Up and Governing Across: Transnational Governance and Environmental Protection". In *Journal of European Public Policy*, 4(4): 556–71. Reproduced with permission from Taylor & Francis and D. Vogel.

authorized and has contributed to a significant strengthening of EC environmental regulations. In recent years, the EC has emerged as the world's pace-setter for environmental innovation, led by Germany, its largest and most important member state. Since the early 1970s Japan has been both a major international exporter and has significantly increased its environmental expenditures. During this period, it has accumulated record global trade surpluses, while making substantial progress toward improving domestic environmental quality, especially in the area of air pollution.

The strengthening of domestic environmental standards has not been confined to the world's richest nations. In recent years, Taiwan, South Korea and Singapore – all major exporters – have committed substantially more resources to environmental protection. The compatibility between increased exposure to the global economy and the strengthening of domestic regulatory efforts is also borne out by the experience of Mexico, a developing nation. Since 1986, Mexico has significantly opened up its economy to foreign competition, while between 1988 and 1991 government spending on environmental protection increased tenfold.

[...]

In the case of the European Union, some directives have sought to equalize regulatory requirements within the Union in order to prevent less green nations from taking advantage of the stricter standards of greener ones. But these encompass only a small portion of EC environmental regulations, many of which have little or no impact on the relative costs of producing regionally traded goods. The most pressing source of political conflict over environmental standards in the EC comes not from the interests of southern member states in keeping their standards low in order to attract investment, but from the efforts of northern member states to impose stricter domestic standards which place imports from southern member states at a competitive disadvantage.

Environmental standards are primarily determined by domestic political preferences and interests. They tend to be stronger and better enforced in affluent nations with influential green pressure groups. They also tend to be strengthened during periods of economic prosperity and stabilized or weakened during periods of slower growth. There is no evidence that any relatively affluent nation has *lowered* its existing environmental standards in order to increase the competitiveness of domestic producers, though international economic pressures may well have reduced the rate at which they have been strengthened. In short, the global economy has not interfered with the ability of governments to enact environmental regulations stricter than those of their trading partners with whose products their domestic producers compete.

The Costs of Compliance

Why hasn't increased regional and international competition led regions, nations, or subnational governments to compete with one another by enacting *less* stringent environmental regulations? [...]

Moreover, in light of recent trends in labor markets, it seems puzzling that regulatory policies in rich nations have not followed the same pattern as wages – which have been adversely affected by increased competition from developing nations. [...]

One important reason is that for all but a handful of industries, the costs of compliance with stricter regulatory standards have not been sufficient to force relatively affluent nations or subnational governments to choose between competitiveness and environmental protection. In marked contrast to labor costs, the overall costs of compliance with environmental regulations have been modest. [...] This is not to say that costs are non-existent: many expenditures to improve environmental quality do reduce output and lower the rate of productivity growth. But in the aggregate, increases in national levels of pollution-control expenditures have had little effect on the growth of economic output. [...]

While production standards obviously can and do affect corporate plant location decisions, for most industries the effects are not significant. Within the United States, differences in environmental standards have not been a major factor in plant siting or expansion decisions. Studies of international corporate location decisions reach similar conclusions. For example, only a relatively few heavily polluting industries have relocated their production from the United States to other countries, 'mostly because pollution control expenses alone are generally not large enough a share of total costs to make it worth a company's while to relocate.' Significantly, environmental control costs comprise less than 2 percent of total production cost for most US industries, even though American standards are relatively stringent.

The Organization for Economic Co-operation and Development (OECD) reports that 'very little evidence exists of firms being transferred abroad in order to escape the more stringent environmental regulations at home.' The OECD concludes that the fear that poorer countries would 'deliberately keep environmental standards lax in order to attract investment by becoming pollution havens has [not] materialized ... mostly because pollution control expenditures are generally not a large enough share of total costs to make it worth a company's while to relocate.' Accordingly, 'there is no reason to suppose that international competition for comparative advantage will lead nations to adopt inappropriately low environmental standards.'

[...] Equally importantly, improvements in environmental quality can improve the health, and thus the productivity, of a nation's work-force, in addition to reducing national health-care expenditures. This analysis cannot be pushed too far: nations are not free to impose whatever environmental regulations they wish. For while stricter environmental standards may not make a nation poorer, neither do they make it richer; greater wealth leads to a preference for strong regulatory standards, not the reverse.

[...] While nations with stricter environmental regulations have not experienced lower growth rates than those with laxer ones, neither have those nations with relatively strict standards experienced higher growth rates.

Strengthening regulatory standards

There are two ways in which the dynamics of international competition can contribute to the strengthening of environmental standards. First, stricter regulations can create market opportunities for the export of pollution-control equipment.

These markets are not large. For example, pollution-control equipment accounts for less than one half of 1 percent of total US merchandise exports. But they can be important for particular sectors. For example, owing to their strict emission standards for coal-burning power plants, both Germany and Japan dominate the world market in scrubbers which remove sulfur dioxide from power plant smokestacks.

There is also a second, more subtle way in which stricter regulatory standards can strengthen the international competitiveness of domestic firms. Regulations rarely affect all producers equally: they usually advantage some firms and disadvantage others. Some regulations create a competitive advantage for domestic producers by making it more difficult for foreign producers to sell their products. In fact, knowing or anticipating that the burdens of compliance will fall disproportionately on their international competitors may make domestic producers more willing to support stricter regulations than they would have in the absence of foreign competition.

Examples of 'alliances' between environmentalists and domestic producers abound. [...] The strict automobile emission control requirements supported by German environmentalists during the 1980s protected the domestic market share of German automobile companies, since it was more difficult for French and Italian firms to comply with them. [...]

From this perspective, rather than pressing nations to lower their regulatory standards, more liberal trade policies may actually provide governments with an economic incentive for strengthening them. By contrast, since relatively closed economies can rely on tariffs and quotas to restrict imports, they have less need to adopt protective regulations that advantage domestic producers.

[...] However, there are two mechanisms by which the standards of 'greener' countries can be 'exported' to other, less green ones: one has to do with the terms of market access, the other with international agreements. The remainder of this article describes and assesses their impact.

The California effect

A number of national environmental regulations exhibit what can be described as the 'California effect': they have moved in the direction of political jurisdictions with stricter regulatory standards. The California effect can be illustrated by the history of American automobile emission standards. The 1970 Clean Air Act Amendments specifically permitted California to enact stricter emissions standards than the rest of the United States, an option which California then exercised. Consequently its standards remained stricter than those of any other state. [...]

California has now had America's strictest automotive pollution-control standards for more than three decades. Thus, instead of states with laxer standards undermining those with stricter ones, in the case of automobile emissions precisely the opposite has occurred: California helped to make American mobile emissions standards steadily stronger. Automobile producers had a strong incentive to produce vehicles that complied with California's stricter standards so that they could continue to market their cars in such a large and important market.

[...] The general pattern suggested by this term, the upward ratcheting of regulatory standards in competing political jurisdictions, applies to many national regulations as well. Political jurisdictions which have developed stricter product standards often force foreign producers in nations with weaker domestic standards either to design products that meet those standards, since otherwise they will be denied access to its markets. This, in turn, encourages those producers to make the investments required to produce these new products as efficiently as possible. Moreover, having made these initial investments, they now have a stake in encouraging their home markets to strengthen their standards as well, in part because their exports are already meeting those standards.

Thus the willingness of Germany's automobile manufacturers to support stricter EC standards was in part because of their previous experience in producing vehicles for the American market. It was precisely the firms supplying the largest, wealthiest automobile market in Europe which took the lead in pressuring the EC to adopt the product standards already set by the world's largest, richest market, namely the United States. They made common cause with German environmentalists to demand that Europe adopt American standards. Significantly, half of German automobile sales in the United States are in California, the political jurisdiction with the world's strictest automotive emission standards.

[...]

The pattern of chemical regulation also illustrates how concerns about market access can strengthen regulatory standards. The enactment of the Toxic Substances Control Act by the United States prompted the European Union to enact the Sixth Directive. The EC feared that unless its standards were comparable to those of the United States, it would be deprived of access to one of the world's largest chemical markets. As a result, it established a much stricter system for the introduction and marketing of chemical products. Once again, stricter American standards drove those of its major trading partner *upward*.

The relationship between product standards that disadvantage importers and those which prompt exporters to strengthen their own standards in order to maintain market access must be understood in dynamic terms. The environmental regulatory agenda is a highly fluid one. Rich green nations are continually enacting new regulatory standards. In some cases, these may create only a temporary source of competitive advantage until other nations have adopted them, while in other cases this advantage may prove more enduring. But the result is similar: market incentives can serve to promote the ratcheting upward of regulatory standards.

Exporting Production Standards

The California effect primarily holds for product standards. But product standards constitute only one dimension of environmental regulation; many environmental harms stem from the way a product is produced or processed. In some cases 'greener' nations have used restrictions, or the threat of restrictions, on access to their markets to force their trading partners to change their *production* standards – notwithstanding the fact that such practices violate GATT/WTO rules. Such restrictions have generally been enacted owing to some combination of pressures from domestic firms which want to create a 'level playing field' by imposing additional costs on their international competitors, and environmental groups which want to use trade as leverage to improve the environmental practices of other countries.

For example, the threat of the withdrawal of market access by the EC forced Canada to end its killing of baby seals and has persuaded both the United States and Canada to modify their use of leg-traps to catch fur-bearing animals. The EC's eco-labelling program, because it is based on a 'life-cycle' analysis, explicitly covers the way imported products are produced: many of its provisions are intended to force the EC's trading partners to change their forestry and agricultural practices. Thirteen American laws authorize the use of unilateral sanctions to force America's trading partners to adopt American environmental production standards. All involve efforts to protect animals and marine life outside the legal jurisdiction of the United States. These laws have had a significant impact on the conservation practices of a number of America's trading partners. For example, thanks to the American tuna embargo against Mexico, incidental dolphin deaths by non-American tuna fishing vessels have significantly declined.

In some cases, the impact of the threat of withdrawal of market access has gone beyond specific products. [...] An American threat to impose 'environmental countervailing duties' on goods from nations whose pollution-control standards were laxer than those of the United States played a critical role in strengthening Korean policy-makers to upgrade their nation's environmental standards. In 1994, the EC approved a proposal to modify its Generalized System of Preferences (GSP) to extend additional tariff benefits to 'recipient countries which are able to prove a commitment to international standards of social progress and environmental protection.'

The interest of some developing countries in increasing their access to rich, green country markets has also provided an incentive for the former to strengthen their environmental standards. While the North American Free Trade Agreement (NAFTA) does not formally govern national production standards, the environmental objections raised to NAFTA during the Congressional debates over American approval of the trade agreement played a critical role in intensifying Mexican environmental controls during the early 1990s. [...]

The California effect also has an important non-governmental dimension. Environmental activists in rich countries have frequently targeted particular products that are produced in environmentally harmful ways. In some cases, they have organized boycotts of these products while in others they have applied pressures on multinational firms responsible for their production. A number of these pressures have been highly effective, particularly in the areas of forest and wildlife conservation. International environmental activists based in rich countries have also become an important source of influence on the environmental practices of multinational firms and their subcontractors in many less developed nations. Moreover, 'multinational companies are increasingly adopting the same environmental standards for their plants, regardless of the country in which they operate,' thus helping to promote the export of green country standards to less green ones.

The Limits of Market Pressures

Nevertheless, the significance of market mechanisms in facilitating the export of higher environmental standards is limited. The deliberate use of trade restrictions to force foreign producers to change how they produce their products has been confined to a relatively small number of highly visible and largely 'symbolic' products, usually associated with natural resources. The threat of consumer boycotts by green country consumers or the targets of green activists has likewise been limited to a handful of products, virtually none of which are manufactured goods. [...] The export of green country *product* standards has covered a broader range of products, including chemicals and automobiles, but these standards only affect the environmental impact of the products themselves, not the way they are manufactured. And most involve goods primarily traded among rich countries.

WTO rules have certainly played a role in discouraging rich countries from using production standards to restrict imports from less developed ones on environmental grounds. [...] But the tension between WTO rules and more effective global environmental governance should not be exaggerated. As both the EC's eco-labeling scheme and the provisions of the Montreal Protocol reveal, some production standards can readily be turned into product standards, thus making them WTO consistent. [...]

Finally, much of global production is unaffected by the economic leverage of richer, greener countries. It is either consumed domestically or is exported to other less green countries. As a result, many of the most serious environmental problems in the Third World, such as the destruction of the coral reefs in Asia, deforestation in Latin America and Asia, and air pollution in Latin America and China, remain largely unaffected by the product standards and trade policies of green countries.

The European Community

There is one additional mechanism of international governance: agreements and treaties. [...]

First, the EC has significantly magnified the external environmental impact of its greener member states, most notably Germany, the Netherlands and Denmark. Thanks to the increasing scope of EC environmental regulations and directives, environmental standards have been significantly strengthened throughout the Union, even in poorer member states in which environmental non-governmental organizations (NGOs) enjoy relatively little influence. For much of southern Europe, the EC is the most important cause of any additional resources they have devoted to improving environmental quality. The EC's regulatory rules encompass not only production and product standards for regionally traded products, but a number of other dimensions of environmental quality, such as drinking water quality, the shipment and disposal of hazardous wastes and nature conservation. The EC has also facilitated the ability of its member states to address cross-border environmental problems, such as air and water pollution.

Second, the EC has helped to strengthen global environmental standards. As noted above, it has not only employed its economic leverage to affect the environmental standards of a number of its trading partners, but it has also played an important role in negotiating and strengthening a number of international environmental treaties, including the Montreal Protocol, the Lomé convention (which bans exports of hazardous and radioactive wastes) and the Convention on Long-Range Transboundary Air Pollution. [...]

The key to effective environmental governance at both the regional and global level is the commitment of rich countries: they must be willing both to change their own policies and provide less affluent or green countries with sufficient incentives to modify theirs as well. Many developing nations, including the growing economies of China, India and Indonesia, and the most important Latin American economy, Brazil, remain unwilling to curb trade in endangered species, protect the coral seas, reduce their cutting of hardwood trees, maintain biodiversity or reduce their production of greenhouse gases. They might well change their behavior in response to economic incentives from rich countries, as they did in the case of the Montreal Protocol. But the amount of resources that would be required to be transferred to make them do so is well beyond the political capacity of the EC, the United States and Japan.

In the long run, as many developing nations become more affluent, they are likely to develop both the economic capacity and the political willingness to devote more resources to address their domestic environmental problems. And presumably, they will then enter into regional agreements to address cross-border pollution problems and global treaties to address international ones. But in the short run they are unlikely to make any significant changes in their environmental policies. This is not because international competition is pressuring them to lower their regulatory standards; it is rather that their current level of economic development has made them unwilling to trade off economic growth for environmental quality – especially in those cases where many of their own citizens are not adversely affected by the environmental harms they cause.

This does not preclude rich countries from strengthening their environmental standards, whether acting on their own or in co-operation with other rich countries. The problem is not that poor countries are driving rich country standards downward; it is rather that rich countries lack adequate mechanisms to drive poor country standards sufficiently upward. The problem is not the threat of a 'Delaware effect;' it is rather the limited impact of the 'California effect.' To the extent that the environmental damage caused by the developing countries primarily affects their own citizens or physical environment and is not irreversible, this may not be a serious problem for the global commons, especially if they strengthen their standards as they become more affluent. However, for those international environmental problems which require significant changes in the behavior of poor countries in the short run or which will be exacerbated as they become more affluent, the world confronts a deficit in environmental governance.

18

The WTO and the Undermining of Global Environmental Governance (2000)

Ken Conca

Environmentalists have not always been of the same mind regarding the World Trade Organization (WTO) or the aggressive liberalization of trade. While many have warned about accelerating distorted and unsustainable growth patterns, others have seen opportunities to improve the efficiency of global resource use or to ratchet up national environmental standards where they are weak. But in the wake of the battle in Seattle and five years of experience with the WTO, it is increasingly clear that the hyperliberalization of trade is inimical to the quest for global ecological sustainability in several ways. The WTO has proven to be profoundly anti-environmental both procedurally and substantively, handing down environmentally damaging decisions whenever it has had the chance to do so. Fears of a race to a dirty bottom are proving prescient, and optimism that trade rules can be greened from within has waned appreciably. Moreover, the problem is not just the obvious threat to local environmental quality from the forces of globalizing market pressures. We are also seeing the undermining of global-scale efforts at environmental protection, through the destabilization of several important international environmental regimes and the commodification of critical global cycles and ecosystem services. As a result, environmental opposition in the era of confrontation inaugurated in Seattle is likely to be stronger, more unified, and less willing to tinker on the margins.

Ken Conca. 2000. "The WTO and the Undermining of Global Environmental Governance". In *Review of International Political Economy* 7(3): 484–494. Reproduced with permission from Taylor & Francis and K. Conca.

The Green Critique of the WTO

Advocates often portray aggressively liberalized trade as bringing welfare-enhancing gains rooted in the economic efficiency of comparative advantage. It is ironic that this rationale is so often repeated in a domain where so much of what is happening today is driven by cost externalization. The transportation and communications infrastructures that are central to the explosion of global commerce have been heavily subsidized by national and international public financing. Incentives are manipulated to make sure that manufacturing is shifted to aggressively rule-depleted free trade zones. More than $100 billion in largely unscrutinized export credits and investment guarantees are pumped out annually by national export credit agencies.

Some of the biggest forms of cost externalization are environmental. Shipping all those products all that distance, with massive energy use and attendant pollution, takes a substantial environmental toll that is largely unacknowledged. Even more important external costs come with the strip-mining of forests, soils, biological resources and the various other forms of life-sustaining natural capital. A recent estimate by a group of leading ecological economists placed the value of the earth's 'ecosystem services' – including such critical yet taken-for-granted processes as soil formation, nutrient cycling and habitat maintenance for biodiversity – at $33 trillion annually, well in excess of global GNP.

These distortions are worsened by the WTO's narrow-minded, biased and non-participatory procedures, which stack the deck against reasonable ecological prudence. Important proceedings such as dispute resolution hearings are closed and highly secretive, with no opportunity for stakeholders and public advocates to evaluate the quality of evidence or decisions. Judgments are rendered by trade lawyers and economists with little or no knowledge about environmental problems. The burden of proof is placed squarely on the shoulders of those arguing for environmental precaution. Although these procedural concerns are not unique to environmental issues, they create deep and recurring problems when environmental values and outcomes are at stake. Given the broad array of stakeholders in most environmental disputes, closed procedures guarantee that decisions will be poorly made and illegitimate. And the complex, non-linear ways in which human tampering perturbs ecosystems often make it impossible to demonstrate definitively either harm or the absence of harm. Playing by WTO rules, the first definitive 'proof' of harm will often be irreversible ecosystem collapse.

The Race to a Polluted Bottom

Beyond these serious cost-accounting and procedural distortions, the hyperliberalization of trade generates forms of environmental harm that even the most eco-sensitive rules and procedures would not fully address. Chief among these is the undercutting of national policies for environmental protection. The general logic of trade competitiveness creates intense pressures to weaken environmental regulations which may deter foreign investment or raise production costs for exporters.

Although trade advocates often look skeptically at environmental regulations as environmental protectionism, they remain the only effective means of internalizing the hidden costs of pollution and ecosystem degradation. [...]

There is some debate as to how important environmental considerations may be in causing producers to migrate to areas that have been dubbed 'pollution havens'. What is not in dispute is that the threat to relocate can be an important tool to weaken environmental standards, just as it provides leverage in labor negotiations. To some extent the problem, which plagues a wide array of environmental, health and social standards, is endemic to a world of trade-based economic competition. But WTO rules and procedures clearly exacerbate the problem: to date, the WTO has handed down an anti-environmental decision in every major dispute case where a national environmental regulation has been challenged.

To be sure, environmentalists have not been of a single mind about this problem. Where many fear a race to a polluted bottom, or 'downward harmonization', some have seen instead an opportunity to use trade negotiations to ratchet up national standards where they are weak. During the struggle over the North American Free Trade Agreement, some American environmental organizations argued that NAFTA was a chance to make Mexico a model of environmental protection among developing nations. In the wake of the Uruguay Round of talks within the General Agreement on Tariffs and Trade, some groups pushed for a 'green GATT' round to address trade and environment tensions and, later, for a green working group within the WTO. But it is safe to say that the trend is clearly toward skepticism about greening the trade rules. Experiences such as NAFTA, in which environmental concerns were shunted to a largely ineffective side-agreement, have left little enthusiasm for the idea that trade instruments can be vehicles for affirmative green development in industrialized or developing countries. The WTO has deepened this skepticism, given that its rules and procedures virtually ensure that contested regulations will be judged restraints on trade. [...]

Another reason for mounting skepticism is the recognition that more than just national policies are at risk. The 'race to the bottom' argument is often presented in a David-versus-Goliath context: national policies are under siege from global competitive pressures aided and abetted by the global trading regime. Less recognized, but just as troubling, is a parallel at the international level, in the form of the WTO-based threat to a broad array of international environmental regimes.

[...] [A]greements such as the Montreal Protocol on stratospheric ozone, the Convention on International Trade in Endangered Species, the Kyoto climate accord, the Basel Convention on the hazardous waste trade, and a handful of other multilateral regimes stand as important accomplishments in the quest for sustainability. [...]

Trade measures have been a vital tool for several of these regimes. In some cases, trade itself has been the targeted activity. The Convention on International Trade in Endangered Species controls the import and export of species listed as endangered. The Basel Convention tackles the problem of abuses stemming from the trade in hazardous waste from the OECD to the global south (initially through a system of prior informed consent for waste imports and subsequently through an outright ban on the north–south waste trade). In other cases, trade measures have been an integral part of the political formula for cooperation. The Montreal

Protocol, widely hailed as a model for international environmental regimes, was nearly derailed by a disagreement over whether to regulate production or consumption of the culprit chemicals. Trade provisions were a critical element in breaking this impasse, as well as in creating incentives for non-party states to join the regime.

Perhaps most importantly, trade measures have been an entry point through which to work back upstream to change domestic practices. In both the CITES regime on endangered species and the Basel regime on hazardous wastes, trade regulation has been more than just an end in itself; it has also been an important entry point – indeed, the only entry point – for moving upstream to begin to address fundamental domestic practices of concern. [...]

Finally, there are cases where trade-restricting measures can be important safeguards because trade provides a loophole through which the letter or spirit of environmental commitments is violated. It does a country little good to ban the use of a hazardous chemical such as DDT, for example, if that substance can still be manufactured for export, used abroad, and reimported in the form of pesticide residues in food products. [...]

The WTO creates several obstacles to the use of trade-related mechanisms in international environmental regimes. First, the WTO's mere existence has had a chilling impact on global political imagination. It is difficult to envision the conclusion, in today's economic climate, of an agreement such as the 1973 Convention on International Trade in Endangered Species, which deliberately delegitimizes a lucrative form of international trade. The 1994 amendment to the Basel Convention, which essentially bans the north–south trade in hazardous wastes, probably constitutes the end of an era of targeting the trafficking of environmental hazards. Indeed, the current momentum is in the opposite direction.

We are seeing the reopening to international commerce of areas such as the export of round logs, a battle opponents of deforestation thought had already been won. [...]

Even where established regimes have had some success with trade measures, the threat of a WTO challenge can have a palpable chilling effect. [...]

Commodifying the Commons

Another structural problem of trade liberalization is the destruction of sustainable community resources. Much of the natural capital that constitutes a foundation for economic activity exists because it has been tended across generations by local communities around the world. Despite Garrett Hardin's apocalyptic warning about a 'tragedy of the commons', avoidable only by privatization or state command-and-control regulations, a large and growing body of research shows innumerable instances of local communities sustaining localized commons over long periods of time without the extremes of privatization or state domination. But the often sophisticated systems of contingent access, local monitoring and limits on extraction that surround local fisheries, forests, irrigation systems or grasslands are threatened when these systems are mobilized as tradable commodities. [...]

Advocates of trade liberalization have been fond of arguing that market mechanisms and the gains from trade can elevate incomes and living standards to the point at which societies will demand more environmental protection. [...] These claims, however, are based on a specific form of pollution. There appears to be something akin to a Kuznets curve in the relationship between per-capita incomes and the emissions of a few key air pollutants such as sulphur dioxide; improvements in air quality kick in after a certain per-capita income threshold is reached. But there is no evidence that a similar effect is at work for soils, forests, watersheds, wetlands or other fragile ecosystems and natural services. Rendering these systems and services into tradable commodities without internalizing the social and ecological costs of their exploitation is having devastating consequences, both for nature and for the local communities dependent on it.

[...]

Conclusion

Environmentalists are not of a single mind on how to confront the WTO and the hyperliberalization of trade. Is the WTO best understood as a cause or a symptom? [...] Can the WTO be greened from the inside out, or should the effort go to strengthening environmental regimes and institutions to withstand its pressures? [...] To be sure, there are good and legitimate reasons for environmentalists and others to frame the problem as one of global forces encroaching on local efforts to sustain environmental quality. But the problem must also be seen as the collision of two radically different global visions and the unequally developed institutional expressions of those visions. On the one hand is the aggressive, organized push to bring ever more of the world economy into the trading sphere. Carried to its logical conclusion, it promises the trade-based dismantling of three decades of global environmental rule making and the selling of important dimensions of the global commons. On the other hand is a vision – still fragmented but likely to be reenergized in the wake of Seattle – of global sustainability, grounded in stakeholder participation, ecological honesty in the measurement of costs and value, and prudent precaution in the face of uncertainty.

19

Private Environmental Governance and International Relations: Exploring the Links (2003)

Robert Falkner

This article is concerned with private environmental governance at the global level. It is widely acknowledged that private actors play an increasing role in global environmental politics. Corporations lobby states during negotiations on multilateral environmental agreements (MEAs), featuring prominently in the implementation of international accords. They also interact with each other, as well as with states and other nonstate actors, to create institutional arrangements that perform environmental governance functions. The rise of such private forms of global governance raises a number of questions for the study of global environmental politics: How does private governance interact with state-centric governance? In what ways are the roles/capacities of states and nonstate actors affected by private governance? Does the rise of private governance signify a shift in the ideological underpinnings of global environmental governance? This article explores these questions, seeking a better understanding of the significance of private environmental governance (PEG) for International Relations.

[...]

"Private governance" emerges at the global level where the interactions among private actors, or between private actors on the one hand and civil society and state actors on the other, give rise to institutional arrangements that structure and direct actors' behavior in an issue-specific area. These structuring effects resemble the "public" governing functions of states and intergovernmental institutions, and for this reason the notion of governance, and indeed authority, has been applied to private actors.

Private governance needs to be distinguished from mere cooperation between private actors. Cooperation requires the adjustment of individual behavior to achieve

Robert Falkner. 2003. "Private Environmental Governance and International Relations: Exploring the Links". In *Global Environmental Politics*, 3(2): 72–88. Reproduced with permission from MIT Press.

The Globalization and Environment Reader, First Edition. Edited by Peter Newell and J. Timmons Roberts.
Editorial material and organization © 2017 John Wiley & Sons, Ltd. Published 2017 by John Wiley & Sons, Ltd.

mutually beneficial objectives, and between private actors is a pervasive phenomenon in the global economy. It is mostly of an *ad hoc* nature with a short lifetime. Governance, however, emerges out of a context of interaction that is institutionalized and of a more permanent nature. In a system of governance, individual actors do not constantly decide to be bound by the institutional norms based on a calculation of their interest, but adjust their behavior out of recognition of the legitimacy of the governance system. Cooperation may lead to governance, but more is required than the spontaneous convergence of private actors' interests via the coordinating function of markets.

Private governance has been documented in many global economic sectors. It is also increasing in global environmental protection, at the level of individual firms, industries and cross-sectoral organizations. For example, the US Chemical Manufacturers Association, together with its Canadian counterpart, developed the so-called Responsible Care program in the 1980s to promote environmental and safety principles and codes of management practice within the global chemical industry. Through the market clout of American MNCs such as DuPont and Dow, Responsible Care has been exported to a number of developing countries, becoming an important benchmark for developing good practice in the chemical industry. Likewise, the International Organization for Standardization (ISO) created a global standard for environmental management systems (EMS) that provides guidance in the development of environmental management across many industrial sectors and allows individual companies to seek certification. This "ISO 14000 series" has been adopted globally by corporations and regulatory agencies and has become the dominant reference point for developing national or industry-wide EMS.

While interest in private governance has grown more recently, the active involvement of private actors in global governance is not entirely new. Private actors played a substantial role in ordering transnational economic relations in the 19th century, but in the 20th century, with the expansion of the state's regulatory role, first domestically, subsequently in the international system, the provision of global governance came to be associated primarily with public authorities Not surprisingly, perhaps, the re-emergence of private governance is closely related to late-20th century processes of economic globalization and the corresponding restructuring of state functions.

The literature on globalization has thus provided a major vantage point for the study of private governance and authority. Authors such as Susan Strange and DeAnne Julius, and the polemic depiction by anti-globalization campaigners of a globalized economy out of control, suggest the process of globalization is intimately linked with a transfer of power and authority from the public to the private sector. What is missing in this perspective, however, is a better understanding of the more precise connections that exist between globalization and the changing role of private actors. In reviewing the debate on PEG, this article argues that, while the existing literature in International Relations (IR) rightly emphasizes the growing importance of new types of actors in global environmental governance (business actors and social movements) it overstates their autonomy, and underplays the high degree of variation within each type of actor. The following discussion stresses the importance of the relationship of these new actors to other actors and examines three particular claims arising in the context of globalization studies. Each claim suggests that the rise of PEG amounts to a transformational trend in global governance.

The first claim concerns the relationship between globalization and the perceived decline of the nation-state. In this view, private governance indicates a long-term shift away from state-centric models of governance to new forms of authority located in the global economy, with private actors emerging as the new sovereigns. [...]

A second, related, claim links the emergence of private governance with transnationalism and growth in global civil society. The latter is seen to support "activities that shape widespread behavior and influence the way public issues are addressed". Private governance is thus a direct result of pressure exerted by activist groups on corporations. It has become an important instrument in the political toolbox of global civil society in its efforts to promote environmental sustainability. Both the "state in decline" school and the transnationalist approach contribute to the emergence of a "glocalization" perspective on global governance, which sees the interaction between global environmental politics and globalization as giving rise to multi-level governance. Governance is no longer identified solely, or even primarily, with the regime-building activities of states. Instead, multilevel sites of governance emerge out of interactions within the states-system, global civil society and the global economy.

A third, alternative, conceptualization of private governance is found in critical political economy. Following a neo-Gramscian analysis, capitalist forces are seen to be engaging in alliance building processes with a variety of state and civil society actors in an effort to realign the ideological and material bases of the dominant hegemonic order. The rise of private governance signifies a new phase in the ongoing process of re-structuring global hegemony, in which global firms organize to establish environmental standards with a view to shifting the ideological focus in global environmental politics in the direction of market-oriented, deregulatory systems of governance. The emergence of corporate-sponsored environmental regimes thus points to an ideological shift in organizing international responses to the ecological crisis, that ultimately helps to cement the grip by the dominant class over anti-systemic forces.

These three perspectives raise important questions about the significance of PEG for understanding international order and change, suggesting a profound change in the way it is organized. This change affects the roles of states and nonstate actors alike, causing a power shift from the former to the latter. Furthermore, if private governance is indeed becoming more prevalent in global environmental politics, then the possibility of a fundamental shift in the ideological underpinnings of international environmentalism needs to be considered. In the following, these perspectives are examined and the impact of private forms of governance on the roles of states and nonstate actors, as well as the ideological basis for global environmental action, are investigated. I argue that while important changes in the international political economy can be noted, the above perspectives overstate the transformational impact of PEG.

Supplanting, or Complementing, State Authority?

A key question in the study of PEG concerns the relationship between private actors and states. It can be argued that the rise of private forms of governance is intimately linked with a decline in state power and results from the failure of the states-system adequately to govern the global commons. In this perspective, the significance of PEG lies in the support it lends to those arguing for the abandonment of the traditional state-centric model.

[...] Environmental scholars were among the first to point to the eminent role that nonstate actors play in promoting global norms and pressuring states into action. But private actors are usually conceptualized as lobbyists seeking to influence state-centric processes of regime-building. In some cases, private actors have exerted a considerable degree of influence over outcomes, either supporting or hindering progress towards effective environmental governance, as witnessed in the cases of ozone layer protection and climate change respectively. But despite the growing recognition of the involvement of private actors, the conventional notion of governance remains firmly embedded in a state-centric setting, insisting that effective governance depends on state authority in establishing and implementing international regimes.

[...]

A problem, however, is that what might be called the "pure" form of private governance (governance outside the realm of the states-system) is of only limited empirical and conceptual relevance. For most instances of PEG are of the kind that are better described as "mixed" regimes, where "the boundary between public and private spheres is blurred". Hybrid private-public governance emerges out of the interactions of private actors, either with the involvement of states or with the later adoption, or codification, by states and/or intergovernmental organizations. States are not the driving force behind the creation of such governance systems, but lend them strength through official recognition or incorporation into international law.

This mixed nature of PEG can be seen in the case of the ISO 14000 series. [...]

ISO 14000 standards have already proved to be a successful tool in persuading industries around the world to seek ISO certification for their EMS. However, they derive particular strength from the fact that states and international organizations have recognized the ISO standards and lent them additional legitimacy. Several countries, particularly in East Asia and Europe, have adopted ISO 14000 as their official standards; governments are expected to incorporate them into their procurement and international bodies such as the WTO have recognized the voluntary ISO standards as international standards under the WTO system and as being consistent with the Technical Barriers to Trade Agreement.

Thus, private regimes such as ISO standards gain in strength and legitimacy because they are adopted by states and international organizations. More often than not, they are hybrid regimes created by transnational policy networks consisting of industry representatives and regulatory officials. They exist outside the states-system only insofar as the international community has not set comparable standards.

States do, however, exercise considerable influence over such private forms of governance in that they tolerate, and even encourage, their creation and maintenance by the private sector. Simplistic dichotomies between private and public regimes do not help in understanding the dynamics involved in PEG.

The idea that PEG may supplant or undermine the governance function of the states-system is also called into question by the fact that many private regimes are beneficial to states in leaving the burden of implementation in the hands of the private sector. States may actually choose to let industry establish systems of self-regulation where there is no overriding demand for public regulation. In these cases, states are saved from the often complex task of negotiating international standards and do not pay the costs of implementation and compliance. Rather than suffering from a lack of state capacity, as much of the globalization literature suggests, states can therefore be seen to be benefiting from the more widespread use of private governance mechanisms.

Finally, claims about the "state in decline" are misleading in not distinguishing between different states and differential ways in which they are affected by private sector governance. The power of firms clearly has a more constraining effect on the autonomy of the state in developing countries than in the industrialized world. And in the case of PEG, a similar case can be made for arguing that it is primarily developing countries that are left with little capacity to influence, or resist, the setting of international environmental standards by private actors.

[...]

North-South inequality in the setting and implementation of private standards is ubiquitous. Developing country interests regularly find themselves marginalized. Maintaining a sufficient level of involvement for state actors, based on UN-style representation, will therefore be crucial for developing countries in their efforts to redress imbalances in international environmental policy-making. This is not to say that problems of North-South inequality do not plague the state-centric forums of environmental governance, but traditional forums of international policy-making provide Southern states at least with formal equality in the representation of their interests. [...]

This does not claim nothing has changed in the relationship between firms and states; the rise in PEG undoubtedly enhances the position and legitimacy of corporations in GEP. Whether it reduces the power of states at the same time, or signifies an erosion in state capacity, is another question; it cannot be answered in a simple and straightforward manner, but requires more careful analysis of the changing conditions of "stateness" (the institutional centrality of the state) in an era of globalization. It seems clear, however, that the simplistic dichotomy between government and market, and between state-centric and non-state-centric governance at global level, is not helpful in trying to understand the changing dynamics of global environmental governance.

A second set of questions concerns the way in which private governance affects the opportunities for civil society actors in shaping global governance. The focus here is on the interaction between corporations and the environmental movement, particularly the latter's attempts to change the corporate sector's behavior in favor of greater environmental sustainability. [...]

Against the backdrop of this transnationalist conception of global politics, the rise of private governance can be seen as strengthening the position of transnational activist groups in global environmental politics. In this view, important connections exist between the self-regulating activities of corporations and campaigns organized by environmental and consumer groups around the world. The argument is that corporate self-regulation reflects not so much a desire by corporations to govern themselves but a need to respond to public pressure. The campaigning efforts of NGOs are an essential factor in the proliferation of PEG; they push and shove corporations in the direction of environmental sustainability. At the same time, private governance helps empower global civil society in providing activist groups with political levers that exist outside the states-system.

There is indeed growing empirical evidence that NGOs play an important role in the formation of PEG, contributing in two principal ways. First, NGOs target individual firms that they accuse of environmentally damaging behavior, with a view to changing that behavior and creating conditions in which other firms are induced to comply with higher environmental standards. An example of this kind of activity is Greenpeace's campaign against the sinking of Shell's Brent Spar oil platform in the North Sea, which forced the company to abandon its original plan for decommissioning and opt for the more costly alternative of dismantling on land. [...]

Second, NGOs also target entire business sectors, seeking to engage them in a process of establishing sector-specific environmental standards. In this case, NGOs are both a stimulus for and a participant in PEG, and may also play a key role in monitoring compliance. An important example is the global regime to protect forests that has emerged outside the conventional, state-centric realm of environmental regulation. The Forest Stewardship Council (FSC) was launched in 1993 by the World Wide Fund for Nature in response to a lack of effective action by the international community. It establishes criteria for sustainable forest management, certifying companies complying with FSC standards.

The growing involvement of civil society actors in private governance signifies an interesting point of departure in the study of global governance. Some analysts contend that NGOs are empowered by their ability to target global firms in transnational campaigns without having to rely on the established channels of international policy-making. According to this view, environmental activism directed at the corporate sector has opened up new political space that exists outside the confines of the territorially-based states-system. Engaging with private governance mechanisms thus provides NGOs with an alternative form of global environmental activism that is potentially more effective than lobbying states to establish international environmental regulation.

Targeting individual corporations or industry sectors and engaging with firms in a process of global standard setting has become an important form of environmental activism for many NGOs. Yet this trend raises important questions about the nature of the relationship between private actors and activist groups. Some activists have voiced concern about the closeness of this relationship fearing that NGOs are in danger of losing their original identity as civil society actors with campaigns driven by ecological values.

Indeed, these concerns point to critical issues in the conceptualization of the link between private governance and global civil society. First, where environmental NGOs provide the impetus for the creation of private governance, they often do so in an unsystematic, uneven manner, concentrating on those environmental issues that are more likely to support media-intensive public campaigns, as is the case with Greenpeace. It is often large corporations operating at the consumer end of the production chain that are most vulnerable to consumer boycotts and campaigns that dent their reputation. Recent examples of successful campaigns against such firms include the sporting goods manufacturer Nike and the oil company Shell. Given the selective and uneven focus of NGO campaigns, it therefore falls upon public regulatory authorities to ensure adequate global governance. World civic action alone cannot guarantee comprehensive coverage.

Second, the growing willingness of environmental NGOs to engage in a constructive dialogue with corporations and participate in efforts to establish private governance mechanisms has created a new form of interdependence that may limit the scope for independent civil society activism. One aspect of this new interdependence between the private sector and civil society is the growing reliance on corporate funding by some environmental NGOs. Another aspect is the concern that, by working with corporations to create global environmental standards, NGOs are effectively lending legitimacy to these corporations and their business operations. Rather than empowering NGOs, private governance can thus be seen as taming civil society actors.

There is undoubtedly an important link between private governance and global civil society that warrants a transnationalist perspective on the changing conditions of global environmental politics. But to presume that the rise of private governance works in one direction, empowering environmental activists and enhancing the potential for more effective environmental governance, would be misleading. The study of transnationalism needs to be grounded in a political-economic perspective that critically examines the power relationship between private actors and environmental NGOs.

The third, related, dimension of PEG is that it is held to signify a shift not only in authority but also in ideology. In this view, the growing reliance on private governance in global environmental management represents a privileging of a business-friendly, market-oriented approach to environmental politics over a more holistic and ecology-oriented understanding of the relationship between human activity and environmental destruction. The "privatization" of global environmental politics is regarded as a process that undermines established, state-centric, models of democratic accountability in global governance and promotes a deregulatory agenda serving to weaken the transformative power of global environmentalism.

Underlying the trend towards PEG is a change in attitude and strategy in the corporate sector over the last twenty years. In the 1970s and early 1980s, corporate responses to the environmental agenda were largely hostile and consisted of little more than reluctant adaptation. While many companies continue to react in similar fashion, the 1980s saw the emergence of new responses based on proactive and systematic integration of environmental goals into corporate strategy. Having failed to stem the tide of environmental regulation and facing changing consumer attitudes, many corporations began to develop systematic environmental management strategies. Drawing on managerial approaches associated with ecological modernization, corporate leaders embraced the notion that corporate environmentalism can promote "win-win solutions" that further business and environmental interests. A practical manifestation of this was corporations becoming more actively involved in the international political process, seeking not simply to block environmental initiatives but to shape and influence them.

Corporate efforts to shape the global environmental agenda were particularly visible in the run-up to the Rio Earth Summit of 1992. Individual firms and organizations such as the Business Council on Sustainable Development (BCSD) and the International Chamber of Commerce (ICC) lobbied delegates and promoted the idea of a partnership between the private sector, environmentalists and international society in searching for environmental solutions. Putting forward an interpretation of sustainable development that sought to reconcile environmental and business concerns, BCSD and ICC in a sense provided a blueprint for a more market-oriented and self-regulatory model of global environmental governance.

The ideas informing business interpretations of sustainable development center on the notion that markets, if left to their own devices, have the ability to regulate themselves. Environmental governance emerges as a natural outcome of the market process and only in extreme scenarios requires intervention by states to impose regulatory regimes. Under normal circumstances, producers will incorporate environmental concerns into their activities wherever consumers value environmental sustainability, allowing for the price mechanism to establish the optimal level of investment in environmental protection efforts.

[...]

Critics, however, argue that this business interpretation of sustainable development and environmental governance puts at risk the environmental movement's achievement in establishing a political agenda for international environmental issues. By linking environmental policies with the self-regulatory economic agenda, private actors are seen to promote a managerial perspective on global environmental issues that precludes a more radical critique of the world economy as a source of the ecological crisis. In this view, the emergence of PEG represents a shift in the ideological underpinnings of environmental politics towards a corporate conception of state-market relations.

Criticisms of this kind certainly provoke many questions and provide a useful corrective to the belief in the self-healing capacity of global markets. They give rise to an important research agenda that sees private actors as part of a wider global framework of domination based on a mix of economic might and ideological predominance. Neo-Gramscian approaches in IPE, for example, employ the notion of a global hegemonic order, comprising elites from MNCs, state agencies, civil society and academia, which legitimizes a specific model of global political-economic organization and marginalizes alternative political ideologies. Private governance appears to fit well into the neo-Gramscian argument that global hegemony is never a fixed entity, but is constantly undergoing a process of contestation and re-alignment of its central forces. In this view, the growing relevance of private forms of environmental governance suggests a convergence of global hegemonic forces towards a model of environmental governance that favors "market-enabling regimes" over "regulatory regimes."

Yet, the view that the rise of PEG represents an ideological shift in global environmental politics raises two critical problems; it is in danger of overstating the influence of business in setting the global agenda *and* understating the continuity of a fundamentally liberal consensus enshrined in the global environmental agenda. With regard to the role of firms, it is fair to say that private actors have certainly adopted a more proactive role in global environmental politics and are powerful lobbyists in the international bargaining process. But corporate involvement continues to vary considerably, across different sectors and types of business organizations, and is far from promoting an ideologically consistent agenda. As the international politics of ozone, climate and biodiversity demonstrate, business conflict over the objectives and design of global environmental regulations continues to weaken the business case in environmental politics. At the same time, corporations often pursue contradictory objectives when seeking to influence global environmental governance. Global firms may wish to achieve harmonization of environmental standards while national firms continue to oppose them; and although favoring market-consistent regulation in principle, many firms that have successfully adapted to command-and-control regulations often find it in their economic interest to preserve such traditional, state-centric, forms of governance.

Moreover, the notion that we are experiencing an ideological shift in environmental politics tends to understate the continuity of a liberal orientation in global environmental governance. The rise of private governance has undoubtedly strengthened the place of liberal ideas of self-regulation in environmental politics, particularly since the 1992 Rio Earth Summit. But to suggest that this represents fundamental change in the ideological underpinnings of global governance underestimates the extent to which the institutionalized praxis of environmental protection has come to reflect liberal political and economic ideas. [...]

Private governance has become a reality in global environmental politics that few analysts deny. Its significance for International Relations, however, remains contested in contemporary debates about globalization and international order. There are good reasons to suggest that the rise of private actors in environmental governance points to an ongoing erosion of state capacity, empowerment of global civil society and shift in the ideological underpinnings of global environmental governance.

However, closer analysis of the phenomenon of private governance reveals the more complex connections that exist between the "privatization" of environmental governance and shifts in the relationship between firms, states and global civil society. The new agenda in global governance is defined by an intricate private-public nexus in which private and public authorities work hand-in-hand to redefine the parameters of global policy-making. Environmental activists' groups assume a larger role in shaping global agendas and pressuring private actors into action, but their involvement in private governance also serves to alter their role and identity as nonstate actors. And PEG not only strengthens the predominant liberal paradigm in the ideational structure contained in the global environmental agenda, but promotes a model of global self-regulation that benefits the interests of powerful MNCs.

This raises a number of issues that ought to be central to future research on PEG in international relations. First, if the ongoing spread of private governance mechanisms does not suggest a straightforward power shift away from states and towards firms but a more complex interdependence between private and public actors, then the public-private mix in environmental governance needs to move center-stage in the study of international environmental politics. Second, given the close involvement of NGOs in private governance, we need to look more carefully at the ways in which global civil society actors are co-opted into self-regulatory efforts, and how this changes their role and influence in the global environmental agenda. Third, if private governance tends to promote a particular international liberal consensus in environmental governance that strengthens the position of MNCs, then we need to pay closer attention to ongoing processes of redefining the legitimacy of public and private actors in global environmental governance.

20

Managing Multinationals: The Governance of Investment for the Environment (2001)

Peter Newell

Introduction: The Regulation of TNCs and the Environment[1]

Transnational companies are increasingly critical players in development. Exporting best practice and initiating great improvements in technology, for some, TNCs are key actors in delivering sustainable development (Schmidheiny, 1992). For others, the mobility of capital and the internationalization of production that make international investment possible, give companies unprecedented freedoms to locate their businesses where it is most profitable to do so, often at the expense of communities and their environment (Madeley, 1999). Of particular concern is the fact that developing countries often experience greater economic and political volatility which means that foreign investors tend to engage in ventures that will yield a high rate of return over a short period, often resulting in environmental devastation and social dislocation (Sauermann, 1986).

Evidence about the relationship between foreign direct investment (FDI) and regulation is mixed and can be used to sustain competing claims of an upgrading effect and a downgrading effect depending on the sector and region and the type of standard under investigation (whether it is labour or environmental for example). It is possible to find examples both of a 'race to the bottom' and of FDI having an upgrading effect (Vogel, 1997, World Bank, 2000). Others have found that more significant than the lowering of standards may be the stalling of the introduction of new environmental regulations (WWF 1999). Whichever view is taken, there can be little doubt that TNCs are increasingly central to environmental decision-making

Peter Newell. 2001. "Managing Multinationals: The Governance of Investment for the Environment". In *Journal of International Development*, 13: 907–919. Reproduced with permission from John Wiley & Sons.

and resource use behaviour. This is because of the importance of their investment decisions for the development paths pursued by countries, the environmental impact of the goods they transfer around the world, and the environmental impact of their production processes. Recognizing this role is key to understanding contemporary interest in approaches to the regulation of TNCs.

This paper looks firstly at the failure of attempts to regulate TNCs at the national and international level by states and international organizations, before considering two approaches to the regulation of TNCs investment practices adopted by NGOs and community organizations. These are firstly, 'civil regulation' (see Newell, 2000; Bendell, 2000), a term used to describe a broad range of strategies increasingly adopted by civil society organizations aimed at holding companies to account for their environmental responsibilities, and secondly, transnational litigation against companies accused of negligence in one of their overseas operations. Both approaches provide interesting insights into the sources and possibilities of non-state regulation in a context of globalization and contribute to our understanding of the prospects of embedding economic activities in social frameworks supportive of development goals.

It is argued that these strategies respond to a perceived 'governance deficit', in that the global power of TNCs is not adequately matched by existing regulatory instruments. It is the limited scope of existing regulation of the environmental impact of companies' activities, which forms the background to attempts by environmental NGOs to create the forms of 'civil regulation' discussed below. They have sought to develop their own mechanisms of corporate accountability by forging alliances with consumers, institutional investors and companies themselves. In the case of foreign direct liability, it is often the absence or breakdown of effective regulation that makes litigation necessary for communities blighted by industrial hazards. Both sets of strategies have the potential to contribute to the regulation of the environmental impact of the activities of transnational companies (TNCs).

The aim of this paper, therefore, is to explore the possibilities and limitations of these different approaches to corporate regulation as mechanisms for promoting responsible investment strategies and deterring social and environmentally destructive practices. Such an exercise helps us both to determine the potential for developing mutually supportive packages of multi-level, formal and informal initiatives on corporate responsibility for development.

Power without Responsibility? The Limits of Existing Regulation

The globalization of production and finance have increased policy and academic attention to the role of regulation in promoting responsible business investment at the national and international level and between public and private partners (Picciotto and Mayne, 1999). This interest focuses on the role of environmental and social obligations within international investment treaties such as the proposed MAI (Multilateral Agreement on Investment) (Ayine and Werksman, 1999), as well as informal 'private' and non-state practices of regulation manifested in codes of conduct and 'stewardship regimes' negotiated between businesses and NGOs (Newell, 2000).

Contemporary interest in regulation is born of concerns about the continued lack of effective regulation of TNCs at the international level. Critics point to the fact that there is a lack of recognition in international environmental agreements of the role of TNCs in causing environmental problems. The issue of TNC regulation was dropped from the UNCED agenda and while Agenda 21 includes recommendations that affect TNCs, it does not take the form of a code of conduct. An international code of conduct to regulate the activities of TNCs has been on the international agenda since the 1970s. The UN Centre for TNCs (UNCTC) was set up in 1973, largely at the request of developing country governments amid concern about the power of TNCs, but was unable to conclude negotiations on a code of conduct. This failure is explained by conflicts of interest between developed and developing countries and the opposition of the United States, in particular, and in 1993 the CTC was restructured to become the Commission on International Investment and Transnational Corporations, housed within UNCTAD. Guidelines and standards promoted by bodies such as the ILO and the OECD are not widely known and therefore rarely used, are entirely voluntary and without sanction, and are outdated, compared even with companies' own codes of conduct (McLaren, 2000). Instead, the importance of these agreements may be that they act as benchmarks for other regulatory initiatives and private codes (Seyfang, 1999). In addition, as Muchlinski notes, 'Although the OECD guidelines are non-binding, they do represent a consensus on what constitutes good corporate behaviour in an increasingly global economy. Furthermore, they are clear that home countries of MNEs have a moral duty to ensure that the standards contained in the guidelines are maintained worldwide' (Muchlinski, 1999, p. 39).

Whilst innovative and ambitious, national and regional attempts to advance the legal debate about the obligations of TNCs when they invest overseas, have also not progressed very far. The European Parliament Resolution on the creation of a Code of Conduct for European MNCs Operating Abroad, which seeks to set standards that EU companies would have to adopt wherever they operate, has been adopted by the European Parliament but is unlikely to progress much further. Political opposition and the principle-driven nature of the resolution will make it difficult to implement its terms concretely (Ward, 2000). Similarly, despite some support for a Bill on the overseas conduct of companies domiciled in Australia, the range of responsibilities it covers and the sanctions it seeks to impose on companies that violate its terms, mean that it will not be passed in the short term (Australian Senate, 2000).[2] At best then, these instruments provide evidence of the expectations state actors have regarding the conduct of TNCs.

Of particular concern is the perceived imbalance between the rights and responsibilities of TNCs. The history of business regulation reveals an imbalance between the promotion and protection of investor rights over investor responsibilities (Muchlinski, 1999), regulation *for* business rather than regulation *of* business. The attempt to create an MAI and the WTO's TRIPs agreement are examples of regulation *for* business aimed at facilitating investment opportunities and creating protection for investments. The TRIPS agreement is part of a broader power-shift in which regional trade organizations, such as NAFTA (North American Free

Trade Agreement), also permit companies to challenge governments and local authorities about restrictions on their activities (Rowen, 1998).

Whilst national regulation and public international law approaches to regulating TNCs help to create frameworks of expectation about the responsibilities of companies to the communities in which they invest, it is clear that they provide a weak level of protection for those most vulnerable to irresponsible investment practices given their non-binding nature and lack of enforcement in most cases.

Civil Regulation: From Confrontation to Collaboration

It is against this background of weak instruments and failed initiatives at the international level that NGOs have begun to target TNCs with increasingly frequency and vigour in recent years. Rather than providing a coherent alternative approach to social regulation, the forms of civil regulation described below amount to a patchwork of activities and campaigns aimed at challenging the environmental impact of TNCs. Civil regulation creates new fora for dialogue and new sets of 'carrots' and 'sticks' to encourage compliance with environmental standards that go further than state-based regulation, but at the same time supplement its weaknesses. In this sense, as Wapner notes, 'The governing capability of global civil society complements but does not replace that of the state system' (Wapner, 1997, p. 67). Taken together, they constitute 'moves', in a Polanyian sense, to re-embed the market within a framework of social norms and expectations about the responsibility corporations have in relation to the communities in which they invest.

A combination of critical and liberal strategies (Newell, 2001a), working with and against companies have been forged which draw on NGOs' assets and bargaining leverage in order to generate new mechanisms of accountability for the conduct of corporations. At the more liberal end of the spectrum, a range of strategies has been adopted aimed at working with businesses to generate reform. Cooperative agreement and the use of the market are what set these approaches apart from the critical strategies discussed later.

Consumer pressure provides one such channel for holding companies to account; the use of the market to express political will and the harnessing of consumer power to the goal of corporate reform. Such pressure embodies both a 'carrot' and a 'stick' for industries targeted by this action. Consumers can both express their support for a business practice considered to be desirable by buying organic produce or fair trade goods, and thereby create a market for it, or they can penalize a company by boycotting products produced in an environmentally damaging way. Examples of campaigns that were successful in changing company behaviour in this way are the CFC boycott directed towards manufacturers of those chemicals (Wapner, 1995) and the boycott of petrol produced by the company Shell over its disposal of the Brent Spar oil rig in the North Sea (Dickson and McCulloch, 1996).

Codes of conduct provide another increasingly popular mechanism for engaging corporations about their responsibilities. In 1989 a coalition of environmental, investor and church interests known as the Coalition for Environmentally Responsible Economies (CERES) met in New York to introduce a ten point environmental code of conduct for corporations. The aim was to provide criteria for auditing the environmental performance of large domestic and multinational industries. The code called on companies to minimize the release of pollutants, conserve non-renewable resources, use sustainable energy sources and use environmental commitment as a factor in appointing members to the board of directors. The principles are known as the *Valdez Principles* (named after the Exxon Valdez disaster in 1989) and have been used by groups such as Friends of the Earth to enlist corporations to pledge compliance. Companies endorsing the CERES principles are required to report annually on their implementation of the principles. The principles have been used to foster shareholder pressure on companies to improve their environmental performance, to help investors decide on socially responsible investments, and as a code with which to praise or criticize corporate behaviour (Wapner, 1995). Wapner argues, 'The CERES Principles represent a new set of institutional constraints on companies and thus another instance of going outside the states system to institutionalise guidelines for widespread and transnational behaviour' (Wapner, 1997, p. 82).

The principles open up new channels of reform and avenues of pressure upon company conduct. They enable companies to claim that their activities are environmentally sound. Whilst they also provide a useful lobbying tool that environmental groups can use to pressure companies to remain faithful to their promises, companies have been able to use them as a way of avoiding government regulation. For example, Humphreys (1997) highlights the case of the Sun company (a petroleum refining company) who have used their endorsement of the Valdez principles to gain credibility when lobbying against environmental legislation in Congress. In addition, codes of conduct provide few channels for verification of compliance with their terms. More generally, codes of conduct are often designed without the participation of those they are intended to benefit and so often fail to have the desired impact because they are not sufficiently targeted to their needs (Barrientos and Orton, 1999). There is also concern that codes of conduct undermine the need for legally binding and state-enforced regulation of MNC investment practices (Kearney, 1999).

Stewardship regimes, which bring together environmental groups, companies and other interested parties to formulate accreditation procedures to identify good corporate conduct, have also begun to develop in recent years. These are more formalized and institutionalized than codes of conduct. They provide an ongoing arena in which dialogue and review take place. The Forestry Stewardship Council provides an interesting example of this form of civil regulation.

The background to the FSC's creation was WWF-UK's decision to pursue an alternative strategy in it's campaign for sustainable forestry; a direct response to the 'lack of commitment and progress being observed at the international policy level' (Murphy and Bendell, 1997, p. 105). Manufacturers' misuse of claims about forestry management led to pressure for the establishment of a standard-setting body with a system for verifying product claims. Hence the Forestry Stewardship Council was established in 1993. The founding group consisted of environmental NGOs, forest industry representatives, community forest groups and forest product certification organizations. The FSC set up an independent forest accreditation programme to alleviate consumer confusion about environmentally friendly wood products. Members of the FSC also agree to nine principles of forestry management. An FSC logo denotes that the product was sourced from an independently certified forest according to FSC principles. There has been a proliferation of such schemes else-where in the world with NGOs initiating buyer groups and FSC working groups. In each case 'a lack of effective government action was a significant factor in making environmental groups turn to the industry itself' (Murphy and Bendell 1997, p. 130).

Each of these strategies, in different ways, provides both positive inducements for reform and rewards for action taken in terms of positive profile and even certification of approval in the case of the FSC. Their aim, therefore, is to promote best practice. As well as guiding and changing behaviour, regulation, if it is to be effective, also has to deter and to provide penalties for non-compliance. This is where critical strat-egies, described below, play a role. Groups pursuing these strategies are more willing to confront a company about its activities and make damaging public claims about them. The issue is not worked out in closed-door meetings between business and NGOs, but in the public arena (through the media or at garage forecourts) aimed at exposing and punishing environmental (and other) abuses. Nevertheless, in as far as the company responds to the criticisms, reforms its behaviour or adopts new working practices; new forms of social regulation are produced.

One example of this has been the growth of organizations devoted towards the surveillance of the activities of TNCs. They expose companies involved in environ-mental degradation and disseminate that knowledge to other activists. There are umbrella groups such as 'Corporate Watch' in the UK, and 'Multinationals Resource Center' in the US as well as sector specific monitors such as 'Oilwatch', which has offices in a number of developing countries in which oil companies operate. Based on the premise that what companies say about their own activities is not to be trusted, and that government surveillance of their operations is limited, TNC monitors seek to deter companies from violating their legal and perceived social obligations by threatening exposure and the activation of campaigns against them.

In recent years, particularly in the US and UK, there has also been a growth in what has been referred to as *shareholder activism* whereby environmental groups buy a small number of shares in a company as a way of obtaining access to the AGM (annual general meeting) and to fora in which they can influence company decision-making. The sponsorship of resolutions at company meetings is aimed at overturning management decisions or at the adoption of a social responsibility measure (Marinetto, 1998). They play on the 'hassle factor', forcing corporations to devote a disproportionate share of their resources to defend a small part of their global operations (Rodman, 1998).

Shell transport and trading, the UK arm of Shell International, had an embarrass-ing confrontation with institutional shareholders in April–May 1997 over its environ-mental (and human rights) record in Nigeria. A group of shareholders holding just 1 per cent of the company called upon the company to improve accountability by establishing new procedures for dealing with environmental and human rights issues (Lewis, 1997). The resolution called for a named member of Shell's committee of managing directors to take charge of environmental and corporate responsibility policies and for an external audit of those policies. The resolution, supported by groups such as WWF and Amnesty International, called on Shell to publish, before the end of the year, a report on its controversial activities in the Niger delta. In March 1997, in an attempt to pre-empt the shareholder motion, Shell revamped its Statement of General Business Principles to include human rights and sustainable development and published its first report on worldwide health safety and environmental activities in an attempt to 'ward off further trouble' (Caulkin, 1997).

Limits of Civil Regulation

The literature on civil regulation suggests that the pressures it creates do have the effect of creating checks and balances on the activities of TNCs (Newell, 2000; Bendell, 2000; Murphy and Bendell, 1997). They have the effect of encouraging private actors to justify their actions to broader public constituencies of share-holders, consumers and civil society at large. The pursuit of profit alone increasingly requires justification. In this sense, the politics that the groups practise contribute towards a new framework of ethics about how companies should view their responsibilities to the communities in which they invest and their impact upon the environment.

Clearly, however, civil regulation does not amount to an adequate or appropriate replacement for regulation at the state or international level. The NGOs engaging with the corporate sector in this way have neither the mandate nor the legitimacy to represent broader publics. Allowing the small section of society that NGOs represent to define the public interest in corporate regulation is highly problematic. Some strategies depend upon large-scale popular support in order to make an impact. Boycotts in particular, if they are to be successful, have to be undertaken by a significant number of people in different markets if TNCs are to take them seriously. Private collaborations between NGOs and companies, on the other hand not open to wider participation and scrutiny, are more likely to fuel concerns about representation.

At present, civil regulation is *ad hoc* and limited in geographical scope, as well as focused on particular TNCs. To be effective, the boycotts have to be adopted in those markets of greatest importance to the TNC. Fortunately for the environmental movement, many of these TNCs that have been the target of consumer action have been dependent for their profit margins on success in markets in the west, where organized mobilization around environmental concerns is currently strongest. Often, however, there are fewer checks and balances in place to restrain perceived 'deviant behaviour' in the developing world, and if the pressures for reform originate from outside the host country, from Western NGOs, they can be regarded as interference.

As an effective form of regulation, it is also clear that many TNCs are relatively insulated from NGO campaigns, often those whose activities have the greatest environmental impact. Rodman shows in his discussion of NGO pressure on TNCs investing in Burma, that the oil companies have been 'the most impervious to non-governmental pressures' (Rodman, 1998, p. 29). The conflict over Shell's operations in Nigeria also demonstrated the failure of activists to exact a price high enough to elicit compliance with their demands (Rodman, 1998, p. 36). Shell's access to technology, expertise and distribution networks cannot easily be replaced by companies from other regions, encouraging the host nation to provide extra inducements to ensure the company stays. Campaigns likely to be most successful are those targeted against particular projects which are of negligible value to the overall operations of the company, so that fear of loss of profits and damage to reputation in other (more important) markets make the targeted operation a liability. Only those TNCs vulnerable to NGO pressure and where consumer preference really matters, are being affected by these strategies. In this sense the scope of the surveillance is restricted to 'easy' targets.

Litigation against TNCs

Given the limitations of both international law and civil regulation as instruments of corporate social regulation, there is a pressing need to look at what role litigation can play in defending the poor where companies are exposing people to environmental risks. For while international law may set standards and generate expectations, and civil negotiation supplies additional incentives and disincentives to conform to these, when companies consciously violate standards or act negligently, litigation has a role to play. Moreover, a number of recent high-profile cases of transnational environmental litigation (foreign direct liability) suggest that holding parent companies to account for the conduct of their subsidiaries, wherever they may operate, provides a potentially vital channel for ensuring that TNCs do not exploit lower environmental standards and poor enforcement regimes at the expense of workers and their environment. It offers a possible vehicle for internationalising standards of protection.

Foreign direct liability refers to two approaches to holding companies legally accountable in their home jurisdiction for negative environmental or health and safety impacts, or complicity in human rights abuses in developing countries where they operate (Ward, 2000, p. 2). Firstly, appeals have been made to use the *Alien Tort Claims Act* of 1789 in the US, which gives district courts the power to hear civil claims from foreign citizens for injuries caused by action 'in violation of the law of nations or a treaty of the United States'. Actions for compensation are based on allegations of corporate complicity in violations of human rights or principles of international environmental law. Examples include litigation against Texaco over environmental damage in Ecuador (Wray, 2000) and Shell, in relation to human rights abuses in Nigeria (Ward, 2000). Key to the successful use of the *Alien Tort Claims Act* is demonstrating that through a 'symbiotic' relationship with the state, a company is culpable for a violation of international law. The case brought against Unocal for the use of forced labour on their gas pipeline project in Burma, for example, had to demonstrate evidence of clear complicity with the state's use of forced labour.

A second type of case has also been brought against parent companies in the UK, Australia and Canada, claiming that they have a responsibility to ensure that home country standards of care apply to subsidiaries, wherever they may be based. A few landmark settlements have been won in this regard, setting important legal precedents. In the Thor case (*Sithole and Others v Thor Chemicals Holdings Ltd*), 20 workers who suffered potentially lethal mercury poisoning in a factory in South Africa won substantial damages (£1.3 million) from the UK parent company because of negligent design, transfer and supervision of an intrinsically hazardous process. In a case brought against Cape plc by workers at their asbestos plant in South Africa (*Lubbe et al v Cape plc*) for negligence, the issue was not that the company had breached British or South African law, but that knowing the harmful effects of asbestos (given the levels accepted in Britain), the company adopted lower standards in South Africa.

The benefits of bringing such cases include the possibility of generating positive reforms. For example, despite the failings of the case brought against Union Carbide for the Bhopal gas leak disaster, in terms of the way it was handled by the Indian government and the amount of compensation that was settled upon, Sripada (1989) argues, the Bhopal incident has prompted action by governments and corporations. Following the case, TNCs everywhere have been under greater popular and government pressure to disclose information regarding environmental impact and safety and to put in place proper risk assessment and avoidance measures. Governments, in turn, have responded by promulgating new environmental legislation or by making existing legislation more stringent. Even if not successful in adequately compensating the victims of corporate negligence, therefore, the act of bringing cases against TNCs can prompt positive reforms.

On the other hand, there are many limitations to using litigation as a strategy for holding companies to account. Legal strategies often reduce complex social problems to questions of monetary compensation. The legal illiteracy of the poor alienates potential users of the law and poorer communities often express distrust and suspicion towards the legal system and the lawyers whom they feel often exploit the plight of the poor for their own ends. In the aftermath of the Bhopal gas leak, US lawyers descended on the slum dwellings of the city, looking for plaintiffs to bring a case against Union Carbide (on the condition that the lawyer receives a substantial sum of any award by the Court). This incident, in particular, has heightened calls for a code of conduct among the legal profession to avoid future irresponsible practice along these lines (Anderson and Ahmed, 1996).

In addition, a key problem in bringing legal suits for negligence on health and environmental grounds, is identifying cause–effect relationships between manifested effects and particular pollutants, as well as deciphering direct from indirect effects. Common law traditions, in particular, establish high requirements for scientific evidence. The technical nature of the industrial processes and the fact that the burden of proof rests on the plaintiff to establish that an environmental standard has been violated, by recourse to independent and reliable technical and scientific data, excludes all but the most wealthy or technically competent. Added to this are concerns about the level of funds required to sponsor such cases and to cover the payment of fees to the defendant in the event that the case is unsuccessful. Intimidation by governments against communities considering bringing cases has also been a key deterrent, especially where governments have often created strong incentives for companies to locate there. George Frynas's work on Shell in Nigeria (Frynas, 1998), for example, shows how threats to the personal security of potential plaintiffs have deterred them from bringing cases against the company in seeking compensation for damage to their lands and loss of livelihood earnings.

Community legal actions are often rejected on the grounds that they do not represent the specific grievances of individuals involved in the case. In Ecuador, for example, unlike the 'class action' system in the US, Courts abide strictly by the principle of direct interest in a case. Activist Norman Wray, engaged in a case against Texaco sums up the situation thus; 'in practice if the trial goes on in Ecuador, the 30 thousand people that constitute this class action suit, have to sue individually ... This will provoke chaos in the civil court of Lago Agrio' (Wray, 2000, p. 6). India, on the other hand, has an innovative system of public interest litigation in which organizations and individuals, not part of the affected class, can represent them (Cottrell, 1992; Anderson and Ahmed, 1996). Nevertheless, in mass tort cases, where large sections of a poor community have been affected by a damaging company investment, issues of who is entitled to speak on behalf of the victims serve to stall or slow the legal process.

The common law legal doctrine of *forum non conveniens* has been the principal means by which transnational cases against companies have been stalled. Whilst the choice of forum is normally the prerogative of the plaintiff, the defendant can invoke the principle to claim that the proposed forum is inconvenient, where there is another 'clearly and distinctly more appropriate forum' where justice between the parties will be done. Plaintiffs often argue that, rather than deterring plaintiffs from 'forum-shopping' in order to access higher levels of compensation, this doctrine allows companies to engage in 'reverse forum-shopping' to evade their obligations in their home country. The World Development Movement argues, 'such shopping around [*by plaintiffs*] is not the reason people from developing countries bring cases to Britain or the US. For most of them, it is their only hope of obtaining justice. The choice is not therefore between different levels of compensation, but between justice and no justice at all' (WDM, 1998, p. 7). Issues raised above, such as fear of persecution, delays in local courts and lack of funding are more probable reasons for foreign plaintiffs pursuing cases in Northern courts.

The underdevelopment of the legal personality of corporations means that different components of TNCs are legally accountable only to the laws of the country in which they are operating. This makes it necessary for campaigners involved in transnational litigation to 'pierce the corporate veil' in demonstrating a clear chain of command-between the headquarters of a company and its subsidiaries. Difficult in any tort case, it becomes very difficult indeed when parent companies often claim they are merely stock or shareholders and that they are only connected for book-keeping purposes. Where a plant design or technology has been designed and exported by the parent company for use in a subsidiary country, in full knowledge of the potential dangers associated with its use, the connections are easier to establish (as in the *Thor* case discussed above). Nevertheless, it is difficult for plaintiffs to identify units within the company that were chiefly responsible for making key decisions. The Indian government made this point to the US Court hearing the Bhopal case; 'Persons harmed by the acts of a multinational corporation are not in a position to isolate which unit of the enterprise caused the harm, yet it is evident that the multinational enterprise that caused the harm is liable for such harm' (Baxi and Thomas, 1986).

As a strategy for addressing the immediate needs of communities affected by damaging investments, litigation is often viewed as a last resort option because of the slowness, (often up to two years for preliminary appeals, two years substantive trial and two years appellate proceedings) complexity and costs of the process and the uncertain nature of the outcomes. For many of the reasons outlined above, pursuing cases against TNCs through foreign courts is not a realistic strategy for most communities. Working with TNCs to avoid these problems in the first place, undertaking impact assessments, agreeing standards or negotiating conditions on investments may avoid the need for these cases. Many companies, concerned for their reputation, will respond to such an approach. The problem comes with 'rogue' companies, those intent on exploiting lower standards in countries where governments are either unwilling or unable to ensure that adequate safeguards are put in place. This is where a legal approach may be necessary. The suitability of litigation will rest upon the type of change being sought; prevention, exposure, or compensation. The goal will determine the point at which legal remedies stop being useful and informal patterns of soft or civil regulation become important, or perform useful supplementary functions.

The current popularity of *forum non conveniens* as grounds for not hearing cases in foreign courts, the difficulty of using the *Alien Tort Claims Act* and, in many cases, the impenetrability of the corporate veil, means that companies looking to exploit lower environmental and social standards in developing countries can often do so without fear of meaningful legal redress. Multi-pronged, multi-level legal and non-legal strategies combining formal and informal mechanisms that reinforce a system of obligations for TNCs are needed to reverse this situation. From a development perspective, in which socially and environmentally responsible business practice is the goal, achieving a 'deterrent effect' is critical, whereby companies build safeguards into their operations for fear of the penalties they may accrue for acting irresponsibly. This was an issue raised in the Bhopal case, for example, where a call was made for damages 'sufficient to deter' Union Carbide and all TNCs 'involved in similar business activities' from 'wilful, malicious and wanton disregard of the rights and safety of the citizens of India' (Baxi and Dhandra, 1990). As well as securing short-term compensation, this surely has to be the aim of litigation; not just making companies liable for their activities wherever they happen to be based, but ensuring that weaker systems of governance or enforcement in developing countries, which expose the poor and their environment to risks that would not be acceptable in the North, are not a legitimate basis for comparative advantage.

Conclusion

This paper provides a critical assessment of the benefits and limitations of three types of approach to corporate regulation. Starting with traditional mechanisms of formal regulation of corporate activity, it was argued that most initiatives at the international level, and by individual countries to create legislation regulating the conduct of their TNCs overseas, are either severely limited or have not progressed very far. Instead, it was suggested, there is an imbalance between the rights and responsibilities of TNCs that provides the impetus for the alternative strategies that are discussed in this paper. These were firstly civil society-based approaches to business regulation, aimed, in different ways, at holding companies to account for their social and environmental responsibilities by mobilizing the public and their consumer power towards that end. It was suggested that while they usefully generate new expectations about the responsibilities of corporations when they invest in developing countries, and do appear to engage many larger companies concerned for their brand names, they provide only a limited means of surveillance, such that the worst polluters and violators often escape attention. Secondly, the role of transnational litigation was discussed as a further means by which checks and balances on the impacts of investment can be created. It was argued that while important precedents have been set, and changes brought about through out of court settlements or indirect pressures on other companies to change their behaviour, litigation is a limited strategy for the poor in most settings. For this reason, combinations of formal and informal approaches are likely to be necessary depending on the goal of the action.

Interestingly, a combination of the limitations of civil regulation and transnational litigation, as well as their growing popularity, may generate demands from the public and industry themselves for new international and national binding standards. The limited applicability of foreign direct liability in many legal systems and the confusion surrounding many non-state labelling and certification schemes, has heightened the need for public regulation. In the legal area, there have been moves, for example, to harmonise jurisdictions and to advance negotiations towards a multilateral convention on civil jurisdiction and judgements under the auspices of the Hague Conference on Private International Law (Muchlinski, 2001). The appeal of public regulation is its ability to provide the consistency, transparency and enforceability that many civil regulation approaches lack. The history of weak public regulation of the corporate sector suggests, nevertheless, that it is no panacea. More likely is that we will be faced with a dense and inter-related set of regulatory approaches, both formal and informal, existing at multiple levels from the international down to the local level. The challenge is to ensure the combinations of measures adopted are responsive to the needs of the poor who are most vulnerable to destructive investments.

Notes

1   I use the term transnational companies here to denote the fact that control and decision-making is often concentrated within the western branches of these companies. Given that power, resources and authority are not diffused throughout the organizations, the term 'multi' exaggerates the global scope of the company (see Gill and Law, 1988).

2   There have also been moves within developing countries themselves to recognise the right of citizens to hold TNCs accountable for personal and environmental injuries committed abroad. The NGO coalition AIDA, in Costa Rica, is calling for a bill 'that would officially recognise the right of Costa Rican citizens to bring suits abroad against foreign corporations for environmental and other damages caused in Costa Rica' (cited in Ward, 2000, p. 23).

References

Anderson M, Ahmed A. 1996. Assessing environmental damage under Indian law *REICIEL* 5(4): 335–41.

Australian Senate, 2000. Corporate code of conduct bill: A bill for an act to impose standards on the conduct of Australian corporations which undertake business activities in other countries and for related purposed, drafted by Senator Bourne.

Ayine D, Werksman J. 1999. Implications of the MAI for use of natural resources and land. In *Regulating International Business*, Picciotto S, Mayne R. Macmillan: Basingtoke 126–42.

Barrientos S, Orton L. 1999. *Gender and Codes of Conduct: A Case Study from Horticulture in South Africa*. Christian Aid: London.

Baxi U, Thomas P. 1986. *Mass Disasters and Multinational Liability: The Bhopal Case*. Indian Law Institute: New Delhi.

Baxi U, Dhanda A. 1990. *Valiant Victims and Lethal Litigation*. Indian Law Institute: New Delhi.

Bendell J. (ed.). 2000. *Terms of Endearment: Business, NGOs and Sustainable Development*. Greenleaf Publishers: Sheffield.

Caulkin S. 1997. Amnesty and WWF take a crack at Shell. *The Observer,* May 11.

Cottrell J. 1992. Courts and accountability: Public interest litigation in the Indian high courts. *Third World Legal Studies:* 199–213.

Dickson L, McCulloch A. 1996. Shell, the Brent Spar and Greenpeace: a doomed tryst? *Environmental Politics* 5(1), 122–29.

Frynas G. 1998. Political instability and business: focus on Shell in Nigeria. *Third World Quarterly* 19(3): 457–78.

Gill S, Law D. 1988. *The Global Political Economy*. Harvester/Wheatsheaf: Herts.

Humphreys D. 1997. Environmental accountability and transnational corporations. Paper presented to the International Academic Conference on Environmental Justice: Global ethics for the 21st century, Victoria Australia: University of Melbourne, October 1–3.

Kearney N. 1999. Corporate codes of conduct. The privatised application of labour standards. In *Regulating International Business*, Picciotto S, Mayne R. Macmillan: Basingtoke pp. 205–21.

Lewis W. 1997. Shell to face shareholder vote on ethics. *Financial Times*, April 12.

Madeley J. 1999. *Big Business, Poor People*. Zed Books: London.

Marinetto M. 1998. The shareholders strike back – issues in the research of shareholder activism. *Environmental Politics* 7(3): 125–33.

McLaren D. 2000. The OECD's revised Guidelines for multinational enterprises: a step towards corporate accountability? Friends of the Earth: London.

Muchlinksi P. 1999. A brief history of business regulation, in Picciotto, Sol and Mayne, Ruth (eds). *Regulating International Business: Beyond Liberalization.*

Muchlinski P. 2001. Corporations in international litigation: problems of jurisdiction and the United Kingdom asbestos cases. *International and Comparative Law Quarterly* 50.

Murphy D, Bendell J. 1997. *In the Company of Partners.* Policy Press: Bristol; 105–30.

Newell P. 2000. Environmental NGOs and globalisation: the governance of TNCs. *Global Social Movements* Cohen R, Rai S. (eds). Athlone Press: London; 117–34.

Newell P. 2001a. Environmental NGOs, TNCs and the question of governance. In *The International Political Economy of the Environment: Critical Perspective*, Stevis D, Assetto V. (eds). Lynne Riener: Boulder Co and London.

Newell P. 2001b. Access to environmental justice? Litigation against TNCs in the South. *IDS Bulletin* vol. 32 no. 1 January, pp. 83–94.

Picciotto S, Mayne R. (eds) 1999. *Regulating International Business: Beyond Liberalization.* Macmillan: Basingstoke.

Rodman K. 1998. Think globally, punish locally: non-state actors, MNCs and human rights sanctions. *Ethics and International Affairs* 12.

Rowen A. 1998. Meet the new world government, *The Guardian.* February 13th.

Sauermann D. 1986. The regulation of multinational corporations and Third World Countries *South African Yearbook of International Law* 55.

Schmidheiny S. 1992. *Changing Course: A Global Business Perspective on Development and the Environment.* MIT Press: Cambridge MA.

Seyfang G. 1999. Private sector self-regulation for social responsibility: mapping codes of conduct. Working Paper No. l Social Policy Research Programme, DfID/UEA.

Sripada S. 1989. The multinational corporations and environmental issues. *Journal of the Indian Law Institute* 31(4): 534–52.

Vogel D. 1997. Trading up and governing across: transnational governance and environmental protection. *Journal of European Public Policy* 4.

Wapner P. 1995. *Environmental Activism and World Civic Politics.* SUNY: New York.

Wapner P. 1997. Governance in global civil society, *Global Governance*, Oran Y, Oran R. (eds). MIT Press: Cambridge MA, 67.

Ward H. 2000. Foreign direct liability: exploring the issues. FDL Workshop Background Paper, RIIA, London.

World Bank, 2000. Is globalization causing a race to the bottom in environmental standards? Briefing Paper, PREM Economic Policy Group and Development Economics Group, Washington DC.

World Development Movement (WDM). 1998. Law unto themselves: holding multinationals to account, Discussion paper, September, pp. 5–7.

WWF 1999. Foreign direct investment and environment: from pollution havens to sustainable development WWF-UK Report from the OECD Conference, Paris, France, 20/21 September

Wray N. 2000. Texaco document. Center for Economic and Social Rights Quito, Ecuador.

21

Reforming Global Environmental Governance: The Case for a United Nations Environment Organisation (UNEO) (2012)

Frank Biermann

World Politics in the Anthropocene

Over the last two hundred years, humankind has evolved into a planetary force that influences global biogeochemical systems. No longer is the human species a spectator that merely needs to adapt to the natural environment. Humanity itself has become a powerful agent of earth system evolution. In particular global warming is proceeding rapidly. The snowfields on the Kilimanjaro might melt within a few decades, and the ice cover on the Arctic Ocean has shrunk by over 30 percent since satellite observations begun in 1979. Some scientists warn that major disruptions in the earth system could occur within this century. The evidence of human influence on all planetary systems is such that stratigraphy experts are prepared today to formally classify the present time as a distinct epoch in planetary history, the "Anthropocene".

This development poses one of the largest governance challenges ever. Policymakers in the twentieth century gained much experience in managing confined ecosystems, such as river basins, forests, or lakes. In the twenty-first century, they are faced with one of the largest political problems humankind has had to deal with: protecting the entire system earth, including most of its subsystems, and building stable institutions that guarantee a safe transition and a co-evolution of natural and social systems at planetary scale. I call this the challenge of earth system governance, as a new paradigm to describe this particular challenge of planetary coevolution of humans and nature.

Frank Biermann. 2012. "Reforming Global Environmental Governance: The Case for a United Nations Environment Organisation". SDG Stakeholder Forum. pp. 4–12. Reproduced with permission from F. Biermann.

This governance challenge is a core task for governments and civil society organizations, for local actors and national alliances, for public and private agents alike. Importantly, it is a challenge for effective international collaboration. There are a number of central actors here, including the numerous international organizations, ranging from the many specialized agencies of the United Nations to the hundreds of secretariats to international environmental treaties. International organizations are crucial in many ways. They influence governance through funding and administration of research, the synthesis of scientific findings, the development of policy proposals, problem frames and policy assessments, and eventually through the distribution of this knowledge to stakeholders, from national governments to individual citizens. International organizations also influence earth system governance through the creation, support and shaping of norm-building processes. This is in particular the role of the staff of treaty secretariats, which organize meetings, set agendas and report to the conferences of the parties. International bureaucracies are crucial in shaping procedures, providing arenas for negotiations and framing inter- and transnational processes of bargaining and arguing. Last but not least, international organizations are important in helping countries to implement international agreements, for example by supporting administrative capacity in many countries.

In short, international organizations are important agents in earth system governance. Their role is vital. However, recent research also indicates that the overall system of international organizations in this domain falls short of its potential. For one, the community of international organizations and programs in earth system governance is highly fragmented, with most major international agencies running their own environmental programs, along with several hundred larger or smaller convention secretariats, with little effective coordination. In addition, earth system governance is not accountable to one international bureaucracy that is solely devoted to supporting international governance processes in this area. This situation has led to a debate in academia and policy circles on the need for a larger integrated organization, such as a "world environment organization" or a "UN environment organization." In this paper, I summarize this debate and lay out my own vision on why a UN Environment Organization, based on the current UNEP, is an important building block for successful international cooperation. I believe that 2012 will be a crucial year to set into motion the necessary negotiation and planning processes to upgrade UNEP to a UN specialized agency.

Forty Years of Debate on a World Environment Organization

Proposals to create an international agency on environmental protection have been debated for now over forty years. The first proposal for such an organization dates back to US foreign policy strategist George F. Kennan (1970), who argued for an

International Environmental Agency encompassing "a small group of advanced nations." Several authors supported this idea at that time. As one outcome of this debate, the United Nations established in 1973 the United Nations Environment Programme (UNEP), following a decision adopted at the 1972 Stockholm Conference on the Human Environment. UNEP is not an intergovernmental organization, but a subsidiary body of the General Assembly reporting through the Economic and Social Council. The creation of a UN environment program was a more modest reform than the strong international environmental organization that some observers had called for at that time. Nonetheless, this reform altered the context of the organizational debate in international environmental politics – and effectively halted it.

The debate about a larger, more powerful agency for global environmental policy was revived in 1989. The Declaration of The Hague, initiated by the governments of The Netherlands, France and Norway, called for an authoritative international body on the atmosphere that would include a provision for effective majority rule. Although not representative of the international community at the time, the declaration helped to trigger more proposals for a world environment organization that could replace UNEP. At the 1997 Special Session of the UN General Assembly on environment and development, Brazil, Germany, Singapore, and South Africa submitted a joint proposal for a "global umbrella organization for environmental issues, with the United Nations Environment Programme as a major pillar." The broadening of the debate in the late 1990s resulted in a variety of new views about what a world environment organization should or should not do.

More skeptical voices and critics of a new organization came also forward. The former head of the secretariat to the Convention on Biological Diversity, Calestous Juma, argued that advocates of a central authority divert attention from more pressing problems and fail to acknowledge that centralizing institutional structures is an anachronistic paradigm. Sebastian Oberthür and Thomas Gehring supported these concerns based on institutional theory. Konrad von Moltke or Adil Najam argued in favor of decentralized institutional clusters to deal with diverse sets of environmental issues rather than entrusting all problems to one central organization.

In recent years, the debate has been given new impetus by the diplomatic effort of France to create a UN Environment Organization. In 2003, the French government circulated a proposal to transform UNEP into an "Organisation spécialisée des Nations Unies pour l'environnement," which followed up on earlier French initiatives to replace UNEP by a "world environment organization." This proposal has been emphasized by the 2007 Paris Call for Action during the Citizens of the Earth Conference for Global Ecological Governance, and supported by an intergovernmental "Group of Friends of the UN Environment Organization." A consultative process within the UN system explored the possibility of a more coherent institutional framework for the environmental activities in the UN system. After a series of consultations with country delegations, members of the UN Secretariat and secretariats of multilateral environmental agreements, as well as with scientists, business leaders and non-governmental organizations, the process summarized several proposals on how to address the shortcomings in international environmental governance. Amongst these proposals is the establishment of a UN Environment Organization.

Three Models of a World Environment Organization

Virtually all proposals for a world environment organization can be categorized in three ideal type models, which differ regarding the degree of change that is required. First, the least radical proposals advise upgrading UNEP to a specialized UN agency with full-fledged organizational status. Proponents of this approach have referred to the World Health Organization or the International Labor Organization as suitable models. Other agencies operating in the environmental field would neither be integrated into the new agency nor disbanded. The new agency in this model is expected to improve the facilitation of normbuilding and norm-implementation processes. This strength would in particular derive from an enhanced mandate and better capabilities of the agency to build capacities in developing countries. This differs from UNEP's present "catalytic" mandate that prevents the program from engaging in project implementation. Furthermore, additional legal and political powers could come with the status of a UN special agency. For example, its governing body could approve by qualified majority vote certain regulations that could be binding, under certain conditions, on all members (comparable to the International Maritime Organization), or could adopt drafts of legally binding treaties negotiated by sub-committees under its auspices (comparable to the International Labor Organization). Such powers would exceed those entrusted to UNEP, which cannot adopt legal instruments.

Second, some observers argue for a more fundamental reform to address the substantive and functional overlap between the many international institutions in global environmental governance. These advocates of a more centralized governance architecture call for the integration of several existing agencies and programs into one all-encompassing world environment organization. Such an integration of environmental regimes could loosely follow the model of the World Trade Organization, which has integrated diverse multilateral trade agreements. According to some scholars, this integration could even include established intergovernmental organizations, although historic evidence suggests that this goes beyond the politically conceivable.

The third and most far-reaching model is that of a hierarchical intergovernmental organization on environmental issues that would be equipped with majority decision-making as well as enforcement powers vis-à-vis states that fail to comply with international agreements on the protection of global commons. The Hague Declaration of 1989 seemed to have veered in the direction of an environmental agency with sanctioning powers, and at the end of the 1980s, New Zealand had suggested establishing an "Environment Protection Council," whose decisions would be binding. Yet support for such a powerful international agency remains very scarce. Most scholars have focused in recent years on reform proposals that are feasible in the current political context.

Rio Plus 2012: The Case for Getting Serious about a United Nations Environment Organization

While a world environment organization is still not a reality after forty years of debate, the idea of creating such a new agency is one of the most long-standing, and most vivid, reform debates in the field of globalization and the governance of its environmental impacts. With more than fifty nations now firmly behind a concrete proposal for a UN Environment Organization, the establishment of a new agency, based on the existing UN Environment Programme, becomes more likely, at least in the medium term. Yet the extent to which this new agency would in fact advance the effectiveness of earth system governance, is certain to remain a hotly debated issue. I have participated in this debate for fifteen years by now (see in particular Biermann 2000), and continue to believe that a world environment organization, or a United Nations Environment Organization, as the most recent proposals call it, would improve the overall effectiveness of earth system governance in a variety of ways. In my view, upgrading UNEP to a specialized UN agency would follow the long-standing policy of functional specialization within the UN system, with the United Nations Organization as the focal point among numerous independent organizations for specific issues, such as food and agriculture (FAO, established in 1945); education, science, and culture (UNESCO 1945); health (WHO, 1946); civil aviation (ICAO, 1944); or meteorology (WMO, 1947). While some specialized organizations are much older than the United Nations itself (for instance the Universal Postal Union, created in 1874), most were founded simultaneously with the establishment of the United Nations, since it was felt at that time that the vast number of issues in the economic, social or technical fields would "overstretch" the world body. Environmental problems, however, were no concern in 1945, with the term "environment" not even appearing in the UN Charter. It was only in 1972 that UNEP was set up as a mere program, without legal personality, without budget, and – according to its founding instruments – with only a "small secretariat." UNEP is no comparison to the other specialized organizations that can avail themselves of more resources and hence influence.

The establishment of a UN specialized agency on environmental issues could strengthen global norm-building and institutionalization. One example of how this could work is the International Labor Organization. ILO has developed a comprehensive body of "ILO conventions" that come close to a global labor code. In comparison, current earth system governance is far more disparate and cumbersome in its norm-setting processes. The general assembly of a UN Environment Organization could adopt draft treaties that have been negotiated by subcommittees under its auspices and that would then be opened for signature within UNEO headquarters. The ILO Constitution requires its parties in article 19.5 to submit, within one year, all treaties adopted by the ILO General Conference to the respective national authorities (such as the parliament) and to report to the organization on progress in the ratification process. This goes much beyond the powers of the UNEP Governing Council, which can initiate intergovernmental negotiations, but cannot adopt legal instruments on its own.

A UN Environment Organization could also be enabled to approve by qualified majority vote certain regulations, which are then binding on all members, comparable to article 21 and 22 of the WHO Constitution. Within the WHO system, certain regulations – for instance on various sanitary and quarantine requirements, nomenclatures, or safety or labeling standards – enter into force for all states after adoption by the Health Assembly with the exception of states that have notified the organization of rejection or reservations within a certain period.

Upgrading UNEP to a UN Environment Organization could moreover ameliorate a coordination deficit in earth system governance. Norms and standards in each area of environmental governance are created by distinct legislative bodies – the conferences of the parties to various conventions – with little respect for repercussions and links with other fields. While the decentralized negotiation of rules and standards in separate functional bodies may be defensible, this is less so regarding the organizational fragmentation of the various convention secretariats, which have evolved into quite independent bureaucracies with strong centrifugal tendencies. In addition, most specialized organizations and bodies, such as the UN Food and Agriculture Organization (FAO) or the UN Organization for Industrial Development (UNIDO), have initiated their own environmental programs independently from each other and with little policy coordination among themselves and with UNEP.

This problem is well known. The attempt to network individual organizations, programs and offices has been ongoing since 1972, when a first coordinating body was set up within the United Nations. This and its successors, however, have lacked the legal authority to overcome the special interests of individual departments, programs, and convention secretariats. For earth system governance, no central anchoring point exists that could compare to WHO or ILO in their fields. Instead, there is an overlap in the functional areas of several institutions. An international center with a clear strategy to ensure worldwide environmental protection is thus the need of the hour. Just as within nation states, where environmental policy was strengthened through introduction of independent environmental ministries, earth system governance could be made stronger through an independent UN Environment Organization that helps to contain the special interests of individual programs and organizations and to limit duplication, overlap and inconsistencies.

Governments could also empower the new agency to coordinate multilateral environmental agreements (generally by a decision of the respective conferences of the parties). The constitutive treaty of the organization could provide general principles for multilateral environmental treaties as well as coordinating rules that govern the organization and its relationship with the issue-specific environmental regimes.

Following WTO usage, environmental regimes covered by the UN Environment Organization could be divided into "multilateral" and "plurilateral" environmental agreements. For "multilateral" agreements, ratification would be compulsory for any new member of the organization, while "plurilateral" agreements would still leave members the option to remain outside. The multilateral agreements would thus form the "global environmental law code" under the UN Environment Organization, with the existing conferences of the parties being transformed into subcommittees under the UNEO Assembly. This would enable the UNEO Assembly to develop a common reporting system for all multilateral environmental agreements; a common dispute settlement system; mutually agreed guidelines that could be used – based on an inter-agency agreement – for the environmental activities of the World Bank and for environmentally-related conflicts regulated under the WTO dispute settlement system; as well as a joint system of capacity-building for developing countries along with financial and technological transfer.

Apart from regime building and norm setting, a UN Environment Organization could also improve the overall implementation of earth system governance, for example by a common comprehensive reporting system on the state of the environment and on the state of implementation in different countries, as well as by stronger efforts in raising public awareness. At present, several environmental regimes require their parties to report on their policies, and a few specialized organizations collect and disseminate valuable knowledge and promote further research. Yet there remains a sizeable lack of coordination, bundling, processing, and channeling of this knowledge in a policy-oriented manner. Most conventions still have different reporting needs and formats, with a certain amount of duplication. The current system is burdensome especially for developing countries, since the myriad reporting systems siphon off administrative resources that governments could use for other purposes. All reporting requirements could be streamlined into one single report to be dispatched to one single body, such as a UN Environment Organization. Instead of adding another layer of bureaucracy, a UN Environment Organization could provide a level of streamlining and harmonization that would reduce the current administrative burden, in particular for developing countries.

Importantly, a UN Environment Organization could help in particular smaller developing countries in making their participation in earth system governance stronger and more effective. One problem is that the current organizational fragmentation and inadequate coordination causes special problems for developing countries. Individual environmental agreements are negotiated in a variety of places. Recent conferences on climate change, for example, were hosted in a circular movement covering four continents, from Berlin in 1995 to Geneva, Kyoto, Bonn, Buenos Aires, The Hague, Marrakech, New Delhi, Milan, Buenos Aires, Montreal, Bali, Poznan, Copenhagen, and in 2010 Cancun.

Smaller developing countries lack the resources to attend all these meetings with a sufficient number of well-qualified diplomats and experts. Often, even larger countries need to rely on their local embassy staff to negotiate highly complex technical regulations on the environment. This system of a "travelling diplomatic circus" distinguishes earth system governance from many other policy fields, where negotiations are held within the assembly of an international agency at its seat. The creation of a UN Environment Organization could thus help developing countries to build up specialized "environmental embassies" at the seat of the new organization. This would reduce their costs and increase their negotiation influence. The same could be said for nongovernmental organizations, which could participate in global negotiations within the UNEO Assembly and its committees at lower costs.

Decision-making procedures based on North-South parity – that is, veto rights for the South (and the North) as a group – could ensure that the UN Environment Organization would not evolve into a new form of eco-colonialism, as many Southern actors and observers may fear. One solution could be a double-weighted majority system in the UNEO Assembly, comparable to that of the Montreal Protocol as amended in 1990 or of the Global Environment Facility as reformed in 1994. In both institutions, decisions require the assent of two thirds of members that must include the simple majority of both developing and developed countries (or, in the case of the GEF, sixty percent of the states participating and sixty percent of the financial contributions). Given that the concept of double-weighted voting has been developed in the environmental field, it seems to be a good basis for voting within the UNEO Assembly.

Some have argued that the environment is too complex an issue to shape the mandate for a single organization, and have hence proposed a "world organization on sustainable development" that would build on a merger (and upgrade) of UNEP and UNDP (at least). I view this option as problematic. It would be a marriage of unequals that is likely to harm environmental interests in the long run without strengthening development goals. First, UNDP and UNEP are unequal regarding their sheer size and resources. Taking into account the twelvefold larger core budget of UNDP vis-à-vis the UNEP Environment Fund as well as a ratio of roughly four to one in professional staff, merging both programs would come close to the dissolution of UNEP within the significantly larger UNDP. This could result either in a strengthening of environmental goals within the development community or in the slow degrading of environmental goals in a larger new, development-oriented agency. Both UNEP and UNDP are marked by distinct organizational cultures tuned to the goals of the respective programs. Given differences in size and resources, it is difficult to believe that the much smaller "environmental" community will eventually prevail in changing the much larger "development" community within an overall new organization. It seems certain that the strength and independence of environmental concerns will be weakened over time.

This is in the interest of neither North nor South, since functional differentiation in governance systems between socio-economic development and environmental protection makes sense. Hardly any country has opted for the administrative merger of "economic development" and "environmental protection" as policy areas at the national level. Most countries maintain the differentiation between economic or development ministries, and environmental ministries. This experience at the national level illustrates that environmental policy indeed can, and should, be addressed by one administrative unit. It is not clear why administrative functional differentiation should differ at the international level. Most international organizations and national ministries have clearly defined mandates for their respective policy areas, and it is theoretically not difficult to demarcate the responsibilities of a new international organization for the environment. All this advises against the merger of UNEP and UNDP into one program or organization.

UNEP and UNDP are also unequal regarding their functions within their respective governance areas. UNEP has an important role in agenda-setting and knowledge-management, for example with a view to the initiation of new treaties, the organization of international diplomatic conferences, the training of national administrative and legal personnel, or the initiation, synthesis and dissemination of new knowledge, regarding both fundamental and applied environmental science. UNDP's core functions, on the other hand, are operational. It is mandated to generate and implement projects, with less regard to international standard setting or knowledge-generation. A merger of UNDP and UNEP hence runs the risk that the different functions of UNEP will lose influence within such a larger new agency.

If, on the other hand, a world organization on sustainable development would imply merely the upgrading of UNEP to an international organization with this name, while leaving other bodies – including UNDP or the World Bank – untouched, it is unclear what consequences the choice of the organization's name – "sustainable development" instead of "environment" – would have. This could reduce the overarching concept of "sustainable development" to a new yet deluding label for environmental protection. In sum, a world organization on sustainable development would be either ill advised if it implies the integration of UNEP and UNDP, or a misuse of a key concept of North-South relations if it merely implies giving a new name to an essentially environmental organization.

This does not imply that a UN Environment Organization should address environmental policy as unrelated to the larger quest for development. A UN Environment Organization would aim at the preservation of environmental resources *within* the development process, not unlike the role of environmental ministries in developing countries. A UN Environment Organization should not be seen in juxtaposition of environment *and* development, but rather within a framework of environment *for* development. The UN Environment Organization constitution would hence have to encompass more than purely environmental rules, but address the development concerns of the South as well. Therefore, general principles such as the right to development, the sovereign right over natural resources within a country's jurisdiction or the principle of common but differentiated responsibilities and capabilities need to be integrated into the constitutive instrument of the UN Environment Organization.

Summing Up

In sum, even though international organizations and bureaucracies play important roles in earth system governance, the current system of international organization and of international bureaucracies lacks effectiveness. This is partially due to a lack of standing of the core agencies in this respect and the overall fragmentation of earth system governance. I have laid out in this paper a proposal for upgrading UNEP to a United Nations Environment Organization. The establishment of a UN Environment Organization would improve coordination of earth system governance; pave the way for the elevation of environmental policies on the agenda of governments, international organizations and private organizations; assist in developing the capacities for environmental policy in African, Asian and Latin American countries; and strengthen the institutional environment for the negotiation of new conventions and action programs as well as for the implementation and coordination of existing ones. Naturally, a UN Environment Organization as outlined here cannot solve all problems of environmental degradation. It can only be a partial contribution. Yet this should not result in a rejection of reform. A United Nations Environment Organization is no silver bullet. But its creation will be an important building block in improving the overall effectiveness of our efforts to protect the biogeochemical systems of the planet.

Part V
Can Globalization be Greened?

Introduction

The previous section sought to explore the extent to which globalization could be governed for the protection of the environment and how that might be done. This section brings together a contrasting set of views about whether or not the idea of greening a global, capitalist economy represents a contradiction in terms. In other words, the debate is less about what type of regulation or governance might be best, and more about whether the very model of development presumed by a globalizing economy is compatible with the achievement of sustainability.

For critics, as the first piece in this section by *The Ecologist* magazine editors make clear, the global economy is reorganizing societies and ecologies to meet the needs of the market, transforming them into expendable resources for exploitation, and in so doing is undermining institutions and cultures that protect common properties. From this perspective globalization cannot be greened because its globalizing, expansionist and extractivist project is at odds with the pursuit of sustainability. States are seen as handmaidens of global business, such that effective and democratic responses to environmental threats will have to come from below, by resisting incursions into the commons and respecting common property. This is about asserting and defending resource rights, not as inalienable property rights, but rather as a collective local stewardship responsibility. The environmental movement therefore needs to align itself with community-based struggles for environmental justice and control over resources, challenging the ideology of growth, and strengthening the "weapons of the weak" (Scott, 1985) that enable everyday resistance to further "enclosure of the commons."

Richard Falk is likewise critical of what he calls "top-down" globalization, the pursuit of a neoliberal agenda by a privileged global elite, and subject to the discipline of global capital. Rather than focus on community-based struggles alone,

The Globalization and Environment Reader, First Edition. Edited by Peter Newell and J. Timmons Roberts.
Editorial material and organization © 2017 John Wiley & Sons, Ltd. Published 2017 by John Wiley & Sons, Ltd.

however, he draws on a range of environmental and non-environmental examples of what he calls "globalization from below." By this he means transnational activism aimed at holding governments, corporations, and international institutions to account, opening spaces for participation, to protect global public goods and resist the more insidious aspects of globalization. Falk concludes by suggesting that the competition between "top-down" and "bottom-up" globalization "is not a zero-sum rivalry, but rather one in which the transnational democratic goals are designed to reconcile global market operations with the wellbeing of peoples and with the carrying capacity of the earth." In this sense his stance is less radical and critical than that of *The Ecologist*, since he suggests "There is nothing inherently wrong with encouraging economies of scale and the pursuit of comparative advantage so long as the social, environmental, political and cultural effects are mainly beneficial." For him the pendulum has swung too far towards the promotion of economic growth at any cost while disregarding adverse social and environmental effects. It is about fighting for the survival of the "compassionate state": an oxymoron for critics of the role of state in accelerating environmental crises. But he situates it as part of an emerging set of shared world order values: minimizing violence, maximizing economic wellbeing, realizing social and political justice, and upholding environmental quality social contracts that restore balance to the interests of people and those of markets.

Falk is optimistic, therefore, about the prospects that ecological constraints of various sorts will induce the market to send a variety of signals that demand a negotiated transition to managed economic growth in the interest of sustainability. This, he hopes, would form the basis of a new global social contract.

Alisdair Young meanwhile takes aim at environmentalists and academics (such as Ken Conca in the previous section) who in his view exaggerate the power of global economic institutions such as the WTO and who overestimate these institutions' ability to limit progressive environmental regulation. In doing so, Young argues environmentalists end up absolving states of responsibilities for protecting the environment, whereas it is states that negotiate trade agreements, enforce rules, and (in many cases) are accountable to publics. Environmentalists may be creating a self-fulfilling prophecy by exaggerating the constraint imposed upon national governments by the WTO and so run the risk of actually discouraging the very regulations they favor. He suggests "By proclaiming that international rules are hostile to public health and environmental protection they give the opponents of regulation an additional argument to use in the domestic debate and give reluctant governments another excuse not to act." Far from making sure trade rules trump environmental regulations and ensuring a race to the bottom, he argues the WTO can be an institution capable of realizing progressive environmental change. Far from constraining policy autonomy, Young argues that governments have relative freedom to adopt whatever public health and environmental protection rules they see fit. In this market liberal view (see Clapp and Dauvergne chapter in Part III) then there is no contradiction between the organization of a global economy along capitalist lines and the realization of sustainable development. Hence while acknowledging that the concerns of environmentalists are not without some foundation, he feels they are ultimately "picking the wrong fight."

Next up are Magdoff and Foster, who argue passionately that discussions about governing, regulating or managing globalization for the benefit of the environment or the poor are fundamentally misguided. They point to the capitalist system and its growth imperatives towards ever expanding production and consumption as the source of the problem, since a system geared towards exponential growth will inevitably transgress planetary boundaries. Most environmental problems are either caused, or made much worse, they suggest, by the workings of our economic system. Even such issues as population growth and technology are best viewed in terms of their relation to the socioeconomic organization of society. In this sense ecological destruction is built into the inner nature and logic of our present system of production. This means "solutions" proposed for environmental devastation, which would allow the current system of production and distribution to proceed unabated, inevitably fail. The focus of their critique is those environmentalists who criticize the system and its "market failures" but end up promoting a more tightly controlled "humane" and non-corporate capitalism, instead of getting outside the box of capitalism. Contrary to those that think that capitalism can and should be reformed, they argue for a dynamic, multifaceted struggle for a new cultural compact and a new productive system organized along socialist or communal lines, aimed at enhancing democratic control over production to ensure it exists within ecological limits.

Beyond the broader claims about the sustainability or otherwise of capitalism, Steinberger et al. then show in a more quantitative fashion how ecology and economy are intertwined in flows around the global economy. They use new consumption-based measures of national carbon emissions to explore the relationship between human development and carbon. Consumption-based accounting corrects the way greenhouse gas emissions are usually counted (as territorial emissions) by adding the emissions generated to produce imported goods and services, while subtracting those generated to produce exports. Carbon is embodied in the import and export of goods around the world. This hugely complicates the task of allocating the responsibility for addressing climate change, when there is increasingly less of a relationship between where something is produced and where it is consumed.

Their focus is on which societies have created high levels of human development (as measured by long life expectancy) with relatively low levels of carbon emissions. Importantly, they find that despite strong international trends, there is no deterministic industrial development trajectory. There is instead great diversity in pathways, and national histories do not necessarily follow the global trends, despite the fact that all countries are linked by global trade and rely to a large extent on similar technologies. There is evidence of a relative, but not absolute, decoupling of socioeconomic gains from carbon-intensive processes. In this sense their piece offers a more nuanced and contingent and possibly optimistic account than that provided by Magdoff and Foster. As they put it: "the findings provide hope that national choices and pathways matter, and policies are available that do not prioritize growth at the expense of climate stability and a long life for our societies."

This long-standing debate about the relationship between globalization and the environment has been given a new lease of life around concepts such as the "green economy" and "green growth" promoted by institutions such as the OECD, G8, and World Bank. As UNEP puts it in their report on "Towards a Green Economy," we have seen the "idea of a 'green economy' float out of its specialist moorings in environmental economics and into the mainstream of policy discourse," as witnessed in the words of heads of state and finance ministers, in the text of G20 communiqués and in the Rio+20 document "The Future We Want." Though borne of a legitimacy crisis caused by the confluence of financial, social and environmental crises, the report also draws attention to increasing evidence of a way forward, a new economic paradigm – one in which material wealth is not delivered at the expense of growing environmental risks, ecological scarcities, and social disparities. These are the foundations of the green economy. As with ecological modernization discussed earlier in the book (see Mol in Part I), it seeks to reconcile growth with sustainability by arguing that the green economy offers vast opportunities for employment, investment, technological innovation, and so on.

Sustainability, in sum, is repositioned as an opportunity as much as a threat, as long as the right enabling conditions are put in place. For governments, it affords the chance to reduce subsidies on fossil fuels, to re-direct public investment through a "green new deal" aimed at creating employment in the low carbon economy, and by greening public procurement. For the private sector, it means seizing the opportunity to engage early in the transitions taking place across a number of key sectors, and responding to policy reforms and price signals through higher levels of financing and investment. Politically, the report aims to debunk what it refers to as several myths and misconceptions about greening the global economy, around the trade-offs between growth and sustainability and so to respond to the sort of critiques outlined in some of the other pieces in this section.

The final piece in this section and the volume takes issue with these claims, and brings us back to the politics of green transformations (Scoones et al., 2015). Its point of departure is the fact that "None of the green economy strategy papers – from OECD to UNEP – tackles the issues of power and distribution of resources." It is critical of the obsession with technological innovation and efficiency as a cure-all for ecological crises, while overlooking the scope for negative and feedback effects unless absolute de-coupling of wealth generation from resource use takes place. It argues that while the green economy certainly presents opportunities for business in terms of new markets, investment and innovation opportunities, real "greening" will never be achieved while the rest – indeed the majority – of the global economy operates along business-as-usual lines.

Contrary to the UNEP report, pricing and financializing nature are, in this view, not the way to facilitate green transformations that require more structural changes in how the global economy is organized. It also places strong emphasis on the rights, implications and questions of global environment justice that arise when resources are re-classified as "natural capital" to be conserved or destroyed by those who own it (Sikor and Newell, 2014). In other words while it remains immensely profitable to extract and burn the resources driving us towards an uninhabitable planet and businesses, governments and international institutions do little to restrain this, talk of a green economy is at best optimistic, and at worse outright naive and dangerously fanciful.

References

Scoones, I., Leach, M., and Newell, P. (eds) (2015) *The Politics of Green Transformations*, Routledge, London.

Scott, J. (1985) *Weapons of the Weak: Everyday Forms of Peasant Resistance*, Yale University Press, New Haven, CT.

Sikor, T. and Newell, P. (2014) "Globalizing environmental justice?," *Geoforum*, 54, 151–157.

22

Whose Common Future: Reclaiming the Commons (1994)

The Ecologist

I. The Commons

THIS PAPER DESCRIBES how one of the main forces underlying evictions in both urban and rural areas is the enclosure of land and other resources which had previously been managed by local communities. This enclosure not only destroys homes, settlements and (in many instances) livelihoods but also undermines the institutions and cultural patterns that protected "common properties". The paper argues that environmentalists should support people and their community organizations in their efforts to reclaim the right to use, maintain and control local resources.

[...]

a. An Everyday Reality

[...] For many people in the West, the word "commons" carries an archaic flavor: that of the medieval village pasture which villagers did not own but where they had rights to graze their livestock. Yet, for the vast majority of humanity, the commons is an everyday reality. [...] In the Philippines, Java and Laos, irrigation systems are devised and run by villagers themselves, the water rights being distributed through rules laid down by the community. Even in the North, there are communities which still manage their forests, pastures, water supplies and fisheries jointly.

Moreover, new commons are constantly being born, even among what might seem the most fragmented communities. In the inner cities of the US, black commu-

The Ecologist. 1993. "Whose Common Future? Reclaiming the Commons". *Environment and Urbanization*, 6(1): 106–130. Reproduced with permission from Sage.

nities' dialects express concepts that the language taught in state schools cannot touch. At toxic dump sites and around proposed nuclear plants in France, Switzerland, and elsewhere, people have insisted on their "rights" to keep the earth and air around their communities free from the threat of poisonous and radioactive substances, damning the economic and "public" rationality which dictates that their homes are "objectively" the best locations for waste sinks. For them, the sentiments expressed by an elder of a Brazilian tribe, despite the religious language in which they are couched, cannot be completely unrecognizable:

> "The only possible place for the Krenak people to live and to re-establish our existence, to speak to our Gods, to speak to our nature, to weave our lives, is where God created us. We can no longer see the planet that we live upon as if it were a chess-board where people just move things around."

b. The Commons Neither Public nor Private

Despite its ubiquity, the commons is hard to define. It provides sustenance, security and independence, yet (in what many Westerners feel to be a paradox) typically does not produce commodities. Unlike most things in modern industrial society, moreover, it is neither private nor public: neither business firm nor state utility neither jealously guarded private plot nor national or city park. Nor is it usually open to all. The relevant local community typically decides who uses it and how.

The unlimited diversity of commons also makes the concept elusive. While all commons regimes involve joint use, what they define access to is bewilderingly varied: for example, trees, forests, land, minerals, water, fish, animals, language, time, radio wavelengths, silence, seeds, milk, contraception and streets.

More fruitful than attempts to define regimes through their domains are attempts to define them through their social and cultural organization: for example local or group power, distinctions between members and non-members, rough parity among members, a concern with common safety rather than accumulation, and an absence of the constraints which lead to economic scarcity. Even here, however, it would be a mistake to demand too much precision. For example, what does the "local" in "local power" mean? In Shanxi province in China, communal forests were owned by villages, several villages together, or clans. In India, the relevant bodies may be caste groups, while for Switzerland's city forests, it is "citizenship" (election to a given community) that counts.

Similarly, what does the "power" in "local power" consist of? Sometimes it is the power to exclude outsiders or to punish them if they abuse the commons. Often this power lays the foundation for an additional structure of internal rules, rights, duties and beliefs which mediates and shapes the community's own relationship with its natural surroundings. Sometimes the meshes of power internal to commons regimes give rise to notions of "property" or "possession" but, in many cases the relevant group does not regard itself as owning, but rather as owned by, or as stewards of, water or land.

c. Perception of Scarcity

A further characteristic often ascribed to the commons is that, unlike resources in the modern economy, it is "not perceived as scarce". This is not only because many things available as commons, such as silence, air or genetic diversity, will renew themselves continually until deliberately made scarce by the encroachment of outside political actors. More importantly, the needs which many commons satisfy are not infinitely expanding. They are not determined by a growth oriented external system producing goods and services, but rather are constantly adjusted and limited by the specific commons regime itself, whose physical characteristics remain in everyone's view. Without the race between growth and the scarcity which growth creates, there can thus be a sense of "enoughness". Even where produce from the commons is sold, the "needs" defined by consumerism and external market demand for goods and services will be subject to internal revision.

d. The Worldly Commons

Despite their resolutely local orientation and resistance to being swallowed up by larger systems, commons regimes have never been isolated in either space or time. Nor have their social organizations ever been static. Commons regimes welcome, feed upon and are fertilized by contact, and evolve just like any other social institution. Communities maintaining commons often work out arrangements over larger geographical areas with other groups. For example, in the Philippines, competing claims to water rights among different *zanjaras*, or communal irrigation societies, have customarily been decided by inter-village councils composed of *zanjara* officers and family elders in the community.

Systems of common rights, in fact, far from evolving in isolation, often owe their very existence to interaction and struggle between communities and the outside world. It is arguably only in reaction to invasion, dispossession or other threats to accustomed security of access that the concept of common rights emerges. Today, such rights are evolving where access to seeds, air and other resources previously taken for granted is being challenged through commoditization, legal enclosure or pollution.

e. Defining Oneself

Each commons regime may be as different culturally from the next as all are from, say, a factory. But it is not only their cultural diversity that makes such regimes difficult to "capture" in technical or universal terms. Ivan Illich makes this point when he says that the "law establishing the commons was unwritten, not only because people did not care to write it down, but because what it protected was a reality much too complex to fit into paragraphs." This is somewhat inexact; commons rules are sometimes written down; and where they are not, this is not so much because what they protect is complex as because the commons requires an open-endedness, receptiveness and adaptability to the vagaries of local climate, personalities, consciousness, crafts and materials which written records cannot fully express. But Illich's point is important. What makes the commons work, like the skills of wheelwrights, surgeons or machinists, cannot easily be encoded in written or other fixed or "replicable" forms useful to cultural outsiders. These forms can make some of the workings of commons regimes "visible" to such outsiders but have generally functioned to transfer local power outside the community at the expense of commons regimes.

In this and other respects, the concept of the commons flies in the face of the contemporary wisdom that each spot on the globe consists merely of coordinates on a global grid laid out by state and market: a uniform field which determines everyone's and everything's rights and roles. "Commons" implies the right of local people to define their own grid, their own forms of community respect for watercourses, meadows or paths; to resolve conflicts their own way; to translate what enters their ken into the personal terms of their own dialect; to be "biased" against the "rights" of outsiders to local "resources" in ways usually unrecognized in modern laws; to treat their home not simply as a location housing transferable goods and chunks of population but as irreplaceable and even to be defended at all costs.

f. No Free-for-all

For many years, governments, international planning agencies (and many conservationists) have viewed commons regimes with deep hostility. Nothing enrages the World Bank more, for example, than the "Not-In-My-Back-Yard" or "NIMBY" mentality which so many communities display in defending their commons against dams, toxic waste dumps, polluting factories and the like. Many conservationists and delegates to the United Nations "Earth Summit" in Rio de Janeiro in 1992, similarly, view local control over land, forests, streams and rivers as a recipe for environmental destruction. The only way to secure the environment, they say, is to put a fence around it, police it and give it economic value through development.

In defence of such views, development agencies have played upon two related confusions. The first, promulgated most famously in the 1960s by Garrett Hardin and others, is the myth of the "tragedy of the commons". According to Hardin, any commons (the example he used was a hypothetical rangeland) "remorselessly generates tragedy" since the individual gain to each user from overusing the commons will always outweigh the individual losses he or she has to bear due to its resulting degradation. As many critics have pointed out, however, and as Hardin himself later acknowledged, what he is describing is not a commons regime, in which authority over the use of forests, water and land rests with a community, but rather an *open access* regime, in which authority rests nowhere; in which there is no property at all; in which production for an external market takes social precedence over subsistence; in which production is not limited by considerations of long-term local abundance; in which people "do not seem to talk to one another"; and in which profit for harvesters is the only operating social value.

g. Tending the Commons

The difference is critical. Far from being a "free-for-all", use of the commons is closely regulated through communal rules and practices. For example, amongst the *Barabaig*, a semi-nomadic pastoralist group in Tanzania, rights of use and access to land are variously invested in the community, the clan and individual households. As Charles Lane explains "the *Barabaig* recognize that, to make efficient use of resources, access to grazing needs to be controlled to prevent exploitation beyond the capacity to recover. Although surface water is universally accessible to everyone, its use is controlled by rules…water sources must not be diverted or contaminated… A well becomes the property of the clan of the man who digs it. Although anyone may draw water for domestic purposes from any well, only clan members may water their stock there." Whether land is privately or collectively owned, there are rules ensuring that the use made of it is not detrimental to the community as a whole, while certain species of tree are regarded as sacred for the same reason. Disputes, which are rare, are resolved by a public assembly of all adult males, though sometimes in the case of a particularly difficult issue a special committee is formed. There is a parallel council of women, who also have property rights over land and animals, and occasionally may be the head of a family. Women have jurisdiction in matters concerning offences by men against women and in matters concerning spiritual life. [...] At a regional level, a similar council oversees the movement of herds and people to ensure that there is no overgrazing.

h. The Tragedy of Enclosure

A second confusion that muddies the debate over the commons is between environmental degradation which can be attributed to commons regimes themselves and that which typically results from their breakdown at the hands of more global regimes. As many authors have pointed out, "tragedies of the commons" generally turn out on closer examination to be "tragedies of enclosure". Once they have taken over land, enclosers, unlike families with ties and commitments to the soil, can mine, log, degrade and abandon their holdings, and then sell them on the global market without suffering any personal losses. It is generally enclosers rather than commoners who benefit from bringing ruin to the commons.

i. Commons Regimes and their Natural Surroundings

None of this is to suggest that all commons regimes are always capable of preventing degradation of forests, fisheries or land indefinitely. But as Martin Khor of Third World Network puts it, "…local control, while not necessarily sufficient for environmental protection, is necessary, while under state control the environment necessarily suffers."

One reason why local control is essential is that, as Richard O'Connor has argued, "…the environment itself is local: nature diversifies to make niches, enmeshing each locale in its own intricate web. Insofar as this holds, enduring human adaptations must also ultimately be quite local." Biological diversity, for example, is related to the degree to which one locale is distinct from the next in its topography and natural and human history. It is best preserved by societies which nourish those local differences – in which the traditions and natural history of each area interact to create distinctive systems of cultivation and water and forest use.

This local orientation is displayed *par excellence* in small commons regimes. As Elinor Ostrom notes:

> "Small-scale communities are more likely to have the formal conditions required for successful and enduring collective management of the commons. Among these are the visibility of common resources and behaviour toward them; feedback on the effects of regulations; widespread understanding and acceptance of the rules and their rationales; the values expressed in these rules (that is, equitable treatment of all and protection of the environment); and the backing of values by socialization, standards, and strict enforcement."

A second reason why local control is important is that where people rely directly on their natural surroundings for their livelihood, they develop an intimate knowledge of those surroundings which informs their actions. The *Barabaig*, for example, fully understand that if cattle were to be kept permanently on pastures near local water sources, the land would quickly become degraded.

> "As herds of livestock are brought to the river margins every day, whatever the season, they know that the forage there is needed by those who are watering their stock. If others are allowed to permanently graze it, this forage would soon be depleted and not available to those who go there to draw water. This would ultimately result in destruction of the land through over-grazing and damage from concentration of hoof traffic. The *Barabaig*, therefore, have a customary rule that bans settlement at the river margins and denies horders the right to graze the forage if they are not there to water their stock."

The key to the success of commons regimes lies in the limits that its culture of shared responsibilities place upon the power of any one group or individual. The equality which generally prevails in the commons, for example, does not grow out of any ideal or romantic preconceived notion of *communitas* any more than out of allegiance to the modern notion that people have "equal rights". Rather, it emerges as a by-product of the inability of a small community's élite to eliminate entirely the bargaining power of any one of its members, the limited amount of goods any one group can make away with under the others' gaze, and the calculated jockeying for position of many individuals who know each other and share an interest both in minimizing their own risks and in not letting any one of their number become too powerful.

Changes in the power base of a local élite or increases in effective community size entailed by integration into a global social fabric can rapidly undermine the authority of the commons. The sense of shame or transgression so important to community controls as well as the monitoring of violations themselves, is diluted or denatured by an increase in numbers, while envy of outsiders unconstrained by those controls flourishes. At some point, "…the breakdown of a community with the associated collapse in concepts of joint ownership and responsibility can set the path for the degradation of common resources in spite of abundance."[1]

It is precisely this process that development fuels. The expansion of modern state, international and market institutions entails a shrinking space for the commons. Today, virtually all "human communities are encapsulated within or fully integrated into larger socio-political systems" as are their "local systems of resources use and property rights",[2] making enclosure an ever-present threat. As political, social and ecological boundaries are erased, control is centralized or privatized, skills are made obsolete, people put at the service of industry or made redundant, and land is commercialized or placed under management. As their environments are destroyed or degraded, their power eroded or denied, and their communities threatened, millions are now demanding a halt to the development process. As the social activist Gustavo Esteva writes, "…if you live in Rio or Mexico City, you need to be very rich or very stupid not to notice that development stinks… We need to say 'no' to development, to all and every form of development, and that is precisely what the social majorities – for whom development was always a threat – are asking for." For them, the struggle is to reclaim, defend or create their commons and with it the rough sense of equity that flows from sharing a truly common future.

II. Development as Enclosure

a. The Establishment of the Global Economy

THE CREATION OF empires and states, business conglomerates and civic dicta-torships – whether in pre-colonial times or in the modern era – has only been possible through dismantling the commons and harnessing the fragments deprived of their old significance, to build up new economic and social patterns that are responsive to the interests of a dominant minority. The modern nation state has been built only by stripping power and control from commons regimes and creating structures of governance from which the great mass of humanity (particularly women) are excluded. Likewise, the market economy has expanded primarily by enabling state and commercial interests to gain control of territory that has traditionally been used and cherished by others, and by transforming that territory – together with the people themselves – into expendable "resources" for exploitation. By enclosing forests, the state and private enterprise have torn them out of fabrics of peasant subsistence; by providing local leaders with an outside power base, unaccountable to local people, they have undermined village checks and balances; by stimulating demand for cash goods, they have impelled villagers to seek an ever wider range of things to sell. Such a policy was as determinedly pursued by the courts of Aztec Mexico, the feudal lords of West Africa, the factory owners of Lancashire and the British Raj as it is today by the International Monetary Fund or Coca-Cola Inc.

Only in this way has it been possible to convert peasants into labour for a global economy, replace traditional with modern agriculture, and free up the commons for the industrial economy. Similarly, only by atomizing tasks and separating workers from the moral authority, crafts and natural surroundings created by their communities has it been possible to transform them into modern, universal individuals susceptible to "management". In short, only by *deliberately* taking apart local cultures and reassembling them in new forms has it been possible to open them up to global trade.

To achieve that "condition of economic progress", millions have been marginalized as a calculated act of policy, their commons dismantled and degraded, their cultures denigrated and devalued and their own worth reduced to their value as labour. Seen from this perspective, many of the the processes that now go under the rubric of "nation-building", "economic growth", and "progress" are first and foremost processes of expropriation, exclusion, denial and dispossession. In a word, of enclosure. As the numbers of landless multiply, so one dispossession leads to another; farmers move from one area enclose someone else's land elsewhere, often encouraged to do so by government sponsored migration schemes or by patron-client networks.

[...]

b. Urban Enclosure in the North

While the commons in the rural South is threatened by development, in the urban North it is threatened by redevelopment. As the commercial hub of the city expands and the radial road system broadens, poorer neighbourhoods and communities are characterized as slums or run-down inner-city areas and targeted for urban renewal. Of the innumerable conflicts and tensions that fill the pages of daily newspapers, a sizeable proportion are rooted in the resistance of an urban community to the forces of enclosure.

City Centres. Like the "improvement" of agricultural land, the redevelopment of urban space is driven by the need to extract an ever-higher rent from a given area. The centres of our cities and towns have been the arena of a battle between powerful interests who wish to enclose public space and the communities who will be thereby displaced. City blocks – long-established communities of homes, shops and work-places – are systematically bought up by syndicates of wealthy redevelopers, razed to the ground and replaced by spectacular tower-blocks and sprawling "complexes" of superhuman dimensions. Millions of square metres of office space are constructed, not to answer any human need but to generate profit. Sometimes, as in the case of Centrepoint Tower in London, they remain empty for years, or even decades, since they gain more value as enclosed land than they could do by being rented. In other cases, developers miscalculate the market and have to be bailed out, as in London's showpiece Canary Wharf scheme. The communities displaced by these develop-ments, though they put up a fight, are often no match for the steamroller of commerce, and are frequently dispersed to soulless housing estates or to dormitory suburbs of enclosed rural land, leaving only a rump of marginalized squatters prepared to resist to the end.

Shops. In tandem with the redevelopment of town centres, there has been a progressive enclosure of what is now known as the retail sector. As high-streets are transformed into malls, pedestrian precincts and shopping centres, rents rise to a height only affordable by national and international chains of shops, often masquer-ading under two or three different names, but selling the same restricted range of internationally distributed products. The small outlets which supply local, fresh, handmade, secondhand or unusual products – in fact anything that does not benefit from economies of scale – are unable to afford the rents. The hitherto public forum of the market-place is transformed into a privately owned precinct, managed by a business syndicate or a corporation such as British Telecom or even the Church of England. Sometimes, these places are locked up in evening or placed out of bounds to "undesirable" individuals who are thus, in effect, barred from their own city centre.

Streets. The most ubiquitous enclosure of the public domain has been in the street, where the principal agent of enclosure has not been a capitalist élite, but a technology with "democratic" pretensions, namely the motor car. Whereas the street until early this century [the twentieth] was an arena for social intercourse, for commercial exchange, for idle dalliance and for banter and play, it has now become mainly a thor-oughfare for expensive, polluting and dangerous automobiles transporting busy citi-zens from A to B and then back to A again. Without doubt, those who have suffered most from this enclosure have been children, many of whom are virtually held prisoner in their own house; and by association their exasperated parents.

Although the motor car has been effective, in the main, at clearing human activity off the streets and enclosing it in pedestrian precincts, hypermarkets and leisure centres, people still strive to recreate urban commons. An army of officials – police, social workers, planning officers – are therefore employed to "keep people off the streets": to clamp down on unlicensed street dealing, unofficial advertising (bill-sticking and graffiti), open air festivities and games, disorderly assembly, begging and loitering. It is in the so-called deprived inner-city areas that the commons is often the most resilient; and it is these deprived areas that are most frequently targeted for enclosure and redevelopment.

III. The Encompassing Web

a. The Ramifications of Enclosure

BECAUSE HISTORY'S BEST-known examples of enclosure, involved the fencing in of common pasture, enclosure is often reduced to a synonym for "expropriation". But enclosure involves more than land and fences, and implies more than simply privatization or takeover by the state. It is a compound process which affects nature and culture, home and market, production and consumption, germination and harvest, birth, sickness and death. It is a process to which no aspect of life or culture is immune.

The *Oxford English Dictionary* offers a general definition of enclosure – to "insert within a frame", Enclosure tears people and their lands, forests, crafts, technologies cosmologies out of the cultural framework in which they are embedded and tries to force them into a new framework which reflects and reinforces the values and interests of newly-dominant groups. Any pieces which will not fit into the new framework are devalued and discarded. In the modern age, the architecture of this new framework is determined by market forces, science, state and corporate bureaucracies, patriarchal forms of social organization, and ideologies of environmental and social management.

Land, for example, once it is integrated into a framework of fences, roads and property laws, is "disembedded" from local fabrics of self-reliance and redefined as "property" or "real estate". Forests are divided into rigidly defined precincts – mining concessions, logging concessions, wildlife corridors and national parks – and transformed from providers of water, game, wood and vegetables into scarce exploitable economic resources. Today they are on the point of being enclosed still further as the dominant industrial culture seeks to convert them into yet another set of components of the industrial system, redefining them as "sinks" to absorb industrial carbon dioxide and as pools of "biodiversity". Air is being enclosed as economists seek to transform it into a marketable "waste sink"; and genetic material by subjecting it to laws which convert it into the "intellectual property" of private interests.

People too are enclosed as they are fitted into a new society where they must sell their labour, learn clock-time, and accustom themselves to a life of production and consumption; groups of people are redefined as "populations", quantifiable entities whose size must be adjusted to take pressure off resources required for the global economy. Women are enclosed by consigning them to the "unproductive" periphery of a framework of industrial work which they can only enter by adopting "masculine" values and ways of being, thinking and operating. Skills, too, are enclosed, as are systems of knowledge associated with local stewardship of nature.

b. New Values

Enclosure inaugurates what Ivan Illich has called "a new ecological order." It upsets the local power balance which ensured that survival was "the supreme rule of common behaviour, not the isolated right of the individual." It scoffs at the notion that there can be "specific forms of community respect" for parts of the environment which are "neither the home nor wilderness," but lie "beyond a person's threshold and outside his possession" – the woods or fields, for example, that secure a community's subsistence, protect it from flood and drought, and provide spiritual and aesthetic meaning.

Instead, enclosure transforms the environment into a "resource" for national or global production – into so many chips that can be cashed in as commodities, handed out as political favours and otherwise used to accrue power. The sanctions on exploitation imposed by commons regimes in order to ensure a reliable local subsistence form local nature are now viewed "simply as constraints to be removed."

Control over those resources is assigned to actors outside the community. Most obviously, land – and in particular, the best-quality land – is concentrated in proportionately fewer and fewer hands. Enclosure of water and other resources has also generated scarcity and conflict. Large-scale irrigated plantations, for example, deny water to local farmers who work outside the plantation system. In central India "… whilst staple crops in the drought stricken areas…are denied water, the sugar-cane fields and grape vines are irrigated with scarce groundwater. A soil water drought has been created not by an absolute scarcity of water but by the preferential diversion of a limited water supply." In cities, meanwhile, people without motor cars are progressively shut out from access to the street. [...]

Enclosure thus cordons off those aspects of the environment that are deemed "useful" to the encloser – whether grass for sheep in sixteenth century England or stands of timber for logging in modern-day Sarawak – and defines them, and them alone, as valuable. A street becomes a conduit for vehicles: a wetland field to be drained; flowing water, a wasted asset to be harnessed for energy or agriculture. Instead of being a source of multiple benefits, the environment becomes a one-dimensional asset to be exploited for a single purpose – that purpose reflecting the interests of the encloser, and the priorities of the wider political economy in which the enclose operates.

c. New Forms of Exchange

Enclosure reorganizes society to meet the overriding demands of the market. It demands that production and exchange conform to rules that reflect the exigencies of supply and demand, of competition and maximization of output, of accumulation and economic efficiency.

In the commons, activities we now call "economic" are embedded in other activities. The planting of fields or the harvesting of crops cannot be reduced to acts of production: they are also religious events, occasions for celebration for fulfilling communal obligations and for strengthening networks of mutual support. Farming, for example, is carried out not to maximize production – though a healthy crop is always welcome but to feed the gods, enable cultural practices to continue with dignity, or minimize risk to the community as a whole, not least by strengthening networks of mutual support. Thus, when enclosure begins people feel threatened not only by material expropriation but by the cultural and personal humiliations that inevitably accompany it. Unsurprisingly, much of their resistance against enclosure is also developed and codified in non-economic forms: gossip, songs, jokes, rumours, drama and festivals.

Because economic relations need not be crucial to survival in commons regimes, they generally take a back seat to other social relationships. *Homo economicus* – the obsessively rent-maximizing archetype around whose supposed universality modern economic theory has been constructed – might in fact be unable to scratch together a living in many commons regimes. Unwilling to share with neighbours in times of dearth or to "waste time" in "unprofitable" labour-sharing, rituals of reciprocity, craft acquisition, gossip and the like, he or she could well be cut off from the community support needed to make ends meet.

As production and exchange are enclosed by the market, economic activity is cordoned off from other spheres of social life, bounded by rules that actively undermine previous networks of mutual aid. As Gerald Berthoud observes:

> "The market tends to become the only mode of social communication, even between those who are intimately connected. Within this universe of generalized commodities, it becomes logical that individuals increasingly become strangers to one another. Even for those who are culturally and socially close, the market mentality maintains a distance between them, almost as if close and distant relationships had become indistinguishable."

In an undiluted market economy, access to food, for example, is no longer dependent on being part of – and contributing to – a social network; instead, food goes to those who have the money to buy it. Only those who, in the economists' jargon, have the income to translate their biological needs into effective demand get to eat. In the global supermarket, people earning perhaps 100 dollars a year – if they are lucky – must compete for the same food with people earning 100 dollars a week, 100 dollars an hour, or even 100 dollars a minute.

d. New Roles

Enclosure redefines community. It shifts the reference points by which people are valued. Individuals become "units" whose "value" to society is defined by their relationship to the new political entity that emerges from enclosure. Increasing numbers of people do not have access to the environment, the political process, the market or the knowledge they need.

Enclosure ushers in a new political order. When the environment is turned over to new uses, a new set of rules and new forms of organization are required. Enclosure redefines how the environment is managed, by whom and for whose benefit. Old forms of environmental management are forced into redundancy or vilified, derided or outlawed.

Enclosure not only redefines the forum in which decisions and made but also redefines whose voice counts in that forum. In order to place management in the hands of "others", whose allegiances and sources of power lie outside the community, it cuts knowledge off from local ethics. As Tariq Banuri and Frédérique Apffel-Marglin note:

> "Local knowledge is bound by time and space, by contextual and moral factors. More importantly, it cannot be separated from larger moral or normative ends…Once knowledge is meant to be universally applicable, it begins to gravitate into the hands of experts or professionals, those 'conspiracies against the laity', as George Bernard Shaw once called them, whose interests in acquiring, creating, promoting, or acting upon the basis of such knowledge begins more and more to be motivated by internal professional considerations, rather than by normative social implications. In fact under these circumstances, the activity can often become an end in itself and become unmoored from its narrow technical objectives."

Enclosure opens the way for the bureaucratization and enclosure of knowledge itself. It accords power to those who master the language of the new professionals and who are versed in its etiquette and its social nuances. It creates a new language of power, inaccessible to those who have not been to school or to university, who do not have professional qualifications, who cannot operate computers, who cannot fathom the apparent mysteries of a cost-benefit analysis, or who refuse to adopt the forceful and inflexible tones of an increasingly "masculine" world.

In that respect, as Illich notes, "…enclosure…is as much in the interest of professionals and of state bureaucrats as it is in the interests of capitalists." For as local ways of knowing and doing are devalued or appropriated and as vernacular forms of governance are eroded, so state and professional bodies are able to insert themselves within the commons, taking over areas of life that were previously under the control of individuals, households and the community. Enclosure "…allows the bureaucrat to define the local community as impotent to provide for its own survival." It invites the professional to come to the "rescue" of those whose own knowledge is deemed inferior to that of the encloser. It provides a tool for control.

e. Enclosure as Control

Enclosure is thus a change in the networks of power which enmesh the environment, production, distribution, the political process, knowledge, research and the law. It reduces the control of local people over community affairs. Whether female or male, a person's influence and ability to make a living depends increasingly on becoming absorbed into the new policy created by enclosure, on accepting – willingly or unwillingly – a new role as a consumer, a worker, a client or an administrator, on playing the game according to new rules. The way is thus cleared for cajoling people into the mainstream, be it through programmes to bring women "into development", to entice smallholders "into the market" or to foster paid employment.

Those who remain on the margins of the new mainstream, either by choice or because that is where society has pushed them, are not only deemed to have little value: they are perceived as a threat. Thus it is the landless, the poor, the dispossessed who are blamed for forest destruction; their poverty which is held responsible for "overpopulation"; their protests which are classed as subversive and a threat to political stability. And because they are perceived as a threat, they become objects to be controlled, the legitimate subjects of yet further enclosure. Witness the measures taken by the Tanzanian authorities to curb street-traders. After the Human Resources Deployment Act in 1983:

> "Those who could not produce proper identification were to be resettled in the countryside. In the Dar es Salaam region, all unlicensed, self-employed people, including fish sellers, shoe repairmen, tailors, etc., were to be considered 'idle and disorderly' and treated as 'loiterers'. President Nyerere ordered the Prime Minister to be 'bold' in implementing the Act, saying: 'If we don't disturb loiterers, they will disturb us.' The loiterers were compared with economic saboteurs and racketeers 'whom the nation has declared war on.'"

From the dispossessed beggars of sixteenth century England to the illegal settlers in São Paulo, people have been defined as too poor, too dependent, too inarticulate, too marginal to be of "use" to mainstream society. They are shunted from one place to another as further areas are enclosed or, as on the case of the street children of Brazil, they are simply murdered. Enclosure creates, as one New Guinea villager has put it, "rubbish people" – in the North no less than in the South.

f. Conceptual Trapping: the Enclosure of Language and Culture

Enclosure defines power. But it involves more than the taking over of public office, natural resources or markets by one group at the expense of another. By "taking something out of one social frame and forcing it into a new one," by redefining meanings, enclosure involves something akin to translation.

When a concept is enclosed in the context of a radically alien language, something is inevitably "lost in translation". When what is lost is essential to the identity and livelihoods of a group, yet they are unable to use their native language to regain or defend it, their defences are weakened and they become victims. For women who have to use a language such as contemporary English with patriarchal elements and assumptions, there is often "nowhere to go in the language", no words or ways to express what is essential for them to express.

[...]

People who would oppose dams, logging, the redevelopment of their neighbourhoods or the pollution of their rivers are often left few means of expressing or arguing their case unless they are prepared to engage in a debate framed by the languages of cost-benefit, analysis, reductionist science, utilitarianism, male domination – and, increasingly, English. Not only are these languages in which many local objections – such as that which holds ancestral community rights to a particular place to have precedence over the imperatives of "national development" – appear disreputable. They are also languages whose use allows enclosers to eavesdrop on, "correct" and dominate the conversations of the enclosed.

This process of conceptual trapping has gathered pace through the eras of state formation, colonialism, economic development and, now, environmental management. None of these dominant systems can afford a "live and let live" attitude towards the thousands of other, more or less independent languages which make up the social universe. They must expand to global scale; other systems with their messy multitude of goals and ways of settling conflicts just get in the way. When they do, they are enclosed – squeezed into the new, overarching system, constricting those within them in the process. All conflict is settled by criteria determined by the enclosers.

This conceptual trapping is justified morally by persuading people that they have no right to refuse to abide by an alien translation of their words, practices and ways of life. Enclosure claims that its own social frame, its language, is a universal norm, an all-embracing matrix which can assimilate all others. Whatever may be "lost in translation" is supposedly insignificant, undeveloped or inferior to what is gained. As Stephen Marglin points out:

> "What it cannot comprehend and appropriate, it not only cannot appreciate, it cannot tolerate…In the encounter of modern knowledge with [vernacular knowledge], the real danger is not that modern knowledge will appropriate [vernacular knowledge] but that it will do so only partially and will return this partial knowledge…as the solid core of truth extracted from a web of superstation and false belief. What lies outside the inter-section of modern knowledge and [vernacular knowledge] risks being lost altogether."

Because they hold themselves to be speaking a universal language, the modern enclosers who work for development agencies and governments feel no qualms in presuming to speak for the enclosed. They assume reflexively that they understand their predicament as well as or better than the enclosed do themselves. It is this tacit assumption that legitimizes enclosure in the encloser's mind – and it is an assumption that cannot be countered simply by transferring the visible trappings of power from one group to another.

IV. Reclaiming the Commons

a. The Commons Resurgent

IN SEEKING TO defend their local land, to restore the damage done to it and to thwart the strategies of would-be enclosers, community groups opposed to toxic dumping or movements such as Chipko are part of a long tradition. Throughout history commons regimes have resisted the enclosure of the forests, rangelands, fields, fishing grounds, lakes, streams, plants and animals that they rely upon to maintain their ways of life and ensure their well-being. Such resistance has taken many forms, and its focus has been as various as the commons being defended. Machinery has been sabotaged, hay ricks burned, landlords and officials satirized and threatened, experts lampooned, loyalties shifted and bureaucratic defences tested in an endless flow of effort to stall enclosure. Whether overt or subterranean, thwarted or beaten down, channeled into ideology or action, this resistance has been opportunistic, pragmatic and resourceful. Frequently using local traditions as an arsenal, constantly faced with reversals, it always finds fresh ground to fight from, some of it created by the very systems in opposition to which it must constantly transform and renew itself. Willing to adapt new developments to its own purposes, it is nonetheless uncompromising when the bounds it has set are overstepped.

It is partly through such resistance that the ideology of economic growth as the only concrete solution to poverty, inequality and hardship is slowly being dismantled. Millions of people in both the South and the North who know first-hand of its false promise need no convincing. Whilst most participants in the Earth Summit (UNCED) and similar forums are interested only in "solutions" that will permit industrial growth to continue, the movements that have been spawned through resistance to enclosure are carving out a very different path. Their demands centre not on refining market mechanisms, nor incorporating text-book ecology into economics, nor on formulating non-legally binding treaties, but on reclaiming the commons; on re-appropriating the land, forests, streams and fishing grounds that have been taken from them; on re-establishing control over decision-making; and on limiting the scope of the market. In saying "no" to a waste dump, a dam, a logging scheme or a new road, they are saying "yes" to a different way of life; "yes" to the community's being able to decide its own fate; "yes" to the community's being able to define itself.

What begins as a fight against one form of enclosure – a proposed incinerator, perhaps, or a plantation scheme often becomes part of a wide struggle to allow the community to define its own values and priorities. As Triana Silton noted of the movement to oppose toxic wastes in the United States:

> "Many community groups have moved from simply fighting off an incinerator to looking around at themselves, at the community they are part of, identifying what they don't like and attempting to solve those problems. The empowerment that accompanies as success, whether that success is having your voice heard or actually stopping the facility, allows people to have some control over the things that happen to them."

b. Defending the Commons

Often making use of what James Scott calls the "weapons of the weak", groups, communities and individuals the world over are successfully resisting the web of enclosure and reclaiming a political and cultural space for the commons. The search is generally not for "alternatives" in the sense that Western environmentalists might use the term: rather it is to rejuvenate what works, to combine traditional and new approaches and to develop strategies that meet local needs. In that respect, the debate is not over such technocratic issues as **how** to conserve soil or **what** species of tree to plant – for those who rely on the commons, the starting point for address- ing such questions is usually, "Let's see what has worked in the past and build on that" – but rather over how to create or defend open, democratic community institutions that ensure people's control over their own lives.

In India, Chipko is only one of thousands of popular movements that have challenged enclosure. Widespread mobilizations against hydropower programmes that are displacing thousands of communities and flooding their farmlands and forests have sprung up all over the country. In September 1989, a rally of some 60,000 people against "destructive development" was held at Harsud in the Narmada Valley, the site of one of India's largest hydropower projects. The slogan of the march was "Our Villages, Our Rule". Mass marches of protesters have led, in some places, to the cancellation of proposed dams and, in others have resulted in police firings and deaths.

For other groups and communities, the focus of their struggle is not the defence of an existing commons but the reclaiming of those commons that have been enclosed or, in other cases, the taking over of territory on which to build a new com- mons. In Brazil, disillusionment with the government's abject failure to implement its promised programme of land reform has led to land "takeovers" by peasants. […]

In the North, moves to reclaim the commons are often closely linked to attempts to disengage from the wider market, by networks of exchange over which a community or group has control. One example is to be found in the Community Supported Agriculture (CSA) movement, now taking root in Europe, the US and Japan. The special feature of CSA initiatives is that the community or a specific group of people from one local area agrees to share the risks and respon- sibilities of food production with the farmer. In some instances, a detailed budget for the farm is drawn up on an annual basis, which includes wages for those working on the land, and then the costs are shared by the community which the farm will support. Sometimes this done on the basis of pledges made at a meeting at the beginning of the season, the amount pledged varying according to the ability to pay. One of the advantages for farmers is that they start to get paid as soon as the crops are planted, rather than having to wait until crops are harvested before they receive any return.

Because farmers know that their income is guaranteed and that they are growing produce for people and not for the market, they tend to grow a much wider variety of produce, and aim to provide what people want, instead of concentrating on the crops that give the highest returns. This diversity of crops creates conditions which are favourable for companion planting, and encourages the kind of integrated crop- ping practices which make crop failures less likely. The active involvement of share- holders in farm work is encouraged, a principle aim being to "reconnect" with the land those whose primary activities lie outside farming. This building up of a community sensitive to the vagaries of nature means that other related issues – such as land-ownership, conservation, recycling, and use of natural resources – become topics that are considered and discussed. Moreover, the tying of production and consumption to a community level has the potential to create extra jobs in processing, local transport and retailing. These activities tend to put the heart back into a community, whereas the types of jobs which might be lost, such as long-distance truck driving, tend to take people and work out of the community.

c. The Balance of Power

If there is a common denominator to the initiatives and struggles described above, it is not that they share a uniform "vision" of the future, or adhere to a single "blueprint" for change, but rather that they are all, in their many and various ways, attempts by local people to reclaim the political process and to re-root it within the local community. The central demand made by group after group is for authority to be vested in the community – not in the state, local government, the market or the local landlord, but in those who rely on the local commons for their livelihood. As such, the struggle is for more than the mere recognition of rights over the physical commons: critically, it is also a struggle to restore or to defend the checks and balances that limit power **within** the local community.

As we have seen, enclosure fatally undermines the institutions and cultural patterns that prevent any one group within the commons from monopolizing power and imposing its will upon the community. The door has been opened to personal gain at the expense of the community's security, both social and environmental.

But the emergence of local élites does not mean that the commons has been shattered: the community often maintains features typically associated with the commons – networks of mutual aid, a limited market, production primarily for use rather than exchange, an emphasis on reciprocity and redistribution rather that accumulation, the extended family as the basic unit of socialization and production or an ideology that stresses harmonious relations with nature. And in numerous instances, local people have begun to evolve their own institutions, accountable to the community as whole, to redress the imbalance in power and to reclaim control of the commons.

Across the world, grassroots movements are working to open up more space for the commons by denying that any single social whole – whether culture, language, livelihood, art, theory, science, gender, race or class – has a right to assert privileged status over, and thus to enclose, all others of its type. They are creating space where, on the contrary, the local community has the right to decide its own future: the right to refuse to have to abide by an alien translation of its own words and practices; the right to its own culture.

Key to the struggle is the building up of open and accountable institutions that restore authority to commons regimes – a struggle which requires increasing the bargaining power of those who are currently excluded or marginalized from the political process and eroding the power of those who are currently able to impose their will on others. Only in this way – when all those who will have to live with a decision have a voice in making that decision – can the checks and balances on power that are so critical to the workings of the commons be ensured.

Achieving that political order requires promoting the virtues of receptivity, flexibility, patience, open-mindedness, non-defensiveness, humour, curiosity and respect for the opinions of others as a counterweight to the formulas, principles, translations or "limits" which trap people in single languages. It involves legitimizing a type of rational decision-making and self-correction which emphasizes not the application of pre-determined methods, technical vocabularies, "objective" data and yardsticks – the machinery of enclosure – but the indispensability of open-ended conversation, a willingness to listen and learn, to change one's view and to work at achieving a consensus.

For those who are used to imposing their will and languages on others, or who see the environmental threats facing humanity as so overwhelming that only centralized decision-making by cliques of experts can meet the task in hand, the call for community control is at best a threat to the power, at worst a recipe for indecision and muddling through to ecological disaster. But the evidence is overwhelming that local-level institutions in which power is limited and the common right to survival is the preoccupation of all are the best means of repairing the damage done through enclosure. Equally overwhelming is the evidence that "non-local, state-management systems are both costly and often ineffective."

d. Everyday Commons

It is a mistake to see acts of resistance and reclamation solely as the province of those active in party politics, or of those whose "backs are against the wall". On the contrary, resistance to enclosure takes place in countless everyday ways in both the South and the North. Acquiescent behaviour towards enclosers, and feigned ignorance or incompetence in their presence, allow individuals to retain their own sense of dignity by mocking the stereotypes that have been imposed upon them. As an Ethiopian proverb has it, "When the great lord passes, the wise peasant bows deeply and silently farts." Feigned acquiescence and subservience, by relaxing enclosers' scrutiny, also makes it easier for ordinary people to find social and physical spaces where they can develop criticisms and alternatives to the dominant order. When workers on a site politely acknowledge the pontifications of a visiting expert in their presence, but laughingly ignore them once they have gone, the workers are asserting the validity of their own practical knowledge. Even humble actions, such as deliberately choosing local produce, buying jumble and second-hand furniture or saving jam-jars for home produce stalls, are ways in which people express their dissatisfaction with the enclosed world of consumerism and reclaim an element of control.

These small actions do not make headlines and may not even be noticed by the dominant groups within society; but they help empower individuals and communities and they create the confidence and vision to resist still further, whenever opportunities to do so present themselves. Indeed, as the structures of enclosure begin to falter and break down under the stress of economic recession, international debt, popular protest and everyday resistance to the anonymity of industrialization, new life is breathed into even the most seemingly dismal communities as people rediscover the value of coming together to resolve their problems. As Gustavo Esteva enthusiastically records for Mexico City:

> "With falling oil prices, mounting debts, and the conversion of Mexico into a free trade zone, so that trans-national capital can produce Volkswagen 'Beetles' in automated factories for export to Germany, the corruption of our politics and the degradation of Nature – always implicit in development – can finally be seen, touched and smelled by everyone. Now the poor are responding by creating their own moral economy. As Mexico's Rural Development Bank no longer has sufficient funds to force peasants to plant sorghum for animal feed, many have returned to the traditional inter-cropping of corn and beans, improving their diets, restoring some village solidarity and allowing available cash to reach further. In response to the decreasing purchasing power of the previously employed, thriving production cooperatives are springing up in the heart of Mexico City. Shops now exist in the slums that reconstruct electrical appliances: merchants prosper by imitating foreign trademarked goods and selling them as smuggled wares to tourists. Neighbourhoods have come back to life. Street stands and tiny markets have returned to corners from where they disappeared long ago. Complex forms of non-formal organization have developed, through which the *barrio* (village) residents create protective barriers between themselves and intruding development bureaucracies, police and their officials; fight eviction and the confiscation of their assets; settle their own disputes and maintain public order."

The erosion of the global economy, far from being a disaster, ushers in a new era of opportunities – the opportunity to live with dignity, the opportunity for communities to define their own priorities and identities, to restore what development has destroyed and to enjoy lives of increased variety and richness.

V. A Concluding Remark

IT IS CUSTOMARY to conclude with policy recommendations. We are not going to do so. Our reasons are many but two of them have been expressed admirably (although in another context) by Philip Raikes in the introduction to his book *Modernizing Hunger*:

> "It becomes increasingly difficult to say what are practical suggestions, when one's research tends to show that what is politically feasible is usually too minor to make any difference, while changes significant enough to be worthwhile are often unthinkable in practical political terms. In any case, genuine practicality in making policy suggestions requires detailed knowledge of a particular country or area: its history,

culture, vegetation, existing situation, and much more besides. Lists of general 'policy conclusions' make it all too easy for the rigid-minded to apply them as general recipes, without thought, criticism or adjustment for circumstances."

Like Raikes's book, this paper [...] is "full of implicit conclusions" and explicit demands, but to formulate them as "policy recommendations" would be to go against the case we have attempted to make. It would suggest that there is a single set of principles for change; and that today's policy makers, whether in national governments or international institutions, are the best people to apply them. We reject that view.

A space for the commons cannot be created by economists, development planners, legislators, "empowerment" specialists or other paternalistic outsiders. To place the future in the hands of such individuals would be to maintain the webs of power that are currently stifling commons regimes. One cannot legislate the commons into existence; nor can the commons be reclaimed simply by adopting "green techniques" such as organic agriculture, alternative energy strategies or better public transport – necessary and desirable though such strategies often are. Rather, commons regimes emerge through ordinary people's day-to-day resistance to enclosure, and through their efforts to regain the mutual support, responsibility and trust that sustain the commons.

That is not to say that one can ignore policy makers or policy-making. The depredations of trans-national corporations, international bureaucracies and national governments cannot be allowed to go unchallenged. But the environmental movement has a responsibility to ensure that in seeking solutions, it does not remove the initiative from those who are defending their commons or attempting to regenerate common regimes. It is a responsibility it should take seriously.

Notes

1   Berkes, F. and D. Feeny (1990), "Paradigms lost: changing views on the use of common property resources". *Alternatives*, Vol. 17, No. 2, page 50.
2   McCay, B.J. and J.M. Acheson (1987), *The Question of the Commons*, University of Arizona, Tucson.

23

Resisting 'Globalisation-from-above' Through 'Globalisation-from-below' (1997)

Richard Falk

I. A Normative Assessment of Globalisation

Globalisation, with all of its uncertainties and inadequacies as a term, does usefully call attention to a series of developments associated with the ongoing dynamic of economic restructuring at the global level. The negative essence of this dynamic, as unfolding within the present historical timeframe, is to impose on governments the discipline of global capital in a manner that promotes economistic policy making in national arenas of decision, subjugating the outlook of governments, political parties, leaders and elites and often accentuating distress to vulnerable and disadvantaged regions and peoples.

Among the consequences is a one-sided depoliticising of the state as neoliberalism becomes 'the only game in town', according to widely accepted perceptions that are dutifully disseminated by the mainstream media to all corners of the planet. Such a neoliberal mind-set is deeply opposed to social public sector expenditures devoted to welfare, job creation, environmental protection, health care, education, and even the alleviation of poverty. To a great extent, these expenditures are entrenched, and difficult to diminish directly because of legal obstacles and citizen backlash, as well as varying degrees of electoral accountability in constitutional democracies. Nevertheless, the political tide is definitely running in the neoliberal direction, and will continue to do so as long as the public can be induced to ingest the pill of social austerity without reacting too vigorously. To date, the mainstream has been generally pacified, especially as represented by principal political parties, and what reaction has occurred has too often been expressed by a surge of support

Richard Falk. 1997. "Resisting 'Globalisation-from-above' through 'Globalisation-from-below'". In *New Political Economy*, 2(1): 17–24. Reproduced with permission from Taylor & Francis and R. Falk.

for nativist, right-wing extremism that indicts global capital and blames immigrants for high unemployment and stagnant wages.

This set of circumstances, if not properly modified, presages a generally grim future for human society, including a tendency to make alternative orientations towards economic policy appear irrelevant; to the extent believed, this induces a climate of resignation and despair. To the extent that normative goals continue to be affirmed within political arenas, as is the case to varying degrees with human rights and environmental protection, their substantive claims on resources are treated either as an unfortunate, if necessary, burden on the grand objectives of growth and competitiveness or as a humanitarian luxury that is becoming less affordable and acceptable in an integrated market-driven world economy.

Indeed, one of the obvious spillover effects of the mind-set induced by globalisation is to exert strong downward pressure on public goods expenditures, especially those with an external or global dimension. The financial strains being experienced by the United Nations, despite the savings associated with the absence of strategic rivalry of the sort that fuelled the Cold War arms race, is emblematic of declining political support for global public goods, and runs counter to the widespread realisation that the growing complexity of international life requires increasing global capabilities for coordination and governance, at minimum for the sake of efficiency.[1]

In the context of international trade, both domestic labour and minority groups in rich countries of the North mount pressure to attach human rights and environmental conditionalities to trade considerations, whereas business and financial elites resist such advocacy (unless they happen to be operating outside the global marketplace, and hence have an anachronistic territorial, statist outlook on sales and profits) as it diminishes their 'out-sourcing' opportunities to take advantage of dramatically lower labour costs and weaker regulatory standards in most of the South.

Economic globalisation has also had some major positive benefits, including a partial levelling-up impact on North–South relations and a rising standard of living for several hundred million people in Asia, which has included rescuing many millions from poverty. Indeed, according to recent UNDP figures the proportion of the poor globally, but not their absolute number, has been declining during the past several years. There are some indications that after countries reach a certain level of development, especially in response to the demands of an expanding urban middle class, pressures mount to improve workplace and environmental conditions. Such governments also become more confident actors on the global stage, challenging inequities and biases of geopolitical structures; Malaysia typifies such a pattern. There is nothing inherently wrong with encouraging economies of scale and the pursuit of comparative advantage so long as the social, environmental, political and cultural effects are mainly beneficial. What is objectionable is to indulge a kind of market mysticism that accords policy hegemony to the promotion of economic growth, disregarding adverse social effects and shaping economic policy on the basis of ideological certitudes that are not attentive to the realities of human suffering.

Globalisation is also historically influenced by several contingent factors that intensify these adverse human effects, i.e. the social costs of the process. First of all, in the current period globalisation is proceeding in an ideological atmosphere in which neoliberal thinking and priorities go virtually unchallenged, especially in the leading market economies; the collapse of the socialist 'other' has encouraged capitalism to pursue its market logic with a relentlessness that has not been evident since the first decades of the industrial revolution. Second, this neoliberal climate of opinion is reinforced by an anti-government societal mood that is composed of many elements, including a consumerist reluctance to pay taxes; an alleged failure by government to be successful when promoting social objectives; a 'third wave' set of decentralising technological moves that emphasise the transformative civilisa-tional role of computers and electronic information; and a declining capacity of political parties to provide their own citizenry with forward-looking policy proposals. Third, the policy orientation of government has also grown steadily more business-focused, reflecting the decline of organised labour as a social force, result-ing in the serious erosion of the perceived threat of revolutionary opposition from what Immanuel Wallerstein usefully identifies as 'the dangerous classes'.[2] In addition, the mobility of capital is increasing in a world economy that is much more shaped by financial flows and the acquisition of intellectual property rights than it is by manufacturing and trade in tangible goods and services. Fourth, the fiscal impera-tives of debt and deficit reduction in the interests of transnational monetary stability reinforce other aspects of globalisation. Fifth, this unfolding of globalisation as an historical process is occurring within an international order that exhibits gross inequalities of every variety, thereby concentrating the benefits of growth upon already advantaged sectors within and among societies and worsening the relative and absolute condition of those already most disadvantaged. The experience of sub-Saharan Africa is strongly confirmatory of this generalisation.[3]

Thus it is that globalisation in *this* historical setting poses a particular form of normative challenge that is distinctive and different from what it would be in other globalising circumstances. The challenge being posed is directed, above all, at the survival of, and maybe the very possibility of sustaining, the compassionate state, as typified by the humane achievements of the Scandinavian countries up through the 1980s and by the optimistic gradualism of social democratic approaches to politics.[4] The impacts attributed to globalisation have been strongly reinforced by the most influential readings given to the ending of the Cold War, discrediting not only utopian socialism, but any self-conscious societal project aimed at the betterment of living conditions for the poor or regarding the minimising of social disparities as generally desirable.

These ideological and operational aspects of globalisation are associated with the way transnational market forces dominate the policy scene, including the significant cooptation of state power. This pattern of development is identified here as 'globali-sation-from-above', a set of forces and legitimating ideas that is in many respects located beyond the effective reach of territorial authority and that has enlisted most governments as tacit partners. But globalisation, so conceived, has generated criticism and resistance, both of a local, grassroots variety, based on the concrete-ness of the specifics of time and place – e.g. the siting of a dam or nuclear power plant or the destruction of a forest – and on a transnational basis, involving the linking of knowledge and political action in hundreds of civic initiatives. It is this latter aggregate of phenomena that is described here under the rubric of 'globalisation-from-below'.[5]

Given this understanding it is useful to ask the question – what is the normative potential of globalisation-from-below? The idea of normative potential is to conceptualise widely shared world order values: minimising violence, maximising economic well-being, realising social and political justice, and upholding environmental quality.[6] These values often interact inconsistently, but are normatively coherent in the sense of depicting the main dimensions of a widely shared consensus as to the promotion of benevolent forms of world order, and seem at odds in crucial respects with part of the orientation and some of the main impacts of globalisation-from-above in its current historical phase. In all probability, globalisation-from-above would have different and generally more positive normative impacts if the prevailing ideological climate was conditioned by social democracy rather than by neoliberalism or if the adaptation of the state was subject to stronger countervailing societal or transnational pressures of a character that accorded more fully with world order values. This historical setting of globalisation exhibits various tendencies of unequal significance, the identification of which helps us assess whether globalisation-from-below is capable of neutralising some of the detrimental impacts of globalisation-from-above. A further caveat is in order. The dichotomising distinction between above and below is only a first approximation of the main social formations attributable to globalisation. Closer scrutiny suggests numerous cross-cutting diagonal alignments that bring grassroots forces into various positive and negative relationships with governmental and neoliberal policies. Coalition possibilities vary also in relation to issue area. For instance, transnational social initiatives with respect to economic and social rights may be affirmed by some governments, while comparable initiatives directed at environmental protection or disarmament would appeal to other governments.

II. The New Politics of Resistance in an Era of Globalisation

Political oppositional forms in relation to globalisation-from-above have been shaped by several specific conditions. First, there is the virtual futility of concentrating upon conventional electoral politics, given the extent to which principal political parties in constitutional democracies have subscribed to a programme and orientation that accepts the essential features of the discipline of global capital. This development may not persist if social forces can be mobilised in such a way as to press social democratic leaderships effectively to resume their commitment to the establishment of a compassionate state, and such an outlook proves to be generally viable in the context of governing. To succeed, except under special circumstances, would imply that globalisation-from-above was not structurally powerful enough to prevent defections at the unit level of the state. Of course, variations of constraining influence arise from many factors, including the ideological stance of the leadership, efficiency in handling the social agenda, disparities in wealth and income, and the overall growth rates of the national, regional and global economies. The main conclusion remains. Resistance to economic globalisation is not likely to be effective if it relies on national elections to gain influence and change the role of government on matters of political economy.

Second, criticism of economic globalisation at the level of societal politics is unlikely to have a major impact on public and elite opinion until a credible alternative economic approach is fashioned intellectually, and such an alternative approach has enough mobilising effect on people that a new perception of the 'dangerous classes' – which this time is not likely to be the industrial working class – re-enters discourse, again making economic and political elites nervous enough about their managerial ability to contain opposition to begin seriously entertaining more progressive policy options. In such an altered atmosphere it is easy to imagine the negotiation of social contracts that restore balance to the interests of people and those of markets.

Third, aside from the re-emergence of dangerous classes, there are prospects that ecological constraints of various sorts will induce the market to send a variety of signals calling for a negotiated transition to managed economic growth in the interest of sustainability. Under these conditions, with limits on growth being required for both environmental reasons and middle-term business profitability, it may be possible at some now unforeseen point in the future to reach a series of agreements on a regional basis, and perhaps even globally, that amount to a global social contract. The objective of such an instrument, which would not need to be formally agreed upon, would be to balance anxieties about the carrying capacity of the earth against a range of social demands about securing the basic needs of individuals and communities, quite possibly on a regional level.

Fourth, globalisation-from-above is definitely encouraging a resurgence of support for right-wing extremism, a varied and evolving array of political movements that may scare governments dominated by moderate outlooks into rethinking their degree of acquiesence to the discipline of global capital. Electoral results in several European countries, including Austria and France, reveal both growing support for the political right and a turn to the far right by citizens faced with the fiscal symptoms of economic globalisation, including cutbacks in social services, high interest rates, capital out-flows and instability in employment and prospects. Will national political parties and governments be able to recover their legitimacy and authority by responding effec-tively to this challenge without successfully modifying the global setting and its current impact on the policy-making process?

Fifth, will labour militancy become somewhat more effective and socially visible as it shifts its focus from industrial age priorities of wages and workplace conditions to such emerging concerns as downsizing, out-sourcing and job security? There are also possibilities of engaging wider constituencies than organised labour in this struggle, individuals and groups that are feeling some of the negative effects of globalising tendencies. Jacques Chirac seemed sufficiently shaken by the

December 1995 large-scale work-stoppages and demonstrations that he partially reversed ideological course, at least rhetorically, and suddenly called for the creation of 'a social Europe', which was a retreat from a basic tenet of neoliberalism and thus provided a psychological victory for the perspectives favouring globalisation-from-below. Subsequent demonstrations and strikes in France appear to be generalised societal, especially urban, reactions against the austerity budget being implemented by the government so as to qualify the country for participation in plans to establish currency and monetary union within the framework of the European Union. But rhetorical victories do not necessarily produce adjustments in policy, particularly if the structures that underpin the neoliberal approach are strong and elusive, as is the case with the world economy. In retrospect, Chirac's conversion to the cause of a social Europe seems like little more than a tactical manoeuvre designed to gain more operating room, comparable perhaps to George Bush, the arch realist, momentarily extolling the virtues of the United Nations during the Gulf crisis and proclaiming a new world order. After the crisis passed, so did the opportunistic embrace Bush had made of a more law-orientated system of security for international society.

Another indicative development with respect to labour is a renewed recourse to the strike weapon as a means for working people to resist globalisation. Organised labour, despite economic growth in the North, has not been able to share in the material benefits of a larger economic pie because of the impinging effects of competitiveness and fiscal austerity, and in numerous economic sectors it has been losing jobs and facing a continuous threat of industrial relocation. The General Motors strike of October 1996 in Canada may be a harbinger of both a new wave of labour militancy and a new agenda of grievances. The strike focused on precisely these issues, involving a direct challenge to the approach of the managers of economic globalisation. It is symbolically, as well as intrinsically, important, suggesting a new direction of emphasis in the labour movement that has all sorts of potential for transnational cooperative activities across societies whose workers have benefited from globalisation, but whose working conditions are miserable in a variety of respects.

Sixth, and informing the whole process of globalisation, whether from above or below, is the weakening of control by the state over identity politics, with a variety of positive and negative consequences. Transnational networks of affiliation in relation to gender, race and class have become more tenable, although confusingly they coexist with an ultra-nationalist backlash politics that seeks to reappropriate the state for the benefit of traditional ethnic identities. In important respects, backlash politics represents the inversion of globalisation-from-below, i.e. a repudiation of globalisation-from-above by a reliance on the protectionist capabilities of the state, a tactic that has generally been an economic failure, most spectacularly in relation to the experience of the Soviet bloc countries in the latter stages of the Cold War. In contrast, China, with its opening to the forces of globalisation-from-above, while suppressing those associated with globalisation-from-below, has enjoyed spectacular economic success, although at high human costs. The main point, however, is that the democratic spaces available to resist globalisation-from-above tend to be mainly situated at either local levels of engagement or transnationally. One very visible siting has been in relation to global conferences under the auspices of the United Nations on a variety of policy issues, including environment, development, human rights, the role of women, the social responsibilities of government, population pressures and problems of urban life and habitat. What has been impressive has been the creative tactics used by transnational participating groups, denied formal access because of their lack of statist credentials, yet exerting a considerable impact on the agenda and substantive outcomes of inter-governmental activities, and at the same time strengthening transnational links. Starting with the Rio Conference on Environment and Development in 1992, through the 1993 Vienna Conference on Human Rights and Development, the 1994 Cairo Conference on Population and Development, the 1995 Social Summit in Copenhagen and the Beijing Conference on Women and Development, to the 1996 Istanbul Conference on Habitat and Development, there has been a flow of gatherings that acknowledged to varying degrees the emergent role of globalisation-from-below. These events were early experiments in a new sort of participatory politics that had little connection with the traditional practices of politics within states, and could be regarded as fledgling attempts to constitute 'global democracy'.

Such developments, representing a definite effort to engage directly both statist and market forces, produced their own kind of backlash politics. At first, at Rio and Vienna, the effort was a cooptive one, acknowledging the participation of globalisation-from-below as legitimate and significant, yet controlling outcomes. But later on, at Cairo, Copenhagen and Beijing, the more radical potentialities of these democratising forces were perceived as adversaries of the neoliberal conception of political economy, and the format of a global conference open to both types of globalisation began to be perceived as risky, possibly an early sighting of the next wave of revolutionary challenge, the rebirth of dangerous classes in the sense earlier reserved for the labour movement.

If this assessment of action and reaction is generally accurate it suggests the probability of several adjustments. To begin with, there may emerge a reluctance to finance and organise global conferences under the banner of the United Nations that address non-technical matters of human concern. There will be a search for new formats by forces associated with globalisation-from-below, possibly increasing the oppositional character of participation, creating a hostile presence at meetings of the Group of Seven or at the annual meetings of the Board of Governors of the IMF or World Bank, possibly organising tribunals of the people to consider allegations against globalisation-from-above. In effect, if the challenge of globalisation-from-below is to become dangerous enough to tempt those representing globalisation-from-above to seek accommodation, new tactics will have to be developed. One direction of activity that is easier to organise is to concentrate energies of resistance at the regional levels of encounter, especially in Europe and Asia-Pacific, at inter-governmental gatherings devoted to expanding relative and absolute growth for the region *vis-à-vis* the global economy. The Third World Network, based in Penang, has been very effective in educating the cadres of resistance to globalisation-from-above about adverse effects and encouraging various types of opposition. Otherwise, resistance to globalisation-from-above and the ascendancy of market forces is likely to be ignored.

Seventh, it has become necessary to formulate a programmatic response to this pattern of action and reaction between those political tendencies seeking to embody the logic of the market in structures of global economic governance, such as the World Trade Organization and the Bretton Woods institutions, and the transnational political forces seeking to realise the vision of cosmopolitan democracy.[7] More directly, militant tactics may also be selectively employed to supplement the regulatory efforts, feeble at best, of national governments. Such a dynamic was initiated successfully by Greenpeace two years ago to reverse a decision by Shell Oil, approved by the British government, to sink a large oil rig named Brent Spar in the North Sea. The issue here was one of environmental protection, but the tactic of consumer leverage is potentially deployable in relation to any issue that finds its way onto the transnational social agenda. What induced the Shell turnaround – although it never conceded the possible environmental dangers of its planned disposal of the oil rig – was the focus of the boycott on Shell service stations, especially those located in Germany. Indeed, the impact of this initiative was so great that both the *Wall Street Journal* and the *Financial Times* editorialised against Greenpeace, complaining that it had become 'an environmental superpower'.

At this stage, the politics of resistance in this emergent era of globalisation are in formation. Because of the global scope, combined with the unevenness of economic and political conditions, the tactics and priorities will be diverse, adapted to the local, national and regional circumstances. Just as globalisation-from-above tends towards homogeneity and unity, so globalisation-from-below tends towards heterogeneity and diversity, even tension and contradiction. This contrast highlights the fundamental difference between top-down hierarchical politics and bottom-up participatory politics. It is not a zero-sum rivalry, but rather one in which the transnational democratic goals are designed to reconcile global market operations with the well-being of peoples and with the carrying capacity of the earth. Whether such a reconciliation is possible is likely to be the most salient political challenge at the dawn of a new millennium.

Notes

1   See two recent reports of global commissions of eminent persons, published as *Our Global Neighbourhood* by the Independent Commission on Global Governance (Oxford University Press, 1995); and *Caring for the Future* by the Independent Commission on Population and the Quality of Life (Oxford University Press, 1996).
2   Immanuel Wallerstein, *After Liberalism* (New Press, 1995), pp. 1–8, 93–107.
3   Effectively argued in Smitu Kothari, 'Where are the people? The United Nations, global economic institutions and governance', in: Chris Reus-Smit, Anthony Jarvis & Albert Paolini (Eds), *The United Nations: Between Sovereignty and Global Governance* (Macmillan, 1997).

4   This position is elaborated in Richard Falk, 'An Inquiry into the Political Economy of World Order', *New Political Economy*, vol. 1 (1996), no. 1, pp. 13–26.

5   For initial reliance on this terminology with respect to globalisation, see Richard Falk, 'The making of global citizenship', in: Jeremy Brecher, John Brown Childs & Jill Cutler (eds), *Global Visions: Beyond the New World Order* (South End Press, 1993), pp. 39–50. For a useful and sophisticated overview of globalisation-from-below in the context of transnational environmentalism, see Paul Wapner, *Environmental Action and World Civic Politics* (SUNY Press, 1995).

6   For an attempted clarification of world order values and their interrelations, see Richard Falk, *A Study of Future Worlds* (Free Press, 1975), pp. 11–43.

7   A comprehensive and important effort to formulate such a perspective is to be found in the writings of David Held, *Democracy and the Global Order: From the Modern State to Cosmopolitan Democracy* (Polity Press, 1995), pp. 267–86.

24

Picking the Wrong Fight: Why Attacks on the World Trade Organization Pose the Real Threat to National Environmental and Public Health Protection (2005)

Alasdair R. Young

The World Trade Organization (WTO) has existed for more than 10 years. As the mass demonstrations at the WTO Ministerial in Seattle in December 1999 illustrated, it has become a lightning rod for much anti-globalization sentiment. One of the principal reasons for this is concern that national rules – especially those protecting the environment and public health – may be overturned because they are incompatible with the WTO's rules.

I argue that while these concerns are not totally unfounded, they are exaggerated. A central reason for this exaggeration is that some environmental and consumer advocates discount the pivotal role of governments in the dispute resolution process. Governments agreed to the multilateral rules in the first place. Governments decide which market access barriers to pursue and how aggressively. Governments determine how to comply with WTO judgments that go against them.

Furthermore, I argue that by exaggerating the constraint imposed upon national governments by the WTO, consumer and environmental advocates run the risk of actually discouraging the very regulations they favor. By proclaiming that international rules are hostile to public health and environmental protection they give the opponents of regulation an additional argument to use in the domestic debate and give reluctant governments another excuse not to act. They, therefore, may be creating a self-fulfilling prophecy and contributing to a so-called "regulatory chill."

[...]

Alasdair R. Young. 2005. "Picking the Wrong Fight: Why Attacks on the World Trade Organization Pose the Real Threat to National Environmental and Public Health Protection". In *Global Environmental Politics*, 5(4): 47–72. Reproduced with permission from MIT.

There is extensive concern that the WTO's rules and free trade ethos inhibit the development of effective global environmental governance. It is with respect to national environmental and public health rules, however, that the WTO's dispute settlement process comes into play and where there is the potential for WTO rules to roll back national rules, as well as to inhibit their development [...].

Environmental organizations in developed countries, in particular, have serious concerns about the potential of WTO obligations to adversely affect national rules. A WWF-UK discussion paper, for example, states that the WTO and regional integration projects are "threatening ... legitimate national policies in the areas of health and the environment." The Canadian nongovernmental organization West Coast Environmental Law contends that "... [t]he primary goal of trade law is to limit government law making and regulatory authority" and that "... trade dispute processes have now become a popular weapon for attacking environmental and conservation measures in Canada, the US and Europe." The San-Francisco-based Earthjustice Legal Defense Fund states that the WTO's rules "treat [health and environmental] protections as obstacles to trade that should be eliminated [...]".

Two central worries underpin these concerns about the WTO. First, that foreign firms, acting through their national governments, will use the WTO to challenge existing domestic rules. Second, that fear of such challenges will make governments reluctant to adopt strict public health or environmental regulations – creating a so-called "regulatory chill."

I contend that these attacks aimed at abolishing the WTO may actually exacerbate the impact of the WTO on domestic regulation by discouraging the adoption of new rules. By exaggerating the threat that the WTO poses to national regulation, the very champions of such regulation are playing into the hands of their opponents. [...]

[...] [I]t matters less whether the WTO strictly constrains national regulatory autonomy than whether political actors believe it does, and so do not act, or invoke it in order to avoid paying a political price for not taking popular action. Lori Wallach and Patrick Woodall provide numerous anecdotes of government action not taken for fear of WTO censure. Whether this is causal or not is debatable, but there are indications of policy makers, even those favorably inclined towards environmental and public health regulation, echoing the view that the WTO is inherently hostile to such measures. Further, governments frequently seek to shift blame for costly or unpopular domestically-motivated measures to international institutions [...] with regard to the European Union and the International Monetary Fund, in particular. It is a short logical step from blaming international institutions for having to adopt unpopular measures and blaming them for not being able to adopt popular ones. Consequently, those environmental and consumer groups that persistently build the WTO up as the enemy of environmental and public health regulation run the risk of either persuading policy makers that adopting environmental and public health measures is futile or making more credible their excuses for not adopting popular policies. Thus activists' attacks on the WTO risk contributing to the "regulatory chill" that they claim the WTO causes.

Why the Concerns? (or What's New about the WTO?)

Although overselling the WTO's antipathy to environmental and public health regulations may be counterproductive, the concerns of these environmental and consumer groups are not without some foundation. The Uruguay Round of multilateral trade negations that led to the creation of the WTO in 1995 introduced some major changes to how the multilateral trading system operates. These changes involved extending the breadth of issues covered by multilateral rules and making those multilateral rules more binding on the members. In doing so, the Uruguay Round made multilateral trade rules more challenging to domestic policy autonomy.

In particular, the Uruguay Round increased the extent to which multilateral rules apply to national measures that have implications for trade even if that is not their purpose, such as regulations. This is particularly the case with rules affecting food safety and plant and animal health, which are covered by the Sanitary and Phytosanitary (SPS) Agreement, which is more proscriptive than most WTO agreements. It encourages governments to adopt a science-based approach and to harmonize standards based on those developed by international standards organizations, such as the Codex Alimentarius Commission. [...]

During the Uruguay Round trade-related environmental issues were addressed in the General Agreement on Trade in Services, and in the Agreements on Agriculture, SPS, Subsidies and Countervailing Measures and Trade Related Intellectual Property Rights. [...]

In particular, the Uruguay Round made the new and existing rules, particularly Article III of the General Agreement on Tariffs and Trade, which prohibits discrimination against foreign goods, more constraining through the introduction of binding dispute settlement. In the WTO agreements the participating governments effectively delegated the binding adjudication of disputes to a third-party body. They also formalized a system in which an aggrieved party can punish non-compliance with a Dispute Settlement Body (DSB) judgment by imposing trade sanctions. These changes mean that the multilateral rules now have teeth.

[...]

Any compromise of domestic autonomy is objectionable in principle to those environmental and consumer groups most concerned about the WTO, but all seem to consider the development of the WTO to be extremely worrying for two related, but distinct, reasons: 1) a selective reading of the agreements, which assumes that the interests of free trade will prevail over other considerations; 2) an assumption that governments are simply the agents of big business. The assumption that governments are agents of big business supports the view that the multilateral rules have been negotiated to the benefit of free trade above all other considerations and anticipates that governments will aggressively prosecute all foreign regulatory measures that impede trade.

Environmental and consumer groups' concern about the WTO is based on an often selective reading of the WTO agreements. This involves both interpreting the agreements' provisions in an extremely constraining way and ignoring or discounting the exception clauses, which are intended to permit governments to pursue public policy objectives. [...]

It is worth noting, however, that both the TBT and SPS Agreements explicitly state that governments have the right to regulate to protect human, animal and plant life and health [...]. Further, the GATT contains a general exception clause Article XX, which expressly permits governments to pursue measures to protect the environment and human health so long as they are not arbitrary, unjustified or are a disguised restriction on international trade. These exceptions reveal that the governments that negotiated the multilateral trade rules have sought to strike a balance between permitting protection of consumers and the environment while prosecuting disguised protectionism.

The environmental and consumer groups' dire interpretations of the WTO's rules are supported by a refrain of cases in which states' environmental or consumer protection measures have been found to be incompatible with WTO rules. [...]

Those environmental and consumer groups that are worried about the WTO tend to exaggerate the extent to which WTO rules impinge upon national regulation. They tend to take a ruling in favor of the complaint(s) as proof that the WTO's rules are stacked against regulation, while only fairly technical aspects of the measures have usually been found to be incompatible with WTO rules, while important principles have been upheld. The EU's ban on hormone-treated beef, for example, was found to be incompatible with the EU's multilateral obligations because it was not based on an adequate risk assessment and it was permanent (not temporary, so the precautionary clause of the SPS Agreement did not apply). The WTO's Appellate Body, however, upheld the important principle that a polity may set what level of risk it finds acceptable. [...]

The anti-WTO activists also tend to neglect or discount contradictory cases. While environmentalists made much of the WTO's ruling against the US government's ban on shrimp caught without turtle-excluding nets (DS58, 61), they were largely silent on the WTO ruling up-holding the US government's relatively minor adjustments to the measure. The case against the WTO also tends to ignore, or dismiss as a fluke, the Asbestos case (DS135) in which a French ban on asbestos products was upheld by the WTO even though it impeded trade, because it was justified under Article XX.

[...]

Environmental and Public Health Complaints in Context

Significantly, the anti-WTO activists' refrain of cases is virtually the sum total of serious complaints involving animal, plant or human health or environmental protection regulations. [...] The vast majority of these complaints have not progressed beyond the consultation phase for years, an indication that the dispute is effectively dormant.

Arguably, the high success rate of challenges to environmental and public health protection measures [...], has less to do with an imbalance in the WTO in favor of free trade, as the anti-WTO activists contend, than to do with case selection. Arguably, WTO members have challenged only poor regulations, which are either disguised protectionism or use inappropriate tools to achieve their intended objective. Governments being selective about which national rules to challenge would help to account for the relatively small number of complaints and smaller number of adjudications concerning public health and environmental regulations.

Considering the vast range of regulations that have *not* been challenged supports this contention. For example, the European Commission recently identified 121 European Union rules that affect imports of animals and animal products. Such measures are, to some extent, barriers to trade. In contrast to these 121 rules affecting imports of animals and animal products, only 29 EU measures concerning all aspects of food safety, animal and plant health (a broader category) have been raised by the EU's trading partners [...], and formal WTO complaints have been initiated against only two such measures (beef hormones and genetically modified crops). Thus the overwhelming majority of EU measures protecting consumer safety and plant and animal health, even of those that impede trade, have not even been questioned by the EU's trading partners, let alone challenged before the WTO.

The EU's experience is not unique. As of November 2003, 183 national food safety and animal and plant health measures had been raised in the SPS Committee, surely a tiny fraction of such measures adopted by all 148 WTO members over more than 10 years. [...]

Examining measures that fall under the SPS Agreement is a particularly appropriate test of the threat posed by WTO rules to domestic regulation. First, the Agreement covers issues at the heart of consumer and environmental protection – human, animal and plant life. Second, the SPS Agreement establishes stricter disciplines than the TBT Agreement, the other specific multilateral discipline on regulatory policy. If WTO rules should bite on regulation anywhere, it should be here. Consequently, this analysis suggests that the vast majority of food safety issues, and by extension other social regulations that impede trade, are not challenged under WTO rules.

The conclusion that public health and environmental protection measures are only challenged exceptionally, suggests that the common assumption that governments are simply the agents of big business is flawed. If they were, we should expect to see many more trade disputes challenging the many national rules that impede trade.

[...]

The preceding discussion has demonstrated that governments often do not pursue foreign trade barriers through the WTO, even if business interests have complained about them. One possible reason for this is that other business interests might oppose such action. Such opposition, however, is rare, as initiating a trade dispute only very occasionally imposes costs on other domestic actors; the costs of adjustment normally fall only on the other country. Consequently, the concerns of governments themselves are the key to understanding why some complaints are pursued and others are not.

[...] [There are] a number of considerations that encourage governments to be cautious when pursuing WTO complaints, especially when regulatory measures are at issue. These include: not wanting to jeopardize other foreign policy objectives, wanting to win, and wanting to avoid inadvertently constraining their own policy autonomy.

The principal participants in WTO dispute settlement have extensive and often intense political relationships with other countries in the world. Initiating a trade dispute may disrupt those relationships. For this reason many export-oriented firms dislike trade disputes because they sour the economic environment. Governments likewise may wish to avoid antagonizing important partners. [...]

When initiating a WTO complaint a government also has to be careful that it does not end up scoring an own-goal by winning a WTO complaint that also applies to its own rules. Because of the importance of precedence within the WTO's legal framework, a government needs to have an eye on whether a successful challenge to a foreign government's rule might establish a precedent that applies to its own policies. The Commission is also reluctant to challenge other governments' rules on product labels, as the EU has adopted quite onerous labeling requirements for genetically modified foods, or on export subsidies. [...]

As this discussion suggests, there are a number of reasons why members of the WTO might not pursue a regulatory measure even if they are under pressure from business interests to do so. The governments' "gatekeeping" role, therefore, significantly restricts the number of regulatory measures that are challenged before the WTO, thereby limiting the impact of multilateral obligations on national rules.

Another problem with many environmental and consumer groups' critiques of the WTO, is that they do not consider what actual policy changes have followed from the adverse WTO judgments they cite. Even if a complaint is initiated and the complainant wins, the respondent government may well be able to comply with its international obligations without fundamentally undermining the original objective of the measure.

Although most governments have complied with most adverse WTO judgments, they have tended to do so in ways that mitigate the impact of the adverse judgement. This is the case even with most of the activists' *causes célèbres*. Although the US government revised its methodology for establishing compliance with its rules on conventional gasoline in order to eliminate the discrimination against foreign producers, this did not adversely affect the measure's capacity to promote cleaner air. Arguably the adjustments the US government made to its ban on imported shrimp not caught using turtle-excluding nets in response to the WTO's adverse ruling actually made the rule more effective at achieving its environmental objective, because it is now more focused on protecting turtles and less on protecting the US shrimping industry. The WTO's adverse judgment on the EU's ban on hormone treated beef and even the subsequent imposition of sanctions by Canada and the US have had no practical effect on the ban. [...]

Such limited changes to public health and environmental protection regulations, even in the face of trade sanctions, reflect that the measures originally resulted from domestic political pressures. [...] A WTO ruling only starts this process. It does not determine its conclusion. As the preceding discussion suggests, this domestic political process has tended to preserve the crucial public health or environmental protection objectives of the challenged measures.

Even if the preceding argument is incorrect and the WTO is as intrusive and overbearing as its opponents claim, there is still no reason why this should provoke a regulatory "chill." As there is no right under WTO law to damages suffered while a WTO-inconsistent measure is in place, the only cost to adopting a WTO-inconsistent measure is that of defending it before the WTO. Consequently, it makes sense for governments to adopt whatever public health and environmental protection rules they see fit. If, and only if, such a measure is challenged by others does the government need to decide whether it is worth defending, both a legal and political calculation. Even if the measure is ultimately overturned, either as the result of the government deciding to acquiesce or because of an adverse WTO judgment, in the meantime the polity has enjoyed whatever protective benefits the measure provides. Consequently, it does not make sense for a government to self censor and refuse to adopt a measure for fear that it might be challenged before the WTO.

Conclusions

The WTO is a new form of governance and it represents a new trade-off between the benefits of increased compliance by others and the disadvantages of decreased policy autonomy at home. As a result, there is good reason to regard it with circumspection.

Depicting the WTO's rules as favoring free trade over all else, as some environmental and consumer groups are wont to do, however, is distorting, and in a dangerous way. There are three reasons why their critique is overstated. First, the rules are not as pro-free-trade as they depict. Because the governments of the advanced developed countries have duties to their citizens, on whom they rely for re-election, they were and are sensitive to the trade-off between increasing the compliance of others and reducing their own autonomy. [...] This is evident in the WTO's judgments to date, which, while finding fault with aspects of most of the few public health and environmental protection measures brought before it, have supported their objectives and demonstrated deference for national regulators.

Second, the high proportion of successful challenges to regulatory measures before the WTO is due less to the nature of the WTO's rules than to the careful selection of the few complaints brought. Governments have tended to challenge only poorly developed regulations. This is because governments weigh carefully the decision to initiate trade disputes, because doing so incurs costs beyond simply the resources required. Not least among these considerations when it comes to regulatory measures is a desire to avoid establishing a precedent against a foreign rule that may affect their own policies.

Third, when confronted with an adverse WTO judgment, governments have tended to seek to comply without fundamentally altering the objectives of the policy in question. This reflects the underlying political process that produced the measure in the first place. Although an adverse WTO judgment alters the domestic political balance, it does not wholly transform it. As a consequence, compliance with adverse WTO judgments against public health and environmental regulations has been more of style than of substance. [...]

By exaggerating the extent to which the WTO constrains national regulatory autonomy, environmental and consumer activists risk contributing to the regulatory chill that they claim the WTO causes. They are feeding the myth that action to protect consumers or the environment is futile because it will ultimately be undone by the WTO. This only aids the opponents of regulation. Rather than demonizing the WTO, consumer and environmental advocates should concentrate on winning the debate for regulation at home.

25

What Every Environmentalist Needs to Know About Capitalism (2010)

Fred Magdoff and John Bellamy Foster

For those concerned with the fate of the earth, the time has come to face facts: not simply the dire reality of climate change but also the pressing need for social-system change. The failure to arrive at a world climate agreement in Copenhagen in December 2009 was not simply an abdication of world leadership, as is often suggested, but had deeper roots in the inability of the capitalist system to address the accelerating threat to life on the planet. Knowledge of the nature and limits of capitalism, and the means of transcending it, has therefore become a matter of survival.

[...]

It is our contention that most of the critical environmental problems we have are either caused, or made much worse, by the workings of our economic system. Even such issues as population growth and technology are best viewed in terms of their relation to the socioeconomic organization of society. Environmental problems are not a result of human ignorance or innate greed. They do not arise because managers of individual large corporations or developers are morally deficient. Instead, we must look to the fundamental workings of the economic (and political/social) system for explanations. It is precisely the fact that ecological destruction is built into the inner nature and logic of our present system of production that makes it so difficult to solve.

In addition, we shall argue that "solutions" proposed for environmental devastation, which would allow the current system of production and distribution to proceed unabated, are not real solutions. In fact, such "solutions" will make things worse because they give the false impression that the problems are on their way to being overcome when the reality is quite different. The overwhelming environmental problems facing the world and its people will not be effectively dealt with until we

Fred Magdoff and John Bellamy Foster. 2010. "What Every Environmentalist Needs to Know About Capitalism". In *Monthly Review*, 61(10): 1–30. Reproduced with permission from Monthly Review.

institute another way for humans to interact with nature – altering the way we make decisions on what and how much to produce. Our most necessary, most rational goals require that we take into account fulfilling basic human needs, and creating just and sustainable conditions on behalf of present and future generations (which also means being concerned about the preservation of other species).

Characteristics of Capitalism in Conflict with the Environment

The economic system that dominates nearly all corners of the world is capitalism, which, for most humans, is as "invisible" as the air we breathe. We are, in fact, largely oblivious to this worldwide system, much as fish are oblivious to the water in which they swim. It is capitalism's ethic, outlook, and frame of mind that we assimilate and acculturate to as we grow up. Unconsciously, we learn that greed, exploitation of laborers, and competition (among people, businesses, countries) are not only acceptable but are actually good for society because they help to make our economy function "efficiently."

Let's consider some of the key aspects of capitalism's conflict with environmental sustainability.

Capitalism Is a system that Must Continually Expand

No-growth capitalism is an oxymoron: when growth ceases, the system is in a state of crisis with considerable suffering among the unemployed. Capitalism's basic driving force and its whole reason for existence is the amassing of profits and wealth through the accumulation (savings and investment) process. It recognizes no limits to its own self-expansion – not in the economy as a whole; not in the profits desired by the wealthy; and not in the increasing consumption that people are cajoled into desiring in order to generate greater profits for corporations. The environment exists, not as a place with inherent boundaries within which human beings must live together with earth's other species, but as a realm to be exploited in a process of growing economic expansion.

Indeed, businesses, according to the inner logic of capital, which is enforced by competition, must either grow or die – as must the system itself. There is little that can be done to increase profits from production when there is slow or no growth. Under such circumstances, there is little reason to invest in new capacity, thus closing off the profits to be derived from new investment. There is also just so much increased profit that can be easily squeezed out of workers in a stagnant economy. Such measures as decreasing the number of workers and asking those remaining to "do more with less," shifting the costs of pensions and health insurance to workers, and introducing automation that reduces the number of needed workers can only go so far without further destabilizing the system. If a corporation is large enough it can, like Wal-Mart, force suppliers, afraid of losing the business, to decrease their prices.

But these means are not enough to satisfy what is, in fact, an insatiable quest for more profits, so corporations are continually engaged in struggle with their competitors (including frequently buying them out) to increase market share and gross sales.

It is true that the system can continue to move forward, to some extent, as a result of financial speculation leveraged by growing debt, even in the face of a tendency to slow growth in the underlying economy. But this means, as we have seen again and again, the growth of financial bubbles that inevitably burst.[1] There is no alternative under capitalism to the endless expansion of the "real economy" (i.e., production), irrespective of actual human needs, consumption, or the environment.

One might still imagine that it would be theoretically possible for a capitalist economy to have zero growth, and still meet all of humanity's basic needs. Let's suppose that all the profits that corporations earn (after allowing for replacing worn out equipment or buildings) are either spent by capitalists on their own consumption or given to workers as wages and benefits, and consumed. As capitalists and workers spend this money, they would purchase the goods and services produced, and the economy could stay at a steady state, no-growth level (what Marx called "simple reproduction" and has sometimes been called the "stationary state"). Since there would be no investment in new productive capacity, there would be no economic growth and accumulation, no profits generated.

There is, however, one slight problem with this "capitalist no-growth utopia": it violates the basic motive force of capitalism. What capital strives for and is the purpose of its existence is its own expansion. Why would capitalists, who in every fiber of their beings believe that they have a personal right to business profits, and who are driven to accumulate wealth, simply spend the economic surplus at their disposal on their own consumption or (less likely still) give it to workers to spend on theirs – rather than seek to expand wealth? If profits are not generated, how could economic crises be avoided under capitalism? To the contrary, it is clear that owners of capital will, as long as such ownership relations remain, do whatever they can within their power to maximize the amount of profits they accrue. A stationary state, or steady-state, economy as a stable solution is only conceivable if separated from the social relations of capital itself.

Capitalism is a system that constantly generates a reserve army of the unemployed; meaningful, full employment is a rarity that occurs only at very high rates of growth (which are correspondingly dangerous to ecological sustainability). Taking the US economy as the example, let's take a look at what happens to the number of "officially" unemployed when the economy grows at different rates during a period of close to sixty years.

[...]

What, then, do we see in the relationship between economic growth and unemployment over the last six decades?

1 During the eleven years of very slow growth, less than 1.1 percent per year, unemployment increased in each of the years.
2 In 70 percent (nine of thirteen) of the years when GDP grew between 1.2 and 3 percent per year, unemployment also grew.

3   During the twenty-three years when the US economy grew fairly rapidly (from
    3.1 to 5.0 percent a year), unemployment still increased in three years and
    reduction in the percent unemployed was anemic in most of the others.
4   Only in the thirteen years when the GDP grew at greater than 5.0 percent annu-
    ally did unemployment not increase in any of these years.

[...] It is clear that, if the GDP growth rate isn't substantially greater than the increase
in population, people lose jobs. While slow or no growth is a problem for business
owners trying to increase their profits, it is a disaster for working people.

What this tells us is that the capitalist system is a very crude instrument in
terms of providing jobs in relation to growth – if growth is to be justified by
employment. It will take a rate of growth of around 4 percent or higher, far above
the average growth rate, before the unemployment problem is surmounted in
US capitalism today. Worth noting is the fact that, since the 1940s, such high
rates of growth in the US economy have hardly ever been reached except in
times of wars.

Expansion Leads to Investing Abroad in Search of Secure Sources of Raw Materials, Cheaper Labor, and New Markets

As companies expand, they saturate, or come close to saturating, the "home" market
and look for new markets abroad to sell their goods. In addition, they and their
governments (working on behalf of corporate interests) help to secure entry and
control over key natural resources such as oil and a variety of minerals. We are in the
midst of a "land-grab," as private capital and government sovereign wealth funds
strive to gain control of vast acreage throughout the world to produce food and
biofuel feedstock crops for their "home" markets. It is estimated that some thirty
million hectares of land (roughly equal to two-thirds of the arable land in Europe),
much of them in Africa, have been recently acquired or are in the process of being
acquired by rich countries and international corporations.[2]

This global land seizure (even if by "legal" means) can be regarded as part of the
larger history of imperialism. The story of centuries of European plunder and expansion is well documented. The current US-led wars in Iraq and Afghanistan follow
the same general historical pattern, and are clearly related to US attempts to control
the main world sources of oil and gas.[3]

Today multinational (or transnational) corporations scour the world for
resources and opportunities wherever they can find them, exploiting cheap labor in
poor countries and reinforcing, rather than reducing, imperialist divisions. The
result is a more rapacious global exploitation of nature and increased differentials
of wealth and power. Such corporations have no loyalty to anything but their own
bottom lines.

A system that, by Its Very Nature, Must Grow and Expand Will Eventually Come Up Against the Reality of Finite Natural Resources

The irreversible exhaustion of finite natural resources will leave future generations without the possibility of having use of these resources. Natural resources are used in the process of production – oil, gas, and coal (fuel), water (in industry and agriculture), trees (for lumber and paper), a variety of mineral deposits (such as iron ore, copper, and bauxite), and so on. Some resources, such as forests and fisheries, are of a finite size, but can be renewed by natural processes if used in a planned system that is flexible enough to change as conditions warrant. Future use of other resources – oil and gas, minerals, aquifers in some desert or dryland areas (prehistorically deposited water) – are limited forever to the supply that currently exists. The water, air, and soil of the biosphere can continue to function well for the living creatures on the planet only if pollution doesn't exceed their limited capacity to assimilate and render the pollutants harmless.

Business owners and managers generally consider the short term in their operations – most take into account the coming three to five years, or, in some rare instances, up to ten years. This is the way they must function because of unpredictable business conditions (phases of the business cycle, competition from other corporations, prices of needed inputs, etc.) and demands from speculators looking for short-term returns. They therefore act in ways that are largely oblivious of the natural limits to their activities – as if there is an unlimited supply of natural resources for exploitation. Even if the reality of limitation enters their consciousness, it merely speeds up the exploitation of a given resource, which is extracted as rapidly as possible, with capital then moving on to new areas of resource exploitation. When each individual capitalist pursues the goal of making a profit and accumulating capital, decisions are made that collectively harm society as a whole.

The length of time before nonrenewable deposits are exhausted depends on the size of the deposit and the rate of extraction of the resource. While depletion of some resources may be hundreds of years away (assuming that the rate of growth of extraction remains the same), limits for some important ones – oil and some minerals – are not that far off. For example, while predictions regarding peak oil vary among energy analysts – going by the conservative estimates of oil companies themselves, at the rate at which oil is currently being used, known reserves will be exhausted within the next fifty years. The prospect of peak oil is projected in numerous corporate, government, and scientific reports. The question today is not whether peak oil is likely to arrive soon, but simply how soon.[4]

Even if usage doesn't grow, the known deposits of the critical fertilizer ingredient phosphorus that can be exploited on the basis of current technology will be exhausted in this century.[5]

Faced with limited natural resources, there is no rational way to prioritize under a modern capitalist system, in which the well-to-do with their economic leverage decide via the market how commodities are allocated. When extraction begins to decline, as is projected for oil within the near future, price increases will put even more pressure on what had been, until recently, the boast of world capitalism: the supposedly prosperous "middle-class" workers of the countries of the center.

The well-documented decline of many ocean fish species, almost to the point of extinction, is an example of how renewable resources can be exhausted. It is in the short-term individual interests of the owners of fishing boats – some of which operate at factory scale, catching, processing, and freezing fish – to maximize the take. Hence, the fish are depleted. No one protects the common interest. In a system run generally on private self-interest and accumulation, the state is normally incapable of doing so. This is sometimes called the tragedy of the commons. But it should be called the tragedy of the private exploitation of the commons.

The situation would be very different if communities that have a stake in the continued availability of a resource managed the resource in place of the large-scale corporation. Corporations are subject to the single-minded goal of maximizing short-term profits – after which they move on, leaving devastation behind, in effect mining the earth. Although there is no natural limit to human greed, there are limits, as we are daily learning, to many resources, including "renewable" ones, such as the productivity of the seas. (The depletion of fish off the coast of Somalia because of overfishing by factory-scale fishing fleets is believed to be one of the causes for the rise of piracy that now plagues international shipping in the area. Interestingly, the neighboring Kenyan fishing industry is currently rebounding because the pirates also serve to keep large fishing fleets out of the area.) [...]

A System Geared to Exponential Growth in the Search for Profits Will Inevitably Transgress Planetary Boundaries

The earth system can be seen as consisting of a number of critical biogeochemical processes that, for hundreds of millions of years, have served to reproduce life. In the last 12 thousand or so years the world climate has taken the relatively benign form associated with the geological epoch known as the Holocene, during which civilization arose. Now, however, the socioeconomic system of capitalism has grown to such a scale that it overshoots fundamental planetary boundaries – the carbon cycle, the nitrogen cycle, the soil, the forests, the oceans. More and more of the terrestrial (land-based) photosynthetic product, upwards of 40 percent, is now directly accounted for by human production. All ecosystems on earth are in visible decline. With the increasing scale of the world economy, the human-generated rifts in the earth's metabolism inevitably become more severe and more multifarious. Yet, the demand for more and greater economic growth and accumulation, even in the wealthier countries, is built into the capitalist system. As a result, the world economy is one massive bubble.

There is nothing in the nature of the current system, moreover, that will allow it to pull back before it is too late. To do that, other forces from the bottom of society will be required.

Capitalism Is Not Just an Economic System – It Fashions a Political, Judicial, and Social System to Support the System of Wealth and Accumulation

Under capitalism people are at the service of the economy and are viewed as needing to consume more and more to keep the economy functioning. The massive and, in the words of Joseph Schumpeter, "elaborate psychotechnics of advertising" are absolutely necessary to keep people buying.[6] Morally, the system is based on the proposition that each, following his/her own interests (greed), will promote the general interest and growth. Adam Smith famously put it: "It is not from the benevolence of the butcher, the brewer, or the baker that we expect our dinner, but from their regard to their own interest."[7] In other words, individual greed (or quest for profits) drives the system and human needs are satisfied as a mere by-product. Economist Duncan Foley has called this proposition and the economic and social irrationalities it generates "Adam's Fallacy."[8]

The attitudes and mores needed for the smooth functioning of such a system, as well as for people to thrive as members of society – greed, individualism, competitiveness, exploitation of others, and "consumerism" (the drive to purchase more and more stuff, unrelated to needs and even to happiness) – are inculcated into people by schools, the media, and the workplace. The title of Benjamin Barber's book – *Consumed: How Markets Corrupt Children, Infantilize Adults, and Swallow Citizens Whole* – says a lot.

The notion of responsibility to others and to community, which is the foundation of ethics, erodes under such a system. In the words of Gordon Gekko – the fictional corporate takeover artist in Oliver Stone's film *Wall Street* – "Greed is Good." Today, in the face of widespread public outrage, with financial capital walking off with big bonuses derived from government bailouts, capitalists have turned to preaching self-interest as the bedrock of society from the very pulpits. On November 4, 2009, Barclay's Plc Chief Executive Officer John Varley declared from a wooden lectern in St Martin-in-the-Fields at London's Trafalgar Square that "Profit is not Satanic." Weeks earlier, on October 20, 2009, Goldman Sachs International adviser Brian Griffiths declared before the congregation at St Paul's Cathedral in London that "The injunction of Jesus to love others as ourselves is a recognition of self-interest."[9]

Wealthy people come to believe that they deserve their wealth because of hard work (theirs or their forbearers) and possibly luck. The ways in which their wealth and prosperity arose out of the social labor of innumerable other people are downplayed. They see the poor – and the poor frequently agree – as having something wrong with them, such as laziness or not getting a sufficient education. The structural obstacles that prevent most people from significantly bettering their conditions are also downplayed. This view of each individual as a separate economic entity concerned primarily with one's (and one's family's) own well-being, obscures our common humanity and needs. People are not inherently selfish but are encouraged to become so in response to the pressures and characteristics of the system. After all, if each person doesn't look out for "Number One" in a dog-eat-dog system, who will?

Traits fostered by capitalism are commonly viewed as being innate "human nature," thus making a society organized along other goals than the profit motive unthinkable. But humans are clearly capable of a wide range of characteristics, extending from great cruelty to great sacrifice for a cause, to caring for non-related others, to true altruism. The "killer instinct" that we supposedly inherited from evolutionary ancestors – the "evidence" being chimpanzees' killing the babies of other chimps – is being questioned by reference to the peaceful characteristics of other hominids such as gorillas and bonobos (as closely related to humans as chimpanzees).[10] Studies of human babies have also shown that, while selfishness is a human trait, so are cooperation, empathy, altruism, and helpfulness.[11] Regardless of what traits we may have inherited from our hominid ancestors, research on pre-capitalist societies indicates that very different norms from those in capitalist societies are encouraged and expressed. As Karl Polanyi summarized the studies: "The outstanding discovery of recent historical and anthropological research is that man's economy, as a rule, is submerged in his social relationships. He does not act so as to safeguard his individual interest in the possession of material goods; he acts so as to safeguard his social standing, his social claims, his social assets."[12] In his 1937 article on "Human Nature" for the *Encyclopedia of the Social Sciences,* John Dewey concluded – in terms that have been verified by all subsequent social science – that:

> The present controversies between those who assert the essential fixity of human nature and those who believe in a greater measure of modifiability center chiefly around the future of war and the future of a competitive economic system motivated by private profit. It is justifiable to say without dogmatism that both anthropology and history give support to those who wish to change these institutions. It is demonstrable that many of the obstacles to change which have been attributed to human nature are in fact due to the inertia of institutions and to the voluntary desire of powerful classes to maintain the existing status.[13]

Capitalism is unique among social systems in its active, extreme cultivation of individual self-interest or "possessive-individualism."[14] Yet the reality is that non-capitalist human societies have thrived over a long period – for more than 99 percent of the time since the emergence of anatomically modern humans – while encouraging other traits such as sharing and responsibility to the group. There is no reason to doubt that this can happen again.[15]

The incestuous connection that exists today between business interests, politics, and law is reasonably apparent to most observers.[16] These include outright bribery, to the more subtle sorts of buying access, friendship, and influence through campaign contributions and lobbying efforts. In addition, a culture develops among political leaders based on the precept that what is good for capitalist business is good for the country. Hence, political leaders increasingly see themselves as political entrepreneurs, or the counterparts of economic entrepreneurs, and regularly convince themselves that what they do for corporations to obtain the funds that will help them get reelected is actually in the public interest. Within the legal system, the interests of capitalists and their businesses are given almost every benefit.

Given the power exercised by business interests over the economy, state, and media, it is extremely difficult to effect fundamental changes that they oppose. It therefore makes it next to impossible to have a rational and ecologically sound energy policy, health care system, agricultural and food system, industrial policy, trade policy, education, etc.

[...]

Proposals for the Ecological Reformation of Capitalism

There are some people who fully understand the ecological and social problems that capitalism brings, but think that capitalism can and should be reformed. According to Benjamin Barber: "The struggle for the soul of capitalism is…a struggle between the nation's economic body and its civic soul: a struggle to put capitalism in its proper place, where it serves our nature and needs rather than manipulating and fabricating whims and wants. Saving capitalism means bringing it into harmony with spirit – with prudence, pluralism and those 'things of the public'… that define our civic souls. A revolution of the spirit."[16] William Greider has written a book titled *The Soul of Capitalism: Opening Paths to a Moral Economy*. And there are books that tout the potential of "green capitalism" and the "natural capitalism" of Paul Hawken, Amory Lovins, and L. Hunter Lovins.[17] Here, we are told that we can get rich, continue growing the economy, and increase consumption without end – and save the planet, all at the same time! How good can it get? There is a slight problem – a system that has only one goal, the maximization of profits, has no soul, can never have a soul, can never be green, and, by its very nature, it must manipulate and fabricate whims and wants.

There are a number of important "out of the box" ecological and environmental thinkers and doers. They are genuinely good and well-meaning people who are concerned with the health of the planet, and most are also concerned with issues of social justice. However, there is one box from which they cannot escape – the capitalist economic system. Even the increasing numbers of individuals who criticize the system and its "market failures" frequently end up with "solutions" aimed at a tightly controlled "humane" and non-corporate capitalism, instead of actually getting outside the box of capitalism. They are unable even to think about, let alone promote, an economic system that has different goals and decision-making processes – one that places primary emphasis on human and environmental needs, as opposed to profits.

Corporations are outdoing each other to portray themselves as "green." You can buy and wear your Gucci clothes with a clean conscience because the company is helping to protect rainforests by using less paper.[18] *Newsweek* claims that corporate giants such as Dell, Hewlett-Packard, Johnson & Johnson, Intel, and IBM are the top five green companies of 2009 because of their use of "renewable" sources of energy, reporting greenhouse gas emissions (or lowering them), and implementing formal environmental policies and good reputations.[19] You can travel wherever you want, guilt-free, by purchasing carbon "offsets" that supposedly cancel out the environmental effects of your trip.

Let's take a look at some of the proposed devices for dealing with the ecological havoc without disturbing capitalism.

Better Technologies that Are More Energy Efficient and Use Fewer Material Inputs

Some proposals to enhance energy efficiency – such as those to help people tighten up their old homes so that less fuel is required to heat in the winter – are just plain common sense. The efficiency of machinery, including household appliances and automobiles, has been going up continually, and is a normal part of the system. Although much more can be accomplished in this area, increased efficiency usually leads to lower costs and increased use (and often increased size as well, as in automobiles), so that the energy used is actually increased. The misguided push to "green" agrofuels has been enormously detrimental to the environment. Not only has it put food and auto fuel in direct competition, at the expense of the former, but it has also sometimes actually decreased overall energy efficiency.[20]

Nuclear Power

Some scientists concerned with climate change, including James Lovelock and James Hansen, see nuclear power as an energy alternative, and as a partial technological answer to the use of fossil fuels; one that is much preferable to the growing use of coal. However, although the technology of nuclear energy has improved somewhat, with third-generation nuclear plants, and with the possibility (still not a reality) of fourth-generation nuclear energy, the dangers of nuclear power are still enormous – given radioactive waste lasting hundreds and thousands of years, the social management of complex systems, and the sheer level of risk involved. Moreover, nuclear plants take about ten years to build and are extremely costly and uneconomic. There are all sorts of reasons, therefore (not least of all, future generations), to be extremely wary of nuclear power as any kind of solution. To go in that direction would almost certainly be a Faustian bargain.[21]

Large-Scale Engineering Solutions

A number of vast engineering schemes have been proposed either to take CO_2 out of the atmosphere or to increase the reflectance of sunlight back into space, away from earth. These include: *Carbon sequestration schemes* such as capturing CO_2 from power plants and injecting it deep into the earth, and fertilizing the oceans with iron so as to stimulate algal growth to absorb carbon; and *enhanced sunlight reflection schemes* such as deploying huge white islands in the oceans, creating large satellites to reflect incoming sunlight, and contaminating the stratosphere with particles that reflect light.

No one knows, of course, what detrimental side effects might occur from such schemes. For example, more carbon absorption by the oceans could increase acidification, while dumping sulphur dioxide into the stratosphere to block sunlight could reduce photosynthesis.

Also proposed are a number of low-tech ways to sequester carbon such as increasing reforestation and using ecological soil management to increase soil organic matter (which is composed mainly of carbon). Most of these should be done for their own sake (organic material helps to improve soils in many ways). Some could help to reduce the carbon concentration in the atmosphere. Thus reforestation, by pulling carbon from the atmosphere, is sometimes thought of as constituting negative emissions. But low-tech solutions cannot solve the problem given an expanding system – especially considering that trees planted now can be cut down later, and carbon stored as soil organic matter may later be converted to CO_2 if practices are changed.

Cap and Trade (Market Trading) Schemes

The favorite economic device of the system is what are called "cap and trade" schemes for limiting carbon emissions. This involves placing a cap on the allowable level of greenhouse gas emissions and then distributing (either by fee or by auction) permits that allow industries to emit carbon dioxide and other greenhouse gases. Those corporations that have more permits than they need may sell them to other firms wanting additional permits to pollute. Such schemes invariably include "offsets" that act like medieval indulgences, allowing corporations to continue to pollute while buying good grace by helping to curtail pollution somewhere else – say, in the third world.

In theory, cap and trade is supposed to stimulate technological innovation to increase carbon efficiency. In practice, it has not led to carbon dioxide emission reductions in those areas where it has been introduced, such as in Europe. The main result of carbon trading has been enormous profits for some corporations and individuals, and the creation of a subprime carbon market.[22] There are no meaningful checks of the effectiveness of the "offsets," nor prohibitions for changing conditions sometime later that will result in carbon dioxide release to the atmosphere.

What Can Be Done Now?

In the absence of systemic change, there certainly are things that have been done and more can be done in the future to lessen capitalism's negative effects on the environment and people. There is no particular reason why the United States can't have a better social welfare system, including universal health care, as is the case in many other advanced capitalist countries. Governments can pass laws and implement regulations to curb the worst environmental problems. The same goes for the environment or for building affordable houses. A carbon tax of the kind proposed by James Hansen, in which 100 percent of the dividends go back to the public, thereby encouraging conservation while placing the burden on those with the largest carbon footprints and the most wealth, could be instituted. New coal-fired plants (without sequestration) could be blocked and existing ones closed down.[23] At the world level, contraction and convergence in carbon emissions could be promoted, moving to uniform world per capita emissions, with cut-backs far deeper in the rich countries with large per capita carbon footprints.[24] The problem is that very powerful forces are strongly opposed to these measures. Hence, such reforms remain at best limited, allowed a marginal existence only insofar as they do not interfere with the basic accumulation drive of the system.

Indeed, the problem with all these approaches is that they allow the economy to continue on the same disastrous course it is currently following. We can go on con-suming all we want (or as much as our income and wealth allow), using up resources, driving greater distances in our more fuel-efficient cars, consuming all sorts of new products made by "green" corporations, and so on. All we need to do is support the new "green" technologies (some of which, such as using agricultural crops to make fuels, are actually not green!) and be "good" about separating out waste that can be composted or reused in some form, and we can go on living pretty much as before – in an economy of perpetual growth and profits.

The very seriousness of the climate change problem arising from human-generated carbon dioxide and other greenhouse gas emissions has led to notions that it is merely necessary to reduce carbon footprints (a difficult problem in itself). The reality, though, is that there are numerous, interrelated, and growing ecological problems arising from a system geared to the infinitely expanding accumulation of capital. What needs to be reduced is not just *carbon footprints,* but *ecological foot-prints,* which means that economic expansion on the world level and especially in the rich countries needs to be reduced, even cease. At the same time, many poor countries need to expand their economies. The new principles that we could pro-mote, therefore, are ones of sustainable human development. This means *enough* for everyone and no more. Human development would certainly not be hindered, and could even be considerably enhanced for the benefit of all, by an emphasis on sustainable human, rather than unsustainable economic, development.

Another Economic System Is Not Just Possible – It's Essential

The foregoing analysis, if correct, points to the fact that the ecological crisis cannot be solved within the logic of the present system. The various suggestions for doing so have no hope of success. The system of world capitalism is clearly unsustainable in: (1) its quest for never ending accumulation of capital leading to production that must continually expand to provide profits; (2) its agriculture and food system that pollutes the environment and still does not allow universal access to a sufficient quantity and quality of food; (3) its rampant destruction of the environment; (4) its continually recreating and enhancing of the stratification of wealth within and bet-ween countries; and (5) its search for technological magic bullets as a way of avoid-ing the growing social and ecological problems arising from its own operations.

The transition to an ecological – which we believe must also be a socialist – economy will be a steep ascent and will not occur overnight. This is not a question of "storming the Winter Palace." Rather, it is a dynamic, multifaceted struggle for a new cultural compact and a new productive system. The struggle is ultimately against the *system of capital.* It must begin, however, by opposing the *logic of capital,* endeavoring in the here and now to create in the interstices of the system a new social metabolism rooted in egalitarianism, community, and a sustainable relation to the earth. The basis for the creation of sustainable human development must arise *from within* the system dominated by capital, *without being part of it,* just as the bourgeoisie itself arose in the "pores" of feudal society.[25] Eventually, these initiatives can become powerful enough to constitute the basis of a revolutionary new movement and society.

All over the world, such struggles in the interstices of capitalist society are now taking place, and are too numerous and too complex to be dealt with fully here. Indigenous peoples today, given a new basis as a result of the ongoing revolutionary struggle in Bolivia, are reinforcing a new ethic of responsibility to the earth. La Vía Campesina, a global peasant-farmer organization, is promoting new forms of eco-logical agriculture, as is Brazil's MST (Movimento dos Trabalhadores Rurais Sem Terra), as are Cuba and Venezuela. Recently, Venezulean President Hugo Chávez stressed the social and environmental reasons to work to get rid of the oil-rentier model in Venezuela, a major oil exporter.[26] The climate justice movement is demanding egalitarian and anti-capitalist solutions to the climate crisis. Everywhere radical, essentially anti-capitalist, strategies are emerging, based on other ethics and forms of organization, rather than the profit motive: ecovillages; the new urban environment promoted in Curitiba in Brazil and elsewhere; experiments in perma-culture, and community-supported agriculture, farming and industrial cooperatives in Venezuela, etc. The World Social Forum has given voice to many of these aspira-tions. As leading US environmentalist James Gustave Speth has stated: "The inter-national social movement for change – which refers to itself as 'the irresistible rise of global anti-capitalism' – is stronger than many may imagine and will grow stronger."[27]

The reason that the opposition to the logic of capitalism – ultimately seeking to displace the system altogether – will grow more imposing is that there is no alternative, if the earth as we know it, and humanity itself, are to survive. Here, the aims of ecology and socialism will necessarily meet. It will become increasingly clear that the distribution of land as well as food, health care, housing, etc. should be based on fulfilling human needs and not market forces. This is, of course, easier said than done. But it means making economic decisions through democratic processes occurring at local, regional, and multiregional levels. We must face such issues as: (1) How can we supply everyone with basic human needs of food, water, shelter, clothing, health care, educational and cultural opportunities? (2) How much of the economic production should be consumed and how much invested? and (3) How should the investments be directed? In the process, people must find the best ways to carry on these activities with positive interactions with nature – to improve the ecosystem. New forms of democracy will be needed, with emphasis on our responsibilities to each other, to one's own community as well as to communities around the world. Accomplishing this will, of course, require social planning at every level: local, regional, national, and international – which can only be successful to the extent that it is *of and by*, and not just ostensibly *for*, the people.[28]

An economic system that is democratic, reasonably egalitarian, and able to set limits on consumption will undoubtedly mean that people will live at a significantly lower level of consumption than what is sometimes referred to in the wealthy countries as a "middle class" lifestyle (which has never been universalized even in these societies). A simpler way of life, though "poorer" in gadgets and ultra-large luxury homes, can be richer culturally and in reconnecting with other people and nature, with people working the shorter hours needed to provide life's essentials. A large number of jobs in the wealthy capitalist countries are nonproductive and can be eliminated, indicating that the workweek can be considerably shortened in a more rationally organized economy. The slogan, sometimes seen on bumper stickers, "Live Simply so that Others May Simply Live," has little meaning in a capitalist society. Living a simple life, such as Helen and Scott Nearing did, demonstrating that it is possible to live a rewarding and interesting life while living simply, doesn't help the poor under present circumstances.[29] However, the slogan will have real importance in a society under social (rather than private) control, trying to satisfy the basic needs for all people.

Perhaps the Community Councils of Venezuela – where local people decide the priorities for social investment in their communities and receive the resources to implement them – are an example of planning for human needs at the local level. This is the way that such important needs as schools, clinics, roads, electricity, and running water can be met. In a truly transformed society, community councils can interact with regional and multiregional efforts. And the use of the surplus of society, after accounting for people's central needs, must be based on their decisions.[30]

The very purpose of the new sustainable system, which is the necessary outcome of these innumerable struggles (necessary in terms of survival and the fulfillment of human potential), must be to satisfy the basic material and non-material needs of all the people, while protecting the global environment as well as local and regional ecosystems. The environment is not something "external" to the human economy, as our present ideology tells us; it constitutes the essential life support systems for all living creatures. To heal the "metabolic rift" between the economy and the environment means new ways of living, manufacturing, growing food, transportation and so forth.[31] Such a society must be sustainable; and sustainability requires substantive equality, rooted in an egalitarian mode of production and consumption.

Concretely, people need to live closer to where they work, in ecologically designed housing built for energy efficiency as well as comfort, and in communities designed for public engagement, with sufficient places, such as parks and community centers, for coming together and recreation opportunities. Better mass transit within and between cities is needed to lessen the dependence on the use of the cars and trucks. Rail is significantly more energy efficient than trucks in moving freight (413 miles per gallon fuel per ton versus 155 miles for trucks) and causes fewer fatalities, while emitting lower amounts of greenhouse gases. One train can carry the freight of between 280 to 500 trucks. And it is estimated that one rail line can carry the same amount of people as numerous highway lanes.[32] Industrial production needs to be based on ecological design principles of "cradle-to-cradle," where products and buildings are designed for lower energy input, relying to as great degree as possible on natural lighting and heating/cooling, ease of construction as well as easy reuse, and ensuring that the manufacturing process produces little to no waste.[33]

Agriculture based on ecological principles and carried out by family farmers working on their own, or in cooperatives and with animals, reunited with the land that grows their food has been demonstrated to be not only as productive or more so than large-scale industrial production, but also to have less negative impact on local ecologies. In fact, the mosaic created by small farms interspersed with native vegetation is needed to preserve endangered species.[34]

A better existence for slum dwellers, approximately one-sixth of humanity, must be found. For the start, a system that requires a "planet of slums," as Mike Davis has put it, has to be replaced by a system that has room for food, water, homes, and employment for all.[35] For many, this may mean returning to farming, with adequate land and housing and other support provided.

Smaller cities may be needed, with people living closer to where their food is produced and industry more dispersed, and smaller scale.

Evo Morales, President of Bolivia, has captured the essence of the situation in his comments about changing from capitalism to a system that promotes "living well" instead of "living better." As he put it at the Copenhagen Climate Conference in December 2009: "Living better is to exploit human beings. It's plundering natural resources. It's egoism and individualism. Therefore, in those promises of capitalism, there is no solidarity or complementarity. There's no reciprocity. So that's why we're trying to think about other ways of living lives and living well, not living better. Living better is always at someone else's expense. Living better is at the expense of destroying the environment."[36]

The earlier experiences of transition to non-capitalist systems, especially in Soviet-type societies, indicate that this will not be easy, and that we need new conceptions of what constitutes socialism, sharply distinguished from those early abortive attempts. Twentieth-century revolutions typically arose in relatively poor, underdeveloped countries, which were quickly isolated and continually threatened from abroad. Such post-revolutionary societies usually ended up being heavily bureaucratic, with a minority in charge of the state effectively ruling over the remainder of the society. Many of the same hierarchical relations of production that characterize capitalism were reproduced. Workers remained proletarianized, while production was expanded for the sake of production itself. Real social improvements all too often existed side by side with extreme forms of social repression.[37]

Today we must strive to construct a genuine socialist system; one in which bureaucracy is kept in check, and power over production and politics truly resides with the people. Just as new challenges that confront us are changing in our time, so are the possibilities for the development of freedom and sustainability.

When Reverend Jeremiah Wright spoke to *Monthly Review*'s sixtieth anniversary gathering in September 2009, he kept coming back to the refrain "What about the people?" If there is to be any hope of significantly improving the conditions of the vast number of the world's inhabitants – many of whom are living hopelessly under the most severe conditions – while also preserving the earth as a livable planet, we need a system that constantly asks: "What about the people?" instead of "How much money can I make?" This is necessary, not only for humans, but for all the other species that share the planet with us and whose fortunes are intimately tied to ours.

Notes

1   For treatments of the role of speculation and debt in the US economy, see John Bellamy Foster and Fred Magdoff, *The Great Financial Crisis* (New York: Monthly Review Press, 2009) and Fred Magdoff and Michael Yates, *The ABCs of the Economic Crisis* (New York: Monthly Review Press, 2009).

2   "Fears for the World's Poor Countries as the Rich Grab Land to Grow Food," *Guardian*, July 3, 2009; "The Food Rush: Rising Demand in China and West Sparks African Land Grab," *Guardian*, July 3, 2009.

3   For a brief discussion of European expansion, see Harry Magdoff and Fred Magdoff, "Approaching Socialism," *Monthly Review* 57, no. 3 (July–August 2005), 19–61. On the relation of oil and gas to the wars in Iraq and Afghanistan, see Michael T. Klare, *Rising Powers, Shrinking Planet* (New York: Metropolitan Books, 2008).

4   British Petroleum, *BP Statistical Review of World Energy,* June 2009, http://bp.com; John Bellamy Foster, *The Ecological Revolution* (New York: Monthly Review Press, 2009), 85–105.

5   David A. Vaccari, "Phosphorus Famine: A Looming Crisis," *Scientific American,* June 2009:54–59.

6   Joseph A. Schumpeter, *Business Cycles* (New York: McGraw Hill, 1939), vol. 1, 73.

7   Adam Smith, *The Wealth of Nations*, (New York: Modern Library, 1937), 14.

8   Duncan K. Foley, *Adam's Fallacy* (Cambridge, MA: Harvard University Press, 2006).

9   "Profit 'Is Not Satanic,' Barclays Says, after Goldman Invokes Jesus," Bloomberg.com, November 4, 2009.

10   Frans de Waal. "Our Kinder, Gentler Ancestors," *Wall Street Journal,* October 3, 2009.

11   J. Kiley Hamlin, Karen Wynn, and Paul Bloom, "Social Evaluation by Preverbal Infants," *Nature* 50, no. 2 (November 22, 2007), 557–559; Nicholas Wade. "We May be Born with an Urge to Help," *New York Times*, December 1, 2009. Some recent research in this regard is usefully summarized in Jeremy Rifkin, *The Empathic Civilization* (New York: Penguin, 2009), 128–34.

12   Karl Polanyi, *The Great Transformation* (Boston: Beacon, 1944), 46.

13   John Dewey, *Selections from the Encyclopedia of the Social Sciences* (New York: Macmillan, 197), 536.

14   See C. B. Macpherson, *The Political Theory of Possessive Individualism* (Oxford: Oxford University Press, 1962).

15   For a fuller discussion of these issues see Magdoff and Magdoff, "Approaching Socialism," 19–23.

16   Benjamin Barber, "A Revolution in Spirit," *The Nation,* February 9, 2009, http://
      thenation.com/doc/20090209/barber.

17   Paul Hawken, Amory Lovins, and L. Hunter Lovins, *Natural Capitalism* (Boston: Little,
      Brown and Co., 1999). For a detailed critique of the ideology of "natural capitalism," see F.E.
      Trainer, "Natural Capitalism Cannot Overcome Resource Limits," http://mnforsustain.org.

18   "Gucci Joins Other Fashion Players in Committing to Protect Rainforests," *Financial
      Times,* November 5, 2009.

19   Daniel McGinn, "The Greenest Big Companies in America," *Newsweek,* September 21,
      2009. http://newsweek.com.

20   Fred Magdoff, "The Political Economy and Ecology of Biofuels," *Monthly Review* 60, no.
      3 (July–August 2008), 34–50.

21   James Lovelock, *The Revenge of Gaia* (New York: Perseus, 2006), 87–105, Hansen,
      Storms of My Grandchildren, 198–204. On the continuing dangers of nuclear power,
      even in its latest incarnations, see Robert D. Furber, James C. Warf, and Sheldon C. Plot-
      kin, "The Future of Nuclear Power," *Monthly Review* 59, no. 9 (February 2008), 38–48.

22   Friends of the Earth, "Subprime Carbon?" (March 2009), http://foe.org/suprime carbon,
      and *A Dangerous Obsession* (November 2009), http://foe.co.uk; James Hansen, "Wor-
      shipping the Temple of Doom" (May 5, 2009), http://columbia.edu; Larry Lohman,
      "Climate Crisis: Social Science Crisis," forthcoming in M. Voss, ed., *Kimawandel*
      (Wiesbaden: VS-Verlag), http://tni.org//archives/archives/lohmann/sciencecrisis.pdf.

23   See Hansen, *Storms of My Grandchildren,* 172–177, 193–194, 208–222.

24   See Aubrey Meyer, *Contraction and Convergence* (Devon: Schumacher Society, 2000);
      Tom Athansiou and Paul Baer, *Dead Heat* (New York: Seven Stories Press, 2002).

25   Karl Marx and Frederick Engels, *Collected Works* (New York: International Publishers,
      1975), vol. 6, 327; Karl Marx, *Capital,* vol. 3 (London: Penguin, 1981), 447–448.

26   "Chávez Stresses the Importance of Getting Rid of the Oil Rentier Model in Venezuela,"
      MRzine, http://mrzine.org (January 11, 2010).

27   James Gustave Speth, *The Bridge at the Edge of the World* (New Haven: Yale University
      Press, 2008), 195.

28   On planning, see Magdoff and Magdoff, "Approaching Socialism," 36–61.

29   See Helen and Scott Nearing, *Living the Good Life* (New York: Schocken, 1970). Scott
      Nearing was for many years the author of the "World Events" column in *Monthly Review.*

30   See Iain Bruce, *The Real Venezuela* (London: Pluto Press, 2008), 139–175.

31   On the metabolic rift, see Foster, *The Ecological Revolution,* 161–200.

32   C. James Kruse, et al., "A Modal Comparison of Domestic Freight Transportation Effects
      on the General Public, Center for Ports and Waterways," Texas Transportation Institute,
      2007; http://americanwaterways.com; Mechanical Database website, Rail vs. Truck
      Industry, accessed; http://mechdb.com January 17, 2010.

33   William McDonough and Michael Braungart, *Cradle to Cradle* (New York: North Point
      Press, 2002).

34   See Miguel A. Altieri, "Agroecology, Small Farms, and Food Sovereignty," *Monthly
      Review* 61, no. 3 (July–August 2009), 102–113.

35   Mike Davis, *Planet of the Slums* (London; Verso, 2007).

36   Interview of Evo Morales by Amy Goodman, *Democracy Now,* December 17, 2009,
      http://democracynow.org/2009/12/17/bolivian_president_evo_morales_on_climate.

37   See Paul M. Sweezy, *Post-Revolutionary Society* (New York: Monthly Review Press, 1980).

26

Pathways of Human Development and Carbon Emissions Embodied in Trade (2012)

Julia K. Steinberger, J. Timmons Roberts, Glen P. Peters, and Giovanni Baiocchi

It has long been assumed that human development depends on economic growth, that national economic expansion in turn requires greater energy use and, therefore, increased greenhouse-gas emissions. These interdependences are the topic of current research. Scarcely explored, however, is the impact of international trade: although some nations develop socio-economically and import high-embodied-carbon products, it is likely that carbon-exporting countries gain significantly fewer benefits. Here, we use new consumption-based measures of national carbon emissions [1] to explore how the relationship between human development and carbon changes when we adjust national emission rates for trade. Without such adjustment of emissions, some nations seem to be getting far better development 'bang' for the carbon 'buck' than others, who are showing scant gains for disproportionate shares of global emissions. Adjusting for the transfer of emissions through trade explains many of these outliers, but shows that further socio-economic benefits are accruing to carbon-importing rather than carbon-exporting countries. We also find that high life expectancies are compatible with low carbon emissions but high incomes are not. Finally, we see that, despite strong international trends, there is no deterministic industrial development trajectory: there is great diversity in pathways, and national histories do not necessarily follow the global trends.

Seriously addressing climate change requires drastically cutting carbon emissions. To 'avoid dangerous climate change' [2] would require rapid reductions in emissions, from 1.2 tC per capita on average in 2005 (ref. 3) to well below 1tC per capita by 2050, with proposals ranging from 0.35 to 0.2tC per capita (refs 4, 5). These emission reductions, however, need to be achieved in an equitable manner [2]. The implica-

Julia K. Steinberger, J. Timmons Roberts, Glen P. Peters, and Giovanni Baiocchi. 2012. "Pathways of Human Development and Carbon Emissions Embodied in Trade". In *Nature Climate Change*, 2(2): 81–85. Reproduced with permission from Nature Publishing Group.

tions of such reductions for national economies and human development are at the core of international disagreements over addressing climate change. As a result, the empirical links between fossil-fuel-based energy and economic and human progress are now central topics of research [6–10]. High life expectancy is attainable at ever-declining levels of income [11], and economic growth is increasingly challenged as the precondition of development [12]. Moreover, human development has been steadily decoupling from energy and carbon emissions [13].

Recently, the relative decarbonization of wealthy nations' economies has been questioned, because these countries may be benefiting not only from the carbon emitted within their national territory (which are recorded in national and international statistics), but also from the carbon emissions embodied in the goods and services they import [1, 14–18]. Several pioneering studies based on environmentally extended input-output methodologies have recently provided the first robust estimates of international trade-corrected consumption-based carbon [14, 15] and greenhouse-gas emissions [16]. Conventional carbon accounting covers emissions occurring in the country's territory, and these are the basis of the Kyoto Protocol agreements. Consumption-based accounting corrects territorial emissions by adding emissions generated to produce imported goods and services, and subtracting those generated to produce exports. This method has now been extended to estimate consumption-based emissions for a large set of countries in the time span 1990–2008 (ref. 1).

This Letter focuses on differences between consumption-based and territorial emissions in their relation to human development. The underlying factors causing certain countries to be net importers or exporters of carbon are thus beyond its scope. In fact, the drivers of traded carbon and energy have proved elusive, and cannot simply be ascribed to higher environmental standards or cleaner production patterns in one country or region driving carbon-intensive production to another [17, 18].

Our hypothesis is that consumption-based emissions, which include the carbon embodied in all goods and services consumed in a country, should reflect the socio-economic benefits (measured by life expectancy and income) accruing from these emission processes better than territorial emissions. It has already been shown that carbon emissions per unit gross domestic product (GDP) converge to similar values in a consumption perspective [19].

It is currently unknown, however, how consumption-based emissions related to life expectancy and income. Figure 26.1 shows the relationship between carbon emissions and life expectancy and GDP per capita, with and without corrections for carbon embodied in trade (using consumer emissions from ref. 1). In Fig. 26.1, we show countries and regions as horizontal arrows moving from territorial to consumption-based carbon emissions. The start of the arrow thus corresponds to conventional national accounting (such as was used in the Kyoto Protocol), whereas the centre of head of the arrow takes into account the emissions embodied in trade. Carbon-exporting countries move from right to left ([lighter] arrows, solid lines), and carbon-importing countries move from left to right (dashed lines). Countries whose total emissions are mostly unaffected by trade are shown as circles. The area of the points is proportional to population.

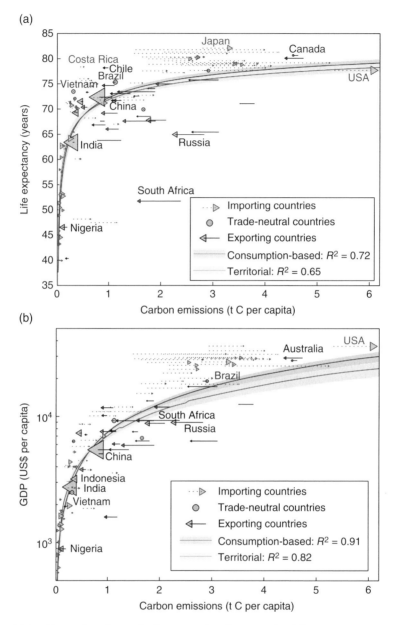

Figure 26.1   Correcting for trade: how moving from territorial to consumption-based emissions changes the relation between carbon and human development. **a,b,** Each arrow represents a country/region moving horizontally from territorial (arrow base) to consumption-based (centre of arrowhead) carbon emissions, in the year 2004. The vertical axes are life expectancy (**a**) and income (**b**). The arrowhead size represents national population. [...]

As expected, both territorial and consumption-based carbon emissions are highly correlated to the human development indicators shown in Fig. 26.1. However, the shape and strength of the relationship between carbon and income is very different from the one between carbon and life expectancy. Carbon emissions scale roughly proportionally with income, with a high goodness of fit, whereas life expectancy grows with carbon emissions in the lower range, but then seems to decouple, reaching a level where higher emissions do not generate much benefit, and has a lower goodness of fit. These different behaviours can be seen in Fig. 26.1: life expectancy has a turning point, which is absent for income (the income–carbon plot is linear in log–log space). Adjusting emissions for international trade tends to move the countries closer to the fit curves and improves the goodness of fit R^2. Countries that are above (same carbon emissions, higher socio-economic performance), or to the left (same socio-economic performance, lower carbon emissions), of others in Fig. 26.1 are more carbon efficient in delivering socio-economic wellbeing to their populations.

Most of the carbon-exporting countries and regions are grouped at intermediate life expectancy (between 63 and 75 years) and income (between US$2,000 and US$12,000 per capita). They perform worse than non-exporting countries and the global trend, in terms of socio-economic achievement given their level of carbon emissions. Even when their emissions are corrected for the embodied carbon in international trade, most of them are still below other countries and the global trend. This result indicates that there is a systematic disadvantage, in terms of socio-economic benefits, for carbon-exporting economies. In addition to China and India, which are relatively close to the global trend, these countries are mainly from the former Soviet Union, Eastern Europe, Middle East, and South Africa. They are the fossil fuel-exporting and raw material-exporting economies. This suggests the double negative of specializing in natural resource extraction and earlier stages of processing and manufacturing [20, 21], and can be interpreted as evidence for the environmentally unequal exchange theory [22].

The carbon-importing countries, in contrast, are an extremely diverse group. They consist of high-socio-economic-status OECD (Organisation for Economic Co-operation and Development) countries (life expectancies above 75 years and national average income above US$12,000 per capita), some intermediate countries from Asia and Latin America and most of the countries with low socio-economic status (life expectancies below 63 years, income below US$2,000 per capita), which are overwhelmingly African. The membership of the carbon-importing club thus consists of two extremes: the most socio-economically well off, and the poorest of the poor. The plight of development is particularly acute for the poorest countries, which are constrained to import not just energy itself, but also carbon-intensive goods and services from the global market, sometimes relying on large amounts of foreign assistance for this purpose [23]. These countries are thus doubly vulnerable to price increases in fossil fuels.

Importantly, at lower incomes and carbon emissions the consumption-based fit curve lies below the territorial ones (although this difference is not visible in Fig. 26.1b, because of the steepness of the curves; see Supplementary Information for details). This indicates that low income levels require higher carbon emissions than previously thought, when trade is taken into consideration. The leftwards shift of carbon-exporting middle-income economies, and rightwards shift of importing high-income countries, tends to dispel the apparent 'environmental Kuznets curve', according to which, at very high levels of income, economic growth results in a decline of emissions. This supports the finding that the environmental Kuznets curve for carbon per capita, already contested for territorial emissions [24], does not exist after correcting for embedded carbon emissions of imports [14, 25, 26]. Indeed, the monetary wealth achieved by most OECD countries corresponds to consumption-based carbon emissions significantly above the territorial emissions taken into account by the Kyoto Protocol [1].

Consumption-based emissions are consequently the most appropriate for comparison with human development. The three-variable plot (Fig. 26.2) enables the simultaneous visualization of life expectancy, consumption-based emissions and income, and thus summarizes important global patterns and variation in 2004. A life expectancy between 75 and 80 years of age was achieved by countries with emissions ranging from a modest 0.5 tC per capita for Costa Rica to 6.2 tC per capita for the United States. The income range for these countries was also extreme, from US$4,500 (Albania) to US$36,000 per capita (United States again). If we zoom in on the countries with lifespan of over 70 years and less than 1 tC per capita (the 'Goldemberg corner' [13]), we see a large range in possible incomes, from US$2,500 to US$12,000 per capita. The countries in this virtuous group are geographically diverse: from Latin America, Asia, Eastern Europe and North Africa.

The large range in carbon emissions and incomes at the highest life expectancies could be seen as good news. However, there is a clear pattern within these ranges: the countries at the lowest carbon ranges of their life-expectancy cohort are also the ones at the lowest incomes. This suggests that higher incomes make lower carbon profiles difficult, especially if we factor in embodied carbon in imports.

Our final objective is to move beyond global trends to find examples of countries with more sustainable pathways of economic and social development, and to assess whether their relative sustainability holds up even when their emissions from the import of goods and services are taken into account.

We address this question by observing the development trajectories of 13 key countries and regions from 1990 to 2005, in terms of our four variables: life expectancy, income and per capita carbon emissions (both territorial and consumption based), and comparing these trajectories with the global trend lines. The countries in Fig. 26.3 were selected for geographical diversity, size and interest, and they represent over half of the world's population and carbon emissions.

Although the typical trajectory in Fig. 26.3 is one of growth in all three dimensions, the Russian Federation and many African countries suffered decreases in life expectancy over the period, due to political and economic collapse and the AIDS epidemic respectively. The trajectories in Fig. 26.3 are thus upwards, except when indicated otherwise. The UK experienced a significant decrease in its territorial emissions per capita, although emissions grew when embodied emissions in trade were considered [27, 28]. For some countries, the trajectories show the consequences of political upheaval (Russian Federation) and economic crises (Chile, Japan).

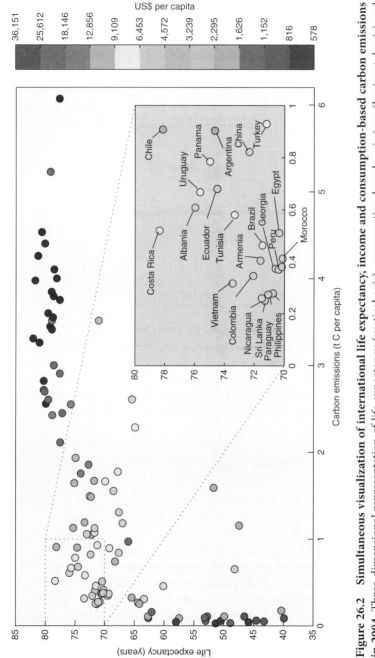

Figure 26.2   Simultaneous visualization of international life expectancy, income and consumption-based carbon emissions in 2004. Three-dimensional representation of life expectancy (vertical axis), consumption-based emissions (horizontal axis) and income (colour scale [see online article for colour scale]). The inset is the 'Goldemberg corner', with life expectancy over 70 years and less than one tonne of carbon emissions per capita. The highest life-expectancy levels are attained at a wide range of carbon emissions and incomes.

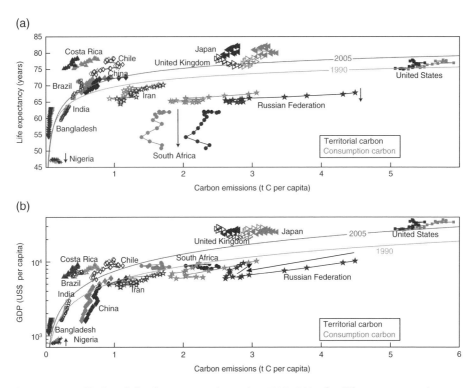

Figure 26.3   National development trajectories 1990–2005 for life expectancy, income and territorial and consumption-based emissions. a,b, Territorial-emission trajectories are dark grey; consumption-based ones are pale grey, shown for life expectancy (**a**) and income (**b**), and contrasted with the global fit curves for consumption-based carbon in 1990 and 2005. The trajectories are upwards except when the arrows indicate otherwise. South Africa's trajectory in **b** is clockwise.

Overall, the development trajectories in Fig. 26.3 are consistent with the trends seen in Figs 26.1 and 26.2: high life expectancy is attainable at a large range of carbon emissions, whereas income is much more closely linked with carbon. However, and perhaps surprisingly, several countries do not follow the global trends (shown for 1990 and 2005, consumption-based emissions): in general, the growth in socio-economic benefits is larger than the growth in carbon emissions could account for, if the trend curves were followed. This explains why the global trend curves are steadily moving upwards, as we have shown previously [13]. This is evidence of relative, but not absolute, decoupling of socio-economic gains from carbon-intensive processes. Moreover, the diversity of development pathways shown in Fig. 26.3 is evidence that there is no deterministic single development trajectory, despite the fact that all the countries shown are linked by global trade and rely to a large extent on similar technologies.

Ideally, nations could achieve all three of the objectives required for sustainable development: low carbon emissions, high life expectancy and high income. However, the evidence from our analysis demonstrates that it is indeed possible to achieve

Table 26.1 Regression results for the trend curves shown in Figs 26.1 and 26.3

	Number of countries/regions and fraction of global population	Year	Emission accounting	R^2	Ordinate at origin a	Slope b	Saturation value
Fig. 26.1a: life expectancy	109; 99.1%	2004	Territorial	0.65	2.92(0.02)	−0.23 (0.02)	90.03
			Consumption based: MRIO	0.72	2.89 (0.02)	−0.26 (0.02)	90.03
Fig. 26.1b: income	106; 97.9%	2004	Territorial	0.82	8.85 (0.05)	0.68 (0.03)	
			Consumption based: MRIO	0.91	8.91 (0.03)	0.77 (0.02)	
Fig. 26.3a: life expectancy	108; 98.9%	1990	Consumption based: TSTRD	0.78	2.85 (0.02)	−0.24 (0.01)	86.8
	109; 99.1%	2005		0.71	2.91 (0.02)	−0.27 (0.02)	90.5
Fig. 26.3b: income	104; 97.5%	1990	Consumption based: TSTRD	0.81	8.59 (0.06)	0.70 (0.04)	
	105; 97.9%	2005		0.90	8.92 (0.03)	0.77 (0.03)	

Values in parentheses are the standard errors of the coefficients.

simultaneous environmental and social sustainability (in the form of lower carbon emissions and high life expectancy), but only at levels of income below US$12,000 per capita (Fig. 26.2). Indeed, the coupling between economic activity and carbon emissions (Fig. 26.1b) is stronger than the correlation between life expectancy and carbon emissions (Fig. 26.1a), or between life expectancy and income. This enables certain combinations of desirable outcomes, but not all: high life expectancies and high incomes are compatible, so are high life expectancies and low carbon emissions, but economic and environmental goals seem to be at odds with each other, at least at the highest levels of GDP per capita.

In other words, a moderate income is currently a necessary (but not sufficient) requirement for environmental sustainability: 'necessary' because no high-income country has carbon emissions below 1 tC per capita when correcting for embodied carbon in imports; 'not sufficient' because moderate incomes do not guarantee either high life expectancy or low carbon emissions.

This study suggests avenues for further research. The causal factors underlying development pathways need to be explored to identify viable low-carbon transitions going forward. A better understanding of the obvious regional differences in the national trajectories seen in Fig. 26.3 is of clear interest. There is much further work to do on scenarios, projecting current trends of nations and groups of nations that are moving in a measurable direction. What will the structure of global pathways look like if these countries continue in the directions they are heading? Can this approach better inform socio-economic elements of global climate models? The implications of these findings are substantial, then, both for climate modellers and for development planners. For planners and decision-makers, the findings provide hope that national choices and pathways matter, and policies are available that do not prioritize growth at the expense of climate stability and a long life for our societies.

References

1   Peters, G. P., Minx, J. C., Weber, C. L. & Edenhofer, O. Growth in emission transfers via international trade from 1990 to 2008. *Proc. Natl Acad. Sci. USA* 108, 8903–8908 (2011).

2   UNFCCC *United Nations Framework Convention on Climate Change* (United Nations, 1992); available at http://unfccc.int/resource/docs/convkp/conveng.pdf.

3   Boden, T. A., Marland, G. & Andres, R. J. *Global, Regional, and National Fossil-Fuel CO_2 Emissions* (Carbon Dioxide Information Analysis Center (CDIAC), Oak Ridge National Laboratory, US Department of Energy, 2009).

4   Meinshausen, M. *et al.* The RCP greenhouse gas concentrations and their extensions from 1765 to 2300. *Climatic Change* 109, 213–41 (2011).

5   Baer, P., Athanasiou, T. & Kartha, S. in *The Right to Development in a Climate Constrained World: The Greenhouse Development Rights Framework* 1–95 (Heinrich Böll Foundation, Christian Aid, EcoEquity and the Stockholm Environment Institute, 2007); available at http://ecoequity.org/docs/TheGDRsFramework-first.pdf.

6   Cottrell, F. *Energy and Society. The Relation between Energy, Social Change, and Economic Development* (McGraw-Hill Book Company, 1955).

7   Mazur, A. & Rosa, E. Energy and life-style. *Science* 186, 607–10 (1974).

8   UNDP *Energy as an Instrument for Socio-Economic Development* (United Nations Development Programme, 1995).

9   Goldemberg, J. & Johansson, T. B. in *World Energy Assessment. Overview 2004 Update* 1–85 (United Nations Development Programme, United Nations Department of Economic and Social Affairs and the World Energy Council, 2004); available at http://www.undp.org/energy/weaover2004.htm.

10 Wilkinson, P., Smith, K. R., Joffe, M. & Haines, A. A global perspective on energy: Health effects and injustices. *Lancet* 370, 965–78 (2007).

11 Preston, S. H. The changing relation between mortality and level of economic development. *Int. J. Epidemiol.* 36, 484–90 (2007).

12 UNDP *Human Development Report 2010. The Real Wealth of Nations: Pathways to Human Development* (United Nations Development Programme, 2010).

13 Steinberger, J. K. & Roberts, J. T. From constraint to sufficiency: The decoupling of energy and carbon from human needs, 1975–2005. *Ecol. Econ.* 70, 425–33 (2010).

14 Peters, G. P. & Hertwich, E. G. CO_2 embodied in international trade with implications for global climate policy. *Environ. Sci. Technol.* 42, 1401–7 (2008).

15 Davis, S. J. & Caldeira, K. Consumption-based accounting of CO_2 emissions. *Proc. Natl Acad. Sci. USA* 107, 5687–92 (2010).

16 Hertwich, E. G. & Peters, G. P. Carbon footprint of nations: A global, trade-linked analysis. *Environ. Sci. Technol.* 43, 6414–20 (2009).

17 Levinson, A. Offshoring pollution: Is the United States increasingly importing polluted goods? *Rev. Environ. Econ. Policy* 4, 63–83 (2010).

18 Peters, G. P. Policy update: Managing carbon leakage. *Carbon Manage.* 1, 35–7 (2010).

19 Caldeira, K. & Davis, S. J. Accounting for carbon dioxide emissions: A matter of time. *Proc. Natl Acad. Sci. USA* 108, 8533–4 (2011).

20 Roberts, J. T. & Parks, B. C. *A Climate of Injustice. Global Inequality, North–South Politics, and Climate Policy* (MIT Press, 2007).

21 Dicken, P. *Global Shift: Mapping the Changing Contours of the World Economy Sixth Edition* (Sage, 2010).

22 Bunker, S. G. Modes of extraction, unequal exchange, and the progressive underdevelopment of an extreme periphery: The Brazilian Amazon, 1600–1980. *Am. J. Sociol.* 89, 1017–64 (1984).

23 Unruh, G. C. & Carrillo-Hermosilla, J. Globalizing carbon lock-in. *Energ. Policy* 34, 1185–97 (2006).

24 Stern, D. Between estimates of the emissions-income elasticity. *Ecol. Econ.* 69, 2173–82 (2010).

25 Rothman, D. S. Environmental Kuznets curves – real progress or passing the buck? A case for consumption-based approaches. *Ecol. Econ.* 25, 177–94 (1998).

26 Suri, V. & Chapman, D. Economic growth, trade and energy: Implications for the environmental Kuznets curve. *Ecol. Econ.* 25, 195–208 (1998).

27 Wiedmann, T. *et al.* A carbon footprint time series of the UK – results from a Multi-Region Inpu–Output model. *Econ. Syst. Res.* 22, 19–42 (2010).

28 Baiocchi, G. & Minx, J. C. Understanding changes in the UK's CO_2 emissions: A global perspective. *Environ. Sci. Technol.* 44, 1177–84 (2010).

29 UN *World Urbanization Prospects: The 2007 Revision* (United Nations, Department of Economic and Social Affairs, Population Division, 2008).

30 The World Bank *World Development Indicators* (World Bank, 2010); available at http://data.worldbank.org/data-catalog.

27

Introduction to *Towards a Green Economy: Pathways to Sustainable Development and Poverty Eradication* (2012)

United Nations Environment Programme (UNEP)

Setting the Stage for a Green Economy Transition

From Crisis to Opportunity

The last two years have seen the idea of a "green economy" float out of its specialist moorings in environmental economics and into the mainstream of policy discourse. It is found increasingly in the words of heads of state and finance ministers, in the text of G20 communiques, and discussed in the context of sustainable development and poverty eradication.

This recent traction for a green economy concept has no doubt been aided by widespread disillusionment with the prevailing economic paradigm, a sense of fatigue emanating from the many concurrent crises and market failures experienced during the very first decade of the new millennium, including especially the financial and economic crisis of 2008. But at the same time, there is increasing evidence of a way forward, a new economic paradigm – one in which material wealth is not delivered perforce at the expense of growing environmental risks, ecological scarcities and social disparities.

Mounting evidence also suggests that transitioning to a green economy has sound economic and social justification. There is a strong case emerging for a redoubling of efforts by both governments as well as the private sector to engage in such an economic transformation. For governments, this would include leveling the playing field for greener products by phasing out antiquated subsidies, reforming policies and providing new incentives, strengthening market infrastructure

UNEP. 2012. *Towards a Green Economy: Pathways to Sustainable Development and Poverty Eradication.* Nairobi: United Nations Environment Programme. pp. 14–24. Reproduced with permission from UNEP.

and market-based mechanisms, redirecting public investment, and greening public procurement. For the private sector, this would involve understanding and sizing the true opportunity represented by green economy transitions across a number of key sectors, and responding to policy reforms and price signals through higher levels of financing and investment.

An Era of Capital Misallocation   Several concurrent crises have unfolded during the last decade: climate, biodiversity, fuel, food, water, and more recently, in the global financial system. Accelerating carbon emissions indicate a mounting threat of climate change, with potentially disastrous human consequences. The fuel price shock of 2007–2008 and the related skyrocketing food and commodity prices, reflect both structural weaknesses and unresolved risks. Forecasts by the International Energy Agency (IEA) and others of rising fossil fuel demand and energy prices suggest an ongoing dependence as the world economy struggles to recover and grow.

Currently, there is no international consensus on the problem of global food security or on possible solutions for how to nourish a population of 9 billion by 2050. [...] Freshwater scarcity is already a global problem, and forecasts suggest a growing gap by 2030 between annual freshwater demand and renewable supply. The outlook for improved sanitation still looks bleak for over 1.1 billion people and 844 million people still lack access to clean drinking water. Collectively, these crises are severely impacting the possibility of sustaining prosperity worldwide and achieving the Millennium Development Goals (MDGs) for reducing extreme poverty. They are also compounding persistent social problems, such as job losses, socio-economic insecurity, disease and social instability.

The causes of these crises vary, but at a fundamental level they all share a common feature: the gross misallocation of capital. During the last two decades, much capital was poured into property, fossil fuels and structured financial assets with embedded derivatives. However, relatively little in comparison was invested in renewable energy, energy efficiency, public transportation, sustainable agriculture, ecosystem and biodiversity protection, and land and water conservation.

Most economic development and growth strategies encouraged rapid accumulation of physical, financial and human capital, but at the expense of excessive depletion and degradation of natural capital, which includes the endowment of natural resources and ecosystems. By depleting the world's stock of natural wealth – often irreversibly – this pattern of development and growth has had detrimental impacts on the well-being of current generations and presents tremendous risks and challenges for the future. The recent multiple crises are symptomatic of this pattern.

Existing policies and market incentives have contributed to this problem of capital misallocation because they allow businesses to run up significant, largely unaccounted for, and unchecked social and environmental externalities. To reverse such misallocation requires better public policies, including pricing and regulatory measures, to change the perverse incentives that drive this capital misallocation and ignore social and environmental externalities. At the same time, appropriate regulations, policies and public investments that foster changes in the pattern of private investment are increasingly being adopted around the world, especially in developing countries (UNEP 2010).

Why is this Report Needed Now?   UNEP's report, *Towards a Green Economy*, aims to debunk several myths and misconceptions about greening the global economy, and provides timely and practical guidance to policy makers on what reforms they need to unlock the productive and employment potential of a green economy.

Perhaps the most prevalent myth is that there is an inescapable trade-off between environmental sustainability and economic progress. There is now substantial evidence that the greening of economies neither inhibits wealth creation nor employment opportunities. To the contrary, many green sectors provide significant opportunities for investment, growth and jobs. For this to occur, however, new enabling conditions are required to promote such investments in the transition to a green economy, which in turn calls for urgent action by policy makers.

A second myth is that a green economy is a luxury only wealthy countries can afford, or worse, a ruse to restrain development and perpetuate poverty in developing countries. Contrary to this perception, numerous examples of greening transitions can be found in the developing world, which should be replicated elsewhere. *Towards a Green Economy* brings some of these examples to light and highlights their scope for wider application.

UNEP's work on green economy raised the visibility of this concept in 2008, particularly through a call for a Global Green New Deal (GGND). The GGND recommended a package of public investments and complementary policy and pricing reforms aimed at kick-starting a transition to a green economy, while reinvigorating economies and jobs and addressing persistent poverty. Designed as a timely and appropriate policy response to the economic crisis, the GGND proposal was an early output from the United Nations' Green Economy Initiative. This initiative, coordinated by UNEP, was one of the nine Joint Crisis Initiatives undertaken by the Secretary-General of the UN and his Chief Executives Board in response to the 2008 economic and financial crisis.

Towards a Green Economy – the main output of the Green Economy Initiative – demonstrates that the greening of economies need not be a drag on growth. On the contrary, the greening of economies has the potential to be a new engine of growth, a net generator of decent jobs and a vital strategy to eliminate persistent poverty. The report also seeks to motivate policy makers to create the enabling conditions for increased investments in a transition to a green economy in three ways.

First, the report makes an economic case for shifting both public and private investment to transform key sectors that are critical to greening the global economy. It illustrates through examples how added employment through green jobs offsets job losses in a transition to a green economy.

Second, it shows how a green economy can reduce persistent poverty across a range of important sectors – agriculture, forestry, freshwater, fisheries and energy. Sustainable forestry and ecologically friendly farming methods help conserve soil fertility and water resources. This is especially critical for subsistence farming, upon which almost 1.3 billion people depend for their livelihoods.

Third, it provides guidance on policies to achieve this shift by reducing or eliminating environmentally harmful or perverse subsidies, addressing market failures created by externalities or imperfect information, creating market-based incentives, implementing appropriate regulatory frameworks, initiating green public procurement and by stimulating investment.

What is a Green Economy?

UNEP defines a green economy as one that results in "improved human well-being and social equity, while significantly reducing environmental risks and ecological scarcities". In its simplest expression, a green economy is low-carbon, resource efficient, and socially inclusive. In a green economy, growth in income and employment are driven by public and private investments that reduce carbon emissions and pollution, enhance energy and resource efficiency, and prevent the loss of biodiversity and ecosystem services.

These investments need to be catalysed and supported by targeted public expenditure, policy reforms and regulation changes. The development path should maintain, enhance and, where necessary, rebuild natural capital as a critical economic asset and as a source of public benefits. This is especially important for poor people whose livelihoods and security depend on nature.

The key aim for a transition to a green economy is to enable economic growth and investment while increasing environmental quality and social inclusiveness. Critical to attaining such an objective is to create the conditions for public and private investments to incorporate broader environmental and social criteria. In addition, the main indicators of economic performance, such as growth in Gross Domestic Product (GDP) need to be adjusted to account for pollution, resource depletion, declining ecosystem services, and the distributional consequences of natural capital loss to the poor.

A major challenge is reconciling the competing economic development aspirations of rich and poor countries in a world economy that is facing increasing climate change, energy insecurity and ecological scarcity. A green economy can meet this challenge by offering a development path that reduces carbon dependency, promotes resource and energy efficiency and lessens environmental degradation. As economic growth and investments become less dependent on liquidating environmental assets and sacrificing environmental quality, both rich and poor countries can attain more sustainable economic development.

The concept of a green economy does not replace sustainable development; but there is a growing recognition that achieving sustainability rests almost entirely on getting the economy right. Decades of creating new wealth through a "brown economy" model based on fossil fuels have not substantially addressed social marginalisation, environmental degradation and resource depletion. In addition, the world is still far from delivering on the Millennium Development Goals by 2015. The next section looks at the important linkages between the concept of a green economy and sustainable development.

A Green Economy and Sustainable Development   In 2009, the UN General Assembly decided to hold a summit in Rio de Janeiro in 2012 (Rio+20) to celebrate the 20th anniversary of the first Rio Earth Summit in 1992. Two of the agenda items for Rio+20 are, "Green Economy in the Context of Sustainable Development and Poverty Eradication", and "International Framework for Sustainable Development". With the green economy now firmly established on the international policy agenda, it is useful to review and clarify the linkages between a green economy and sustainable development.

Most interpretations of sustainability take as their starting point the consensus reached by the World Commission on Environment and Development (WCED) in 1987, which defined sustainable development as "development that meets the needs of the present without compromising the ability of future generations to meet their own needs".

Economists are generally comfortable with this broad interpretation of sustainability, as it is easily translatable into economic terms: an increase in well-being today should not result in reducing well-being tomorrow. That is, future generations should be entitled to at least the same level of economic opportunities – and thus at least the same level of economic welfare – as is available to current generations.

As a result, economic development today must ensure that future generations are left no worse off than current generations. Or, as some economists have succinctly expressed it, per capita welfare should not be declining over time. According to this view, it is the total stock of capital employed by the economic system, including natural capital, which determines the full range of economic opportunities, and thus well-being, available to both current and future generations.

Society must decide how best to use its total capital stock today to increase current economic activities and welfare. Society must also decide how much it needs to save or accumulate for tomorrow, and ultimately, for the well-being of future generations.

However, it is not simply the aggregate stock of capital in the economy that may matter but also its composition, in particular whether current generations are using up one form of capital to meet today's needs. For example, much of the interest in sustainable development is driven by concern that economic development may be leading to rapid accumulation of physical and human capital at the expense of excessive depletion and degradation of natural capital. The major concern is that by irreversibly depleting the world's stock of natural wealth, today's development path will have detrimental implications for the well-being of future generations.

One of the first economic studies to make the connection between this capital approach to sustainable development and a green economy was the 1989 book *Blueprint for a Green Economy*. The authors argued that because today's economies are biased towards depleting natural capital to secure growth, sustainable development is unachievable. A green economy that values environmental assets, employs pricing policies and regulatory changes to translate these values into market incentives, and adjusts the economy's measure of GDP for environmental losses is essential to ensuring the well-being of current and future generations.

As pointed out by the *Blueprint for a Green Economy* authors, a major issue in the capital approach to sustainable development is whether substitution among different forms of capital – human capital, physical capital and natural capital – is possible. A strong conservationist perspective might maintain that the natural component of the total capital stock must be kept intact, as measured in physical terms. However, this may be questioned in practice, especially in the context of developing countries, if natural capital is relatively abundant while physical and human capital needs to be developed to meet other human demands. This type of substitution reflects the unfortunate reality that the creation of physical capital – for example roads, buildings and machinery – often requires the conversion of natural capital. While substitution between natural capital and other forms of capital is often inevitable, there is often room for efficiency gains. There is also a growing recognition of environmental thresholds that would constrain substitution beyond minimum levels needed for human welfare.

Yet, there has always been concern that some forms of natural capital are essential to human welfare, particularly key ecological goods and services, unique environments and natural habitats, and irreplaceable ecosystem attributes. Uncertainty over the true value of these important assets to human welfare, in particular the value

Table 27.1 Natural capital: Underlying components and illustrative services and values

Biodiversity	Ecosystem goods and services (examples)	Economic values (examples)
Ecosystems (variety & extent/area) Species (diversity & abundance) Genes (variability & population)	• Recreation • Water regulation • Carbon storage • Food, fiber, fuel • Design inspiration • Pollination • Medicinal discoveries • Disease resistance • Adaptive capacity	Avoiding greenhouse gas emissions by conserving forests: US$ 3.7 trillion (NPV) Contribution of insect pollinators to agricultural output: ~US$ 190 billion/year 25–50% of the US$ 640 billion pharmaceutical market is derived from genetic resources

that future generations may place on them if they become increasingly scarce, further limits our ability to determine whether we can adequately compensate future generations for today's irreversible losses in such essential natural capital. This concern is reflected in other definitions of sustainable development. For example, in 1991, the World Wide Fund for Nature, the International Union for Conservation of Nature (IUCN), and UNEP interpreted the concept of sustainable development as "improving the quality of human life within the carrying capacity of supporting ecosystems".

As this definition suggests, the type of natural capital that is especially at risk is ecosystems. As explained by Partha Dasgupta "Ecosystems are capital assets. Like reproducible capital assets … ecosystems depreciate if they are misused or are overused. But they differ from reproducible capital assets in three ways: (1) depreciation of natural capital is frequently irreversible (or at best the systems take a long time to recover); (2) except in a very limited sense, it isn't possible to replace a depleted or degraded ecosystem by a new one; and (3) ecosystems can collapse abruptly, without much prior warning."

Rising ecological scarcity is an indication that we are irrevocably depleting ecosystems too rapidly, and the consequence is that current and future economic welfare is affected. An important indicator of the growing ecological scarcity worldwide was provided by the *Millennium Ecosystem Assessment* (MEA) in 2005, which found that over 60 per cent of the world's major ecosystem goods and services covered in the assessment were degraded or used unsustainably.

Some important benefits to humankind fall in this category, including fresh water; capture fisheries; water purification and waste treatment; wild foods; genetic resources; biochemicals; wood fuel; pollination; spiritual, religious and aesthetic values; the regulation of regional and local climate; erosion; pests; and natural hazards. The economic values associated with these ecosystem services, while generally not marketed, are substantial (see Table 27.1 [on p. 411]).

One major difficulty is that the increasing costs associated with rising ecological scarcity are not routinely reflected in markets. Almost all the degraded ecosystem goods or services identified by the *Millennium Ecosystem Assessment* are not marketed. Some goods, such as capture fisheries, fresh water, wild foods, and wood fuel, are often commercially marketed, but due to the poor management of the biological resources and ecosystems that are the source of these goods, and imperfect information, the market prices do not reflect unsustainable use and overexploitation.

Nor have adequate policies and institutions been developed to handle the costs associated with worsening ecological scarcity globally. All too often, policy distortions and failures compound these problems by encouraging wasteful use of natural resources and environmental degradation. The unique challenge posed by rising ecological scarcity and inefficient resource and energy use today is to overcome a vast array of market, policy, and institutional failures that prevents recognition of the economic significance of this environmental degradation.

Reversing this process of unsustainable development requires three important steps. First, as argued by the *Blueprint for a Green Economy* authors, improvements in environmental valuation and policy analysis are required to ensure that markets and policies incorporate the full costs and benefits of environmental impacts. Environmental valuation and accounting for natural capital depreciation must be fully integrated into economic development policy and strategy. As suggested above, the most undervalued components of natural capital are ecosystems and the myriad goods and services they provide. Valuing ecosystem goods and services is not easy, yet it is fundamental to ensuring the sustainability of global economic development efforts.

A major international research effort supported by UNEP, the Economics of Ecosystems and Biodiversity (TEEB), is illustrating how ecological and economic research can be used to value ecosystem goods and services, as well as how such valuation is essential for policy making and investments in the environment.

Second, the role of policy in controlling excessive environmental degradation requires implementing effective and appropriate information, incentives, institutions, investments and infrastructure. Better information on the state of the environment, ecosystems and biodiversity is essential for both private and public decision making that determines the allocation of natural capital for economic development. The use of market-based instruments, the creation of markets, and where appropriate, regulatory measures, have a role to play in internalising this information in everyday allocation decisions in the economy. Such instruments are also important in correcting the market and policy failures that distort the economic incentives for improved environmental and ecosystems management.

However, overcoming institutional failures and encouraging more effective property rights, good governance and support for local communities, is also critical. Reducing government inefficiency, corruption and poor accountability are also important in reversing excessive environmental degradation in many countries. But there is also a positive role for government in providing an appropriate and effective infrastructure through public investment, protecting critical ecosystems and biodiversity conservation, creating new incentive mechanisms such as payment for ecosystem services, fostering the technologies and knowledge necessary for improving ecosystem restoration, and facilitating the transition to a low-carbon economy.

Third, continuing environmental degradation, land conversion and global climate change affect the functioning, diversity, and resilience of ecological systems and the goods and services they supply. The potential long-term impacts of these effects on the health and stability of ecosystems are difficult to quantify and value. Increasing collaboration between environmental scientists, ecologists and economists will be required to assess and monitor these impacts. Such interdisciplinary ecological and economic analysis is also necessary to identify and assess the welfare consequences for current and future generations from increasing ecological scarcity. Further progress in reversing unsustainable development calls for more widespread interdisciplinary collaboration to analyse complex problems of environmental degradation, biodiversity loss and ecosystem decline.

Interdisciplinary research also needs to determine the thresholds that should govern the transformation of specific types of natural capital into other forms of capital. For example, how much forestland is allowed for conversion into farmland, industrial use or urban development in a given area? How much underground water is allowed for extraction each year? How much and what fish species can be caught in a given season? Which chemicals should be banned from production and trading? And more important, what are the criteria for setting these thresholds? Once these standards are established, incentive measures at national or international levels can be devised to ensure compliance.

The other key to balancing different forms of capital recognises that substitutability is a characteristic of current technologies. Investing in changing and substituting these technologies can lead to new complementarities. Most renewable energy sources, such as wind turbines or solar panels, considerably reduce the amount of natural capital that is sacrificed in their construction and the lifetime of their operation, compared to fossil fuel burning technologies. Both of these types of solutions – setting thresholds and altering technologies – are important for achieving a green economy.

In sum, moving towards a green economy must become a strategic economic policy agenda for achieving sustainable development. A green economy recognises that the goal of sustainable development is improving the quality of human life within the constraints of the environment, which include combating global climate change, energy insecurity, and ecological scarcity. However, a green economy cannot be focused exclusively on eliminating environmental problems and scarcity. It must also address the concerns of sustainable development with intergenerational equity and eradicating poverty.

A Green Economy and Eradicating Poverty   Most developing countries, and certainly the majority of their populations, depend directly on natural resources. The livelihoods of many of the world's rural poor are also intricately linked with exploiting fragile environments and ecosystems. Well over 600 million of the rural poor currently live on lands prone to degradation and water stress, and in upland areas, forest systems, and drylands that are vulnerable to climatic and ecological disruptions. The tendency of rural populations to be clustered on marginal lands and in fragile environments is likely to be a continuing problem for the foreseeable future, given current global rural population and poverty trends. Despite rapid global urbanisation, the rural population of developing regions continues to grow, albeit at a slower rate in recent decades. Furthermore, around three-quarters of the developing world's poor still live in rural areas, which means about twice as many poor people live in rural rather than in urban areas.

The world's poor are especially vulnerable to the climate-driven risks posed by rising sea levels, coastal erosion and more frequent storms. Around 14 per cent of the population and 21 per cent of urban dwellers in developing countries live in low elevation coastal zones that are exposed to these risks. The livelihoods of billions – from poor farmers to urban slum dwellers – are threatened by a wide range of climate-induced risks that affect food security, water availability, natural disasters, ecosystem stability and human health. For example, many of the 150 million urban inhabitants, who are likely to be at risk from extreme coastal flooding events and sea level rise, are likely to be the poor living in cities in developing countries.

As in the case of climate change, the link between ecological scarcity and poverty is well-established for some of the most critical environmental and energy problems. For example, for the world's poor, global water scarcity manifests itself as a water poverty problem. One-in-five people in the developing world lacks access to sufficient clean water, and about half the developing world's population, 2.6 billion people, do not have access to basic sanitation. More than 660 million of the people without sanitation live on less than US$ 2 a day, and more than 385 million on less than US$ 1 a day. Billions of people in developing countries have no access to modern energy services, and those consumers who do have access often pay high prices for erratic and unreliable services. Among the energy poor are 2.4 billion people who rely on traditional biomass fuels for cooking and heating, including 89 per cent of the population of Sub-Saharan Africa; and, the 1.6 billion people who do not have access to electricity.

Thus, finding ways to protect global ecosystems, reduce the risks of global climate change, improve energy security, and simultaneously improve the livelihoods of the poor are important challenges in the transition to a green economy, especially for developing countries.

As this report demonstrates, a transition to a green economy can contribute to eradicating poverty. A number of sectors with green economic potential are particularly important for the poor, such as agriculture, forestry, fishery and water management, which have public goods qualities. Investing in greening these sectors, including through scaling up microfinance, is likely to benefit the poor in terms of not only jobs, but also secure livelihoods that are predominantly based on ecosystem services. Enabling the poor to access microinsurance coverage against natural disasters and catastrophes is equally important for protecting livelihood assets from external shocks due to changing and unpredictable weather patterns.

However, it must be emphasised that moving towards a green economy will not automatically address all poverty issues. A pro-poor orientation must be superimposed on any green economy initiative. Investments in renewable energy, for example, will have to pay special attention to the issue of access to clean and affordable energy. Payments for ecosystem services, such as carbon sequestration in forests, will need to focus more on poor forest communities as the primary beneficiaries. The promotion of organic agriculture can open up opportunities, particularly for poor small-scale farmers who typically make up the majority of the agricultural labour force in most low-income countries, but will need to be complemented by policies to ensure that extension and other support services are in place.

In sum, the top priority of the UN MDGs is eradicating extreme poverty and hunger, including halving the proportion of people living on less than US$ 1 a day by 2015. A green economy must not only be consistent with that objective, but must also ensure that policies and investments geared towards reducing environmental risks and scarcities are compatible with ameliorating global poverty and social inequity.

Pathways to a Green Economy

If the desirability of moving to a green economy is clear to most people, the means of doing so is still a work in progress for many. This section looks at the theory of greening, the practice and the enabling conditions required for making such a transition. However, before embarking on this analysis, the section frames the dimensions of the challenge.

How Far Is the World from a Green Economy?   Over the last quarter of a century, the world economy has quadrupled, benefiting hundreds of millions of people. However, 60 per cent of the world's major ecosystem goods and services that underpin livelihoods have been degraded or used unsustainably. This is because the economic growth of recent decades has been accomplished mainly through drawing down natural resources, without allowing stocks to regenerate, and through allowing widespread ecosystem degradation and loss.

[...]

For the first time in history, more than half of the world population lives in urban areas. Cities now account for 75 per cent of energy consumption and of carbon emissions.[1] Rising and related problems of congestion, pollution and poorly provisioned services affect the productivity and health of all, but fall particularly hard on the urban poor. With approximately 50 per cent of the global population now living in emerging economies that are rapidly urbanising and developing, the need for green city planning, infrastructure and transportation is paramount.

The transition to a green economy will vary considerably among nations, as it depends on the specifics of each country's natural and human capital and on its relative level of development. As demonstrated graphically, there are many opportunities for all countries in such a transition (see Box 27.1). Some countries have attained high levels of human development, but often at the expense of their natural resource base, the quality of their environment, and high greenhouse gas (GHG) emissions. The challenge for these countries is to reduce their per capita ecological footprint without impairing their quality of life.

Other countries still maintain relatively low per capita ecological footprints, but need to deliver improved levels of services and material well-being to their citizens. Their challenge is to do this without drastically increasing their ecological footprint. As the diagram illustrates, one of these two challenges affects almost every nation, and globally, the economy is still very far from being green.

Box 27.1   Towards a green economy: A twin challenge

Many countries now enjoy a high level of human development – but at the cost of a large ecological footprint. Others have a very low footprint, but face urgent needs to improve access to basic services such as health, education, and potable water. The challenge for countries is to move towards the origin of the graph, where a high level of human development can be achieved within planetary boundaries.

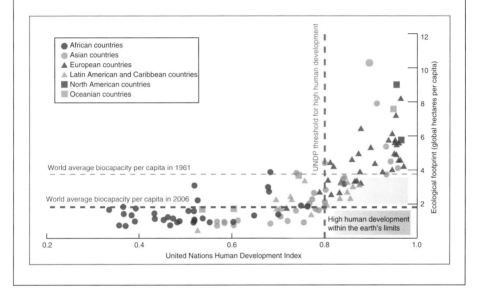

Enabling Conditions for a Green Economy   To make the transition to a green economy, specific enabling conditions will be required. These enabling conditions consist of national regulations, policies, subsidies and incentives, as well as international market and legal infrastructure, trade and technical assistance. Currently, enabling conditions are heavily weighted towards, and encourage, the prevailing brown economy, which depends excessively on fossil fuels, resource depletion and environmental degradation.

For example, price and production subsidies for fossil fuels collectively exceeded US$ 650 billion in 2008. This high level of subsidisation can adversely affect the adoption of clean energy while contributing to more greenhouse gas emissions. In contrast, enabling conditions for a green economy can pave the way for the success of public and private investment in greening the world's economies. At a national level, examples of such enabling conditions are: changes to fiscal policy, reform and reduction of environmentally harmful subsidies; employing new market-based instruments; targeting public investments to green key sectors; greening public procurement; and improving environmental rules and regulations, as well as their enforcement. At an international level, there are also opportunities to add to market infrastructure, improve trade and aid flows and foster greater international cooperation.

At the national level, any strategy to green economies should consider the impact of environmental policies within the broader context of policies to address innovation and economic performance.[2] In this view, government policy plays a critical role within economies to encourage innovation and growth. Such intervention is important as a means for fostering innovation and for choosing the direction of change.

For some time, economists such as Kenneth Arrow have shown that competitive firms and competitive markets do not necessarily produce the optimal amount of innovation and growth within an economy.[3] Public intervention within an economy is therefore critically important for these purposes. This is because industries in competitive markets have few incentives to invest in technological change or even in product innovation, as any returns would be immediately competed away. This is one of the best-known examples of market failure in the context of competitive markets, and provides the rationale for various forms of interventions.

Examples of spurring growth and innovation can be seen from histories of many recently emerged economies. In the 1950s and 1960s, the Japanese and South Korean governments chose the direction of technological change through importing the technology of other countries. This changed in the 1970s when these economies shifted to aggressive policies for encouraging energy-efficient innovation. Shortly afterwards, Japan was one of the leading economies in the world in terms of research and development (R&D) investment in these industries.[4] This pattern of directed spending and environmental policies is being repeated today across much of Asia. The cases of South Korea and China in particular are illustrative, where a large proportion of their stimulus packages was directed at a "green recovery" and has now been instituted into longer-term plans for retooling their economies around green growth.

Thus, moving towards a green development path is almost certainly a means for attaining welfare improvements across a society, but it is also often a means for attaining future growth improvement. This is because a shift away from basic production modes of development based on extraction and consumption and towards more complex modes of development can be a good long-term strategy for growth. There are several reasons why this shift might be good for long-term competitiveness as well as for social welfare.

First, employing strong environmental policies can drive inefficiencies out of the economy by removing those firms and industries that only exist because of implicit subsidies in under-priced resources. The free use of air, water and ecosystems is not a value-less good for any actor in an economy and amounts to subsidising negative net worth activities. Introducing effective regulation and market-based mechanisms to contain pollution and limit the accumulation of environmental liabilities drives the economy in a more efficient direction.

Second, resource pricing is important not just for the pricing of natural capital and services, but also for pricing of all the other inputs within an economy. An economy allocates its efforts and expenditures according to relative prices, and under-priced resources result in unbalanced economies. Policy makers should be targeting the future they wish their economies to achieve, and this will usually require higher relative prices on resources. An economy that wishes to develop around knowledge, R&D, human capital and innovation should not be providing free natural resources.

Third, employing resource pricing drives investments into R&D and innovation. It does so because avoiding costly resources can be accomplished by researching and finding new production methods. This will include investment in all of the factors (human capital and knowledge) and all of the activities (R&D and innovation) listed above. Moving towards more efficient resource pricing is about turning the economy's emphasis towards different foundations of development.

Fourth, these investments may then generate innovation rents. Policies that reflect scarcities that are prevalent in the local economy can also reflect scarcities prevalent more widely. For this reason, a solution to a problem of resource scarcity identified locally (via R&D investments) may have applicability and hence more global marketability. The first solution to a widely experienced problem can be patented, licensed and marketed widely.

Fifth, aggressive environmental regulation may anticipate future widely-experienced scarcities and provide a template for other jurisdictions to follow. Such policy leadership can be the first step in the process of innovation, investment, regulation and resource pricing described above.

In sum, the benefits from a strong policy framework to address market failures and ecological scarcities will flow down the environment pathway that comes from altering the direction of an economy. Policies and market-based mechanisms that enhance perceived resource prices creates incentives to shift the economy onto a completely different foundation – one based more on investments in innovation and its inputs of human capital, knowledge, and research and development.

How to Measure Progress Towards a Green Economy It is difficult, if not impossible, to manage what is not measured. Notwithstanding the complexity of an overall transition to a green economy, appropriate indicators at both a macroeconomic level and a sectoral level will be essential to informing and guiding the transition.

To complicate matters, conventional economic indicators, such as GDP, provide a distorted lens for economic performance, particularly because such measures fail to reflect the extent to which production and consumption activities may be drawing down natural capital. By either depleting natural resources or degrading the ability of ecosystems to deliver economic benefits, in terms of provisioning, regulating or cultural services, economic activity is often based on the depreciation of natural capital.

Ideally, changes in stocks of natural capital would be evaluated in monetary terms and incorporated into national accounts. This is being pursued in the ongoing development of the System of Environmental and Economic Accounting (SEEA) by the UN Statistical Division, and the World Bank's adjusted net national savings methods. The wider use of such measures would provide a better indication of the real level and viability of growth in income and employment. Green Accounting or Inclusive Wealth Accounting are available frameworks that are expected to be adopted by a few nations[5] initially and pave the way for measuring the transition to a green economy at the macroeconomic level.

How Might a Green Economy Perform Over Time?   In this report, the macro-economic Threshold 21 (T21) model is used to explore the impacts of investments in greening the economy against investments in business as usual. The T21 model measures results in terms of traditional GDP as well as its affects on employment, resource intensity, emissions, and ecological impacts.

The T21 model was developed to analyse strategies for medium to long-term development and poverty reduction, most often at the national level, complementing other tools for analysing short-term impacts of policies and programmes. The model is particularly suited to analysing the impacts of investment plans, covering both public and private commitments. The global version of T21 used for purposes of this report models the world economy as a whole to capture the key relationships between production and key natural resource stocks at an aggregate level.

The T21 model reflects the dependence of economic production on the traditional inputs of labour and physical capital, as well as stocks of natural capital in the form of resources, such as energy, forest land, soil, fish and water. Growth is thus driven by the accumulation of capital – whether physical, human or natural – through investment, also taking into account depreciation or depletion of capital stocks. The model is calibrated to reproduce the past 40-year period of 1970–2010; simulations are conducted over the next 40-year period, 2010–2050. Business-as-usual projections are verified against standard projections from other organisations, such as the United Nations Population Division, World Bank, OECD, the International Energy Agency, and the Food and Agriculture Organization.

The inclusion of natural resources as a factor of production distinguishes T21 from all other global macroeconomic models. Examples of the direct dependence of output (GDP) on natural resources are the availability of fish and forest stocks for the fisheries and forestry sectors, as well as the availability of fossil fuels to power the capital needed to catch fish and harvest timber, among others. Other natural resources and resource efficiency factors affecting GDP include water stress, waste recycle and reuse and energy prices[6].

Based on existing studies, the annual financing demand to green the global economy was estimated to be in the range US$ 1.05 to US$ 2.59 trillion. To place this demand in perspective, it is about one-tenth of total global investment per year, as measured by global Gross Capital Formation. Taking an annual level of US$ 1.3 trillion (2 per cent of global GDP) as a reference scenario, varying amounts of investment in the 10 sectors covered in this report were modelled to determine impact on growth, employment, resource use and ecological footprint. The results of the model, presented in more detail in the modelling chapter [in the original], suggest that over time investing in a green economy enhances long-term economic performance. Significantly, it does so while enhancing stocks of renewable resources, reducing environmental risks, and rebuilding capacity to generate future prosperity. These results are presented in a disaggregated form for each sector to illustrate the effects of this investment on income, employment and growth, and more comprehensively, in the modelling chapter [in the original].

[...]

Notes

1 For a critique of these figures, see Satterthwaite's "Cities' contribution to global warming: notes on the allocation of greenhouse gas emissions" *Environment and Urbanization*, 20 (2): 539–49.
2 This point has been debated since at least the time of the initial statement of the Porter Hypothesis. Porter argued then that environmental regulation might have a positive impact on growth through the dynamic effects it engendered within an economy.
3 It has been known since at least the time of the seminal work of Kenneth and the structural work of Kamien and Schwartz that competitive firms and competitive markets need not produce the optimal amount of innovation and growth within an economy.
4 By 1987, Japan was the world leader in R&D per unit GDP (at 2.8 per cent) and the world leader in the proportion of that spent on energy-related R&D (at 23 per cent).
5 World Bank, together with UNEP and other partners, have recently (at Nagoya, CBD C0P-10, October 2009) announced a global project on Ecosystem Valuation and Wealth Accounting which will enable a group of developing and developed nations to test this framework and evolve a set of pilot national accounts that are better able to reflect and measure sustainability concerns.
6 The T21 analysis purposely ignores issues such as trade and sources of investment financing (public vs private, or domestic vs foreign). As a result, the analysis of the potential impacts of a green investment scenario at a global level are not intended to represent the possibilities for any specific country or region. Instead, the simulations are meant to stimulate further consideration and more detailed analysis by governments and other stakeholders of a transition to a green economy. [...]

28

Critique of the Green Economy: Toward Social and Environmental Equity (2012)

Barbara Unmüßig, Wolfgang Sachs, and Thomas Fatheuer

Since the Rio Earth Summit in 1992 the world has experienced a series of financial and economic crises, such as those in Asia (1997/1998) and Argentina (1998/2001); in March 2000 the New Economy bubble burst and the failure of Lehman Brothers in September 2008 triggered the biggest financial and economic crisis since the Second World War. [...] The state of the financial markets, however, along with the various environmental and social crises, has prompted a revival of criticism directed at capitalism and growth. Calls for a different economic paradigm are intensifying and discussion of the need for new models of prosperity and alternative lifestyles is not confined to niche segments of society or academic circles. Criticism of the very basis of the production and consumption patterns of industrialized society is clearly on the increase and the search for alternatives is back on the agenda.

Alongside the discussion of issues of principle, the debate on the green economy is gathering pace. Hitherto spearheaded largely by environmentalists and green parties, the green economy is now a concept espoused by the European Union (EU), the Organisation for Economic Co-operation and Development (OECD), the various organizations of the United Nations (UN), by think tanks, universities and sections of the business community itself. The starting point of all deliberations on the green economy is the impending threat of climate change and resource scarcity ("peak oil," "peak water," "peak land"). Decarbonizing the global economy – preferably within the two-degree warming corridor, with extensive investment in resource efficiency and renewables – is a declared objective of all protagonists of a green economy. None of them consider the "business-as-usual" scenario to be an option.

Barbara Unmüßig, Wolfgang Sachs, and Thomas Fatheuer. 2012. *Critique of the Green Economy: Toward Social and Environmental Equity*. pp. 22–34, 35–41. Reproduced with permission from B. Unmüßig.

This is an assertion repeated over and over in the plethora of publications and studies centered on the idea of the green economy.

This welcome common ground very soon reveals itself to be riddled with fault lines. This is evident even in the great variety of terms in circulation, which often cause confusion over concepts. The United Nations Environment Programme, UNEP, speaks of the "green economy," while the OECD and the World Bank refer sometimes to sustainable growth and at other times to green growth. There is also talk of "greening the economy." Meanwhile the idea of a "Green New Deal," which was introduced into the debate during the global economic crisis of 2008 – primarily by UNEP – to stimulate "greener" economic recovery packages, may have lost some of its sheen internationally, but it remains a topic of discussion, especially among German and European Greens. Considerable technological hopes are also being pinned on the bio-economy, which many believe will promote the transition from an oil-based economy to a bio-based one. Bio-economy strategies are currently being driven forward by the German government and the Obama administration in the USA. While there is a certain degree of overlap between bio-economy and green economy issues, a conceptual distinction needs to be drawn between the two. The UNEP and OECD proposals are explicitly contributions towards the Rio+20 conference, at which it is envisaged that a "green economy roadmap" will be adopted. "Sustainable development," the buzzword at Rio 1992, may well be displaced in 2012 by the "green economy."

All these terms conceal very disparate estimates of the levels of economic growth and natural resource use the planet can still sustain, and of how much of these would be needed to reduce poverty. Equally diverse are the views on who should benefit from the green economy. Should it be the growing global middle classes? The McKinsey Global Institute talks of three billion consumers joining the middle classes in the coming years. This thinking focuses on the fear that important mineral and natural resources are dwindling too quickly. The answer lies not in changing consumption patterns and lifestyles, a kind of "disarmament program" for resource use. Instead, the solution being proposed is to increase productivity and efficiency through technological innovation, but also to improve the availability of resources. Using green economic policies to combat the poverty affecting more than two billion people is closer to the thinking of the UNEP Green Economy Initiative. Who should benefit from the green economy? All of humanity? And how can we ensure that we keep the green economy within ecological limits? This leads us to the question of "how?" By what means? Using what instruments and what measures?

The Green Economy According to UNEP

UNEP has positioned itself as the leading player in elaborating the idea of the green economy [with] its report "Towards a Green Economy" [...]. UNEP defines the green economy as one that results in improved human wellbeing and social equity, while significantly reducing environmental risks and ecological scarcities and facilitating sustainable resource management. The report notes that all global problems have a common basis, namely the misallocation of capital: during the past two decades, it says, most capital has been poured into property, fossil fuels and financial market products including derivatives. By comparison, relatively little has been invested in renewable energy, energy efficiency, public transport, sustainable agriculture and conservation of ecosystems, biodiversity and water resources.

UNEP therefore advocates targeted investment in ten key economic sectors (including energy, agriculture, urban development, water, forestry, fisheries and ecosystem services), with a view to enabling a rapid and effective transition to greener and more poverty-focused development, and underpins its arguments with an impressive array of facts and econometric calculations. It proposes spending two percent of current global GDP (equivalent to approximately USD1.3 billion) annually to finance these investments. UNEP believes that this investment would be sufficient to provide an effective stimulus for a lower-carbon, more resource-efficient global economy. UNEP in this regard remains true to its mandate as a program and contents itself with identifying economic niches rather than setting out ideas for structural changes that might result, for example, in a moratorium on the development of new oil and gas fields. Trade regulations, it says, should help to favor environmental goods and services on the world market. Yes, even UNEP calls for this. However, the UNEP report has little to say on how trade regulations would need to be designed in order to decarbonize the global economy and make it more resource-efficient. [...] One of the most important and far-reaching demands made by UNEP is its call for the abolition of environmentally and socially harmful subsidies in the agricultural and transport sectors and for coal and oil. National governments are viewed as vital regulators; it will not be possible to implement the green economy without clear statutory provisions and national regulatory frameworks.

Monetizing Nature – A Way Out of the Ecosystem Crisis?

One of the polemical slogans in the debate around Rio+20 is "monetizing nature." In the eyes of Pablo Solón, former Bolivian ambassador to the UN and an influential intellectual in Latin America, the green economy is in essence an attempt to establish a new way of commercializing nature. "Not only does it seek to commodify materials from nature, but also nature's processes and functions. For example, in future timber will not be the only forest commodity to be up for sale; forests' CO_2-binding potential will also be a marketable commodity."

In recent years UNEP has indeed been a leader in the debate on the revaluation of nature, which includes the use of market-based instruments to help preserve ecosystems. Whether in the context of forest conservation or biodiversity in general, UNEP seeks to protect ecosystems by valuing the services they perform both for humanity as a whole and for people whose lives depend directly on them (and, for example, incorporating these valuations into calculations of gross national product). However, UNEP also wants to assign an economic market value to ecosystem services and invest in them in the long term: "A green economy values and invests in natural capital." In UNEP's view, ecosystem services are seriously undervalued as economic factors: "These so-called ecosystem services mainly take the form of public goods and services whose economic invisibility has been, up to now, a key reason for their undervaluation, mismanagement and ultimately loss." A green economy must increase this "natural capital." This is a reformulation of the old idea that it is easier to protect ecosystems and biodiversity if it costs money to use them. The economization of climate protection began some time ago with emissions trading and the Clean Development Mechanism, but – except in Europe – no concomitant emissions reduction policy was put in place.

As the public coffers are already empty in the wake of the recent financial and economic crises, it is UNEP's view that additional market incentives are needed to encourage the private sector to invest in environmental conservation. Since the climate negotiations in Bali in 2007, REDD (Reducing Emissions from Deforestation and Degradation) has therefore been regarded as a promising instrument for global forest protection. For UNEP it is a unique opportunity to transform non-sustainable forest use (logging for the timber trade and livestock production) into green use by shifting the emphasis onto ecosystem services (soil conservation, water resources, biodiversity), for which payment is then required.

The prospect of turning nature conservation into a source of profit has captivated economists and nature conservationists alike and raises understandable hopes: "If we were at last able to capture the value of ecological services, and especially the services of natural ecosystems, in other words, to incorporate them into our pricing systems, this would be a major key to securing our future".

But what exactly does it mean to "capture the value of ecosystems"? Not all monetization pathways lead straight to commodification of the natural environment. Establishing monetary value – even approximately – is for example important when it comes to measuring damage. What penalties should be imposed on the operators of Deepwater Horizon for the damage to ecosystems in the deep ocean in the Gulf of Mexico? What damage is caused by a ship that ploughs through a coral reef? It certainly also makes sense to weigh up whether, for example, it is more costly to invest in water treatment or in the protection of water sources. According to TEEB (The Economy of Ecosystems and Biodiversity), an initiative spearheaded by UNEP putting a price on nature would make life easier for decision-makers in politics and industry, and moreover, do it in a language that they understand. It would help businesses to recognize risks and enable politicians to perceive the hidden costs and long-term consequences of their actions.

Advocates of the monetization of nature rarely spare a thought for the social context within which "ecosystem services" are provided; indeed, such terms all but obscure the social context. After all, it is not industrious nature itself that is to receive payment for ecosystem services, but its owner. But many of the last intact ecosystems are located in areas occupied by indigenous peoples and local communities. Their traditional ownership rights are jeopardized by new market-based instruments. The most vigorous critics of the UNEP concept point out that natural resources are being commodified in order to make them more attractive to the private sector, thus making them vulnerable to commercial exploitation. Capitalizing on "ecosystem services" has come under fierce attack as a new stage in the privatization and commercialization of the natural environment. Instead of joining forces with local inhabitants to protect natural resources from commercial exploitation, so the accusation goes, business is turning nature into a commodity and not infrequently driving out the local population.

Little attention has so far been given to the tendency to turn all types of natural resources into tradable goods, thereby tying resources such as soil, water and forests even more tightly into monetary loops and trading them as commodities on the global financial markets via financial instruments and products such as derivatives. In the search for new investment opportunities, it is not only raw materials and food markets that are to be rendered attractive to profit-seekers, but also soils and forests, and most notably their capacity for storing CO_2. Assigning a monetary value to ecosystem services or to the environmental costs of climate change (e.g. by way of CO_2 emissions trading) or biodiversity loss opens the floodgates to the financialization of natural capital. "Climate and environment policy are being made compatible with financial speculation," according to the analysis of Elmar Altvater. Since we are dealing with an all-out wave of financialization, we need a comprehensive and nuanced debate on the "economics of ecosystems and biodiversity" that is being aggressively promoted by UNEP. The debate needs to be nuanced because the search for solutions in the climate, resource and poverty crisis is not well served by dismissing all aspects of the green economy and all market-based instruments out of hand as "greenwashing," green capitalism or as a wolf in green sheep's clothing, a view expressed increasingly vociferously in the run-up to the Rio conference.

Green Growth According to the OECD

The OECD [...] has been debating a greener growth approach since 2009. In May 2011 it presented its strategy for achieving this in *Towards Green Growth*. The starting point for the OECD's deliberations is the risk of climate change and concerns about the drastic decline in certain resources, unchecked biodiversity loss, overfishing, and the growing scarcity of land and water. "We need green growth because risks to development are rising as growth continues to erode natural capital," states that OECD report. New sources of growth can be opened up through increased productivity (efficient use of energy and resources), through innovation (new ways of creating value and addressing environmental problems) and through new markets (stimulating demand for green technologies, goods and services). The strategy for green growth is intended to be a lens for "looking at growth" and avoiding "crossing critical local, regional and global environmental thresholds". By pushing these frontiers outwards, innovation can help to "decouple growth from natural capital depletion". Investing in more efficient use of natural capital is therefore viewed as essential for securing raw material and resource inputs for the economy. Internalization of environmental costs (e.g. setting a high price for CO_2) is advocated as an incentive for innovation, as is the removal of subsidies that damage the environment.

Development of renewable energies and environmental technologies will create many millions of new jobs – the OECD estimates that up to 20 million new jobs could be created worldwide by 2030 in the field of renewable energy generation and distribution.

There are several notable features in this green growth strategy, particularly the call for rigorous internalization of environmental costs, as well as the comment that "not every situation lends itself to market instruments" and that "in certain cases well-designed regulation […] may be more appropriate or an important complement to market instruments". As might be expected, the familiar ordoliberal principle of establishing a framework that creates confidence and security and makes planning possible is also reflected in the OECD strategy. If, as is planned, this strategy is now taken on board in OECD country reports and additional sector studies are conducted to bring greater clarity, then progress will have been achieved compared to a blanket "growth at all costs" strategy.

In line with the OECD strategy, the McKinsey Global Institute published a paper on the "resource revolution" in November 2011. Here too, the focal point of the paper is the warning that resource scarcity will a) lead to very high and volatile prices, and b) mean that important production factors may no longer be available at all. The only answer is productivity, efficiency, innovation and investment to the tune of billions targeted especially at the "resource system" to ensure that future demand for resources can be met. The "challenges," in other words the high costs of energy and raw materials, are contrasted with the great variety of economic "opportunities" that can inject new vitality into the economy.

Bio-economy – The Rise of the Bio-masters

Bio-economy is a relatively new concept that is cropping up with increasing frequency and often in the context of the green economy. The bio-economy focuses similarly on technological innovation to enhance efficiency and the use of natural resources for food, energy, pharmaceuticals and the chemicals industry.

The German government's "National Research Strategy BioEconomy 2030" is "striving towards a natural cycle oriented, bio-based economy that is in accordance with technology and ecology" and as a knowledge-based bio-economy uses biological processes – from the level of genes to the entire ecosystem. The complex building blocks and blueprints of biological systems need to be better understood in order to be better able to exploit them technologically "for the benefit of mankind and the environment". The aim of the bio-economy is to develop these components technologically to make them more efficient and more "sustainable." This approach also seeks to include economic, environmental and social aspects and consideration of entire value chains. The objective is to shift from an oil-based to a bio-based economy. At the same time the international competitiveness of Germany's chemical and pharmaceutical industry, biotechnology companies, and small and medium-sized seed companies and plant breeders operating transnationally will be maintained and enhanced. German government research funding is being greatly expanded in order to provide fresh impetus for technological innovation.

In Washington, too, the White House has released a "National Bioeconomy Blueprint" (April 2012). It follows on from the 2009 report by the US National Research Council, *A New Biology for the 21st Century*, and highlights the potential of technological innovation for health and food in the future, emphasizing the importance of research to free the USA from its dependency on oil and enable production of new, non-oil-based goods. Research to boost competitiveness is also at the forefront of the US strategic program. Financial resources for research and investment in future technologies need to be integrated and mobilized at an entirely new level for this purpose, including by developing public-private partnerships and a regulatory framework that creates a positive environment for the market (e.g. safe-guarding property rights by means of patents etc.). US income from various biotech-nologies (excluding the agricultural sector) was already estimated at as much as USD100 billion in 2010. The high growth rate of the US bio-economy is put down to the multitude of possibilities opened up by biotechnologies, genetic engineering and genomics. Synthetic biology – in other words direct alteration and use of micro-organisms and plants, re-design of proteins in organisms, and access to and management of important bio-information – is considered to be the most crucial field of activity for the future.

Who are the "bio-masters" of tomorrow? This is the question posed in view of developments relating to the green economy and in particular in the bio-sciences and bio-economy by the non-governmental organization ETC Group, which for many years now has turned the spotlight on the corporate strategies of the major multinationals in the energy, chemicals, pharmaceuticals and food sectors. In the 21st century, says the ETC Group, biology will take on the role that was played by fossil fuels in the past 200 years of industrialization. The desire to control so-called green fuels and crucial food plants by way of high-yielding varieties or genetically modified seed is driving the corporate policy of major industry players such as Monsanto, Procter & Gamble, Chevron and BASF. Big Energy, Big Pharma, Big Food, and Big Chemical are constantly entering into new alliances and creating new technology platforms, according to ETC Group research. Interest in every form of life and biomass – from algae to sugar beet – has increased dramatically in recent years. Everything is being considered in the search for new industrial products that could reduce dependency on, and ultimately entirely replace, petroleum-based chemicals and ensure control of food production. Producing synthetic DNA is the ultimate aim of synthetic biology; this is seen as the biggest future growth market.

A handful of large transnational corporations in the USA, Europe, Japan, China, and other Asian economies are striving to gain strategic control of entire value chains – genetic and technical information, production processes, and production factors such as energy, biomass, water and land. As far as they are concerned, this is the goal of the present technological innovations. In the absence of political action to prevent it, there is a clear and alarming tendency here towards concentration of power. This can be seen in the food sector; most food production and marketing is controlled by a few large agricultural companies and the agricultural industry. Production of fertilizers, pesticides, seed and genetically modified seed is largely concentrated in the hands of a few conglomerates – the same ones that control the global food market.

The powerful seed, fertilizer and pesticide lobby is intent on securing market power in this area for itself. Its representatives exert increasing influence on policy-making everywhere in the world. This is why access to intellectual property rights is part of the repertoire of economic negotiations and of innumerable bilateral trade agreements between industrialized and developing countries. Small farmers and rural workers rarely have the power to defend themselves against the conditions imposed by global corporations. Robust farmers' organizations able to negotiate in the interests of smallholder farmers are lacking, as are trade unions to represent the rights of rural employees.

Sadly, this concentration of power is not on any political agenda. In the political sphere and among the general public there is little awareness that the problem even exists. No political lessons are being learned from the concentration of power in the hands of large financial market players and "systemic banks," which have used it to extort political capital (they are "too big to fail"). On the contrary: in global competition what matters is for players to position themselves rapidly and strategically with bio-economic and green innovations. In this context governments are supporting large corporations and small and medium-sized businesses with a transnational presence by providing financial and research-oriented incentives and programs, and by helping safeguard proprietary rights (from land to patents) they are encouraging this private-sector run on all sorts of resources and the code of life itself.

Technological innovations and efficiency will continue to point the way towards a more resource-efficient economy in future and help to push back ecological limits. However, every strategy for a green economy or a new bio-economy should be asking the question: technology and innovation, yes, but for whom? Who controls them? What are the potential social and ecological consequences? Are they adequate, or are they merely a strategy to avoid or delay a long-overdue turnaround towards a "policy of less"? These questions are quite rightly becoming an area of growing controversy between governments, industry and civil society.

None of the green economy strategy papers – from OECD to UNEP – tackles the issues of power and distribution of resources. They are simply omitted. Clearly, as far as these organizations are concerned, all new initiatives and programs take place in an arena where power and interests do not exist. Both organizations – UNEP more explicitly so than the OECD – support the role of the state as a framework-setting institution whose task it is to remove environmentally harmful subsidies, formulate legislative standards, implement sustainable industrial policy and above all promote research. Drastic command-and-control measures to limit energy and resource consumption ("caps," large-scale nature conservation measures, bans on resource extraction in sensitive ecosystems such as the Arctic or the deep ocean) are no longer seriously considered as policy options. Setting limits scarcely features as a priority, let alone a requirement, in the minds of the protagonists of the green economy.

Technology and Efficiency as a Cure-all

In every transformation strategy and every concept of a green economy, pride of place goes to technological innovation. Such innovation is seen as the way to enhance the productivity of resource use and find substitutes for scarce resources. Actual and potential negative social and environmental effects are overlooked, especially in the case of large-scale technological solutions. Not everything that is regarded as helping to combat climate change – ocean fertilization, vast mirrors in space, nuclear power, mega-dams – can be considered socially and environmentally acceptable. The same goes for genetic engineering, which, it is claimed, will help overcome the food crisis. The consequences of such technologies for humans and the environment are sadly not being assessed with appropriate care and weighed up politically. It is therefore a matter of urgency to include assessment of all aspects of the consequences of technology on the political agenda. In the light of the interwoven nature of global economics, it is no longer enough to do this at national level. In this regard, Rio+20 could pave the way for an initiative at UN level for assessing the consequences of different technologies.

A resource and efficiency revolution – this seems to have become the be-all and end-all, the mantra of our time. The greatest hope rests on decoupling gross domestic product (GDP) from resource use; this is part of the credo that the environmental and food crisis can be halted by means of technology. Decoupling is crucial, and reducing resource consumption in absolute terms is urgent. But the question is, how can this be achieved?

The first answer is efficiency – by using energy and materials more efficiently. More than 90 percent of all materials and energy mobilized for the manufacture of consumer goods are consumed well before the finished product stage – e.g. waste material excavated in the mining industry, waste heat from power plants, soil loss in mechanized farming, waste from timber or metal processing, grain in livestock farming, water in metal finishing, and transport costs associated with fuel supply. The lower its resource use, the more eco-efficient an economy is. A great deal can be achieved using alternative technologies, processes and products that drastically reduce the consumption of energy and materials. An efficiency strategy will have great potential if supportive policy measures – such as statutory standards, reduced subsidies for fossil-fuel-based products, efficiency standards for housing, machinery and equipment – are also put in place.

However, attention must be paid to the rebound effect. This is the effect that occurs if efficiency improvements enable other resource-intensive activities to take place, thereby negating any saving or efficiency gain. There are some notorious examples of this: the benefits of more efficient heating systems being lost as a result of living space being increased; the benefits of more efficient engines being eroded by an increase in vehicle weight and speed; the benefits of more efficient production lines being cancelled out by expansion and an increase in the vertical range of production. This phenomenon particularly affects those situations referred to as win-win scenarios that promise environmental benefits in tandem with economic gains: these in a sense have a "built-in" rebound effect due to the higher financial gains. Moreover, it is emerging economies that are worst affected by the rebound effect, since they are starting from a lower base in terms of equipment and machinery.

The efficiency revolution is nevertheless touted as the *ultimate* panacea, despite the fact that more recent research has shown that various rebound effects – financial, material and quantitative as well as psychological – will prevent consumption from staying within ecological limits. To date, according to a report published in December 2011 by the German government's study commission on "Growth, Wealth, Quality of Life," "economy-wide analyses of the causal effects of efficiency on resource use have been few and far between." [...] [T]he authors state "as regards the decoupling strategy, what stands out the most is that although consumption of certain resources has increased less rapidly than GDP (*relative* decoupling), the number of cases where there has been an absolute reduction in resource consumption (*absolute* decoupling) is close to zero". The conclusion: more efficient use of resources must go hand in hand with more moderate goals; unless there is a revolution in terms of sufficiency, the efficiency revolution lacks direction.

The second answer is consistency – by switching to more environmentally sound technologies. While still including an efficiency strategy, more sophisticated concepts of a green economy place considerable importance on a strategy of consistency, in other words on ensuring that industry is compatible with the natural environment. How can we exploit nature without destroying it? Technologies from the pre-fossil fuel era may provide clues: the three-field crop rotation system, timber-frame construction, windmills, sailing ships. They always follow a similar logic. Humans must learn to fit in with natural flows before they can harness and manage them for their own benefit. Today, however, in the post-fossil fuel era, we have a different arsenal of technologies at our disposal. Biotechnology and informatics, bionics and engineering can also operate according to this same logic: making clever use of nature without impairing its regenerative capacities. Renewable energies are the most prominent example of this type of strategy; organic farming is another. Wind, solar power and geothermal energy, just like micro-organisms and nutrients, are all natural flows which in principle may be harnessed for the benefit of humans without destroying them. Compared to the efficiency strategy, a consistency strategy has the distinct advantage that the direction of technological development is a sustainable one, while efficiency strategies may lead down a blind alley.

The downside is that the consistency strategy very quickly comes up against constraints if applied on a large scale. Even renewable energy and resources, after all, are not limitless; most notably, there is very little scope for expanding the total land available for bio-energy and biomass production without putting food production and nature conservation at risk. We have known for a long time that finding a substitute for a scarce resource is no straightforward matter. For example, available arable land has fallen from 0.45 ha per capita to less than 0.25 ha in recent decades. And there is more: the more technology is integrated into natural cycles, the more effectively natural rhythms and capacities act as a brake on excessive demands on their performance, unless fossil fuels are once again resorted to. Neither efficiency nor consistency strategies will be able to achieve their objectives unless accompanied by the principle of sufficiency – prosperity with moderation instead of unbridled excess. This, however, is conspicuously absent from all of the green economy concepts.

A Blind Spot: Human Rights

In all green economy or bio-economy scenarios, political, social, economic and cultural rights are largely left out of the picture. It is all the more serious, then, that (other than making reference to labor market effects) none of the deliberations on a green economy include considerations relating to human rights, issues of distribution or democratic rights of participation as key components of a green economy. Surely one might reasonably expect a UN body such as the United Nations Environment Programme to integrate into its thinking on a green economy the most important standards and parameters of international environmental law and human rights. Who else is supposed to bring together the principles, rights and standards newly enshrined in international law (polluter-pays principle, precautionary principle, right to water, right to food), if not the United Nations? [...] The social dimension is viewed almost exclusively from the angle of the labor market and potential poverty reduction. But social and political rights are much broader than this. Governments have an obligation to enforce them and businesses are required to implement them. The green economy needs a clear social compass with distributive policies favoring ordinary people and the poorest fifth of the population in every society, and favoring the poor and very poor in developing countries and emerging economies. Democratic control and social participation as the basis for economic action are blind spots. None of the current documents – from UNEP to the OECD – covers these adequately or even in outline.

Sadly, the unholy alliance of governments of industrialized countries, developing countries and emerging economies is united on this issue too: human rights and democratic principles all too often fall by the wayside when it comes to defending the interests of economically powerful lobby groups and countries' national interests. The industrialized countries, for example, are not particularly interested in the day-to-day consequences of climate change for human rights or the social consequences of bilateral trade agreements – as long as they do not occur at home. And emerging economies and developing countries (together with some companies based in industrialized nations) still show woefully little interest in ensuring that their populations enjoy social standards, employment rights and democratic participation. [...]

The basic tenet of a human rights perspective could be summarized as follows: survival takes precedence over a better life. General human rights take priority over a higher standard of living – in the North as well as in the South. In times of large-scale shortages, environment and resource policy also determines who gets how much of the global environmental space. At present this space is divided up with a startling lack of equity. In the absence of a distribution system that is equitable in terms of resource and climate aspects, the closer resource use or atmospheric pollution gets to the limits of sustainability, the smaller the share left for the marginalized majority of the Earth's inhabitants. In order to give precedence to basic needs, therefore, a more cosmopolitan resource and environment policy needs to promote a reduction in consumption of resources in industrialized countries. Around one third of the world's population depends on direct access to natural resources. They often derive their livelihood from ecosystems such as savannahs, forests, rivers, lakes, fields and coastal areas whose resources are even more highly sought after by public and private-sector firms. Natural and cultural spaces are being lost irretrievably on an almost daily basis. This situation is unlikely to change unless demand for natural resources is significantly reduced. [...] In short, "resource-light" production and consumption patterns are the basis for global resource management that is compatible with human rights.

All concepts relating to the green economy place the economic sphere at the centre of any debate on future viability. According to this view, we can only save the planet with the economy, not against it. So do all solutions revolve around *Homo oeconomicus* once again? If we are looking for new models for society that accept human rights, equity, cultural diversity and democratic participation as fundamental principles while at the same time aiming to stay within ecological limits, we are tasked with nothing less than reinvention of the modern age.

Blueprint For an Economy of Moderation

No matter what angle one considers it from, a green economy must find an alternative to the lack of moderation that has accompanied industrialization. The fossil economy has grown out of all proportion to nature and is bringing the biosphere to its knees. And it is not just the physical size of the fossil economy that needs to be addressed; the scale of the social impacts of the economic system must also be reviewed. Just as a new balance between the economy and the natural world is needed, so must a new equilibrium between the economy and the social order be found. It is hard to see how an economy could contain its resource flow within physical limits without placing social limits on the expansion of the economic system. It is impossible to abandon the world of fossil fuels and leave the mental world untouched. Technology must have a counterpart in the social culture, and vice versa. In short: without a moderate economy there can be no green economy.

At the 1992 Rio Earth Summit there was at least a hint of social reform linked to reduction of pressures on the natural environment. Under the slogan "sustainable production and consumption patterns," Agenda 21 called on countries and communities worldwide to work towards an economic style that encompasses all countries, rich and poor, without driving the biosphere to ruin. Since then, however, attention has become focused on the introduction of sustainable, efficient and environmentally friendly production patterns; changing the consumption patterns of the world's middle and upper classes has been neglected. Discussion no longer centers on the major hindrance to sustainability represented by the space-hungry, material-intensive lifestyle of the affluent population. If social inequality around the globe receives any mention in the strategies of the green economy, thoughts turn immediately to tackling poverty. Leaving the poor the forests and the fish, the pastures and the fields and sparing them from mines and oil extraction – so far, so good. But can the task of alleviating poverty be separated from alleviating wealth?

An Economy of Sufficiency

The green economy as we understand it must foster not only technical innovation but also the art of restraint. Too many goods, too much speed, excessive distances, an overdose of stress at work and too many areas of life, such as school and culture, where the maxims of competitiveness and efficiency hold sway – moderation is alien to today's economy. That is why for us the art of restraint is part of the vision of a viable economy. There is no evading the question of "How much is enough?" The right balance between excess and deprivation is to be found in sufficiency. On the one hand sufficiency targets excess, because excess burdens individuals and society with all sorts of costs. And on the other it targets deprivation, because many people are without the bare necessities of life. The global middle classes are often afflicted by excess, while the majority of the world's population suffers from deprivation.

The idea of sufficiency must form part of the concept of the green economy, just as the idea of "more and more" was built into the fossil economy. Over the last 200 years the economy has freed itself from its natural and social bounds; now it must impose political bounds on itself for the sake of both nature and society. The economics of the last two centuries have been driven by an imperative of constant increase; now we must turn our minds to economic disarmament and rediscover an economy of moderation. In environmental terms this means that, in order for the economic system to be transformed, sufficiency (wealth in moderation) must take its place alongside efficiency (the smart use of resources) and consistency (compatibility between industry and nature). "Better," "different" and "less" are the triumvirate of sustainability.

We know from everyday experience that self-restraint can be beneficial. Too much food makes us lethargic and is bad for our health; too much sport is addictive and puts the body under stress. It is possible to have too much of a good thing. In the same way the benefits of the fossil economy can backfire. In terms of time it offers great speeds – which, however, frequently end in queues and traffic jams. Geographically it creates global networks, for which the price to be paid is the decline of the local economy. And finally it produces an almost infinite range of goods, which in turn contribute to satiety and the accumulation of waste. That a high standard of living does not necessarily result in a high quality of life – indeed, that an excessive standard of living can reduce quality of life – is one of the lessons that affluent societies are now having to learn. In view of this the aim of the sufficiency perspective is to remove excess and bloating so that suppressed quality of life can come into its own. This opens up the prospect of a double dividend: lower economic output not only saves resources but also makes space for a better life.

Slower speeds. When one considers that high speeds are disproportionately heavy on resources, it makes sense to introduce self-restraint as a design principle. For example, cars, trains and – in a different way – airplanes too can be designed for moderate speeds. Thus a cautiously engineered fleet of cars in which no vehicle can exceed a maximum speed of, let us say, 120 kilometers per hour uses significantly less fuel and can adopt a different approach to materials, weight, safety features and styling; in other words, it allows a new generation of automobile technology. In similar fashion, trains can be limited from the design side to around 250 kilometers per hour – a threshold beyond which energy costs rise disproportionally. The design of cautiously engineered vehicles and drive units is the technical expression of the 21st century's utopian vision of living elegantly within natural boundaries.

More regionalization. Speed leads to greater distances. That is why fossil-driven acceleration has led to the development of far-reaching networks at national, continental and global level. First the railway and the truck, then the airplane and the container ship and finally the Internet have dissolved local connections in business and everyday life and replaced them with links to supra-local and supra-national centers, usually in faraway places. Grapes come from Chile, computers from Taiwan, and even the ingredients of one's organic muesli have already travelled hundreds if not thousands of kilometers. In the process the regions, the local communities, become little more than platforms for the implementation of supra-local sales and production strategies. But environmentally friendly wealth will have to strike a new balance between distance and closeness. It is obvious that supply systems with less intensive transport requirements will be needed if we are to prepare for the end of the age of cheap oil. In addition, a green economy must be in tune with natural cycles; it must obtain and process energy resources, building materials, textiles and food from regional ecosystems. To a certain extent this revives the material basis for a regionally focused economy. After the triumph of globalization, we await the renaissance of the regions.

Considered consumption. This renaissance is good news for a society that wants to reduce the total quantity of handled goods to non-harmful levels. For it is essential to ask whether there is any sense in an economic system that at times of widespread scarcity uses valuable natural resources to satisfy ever more needs via market products, offers a hundred variants of each market product and allows all one hundred variants to quickly become obsolete so that they can be replaced with brand new products. However – does this need to be emphasized? – a strategy of quantitative sufficiency is at cross-purposes with the drivers of a type of capitalism that is programmed for survival of the fittest: only those who succeed in adding value in the face of a falling number of goods can hope to remain viable. It is also becoming apparent that by endlessly generating wants the consumption society is departing from its real purpose of improving people's lives. Over-abundance and obsolescence cycles tend to overtax people's ability to maintain perspective and take decisions. Everyone would do well to learn a completely new skill – to reject things, select things, to say no. "Nothing in excess" – over the past two and a half thousand years the ancient motto of Delphi can rarely have been as apt as it is in the present era of the hyperconsumption society.

Social Commons as an Economic Factor

In all the old industrial countries the times of high economic growth are past. Experts now argue over whether we should expect a slight rise in economic output year on year or zero growth punctuated by upswings and downswings. Yet that takes no account of the green transformation of society and the economy. A strategy of eco-efficiency ("better"), environmental sustainability ("different") and self-restraint ("less") has fewer prospects of growth. In a post-growth society the renewable sectors of the economy will need to grow while the fossil ones shrink, but on balance it must be assumed that in the long term growth rates will be negative.

How will a non-growing economy work, if everyone has a lower income than before? To this key question, which will define the next few decades, there are broadly speaking two answers – a reactionary one and a progressive one. The reactionary answer involves enduring a period of loss of growth accompanied by increasing inequality, social exclusion and impoverishment. The progressive one sees us investing in a new model of wealth that ensures that everyone has enough, because it is based on a different equilibrium between the economy and society. The progressive answer does not just fall from the sky; we must prepare for it over the forthcoming years and decades. Strengthening society as against the economy needs new types of infrastructure for different ways of thinking.

The commons are a fundamental feature of our present reality. People can only survive and thrive if they have access to nature, to family and friends, and to language and culture. While this may seem obvious, it is hard to find a public and political language in which to talk about the commons. If we speak of the economy, the concepts of the market and the state dominate everything else. If we speak of politics, what comes to mind is the polarization of right and left.

Hardly anyone mentions the commons – as though nothing of significance exists outside the market and the state. These two concepts are like two communicating tubes: a lot of market on one side and not much state on the other; not much market on one side and a lot of state on the other. Yet historians and anthropologists have long been at pains to point out that exchanging goods via the market or via the state are only two ways in which goods can be distributed – there is a third way: exchange in the community. The first way is governed by the principle of competition and the second by the principle of planning, while in the third the emphasis is on mutuality. In any society the three distributive principles usually mingle, but over the last two centuries something new has happened: the principle of mutuality has steadily lost ground. Since Adam Smith the relationship between the market and the state, between competition and planning, has become the main dispute, while the principle of mutuality has become the big loser. Social groups such as families, relatives, neighborhoods, networks of friends, cooperatives and similar economic forms have been sucked into a vortex of decline from which by turns the market and the state have emerged victorious.

In a post-growth society this development must be reversed. Or rather: it must move forwards. The commons are another source of wealth in addition to the market and the state. They form the basis of social communities, especially at four levels:

- *Firstly*, at the natural level all humans depend on water, forests, soil, fishing grounds, species diversity, countryside, air and the atmosphere and on the life processes embedded in them. As biological beings they have a right to natural assets, regardless of and with precedence over any private ownership of natural stocks.
- *Secondly*, at the social level places such as squares, parks, courtyards and public gardens, as well as post-work leisure, holidays and free time, are essential if social networks are to develop.
- *Thirdly*, as far as the cultural level is concerned, it is obvious that language, memory, customs and knowledge are basic to the creation of any material or non-material product. As cultural beings, the spirits and fates of every person ultimately rely on the achievements of others.
- And finally, *fourthly*, at the digital level: production and exchange on the Internet work best if access to stored data is not impeded. For free navigation in the virtual world it is important that neither software codes nor the wealth of uploaded documents, sounds and pictures are locked away by excessive property claims.

Restoring the strength of the commons requires a different perspective on the economy. What actually is property? And what legitimates the ownership of property? What sounds like a philosophical discussion has practical consequences. If the concept of property does not discriminate clearly between possession and use there is little hope either for the shepherd who lets his sheep graze here one day and there the next, or for the Internet surfer who downloads articles and pictures. And what actually is competition? If competition is understood as "co-striving" (and the German word for competition, "Konkurrenz," has the same Latin root as the English "concur") rather than as "survival of the fittest," then small traders and software specialists can breathe again. And what does creating value actually mean? If it means only monetary value created by selling goods and services, then work in the home, neighborhood services, community organizations and peer groups are left out in the cold. And – the most fundamental question of all – what actually is money? If we make no distinction between money as a means of exchange and credit and money as a means of enrichment and speculation, the whole economy is listing dangerously – in nautical terms it is a disaster waiting to happen.

Looking at the economy from a different angle reveals important aspects that could be relevant to a no-growth economy. Alongside the formal economy there is a relational economy that is concerned not with material things but with relationships between people. The ambit of the relational economy is wide and can range from traditional associations such as sports clubs and church communities, together with businesses of the classical type such as shops and repair services, to post-modern manifestations such as car-sharing schemes and community solar energy projects. Different forms of commitment can arise: friendships, self-help groups and neighborhood services as well as welfare organizations, local businesses and Internet services. Forms of the relational economy can be found in different sectors: relating to food, the care of the sick and elderly, service provision and everyday needs, and in sports and entertainment.

At the core is an economy that is built on social relationships, a "care economy." It cares for children, young people, the sick and the elderly. It brings together parents, educators and carers of all types. Of course it also demonstrates the difficulties that a relational economy has to contend with: care work, family relationships, local communities and private organizations will need to be financially and structurally reorganized. This reorganization must also extend to relationships between the genders if the inherited gender-based division of labor that is predicated on gender hierarchy is not to become even more firmly entrenched. The "care economy," and with it the whole concept of the relational economy, will be derailed if men and women do not participate equally. Caring must undergo a political and social revaluation. In the process, paid and unpaid work must be redistributed – not just between the genders, but primarily so.

Moreover, the relational economy appeals to different motives and norms than the market and the state. Competition and achievement, routine and loyalty certainly occur and can be a component of the social commons, but they can never replace voluntary action and self-organization, cooperation and enterprise. Whether in the development of Wikipedia or of urban community gardens or in the running of old people's clubs and nursery schools – the virtue of cooperation is writ large. Cooperation, with all the attendant difficulties, is held in higher regard than competition, shared curiosity is valued more than hoarding egotism. Things are more successful if they are done with passion, commitment and a sense of responsibility – this is an old lesson that classical business administration has been slow to learn.

How can an economy function without growing? This is a big question that cannot be answered without considering the hidden dimensions of wealth – and in particular of the care economy. One of these dimensions is the social commons. Although private wealth is the most frequently highlighted aspect of wealth, all the variants of community wealth are just as important. Moreover, they harbor the opportunity of creating forms of a "distributed economy" based on the model of distributed energy production – in other words, forms of local production that are linked, globally if necessary, via the Internet. Above all, though, it has become possible to imagine a form of wealth with less money. Because in the social commons services are not provided for monetary reasons, but out of a sense of community spirit, interest or solidarity, needs can be met with a lesser investment of money. For example, just as Wikipedia would be unaffordable if all the authors and editors had to be paid a fee, older people in a housing project provide caring services for each other that could never be paid for from public care budgets. The reinvention of the commons is therefore vital to the creation of an economic order for the 21st century that has been freed from the dictate of growth.

[…]

Index

References to notes are entered as, for example, 329n. References to tables are in bold, e.g. **210**.